FINDERS KEEPERS?

HENRY L. DOHERTY, oil tycoon and campaigner for unitization
Denver Public Library, Western History Collection

FINDERS KEEPERS?

*How the Law of Capture
Shaped the World Oil Industry*

TERENCE DAINTITH

RFF PRESS
RESOURCES FOR THE FUTURE

Washington, DC • London

First published in 2010 by RFF Press, an imprint of Earthscan

Earthscan LLC, 1616 P Street, NW, Washington, DC 20036, USA
Earthscan Ltd, Dunstan House, 14a St Cross Street, London EC1N 8XA, UK
Earthscan publishes in association with the International Institute for Environment and Development

For more information on RFF Press and Earthscan publications, see www.rffpress.org and www.earthscan.co.uk or write to earthinfo@earthscan.co.uk

ISBN: 978-1-933115-84-9 (hardback)
ISBN: 978-1-933115-83-2 (paperback)

Copyedited by Joyce Bond
Typeset by OKS
Cover design by Ellen A. Davey

Cover photo: the Phillips and Woodford Wells, Oil Creek, PA, 1862 – the first documented case of two wells on different properties capturing oil from the same source. Drake Well Museum and Archive, Titusville PA.

Library of Congress Cataloging-in-Publication Data

Daintith, Terence.
  Finders keepers : how the law of capture shaped the world oil industry / Terence Daintith.
       p. cm.
    Includes bibliographical references and index.
    ISBN 978-1-933115-84-9 (hardback : alk. paper) – ISBN 978-1-933115-83-2 (pbk. : alk. paper)
    1. Petroleum law and legislation.
  I. Title.
  K3915.D35 2010
  343'.0772–dc22   2010000843

A catalogue record for this book is available from the British Library.

At Earthscan we strive to minimize our environmental impacts and carbon footprint through reducing waste, recycling and offsetting our CO_2 emissions, including those created through publication of this book. For more details of our environmental policy, see www.earthscan.co.uk.

Printed and bound in the U.S. by Edwards Brothers, Inc.

About Resources for the Future *and* RFF Press

Resources for the Future (RFF) improves environmental and natural resource policymaking worldwide through independent social science research of the highest caliber. Founded in 1952, RFF pioneered the application of economics as a tool for developing more effective policy about the use and conservation of natural resources. Its scholars continue to employ social science methods to analyze critical issues concerning pollution control, energy policy, land and water use, hazardous waste, climate change, biodiversity, and the environmental challenges of developing countries.

RFF Press supports the mission of RFF by publishing book-length works that present a broad range of approaches to the study of natural resources and the environment. Its authors and editors include RFF staff, researchers from the larger academic and policy communities, and journalists. Audiences for publications by RFF Press include all of the participants in the policymaking process—scholars, the media, advocacy groups, NGOs, professionals in business and government, and the public. RFF Press is an imprint of **Earthscan**, a global publisher of books and journals about the environment and sustainable development.

CONTENTS

FIGURES AND TABLES

PREFACE AND ACKNOWLEDGMENTS

The story this book aims to tell is of how a legal rule has influenced the development of a key international industry. The industry is the oil industry, and the rule, known as the law of capture or rule of capture, says that oil and gas become the property of the person who recovers them by drilling on land he or she owns or has lawful access to, even if that oil and gas may have migrated from under adjoining lands. At first thought, this may seem like just one of a multitude of rather mundane and technical rules of property law; in practice, however, the choice between acceptance and rejection of this particular rule has been crucial to the way the oil industry has developed. This is true not just of the United States, but of oil-producing countries generally. A different property rule would have resulted in a different industry, indeed a different world. Although people in and around the U.S. oil industry tend to think of capture as a peculiarly American institution, it was a rule that, in the early years of the industry at least, enjoyed wide international acceptance. One of the aims of this book is to show why, despite this common beginning, the rule today is of marginal importance elsewhere yet remains the foundation of the complex legal structure that regulates the domestic U.S. industry.

As capture is a legal rule, it is natural that much of the material for this account should be drawn from legislative and judicial decisions applying it, restricting it, negating it, or interpreting it. But this is not a legal text: my concern is not to defend or criticize these decisions on grounds of their legal or constitutional correctness, but to show how they came to be adopted and what their effects were. The emphasis is on the political, economic, and industrial environment in which those decisions were taken and implemented, and at all times I have tried to ensure that the legal decisions and even the formal legal reasoning with which they may have been supported are presented in terms accessible to any reader who has some understanding of or interest in the industry. One of the questions that the book seeks to present to that reader, and indeed to the legal reader, is precisely whether such formal legal reasoning has been of much or any importance to the processes of selecting, applying, elaborating, and restricting the rule.

In tracing the history of capture in the oil industry, I have moved back and forth between the American experience and that of other countries. Chapters 1 to 3 and 7 to 9 aim to provide a linear account of how the domestic U.S. industry developed under the rule of capture. The remaining chapters offer a broader picture, which may not only demonstrate the influence of the rule in other places, but also make American readers aware of roads not taken, indeed roads never noticed, in the course of their industry's 150-year journey.

I should like to express warm appreciation to the board of the Australian Resources and Energy Law Association (AMPLA), who provided a research grant that enabled me to pursue archive and library research in a variety of locations. I am also indebted to the helpers who tracked down sources in other places: Yee-Fui Ng in Canberra, Nichola Daintith in Munich, Alexandrea Thompson in New York, and Edward Daintith in Vienna. Librarians who helped me beyond the call of duty were Susan Beates at the Drake Well archive in Titusville, Pennsylvania, and Catherine Cosgrove at the Energy Institute Library and Katherine Read at the Institute of Advanced Legal Studies Library, both in London. For translations, I am most grateful to Edward Daintith, Marianne Everett, and Yuri Kushko.

Owen Anderson of the University of Oklahoma and Michael Crommelin of the University of Melbourne read the entire text in draft and made many valuable suggestions. Other sources of improvement were the detailed comments of three anonymous reviewers, as well as the challenging critique offered by Jacqueline Weaver of the University of Houston. Many others helped in providing information or pointing to sources, notably Nigel Bankes, Phillippe Bergot, Jessica Davies, Alison Frank, Richard Healey, Geoff Hewitt, Adrian Hill, Alexandra Lamont, John Lowe, Dagfin Nygard, David Roby and his colleagues at the Alaska Oil and Gas Conservation Commission, Gavin Ryan, and Rose Villazor. Special thanks are also due to John Lowe at Southern Methodist University in Dallas, who

gave me the chance to test some of the ideas in the
academic legal audiences in that city. William Brice,
Institute, kindly offered a similar opportunity with l
publishing an earlier version of Chapter 3 in Volume 8
Industry History. In addition, an early draft of the final c
meeting of the Academic Advisory Group of the Intern
Energy and Infrastructure Section in Abuja, Nigeria, ii
grateful to Barry Barton for making this happen.

In the course of a lengthy publishing career, I have not previously had the good
fortune to receive the level of expert and thoughtful support and guidance offered
on this occasion by Don Reisman of RFF Press, for which I should like to express
particular thanks. Along with the other contributions mentioned above, this did
much to sustain me in the daunting task of writing, as a non-American, about an
industry, and about principles of its legal regulation, that Americans, with some
justice, regard as very much their own. The reader will decide whether those who
provided all this encouragement and help were, as things turned out, well advised
to do so.

Terence Daintith

A NOTE ON REFERENCES, WEIGHTS, MEASURES, AND VALUES

Any book written with the hope that it may be read by people from a range of disciplinary backgrounds has to deal with the problem of satisfying the varying conventions of those disciplines for the referencing of material. Lawyers like to see all their references spelled out in detail in notes at the foot of the page—notes that sometimes have a disturbing tendency to swell and rise up the page until they engulf the text. Social scientists are content with parenthetical insertions in the text in summary form, referring to a list of references at the end of the book. Historians, who seem able to consult a book in several different places simultaneously, favor endnotes rather than footnotes, which in their turn refer the reader on to a fully detailed bibliography. And the general reader—on the chance that he or she can be lured into reading the book—may not want to be distracted by references at all.

The referencing method I have adopted represents a compromise among these conventions, which, if it risks satisfying nobody completely, has at least the merit of keeping the pages reasonably uncluttered and concentrating detailed references in a section at the end of the book. Footnotes are mostly confined to abbreviated author-date citations, sufficient to identify the work in the references section, along with page numbers where appropriate; I have resisted so far as I can the lawyer's predilection for the use of footnotes as a vehicle for exposition and even argument. Exceptionally, I have provided full footnote references to judicial decisions, whose citation is complicated by the fact that they may be found in more than one series of reports, with different volume numbers and paginations.

Quantitative information is not a central concern of this book, but it is important at a number of points to have some notion of orders of magnitude, not least as among petroleum activities in different countries and at different times. Getting a clear view of such issues is made more difficult by the lack of standardization of the measures relevant to such activities, particularly in the early days of the industry. At a time when Americans measured their petroleum by volume, in barrels, others measured by weight: Romanians in tonnes, Russians in poods, and Burmese in viss. Conversions are bedeviled by the facts both that the weight of a given volume of crude oil may vary considerably according to its type, and that the underlying basic measures used may also vary from place to place: an imperial gallon, for example, is 20 percent larger than a U.S. gallon, so the 42-gallon U.S. barrel measure for oil is in fact smaller than the 40-gallon imperial barrel measure that replaced the viss in Burma.

Wherever possible in the text, I have provided a conversion of oil quantities to U.S. barrels, using where necessary the weight/volume conversion of 1 metric tonne to 7.4 U.S. barrels. There is a degree of arbitrariness in this, but not such as to falsify the broad comparisons being offered. I have also, in the text, converted

Metric	Other	U.S.
Length		
1 meter		1.0936 yards
1 kilometer		0.6214 mile
1.89 meters	1 klafter (Austria)	2.067 yards
Area		
1 sq. meter		1.196 sq. yards
1 hectare		2.4711 acres
1 sq. kilometer		0.3861 sq. miles
4.55 sq meters	1 sq. sazhen (Russia)	5.444 sq. yards
1.1 hectare	1 dessiatine (Russia)	2.7 acres
Weight		
1 tonne		1.1023 tons
1.016 tonnes	1 ton (UK)	1.12 tons
16.38 kilograms	1 pood or pud (Russia)	36.11 pounds
1.66 kilograms	1 viss (Burma)	3.65 pounds

Table 1. Measures Used in This Book

unusual or out-of-date measures to current U.S. measures, but I have not offered U.S.-to-metric conversions or vice versa. Such conversions of the main measures are set out for convenience in Table 1, along with those of the more exotic measures referred to above.

I have also tried where possible to give currency conversions to U.S. monetary units as at the equivalent date, relying principally on the tables at www.measuringworth.org.

For Chris, at last

PART I
THE BEGINNINGS OF THE RULE OF
CAPTURE IN THE UNITED STATES

CHAPTER 1

THE RULE OF CAPTURE: NAMING AND BLAMING

AN AMERICAN PARABLE

Excitement at Pac-Bell Park, the home of the San Francisco Giants baseball team, ran unusually high on October 7, 2001. This was the final game of the year for the second-place Giants, and their big hitter Barry Bonds was trying to advance the home run record that he had set only two days before, when he broke Mark McGwire's single season mark by hitting his 71st and 72nd home runs. Many of the fans who had tickets for the arcade section of the stadium—Bonds's preferred destination for big hits—came equipped with baseball mitts, in the hope of being the one to catch his home run ball. Non-American readers should realize that when you catch a record home run ball, you do not throw it back so that play can continue; you keep it and—unless you are rich and sentimental—later offer it for sale. The ball that Mark McGwire hit for his 70th home run sold for more than $3 million. Major league baseball clubs in effect treat a ball as abandoned once it is hit out of the playing area.[1]

---

[1] Finkelman 2002.

Barry Bonds hit his home run in his first at bat. As the ball sailed into the arcade, it was Alex Popov who managed to connect with his glove and pull the ball down. But he was unable to get complete control of it before he was submerged under a mass of struggling fans, who grabbed, hit, and kicked him. In this melee, Popov lost his hold on the ball, which eventually appeared in the mitt of another fan, Patrick Hayashi. Over Popov's protests, security staff surrounded Hayashi and took him to official premises at the ground, where he was recognized as the successful capturer of the ball.

Popov did not let the matter rest there; he sued Hayashi for the wrongful taking of the ball. After hearing large numbers of witnesses give conflicting evidence about what happened in the melee, the court concluded that both men had a good and equal claim to the ball, granted each of them an equal and undivided interest in it, and ordered that it be sold and the proceeds divided between them.[2] Sadly for the parties, the length of time that had elapsed and the allegations of lying and bad faith traded between them in the courtroom seriously tainted the ball as a souvenir, and the fact that by this time Bonds's home run prowess was being alleged to stem from illegitimate use of steroids did not help either. At auction, the ball yielded only $300,000; Popov's share did not even pay his legal costs.

Baseballs might seem to have little in common with the oil and gas resources that have been the essential fuel of economic development since the late nineteenth century, but this cautionary tale of ferocious and mutually destructive competition for possession of a prized resource replicates in miniature a parallel story played out, on a much greater scale and with much more dramatic consequences, over the entire century and a half of modern petroleum history. This is the story of how the oil industry in the United States—and indeed, in many other countries of the world—has been shaped by the operation of the same principle of law that underlay the legal dispute in *Popov v. Hayashi*: that is, the principle of property law that gives ownership of an unowned object to the person who first reduces it to possession.

Commonly known as the "rule of capture" or "law of capture" (the expressions are interchangeable) and boasting a pedigree that takes it back to the writings of Roman law commentators two millennia ago,[3] the principle assumed particular importance in the United States, where the process of westward expansion constantly opened up new resources that might be available for appropriation by the prompt and energetic. As individual ownership by European settlers replaced the communal enjoyment of resources practiced by earlier inhabitants, scope for the operation of the rule was steadily reduced, but it continued to be important

---

[2] *Popov v. Hayashi* (Superior Court, San Francisco, December 18, 2002).

[3] Drummond et al. 2004: 1–51.

in relation to resources to which it was difficult for individuals to assert a permanent and effective claim in the absence of actual physical possession. Wildlife, fisheries, and flows of water offer familiar examples. Ecologists and economists have emphasized the dangers of wasteful exploitation, and premature exhaustion, of such common resources, reasoning that the failure or inability of the law to apportion individual rights to them exposes them to a competitive and unsustainable competition for possession, engendering, in Garret Hardin's famous phrase, the "tragedy of the commons."[4]

THE RULE OF CAPTURE IN RELATION TO OIL AND GAS

In this book, I examine the application of this "rule of capture" to oil and gas. How a rule dealing with unowned property comes to apply to something as valuable as oil and gas clearly deserves a little explanation.

Oil and gas, we now know, are produced from sediments rich in decayed plant and animal matter. Over millions of years, such sediments are compacted and heated as they are overlain and driven downward by the deposition of new layers, a process that produces chemical transformation into hydrocarbons in the form of oil and gas. The expansion attendant on this process drives the hydrocarbons into the pore spaces of neighboring reservoir rocks, typically sandstones and limestones. If these permeable rock reservoirs are surrounded by impermeable rock layers, the oil and gas will be trapped and held; if not, they will be dissipated through the subsoil, eventually reaching the surface in the form of oil or gas seepages or bituminous deposits. Several different types of reservoirs are now distinguished, depending on the nature of the formations that operate to hold the hydrocarbons in reservoir rock. These include anticlines, folds or domes in the earth's surface that may trap hydrocarbons as they rise under pressure; structural traps, created by the fracture and sliding of rock masses; and stratigraphic traps, formed by the juxtaposition of materials of different permeability, as where the sandbars in a buried river gradually form permeable sandstones surrounded by impermeable shales formed from the mud of the riverbed.

What these types of trap have in common is that the oil or gas, or both, that they contain is held under pressure in the pores of the reservoir rock. That pressure may be provided by subsurface water held in the reservoir rock below or, more rarely, beside the hydrocarbon deposits, or by the gas that forms a "cap" on top of the oil in the reservoir or is dissolved in solution within that oil. According to the nature of the principal source of pressure, reservoirs may be categorized as water drive, gas

---

[4] Hardin 1968.

"Capturing" oil

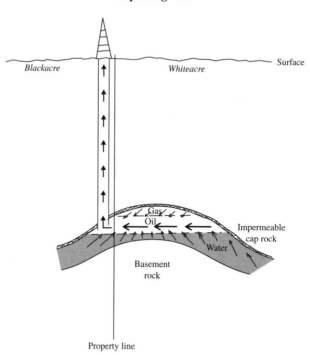

Figure 1-1. The Process of Capture (not to scale)

cap drive, or solution gas drive. When that pressure is released, these fluids will find the quickest way to the surface, and if the release is effected by drilling into the reservoir, that way will be up the drill bore. High pressures along with highly permeable sands through which oil or gas can move quickly produce the spectacular gushers that are a familiar part of oil lore; lower pressures or permeability may produce a steady, if less spectacular, flow or may require assistance by pumping to bring the oil to the surface. In addition, as gas in the reservoir comes out of solution, the oil becomes stickier and flows less freely, needing more pressure, natural or artificial, if it is to be recovered.

There is no reason why the boundaries of the sands in which the oil or gas is trapped should correspond with, or be wholly contained within, the boundaries of the surface landholdings that overlie them. But as soon as the reservoir extends across property lines, the movement of hydrocarbons to the base of the wellbore creates a potential property right problem, as Figure 1.1 indicates.

In a legal system that separates rights in the land surface from rights to the minerals beneath, the fact that oil and gas migrate in this way when the reservoir is pierced *may* cause no problem, if ownership of those substances has been unified in a single pair of hands—usually those of the state. I say "may" because, as we shall see in Chapters 10 and 11, the state may use those rights in ways that make surface divisions relevant again. But in the United States, the world's first great oil-producing power, the rule was, and remains, different: the surface owner is, in the absence of any contrary legal arrangement, also the owner of the subsoil and the minerals within it. What, then, is the legal position when the oil and gas that was under one owner's land migrates up a wellbore drilled in the legitimate exercise of his or her own property rights by a neighbor?

THE RULE OF CAPTURE, ITS CONSEQUENCES, AND ITS CRITICS

The response universally adopted in the United States, in both state and federal law, has been framed in this way by a leading commentator:

> The owner of a tract of land acquires title to the oil and gas which he produces from wells drilled thereon, although it may be proved that part of such oil and gas migrated from adjoining lands.[5]

About the same time, a judge described it as follows:

> The law of capture ... gives the right to produce all of the oil and gas that will flow out of the well on one's land; and this is a property right. And it is limited only by the physical possibility of the adjoining landowner diminishing the oil and gas under one's land by the exercise of the same right of capture.[6]

This rule has been perceived as essentially, one might say quintessentially, American: a rule that places a high value on vigor, on getting there first, on winning one's wealth through free competition. From this perception, it is only a short—but false—step to the assumption that this is a peculiarly American notion, one with no counterpart in other countries' oil industries.[7] In fact, the rule is widely encountered in other legal systems, and one of the aims of this book is to explain why it seems to have mattered elsewhere so much less than in the United States.

Many writers emphasize its crucial importance to the early development of the U.S. oil industry. For the historian Daniel Yergin, the rule was "the most important in shaping the legal context of American oil production, and the very structure of the industry from its earliest days." In his eyes, it was more important

---

[5] Hardwicke 1935: 393.
[6] *Brown v. Humble Oil Co.*, 126 Tex. 296 at 305, 83 S.W. 2d 935 at 940 (1935).
[7] Adelman 1972: 43.

in explaining the race to be first to produce a new field than were lack of geological knowledge, the large and quick rewards obtainable, or the effect of leasing terms imposed by landowners.[8] For the economist Stuart MacDonald, the adoption of the rule was "the single most important factor in the development of American Oil and Gas Law."[9] And two of the leading U.S. scholars of oil and gas law have—with proper lawyerly circumspection—declared that even today, "[t]he rule of capture may be the most important single doctrine of oil and gas law,"[10] a remark cited with approval in a crucial recent capture case in an opinion that called the rule "a cornerstone of the oil and gas industry."[11]

For a rule so important, the rule of capture is singularly unloved. Indeed, it has been subjected to a campaign of vilification that started in the 1920s and has not been abandoned since. The very term "rule of capture" was introduced at that time by those who were convinced that it was the legal rules of property in oil and gas that lay at the root of the tragic waste and disorder of American oil production. The basic evil, which they linked directly with the rule, was the practice of drilling as many wells as possible as quickly as possible after discovery of a new field, and locating them along the boundary lines of one's property, with the idea either of recovering the petroleum under one's neighbor's land as well as under one's own or of protecting oneself from similar predatory behavior by others. When undertaken defensively this was known as "offset drilling" and was an obligation ordinarily imposed on oil and gas lessees.

The unnecessary costs and damage associated with these practices were enormous. An early estimate in 1914 was that overall losses from excessive drilling amounted to some $50 million, at a time when the value of total U.S. production was $214 million.[12] In 1931, it was estimated that 765 more wells than were necessary for efficient drainage had been drilled in the Oklahoma City field, and that these wells, running at full capacity, were capable of producing 20 times what could be absorbed by the market at that time. The same source estimated the unnecessary drilling costs in the Seminole fields in Oklahoma at $70 million.[13] A few years later, notwithstanding the development of conservation measures in a number of states, it was still thought that some 4,000 to 5,000 unnecessary wells were being drilled each year in the United States, at a cost of $80 million to $100 million.[14]

---

[8] Yergin 1991: 32.

[9] MacDonald 2003: 291.

[10] 1 Smith and Weaver 1998: § 1.1(A).

[11] *Coastal Oil and Gas Corp. v. Garza Energy Trust*, 268 S.W. 3d 1, at 13 (Tex. 2008).

[12] Ise 1926: 91, 141.

[13] Marshall and Meyers 1931: 38.

[14] Harrison 1970: 360, citing Ely 1938: 1232.

This spectacular waste of capital and labor was only part of the problem. The need to produce one's oil before one's neighbor did led to production far in excess of demand (an excess of nearly 40 million barrels in the first seven months of 1929)[15] and the consequent collapse of prices. It meant that vast quantities of oil were held in surface storage, leading to fires, pollution, and loss by evaporation, estimated at 20 to 25 percent of production by one 1917 source.[16] Enormous volumes of natural gas, enough to heat large cities, were produced in conjunction with oil, and where no accessible market existed, the gas was simply blown or flared off. The dissipation of the natural reservoir energy furnished by this gas made up to 90 percent of the resources originally in place unrecoverable save by expensive methods of artificial repressurization.[17] In 1980, the *International Petroleum Encyclopedia* recorded that the United States had 88 percent of the world's oil wells ... and 14 percent of worldwide production.[18] Until the mid-1920s, most of the industry accepted this waste as an unfortunate fact of life. It was largely the campaigning efforts of one man, a maverick within the industry, that put it on the public agenda as a problem for political resolution.

This man was Henry L. Doherty, at that time president and self-styled chief engineer of the Cities Service Oil Company, based in Bartlesville, Oklahoma.[19] Doherty's was the classic American story of the advance from rags to riches through hard work and bold decisionmaking. He began his working life at age 12 as an office boy in the Columbus Gas Company in Ohio. Chief engineer at age 20, he had by 1910 acquired a large number of utility companies, from which he created the New York–based Cities Service Company. He took that company into the oil production business in Oklahoma a couple years later.

In 1924, his Cities Service group was the third-largest oil company, after Standard Oil of New Jersey and Harry Sinclair's Consolidated Oil Corporation, though it had suffered a steep decline in profits in the previous three years, largely as a result of the hectic and uncontrolled development of oil fields around Los Angeles including Signal Hill and Huntington Beach. Some have suggested that this experience explains his emergence as the first campaigner from within the industry for the unitization of oil fields—that is to say, their operation as a single unit, regardless of the division of the surface interests lying above them.[20] The link

---

[15] Merrill 1930: 396.
[16] Ball 1917: 3.
[17] Marshall and Meyers 1931: 37–8.
[18] Cited in Libecap 1993: 94.
[19] See generally Nordhauser 1979: 7–16; Olien and Olien 2000: 154–7.
[20] 1 Bradley 1996: 97.

seems plausible: Doherty was a man who pursued his current concerns and enthusiasms with messianic fervor. When acting as director of more than 100 companies in the 1930s, he found time and energy to organize campaigns to eradicate mosquitoes from Manhattan and floodlight the Statue of Liberty.

Whatever prompted his campaign for unitization, as part of it he coined, probably in 1923, the term "law of capture" to describe the common-law rule permitting drainage of oil and gas from under one's neighbor's land.[21] He may not have been quite the first in the industry to associate the word "capture" with property rights in oil—another Oklahoma oilman, E.W. Marland, wrote earlier in 1923 about the landowner's having only "the right to capture" the oil under his land[22]—but by talking of a "law of capture," he was able to draw a powerful comparison between the law of oil and gas and that relating to wild animals, pointing out the wholesale destruction the latter had produced, with complete extinction prevented only by legislation imposing closed seasons and restrictions on marketing. The epithet was clearly meant to be pejorative. Doherty's warning, regularly repeated to the annoyance of his industry colleagues,[23] was that oil was running out and that wasteful exploitation was accelerating the process and could be halted only by compulsory unitization of oil fields.

His prophecy, in the short term, and his remedy, in the longer term, enjoyed far less success than the expression he coined. I shall examine later and in detail how the idea of unitization made its painful way forward in the political and economic maelstrom the industry traversed in the 1930s, a time not of impending shortage but of glut, and how even today it still fails, in the United States, to command unhesitating acceptance as the necessary approach to exploration and production. The expression "law of capture" was, however, readily taken up, as much by the proponents of the existing property rights system for oil and gas as by its adversaries. Within a decade or so, it was the ordinary means of referring to the rule, in use alike in writing by lawyers,[24] engineers,[25] and politicians.[26] As the citation from *Brown v. Humble Oil Co.*, decided in 1935, demonstrates,[27] it quickly came to be used by courts without any negative overtones; indeed, for the Supreme Court of Texas, the law of capture enjoyed the status of a property right,

---

[21] Doherty 1925: 9. He may have first used the term in a memorandum circulated in September 1923 to the board of directors of the American Petroleum Institute: Nordhauser 1979: 11.

[22] Marland 1923.

[23] E.g., at United States. Federal Oil Conservation Board 1926a: 24–33.

[24] Hardwicke 1935. For argument that the use of the term produced unfortunate effects, see Walker 1938: 375, below, at 264.

[25] Oliver 1935.

[26] Pettengill 1936: Ch. 9.

[27] Above, n. 6.

thereby clothing it with a constitutional protection that was doubtless the last thing Doherty and his allies contemplated or desired.[28]

In this period, however, when massive discoveries in Texas and Oklahoma drove American concern over waste and the collapse of prices to new heights, many commentators followed Doherty's line: the rule of capture was stigmatized as a "law of piracy" or "law of the jungle," an "inherent disease,"[29] and an incitement to competitive "delirium."[30] Not everybody joined this chorus. Quite apart from that group of producers who made large amounts of money by exploiting the opportunities it gave them to drain their neighbors' lands, the rule found apologists among economists and, later, lawyers. The economist Joseph Pogue, for example, told an international energy conference in 1938 that, at least up to about 1920, the rule's effects were on balance positive, in that it drove the industry to achieve the rate of expansion that the market demanded.[31] A similar assessment was made in 1946 by Paul Frankel, one of the leading authorities on petroleum economics: "[T]hese somewhat primitive methods were exactly what was needed to make the young industry, in the first instance, aggressive and, in due course, great."[32]

Capture did not, however, cease to be important when the industry entered middle age. Despite the massive increase, in the 1930s and later, of the range and intensity of conservation efforts by state legislators and the administrative commissions they created to regulate the production and transportation of oil and gas, one legal commentator could still write in 1952 that "the impact of the rule of capture upon the fact of the divided interests in minerals presents the major obstacle to scientific development of petroleum-producing formations."[33]

Fifty years later, the rule is still in place and, as later chapters will show, continues to complicate the development of oil and gas under privately owned land. In 2006, such resources accounted for 62.75 percent of U.S. oil production, and 61.64 percent of natural gas production.[34] The rule is hardwired into the mental circuits of domestic oil producers and continues to have its intellectual supporters in the United States, notably among legal specialists who argue that the existence of the rule is a precondition for the efficient operation of the very conservation laws and regulations that limit its operation.[35] It has also been suggested that these regulations produced more waste and less efficiency than

---

[28] See below, Ch. 9, at 263–4 for further discussion of the legal nature of the rule.

[29] All these epithets are collected in Hardwicke 1935: 391–2.

[30] United States. Federal Oil Conservation Board 1930: 18.

[31] Pogue 1938: 236.

[32] Frankel 1969: 19.

[33] Williams 1952: 1156.

[34] United States. Energy Information Administration 2007: Table 1.

[35] Kuntz 1957; Kramer and Anderson 2005: 950–4.

would have followed from the unfettered operation of the rule.[36] Outside the United States, however, lawyers are more likely to echo the unkind epithets of the 1920s and 1930s. For a recent Australian commentator, capture represents the "law of the jungle,"[37] and in a Dutch case decided in 2005, the state's Advocate-General described it to the court as simple "theft."[38]

Certainly plenty of waste and inefficient production occur today in countries where the law of capture has no application. Gas is flared in massive quantities in Middle Eastern countries; design faults in petroleum fiscal and regulatory systems can create incentives for "creaming" easily accessible deposits and leaving the rest in the ground. But at a time of skepticism about the chances of major new oil discoveries and well-grounded fears about the ecological consequences of increased resort to alternative fossil fuels such as oil shale, oil sands, and coal, it is appropriate to investigate a principle to which the United States continues to adhere despite traditionally assigning it the major blame for waste in domestic oil and gas production. Today the United States is by far the largest consumer of the world's finite hydrocarbon resources.[39] In 2007, it accounted for 24.28 percent of world oil consumption (China, the second-largest consumer, accounted for 9.61 percent) and 25.89 percent of world natural gas consumption (in this case, Russia was the runner-up with 17.4 percent). It was also by far the largest importer of oil, with 24.87 percent of total world imports in that year.

In this book, I adopt a historical and comparative approach in reviewing the long and controversial life of the law of capture. I explain how it came to be adopted in the United States (Chapters 2 and 3), explore related experiences elsewhere in order to determine whether this was a distinctively American response to property right problems presented by these minerals (Chapters 4 to 6), and trace the long and turbulent history of U.S. attempts to escape the negative consequences of the rule (Chapters 7 to 9). I also show how the rule has influenced the shape even of petroleum regimes that have purported to discard or neutralize it (Chapters 10 and 11) and examine its place in the federal and international politics of petroleum resources (Chapter 12). A final chapter relates the key elements of this history to general discussions about common resources, in an attempt to explain the remarkable pervasiveness and longevity of the law of capture in this field and assess the justness of the accusation that this judge-made rule is at the root of the industry's past and present problems of waste and overdrilling. The problem, I conclude, lies deeper: it was the uncontrolled exercise of private

---

[36] 1 Bradley 1996: Chs. 3, 4.
[37] Keen 1998: 438.
[38] Spier 2005.
[39] Percentages calculated from BP 2008: 11, 27, 22.

property rights in oil and gas that made the law of capture operate with such disastrous effect, and it is the excessive reverence for such rights that sustains unnecessary obstacles to rational oilfield exploitation in the United States at a time when the rest of the world's oil-producing countries have eliminated private property rights, either totally displacing the rule of capture or fitting it into a broader regime of production control.

BLAMING THE JUDGES

The rule of capture is a common-law rule: that is to say, its authority as a rule of law derives from its adoption, as a basis of decision, by American courts in disputes involving property rights in petroleum. No legislature has ever intervened to frame the rule in statutory terms. So it is understandable that when Henry Doherty and other engineers came to perceive the rule of capture as the root cause of the industry's wasteful behavior, they should blame the judges. And they were forthright in their blaming. Earl Oliver, a petroleum engineer working in E. W. Marland's company, Marland Oil, lashed the judges in a series of papers and presentations starting in 1926. For him, the instability of the industry resulted from an 1875 decision,

> when a Pennsylvania jurist initiated the idea that soon became crystallized into a principle of law, namely, that ownership to [*sic*] oil and gas becomes vested by the act of reduction to possession. ... [W]hen called upon to make a decision on a point on which there was no precedent, fancying he noted some resemblance between its actions and those of wild game, [he] made mention of that resemblance. Other courts being struck by the analogy enlarged upon it and gradually impressed upon oil and gas the existing principles of the law of wild game in so far as it was possible for analogy to run. ... We know how fish, deer, bear and buffalo have disappeared. ... This ... was an abortive principle conceived by an opportunist. It violated centuries of experience as to the type of ownership to property that best serves mankind. It conflicted with economic law. It put a premium on wastefulness rather than efficiency. It was a black sheep among legal principle. It did not harmonize with existing institutions. It did not utilize the predominating traits of human nature without which no law can be economically successful.[40]

The Pennsylvania jurist on the receiving end of this piece of invective was in fact the state's Chief Justice Agnew, who delivered the opinion in the case of

---

[40] Oliver, in United States. Federal Oil Conservation Board 1926a: 93–5. See also Oliver 1930: 721, 1937: 135.

Brown v. Vandergrift.[41] We shall see that Oliver was actually quite wrong in attributing either the principle or the analogy to Agnew. One can sympathize, though, with his assumption that the judges bore responsibility. Judicial attempts to establish coherent rules of property for these troublesome substances had already attracted considerable criticism in learned legal journals, some of it expressed with hardly less force than Oliver's remarks.

For Professor Walter Summers of the University of Kentucky, later the author of one of the standard multivolume works on oil and gas law,[42] the rule (not yet known as the rule of capture when he wrote) represented

> an anomalous exception that destroys the principle [of ownership] itself, forms a rule violative of the plainest principles of justice and equity, acknowledges the weakness of the law to enforce defined rights of property, and makes that relic of barbarism,
>   The simple plan
>   That they should take who have the power,
>   And they should keep who can
> the basis of the law of property in oil and gas.[43]

A year later, James Veasey, who was general counsel to the Carter Oil Company, an Oklahoma subsidiary of Standard Oil of New Jersey, and in the 1920s and 1930s one of the most influential of oil industry lawyers, waded into the attack in his turn, mocking the judges for their scientific ignorance and their seduction by romantic analogies. He accused them, in their development of the rule, of misunderstanding the nature of oil and gas, notably of failing to apprehend the fact that in their natural state, these elements are trapped in a stable state in reservoirs of porous rock rather than flowing in underground streams; of assuming, on the basis of inadequate evidence, that natural gas, if not oil, might be inexhaustible; and of persisting in these errors long after scientific evidence had shown these beliefs to be unfounded. This last failing was attributed to the blinkered attitude of state courts:

> In the later cases the courts do not receive proof upon the nature of oil and gas, nor have their views in this regard kept pace with the expansion of scientific and practical knowledge upon the subject. Inasmuch as they predicate their conception of the matter upon judicial knowledge alone, the expressions found in the earlier decisions relating to the question are persistently repeated in the later cases. Hence, the error perseveres.[44]

---

[41] 89 Pa. 142 (1875).
[42] Summers 1954.
[43] Summers 1919: 179.
[44] Veasey 1920a: 453–5.

Like Oliver, he accused the early judges of being guided by fanciful and unscientific analogies with the behavior of wild animals, which their successors parroted, thus evading the need for rigorous analysis and perpetuating these errors. Certainly one can point to particular judges who seemed to exist in a bosky arcadia where technology never penetrated, like Justice Smith of the Texas Court of Appeals. In the 1920s, long after the essentials of reservoir mechanics had been generally understood, this judge still appeared to believe that oil and gas "percolate restlessly about under the surface of the earth, even as the birds fly from field to field and the beasts roam from forest to forest"[45] and that "oil in its normal state is of a fugitive nature, restlessly and ceaselessly moving about in the bowels of the earth in response to natural forces and influences which have never been fathomed or mastered by human science."[46]

Few if any other judges were quite so unworldly, nor were they necessarily uncritical of the rule. Indeed, the judgment that stated the principle and implications of the rule of capture with such clarity that it is frequently cited as the leading—though not the first—case on the topic also expressed reservations as to its wisdom. In 1907, in *Barnard v. Monongahela Natural Gas Company*, Judge McIlvaine of the Court of Common Pleas of Washington County, Pennsylvania, put the matter as follows:

> What then has been held to be the law? — it is this, as we understand it, every landowner or his lessee may locate his wells wherever he pleases regardless of the interests of others. He may distribute them over the whole farm or locate them only on one part of it. He may crowd the adjoining farms so as to enable him to draw the oil and gas from them. What then can the neighbor do? Nothing, only go and do likewise. He must protect his own oil and gas. He knows it is wild and will run away if it finds an opening and it is his business to keep it at home. This may not be the best rule, but neither the legislature nor our highest court has given us any better. No doubt many thousands of dollars have been expended "in protecting lines" in oil and gas territory that would not have been expended if some rule had existed by which it could have been avoided.[47]

In bringing the legislature into the picture, as an agency that might have corrected the problems associated with the common-law rule but had failed to do so, Judge McIlvaine suggested a broader target for critique than judges like himself

---

[45] *Medina Oil Development Co. v. Murphy*, 233 S.W. 333 at 335 (Tex. Civ. App. 1921), cited in Walker 1938: 371.

[46] *Texas Pacific Coal and Oil Co v. Comanche Duke Oil Co.*, 274 S.W. 193 at 194 (Tex. Civ. App. 1925), cited in Kellam 1960: 10. This judgment was reversed on appeal.

[47] 216 Pa. 362, at 365, 63 A. 801, at 802.

or his more eminent brethren on the Supreme Court of Pennsylvania ("our highest court").[48] That invitation was taken up in the work that brought the issue out of the specialized spheres of discourse of lawyers and engineers and put it firmly in the public domain: Samuel Pettengill's book *Smoke Screen*, published in 1940. Pettengill, a former congressman from Indiana who had served on a congressional subcommittee examining possible federal oil legislation, had already written a popular book on the problems of overproduction, *Hot Oil* (1936), including a clear exposition of the rule of capture and its effects.[49] *Smoke Screen* was something different, a violent diatribe against the activities of federal government in the United States. Pettengill's targets were government extravagance and over-regulation, but in the middle of his book, he suddenly introduced an accusation of government inaction and neglect. In his words:

> It is probable that no decision by any court in the world's history, unless by some international tribunal, was ever so costly as the one which first legalized the "rule of capture" and set a precedent which other courts followed like sheep. ... The decision forced the industry to be wasteful. It compelled every surface owner over an oil and gas pool to drill, regardless of price or market demand, in order to prevent his neighbor from draining his reserves.[50]

The failure of legislatures to correct this situation meant that government was entirely responsible for the remarkable waste of the nation's petroleum resources. Coming from a member of a committee that had effectively shelved a proposal for corrective federal legislation, this was pretty rich, but Pettengill's book, the highest-selling nonfiction title of its year, was obviously effective in spreading the notion of an industry grimly laboring under the yoke of an ill-adapted legal regime imposed by ignorant judges. His analysis has been echoed many times in accounts of the early days of the industry, which assume a short period of uncertainty about property rights in oil before the courts plucked from the air a fanciful analogy with wild animals and set the industry ineluctably on its wasteful course. In popular[51] and specialized[52] histories, in economic analysis,[53] in

---

[48] The report of the *Barnard* case is frequently but erroneously read as recording an opinion of the Supreme Court of Pennsylvania: Hardwicke 1935: 396–7; Pierce 1983: 1; Weaver 1986: 376, n. 25; Richards, Mitchell et al. 1994: 2; Kramer and Anderson 2005: 920. In fact, the state supreme court, on appeal, simply sustained McIlvaine's judgment without offering any opinion of its own. This error leads Kramer and Anderson to identify "our highest court" as the U.S. Supreme Court.

[49] Pettengill 1936: 72–89.

[50] Pettengill 1940: 96.

[51] O'Connor 1955: 45–6.

[52] Hughes 1993: 5–6.

[53] Zimmermann 1957: 96.

technical papers,[54] and in a vast legal literature,[55] we find this set of assumptions about how the rule of capture came to regulate the operations of the U.S. oil industry.

In the next two Chapters, I explore whether these assumptions are correct. To do this, it is important to look in detail at what these cases did and did not say, at the existing rules of law that might have determined how the judges approached these new and difficult questions, and at whether there were any plausible alternatives to the conclusions they reached. To some extent, this is a matter of formal analysis of caselaw, and nonlawyer readers may be excused for skipping to the conclusions at the end of Chapter 2, where its results are presented and I argue that the early judges were neither as superficial nor as opportunistic in their reasoning as they have been painted. What this legal analysis cannot explain, however, is an awkward lacuna in the "blame the judges" story: the 27 years that elapsed between the drilling of the first commercial oil well near Titusville, Pennsylvania, by "Colonel" Edwin Drake in 1859 and the first time an American court referred to nonliability for drainage of oil and gas from a neighbor's land as a rule of law in 1886. To explain this suspicious gap in the curriculum vitae of the rule of capture, we need to go behind the formal legal utterances of the courts and investigate the views held by people in the industry in those early years about their property rights concerning the substances they were seeking. That is the subject of Chapter 3.

---

[54] Umpleby 1933: 302.
[55] See the extensive list of sources cited by Smith 2004: 1028–9; Craft 1996: 698.

CHAPTER 2

THE LEADING CASES AND THEIR LEGAL BACKGROUND

JUDICIAL POWER AND THE COURT-LAWYER DIALOGUE

Before getting down to cases, it is useful to recall the general principles according to which the law may be declared and developed by judges in the United States and other jurisdictions. Courts, notably the highest appeals courts, are powerful actors in common-law legal systems like those of the United States. By their decisions, they can change the law or adapt it to new circumstances. Many of the most important legal rules and principles in such systems are to be found not in codes or laws enacted by the legislature, but in "unwritten" rules distilled from consistent patterns of judicial decision in cases with relevantly similar facts. Such cases have the status of precedents, and the rules or principles they embody are binding on courts trying similar later cases.

At least, this is true for courts at lower, and usually also equal, levels of superiority in the judicial hierarchy of trial courts and courts of appeals. Courts at higher levels than those whose decisions have produced a rule have the power to modify that rule in a later case that reaches them, or to refuse to apply it in circumstances to which they do not think it appropriate. And to ensure that the development of common-law rules does not become blocked, the highest courts in common-law systems also assert the power to depart from their own previous decisions if they consider them to be wrong or outdated. In common-law systems, judges may also shape and effectively modify the law by changing the interpretations they give of key pieces of legislation and, most important of all, of provisions of the constitution, written or unwritten. It is the existence of this last power that gives the appointment of Supreme Court justices such profound political significance in the United States and has made that court, over certain periods in American history, a key actor in shaping the economic development of the country. Similar developmental and interpretive capacities inhere in the supreme courts of the fifty states.

Civil law systems think differently about the judicial function. They deny—at least in principle—that the judge can make or modify the law; the judge is seen simply as the functionary applying the law to be found in the codes and statutes.[1] In practice, the difference between the two types of system is much less clear, as evidenced by the fact that the judicial hierarchy in civil law systems is topped by a supreme court of appeals recognized as having the authority to provide authoritative interpretation of legal texts and quash ("*casser*" in French, "*cassare*" in Italian) any decision of a lower court based on an incorrect interpretation—whence the title of Cour de Cassation in France, Corte di Cassazione in Italy, and so on. Moreover, France has one extremely important court that operates on the common-law system of building the law through judicial precedent: this is the court competent in administrative law matters, the Conseil d'État.[2]

Despite these judicial powers to modify and develop the law to meet new challenges and circumstances, it would be a mistake to try to explain the way the law has treated capture simply by exploring the thoughts and decisions of judges. Courts cannot choose what cases are put before them and what points of law they are going to address. At most, some senior or supreme courts, such as that of the United States, may possess discretion as to whether they will receive an appeal from a lower court, and the importance of the point of law involved may be a factor in how this discretion is exercised. Even this discretion, familiar in English-language jurisdictions inspired by the common law, is regarded in civil law countries as an unacceptable derogation from the principle of equal access to justice. The exercise of this power to refuse a case normally reflects the view that it is not appropriate to reexamine an existing rule. Where, in contrast, a court is not happy about a rule it is called upon to apply, the best it can do is to signal its dissatisfaction in the hope

---

[1] David 1982: 132–6.

[2] The Conseil d'État (and its predecessor, the Conseil du Roi) have been frequently appealed to in struggles over rights to sources of mineral water in France: see below, Ch. 4, at 98–9, 111–12, 114.

that a higher court may be able and willing to modify it on appeal or in a future decision or, if not, that the legislature may intervene.[3]

Another recipient of such signals is the professional bar: the lawyers who, in advising clients on possible future litigation, may read such remarks as relevant to their chances of success, even in the face of apparently unfavorable legal rules. An even stronger pointer is offered by cases in which one or more judges dissented or where a lower court—especially a lower-level appellate court—provided a reasoned opinion that was overturned at a higher level. Such dissents and opinions may provide material for later argument by resourceful counsel. Thus, they may form a crucial link in a process of legal change and development, because it is lawyers and their clients who decide what cases later courts are going to get. To form a true picture of the beginnings of capture, therefore, we need to understand not just the reasoning of the judges, but the practices and beliefs of the participants in the industry and of the lawyers who advised them, which is the subject of the next chapter.

THE FIRST DECISIONS

Westmoreland & Cambria Natural Gas Co. v. De Witt

The modern consensus among legal scholars is that the leading case on the rule of capture is the decision of the Supreme Court of Pennsylvania in *Westmoreland & Cambria Natural Gas Co. v. De Witt*, delivered on November 11, 1889,[4] just over 30 years after Edwin Drake drilled his famous well. Earl Oliver's 1926 broadside[5] was directed against the 1875 opinion of Chief Justice Agnew in the case of *Brown v. Vandergrift*, but this was clearly a false starting point. Agnew was deciding a familiar type of case, one in which the owner of land was seeking to cancel an oil and gas lease because the lessee had taken no steps to explore or develop the property. Seeing development going on all around him, an owner in this position would want to re-lease his land to a more active operator. Agnew introduced his opinion with some rather confused remarks about the oil industry, designed to show why prompt development was a crucial matter for landowners, so as to justify the use of a remedy—cancellation of the lease—that courts might in ordinary landlord-tenant cases be reluctant to employ. In beginning by referring to oil's

---

[3] As, perhaps, Judge McIlvaine was doing in his opinion in *Barnard v. Monongahela Natural Gas Co.*, above, Ch. 1, at 15; unsuccessfully, as the Supreme Court affirmed his decision without an opinion of its own.

[4] 130 Pa. 235, 18 A. 724; see Kramer and Anderson 2005: 906.

[5] Above, Ch. 1, at 13.

"fugitive and wandering existence within the limits of a particular tract," he may have intended simply to draw attention to the fact that finding oil was a highly uncertain business. He certainly made no allusion to any passage of oil from one owner's tract to another's, but the fact that his phrase was picked up and repeated in the *Westmoreland* judgment has led even the U.S. Supreme Court to assume that he did.[6]

An unpublished 1941 study by James Veasey[7] noted that *Westmoreland* had been referred to by later courts no less than 91 times, a number exceeded only, in the field of oil and gas law, by *Ohio Oil Co. v. Indiana*,[8] the Supreme Court decision that recognized the doctrine of correlative rights and paved the way for the development of oil and gas conservation legislation. Despite its dominant position among the citations, *Westmoreland* is actually one of a cluster of six cases, from four different states, in which the issue of capture was raised between 1886 and 1897. Among these, it was *not* the first to be decided and, unlike several of the others, did *not* directly raise an issue as to rights as between different landowners or their lessees. Its selection as *the* leading case doubtless owes more to the clarity and simplicity of the language used by the court than to any other factor. A look at the facts will explain how the court came to pronounce on the rule of capture and what significance we should attach to its words, after which we can examine the other decisions.

The case arose out of a dispute concerning an oil and gas lease granted to the Westmoreland and Cambria Company by one Brown, presumably the landowner, and came to the Supreme Court of Pennsylvania from the Court of Common Pleas of Westmoreland County, just east of Pittsburgh. This was not part of the so-called Oil Region, where the first discoveries were made in 1859 and immediately thereafter, but lay at the southern end of the "Lower Region" centered on Butler County, where serious and successful development only began in the early 1870s.

The company, as lessees, came to the court to ask that the defendants be restrained from drilling a gas well on the land covered by their lease. De Witt and his colleagues were apparently oilmen to whom Brown had granted a second lease, asserting that the company's lease had been forfeited because of failure to make certain payments at the time envisaged by the lease. The lease required the company to drill a gas well, and it had done so. It was not drawing any gas from the well, but was holding it in reserve. Had this been an oil well, such action could have been prejudicial to the lessor, because it would deprive him of the royalties calculated on actual production, but the lease, as was common at this time,

---

[6] *Brown v. Spilman*, 155 U.S. 665 (1895), at 670.

[7] Veasey 1941: 18.

[8] 177 U.S. 190 (1900), discussed below, Ch. 7, at 181–4.

provided for a fixed rental for gas wells, payable whether they were producing or not. If the case had simply involved interpretation of the payment provisions of the lease, it would not have distinguished itself from large numbers of others on lease payments, such as *Brown v. Vandergrift,* and the *Westmoreland* court in fact treated Brown's contentions about payments as quite without merit. But Brown and the other defendants also raised a highly technical point about the availability of the particular remedy of injunction—an order specifically forbidding the defendants to continue their activities—sought by the company, on the ground that such a remedy was not available to a party that was not in possession of "the premises and rights granted in the lease."

The supreme court held that what was relevant in this case was the possession of the gas or oil contained in, or obtainable through, the land, and that the company, as lessee, clearly held such possession.

> They had put down a well, which had tapped the gas-bearing strata, and it was the only one on the land. They had it in their control, for they had only to turn a valve to have it flow into their pipe, ready for use. ... Brown had no possession of the gas at all. His possession of the soil for purposes of tillage, etc. gave him no actual possession of the gas; and he had no legal possession, for his lease had conveyed that to another.[9]

This conclusion looks obvious once the first step as to the proper object of possession is taken, but to get to it, the court felt it necessary to take a crucial detour in order to address a finding made in proceedings in a lower court that gas, being a mineral, was part of the land while in place, and therefore possession of the land must be possession of the gas. The detour went like this:

> Gas, it is true, is a mineral; but it is a mineral with peculiar attributes, which require the application of precedents arising out of ordinary mineral rights, with much more careful consideration of the principles involved than of the mere decisions. Water also is a mineral: but the decisions in ordinary case of mining rights, etc. have never been held as unqualified precedents in regard to flowing, or even to percolating, waters. Water and oil, and still more strongly gas, may be classed by themselves, if the analogy is not too fanciful, as minerals *ferae naturae.* In common with animals, and unlike other minerals, they have the power and the tendency to escape without the volition of the owner. Their "fugitive and wandering existence within the limits of a particular tract was uncertain," as said by Chief Justice Agnew in *Brown v. Vandergrift,* 80 Pa. St. 147, 148. They belong to the owner of the land, and are part of it, so long as they are on or in it, and are subject to his control; but when they escape, and go into other land, or come under another's control, the title of the

---

[9] 130 Pa. 235 at 250, 18 A. 724 at 725.

former owner is gone. Possession of the land, therefore, is not necessarily possession of the gas. If an adjoining, or even a distant, owner, drills his own land, and taps your gas, so that it comes into his well and under his control, it is no longer yours, but his. And equally so as between lessor and lessee in the present case, the one who controls the gas—has it in his grasp, so to speak—is the one who has possession in the legal as well as in the ordinary sense of the word.[10]

Here, then, is the commonly accepted source both for the common-law principle of the rule of capture, in its application to oil and gas, and for the analogy with wild animals for which courts have been so castigated by later commentators. But a careful reading of the passage must lead to doubt about whether the court's expression both of the principle and of the analogy can sustain the accolade of originality later courts and scholars have conferred. One is struck by the almost offhand manner in which the crucial sentence "[i]f an adjoining, or even a distant, owner, drills his own land, and taps your gas, so that it comes into his well and under his control, it is no longer yours, but his" is introduced. It is not the conclusion of the argument, which remains fixed firmly on rights as between lessor and lessee, but a mere step in the reasoning toward it, and one that the court saw as requiring no support by way of precedent, or even of argument, beyond the fact of the fugacious character of oil, gas, and for that matter water as well. If this principle, that ownership of oil and gas in the ground could be lost by reason of the activities of others on their own land, had been in any way contested or controversial in 1889, it hardly seems likely that the supreme court of the then principal oil-producing state would have treated it so casually.

Wood County Petroleum Co. v. West Virginia Transportation Co.

Although rights as between adjoining landowners were not at issue, the quoted passage in *Westmoreland* had the features that make for "leading case" status: a clear and pithy statement of a rule that later judges could conveniently quote and a picturesque analogy for law professors and their students to chew on. Yet *Westmoreland* was anticipated by three years by the decision of the Supreme Court of Appeals of West Virginia in *Wood County Petroleum Co. v. West Virginia Transportation Co.* in 1886,[11] another lessor–lessee case relating to gas. Here the lease was expressed to be "for the sole purpose of excavating for rock or carbon oil." The lessee, the Transportation Company, drilled a well that produced a small amount of oil, on which it duly paid royalty, and large amounts of gas. Because the

---

[10] *Ibid.*
[11] 28 W Va. 210.

lease did not cover gas, the lessee claimed to be able to take the gas for itself without any accounting for the proceeds to the lessor. The lessor, however, like the lessor in *Westmoreland*, argued that the gas must be his as being part of his land, so that any taking by the lessee must be unlawful. Gas was of increasing economic interest in Wood County at this time, as pipeline networks to supply major cities like Pittsburgh expanded.

This is how the West Virginia court approached the issue:

> While the grant is for the specific purpose of mining for and removing rock or carbon oil, and for none other, still there is necessarily included in this grant all the incidents essential or naturally pertaining to its enjoyment. Included in these are the elements, such as air, light and water. And having the legal right to enter upon and occupy any portion of the premises, the appellant [lessee] could, without becoming a trespasser or incurring any liability to the lessors, use and appropriate anything it might find thereon which is not the property of another, such as animals *ferae naturae*, or waters percolating through the land, even though by such use and appropriation it may deprive another, having an equal right, of the power to do so. These are not the subjects of absolute property and therefore, by the *jurae naturae*, being capable of a qualified ownership only, they belong to him who first appropriates them. ... If the hydro-carbon or natural gas, now in controversy, belongs to the class of things which are incapable of being absolute property, but the subject of qualified property only such as those above mentioned, then it is clear that this gas was not the property of the plaintiff [lessor], and the appellant is not liable for its use and appropriation; but if on the other hand said gas is susceptible of absolute ownership, then it is part of the realty of the plaintiff to which the appellant acquired no right under the said lease, and it is therefore liable to the plaintiff for the value of the same. The important and decisive inquiry in this cause is, therefore, to which category does hydro-carbon gas belong?[12]

For an answer to this question, the court turned to the *Encyclopedia Britannica*, quoting at length from its article on "Gas and Gas Lighting" referring to various occurrences of long-continuing flows of natural gas, from places as far apart as Baku in Russia, Szechuan in China, and neighboring Ohio. From this and more local information, the court drew the conclusion that natural gas "partakes more nearly of the character of air and water than it does of those things which are the subject of absolute property." Part of that character was volatility: "Like water percolating beneath the surface, [natural gas] may, by sinking a well or otherwise, be appropriated for the use of one person on his farm, while the supply may come from an adjoining or many distant farms."

---

[12] *Ibid.* at 215–16.

The right of appropriation of such underground water, the court noted, was absolute, even if the effect should be to drain a neighbor's well. So because the gas was emerging naturally in the course of a lawful operation to get oil (indeed a necessary operation, for if the lessees failed to drill and operate wells, their lease might be forfeited), they had every right to take and use it as they might use the air and water on the property.

This was a much more carefully reasoned decision than that in *Westmoreland*, and it is unfortunate that an unnecessary, if guarded, reference by the court to the possibility that the gas might be "inexhaustible" made its decision the subject of early criticism[13] and has caused it to be remembered chiefly as an example of judicial misapprehension of the nature of hydrocarbons,[14] rather than as the first case in which the analogy between petroleum and water (and more fleetingly, wild animals) was examined with any care and against a background of principle. As with *Westmoreland*, it is notable that the court treated capture by neighbors more as a fact of life than as a principle to be established; it was the lessor–lessee relationship that introduced awkward complications.

THE EARLY NINETIES: VARIATIONS ON A THEME

Acheson v. Stevenson

Curiously, it was only after courts recognized the principle of capture in these lessor–lessee cases that litigation in which neighbors sought to deny the principle started reaching the highest courts of the oil-producing states. In a quartet of decisions in the 1890s, the highest courts of Pennsylvania, Indiana, and Ohio were unanimous in applying the rule of capture to deny relief to landowners or lessees who complained that oil or gas had been drawn from beneath their land. The earliest of these cases, decided like *Westmoreland* by the Supreme Court of Pennsylvania, appears to have been largely neglected by twentieth-century commentators, despite having been the first case anywhere in which the rule of capture was essential to the decision the court reached.

This was the case of *Acheson v. Stevenson*, decided on January 4, 1892.[15] As part of a scheme for dividing land he owned in the town of Franklin, Washington County, into building lots, a Mr. Acheson sold a plot to a Mrs. Effie Schmitz, the conveyance stating that this was "[w]ithout ... the right to drill or mine for

---

[13] See Bryan 1898: 60–63. Bryan's treatise, the first specifically devoted to oil and gas law, is largely a compilation of authorities, in which critical comment is rare.

[14] Merrill 1930: 403. Woodward, however, deals with the property aspect of the case: 1965: 355.

[15] 145 Pa. 228.

petroleum, rock oil, carbon oil, or natural gas, which right is not intended to be conveyed, but is forbidden to both parties." Mrs. Schmitz, however, allowed the defendants to come onto her lot and start drilling a well, where they struck oil. Meanwhile, Acheson had granted an oil lease on nearby land of his, not forming part of his town development scheme, where the lessees had drilled a substantial producing well. Acheson went to court and sought both a permanent prohibition of any drilling on Mrs. Schmitz's land and damages for the unlawful taking of the oil recovered by the defendants. He claimed in court that the purpose of the restriction in his conveyance to Mrs. Schmitz was to protect his land from drainage, and that she knew this; but it was found as fact that she did not. Moreover, the clause was construed as a restriction on enjoyment, rather than a reservation of the oil and gas in Acheson's favor, so that any oil under the land belonged to Mrs. Schmitz (though it was unlawful for her to get it), not to Acheson. On the basis of these findings, the supreme court affirmed the decision of Judge McIlvaine, who had rejected Acheson's claim to damages, holding:

> He [Acheson] is not entitled to the oil drained from his other lands, for the master[16] has found that the purpose of the restriction in Mrs Schmitz' deed was not for the purpose of protecting these lands from drainage by a well on this lot. Oil is a mineral *ferae naturae*, and is part of the land and belongs to its owner only so long as it is in the land and under his control; and as soon as the oil left the land of the plaintiff and flowed on or into the lot of Mrs. Schmitz, it belonged to her, unless some contract or covenant existed between the plaintiff and her by which this rule of property in oil *in situ* was inoperative. The master has found that there was no such contract between them. We must therefore conclude that the plaintiff is not entitled to damages for the oil taken out of the Schmitz well or any part of it.[17]

Acheson did, however, get his permanent injunction prohibiting drilling, but on the basis that this was necessary if the residential value of the lots was to be sustained. Presumably this means that if Mrs. Schmitz's property had not been a town lot, the plaintiff would have been left without remedy notwithstanding capture in clear contravention of the terms of sale. Again, the fact that the court could arrive at such a conclusion without the aid of any authoritative precedent—it did not even cite its own decision in *Westmoreland*—suggests that the notion of capture was not novel, but pretty deeply ingrained.

---

[16] A master is an official appointed in litigation to make findings of fact on technical issues.
[17] 145 Pa. 228 at 238.

Tyner v. People's Gas Co.

Later in the same year, the Supreme Court of Indiana decided cases arising out of the activities of the People's Gas Company in drilling a gas well in the center of the town of Greenfield. The flow being inadequate, the company prepared to "shoot" the well, a familiar but highly dangerous procedure in the early oil industry, involving the explosion of a quantity of nitroglycerin at the foot of the wellbore in order to fracture the petroleum-bearing sands and improve the flow. Among the objectors to this procedure was the plaintiff, Mr. Tyner, who owned the house across the street from the well site. Tyner was successful in obtaining an injunction to prevent the accumulation of nitroglycerin on the site, on the ground that this was a private nuisance, interfering with the comfortable enjoyment of life or property. As the court put it, "To live in constant apprehension of death from the explosion of nitroglycerine is certainly an interference with the comfortable enjoyment of life."[18] He failed, however, to convince the court that an earlier act of "shooting" a well by the company, in September 1889, had caused him actionable damage by creating underground fissures through which gas under his property had flowed to their well. The court, after reviewing authorities on water and citing the core passage from the *Westmoreland* case, held that once the basic rule of capture was accepted, no valid reason could be given why the company might not enlarge its well by the explosion of nitroglycerin therein for the purpose of increasing the flow.[19] The plaintiff's counsel had in fact already admitted, in argument, the applicability of the rule of capture in the absence of such "improvements" to the well—an unlikely concession, again, if the rule had been a recent innovation.

Hague v. Wheeler

In *Hague v. Wheeler*[20] the Supreme Court of Pennsylvania returned to the issue of capture. As in both the *Acheson* and *Tyner* cases, there was an element aggravating the act of capture—in this case, waste. The court held that Hague and the other plaintiffs, who were producing gas from their lease, could not restrain the defendants from draining that lease through an open gas well on their own land, even though they were allowing the gas from that well to escape into the air and making no profitable use of it. The court (which again did not cite its own opinion in *Westmoreland*) explicitly rejected any restriction of the defendants'

---

[18] *Tyner v. People's Gas Co.*, 131 Ind. 408, at 412, 31 N.E. 61, at 62 (1892).

[19] *People's Gas Co. v. Tyner*, 131 Ind. 277, 31 N.E. 59 (1892).

[20] 157 Pa. 324, 27 A. 714 (1893); and see further below, at 40–1.

rights derived from ideas of malice or correlative rights in a common resource, which had been adopted—from the developing law of subterranean waters—in a learned judgment by the court below.

Kelley v. Ohio Oil Co.

Given that these cases had shown that the courts of Pennsylvania and Indiana would tolerate capture, even when "aggravated" by illegality, wastage, or the use of high explosives, it is not surprising that the plaintiff in *Kelley v. Ohio Oil Co.*[21] should, in 1897, have had his claim brusquely rejected by the Supreme Court of Ohio. His complaint was simply one of drainage, of the oil to which he was entitled as a lessee, by lessees of adjoining lands who had drilled wells at 400-foot intervals only 25 feet from the boundary line of the two properties. At one point in the proceedings, he based his claim on an alleged custom of oil operators, when operating adjoining lands, to locate their wells at least 200 feet from the boundary so that drainage from one property to another should not occur—a bold approach, as it directly contradicted a finding as to industry practice of the Ohio Circuit Court in a different case just decided between the same parties, *Ohio Oil Co. v. Kelley*, in 1895.[22] There the custom recognized by the court was "that in order to protect the oil under the premises operated, it was absolutely essential to drill wells close to the boundary lines of the immediate adjoining lands, especially in case the operators of said adjoining lands drill wells close to said boundary lines."

In his own litigation, Kelley's claims about custom were perhaps based on the announced policy of his opponents, at that time the largest oil producer in Ohio, "to avoid the pursuit of that ancient folly of protecting the lines, and to limit the drilling to a large number of acres to the well."[23] It did him no good in the trial court, and he appears to have abandoned the argument at the appeal stage—his counsel's argument makes no mention of it.

On appeal, the supreme court, ignoring other plausible arguments by Kelley's counsel, which I examine later, asked itself simply whether the defendant lessees had the right to drill these wells and answered that "whatever gets into a well belongs to the owner of the well, no matter where it came from. ... The right to drill and produce oil on one's own land is absolute, and cannot be supervised by a court or an adjoining landowner." The possibility of drainage, by wells at any particular distance from a boundary, was too uncertain to be allowed to interfere with "the well-known right which every man has to use his property as he pleases,

---

[21] 57 Ohio St. 317, 49 N.E. 399.

[22] (1895) 9 Ohio C.C.R. 511.

[23] *Petroleum Age* (October 1887): 1756, quoted in Williamson and Daum 1959: 593.

as long as he does not interfere with the legal rights of others," and the drilling of wells on both sides of property lines afforded an ample and sufficient remedy for the supposed grievances complained of. The practice of offset drilling, already well established in leasing practice,[24] thus received its judicial imprimatur.

Kelley's is the only nineteenth-century case in which a landowner or lessee directly attacked the rule of capture by arguing that drainage by ordinary drilling operations on a neighbor's land was an actionable wrong. *Wood County* and *Westmoreland*, as we have seen, were not disputes between neighbors; *Acheson* involved drilling that was unlawful for other reasons; *Tyner* admitted the principle of capture; and *Hague* was based on a claim of unreasonable use by pure waste of gas. The brevity and brutality with which the court dismissed Kelley's case ensured that—so far as I have been able to discover—a claim that ordinary drainage of oil and gas was unlawful would never again be raised in a U.S. court.

THE LEGAL BACKGROUND

The Nature of Property in Oil and Gas

With the exception of the West Virginia court in the *Wood County* case, the judges who issued these decisions were remarkably unforthcoming on the subject of the legal rules and precedents that led them to decide as they did and assert or assume the existence of a rule of capture. The judges were not, however, moving in totally uncharted territory. By the mid-1880s, there had been plenty of litigation on oil and gas matters, particularly in Pennsylvania. Courts had already had to confront the difficulties of dealing with a valuable new substance of an unfamiliar type. None of these cases had directly raised the issue of drainage from one property to another, but several had already presented the question of what kind of rights in oil were held either by the owner of the land under which it lay or the oil producer with whom he or she had concluded an agreement to find and exploit it.

The crucial question, it soon appeared, was whether the title to oil and gas in the ground was a true ownership of a part of the land, like that relating to hard rock minerals, or was simply a right to get, and thereby acquire ownership of, any oil or gas that might lie under the property at a given time—a position sometimes described as "no ownership" and sometimes as "qualified ownership."[25] Classifying the rights of the landowner in this way was important in a wide range

---

[24] Below, Ch. 3, at 76–7.

[25] For early discussions on ownership theory, see Adams 1915; Summers 1919; Simonton 1921; Veasey 1920a; Greer 1923; and for a recent survey, Bennett 2001.

of situations, such as whether guardians of orphans as administrators of their interests, persons holding only a life interest in land, or married women were entitled to grant oil and gas leases; on what basis the oil and gas interest in land should be taxed; or whether and how the oil and gas interest could be separated from other interests in the land. It was also important as part of the basis on which to determine what rights had been granted by landowners to persons exploring for and exploiting oil and gas, and what remedies might be available to such persons who suffered dispossession or invasion of their interests; many of the early Pennsylvania cases discussed in the first oil and gas law treatise, by George Bryan, are concerned with this kind of issue.[26]

The hesitations of the judges on these points are well illustrated by the first Pennsylvania cases. We find Justice Woodward of the Supreme Court of Pennsylvania declaring, in the first reported case in that court after the oil rush started, that petroleum "is part of the land. It is land,"[27] and repeating this position a few years later, now as chief justice, when giving judgment for the supreme court in *Funk v. Haldeman*,[28] saying "[t]hroughout this opinion I have treated oil as a mineral. ... If a mineral, it is part of the land"—which would mean that in its natural state, it was in the ownership and possession of the landowner. But 10 days later, the same court, speaking this time through Justice Strong, opined that "[o]il is a fluid, like water; it is not the subject of property except while in actual occupancy,"[29] which would mean that the landowner needed to appropriate it in some way in order to perfect his or her title to it. Despite this difference of starting points, the court held in both cases that the landowner's grant to an oil and gas operator did not confer any rights in the substances themselves, but was merely an "incorporeal" right; certain remedies that would have been available to a possessor of land could not, therefore, be obtained by the operator. This conclusion clearly troubled Chief Justice Woodward, however: "a right to take land, or any part of land, is not, strictly speaking, an incorporeal hereditament."[30]

Eventually the supreme court, in *Stoughton's Appeal* (1878), came down in favor of the idea of full ownership of oil in the ground. Citing *Funk v. Haldeman*, it held that oil "being a mineral is part of the realty. ... In this it is like coal or any other natural product which *in situ* forms part of the land,"[31] and characterized the lease

---

[26] Bryan 1898: Ch. II.

[27] *Kier v. Peterson*, 41 Pa. 357 (1862).

[28] 53 Pa. 229, at 245–6 (1867).

[29] *Dark v. Johnston*, 55 Pa. 164 (1867).

[30] 53 Pa. 229, at 249.

[31] 88 Pa. 198, at 201. The courts tended to find that oil was owned as part of the land where this was necessary to protect parties with future interests in the land, such as those who would inherit when the current occupant died.

at the center of the litigation as an outright sale of the oil and gas subject to a royalty. Given that these findings had not been contradicted or doubted at any time before the *Westmoreland* case came on, the reasoning in that case is puzzling, to say the least. In response to the view of the lower court that the surface owner must be in possession of the gas because it was "part of the land," the court need have done no more than apply the *Stoughton* finding that the lease represented an outright sale to the lessee of any gas in the ground. Instead, it followed *Stoughton* to the point of saying that gas and similar minerals "belong to the owner of the land, and are part of it"—words that suggest a doctrine of absolute ownership—and then reversed direction in midsentence by declaring that this was only "so long as they are on or in it and are subject to his control," which displaces any notion of ownership in favor of one based on possession. One might have thought that the announcement of two mutually inconsistent views of the nature of property in a substance in the space of a single sentence would appear as the terminus of a subtle chain of reasoning, rather than being supported only by the passing allusions to water and animals offered by the court.

Some other courts, like the West Virginia Supreme Court of Appeals in *Wood County*, avoided this self-contradictory position by the simple holding that oil and gas were not the subject of ownership until recovered. The person who first reduced them to possession, whether as the lessee of the surface owner or, for that matter, the owner or lessee of a neighboring property, thus acquired good title. A number of other states, notably New York, Indiana, and Oklahoma,[32] later adopted this position, which was likewise favored, by reason of its greater coherence, by most of the early academic commentators on oil and gas law.[33]

In law, however, elegance does not always win out over practicality. Despite the critiques of people like Professor Summers,[34] and the unfraternal ridicule to which judges in Indiana later subjected the reasoning of their Pennsylvania colleagues, saying that it was "no less absurd . . . than to say that . . . fish, in their passage up or down a stream of water, become the property of each successive owner over whose land the stream passes,"[35] other state courts followed the Pennsylvania precedent and proclaimed that the rule of capture could somehow coexist with full ownership of oil and gas in place. Generally they did not trouble themselves to explain how this result could come about: thus the Ohio Supreme Court, in *Kelley v. Ohio Oil Co.*, was content to affirm that "[p]etroleum oil is a mineral, and while in the earth

---

[32] *Shepherd v. McCalmont Oil Co.*, 38 Hun. 37 (N.Y. App. Div. 1885), *State v. Ohio Oil Co.*, 150 Ind. 21, 49 N.E. 809 (1898), *Rich v. Doneghey*, 71 Okla. 204, 177 P. 86 (1918).

[33] Adams 1915; Summers 1919; Simonton 1921; Greer 1923. Compare Veasey 1920a.

[34] Above, at 14.

[35] *State v. Ohio Oil Co.*, 150 Ind. at 32, 49 N.E. 809 at 812.

it is part of the realty, and, should it move from place to place by percolation or otherwise, it forms part of that tract in which it tarries for the time being..."

An attempt at a reasoned reconciliation between the rule of capture and the idea that oil could be subject to "absolute ownership" was eventually offered by the courts of Texas. In *Texas Co. v. Daugherty*,[36] where the liability to taxation of an oil lessee depended on whether the lessee had an interest in land, the court sought to relate the two notions in this way:

> A purchaser of [oil and gas] within the ground assumes the hazard of their absence through the possibility of their escape from beneath that particular tract of land, and of course, if they are not discovered the conveyance is of no effect; just as the purchaser of solid minerals within the ground assumes the risk of its absence and therefore a futile venture. But let it be supposed that they have not escaped, and are in repose within the strata beneath the particular tract, and are capable of possession by appropriation from it. There they clearly constitute a part of the realty. Is the possibility of their escape to render them while in place incapable of conveyance, or is their ownership while in that condition, with the exclusive right to take them from the land, anything less than ownership of an interest in the land?

The court's implication that the answer had to be "no" ignored the problem of how you could have full ownership—or indeed, any meaningful ownership at all—of a thing that someone else could take away from you with impunity. But the decision was convenient in simplifying conveyancing and was generally followed in Texas.[37] Many other states continue to apply a similar approach. Verbally, the circle was squared by calling the oil and gas property right a "defeasible" ownership, meaning that you had all the rights of an absolute owner to the oil and gas that was under your land—until it no longer was.

Judicial Analogies: Wild Animals

There must have been some compelling reason for these nineteenth-century American courts to depart either completely, as did those of West Virginia and Indiana, or confusedly and halfheartedly, as did those of Pennsylvania and Ohio, from well-tried principles of the law of mineral property. The ostensible causes were found by those courts in arguments by analogy with other things. While the

---

[36] 107 Tex. 226 (1915).

[37] See *Stephens County v. Mid-Kansas Oil & Gas Co.*, 113 Tex. 160, 254 S.W. 290 (1923), usually regarded as the leading case on the point, but which offers no better explanation.

analogy with subterranean water might appear more compelling, it is that with wild animals that has attracted the greatest attention, and I deal with it first.

The traditional story would have us believe that courts applied the rule of capture to oil and gas because they thought the behavior of oil and gas resembled that of wild animals, and wild animals were subject to the rule of capture. This rendering of the reasoning in the leading cases is both coarse and inaccurate. Certainly, wild animals were subject to the rule of capture, becoming the property of whoever first took firm possession of them. Though the English law Americans brought with them as colonists reserved to the king extensive rights of property in wild animals, and even larger powers of control of hunting,[38] these rights did not survive in the radically different physical and, following independence, political environment in North America. Settlers moving west encountered a landscape teeming with wildlife of every sort. Wild animals and birds were for them not, as today, an object of sport but a nuisance, even a danger, and also an essential resource. Courts were soon led to recognize a general right to acquire property in wild animals by the simple act of capture, and to sweep aside English notions that hunting could be restricted to holders of special privileges. In this, they were doing no more than reapplying a basic principle—that property in things unowned may be acquired by whoever first takes them—that we find fully developed in Roman law.

Roman law conceived of two broad types of property: that which belonged to some particular individual (*res in patrimonium*) and that which did not (*res extra patrimonium*). This latter type of property might be state property, such as roads, ports, or public buildings (*res publicae*); property belonging to people in common—air, running water, the sea (*res communes*); or finally, the property of no one (*res nullius*). Examples of this were unoccupied lands, enemy property, and wild animals, all of which could be appropriated as the property of an individual by *occupatio*, understood as the natural means of taking firm possession of the thing in question.[39]

In the *Wood County* case, the court applied this basic principle to gas, not by comparing the physical characteristics and habits of gas to those of wild animals, but by carefully reviewing the scientific authorities on gas in the *Encyclopaedia Britannica* and establishing that it was more like air and water than like hard minerals, and therefore not a subject of absolute property but only of qualified ownership, flowing from first appropriation. The court referred to wild animals simply as a familiar object of such qualified ownership.

---

[38] Blumm and Ritchie 2005.
[39] See Buckland 1963: 205–8; Epstein 1997: 244–5.

The court in *Westmoreland*, however, did relate the behavior of wild animals more closely to that of oil and gas (and subterranean water as well), pointing out that the one and the other "have the power and the tendency to escape without the volition of the owner." If, however, it had any intention of modeling the rules for oil and gas on those for wild animals, it made a poor job of the matter. Water, oil, and gas, it said, "belong to the owner of the land, and are part of it, so long as they are on or in it, and are subject to his control; but when they escape, and go into other land, or come under another's control, the title of the former owner is gone."

I have already pointed out the incoherence of this "now you own it, now you don't" concept of oil and gas property, and if the court intended this statement to apply to wild animals too (though the reference to being "part of the land" makes this unlikely), it was certainly not a correct statement of the law as it then applied. As just noted, they belonged to no one until captured. The owner of the land on which they were found had no special claim to them. Indeed, early American law was even more liberal to the hunter than its Roman ancestor, moving rapidly in the direction of enlarging the right of capture so as to allow access for hunting even to private land that was not enclosed. This right was recognized in some early state constitutions and was asserted as "undisputed" by some state courts in the early nineteenth century. By the middle of that century, there was a general presumption that landowners who did not post notices of exclusion welcomed hunters to come onto their undeveloped land.[40] Given this strong preference for freedom to take, courts had no difficulty in holding that the hunter, not the landowner, acquired property in the animals taken.[41]

What might have happened if oil and gas law had really been developed by analogy with the law of animals can be seen from the very first reported case in the United States on property in oil and gas, *Hall v. Reed*, decided in Kentucky in 1854.[42] The oil in this case was being produced as a by-product from a salt well. Oil was being regularly encountered in salt wells long before the idea of drilling deliberately for oil occurred to anybody in America, and was generally regarded as nothing but a nuisance, needing to be separated off and usually allowed to run to waste.[43] For the court in *Hall v. Reed*, indeed, it was "a peculiar liquid not necessary nor indeed suitable for the common use of man."

This particular oil, however, seems to have been the subject of more than usual interest. Not only does it appear that the landowner had fitted his well with a pump for the specific purpose of recovering oil, but the defendants had come onto

---

[40] Blumm and Ritchie 2005: 688–90; Lund 1976: 712–14.
[41] *Geer v. Connecticut*, 161 U.S. 519 (1896).
[42] 54 Ky. 479.
[43] Williamson and Daum 1959: 14–16; Price 1947: 674–8.

his land, drawn off some oil, and taken it away, presumably with the idea of selling it for profit and with no apparent claim to be legally entitled to do so. The landowner sued to recover the oil or its value: $4.25. Even at a distance of 150 years, one is bound to admire the chutzpah and initiative of the defendants' counsel, J. F. Bell, faced with the task of justifying acts of his client that a layman might simply describe as theft. He it was who first thought up the wild animal analogy. A landowner, he said, could not get back wild animals taken on his land by a trespasser, because he had no such property in them as would enable him to do this. "[There was] no certainty that he could have used them if the trespasser had not killed them—because they were here today and might have been gone tomorrow—they were fugitive in character, not reduced to possession, and there was no certainty they ever would be."

The analogy with oil, he said, was very strong. "Oil is ever moving, ever escaping, and if the defendants had not obtained that which they put in their barrels, there is no certainty that plaintiffs would ever have gotten one drop of that which was in defendants' barrels." In consequence, while his clients might be liable in damages for the act of trespassing on the plaintiff's land, the oil they had appropriated was theirs, not his.

The court did not think this wild animal analogy worthy of mention. It concentrated instead on an alternative claim that the oil flowed in a subterranean stream, and that the law of surface streams—which would have produced a similar result—should therefore apply. That argument it also rejected on the grounds that the correct analogy was with subterranean water, and that the plaintiff landowner had effectively appropriated the oil by the digging of a well to reach a product that, like subterranean water, was "obtained and reached only by great expense and labour."[44] The court managed to face both ways on the question of whether such evidence of reduction to possession was actually necessary to the landowner's claim, as it also left open the possibility that possession could be assumed on the ground that the oil formed part of the land.[45] Nonetheless, its clear preference for a subterranean water over a wild animal analogy reflects a crucial point: that while wild animals could be captured by anyone anywhere, with no greater or more specialized investment than the purchase of a gun and cartridges, recovery of oil and gas depended on expensive operations of drilling or digging that could be lawfully undertaken only by or with the agreement of the owners of lands under which they "tarried" at any time.

---

[44] 54 Ky. 473, at 491.

[45] Barringer and Adams 1897: 31 and Vandervelde 1980: 354 assume, in my view incorrectly, that this was the only basis for the decision accepted by the court.

There is nothing to indicate that this basic difference was forgotten by the courts in later cases where wild animals were referred to as a familiar subject of a type of property right that required to be perfected by effective possession. The consistent concern of those courts was to protect the party who had undertaken the costly work of drilling for oil against an opponent—whether lessor or trespasser—who had not, and to insist on possession was the key to such protection. It is striking that when the question of capture actually arose in litigation between neighbors, in 1892 and thereafter, references to wild animals were nowhere to be found; the right to drill on, and take oil from, one's own land was apparently too obvious to require bolstering by learned allusions to qualified property rights.

Judicial Analogies: The Law of Subterranean Water

Hall v. Reed likewise prefigured the "leading cases" by addressing the similarities between oil in the ground and subterranean water. The court cited John Bouvier's *Institutes of American Law*, a work heavily influenced by the French Civil Code, for the proposition that the owner of land is entitled to all the advantages arising from it and may use a spring found upon it, like any other property, without regard to the convenience or advantage of others.[46] This rule was received from Roman law into the civil law and was, in France, incorporated into Napoleon's Civil Code in 1804.[47] For the Kentucky court, drilling a well, as opposed to just profiting from a natural spring, reinforced the possessory claim of the owner. What that court did not have to consider was the situation in which the well in question was drilled by another landowner on his or her own land, with the consequence of drying up or reducing the flow of an existing well or spring elsewhere.

This is the situation for which the *locus classicus*, cited by the West Virginia court in the *Wood County* case, was the English decision in *Acton v. Blundell*, dating from 1843.[48] Here the machinery in the plaintiff's cotton mills had for some years been driven by an underground flow of water, which was abruptly cut off when the defendant sunk pits and made drains in the course of nearby coal-mining operations on his own land. The plaintiff, referring to well-known and accepted principles relating to surface streams, invoked a natural right to the flow of the water under his land, claiming that it was his property so long as it was there. The court disagreed. Finding no previous authorities directly in point, it argued from first principles. Subterranean water was quite unlike surface streams, in that

---

[46] (1854) 54 Ky. 479, at 490, citing 2 Bouvier 173. In the second (1870) edition, this passage appears at 1 Bouvier 412.

[47] As art. 641; see further below, Ch. 4, at 96–8.

[48] (1843) 12 M. & W. 324, 152 Eng. Rep. 1223.

the water which feeds [a well] from a neighbouring soil does not flow openly in the sight of the neighbouring proprietor, but through the hidden veins of the earth beneath its surface; no man can tell what changes these underground sources have undergone in the process of time: ... again, no proprietor knows what portion of water is taken from beneath his own soil: how much he gives originally, how much he transmits only, or how much he receives.[49]

If the law of surface streams was inapplicable, policy considerations pointed strongly to denying to persons in the position of the plaintiff an absolute right to subterranean water that would enable them to restrain operations on neighboring land. If this were granted, then,

> by an act which is voluntary on his part, and which may be entirely unsuspected by his neighbour, he may impose on such neighbour the necessity of bearing a heavy expense, if the latter have erected machinery for the purpose of mining, and discovers, when too late, that the appropriation of water has already been made. Further, the advantage on one side and the detriment to the other, may bear no proportion. The well may be sunk to supply a cottage, or a drinking place for cattle, whilst the owner of the adjoining land may be prevented from winning metals and minerals of inestimable value. And lastly, there is no limit of space to which the claim of right to an underground spring can be confined; in the present case, the nearest coal pit is at the distance of half a mile from the well; it is obvious this law must equally apply if there is a distance of many miles.

Chief Justice Tindal's "masterly statement"[50] of the reasons for adopting for subterranean waters a quite different rule of property from that for the waters of surface streams has led to the frequent citation of the decision in American courts, though it was not until the decision of the highest English court, the House of Lords, in *Chasemore v. Richards* in 1859,[51] that the principle he enunciated was definitively established in English law. Indeed *Acton v. Blundell* had been anticipated by decisions of American state courts.

Among these early American cases on subterranean waters, *Greenleaf v. Francis*, decided by the Supreme Court of Massachusetts in 1836,[52] deserves special attention because of the way the behavior of the defendant in looking for water prefigured the early practice of those searching for oil. Mary Greenleaf owned a house with a well in the cellar from which good drinking water was obtained, at least until the defendant Nathaniel Francis, her next-door neighbor, dug a well in

---

[49] *per* Tindal CJ at 12 M. & W. 349, 350.

[50] Budd 1891: 241.

[51] 7 H.L.C. 349; see Getzler 2004: 302–15 for a detailed analysis.

[52] 18 Pick 117.

his own cellar, which had the effect of diverting the flow of water she (or her tenant) had previously enjoyed. Like searchers for oil in years to come, Francis dug his well as close as he possibly could, within the limits of his own property, to his neighbor's productive well—just five feet away, in fact. The court found that in the absence of any restrictive contract with the plaintiff, or specific contrary rule of law, Francis was entitled to do what he did, on the principle that "[e]very one has the liberty of doing in his own ground whatsoever he pleases, even although it should occasion to his neighbor some other sort of inconvenience," citing as authority the civil law writer Jean Domat, whose *Les Loix Civiles dans leur Ordre Naturel* (*The Civil Law in its Natural Order*) was first published in 1694.[53] The plaintiff had argued that Francis was actuated by malice, which, if proven, would have been grounds for sustaining her claim, but it was found, both in the trial court and on appeal, that Francis, having "dug his well, for the purpose of accommodating himself with water, he was not liable for so doing, even if he at the same time entertained hostility towards the plaintiff and a desire to injure her, and these feelings were thereby gratified."

It does not appear that there was any prior case law directly in point on the general issue, and this makes it all the more remarkable that Mrs. Greenleaf's counsel did not attempt to argue, as the plaintiff was to argue in *Acton v. Blundell*, that she had an absolute right to the water in her well. His proposition was, rather, that

> any person may dig a well on his own land, and if in so doing he accidentally and undesignedly drains another well, he is not answerable therefor; but he shall not be permitted to inflict this injury wilfully; and if he, first ascertaining the position of his neighbour's well, places his own in a situation calculated and designed to deprive his neighbour of his water and appropriate it to himself, he will be accountable for the whole injury he thus wilfully inflicts.

It is hardly surprising that the court should not have been tempted by a proposition that would have called, in every case, for inquiries into the state of mind of the defendant. What we should notice is that in 1836 in Massachusetts, a claim to absolute property to the water in a well or spring was not even considered arguable. Some special factor—malice, however defined; express grant; or perhaps long user—had to be present if its capture by others was to be prevented. The idea of the legitimacy of capture seems to have been generally accepted.

---

[53] The court referred to 1 Domat's Civil Law, tit. 12, § 2. The edition used may have been the second English edition of 1737. An American edition was published in 1850: Domat 1850.

Over the rest of the century, the principle enunciated in *Greenleaf v. Francis* and *Acton v. Blundell* was consistently followed almost everywhere in the United States.[54] In some states, it was reinforced by holdings that even malice would not render unlawful the capture of water from another's well or spring.[55] In Pennsylvania, the principle was adopted by the supreme court in a learned opinion in *Wheatley v. Baugh* in 1855,[56] in which the court cited not only Domat but also Justinian's *Digest* to support its propositions. The facts were almost identical to those in *Acton v. Blundell*, though here it was a tannery, not a cotton mill, whose underground water supply was cut off by mining operations. The court also offered a very strong judicial endorsement of the claims of mineral development over other private or commercial interests:

> In conducting extensive mining operations, it is in general impossible to preserve the flow of the subterranean waters through the interstices in which they have usually passed, and many springs must be necessarily destroyed in order that the proprietors of valuable minerals may enjoy their own. The public interest is greatly promoted by protecting this right, and it is just that the imperfect rights and lesser advantage should give place to that which is perfect, and infinitely the most beneficial to individuals and to the community in general.[57]

No doubt the court had in mind the coal-mining operations that were already a staple of Pennsylvania's economy, but it would be surprising if this pro-development stance did not carry over into judicial approaches to the oil industry that was to spring into being in the state just a few years later.[58]

The only state court to refuse to accept the notion of the landowner's near-absolute right to use his or her property in ways that might modify or destroy existing flows of subterranean water to others was that of New Hampshire. In *Bassett v. Salisbury Manufacturing Co.*,[59] the state's superior court argued that to assert an absolute right of abstraction of water in the interfering or developing landowner, based upon his or her ownership of that water as forming part of the soil while present there, was illogical, as it implied exactly the same restrictions on the activity of other landowners as those it was supposed to avoid imposing on the developer. Such a rule, the court said, "must lead in many cases to an interminable struggle for possession or removal of waters in the soil"[60]—a rather accurate

---

[54] Washburn 1862; Budd 1891; Huffcutt 1901; Hatch 1903.

[55] E.g., in Vermont, *Chatfield v. Wilson* (1855) 28 Vt. 49.

[56] 25 Pa. 528.

[57] *Ibid.* at 535.

[58] See generally on nineteenth-century judicial attitudes to development Hurst 1956; Horwitz 1977.

[59] (1862), 43 N.H. 569.

[60] *Ibid.* at 574.

forecast of its later effects in the oil and gas industry. Instead, the court insisted that the proper general rule was

> the rule of reasonable use—of a reasonable exercise of one's own right. The rights of each land-owner being similar, and his enjoyment dependant upon the action of the other land-owners, these rights must be valueless unless exercised with reference to each other, and are correlative. ... What, in any particular case, is a reasonable use or management, is ordinarily a mixed question of law and fact, to be submitted to the jury under the instruction of the court.[61]

Over time, as we shall see,[62] the reasoning of the New Hampshire court gradually won out in other jurisdictions over the "absolute rights" approach of *Acton v. Blundell*. By the end of the first decade of the twentieth century, it had achieved broad but not universal acceptance: Texas followed the *Acton v. Blundell* principle in 1904 and has made no judicial departure from it since.[63] But developments in relation to water appear to have had no direct influence on the evolution of judicial thinking on rights in oil and gas. In general, the water analogy has been offered, whether by counsel or by the court, as a way simply of countering the claim that oil should be treated as part of the land for purposes of determining property rights as between lessor and lessee.[64] Only in *Wood County*, where the court cited Connecticut and Kansas authorities for a rule allowing abstraction, but only so long as it was not malicious or negligent,[65] and notably in *Hague v. Wheeler* in 1893,[66] did the inquiry go beyond the qualified nature of property rights in water to investigate just what these qualifications might be.

Hague v. Wheeler was the case in which a landowner had been persuaded by the plaintiffs to drill a gas well on his land to supply them with gas additional to that produced from their own wells. When negotiations as to the terms on which this supply would be made failed, he simply allowed his gas to escape into the air, thereby draining the reservoir from which the plaintiffs' wells also drew. The lower court made extensive use of cases on rights to percolating water, noting the conflicting views adopted on whether otherwise legal abstraction of water could be vitiated by a malicious motive, and eventually adopted as authoritative a statement

---

[61] *Ibid.* at 577–8.

[62] Below, Ch. 7, at 184–90.

[63] *Houston & Texas Central Railway Co. v. East*, 98 Tex. 146, 81 S.W. 279 (1904); *Sipriano v. Great Springs Waters of America Inc.*, 1 S.W. 3d 75 (Tex. 1999), and generally Drummond et al. 2004.

[64] As in *Hall v. Reed* (by counsel); *Kier v. Peterson* (by counsel); *Dark v. Johnston* (by the court); *Westmoreland* (by the court).

[65] 28 W.Va. at 218.

[66] Above, at 27–8.

by Judge Cooley, in a learned article, that sought to reconcile them by treating as unlawful any abstraction that was not for the "lawful uses" of the landowner effecting it.[67] Finding that the fugitive nature of oil and gas made them, like water, things that, "from the[ir] nature, . . . many must enjoy together," and that the reckless waste of gas here was an injury to all with interests in the reservoir, the court found for the plaintiffs. *Bassett v. Salisbury Manufacturing Co.*, with its test of reasonable use, would have provided the court with a more direct route to its conclusion. This, however, would have made no difference on appeal. Counsel for the defendant indirectly referred to the case as an exception to the general rule, and the supreme court, without explicitly citing *Bassett*, treated the New Hampshire position in relation to water rights as anomalous and not commanding general support. As we have already noted, it robustly rejected the idea that the defendants could be restricted in any way in their disposal of the gas so long as they did not breach any rules of law or injure the property or health of others. Charles Noyes, of the Court of Common Pleas of Warren County, the judge below, thus remained the lone voice pleading for correlative rights in oil and gas until the Supreme Court adopted the notion in *Ohio Oil Co. v. Indiana* in 1900.[68]

Given that judges drew the comparison between oil and subterranean water in the very first case in which the nature of rights in oil had to be decided, *Hall v. Read*, and continued to make such comparisons in the years before *Westmoreland* was decided, it seems reasonable to treat this comparison as the one that operated effectively on their minds when they decided the first capture cases. *Acton v. Blundell* was cited in the *Wood County* judgment, and the Supreme Court of Pennsylvania in *Hague v. Wheeler* treated its counterpart cases in America as authoritative guidance. What is much less easy to assess is the influence water law may have had on practice in the oil industry in its earliest days. Oil was so closely associated with water in the experience of the earliest explorers—coloring the streams into which it seeped with a "beautiful iridescence,"[69] mixed with water as it came to the wellhead, replaced by water as production gave out—that it would be surprising if the basic principles governing subterranean water use, well established by 1859, had not also been present somewhere in the conscious or unconscious minds of those participating in the oil industry, and in the next chapter we shall inquire into this early practice and the understandings behind it.

---

[67] Cooley 1876: 63.
[68] Discussed below, Ch. 7, at 181–4.
[69] Killebrew 1877: 58.

ALTERNATIVE PRINCIPLES

The early industry critics of the courts' first capture decisions paid no heed to this well-established and seemingly apposite body of water law; they preferred to dramatize the issue of capture by invoking the fate of bison and passenger pigeons. Nor did they occupy themselves much in consideration of what, if any, alternative rules of law the courts had available for application. Were there workable rules that the courts rejected in favor of an "opportunistic" use of the rule of capture? Or was there simply no alternative?

Accounting in Equity

As it happens, there was at least one potential alternative. Justice Woodward's opinion in *Kier v. Peterson*, from which I have quoted above, indicated a line of reasoning that, if followed up, might have set the development of petroleum law on an entirely different course. That case, though decided in 1862, arose not as an incident of the brand new oil boom, but—like *Hall v. Read* a few years earlier—as a result of the production of oil as a by-product of drilling for salt. The Kier family's main business was salt well drilling, but Samuel Kier has a strong claim to be regarded as one of the founders of the American oil industry, having carried out some of the earliest activities in the commercial refining of petroleum. In this case, he and Thomas Kier had, since 1837, held a lease from Peterson for the drilling of salt wells on his land, for a royalty of one-twelfth of the salt manufactured. At a certain point, oil began to come up with the salt, and eventually the Kiers started saving this oil and turning it to profit. Peterson sued, claiming that the oil was rightfully his, as the lease gave the Kiers no rights to recover anything but salt. A decision by the District Court of Allegheny County, supported by a "learned and elaborate opinion," went in favor of the plaintiff, but was reversed by a bench of the Supreme Court of Pennsylvania which, according to the report, appeared to contain only three judges.

Justice Reed, speaking for the court, disposed of the case on the simple ground that because the oil was produced from salt wells that had been drilled lawfully, indeed as a matter of obligation, under the terms of the lease, it was the property of the lessee, not the lessor. Justice Woodward concurred in this result but on wholly incompatible reasoning. (The third judge, perhaps in bemusement, dissented from the result without giving an opinion.) As we have seen, Woodward held that oil was part of the land, and as it was not covered by the lease, it never ceased to be the property of Peterson. His position, therefore, was the exact opposite of the West Virginia court in the *Wood County* case.[70] However, the particular remedy sought

---

[70] Above, at 23–5.

by Peterson—which was a specialized remedy, called trover, for the recovery of the oil allegedly wrongfully converted by the Kiers to their own use—was unavailable. To win an action for trover, you had to be not merely the owner of the property at the time of its conversion, but also in possession of it, and this was not the case here, as the Kiers were lawfully in possession by virtue of their lease. But because the *property*—as opposed to its possession—remained with Peterson, he could still obtain compensation for the value of the oil, which was its value at the wellhead— that is, its market value less the cost of the separation and other work done on it by the Kiers. For this purpose, however, he would need to bring a quite different action, by means of a so-called bill in equity. Whether the plaintiff later took up this suggestion and tried again, we do not know.

The reasoning of Justice Woodward can be readily transposed to the ordinary situation of capture between neighboring owners or lessees. In such a situation, the act of drilling on one's own land is lawful, as was the Kiers' by reason of their lease; but its result, as occurred with the Kiers, is to produce oil which is the property of someone else—a finding based on the notion that the oil formed a part of their land. Applying this reasoning, in any state, like Pennsylvania, where oil was viewed as forming part of the land, a landowner or lessor might drill quite lawfully as long as he accounted to his neighbor for the value of any oil produced that demonstrably originated from the neighbor's land. In the event of his failure to do so, the neighbor might have the same remedy as Peterson should have sought: a bill in equity.

Pennsylvania lawyers were likely to have been aware of Woodward's judgment—oddly, though his was only a concurring opinion, it was Woodward's reasoning, not Reed's, that was summarized in the headnote in the report of the case. Why none of them sought to apply his argument in a capture case is something I shall examine in more detail in the next chapter, but we should notice here that it was only in the mid-1880s that we find courts receiving evidence on the issue, essential to the operation of Woodward's proposed remedy, of how much oil produced from a particular well might have been drained from under other properties.

Bradford Oil Co. v. Blair,[71] decided in the same year as the first judicial reference to capture in *Wood County*, was a case of a type that became very familiar: an attempt by a lessor to cancel a oil lease, or get damages for its breach, on the ground that the lessee had failed to show due diligence in developing it, allowing oil to be drained to other properties (which in this and a number of other cases were also in the hands of the same lessee). Blair's lease included an explicit covenant of diligent

---

[71] 113 Pa. 83, 4 Atl. 218 (1886).

development, and he succeeded in obtaining damages for its breach, the Supreme Court approving the lower court's instructions to the jury that

> [i]n case you find that the defendant did not use due diligence in operating plaintiff's premises you will ascertain as well as you can from the evidence how much more oil the plaintiff ought to have received than he actually did receive, and the value of it during the times when it should have been delivered to the plaintiff; and from this you will deduct the cost of producing what he ought to have received at the time and under the circumstances and with the appliances then known. . . .

There was apparently sufficient evidence to enable the jury to fix damages at $7,500. Interestingly, the lower court told the jurors that they "must not allow the plaintiff any damages for the price of oil drained or claimed to be drained from the land by reason of operations on the adjoining lands," which can be read as an expression of judicial opinion—three years before *Westmoreland*—that the lessees were doing nothing intrinsically wrong in draining the plaintiff's land by operations on their adjoining lease.

We know rather more about the evidence on which the master, as finder of fact in the case, was able in *Acheson v. Stevenson* (1892) to quantify Acheson's loss of oil by drainage at 600 barrels, valued at $732. He did this on the basis of expert oil industry testimony, to the effect that

> the drainage as a rule would be greatest in the direction of the best producing well in the immediate vicinity; . . . the distance a well will drain the surrounding territory, depends upon the pressure of the gas and the character of the oil-producing sand; that in good territory, one well is allowed to every five acres; that one well is affected by other wells one hundred and seventy five feet and more apart; and that a big well in rich producing territory, in the vicinity of another big well in the same pool, would be affected more, soon after it came in, than after the first well has failed in its production; that if time were given, one well would drain more than five acres; and that the drilling of the Schmitz well would have a tendency to drain the land of the plaintiff.[72]

Because the supreme court found that there was no liability to the plaintiff for drainage, it did not pronounce on the quality of this evidence. The previous year, in *Duffield v. Rosenzweig*,[73] part of a complex litigation in which the plaintiff struggled to find the right remedy for the assertion of his oil rights under a lease, it had been very unhappy on this score. Having recognized that in the particular circumstances of the case, the plaintiff should have a remedy for the drilling of wells within an area that might have been drained by his own wells, because those

---

[72] (1892) 145 Pa. 228, at 234–5.
[73] 144 Pa. 520, 23 A. 4.

other wells had deprived him of the gas drive necessary to their full potential production, the court reviewed extensive evidence from oil operators familiar with the area and with the local sands as to what proportion of the oil produced by those other wells could otherwise have been taken out through the plaintiff's wells. But having done so, it found that much of it was "of the most unsatisfactory character...to a great degree fanciful, conjectural, and speculative...mere guesses,"[74] and that a different measurement of damage (the reduction in the value of the plaintiff's lease) must be used. A few years later, however, in a case with facts similar to those of *Bradford Oil Co. v. Blair*, the supreme court endorsed a lower court opinion based on evidence as to the likely yields of different wells on the same lease having regard to the differing characteristics of the sands into which they were drilled.[75]

This line of decisions, which runs parallel with the capture cases, shows a steadily increasing sophistication in the evidence offered on the behavior of oil and gas in the reservoir and in the courts' treatment of it, and gives the lie to the suggestion, offered by James Veasey and often since repeated,[76] that judges, at least in Pennsylvania, were in thrall to some fanciful conception of oil and gas as an unpredictable wild animal. They understood the basic mechanics of the oil reservoir[77] and were prepared to quantify the consequences of drainage. Suggestions by judges in capture cases like *Kelley v. Ohio Oil Co.* and *Barnard v. Monongahela Natural Gas Co.* that it would be impossible to assess the amount of drainage should therefore be taken with a large pinch of salt.

Lateral Support

A second alternative to capture was offered by counsel for Kelley in *Kelley v. Ohio Oil Co.* His first concern was to establish the underground situation of the oil in question and thereby convince the court that it should not apply the principles of the percolating water cases. While Kelley's pleadings did not use the term "reservoir," they explicitly claimed that the lands subject to his and the company's leases overlay

> a formation of porous sand or Trenton rock, so-called, which is permeated with valuable mineral oil; that the nature of said mineral oil deposit is such, that when in

---

[74] *Ibid.* at 539–40, 7.

[75] *Kleppner v. Lemon,* (1896) 176 Pa. 502, 35 A. 109: see further below, Ch. 3, at 76–7, and Ch. 7 at 194–7.

[76] Veasey 1920a. For a modern example, see Onorato 1968: 90.

[77] See *Duffield v. Rosenzweig,* 144 Pa. 520, 23 A. 4 (1891), and the lower court opinion in *Hague v. Wheeler,* 157 Pa. 324, 27 A. 714 (1893).

the process of operating, an oil well is drilled from the surface down into and through said oil-bearing rock, and the usual pumping appliances attached to and employed on said well to extract oil therein, the oil will be drawn to said opening from a long distance through said porous rock, and all the oil within a radius of from two hundred to two hundred and fifty feet surrounding such well, will be drawn to and extracted by means of such well, so that in order to drain and exhaust all the oil in the land it is only necessary to drill the wells from four to five hundred feet apart.

Counsel went on to argue that the percolating water cases[78] could not apply where it was known that a single deposit of oil underlay several properties, because those cases were based on the idea that "the existence, origin, movement and course of such waters, and the causes which govern and direct their movements, [were] so secret, occult and concealed, that an attempt to administer any set of legal rules in respect to them would be involved in hopeless uncertainty, and would be, therefore, practically impossible."[79]

Next, he claimed that the Ohio Oil Company, by drilling close to its property lines, had deprived the plaintiff's oil of the lateral support to which it was entitled, and that this withdrawal of support, resulting in the loss of oil from the plaintiff's land, was an actionable wrong. It is worth pausing over this argument, because it represents the only attempt in the American case law, prior to the application to oil and gas of the correlative rights concept in *Ohio Oil Co. v. Indiana*,[80] to find a rational basis for restricting the right of a landowner to use his or her own land so as to produce oil or gas from under a neighbor's. The duty of lateral support appears—implicitly—among the earliest Western laws of which we have a written record, those of the Greek lawgiver Solon, dating from the sixth century BC. Among these, according to Plutarch's *Life of Solon*, was a rule that any ditch or pit dug on one's land must be at least as far away from the boundary as it was deep.[81] By 1897, it was well established, by both English and American cases, that an owner of mineral rights had a duty so to carry out mining operations as not to deprive the surface of support, and that adjoining landowners had reciprocal rights to the continuing *lateral* support by each of the other's land.[82] Kelley's counsel's idea was to apply this rule to subterranean support for oil, as an inherent element of the land.

This was the kind of bright idea that, if accepted, creates a leading case. Here, unfortunately, a few too many obstacles were in the way. Obviously, counsel was

[78] Above, at 36–41.

[79] Quoting from *Frazier v. Brown* (1861) 12 Ohio St. 294, at 311.

[80] Discussed below, Ch. 7, at 181–4.

[81] Plutarch 1845: 105.

[82] *Humphries v. Brogden* (1850) 12 Q.B. 740; *Backhouse v. Bonomi* (1861) 9 H.L.C. 503; Rogers 1864: 455–83.

not going to be able to produce any prior cases that were directly in point, but the cases he did cite did no more than show that in Ohio, the mineral owner had a duty to support the surface.[83] In this case, however, the surface of the neighboring land was totally unharmed, and indeed Kelley, as an oil lessee, had no relevant interest in it anyway. No authorities were available to indicate that lateral support could be claimed *purely* for a subsurface mineral deposit; indeed, there was uncomfortably relevant English authority to suggest that no right of support, even for the surface, could be claimed in respect to a neighbor's subterranean water, so that a landowner could not be prevented from draining his or her land even if this caused damage.[84] This precise point was taken by the Ohio Oil Company's counsel, who argued that an entitlement to lateral support could not exist in relation to a fluid percolating through the earth. Kelley had already asserted that the oil in question here was not a percolating fluid but a stable deposit, but even if the court had been prepared to give attention to this point (which it was not) and had accepted the plaintiff's argument, it would not necessarily have held that a right of lateral support of this kind did or should exist. We shall see in Chapter 5 that an argument similar to Kelley's was made extrajudicially, before a Royal Commission, in Trinidad a few years later and failed to impress.[85]

Nonetheless, these were serious arguments, but the Ohio courts would not listen to them. The lower court refused to hear evidence on the ground that Kelley's pleadings disclosed no cause of action, and the Supreme Court of Ohio confirmed without sending the case back for retrial. All the supreme court had to say in response to Kelley's arguments was that

> whether the oil moves, percolates, or exists in pools or deposits . . . it is property of, and belongs to, the person who reaches it by means of a well, and severs it from the realty and converts it into personalty. While it is generally supposed that oil is drained into wells for a distance of several hundred feet, the matter is somewhat uncertain, and no right of sufficient weight can be founded upon such uncertain supposition, to overcome the well-known right which every man has to use his property as he pleases, so long he does not interfere with the legal rights of others.[86]

It is difficult, reading these dismissive words, to avoid the impression that the principle of capture was already too firmly established in the minds of the judges to be dislodged by whatever alternative rule might be offered in argument and whatever evidence of reservoir mechanics was then available to support it.

---

[83] *Burgner v. Humphrey*, 41 Ohio St. 340 (1884).
[84] *Popplewell v. Hodkinson* (1869) L.R. 4 Ex. 248; 1 Tiffany 1920: 1187; Enever 1947: 48–53.
[85] Below, Ch. 5, at 136–7.
[86] 57 Ohio St. at 328–9; 49 N.E. at 401.

First Appropriation

While we can see in the case law glimmers of two approaches to the drainage problem that might have challenged the rule of capture, a third potential line of argument seems never to have been canvassed at all. This would be to say that the law should protect the *first appropriator* of underground petroleum. The idea is one that has a long and respectable history in the English law relating to surface streams. Sir William Blackstone, whose eighteenth-century *Commentaries* offered a comprehensive view of English common law, propounded the notion that active appropriation of a flow of water, such as for purposes of turning a mill, in itself gave an enforceable right as against those who later sought to abstract some of this flow for their own use.[87] This approach to water rights, though dominant in English law for a few decades, later yielded, there and also in the eastern United States, to notions of shared natural rights of riparian owners to reasonable water use,[88] but it was adopted as the basis of the surface water laws of most of the western states.[89]

A variety of reasons have been suggested for this major departure from the riparian system.[90] One crucial obstacle to the adoption of that system to regulate water use conflicts among the gold miners who occupied much public (federal) land in California in the 1840s and 1850s was that, having no formal title whatsoever to the land they were working, none of them held the riparian rights on which the reasonable use system depended. The California courts thus adopted the miners' own system of protecting prior use of particular quantities of water against the claims of later comers.[91] Homesteaders in arid territory who needed to divert water in order to fulfill their obligations to develop and work their land appear to have adopted similar systems in order to avoid or settle disputes. In addition, the general need for irrigation in these parts of the United States, much greater than in the moister East, argued for the protection of those who, regardless of the situation of their land, had already invested in the diversion of water for its irrigation, as against those who later took up ownership on the banks of the river from which diversion was made.

Prior appropriation of surface water in the West is commonly explained and justified by saying that the clear individual rights it produces are much better suited to the management of scarce water resources that are largely consumed (as by

---

[87] 2 Blackstone 1765–9: 390, 401–3.

[88] See generally Getzler 2004: Chs. 5 and 6, especially at 207–32; Rose 1990; Scott and Coustalin 1995: 850–71; *Tyler v. Wilkinson*, 24 Fed. Cas. 472 (1827).

[89] Scott and Coustalin 1995: 902. Some states have mixed appropriation and riparian systems, and all have substantially modified these basic principles through legislation.

[90] Scott and Coustalin 1995: 901–10.

[91] *Irwin v. Phillips*, 5 Cal. 140 (1855).

irrigation) than is the notion of reasonable access to a common resource by a restricted group of riparian owners, developed for wetter areas where water use (as for powering machinery) employed the flow of the stream without significantly diminishing its volume.[92] This notion of consumption and the fact, not just of occasional scarcity, but of exhaustibility suggest that oil might be a fluid whose production could be governed by a prior appropriation principle: in other words, that the first discoverer of oil or gas should be protected against activities on neighboring land that would have the effect of diminishing the flow obtained.

We shall see in later chapters that prior appropriation is the key principle through which the French have, over a century and a half, regulated competition for sources of mineral water, against a technical and legal background remarkably similar to that prevailing in the early days of the U.S. oil industry,[93] and also that it has strongly influenced the arrangements through which some countries have sought to allocate state-held oil and gas rights for exploitation by private companies.[94] Proposals incorporating the principle of prior appropriation for oil and gas have been put forward from time to time,[95] though so far as I have been able to ascertain, it has never received judicial or legislative consideration as an alternative to the rule of capture. Of course, prior appropriation is itself a form of capture, but one that, insofar as it assured the rights of the *first* to capture, might have appeared an attractive recourse to any who found their production diminished by subsequent drilling on neighboring land. As with the neglect of the approach suggested by Justice Woodward, we need to investigate the attitude and practice of oil operators in order to get some sense of why this road was never taken.

CONCLUSION

By the end of the nineteenth century, the highest courts of West Virginia, Pennsylvania, Indiana, and Ohio—the principal oil- and gas-producing states at that time—had all ruled in favor of the law of capture. Only in West Virginia had this ruling been made on a fully reasoned basis, having regard to the court's view of the nature of the property that might be held in this substance while still in the ground: either a qualified property or no property at all. Indiana, which was to adopt the same view of property, had no reasoned view on capture because, as already noted, the plaintiff had conceded its applicability in the only relevant case.

---

[92] Rose 1990.

[93] Below, Ch. 4.

[94] Below, Ch. 10, at 313–5.

[95] See below, Ch. 9, at 269, n. 133.

The Pennsylvania and Ohio courts had, in effect, treated the rule of capture as so obvious as not to require the support of reason, a fortunate choice given the inconsistency between their view of property rights in oil and gas and the implications of the rule of capture.

In truth, the alternatives to capture had at no time been brought forcefully before the judges in these states. The possibilities inherent in the Woodward opinion in *Kier v. Peterson* were neglected; the precedents for a right of lateral support adduced in *Kelley v. Ohio Oil Co.* were not the most convincing; and first appropriation had not been recognized as a possible means of dealing with claims to property in oil and gas.

A careful reading of the so-called leading cases and the examination of their antecedents lead to several conclusions that are at odds with the conventional history of the legal development of the rule of capture in its application to oil and gas. First, the relevant judgments between 1886 and 1897 treated the rule of capture of oil and gas not as a controversial new rule, but as a well-established principle. Second, there is no evidence that judicial endorsement of the rule in these cases was prompted by fanciful and unscientific views of the nature and behavior of oil and gas underground; the capture cases came at a time when operators understood the general mechanisms of drainage and were presenting evidence based on such understandings in litigation. Third, the question of whether rights in oil depended on reducing it to possession in some way was argued in the very first reported case on property rights in oil, five years before the "official" beginning of the industry in 1859. Fourth, the idea that subterranean water was subject to legitimate capture was by that date almost universally accepted. Fifth, no plausible alternative to the capture principle was argued in a reported drainage case until 1897. Oliver's image of an opportunistic and ignorant judge, at the outset of the industry's development, snatching at a quaint and inappropriate legal analogy to resolve an early property dispute and thereby setting the industry on a destructive path from which it could not escape could hardly be further from the truth.

Even with a more accurate understanding of the circumstances and legal background of the capture cases, it is still remarkable that the issue of drainage of oil and gas from one property to another apparently did not get before the courts until 1892, after more than 30 years of hectic exploration and production activity. It would be extraordinary if a straightforward drainage issue between neighboring producers or landowners had never arisen in all this time. In the next chapter, I explore the industry practices and beliefs that prevailed in its earliest years, with the aim of establishing when and how this issue arose in practice; whether it was in fact litigated but never reached the law reports; and if it was not, how it was dealt with.

CHAPTER 3

PRACTICE AND BELIEF IN THE EARLY PETROLEUM INDUSTRY

INTRODUCTION

Just south of the attractive little town of Titusville, in northwestern Pennsylvania, a state park extends for some 12 miles on either side of a clear stream much frequented by fly fishers and, in high summer, by canoeists also. Traveling the cycle and hiking trails of this beautiful and thickly wooded valley, which narrows and steepens as the stream gets closer to its outfall in the Allegheny River, one could see this as a landscape hardly touched by human hand. But the names in the valley tell another story: the river is Oil Creek; it meets the Allegheny River at Oil City; and the passenger halts on the railway line that hugs the riverbank are Petroleum Center and Drake Well. For this is the birthplace of the U.S. oil industry and the site of the first oil boom—indeed, of the first one or two, if we take into account the busts caused by price collapses at intervals during the industry's first decades, the 1860s and 1870s.

If we are going to get a true perspective on the historical development of the U.S. oil industry—in particular, on the problem of waste and the conservation movement it engendered, and the significance to this of the legal rule of capture—we need to understand the expectations, beliefs, and behaviors of the people who flocked to this valley, to the banks of the Allegheny, and to the nearby valleys running into it, in search of this commodity they thought would make them rich. This is what explains the initial economic and legal structure of the fledgling oil industry and sets the pattern for its future development—and also, I shall argue, offers a persuasive answer to the puzzle of the apparently lengthy legal silence on what we now see as a crucial issue of property rights in oil.

Oil Creek was not given that name as a sign that this was where the modern oil industry began.[1] To the contrary: the industry began here because of the oil seepages that colored—we would now say polluted—the stream and caused it to be so known by the end of the eighteenth century: a reference to it under that name appeared in the *Massachusetts Magazine* in 1789.[2] Collection of oil from these seeps for medical applications, often with the aid of shallow diggings, was a centuries-old practice, associated with and copied from the Seneca Indians who had occupied the territory—hence the name "Seneca oil" frequently encountered in early leases and other documents. But even in a nation which was then—and still is now—enthusiastic for cures and medicines of all kinds, there is a limit to how much oil one can ingest, or rub in, to cure one's ills, so it was not until certain enterprising gentlemen from New York and points east realized the potential of Seneca oil as an illuminant which could replace whale oil, and compete with kerosene manufactured from coal, that the conditions for the creation of the modern industry were set. Even then there remained the not inconsiderable obstacle of producing enough of this oil to change the commercial balance of the market for illuminants. The Pennsylvania Rock Oil Company, the corporate vehicle of our entrepreneurs, began by continuing the established practice of digging on a farm near Titusville where an oil spring had been exploited under lease on a very small scale since 1853. Had they continued by this means, probably nothing much would have happened: oil was being dug in a number of places in the world at this time, sometimes from very deep pits,[3] but nowhere in quantities sufficient to compel the technological shifts that would create the modern industry.

What changed everything, for reasons that still seem slightly mysterious, was the demonstration, on the lands of the Pennsylvania Rock Oil Company in late August 1859, that oil could be found and recovered by drilling rather than digging—and

---

[1] Material in this and the next paragraph draws on Williamson and Daum 1959: Ch 1; Giddens 1947.

[2] Folger 1893: B10. Ise 1926: 6 offers a reference from 1783.

[3] Pearton 1971: 7–8 (Romania) and below, Ch. 6, at 150. Even in the seventeenth century, oil was being recovered by local inhabitants from pits dug to depths of 13 meters near Bologna in Italy: Forbes 1958: 86.

recovered in much greater quantities. This was the achievement of Edwin Drake, recruited by the company to take matters forward at Titusville mainly on the strength of his possession, as a former railroad conductor, of a free rail pass that facilitated his travel to the nearest railhead. Drake, on whom the company, in telegrams to Titusville announcing his coming, bestowed the entirely fictitious rank of "Colonel," had as his key quality a remarkable perseverance in the face of adversity, and having decided that he was going to drill, not dig, for oil on the site, he continued doing so, with the aid of a salt well driller called Billy Smith, long after local respect for his rank had turned to ridicule and the company had ceased to supply him with necessary funds.

When, after months of drilling that took him down only 69 feet, he actually struck oil in late August 1859, it may have been the sheer amazement felt by the community that caused the event to have such a dramatic impact. Finding oil, sometimes in considerable quantities, in wells drilled for salt (and drilled far deeper and more quickly than Drake's) was a familiar phenomenon. These achievements, however, never produced the reaction seen at Drake's well. Though no notice of the find appeared in the press until a *New York Tribune* report a fortnight later, local interest was immediate and sufficient to stoke an oil boom that quickly and durably transformed the region and laid the institutional and infrastructural foundations for a national oil industry.

Oil Creek was not the only location where there were successful attempts to obtain petroleum in quantity at the end of the 1850s and the beginning of the 1860s. A significant find had been made in southern Ontario, Canada, in 1858, though this was by digging, not drilling wells. However, it identified the area as promising and was the precursor of a major oil boom in the early 1860s in the Enniskillen district.[4] Indeed, by 1865, potential investors were being told (with what degree of exaggeration I am not equipped to say) that Canadian oil from Enniskillen was in almost every respect—quality, cost of operation, freedom from regulation, proximity to transportation—superior to the rival Pennsylvania product.[5] Again, development began at almost the same time in western Virginia, in the area that became part of West Virginia when that state seceded in 1863. At least one West Virginia source claims commercial wells were completed there, in Ritchie County, before the Drake Well but were kept quiet by their operators, who had an assured market for the production and were anxious that there should be no inflation of the price of the further land they wished to obtain.[6] A less mysterious well was drilled in 1860 at Burning Springs Run on the Little Kanawha River, and

---

[4] Morritt 1993.
[5] Tyrell 1865.
[6] McKain and Allen 1994: Ch. 1.

a boom ensued that might have rivaled the Pennsylvania oil region's, but for the destabilization of the area as people adopted different sides in the Civil War and the burning of the oil installations in a Confederate raid in 1863.[7]

Though producers and speculators returned in force to the West Virginia fields in the mid-1860s, neither this state nor southern Ontario enjoyed the sustained development and expansion that characterized the industry in Pennsylvania and resulted in that region's activities and problems being by far the best documented in the early years. Published accounts of the area proliferated. The first, Thomas Gale's 80-page pamphlet, *The Wonder of the Nineteenth Century! Rock Oil in Pennsylvania, and Elsewhere*, appeared as early as 1860. Many others followed, often in the form of extended newspaper articles that tended to emphasize the frantic disorder, loose morals, and utter discomfort of the region and the fortitude with which these were suffered by the reporters.[8]

Among more substantial publications that appeared were the contrasting accounts by the Reverend S. J. M. Eaton, *Petroleum: A History of the Oil Region of Venango County, Pennsylvania* (1866), and by William Wright, *The Oil Regions of Pennsylvania* (1865), both of which have supplied important material for this chapter. The contrast could hardly be greater. Eaton was pastor of the Presbyterian church at the Venango county seat of Franklin, and in keeping with his religious calling, was inclined to see God's hand even in the muddy scramble for wealth. The trees might have been stripped from the hillsides and the land covered with inches of oily mud, but Eaton's faith did not waver:

> And now here, in this remote county of Western Pennsylvania, so humble and poor in agricultural resources, God's treasure has been concealed for ages, locked up in the very heart of the eternal rock, awaiting the time of need, and accomplishment of the eternal purposes of Omnipotence. It has oozed forth, in limited quantities, during the lapse of centuries, as if to show us now, that man cannot lay his hand upon the house of God's treasures until his own appointed time. ... [N]ow, through innumerable channels, cut through the living rock by the Creator's hand, and by "paths which no fowl knoweth, and which the vulture's eye hath not seen," is that treasure brought to the earth's surface, just in our time of need. When other supplies are failing, and other resources giving way, we see God's wisdom manifested in opening up new channels.[9]

We should not write off Eaton as a pious eccentric, for his attitude to the resource was long a staple of oil industry thinking. As the president of the

---

[7] Thoenen 1964: Ch 2.

[8] A number of these are collected in Giddens 1947.

[9] Eaton 1866: 61–2.

Tidewater Oil Company said in his address to the 1920 annual meeting of the American Petroleum Institute, "[K]ind Providence never limits the supply of anything so valuable as petroleum."[10]

Wright, a reporter for the *New York Times*, was less convinced of heavenly intervention and devoted a large part of his book, which also had much detailed information on properties, oil wells, and drilling methods, to exposing the sharp practices of company promoters, leasing agents, and others. He styled his book a "searching examination and scathing exposure" of "a system of falsehood and fraud, that might almost be termed *magnificent*,"[11] under which lay a basis of fact that needed to be presented in its true light. Not unnaturally, these general predispositions led Eaton and Wright to comment in rather different terms on some of the key issues presented by oil production activity, not least on the phenomenon that we now call capture but was known at the time as "interference between wells."[12]

Somewhere between these extremes, one might place the indispensable and highly detailed account by Andrew Cone and Walter R. Johns, *Petrolia: A Brief History of the Pennsylvania Petroleum Region, Its Development, Growth, Resources, Etc., from 1859 to 1869* (1870), which attempted a complete inventory of every farm, and its wells, in the Oil Creek and surrounding areas, together with the press coverage offered by regular specialized columns and statistics in the daily *Titusville Morning Herald*, founded in 1865 and still publishing, and the weekly *Oil City Register*, founded in 1862. The abundance of these sources virtually dictates a focus on the Oil Creek region for any inquiry that would elucidate the early practices, understandings, and attitudes of American oilmen, and this chapter concentrates heavily on the region, though not to the exclusion of other areas—notably West Virginia—for which archival and other evidence is available.

FARMERS AND THEIR LAND RIGHTS

The first concern of the more percipient visitors to the Drake Well site was to obtain rights to land which, like that at the well, lay along the flats bordering Oil Creek. By the end of the year, a considerable proportion of the farmland on the flats along the creek, initially considered the most promising territory on the basis of the seeps and of Drake's success in such a location, had either changed hands or become the subject of exclusive rights—usually but not invariably referred to as

---

[10] Quoted by Ise 1926: 410.
[11] Wright 1865: 3–5 (emphasis in original).
[12] Below, 67–71.

leases—to enter and dig or drill for oil (and sometimes also salt and other minerals).

The oil rushes in Pennsylvania and West Virginia differed in a vital respect from the rush for gold in California or silver in Nevada. The land involved was not unsettled public land, as in California,[13] and there was no doubt that the surface landowners to whom it had been granted enjoyed the mineral rights in the subsoil beneath their lands. Under the so-called accession system, adopted alike in Roman law and common law and expressed with some hyperbole in the Latin maxim *Cujus est solum, ejus est usque ad coelum et ad inferos* (Whoever owns the surface owns upward to the skies and downward to the depths), surface ownership implies the holding of all rights in the subsoil beneath the surface and in the airspace above it.[14] Unless, therefore, the person who sells or grants land makes an explicit reservation of the mineral rights, they will pass to the buyer or grantee. In the nineteenth century, the Pennsylvania courts seemed to lean against any implication of such a reservation, as Acheson's difficulties in getting the oil to which he thought himself entitled bear witness.[15] Indeed, the notion of a distinct mineral estate, separable by reservation or express grant, was still being litigated in the middle of the nineteenth century[16] and only received clear judicial backing in Pennsylvania in the case of *Caldwell v. Fulton* in 1858.[17] Certainly there was no reservation, and resulting severance, of mineral rights in this part of Pennsylvania, where the original titles were created to promote agricultural settlement without consideration of the added value that minerals might confer.

Title to Pennsylvania lands north and west of the Ohio and Allegheny rivers traces back to state purchase from local Indian tribes by the treaties of Fort McIntosh and Fort Stanwix in October 1784 and March 1785. Some of these lands in the oil region were granted to soldiers in the War of Independence by way of depreciation certificates and donation certificates issued under an act of 1783, but by far the largest part was disposed of by sale under a further act of 1792. Under the pressure of competing land claims from the Connecticut Company, alleging an entitlement under a royal charter to lands right across northern Pennsylvania, the state government aimed to get individual settlers onto the land, and local governments organized under Pennsylvania law, by selling it at low rates. Few were bold enough, however, to venture into this wild and uninhabited

---

[13] The issues this raised are explored below, Ch. 7, at 211–17.

[14] Bainbridge 1878: Ch. 2 is a contemporary source on the point; an earlier edition was cited in the early oil property case of *Funk v. Haldeman*, 53 Pa. 229 (1867). See Sprankling 2008 for history and criticism of the notion.

[15] *Acheson v. Stevenson*, above, Ch. 2, at 25–6.

[16] Kerr 1894: 254–5; *Green v. Putnam*, 69 Mass. 221 (1851).

[17] 31 Pa. 475.

territory, subject to sanguinary raids by Indians dispossessed by treaty of their traditional hunting grounds, and most of the land (500,000 acres) was eventually sold for cash to a Dutch syndicate, the Holland Land Company, which also made massive purchases in New York State.

Though the company quickly sold on some of its land, the Pennsylvania purchase involved it in endless disputes and litigation, and even threats of violence, since the 1792 act made it a condition of perfecting the purchase of each lot (usually of 400 to 500 acres) that the land should be settled, with a house erected and 2 percent of the acreage cleared within two years. The company thus bought itself the impossible task of settling half a million acres, with the result that those who did take up its land often also claimed more attractive unsettled land nearby on the pretext that the company had failed to perfect its title as prescribed by the act.[18] By the time the oil-fired rush for land and land rights began in 1859, however, these particular title disputes had been effectively settled. Nevertheless, there was still scope for the profitable employment of insider knowledge: one Pennsylvania oil pioneer recounted purchasing land near Oil Creek from a judge, formerly a surveyor, who had been able to identify and claim small parcels of land not taken up by earlier patentees.[19]

Title and boundary problems arising from subsequent transactions did give rise to frequent litigation once the massive value added by oil was appreciated, and such disputes seem to have been a particular problem in the enormously prolific Bradford oilfield in McKean County—developed from the early 1870s onward and supplying, by the early 1880s, the bulk of the world's consumption—where they led to violence and to criminal as well as civil proceedings.[20] I have, however, found no case in which it was suggested that the original surface owner might not be entitled to the mineral, including the oil, rights.

In Pennsylvania in 1859, the fact that the local farmers should be ready to dispose of all or some of their land rights was hardly surprising. This was hardscrabble farming, on poor soil, with crops grown in a few clearings and with the valley slopes largely uncleared of timber, and work as a lumberman or in rafting timber down the Allegheny was often necessary to eke out farm incomes. Visiting journalists, writing highly colored and amusing accounts of oil region conditions to entertain readers in cities like New York, were not always kind to these farmers: one wrote in 1868 that prior to the coming of the oil industry, they

---

[18] See generally Brown 1885: 226–35; Stone 1926: 16–24.
[19] Shippen 2002: 90.
[20] Stone 1926: 182–3. On the development of the Bradford field, see Williamson and Daum 1959: Ch. 15.

"knew very little about farming and still less about anything else."[21] But they proved to be quick learners, at least about money. In the face of the incoming tide of treasure seekers, first from local areas and then, following the New York and other press coverage, from farther afield, farmers generally seem to have extracted prices for their land that reflected in some measure, often in very large measure, the value of the oil that—maybe—lay underneath it. Moreover, they were quick to understand that a lease limited to the oil rights in the land was a far better arrangement than an outright sale: the full use of the land would return to them on the expiration of the lease, and a steady income from an oil-bearing lease could be ensured by the taking of a royalty, a share of the oil produced which was to be delivered by the lessee to the lessor. In the very first modern lease, under which the Drake Well was drilled, royalty was fixed at one-eighth,[22] but before the end of 1859, we find leases in which the royalty rose to one-third if a certain level of production was reached.[23]

In theory, the lease offered farmers two additional advantages over outright sale: it preserved their tillage rights on the land and, by setting aside an area around their farmhouse where no drilling could take place, gave them the means to retain their home and exercise such rights. One wonders, however, how much farming got done in locations like the Oil Creek valley after 1859. One thing that impressed every commentator who came to the region was the forests of oil derricks that were everywhere to be seen.

In 1860, "[f]rom McClintock's [halfway up Oil Creek] to Franklin [on the Allegheny River] one is never out of sight of the *peculiar institution* of this region, viz. the derrick, and in the latter town almost every man has one in his garden."[24] In 1861, the frontage of derricks visible from the river had extended to 30 miles.[25] In 1865, a reporter from the *Boston Journal* went to the boomtown of Pithole, a few miles from the Oil Creek valley, and wrote that he had counted 110 derricks in an area less than a quarter square mile and not a single tree standing.[26] The phenomenon was still evoking wonder in 1868, when a journalist found a new metaphor, describing the bottom lands of Oil Creek as "a wilderness of derricks, which remind you of nothing so much as shipping crowded into some great harbor."[27]

---

[21] Extracted in Giddens 1947: 346.

[22] See, for the text, 2 Boyle (*Derrick's Handbook*) 1900: 191.

[23] Heydrick papers, DW 76.37.19.

[24] Extracted in Giddens 1947: 207–10.

[25] In Morris 1875: 41–43, reprinted in Giddens 1947: 216–17.

[26] Darrah 1972: 21.

[27] Extracted in Giddens 1947: 341.

Even if the spread of the derricks left enough land to farm, it must often have been hopelessly polluted by the vast amounts of oil that regularly flowed unchecked from major new wells, sometimes for days. Small wonder, then, that despite the attractions of a regular royalty, some farmers preferred to make a clean break: like John Blood, who in 1864 sold his farm of 450 acres on Oil Creek outright for $560,000 (which has been calculated as equivalent to at least $30.8 million in today's dollars), taking his family off to Manhattan, where on being refused admission to his chosen hotel—doubtless by reason of his rustic appearance and manners—he made an immediate offer to buy the whole establishment. After a few months of high living, he returned to the oil region to live the rest of his days in calmer splendor in a fine mansion he built in the local county town.[28]

THE CAST OF CHARACTERS

> The lucky strikes in [Butler County, Pennsylvania], and the rapid development of the territory, brought in all classes of people. The heavy capitalist, the experienced operator, the shrewd speculator, the penniless adventurer, the "man who had seen better days," the green novice, the curious tourist, the honest citizen, the common laborer, the tramp, beggar, gambler, sharper, thief, the courtesan, all were there, and jostled each other on the narrow sidewalks.[29]

Within a remarkably short space of time, this motley throng of humanity that surged into the oil regions could be sorted according to an economic class system. Leaving to one side the colorful supporting cast of innkeepers, prostitutes, shopkeepers, teamsters (wagon drivers), oilfield laborers, and the like, we can distinguish four principal roles.

First were the technical service providers, such as steam-engine providers and drilling contractors, usually remunerated under contracts for the services they provided. Given the varying fortunes of producers, those contracts were not always easy to enforce, and a good deal of litigation was recorded at the county courthouses.[30]

Second were the producers, the people who actually tried to make their fortunes by finding and selling oil. Theirs was the riskiest task, for their investment of capital in drilling wells (and estimates for the average cost of a well drilled by steam

---

[28] McLaurin 1896: 140–1.
[29] *History of Butler County* 1883: 134.
[30] For typical examples, see Stralko collection: DW.70.06.504, 679.

power in the mid-1860s range from $5,000[31] or $6,000[32] to $15,000[33]) was subject to both the physical risk of whether the oil was there or not and the economic risk of whether there was a paying market for it. When the price of oil plummeted in late 1861 to some 10 cents a barrel as a result of a number of flowing wells coming on stream, William Phillips, the owner and operator of the prolific Phillips No. 2 Well, was forced to shut it in because the barrels in which he was obliged to deliver his oil to his lessor, Henan James, cost many times more than the oil they contained. James sued for breach of contract in the sum of $112,000 and settled for an increase in Phillips's royalty from a quarter to a half.[34] (Phillips's problem had been foreseen by one of the Heydricks, a prominent family in the region, who in early 1860 reminded a brother who had decided that "the Seneca Oil business is the Ultima Thule of Enterprise and the only plain road to wealth" that he would need to raise enough on the oil found to buy barrels to put it in.[35])

Producers quickly learned to spread their physical risks by taking fractional interests, called working interests, in a number of wells: one-sixteenth in this one, three-sixteenths in that, and so on. We shall see later how they tried to deal with economic risks.

Third, we have the oil capitalists, who had the means to buy or lease substantial tracts of land. The first capitalists were individuals wealthy enough to buy land or take substantial leases and then contemplate the cost of drilling the wells that would be required. The first example was Jonathan Watson, original joint owner of the land on which the Drake Well was drilled, who rode down Oil Creek flats early the next day and secured at least one lease, of the Hamilton McLintock Farm, with others to come later.[36] These leases made Watson rich, but whereas many in his position—Rockefeller the most prominent among them—quickly came to realize that the safest source of oil wealth lay in transportation and refining, Watson never did: he died in poverty, having lost his money in later unsuccessful searches for oil in which he was guided by his wife's Spiritualist faith.[37] Soon groups of such men began entering into informal associations to accumulate the necessary capital; some of the famous early "flowing wells"—that is, wells which did not require pumping like Drake's, but flowed, often uncontrollably, under the pressure of the gas in the reservoir—were drilled by such consortia. An important example is the Noble Well, owned by a large group headed by the curiously named Orange Noble, a

---

[31] Sweet 1865: 90–2, reprinted in Miller 1968: 88–9.

[32] Dodge 1865: 214 (in West Virginia).

[33] Darrah 1972: 16–18 (in Pithole). Darrah includes lease costs in his calculation.

[34] McElwee 2001: 13–17; McLaurin 1896: 140–3.

[35] Heydrick collection: DW 76.37.28.

[36] Kussart 1938: 208; see also Williamson and Daum 1959: 86–7.

[37] Bates 1899: 734; *Titusville Morning Herald*, June 18, 1894.

leading figure in the oil region for a number of years, which was a dry hole when first drilled to 134 feet in 1860 but became a very large producer, at 2,000 to 3,000 barrels a day for many months, when reworked in 1863.[38]

The next step was for such groups to incorporate as companies, thus enabling them to make public calls for capital. This required the intervention of the legislature in each case, as Pennsylvania did not acquire a truly comprehensive incorporation law until 1874; earlier laws covered such areas as manufacturing (1840) and coal and metal mining (1853) but did not extend to the oil business.[39] Special charters were accordingly sought by oil promoters and were granted in large numbers. The same was true of West Virginia, where the legislature incorporated 174 oil companies between 1863 and 1867.[40] These individual incorporation statutes might well contain provisions more favorable to the promoters than those of any general incorporation laws in force. Many other companies active in the oil regions were incorporated in other states: Ida Tarbell, the pioneering investigative historian of the Standard Oil Company, counted a total of 543 oil companies incorporated in the first five years of the industry's existence.[41]

As in every industrial boom, from the English railway boom of the 1840s to the dot-com boom of the 1990s, such companies often functioned purely as a mechanism to transfer the funds of publicly solicited investors into the pockets of the promoters and their friends, without any costly and irksome detours such as would be occasioned by drilling for oil; William Wright devoted an entire chapter of his book to detailing their machinations.[42] The prospectuses of the less scrupulous promoters raised to a new art form the sober and restrained expression of massively exaggerated prospects.

The fourth group were the passive investors, the targets both of the promoters' prose and of the agents and brokers who infested every oil settlement. These were the people who simply wanted to obtain a share of a remunerative oil property while staying as far away from the mud and muck of production as possible. They were, as the cashier of the bank at Parkersburg wrote to a client in January 1861 at the time of the first West Virginia oil discoveries, subject to "a fever little less than the gold fever in California ... Judges, Lawyers, Strangers, Merchants—indeed all classes who have a little means seem to have gone oil mad."[43]

---

[38] Henry 1873: 375–92; and see below at 69–70, 78–9.

[39] Hartz 1948: Ch. II.

[40] McKain and Allen 1994: App. V.

[41] Tarbell 1938: xii. For her history of Standard Oil, see Tarbell 1904.

[42] Wright 1865: 206–27.

[43] Levassor papers, B. Smith to E. Levassor, January 28, 1861.

A month or two later, he reported that this group had been swollen by the addition of "Doctors, Divines, farmers and even the ladies."[44] Such people might buy stock in companies or fractional interests in the royalty rights held by property owners. From the very beginning, those interests were constantly being subdivided for trading and investment purposes, and also as property was passed on through inheritance.

THE LEASING SYSTEM

The leases granted by farmers and other original landowners, though they might cover quite large parcels of land, from 20 or 30 to 100 acres or more, seldom required more of the lessee than the drilling of one or two wells within a few months of the conclusion of the lease, and sometimes not even that. The extraordinary profusion of wells and derricks, already evident only a few months after the Drake Well came in, was due not to the unbridled desire for oil on the part of the first lessees, but to their rapid realization that you did not make money out of oil by producing it, but by subleasing your land to others who would.

Whether as individuals, consortia, or companies, the great majority of capitalists adopted this method of obtaining early returns on their investments.[45] A well or two would ordinarily need to be drilled, often because of the express terms of the lease, but in any event, because some evidence of oil would be needed to attract the investment of others. The initial move, therefore, was to survey as much of the land as the capitalists did not want for themselves, divide it into lots, and sublease. This was the means by which small operators, who might be able to raise funds for only a single well, could get into the game—or into several games, if they took fractional working interests in a number of wells.

Subleasing became the industry norm in a remarkably short space of time. Gale, writing in 1860, referred to it as common practice.[46] John Rynd, a canny farmer who granted a lease of his farm in January 1860 to the omnipresent Jonathan Watson and his partner Jacob Ainger, secured a supplemental agreement the following year providing for the lessees to survey the farm and create and sublease lots, and in 1864 sued them—unsuccessfully—for failing to sublease enough of the

---

[44] *Ibid.*, March 5, 1861. The last-mentioned class of investors took a more active role 40 years later, when the Young Ladies Oil Company was one of those formed to exploit leases at Spindletop in Texas: Olien and Olien 2002: 38–9, and the Women's Pacific Oil Company held a range of properties in California: Rintoul 1976: 50–2.

[45] The economics of this practice are examined in Toyoda 2003: 206–15.

[46] Gale 1860: 22.

land, to the prejudice of his possible royalty take.[47] The Columbia Oil Company, in which Andrew Carnegie was a stockholder, was held up to the world by oil journalists as an unusual company simply because it was said to be developing its 500-acre Story Farm itself, with carefully spaced wells, rather than through leasing.[48] This practice only started, however, after 1865: the annual report of the company for that year shows production from 54 wells, all save 4 of which were on leased lots and represented more than 93 percent of total production.[49]

Subleasing was also a money machine. It was remarkable how effectively, in places where there had been a show of oil and at times when prices were not unduly depressed (the oil price dropped to around 10 cents a barrel in late 1861 as a result of oversupply and the onset of the Civil War), substantial leaseholders could milk their leases by subleasing small lots for large premiums and high royalties. Far more money could be made this way than by actual production.[50] While some of the earliest subdivisions of leaseholds retained quite large lots, subleases of an acre, a half acre, and even less quickly became the norm in promising territory. To get such a lot, a would-be producer might have to pay a premium of $1,000 or even $2,000, and deliver a third to a half of the oil recovered to the sublessor (who, of course, was bound to pass on a fraction to the lessor under his own lease).

A couple of striking examples will indicate the intensity of development this produced. The prospectus of the oil company mounted by the Heydrick brothers in 1865 listed their landholdings and the extent to which these were leased or developed. While most leases were for one acre with a one-well obligation, some at the Heydricks' farm, on the Allegheny River at the mouth of Pithole Creek, were for only a quarter or two-fifths of an acre, with drilling obligations of two or even four wells.[51] Further west, at Tidioute, the owner of Dingley's Acre successfully stipulated for seven wells on an acre of land so precipitous that the legs of the rigs must practically have been intertwined.[52] Of Tidioute generally, the journalist John McLaurin, always one for the arresting phrase, reported that "the wells were jammed so closely that one could walk from Triumph to New London and Babylon [settlements in the area] on the steam-boxes connecting them."[53]

Subleasing, and the division and subdivision of royalty interests and of working interests under leases, got under way during the very earliest days of the industry at Oil Creek. They provided the vehicles for a massive flow of capital into the

---

[47] *Rynd v. Rynd Farm Oil Company,* 63 Pa. 397 (1870); Stralko collection: DW.70.06.770–2.

[48] Wright 1865: 132; Cone and Johns 624–8.

[49] Columbia Oil Company 1865: 16.

[50] Toyoda 2003: 213–15.

[51] Heydrick collection: DW.76.37.3.

[52] Beates 2007: 64–5, citing the *Titusville Morning Herald,* July 19 and 28, 1866.

[53] McLaurin 1896: 200.

industry from people of speculative spirit who had the means to operate, or to invest, only on a small scale. The presence of this vigorous class of small investors was a major reason why development in the United States so far outstripped that in the European oil fields of Romania and Galicia, where, as we shall see in Chapter 6, this class of persons hardly existed and the technological advance necessary for effective development had to be funded by foreign capital. At the same time, this fractionalization of interests, which remained a prominent feature of U.S. oil development for many decades, both created the conditions in which capture would be a major problem, because of the small size of the average holding, and massively complicated the solution of that problem through unitization, because of the very large numbers of people who might hold interests of one kind or another in any given reservoir. The latter issue did not emerge until well after the campaign for unitization led by Henry Doherty got under way in the 1920s.[54]

UNDERSTANDING WHAT WAS BELOW THE SURFACE

As for the link between leasing and subleasing practices and capture, we might conclude, in the light of our *modern* understanding of reservoir geology—the fact that petroleum, prior to drilling, is held in a stable state in reservoir rocks and distributed through the pore spaces of that rock—that their approach to leasing demonstrates a general acceptance among oilmen of the principle of capture from the very first days of the industry. Indeed, we could conclude this even on the basis of the rough understandings of petroleum flows expressed in the industry evidence in *Acheson v. Stevenson* in 1892, when industry witnesses opined that "the distance a well will drain the surrounding territory, depends upon the pressure of the gas and the character of the oil-producing sand; ... in good territory, one well is allowed to every five acres."[55]

Unless everybody had understood that capture was the rule, what driller would have sunk his capital in a well on a one-acre lot, inviting not the risk, but the near certainty, that his neighbors would immediately sue to recover that share of his production which must have been drawn from under the adjacent lots? Such prospects would have rendered small-scale leasing impossible.

An acceptance of capture cannot, however, be deduced quite as easily as this. People in the first decade of the industry did not have even the limited understanding of petroleum geology and reservoir mechanics that is necessary to support this conclusion. The beliefs of "practical men" as to how petroleum was

---

[54] See below, Ch. 9, at 276f.
[55] Above, Ch. 2, at 44.

produced and obtained were quite different and proved remarkably resistant to the steady development of geological understanding, pioneered by the academic community and the public servants responsible for state geological surveys.[56] John Carll, who worked in the Pennsylvania State Geological Service, reported in 1880 his difficulty in convincing oilmen that a large "flowing well" could be sustained simply by the flow of oil through the pore space to the wellbore under the gas and water pressure in the reservoir, and felt it necessary to provide mathematical calculations to prove his point.[57]

Until quite late in the nineteenth century, the beliefs of "practical men" were shaped, as in many other walks of life, by the misinterpretation of experience, whether their own or that of others. The most notorious experience was that of "Uncle" Billy Smith, the salt well driller who actually drilled the Drake Well in 1859. Smith was said to have abandoned drilling on a Saturday when his drill bit dropped a few inches into a subterranean crevice and then stuck.[58] The next day, he found his well full of oil. This piece of information, coupled with earlier experiences with powerful flows of gas when crevices were encountered in drilling salt wells,[59] was enough to support for many years a belief that oil and gas traveled upward through crevices in the rock, sometimes being trapped there by impermeable strata, sometimes finding their way to the surface in the form of seeps of oil or discharges of gas. The theory is widely encountered in the early literature,[60] with diagrams, such as the one from Eaton's book shown in Figure 3-1, to explain the large flowing wells like the Phillips No. 2 and the Noble by positing a system of underground caverns of oil or gas connected by such crevices.[61]

Eaton's drawing is designed to show how a well at c can tap such a cavern by intersecting the crevice $a-b$. In the literature of the 1860s, the contents of such crevices were most commonly spoken of in terms of "veins" of oil.[62] It was not

---

[56] See generally DeGolyer 1961: Ch. 2; Thoenen 1964: Ch. IX.

[57] Carll 1880: 251–3.

[58] Giddens 1972: 59. This story, which appeared in the *Titusville Morning Herald* on November 10, 1880 (reprinted in Giddens 1947: 120), but was presumably in circulation well before that date, finds no support in interviews given by Billy Smith and the son who assisted him (*Titusville Weekly Herald,* January 15, 1880; *Oil City Derrick,* August 27, 1909, both reprinted in Giddens 1947: 72–90). Until the end of the nineteenth century, all oil well drilling was accomplished by repeatedly dropping a heavy drill string down the wellbore to fracture and penetrate the rock; rotary drilling, though in earlier use for water wells, does not appear to have been used for oil before the exploitation of the Corsicana field in Texas in the 1890s: Brantly 1971: 216–20.

[59] Dodge 1865: 181.

[60] Gale 1860: 75: "This is certain, the rock must be broken or it cannot hold oil"; von Millern 1864: 4, 62–8; Cone and Johns 1870: 155f, 184–5; Henry 1873: 375f; Killebrew 1877: 6.

[61] Eaton 1866: 144–6, 255–7.

[62] See sources in nn. 60 and 61, above.

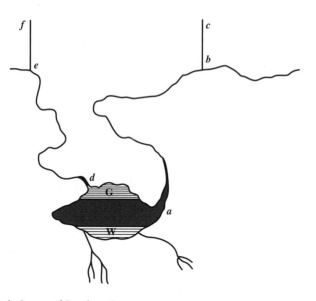

Figure 3-1. An Early Concept of Petroleum Recovery
Source: Eaton 1866: 145

merely a layman's belief, but was seriously espoused by some geologists, one Ebenezer Andrews arguing in a learned paper as late as 1891 that "it would appear to be a law, that the quantity of oil is in direct ratio to the amount of fissures."[63] Practical acceptance of the theory is evidenced by the successful marketing of a "crevice searcher" as a well-drilling accessory.[64]

The crevice or fissure theory had early critics who argued that it was in fact contrary to experience. The self-proclaimed "practical miner" (and occasional poet) Samuel Harries Daddow noted in 1866, in a comprehensive work on mining that formed part of the library of at least one significant oil producer,[65] that the general supposition that oil existed in cracks or fissures running through the strata and extending obliquely or perpendicularly toward the surface was rebutted by the fact that oil was found not randomly, but in particular strata (the "third and fourth sandstones" so regularly alluded to in early industry reporting). He further argued that if oil were held in fissures, it would have solidified to bitumen as its more volatile elements evaporated.[66] For Daddow, oil was the product of gas of volcanic origin deep beneath the earth's crust; this gas liquefied as it rose toward the earth's

---

[63] Cited in DeGolyer 1961: 25. See also Thoenen 1864: 121–2.

[64] Carll 1880: 245.

[65] W. C. Stiles family oil and mining company records.

[66] Daddow and Bannan 1866: 666. For Daddow's poems, see *Trevaro, and Other Occasional Poems* (1853, Pottsville, Pa.).

surface and was eventually trapped in large numbers of discrete cavities in the oil-bearing strata of shale, slate, and mud beneath impervious caprock.

"INTERFERING" WELLS

While Daddow's theory seemed to take an uncertain step toward our modern understanding, it shared with crevice or fissure theory one feature that is highly germane to the rule of capture. This was that the point of contact between the drill and an accumulation of oil was hypothesized as being situated on a line or cavity, not as a point on a continuous plane. If you believed that oil lay not in the pore space of continuous areas of given sandstone strata, but in narrow veins or fissures or in isolated cavities in such strata, you could cheerfully grant and accept even minuscule lease areas whether or not the rule of capture was thought to apply, for the more wells put down on your land, the greater the chance of striking one of these elusive veins. The fact that you were lucky enough to do this, even in close proximity to an existing successful well, need not mean that you were tapping your neighbor's oil; the new well might just have hit a separate but adjacent vein. Such was the reasoning of the optimists among the commentators, among whom we find, as we might expect, the Reverend Eaton:

> As a general thing, wells in the same neighbourhood do not interfere with one another. There are exceptions to this, however, but they are not at present sufficiently numerous to interfere with the rule. In rare instances the same crevice in the rock may be running on the same line with two wells; in such cases there may and will be an interference, unless the cavern or vein be sufficiently capacious to satisfy the demands of both. But in the great majority of cases the wells do not interfere, although not more than fifty feet asunder.[67]

Even more sanguine was J. R. Dodge, of the U.S. Agricultural Service. In vaunting the immense possibilities of development in the West Virginia oilfield, he admitted no problems with capture or with the early exhaustion of the field through overdevelopment.

> While a given well may reasonably be expected to suffer partial exhaustion in a few years, and in some instances a few months, that single well usually drains but a small space—a cavity, imperfectly connected with others by fissures liable to obstruction—or a single crevice, possibly extending a long distance, but entirely

---

[67] Eaton 1866: 88. Compare what Charles Marvin had to say about the Baku oilfield 20 years later, below, Ch. 6, at 162.

unconnected with another parallel to it and a few feet from it. Wells may therefore be increased indefinitely, and if the sources of supply in some of them shall be tapped by others, there will be many still to yield a handsome return.[68]

If even souls of such determinedly cheerful disposition felt constrained to admit, in passing, that there might just be a possibility of tapping of, or interference with, producing wells, we may be fairly sure that there lurked here a problem of some magnitude. Such was indeed the case. Once again it was William Wright who went straight to the heart of the matter:

> The one prime consideration on the part of experienced men is, to plant the derrick on a spot directly in line between two paying wells, where there is doubtless the best chance of striking a good vein. Indeed, without breaking ground, the managers, whose well-springs are thus threatened, may take the alarm, and offer to buy out the newcomer at his own price. For this is one of the methods by which operators sometimes make their fortune.[69]

As many examples adduced by Wright and others show, the notion that a new well might "interfere" with an existing producing well, to the point of totally cutting off its supply of oil, was well understood in the industry at least from 1862. This was when the production from the very prolific Phillips No. 2 well suddenly dropped, some months after the drilling of the Woodford well on a different lease some 20 meters away.

Though the Woodford also began as a prolific flowing well, both were soon reduced to pumping wells producing only a few hundred barrels a day instead of the initial thousands. After a period of destructive competition, in which the tubing of each well was pulled in turn with the idea of flooding the other well with groundwater, followed by retubing and pumping, a compromise was worked out between the owners under which the wells would be pumped together and each well owner would receive one-third of the product of the other well. The various contemporary and later accounts of the incident[70] are so fragmentary and contradictory that this is about all that one can say with certainty, save that, contrary to the assertions of William Wright that "the lawyers were called into settle the dispute" and that there was "much litigation,"[71] no trace can be found of any proceedings having been launched in the relevant county court, that of Venango

---

[68] Dodge 1865: 265.

[69] Wright 1865: 63–4.

[70] 1 Boyle (*Derrick's Handbook*) 1898: 24, 26–7, 29, 39–40; *Titusville Morning Herald*, November 22, 1871; Henry 1873: 232–3; Anon. 1882; McLaurin 1896: 140–1.

[71] Wright 1865: 136–7, 91–3.

Figure 3-2. The Phillips and Woodford Wells
Source: Drake Well Museum and Archive, Titusville, PA

County at Franklin. Indeed, I have found no record of any issue of drainage between neighbors being raised before the court during the period when Venango County was at the center of the oil industry (1859–1870).[72]

A more coherent story emerges regarding the Noble Well,[73] drilled to 145 feet without success in 1860 and then redrilled to 453 feet in 1863, when it produced what were at that time enormous volumes, 3,000 to 4,000 barrels a day. Between these dates, however, the Caldwell Well had been brought in on the neighboring farm, and the effect of the Noble Well was, again, a dramatic reduction in its daily flow of several hundred barrels. The reaction of the owners of the Caldwell was to ask the owners of the Noble, Orange Noble and George Delameter, for a quarter of its production as compensation for their loss. Since this represented a higher daily rate than the Caldwell had ever produced, Noble and Delameter found this unattractive, but when the owners of the Caldwell threatened to pull its tubing, with the likely effect of ruining the Noble Well through water intrusion, a

---

[72] The same finding was apparently made by James Veasey, who did extensive research in his later years, apparently with a view to writing a book rather like this one; he examined the same records but did not report the discovery of any capture cases: Veasey 1941: 172.

[73] Above, at 60–1.

compromise was reached under which the Noble interests bought out the Caldwell well and lease for $145,000. The latter well ceased producing a few months later and was plugged.[74]

Beside these high-profile incidents, which must have become known throughout the oil region, numerous like cases are to be found in the records, both of interference between wells—the most picturesque being that of the so-called Agitator and Sunday Wells on the Rynd Farm, the latter well producing only on Sundays when the Agitator was resting[75]—and of payments to neighbors to stop them provoking water intrusion by pulling tubing from dry or unsatisfactory holes, or to persuade them to keep pumping an unrewarding well. These "arrangements" as they were called, are exemplified by the provision by the Columbia Oil Company of a proportion of the production of some of its wells to the neighboring Dalzell Oil Company, to persuade it to retube an abandoned well that had flooded these Columbia wells,[76] and by the claim of a debtor of the Hammond Oil Company that the oil he had received was part payment for his service in continuing to pump and keep tubed for 30 days a well on his land that was not producing, in order to avoid the flooding of Hammond's producing well, for a consideration of $100 per day.[77]

Once again, we find the Reverend Eaton trying to take a positive view of these exceptions to his God-given scheme of things. Referring to the Phillips–Woodford incident, he wrote:

> This state of affairs has given rise to a number of curious questions in casuistry, or "cases of conscience" as the old fathers called them, not laid down in the books, and that have been generally adjudicated without recourse to courts of law. So far there seems to be a disposition to do justly, to deal equitably with each other, and to consider the business a common one, in which they are all interested. It is something of a feeling that binds people together in new countries, where they feel that mutual concessions and looking after the general welfare is the duty of each individual.[78]

This must have made reassuring reading for any of those "experienced men" whom Wright described as making a handy living by blackmailing producers with threats of pulling tubing close to paying wells, but it certainly did not reflect the general sentiment in contemporary sources, which was that the tapping of producing wells was a common phenomenon, as was their flooding by the

---

[74] Henry 1873: 375–92.

[75] McLaurin 1896: 145–6.

[76] Columbia Oil Company 1865: 12.

[77] *Hammond Oil Co v. Titus* (Court of Common Pleas, Venango County, no. 103 of August Term 1865), Stralko collection DW.70.06.861.

[78] Eaton 1866: 134.

deliberate or negligent withdrawal of tubing from unsuccessful or abandoned wells, and that these were evils that needed to be addressed by common action in the industry or by an appeal to the legislature.

THE CAMPAIGN TO PREVENT THE FLOODING OF WELLS

These two issues, of loss through drainage and loss through flooding, were closely related. An operator who drilled close to a productive well would obviously produce his own well if it successfully tapped the supply to the other, but if it failed to, he had the recourse of threatening to pull his tubing and cause damage. The efforts of the industry in favor of common action or legislative intervention quickly became focused, however, on addressing the problem of the flooding of wells with water, perhaps because at least some lessors and lessees perceived a common interest in preventing something that caused loss to all (as opposed to the transfers of wealth from some operators to others resulting from capture). In one or two locations, therefore, producers and owners of royalty interests took, or at least attempted, collective action to prevent damage by flooding.

At the Tarr Farm, which included the Phillips and Woodford Wells, flooding caused serious damage to a number of wells in 1864, and at a May 1865 meeting, producers and landowners agreed that operative wells must be cased as far down as the second sandstone and be seedbagged[79] at that point, and that idle wells must also be seedbagged at that point to stop the flow of water. Parties would then pump vigorously and without interruption to attempt to restore the flow of oil. If the relevant well owners were absent, casing and seedbagging would be done even without their consent, at the expense, to be paid pro rata, of the parties present at the meeting, with the landowners making the initial advance of the necessary cash. A meeting of Blood Farm interests a few days later reached a similar conclusion and took the further practical step of agreeing on a collective order for the necessary casing.[80] Later that year, wells at the boomtown of Pithole suffered disastrous water flooding (though this was more likely due to massive overdrilling than to pulling of tubing), and a committee of operators was appointed to inspect the steps that had been taken on the Tarr Farm.[81]

---

[79] A seedbag was a doughnut-shaped canvas bag filled with flaxseed or some other absorbent seed, which was lowered so as to surround the drill tubing below the level at which water might enter. Once moistened, the seed swelled to form an impermeable seal.

[80] *Oil City Register*, June 8, 1865: 2.

[81] *Titusville Morning Herald*, November 8, 1865: 4.

Elsewhere, there is no record of such agreements despite comparable problems of widescale flooding, as on the Widow McLintock Farm,[82] and some have suggested that many landowners and royalty interest holders were indifferent to the consequent waste.[83] Few made any effort to regulate the matter by the insertion of appropriate plugging and casing obligations in their leases, a device which, if generalized, would have largely resolved the problem. Landowners and head lessees often had already taken large profits in the form of lease premiums and very high royalties on initial production. William Wright, with his usual perceptiveness, suggested an additional motive for their inaction: that the company promoters who by this time formed an important component of this group were reluctant to address the matter for fear of drawing the attention of the public, and of the financial markets, to an additional risk attached to petroleum investments.[84]

Venango County producers eventually sought the aid of the Pennsylvania legislature. The *Philadelphia Ledger* called for legislative action as early as 1864,[85] and at the end of February 1866, Thomas Hoge, the senator for the district including Venango County, presented a petition from 241 oil well owners in the county and in March introduced a bill "to compel the owners of oil and salt wells to keep them tubed or plugged." The bill was passed by the state senate and transmitted to the Pennsylvania House of Delegates, but only on the last day of the annual session (at this time the legislature sat for only two months in the year), and consequently failed.[86] A further attempt was made the following year, with the introduction of a similar bill in the house, but this too was late in the session, and the bill did not proceed beyond a first reading.[87] Pennsylvania producers had to wait until 1878 for the enactment of a law requiring the plugging of abandoned wells.[88]

West Virginia producers were better treated by their legislature. After a first unsuccessful attempt in 1869, a bill passed both chambers in 1871. Though it preceded the 1878 Pennsylvania act, it was a more sophisticated piece of work. Besides requiring the casing of any well drilled within a mile of another, it made provision for an inspector of wells to be appointed by a circuit court judge, on the application of five or more citizens of an oil-producing county, and gave the inspector the power to enter premises and carry out remedial work on defective

---

[82] McLaurin 1896: 142–3.

[83] Cone and Johns 1870: 168.

[84] Wright 1865: 261.

[85] Article reproduced in von Millern 1864: 82–3. See also Wright 1865: 261.

[86] Pennsylvania, Journal of the Senate 1866: 4, 470, 474, 595.

[87] Pennsylvania, Journal of House of Delegates 1877: 872 (bill no. 1616).

[88] Sayers 1949: 431; Folger 1893: B44–6.

wells, on the application of any oil landowner or of a lessee situated within half a mile of such a well.[89] Comparable casing and plugging laws usually represented the first steps in conservation taken by the legislatures of other oil-producing states.[90]

Oil producers did not cooperate easily. Several attempts in the 1860s and 1870s to improve prices by collective marketing or drilling or production shutdowns were stymied by the failure of enough producers to cooperate.[91] In an individualistic, competitive, and mistrustful industry, it seems highly unlikely that the collective campaign to address the flooding problem would have been sustainable had producers felt they had a remedy in their own hands. Nobody, apparently, thought it worthwhile to pursue the possibility of individual legal redress against negligent or deliberate damage by flooding. Even when the interest holders on the Tarr and Blood Farms felt able to commit funds to collective action to alleviate the problem, legal proceedings do not appear to have entered their minds. They specifically considered what to do about parties who refused to cooperate but were unable to discern a stronger remedy than moral suasion:

> ... regarding anyone who might refuse to unite with those present, ... it was unanimously met by the declaration that any one so refusing or in any way countervailing this movement would be regarded as forfeiting all claims to the consideration of his fellow citizens, and that any such attempt to injure the common property ought to work a foreclosure of his or their leases, and that such conduct should receive the condemnation and reprobation of all persons interested in property connected with the Tarr Farm, its lessors and lessees.[92]

Given that the sort of people who drilled oil wells at that time were precisely those for whom a little condemnation and reprobation were all part of a good day's work, this can hardly have kept noncooperators awake at night, especially as the lease foreclosure threat was rendered empty by the fact that the relevant leases were most unlikely to have regulated the drawing of tubing, casing, and plugging. According to a survey by *The Derrick's Handbook of Petroleum* of the deed books maintained by the oil region counties, the first leases to mention tubing, seedbagging, and plugging were registered only in 1865.[93]

---

[89] Acts of the Legislature of West Virginia 1871, Ch. 126.
[90] Murphy 1949.
[91] Williamson and Daum 1959: 351, 358–60, 430–1.
[92] *Oil City Register,* June 8, 1865: 2.
[93] 2 Boyle (*Derrick's Handbook*) 1900: 202, 199.

REMEDYING CAPTURE PROBLEMS BY LEASE MANAGEMENT

Capture could be seen as the other side of the flooding coin, in that it was only if you failed to tap a neighboring well that you might consider action that would flood it. Yet no movement was mounted against the tapping of wells comparable to that against flooding, even though success in this direction might have attacked the flooding problem, as it were, at its roots. Operators were fully aware of the problem, which was capable of materially affecting the course of development. An 1868 account noted that operators were moving from Shamburg to Pleasantville (both localities not far from Oil Creek) despite the crowdedness of the latter area and the fact that Shamburg had the most productive single wells—perhaps because "very lately several small wells have been drained dry by their larger neighbours, and that has inspired a feeling of distrust."[94] Investors too must have been aware of the issue: the Lisbon Oil Company of Philadelphia thought it worthwhile to announce, in its 1865 prospectus, that "[f]rom the location of most of the boring territory, which runs through the centre of the property, it is impossible for parties operating on either side of the land to tap our wells."[95]

Yet the only plea for action I have found concerning the tapping of wells *per se* appeared in the *Pittsburgh Commercial* of July 21, 1864, reprinting a piece from the *Oil City Register* titled "Facts Concerning the Wells."[96] Its author began by noting that "the interference of one oil well with another, is becoming a common occurrence upon Oil Creek." After reciting a number of cases where new wells had killed or substantially restricted the flow from existing ones, he suggested that some of the interfering wells might have been drilled or reworked deliberately, and with an intent to blackmail, and concluded that "[t]he necessity of some legislative action, to effectually remedy this matter, if such a thing be possible, is keenly felt, and we trust that measures will be taken to check this cut-throat operation. We can see no reason why the law should not protect the man's property from injury by his neighbor, as much in an oil well as anything else."

The author may, however, have weakened his case by his speculations on the state of mind of the parties. While it was "vexatious" and a "great disappointment" for the owner of a producing well when a well drilled near his own "taps it, and turns his golden dreams of wealth into limpid, valueless water ... the true operator takes it coolly. ... if he fails to effect a compromise, or sell out, he seeks another location, and very frequently interferes with someone else in like manner."

---

[94] Extracted in Giddens 1947: 348–50.

[95] Heydrick collection, DW.76.37.135.

[96] I am most grateful to Professor Richard Healey for drawing this to my attention.

If the tapping of wells was for operators truly an affair of swings and roundabouts, it is hardly surprising that there should have been no industry pressure for legislative intervention—which would have been bound to effect an unforeseeable redistribution of gains and losses anyway.

Oil Creek operators can hardly be blamed if they thought and acted in the way our reporter suggested, as it was the greed of sublessors and some landowners that forced them onto lots on which one could hardly drill without the risk of tapping neighboring wells. Still, it should be noted that leasing arrangements could be structured to avoid the capture problem and that some more enlightened lessors and lessees did try to move in this direction. Even in the first years of the industry, some companies tried to avoid difficulties by granting leases or subleases over somewhat larger areas and limiting the number of wells that might be drilled without specific consent, or setting minimum distances between wells and any edge of the lease area that abutted another of the company's leases. Both of these features are found in quite an early lease granted for one of a number of lots in Allegheny Township in 1868, and in West Virginia it was the general practice of the Volcanic Coal and Oil Company, one of the more enlightened owners, to restrict the number of wells that might be drilled on its two-acre leases.[97] At Tidioute, the New York and Alleghany Oil Company leased its property checkerboard fashion so as to make leases more valuable and prevent wells interfering with each other.[98]

This approach might be made to work to the specific advantage of the lessee if it took the form of an undertaking by the lessor not to grant drilling rights to others within a certain distance from the boundaries of the lease. We do sometimes find instances of the creation of such a "zone of protection." *Allison and Evans' Appeal*[99] was a case that turned on the interpretation to be given to a poorly drafted protection clause of this type, and a similar protection clause was unsuccessfully relied upon in the unreported Venango County case of *McCray and Donaghy v. Kepler, Watson and others* (1870)[100] (yet another case featuring Jonathan Watson). Lessors may well have resisted such clauses, however, as potentially restricting their returns from land.[101]

---

[97] Porter farm lease 1868, in Drake Well Museum unclassified lease collection; W. C. Stiles family oil and mining company records, A&M No. 199, Box 3, FF6.

[98] Beates 2007: 61, citing *Titusville Morning Herald,* July 19 and 26, 1866.

[99] 77 Pa. 221 (1874).

[100] Stralko collection DW.70.06.686.

[101] Letter from one Craig, as lessee, to C. W. Heydrick, May 26, 1895, asking if a proposed protection clause was the reason for Heydrick's delay in signing lease: Heydrick collection, DW 76.37.213.

In Chapter 4, which is devoted to the regulation of the exploitation of mineral water sources in France, we shall see that the "zone of protection" concept has been the key instrument for state regulation there, against the background of a civil law system that fully recognizes the rule of capture. Unlike the well spacing laws that began to appear in the United States from 1915 onward,[102] the French "zones of protection" resemble what might have been achieved via lease negotiations, in that each zone is administratively tailored to the specific circumstances of the area, and the achievements and problems of this regime invite consideration of how far protection clauses in leases might have palliated the worst effects of competitive drilling.

The protection from capture that was actually achieved through the leasing system relied on a practice directly contrary to creating zones of protection. Rather than granting lessees buffer zones around their leases, lessors sought to protect their royalties against erosion by drainage of oil and gas into wells on neighboring properties by insisting that the lessees drill additional wells, and in particular, drill wells close to the boundary line opposite any neighboring well that might pose a threat of drainage. As an understanding of how wells might drain an area of land began to develop,[103] cases started appearing, from the early 1880s onward, in which lessors sued their lessees or sought forfeitures of the leases for failure to protect against drainage by drilling wells beyond those expressly provided for by the lease. Pennsylvania courts initially showed little sympathy for these lessors, giving no indication whatsoever that they regarded drainage by neighbors as anything but a familiar risk against which the lessor might have provided by contract.[104] Not until 1896 did a reported case of this kind, *Kleppner v. Lemon*,[105] go the lessor's way, and there it was his own lessee who was drilling on adjacent property.

A parallel evolution occurred in the content of leases themselves, which in the 1880s and 1890s began to include an offset well obligation. The matter still appears, however, to have been one for negotiation and not an automatic obligation. Of four leases granted between 1886 and 1889 by C. W. Heydrick, who was a lawyer with an oil and gas practice as well as a lessor, two had no offset well obligation, one included a quite general one, and the fourth required an offset well only where a paying well was drilled on an adjoining tract within 15 rods (247.5 feet) of the boundary line; the clause did not apply in the case of wells

---

[102] Harrison 1970: 361. See further below, Ch. 9, at 259–68.

[103] See above, Ch. 2, at 43–5, and below, Ch. 7, at 196–7.

[104] *James v. Emory Oil Co.*, 1 Pennypacker 242 (Pa. 1881); *Blair v. Peck*, 1 Pennypacker 247 (Pa. 1881); *McKnight v. Manufacturers' Natural Gas Co.*, 146 Pa. 185, 23 A. 164 (1892).

[105] 176 Pa. 502, 35 A. 109.

drilled on the residue of the tract of which the lease was part.[106] The rather late arrival of the clause is confirmed by the fact that it gets no mention in an analysis of 71 oil and gas leases made between 1859 and 1872, presented in *The Derrick's Handbook of Petroleum* in 1902.[107]

The importance of these clauses diminished in the twentieth century as courts started recognizing an implicit obligation of lessees to protect the leasehold by drilling offset wells.[108] This implied obligation has been stigmatized by at least one leading legal commentator as a much more serious cause of wasteful drilling than the rule of capture itself.[109] This ignores the fact, however, that had the rule of capture not prevailed, the offset drilling obligation would have been unnecessary, since other, less expensive and less risky remedies would have been available where drainage was suspected, such as a legal suit for an injunction and an appropriate share of the production from the offending well. From the standpoint of my argument here, the real importance of the appearance of the offset well obligation, and of the earlier legal attempts to get lessees to drill additional wells, is the evidence thereby offered of a firm industry belief that capture was legitimate and could give rise to no direct remedy.

CONCLUSION: CAPTURE AS THE FIRST PRINCIPLE OF THE INFANT OIL INDUSTRY

I have suggested at a couple of points earlier in this chapter that one should be careful not to assume too readily that early petroleum practice—in particular, the granting of leases over very small areas—of itself demonstrates conclusively that the first lessors and lessees believed the rule of capture governed their operations. As I explained, the prevailing view as to how petroleum existed in its undisturbed state was so different from what scientific investigation has since taught us that arguing from operators' actions to their beliefs about capture is a tricky process. But it is still hard to deny that *some* belief about the legitimacy of capture was crucial to the way the industry first developed. As the preceding discussion shows, there was early recognition that the deliberate tapping of producing wells, by drilling as close as one could get, was common practice; and we find a certain embarrassment, well exemplified in the *Pittsburgh Commercial* article, about drawing a line to distinguish unacceptable from acceptable uses of this technique. Eaton also points

---

[106] Heydrick collection, DW.76.37.204–6, 208.
[107] 2 Boyle (*Derrick's Handbook*) 1902: 190–219.
[108] Below, Ch. 7, at 194–7.
[109] Hardwicke 1935: 418–19.

to this difficulty when he talks about the "curious questions in casuistry" to which the problem of interfering wells gives rise,[110] as does McLaurin when he tells us that "geologists and scientists reveled in the ethics suggested by such interference."[111]

A lawyer is entitled to ask why his own profession should have been so invisible when all this earnest discussion was going on. An anonymous reviewer put this very question in 1873, when asking why the new edition of Professor Washburn's book on easements and servitudes had nothing to say about rights in petroleum deposits. His comments show remarkable prescience:

> We should have supposed that the courts of the great state of Pennsylvania would have had occasion to investigate and decide questions of this character. It is obvious that the analogies governing rights in underground water will be resorted to to settle conflicting claims in petroleum wells: and it is obvious that if the flowing of the fifty-barrel petroleum well may be cut off by an ingenious geologist, who knows how the land lies, the most important rights are to be acquired or lost. This, of course, upon the theory that petroleum percolates. If, however, it flows in streams under the earth, which are well defined, then analogies drawn from rights in natural surface watercourses may govern. If it exists in underground ponds or reservoirs, who can say what are the rights of adjoining proprietors, or whether he shall win the prize in the race of diligence who has the longer pump and the more powerful steam-engine?

One might hazard a guess that this reviewer, who was unaware of the early Pennsylvania cases such as *Funk v. Haldeman*,[112] was not an oil industry specialist. Oilmen were certainly not averse to litigation: cases involving oil leases got into the courts as early as 1860, and the stream of oil and gas litigation has never ceased since.[113] Yet the one idea, expressed or more usually unexpressed, that seems to run through the contemporary discussions of the issue of tapping wells, and is reflected in the reviewer's reference to the "ingenious geologist," is that the sufferer had no legal recourse, even if the tapping could be viewed as "cut-throat" or malicious. Recall that the correspondent of the *Oil City Register*, quoted in the *Pittsburgh Commercial*, started from the premise that property in oil wells was unprotected by law, so that legislative intervention was necessary. An explicit assertion that the well owner was without legal recourse is found in J. T. Henry's detailed account, published in 1873, of the interference of the Noble and Caldwell Wells. This was the case where the first (Noble) well drilled was unsuccessful until redrilled to a

---

[110] 53 Pa. 229 (1867), below, at 88.

[111] McLaurin 1896: 142.

[112] Above, Ch. 2, at 88.

[113] Stralko collection, DW.70.06, *passim*; and for an extreme example, Clark and Halbouty 1952: Ch. 17.

greater depth after the second (Caldwell) well had begun producing, whereupon the former flowed at a much greater rate than its neighbor and substantially reduced the latter's supply. Henry opined:

> Mr. Noble, although not legally bound to pay a single dollar to the owners of the "Caldwell well," yet acknowledged a moral obligation to reimburse them. The Noble well had been located and drilled 134 feet three years before the Caldwell well had been projected, and when it was down, and it was absolutely known that it was drawing the oil from his neighbors, there was no legal obligation resting upon him to make good their loss.[114]

The passage leaves us wondering what importance Henry—and indeed the protagonists—attached to the fact that the Noble Well was located, but not completed, before its neighbor. Would the legal position have been viewed in the same way if the Caldwell had been first in every respect? It is hard to see how the fact that Noble had been first to drill a *dry* hole could bear on the Caldwell's position. The fact that its owners, when it appeared that Noble's offer of compensation would be unsatisfactory to them, refrained—as did the Phillips interests in the Phillips–Woodford incident—from launching any legal process, preferring the familiar threat of drawing their own tubing, thus seems more likely to reflect their view of the general lack of legal recourse of the injured owner.

This behavior of oil producers in Pennsylvania seems especially striking when we look at what was happening on the other side of the country, in the silver mines of Nevada. The rules regulating such mining (I examine their nature in Chapter 8) recognized a party's "extralateral right"—that is, a right to follow one's allotted section of a vein of silver wherever it traveled beneath the earth. This might mean that a mine could run under the claim of another as long as the two mines were accessing separate veins. "Experienced men" in Nevada might therefore be found digging into other people's veins and alleging that they were in fact exploiting a separate vein. Nevada miners, however, did not treat such practice as a basis for "arrangements" or as posing "cases of conscience." They went straight to court and in fact overwhelmed the fledgling Nevada judicial system with the numbers of their cases. Gary Libecap reported in 1978 that 70 percent of district court cases up to 1866 raised such issues, and that the leading mines incurred litigation costs representing 11 percent of production proceeds.[115]

There seems no good reason to suppose that Nevada silver miners came of more litigious stock than Pennsylvania oil producers. While the Pennsylvania preference for self-help may have reflected a considered opinion of the content of the law, it

---

[114] Henry 1873: 386.
[115] Libecap 1978; 1979. On extralateral rights, see further Leshy 1987: 95.

might also be explained by consideration of the *practical* feasibility and utility of legal recourse. One factor that differentiated oil production from hard rock mining, and is easily forgotten today, was the very short life of the average producing well in these first years: not more than 18 months.[116] Winning your case after your well had turned to water would not have been very satisfying.

Moreover, with the fissure theory of petroleum accumulation, rather than modern reservoir theory, as background, capture looks subtly different and much more difficult to prove. If my neighbor's flow of oil is diminished or cut off when I drill nearby, he will have to show that this was my fault and that his well would not have dried up or gone to water anyway. And even if he does overcome this high evidential hurdle, what then? Does the vein run from his land to mine, or vice versa? If Dodge reflected general opinion when he suggested that a "single crevice" might extend "long distances,"[117] who is to say what was the original location of the bulk of the oil produced by either party? And if one followed William Wright's precept and drilled between two flowing wells, the original location of the oil produced from the new well would be impossible to determine. All these considerations must, as a practical matter, have made launching an action for interference a daunting enterprise, though again, the difficulty and uncertainty of determining whether mines were tapping a single mineral vein or separate ones did not deter Nevada litigants.

The frequency with which unsuccessful wells were drilled in close proximity to large flowing ones (in one case reported by Wright, only 11 feet away)[118]— perhaps due to the fact that oil in some of the earliest exploited territories in Pennsylvania was probably held in small stratigraphic traps rather than in extended formations[119]—must have further reinforced feelings that the underground behavior of oil and gas was largely unknowable. Wright in fact calls it "lawless," though with reference to physical, not human, laws.[120] This unknowability was, we should remember, the explicit basis on which mid-nineteenth-century courts in both England and the United States erected the doctrine of capture of subterranean water.[121] It would seem perfectly natural for oil producers to follow the same logic, whether they knew the rules of law on subterranean water or not.

If, in the very beginning, this uncertainty meant that by drilling in close proximity, you "tapped your neighbor's well" rather than "capturing your

---

[116] Williamson and Daum 1959: 159.

[117] Above, at 67–8.

[118] Wright 1865: 91–3; for a contrasting case see Eaton 1866: 133–4.

[119] DeGolyer 1961: 20.

[120] Wright 1865: 91–3.

[121] Above, Ch. 2, at 36–41.

neighbor's oil," the developing literature shows quite an early shift from the language of tapping to that of drainage, implying a notion of some fixed and natural relationship between the surface of land and the oil and gas beneath. Once people recognized drainage, they of course would have recognized capture in the modern sense of the term. An early, though not disinterested, step in this direction is found in the argument of counsel for the complainant Funk in the case of *Funk v. Haldeman*,[122] argued in November 1866. Haldeman and his partners had ratified an agreement allowing Funk to search for and recover oil over defined areas of two farms they had purchased, but a few years afterward, they started drilling for oil themselves within these areas, claiming that Funk's rights were not exclusive. Funk's counsel argued that this would devalue his client's rights: "Oil, like water, is essentially indivisible, and taking it in one place draws it off from all others; and as the owner cannot take oil from our wells, he cannot steal the fluid rights by tapping at a distance."[123] Though the language was still that of "tapping," the admittedly vague notion of oil's subterranean behavior was deployed here to assert a claim to the oil underlying a given area of land.

We have to wait, however, until the next decade to find explicit reference to drainage in the literature. A telling source is a pamphlet issued in 1878 by the Petroleum Producers' Union, which brought together producers' associations from across the oil regions in support of its plan to improve prices by funneling oil sales through the associations, thus giving them the ability to hold quantities off the market to keep prices stable. The pamphlet explains why an alternative approach, a moratorium on drilling, was impracticable: "To a certain extent producers are compelled to produce oil and to sink wells even against their conviction that their operations will work injury to their business. The operations of adjoining owners often compel men to drill their own lands to prevent their being drained by their neighbors."[124]

Two years later, John Carll, the oil expert on the Pennsylvania State Geological Survey, pointed to fear of drainage as a reason why oil producers were so reluctant to disclose well records, a major handicap to the development of better understanding of oilfield geology and reservoir mechanics:

> If he has made a successful venture, the prompt publication of the fact causes an eager crowd to rush in around him on all sides, and he is often obliged in consequences [*sic*] to drill more rapidly than he otherwise would, to protect himself, or in other words to secure his share of oil in the pool which he has discovered—for it is now well known by experience that oil cannot safely be "tanked in the rock" as

---

[122] 53 Pa. 229 (1867).
[123] *Ibid.* at 235.
[124] Petroleum Producers' Union 1878: 9–10.

formerly supposed, to be drawn forth when wanted, if in the meantime wells are drilled and pumped all around the borders of the oil-bearing "tank."

Many farms known to be good, and held in reserve for development when the price of oil should warrant, have been found when subsequently tested, to the chagrin of their owners, to be almost completely drained by the wells on adjoining lands that had been steadily at work during the intervening time in depleting the reserved pool which no farm lines could protect a thousand feet below the surface.[125]

Again, S. F. Peckham, in his 1884 report to the U.S. Congress on the oil industry, wrote that it required only "a moment's reflection" to see that the dangers of drainage compelled early drilling.[126] The appearance, already noted, of cases in the 1880s in which lessors attempted to get leases forfeited for the lessees' failure to protect against drainage shows that this understanding was not confined to geologists but was spreading through the industry—yet at no point before 1897 did it lead to an attempt to get a court to declare that drainage was in itself unlawful.

Working out what people might have thought on the basis of things they did not do and words they did not say is a risky business. But the leasing and drilling practices of the early industry, and the unanimous and continuous acceptance, over several decades of development and change, of the idea that one could have no legal remedy against a neighbor for subterranean loss of oil or damage to a producing well, together refute any notion that the law of capture was a rule imposed on the industry, 30 years after its foundation, by ill-informed judges. Capture, or appropriation, of something whose natural environment and characteristics were almost entirely unknown was from the very beginning the main force driving the industry's participants. As Judge Rufus Stone put it in his 1926 history of McKean County, Pennsylvania, site of the Bradford Field, at one time the largest producing field in the world:

Many years before the Supreme Court decided that oil and gas were of the nature of animals *ferae naturae*, and that possession of the land is not necessarily possession of the oil, the producers of the Bradford District instinctively apprehended that such must be the law. Hence, boundary lines were crowded to bridle the animal before it should escape.[127]

The deepening understanding of the behavior of oil underground and the associated recognition, indeed measurement, of the phenomenon of drainage

---

[125] Carll 1880: 172–3.
[126] Peckham 1884: 91.
[127] Stone 1926: 182.

appear to have done nothing to modify this "instinctive apprehension." The inability of just about everybody connected with the industry to imagine any restraints on capture (or any way in which the industry could be organized so as to function without it) suffices to unlock several puzzles: the near 30-year famine of litigation on the topic; the fact that when the judges finally did refer to the rule of capture, in *Wood County* and *Westmoreland*,[128] it was as nothing more than an uncontroversial link in a chain of reasoning leading elsewhere; and the reason why the only direct challenge to the rule was met with a judgment that contained more indignation than argument.[129]

---

[128] Above, Ch. 2, at 20–25.

[129] *Kelley v. Ohio Oil Co.*, 57 Ohio St. 317, 49 N.E. 399.

PART II
ALTERNATIVES AND PARALLELS

CHAPTER 4

THE MINERAL WATER INDUSTRY IN FRANCE: PROTECTION AND COMPETITION

BACKGROUND

At almost the same time as the peaceful valley of Oil Creek was being turned into a maelstrom of competitive drilling and draining, in another peaceful valley, far away in south-central France, a struggle was developing that put one contemporary observer in mind of "the way they search for oil in the petroleum towns of America."[1] But the object of this struggle, which pitted a local family against the mayor and councilors of the local commune, along with their business associates, was to get possession not of oil, but of a commodity greatly prized in nineteenth-century France: the sources of mineral water that lay beneath the village of La Bourboule and would sustain lucrative activities such as a bathing establishment or the sale of bottled water.

---

[1] Speech by Jules Guérin before the Académie de Médecine in February 1873, cited by Eudel 1911 [2007]: 105.

The *guerre des puits* (war of the wells) carried on with such determination in La Bourboule between 1863 and 1879[2] was not an isolated case. It was one of many competitive struggles for a valuable commercial resource which—even if the curative properties of "Seneca oil" were now understood to be much less important than its other applications—had much in common with oil and gas. Its manifestations at the surface were through clear springs rather than sticky seepages; its underground behavior was no less mysterious than that of oil; but with enough energy, skill, and capital, an entrepreneur might well hope to tap a source and thereby obtain a supply of a commodity that the French had long valued and that was enjoying, by the middle of the nineteenth century, a veritable consumer boom. From the 1830s onward, in fact, anyone in possession of land on which there rose valuable mineral water springs ran the risk that rival operators would appear as owners or lessees of neighboring land and start digging or drilling to capture the same water for bottling or for curative use in a bathing establishment. The method of competition resembled that in the American oilfields, and the main legal issue it raised was exactly the same: did each operator have the right to take any of the fluid rising on his or her land, even if it might have come from under the land of others?

In this chapter, I shall examine the way this issue was dealt with in France, both under the general law of property and by and under legislation that was eventually passed in 1856 after two decades of debate. The story illuminates the rule of capture, as we know it in the oil industry, from several different angles. It demonstrates the antiquity of the rule and shows that American courts were not unusual in treating it as a natural adjunct of property rights in an age of rapid economic development. It also evidences the hesitations and difficulties experienced by the French authorities in their attempts to develop an alternative principle to that of capture, even in support of what was universally then perceived as an important public interest: the widest possible access by the sick to the curative properties of mineral water. These legislative and administrative travails give some hint of the difficulties that were to be expected in the United States once a public interest in conservation was perceived as a perhaps necessary constraint on the exercise of property rights in oil and gas. They are the more remarkable in that mineral water in France, unlike oil and gas in the United States, had long been the subject of close regulatory attention when physical competition for the resource became a serious issue.

To set the legal parallels and divergences in context, I examine in the first few sections of this chapter the economic and physical attributes of mineral water, along with elements of its regulatory history, before analyzing the legal rules

---

[2] Discussed in detail below at 116–8.

through which competitive drilling was first sustained and then—to a limited extent—controlled.

SPAS AND BOTTLES: THE MINERAL WATER INDUSTRY

The mineral water industry is today an important contributor to the French economy. An official paper of 1999[3] estimated the turnover of the industry at some 20 billion francs (€3.05 billion, or $3.12 billion, at 1999 values and exchange rates), of which 65 percent was represented by sales of bottled mineral water and 35 percent by the turnover of the hundred or so French spas. Drinking and bathing in highly mineralized waters remains an important part of French therapeutic culture, with a quarter of the cost of a medically prescribed cure at a spa reimbursed by the country's social security system, and with numerous other persons financing visits as *curistes*[4] from their own resources or staying in spas for purely recreational reasons. From the 1999 paper, we can derive an estimate of more than 1.56 million weeks of presence by *curistes* at spas in 1998 and over 100,000 jobs directly or indirectly sustained by this branch of the industry. The equivalent employment figure for the bottled water sector was more than 30,000. A quarter of bottled mineral water production was exported.

Geography and Hydrology

The sources from which this flow of water derives today number some 400 and are almost all found south and west of a line drawn across France from Metz in the northeast to Bordeaux on the Atlantic coast. It is here that we find the mountainous areas of France, in which a succession of events in the tertiary period, notably the creation of the Alps and Pyrenees and the consequent disturbances to the much older mountains of central France, produced the conditions favorable to the appearance of natural springs of highly mineralized water, often reaching the surface at temperatures substantially higher than those of ordinary subterranean flows. Chaudes-Aigues in Cantal in central France, where water shoots up a fault from a reservoir 2,200 meters down to emerge at a temperature of 82°C (180°F), is the most spectacular example.

The hydrological circuit of heated mineral waters ordinarily comprises an upland capture area where rainwater can penetrate to considerable depths via

---

[3] France. Ministère de l'Économie 1999.

[4] I use this term, which has no convenient English equivalent, to refer to those who visit spas primarily for health, as opposed to recreational, reasons.

fissures in what would otherwise be impermeable rocks (granite, gneiss), before traveling slowly within broken or permeable strata and eventually finding fissures through which it can mount sufficiently rapidly to the surface to retain its heat and avoid excessive dilution from mixture with waters circulating in permeable soils and sands close to the surface. An example is the water of Vichy, where the reservoir strata are thought to lie some 3,000 to 4,500 meters below the surface and to be fed from the mountains of the Chaine des Puys, some 80 kilometers from Vichy itself.[5] Waters of this type may also accumulate significant gas content, becoming charged with CO_2 released from the earth's mantle; the nature and extent of their mineral content depend on the characteristics of the strata through which they travel.

Another type of circuit, perhaps likely to produce cooler waters, can be found in glaciated country like the south shore of Lac Leman, where a reservoir composed of sands trapped between layers of impermeable moraine collects and holds rainfall long enough (around 50 years) for the water issuing from the springs at Evian to acquire its mineral elements.[6] At 50 years, it should be stressed, the waters of Evian are newborns in comparison with deep-strata waters like those of the Pyrenees, for which rainfall-to-emergence periods of 5,000 years (at Cauterets), 14,000 years (at Luchon), and even 40,000 years have been proposed on the basis of radiocarbon dating.[7] It will quickly be appreciated that the underground condition of mineral water (and indeed, of any water stored in deep aquifers) is much closer to that of oil and gas than critics of early judicial linkings of oil and subterranean water have been prepared to allow.[8]

The variable nature of the hydrological circuit, and in particular, of the phase of emergence of mineral water from its reservoir, means that the capture of mineral water by artificial means—the digging or drilling of wells—as opposed to collection from natural springs is a matter of extreme delicacy. The value of a given source of mineral water depends on the mixture of minerals it contains, the gases it carries with it, and the temperature at which it emerges. Digging and drilling in the neighborhood of existing springs (or indeed, in some cases, at considerable distances) can easily have the effect of diverting an existing flow to the surface by offering a more convenient exit for the water without changing its characteristics. Improved flows may indeed result. But it is also possible that such interventions, by allowing greater volumes of nonmineralized subsurface water to dilute the upward flow, may weaken the mineralization of the water or reduce its temperature, to the

---

[5] Chambriard 1999: 18–19. See also, for waters in central France generally, Dolques 2002.

[6] Blavoux 1998.

[7] *Ibid.*

[8] Above, Ch. 1, at 14–17.

point where it becomes worthless for therapeutic or commercial purposes. The growing appreciation of these risks in the course of the nineteenth century was the key factor shaping a process of legislative and judicial qualification of the principle of capture in its application to mineral water resources.

Public Health Regulation, 1605–1823

When that process started in the 1830s, the mineral water industry had already experienced two centuries of governmental interest and regulation, which began with an edict of Henry IV in 1605 establishing a "General Superintendency of the Baths and Mineral Springs of the Kingdom," confided to his principal physician. The superintendent was charged with nominating and supervising local *intendants des eaux* (water supervisors) and improving provision for *curistes*. The burdens of this task were sweetened by the accompaniment of a monopoly over the distribution of mineral water.[9] This early link between mineral water exploitation and medical practice and privileges was consolidated by the promulgation of a decision of the Conseil du Roi (King's Council) dated May 5, 1781, establishing a regime of control of mineral water, from source to final use or consumption, whose broad lines have remained unaltered until the present day.[10] Reconfirmed with modifications and embellishments by each of the regimes that followed the fall of the monarchy, it was comprehensively restated after the Restoration of 1814 in the form of the Royal Ordinance of June 18–July 7, 1823, which, with some modifications introduced by the Imperial Decree of January 28–February 15, 1860, remained in force throughout the nineteenth century.

The key figure in this system was the inspecting physician officially appointed for each bathing establishment or group of establishments, with wide powers of control over both activities at the establishment and the dispatch of water elsewhere. In addition, the ordinance of 1823 required each source of mineral water to be duly authorized on the basis of an analysis of the water produced;[11] records of authorizations provide a clear and precise picture of the extent of interest in commercial exploitation of mineral water at different moments in the nineteenth century and in different locations. Additional powers resided in the *préfet* (prefect) of the relevant *département* (department),[12] who could make

---

[9] Chambriard 1998: 21–2.

[10] See now *Code de la Santé Publique*, arts. L1322-1, R1322-5–R1322-15.

[11] Arts. 1, 2.

[12] After the Revolution, France was divided for administrative purposes into 83 (now 100) *départements*, each governed by a *préfet* as the head of the local administration and the representative of central power.

regulations for the conduct of establishments, approve tariffs, and create additional rules for establishments connected with springs owned by public bodies: the state itself, departments, communes,[13] and also charitable institutions such as hospitals.

The professed objective of all this legislation was to protect the health of the public by ensuring, so far as possible, the authenticity and purity of the waters they drank or bathed in. At the same time, it was a source of public and private enrichment. Like much regulation of the Ancien Régime,[14] the legislation relied upon the creation of monopoly rights, notably in relation to the sale of water elsewhere than at the spring from which it issued, a privilege granted only to a limited number of sales offices in return for an annual fee. In addition, it reflected the medical profession's anxiety to secure effective control over a type of remedy that enjoyed great local popularity in the areas rich in mineral springs and was largely self-prescribed and self-administered. For an entrepreneurially minded doctor, appointment to a post of inspecting physician offered not only a regular stipend, but also chances to profit from the development of the watering places under his supervision. The ideal was to combine the ownership of the springs and associated baths with the functions of official supervision of their operation and the offering of medical services there.

Where bathing establishments owned by the state were operated by private individuals or companies under lease, the inspecting physician was forbidden to take any financial interest in the lease.[15] The government appears to have been less concerned about the cumulation of functions in the private sector, where doctors who discovered or became proprietors of mineral springs were regularly appointed to inspect them until well into the nineteenth century. Thus, Dr. J.-B. Debrest, who acquired a mineral spring at Chateldon in the Puy-de-Dôme in central France around 1770, circulating his own chemical analyses of the waters by way of advertisement, obtained nomination by the royal commission as *intendant* in 1777, and his grandson Dr. Emanuel Debrest, who had become proprietor in 1832, was in turn appointed inspecting physician by the minister of commerce in 1834.[16] More subtle was the approach of Monsieur Choussy-Dubrueil, who in 1828 made an offer to buy the springs and associated baths at La Bourboule (Puy-de-Dôme) from their proprietor, subject to the condition that his brother, Dr. Pierre Choussy, was successful in obtaining appointment as the inspecting

---

[13] The commune is the smallest unit of local government in France. Created at the time of the French Revolution, there were originally some 41,000; today there are still more than 36,000, with a median population (1999 census) of 380 and a median area of 10.73 square kilometers.

[14] The "former order," France's political and social system before the Revolution of 1789.

[15] Arrêté du 21 avril 1800, art. 1(4).

[16] Sarazin 2000.

physician. Dr. Choussy was indeed successful, remaining inspector until his death in 1853 and also managing the baths, of which he became part owner in 1830.[17] Such a combination of public functions and private profit was forbidden by article 12 of the Decree of 1860: with tongue firmly lodged in cheek, the author of the decree's *exposé de motifs* (explanatory note) stated that this was simply for clarification, as it could not be supposed that this principle of economic disinterestedness was ever breached by members of the medical inspection service.

Public Promotion of Development

The interest of the authorities in mineral waters was not simply one of reducing risks to health through the imposition of controls. At all levels—local, regional, and national—there was a desire to promote the development of facilities for *curistes*, through the provision of better buildings for bathing and drinking the waters, more and better accommodation for visitors coming from a distance, and improvement of the springs themselves in both quality and quantity. In part, this desire for development reflected public health concerns. Plenty of early descriptions suggest the rude and insanitary conditions under which springs were kept and used. An official investigation of 1772 produced reports of waters from which some people died because of excessive consumption or which were so misused by the population as to be "more often fatal than healthy," and of baths that were "in such a poor state and so dirty as to inspire horror" or "wretched" and too small.[18]

Other reports from the early part of the century, besides taking up the theme of lack of sanitation,[19] also raised moral issues: promiscuity between the sexes was said to reign at Mont-Dore, in the department of Puy-de-Dôme in central France, especially within the Caesar Bath, with its single basin.[20] (This concern about the low moral tone of bathing establishments actually appeared earlier, in a report by the Florentine Poggi, apostolic secretary at Coutances, the diocese in Normandy where the spa of Forges-les-Eaux is situated, referring to the "innumerable beauties who frequent the baths unaccompanied by husband or relations save an old aunt whose scrutiny is easily escaped." De Ribier, relaying this report in his pamphlet of 1904 on baths and mineral waters under the Ancien Régime, asserts that this reproach cannot be addressed to establishments in Auvergne, "where the manners

---

[17] Roux 1975: 75–85. Subsequent events at La Bourboule are discussed below, 116–8.
[18] Jarrassé 1996.
[19] See Faure 1985 for the area around Saint-Étienne (Loire).
[20] Faure 1994.

are as rigorous as the climate." Clearly he had not examined the departmental archives of Puy-de-Dôme.[21])

Another policy concern was to develop and protect French spas so that they might rival better-known establishments elsewhere, like Spa in what is now Belgium and Carlsbad in Bohemia. The French state has owned some spas for centuries: Vichy, Néris-les-Bains, and Bourbon-l'Archambault, in central France, were fruits of a royal confiscation of lands in 1567; other possessions in northeastern France date from Napoleonic conquests at the beginning of the nineteenth century.

The state's approach to development of this patrimony was at best hesitant. In particular, it dithered between leasing and direct control as the best means of ensuring development and adequacy of service. Napoleon was skeptical of the ability of communes, departments, and even the state to run spas efficiently, and his *arrêté* (decision) of December 27, 1802, provided that bathing establishments were to be leased out rather than run directly by public authorities, unless a specific authorization was obtained from the responsible minister. In fact, a mixture of leasing and direct management continued throughout the nineteenth century: smaller authorities, like communes, that decided to run their own spas often foundered for lack of capital.[22]

The Evolution of the Industry in the Nineteenth Century

Thanks to the requirement for an official authorization for the use of a new source of mineral waters, and the regular returns to the state's supervising authorities, we can trace the development of the exploitation of mineral water in France from early in the nineteenth century.[23] A useful starting point for assessing the development of the industry from this time is the figure of 750 sources in 295 communes recorded by the Mines Administration in 1841, which excluded small springs of no real economic significance. Over the next 50 years, the number of springs recorded on this basis by the Mines Administration rose to 1,412; it reached 1,820 in 1914. These springs were distributed across a proportionally smaller number of communes: 383 in 1892, 443 in 1914.

One can see from these last figures that a process of concentration was going on at least from 1841 as the number of sources grew. New sources were being sought, and found, in communes where springs already existed. This process went hand in

---

[21] de Ribier 1904.

[22] See Penez 1994: 18–20 on Châtel-Guyon, and compare the more positive experience of the departmental establishment not far away at Mont-Dore: Penez 1994; Faure 1994: 28.

[23] See generally Penez 2005: Ch. 1.

hand with the development of facilities, and both were driven by the remarkable increase in the popularity of "taking the waters," sustained throughout the nineteenth century. A tenfold increase in the number of *curistes* between 1822 and 1910 seems quite plausible.[24] From a freely available and often self-prescribed medicament resorted to by local populations (and the occasional rich sufferer or tourist), mineral water springs became the centerpiece of elaborate urban developments designed to offer a comfortable and even luxurious welcome to patients from far and wide, to afford them specialist medical care, and to provide facilities for leisure and diversion that would attract the healthy no less than the ailing. Floating companies to acquire concessions for publicly owned sources, or to purchase private ones, on the promise of ever more elaborate schemes for developing bathing establishments, parks, casinos, hotels, and other amenities, was a favorite sport of promoters. There were, of course, many failures and false starts, but by the end of the century, this *fièvre thermale* (baths fever) had produced a radically changed landscape for the mineral water industry.

When, in 1837, the French legislature first debated proposals to protect existing springs, proponents and opponents of the measure agreed on a figure of only 77 for mineral water establishments: buildings expressly designed for taking the waters by bathing or drinking or both. Eight of these were state-owned, 22 owned by departments or communes, and the rest in private hands. Other counts around this time, however, give a figure of around 120 to 130 *stations* (towns or villages that were watering places), with a much higher proportion of privately owned ones, and since a station could well have more than one establishment, that for establishments should be even higher. Parliamentarians probably had in mind only the best developed. Relating either figure to the Mines Administration's estimate that 295 communes possessed springs at this time makes it clear that the great majority of communes with mineral waters had no associated development worth mentioning. By the end of the century, however, the number of stations had reached nearly 200, which suggests that half the communes possessing sources had a developed station, with a custom-built bathing establishment, hotels, and at least rudimentary tourist attractions.

The popularity, sophistication, and style of these different watering places varied enormously. At all times during the century, the more successful stations exercised a gravitational pull not just on the patient in search of a cure or the tourist in search of diversion, but also on those who saw financial opportunities in mineral water. If you wanted to make money developing a bathing establishment, where better to try than in proximity to facilities that already enjoyed a reputation among the public and the medical profession for the quality of their waters? Opportunities

---

[24] *Ibid.* 32–43.

for acquiring concessions or leases were always limited, and looking for new sources in the vicinity of established ones was often the most attractive option, certainly offering surer returns than investing in the development and marketing of springs that no one hitherto had heard of.

The same logic could be applied to the use of mineral water for bottling and retail sale. Originally a sideline to the development of a bathing establishment, and representing a high-priced product destined for the luxury market, bottled mineral water by the end of the century had become a widely consumed product, meeting a need for pure water at a time when this was not necessarily satisfied by public distribution systems.[25] Certain mineral waters, stemming from high-volume springs and with low levels of mineralization, were particularly suitable for this trade: Evian, Saint-Galmier (the Badoit brand), and Vittel remain as highly successful examples. Again, sources successfully developed for such purposes soon became a point of attraction for explorations by would-be competitors.

PROPERTY RIGHTS AND THEIR REGULATION

General Principles

The conditions of such competition for sources of mineral water were set by the Civil Code promulgated on March 21, 1804. The relevant articles dealt with the matter as a question of private property: under the Ancien Régime, the Crown claimed the bed of navigable rivers as part of the *domaine royal* (royal domain, or Crown lands) under an Ordinance of 1669,[26] but did not consider subterranean waters—or other rivers—to be of sufficient public interest to warrant analogous treatment. The code, in fact, simply carried forward notions that had their origin in Roman law. It adopted the accession principle, stating that the ownership of land included the ownership of what is below it and above it (article 552, first sentence). From this principle, described in discussions during the drafting of the code as "too old and constant a rule not to be well known,"[27] there followed the more specific rules that owners were free to undertake whatever excavations they wished on their land, and take from them whatever products they furnished, subject to laws and regulations relating to mines and *police* (public control) (article 552, third sentence); and that the owner of land with a spring had the right to use the water flowing from it as he or she wished (article 641).

---

[25] Chambriard 1998.
[26] Gaonac'h 1999: 13–14.
[27] See 9 Fenet 1827–9: 138–9.

This last article caused real difficulties to the framers of the code and the official bodies that were called upon to discuss it.[28] Concern was expressed about the situation of landowners who had enjoyed and relied upon a flow of water onto their land from a spring situated on land above, should the proprietor of that land decide to cut off that water and use it entirely for his or her own purposes. The situation of villagers who might be relying on such a supply for their water needs was also evoked. The article also contemplated that an owner might drill, or undertake subsurface works, on his or her land so as to secure a source of water. Scholarly opinion was divided, and law and practice varied in different parts of France, on such questions as whether the inferior proprietor could establish rights to a flow of water by long and notorious usage (prescription) and whether the spring owner's discretion was limited by a requirement that it not be exercised maliciously—the same questions that were to trouble English and American courts later in the century.[29]

The text that emerged in 1804 met these concerns by recognizing that the lower proprietor could obtain rights to a continued flow by 30 years' prescription (article 641, as amended), and that villagers could always insist on the maintenance of a necessary supply of water, though only against payment if they had failed to establish prescriptive rights (article 643). In addition, the courts were given a broad discretion, applicable to both surface and subterranean waters, to adjudicate competing claims to water flow by reconciling the interests of agriculture with respect for property, while respecting local rules and usages (article 645).

What these debates about water rights never touched on, however, was the situation where the owner of a spring found it dried up by reason of another's drilling into or diverting the underground flow that produced it. Nothing appeared to limit the right of the landowner under article 552 to excavate or drill on his or her land to capture underground water, whether percolating at large beneath the surface, following a defined subterranean channel, or trapped in an underground aquifer. Article 641 protected the inferior proprietor who received the runoff from a spring; it did nothing to protect the spring itself from interference. In any competition for water, therefore, the victor would be the one who dug or drilled the deepest well, or whose land was advantageously positioned in relation to the direction of flow of the water, so as to be able to abstract it before it reached a neighbor's land. The French civil courts, in common with those of most other civil law jurisdictions, have seen no reason to adopt a restrictive interpretation of the landowner's right to search for and appropriate water,

---

[28] *Ibid.* 245–314, *passim.*
[29] Above, Ch. 2, at 36–41.

drawing the line only at the purely malicious abstraction of water, done to dry up a neighbor's supply without any purpose of supplying the taker's own water needs.

These malicious appropriation cases happen to concern mineral water, and I look at them in more detail later. Otherwise, any appropriation beneficial to the landowner was likely to find judicial acceptance, even if the true benefit was a purely pecuniary one. In the case of *Commune de Varennes-les-Nevers c. Boignes* in 1861,[30] the town of Nevers had obtained a *déclaration d'utilité publique* (official declaration of public utility) justifying the compulsory acquisition of a freshwater spring which at that time rose on land owned by the commune of Varennes-les-Nevers. Monsieur Boignes, whose land lay above that of the commune, thereupon dug trenches that captured the flow to the spring and diverted it into an existing stream that turned machinery in his factory. Though his motives appear to have been purely mercenary, the Cour de Cassation (Court of Cassation, the highest court in the French judiciary) held that he, and not the commune, was entitled to the indemnity payable by the town for the expropriation of the spring: he had shown both that the flow of water came from his property, and that it was of use to him. The right of a proprietor to drill to get subterranean water, even when it cut off an existing spring, was made explicit by an amendment to article 641 of the code (now appearing as article 641(4)) at the time of a major reform of water law in 1898.

Regulation under the Ancien Régime

Neither the general legal principle nor the judicial approach to it was palatable to those who controlled valuable mineral water resources. The rules of the code constituted an open invitation to would-be competitors to exploit or acquire adjoining lands in the hope of capturing and putting to use some or all of the natural supply. The first attempt to modify the application of what became the code principles dates back to nearly a century before their promulgation—in fact, to 1715. In that year, the owner of the spring and baths at Balaruc, one of the few watering places in France that are low-lying and close to the sea, took legal action to prevent his neighbor, one Mauron, from digging close by and diverting the waters. The case was called in for its own consideration by the Conseil du Roi, which issued decisions in January and December of that year providing for the creation and marking out of a small zone of protection around the springs, in which Mauron (and any other owners of land within it) were forbidden to excavate. The decisions—which were based explicitly on the public interest in access to the springs and baths, and notably the benefit they offered to indigent

---

[30] Cass. civ. December 4, 1860, D.P. 1861.2.149. Some earlier cases are discussed in Nadault de Buffon 1877: 86–95.

sufferers—left open the possibility that Monsieur Mauron might be able to obtain an indemnity for this restriction of his ordinary property rights. When the threat of digging by a neighbor was renewed in 1783, and there was a risk that the civil courts might be called on to decide the matter, the protection zone was confirmed by a further decision of the Conseil, which it explained by explicit reference to the inadequacy of the ordinary legal rules:

> The ordinary courts are less impressed by the advantages of an establishment which is precious to humanity, and more attached to the individual rights of neighboring proprietors. They would fear to sacrifice private interest to the general good, and would decide solely on the basis of the civil law, in a case which ought to be regulated only by the principles of political law (*"droit politique"*).[31]

The protection for the springs of Balaruc was further reinforced by an Imperial Decree of October 7, 1807. A like solicitude was shown by the Conseil for the owner of the source of the mineral waters at Saint Laurent-les-Bains, in the hills west of the Rhone Valley, by a decision in 1736 providing for an expert inquiry with a view to establishing a zone of protection, and meanwhile forbidding any digging by the inhabitants that might damage the source.[32] A third watering place that enjoyed this sort of *ad hoc* protection, in the shape of a decree of the Conseil in 1732, confirmed and extended by an Imperial Decree of June 19, 1804, was the village of Barèges, situated high in the Pyrenees in the "sterile and savage" Bastan valley. As well as a civil hospital, Barèges housed a military hospital where soldiers were sent to recuperate, or die, from their battle wounds. While this may explain its special treatment, it also meant that, in the words of one mid-nineteenth-century commentator, "the combination of these different infirmities does not give this station, the most elevated in Europe, a very festive character."[33]

The Struggle for General Legislation, 1836–1848

Other bathing places, including the state's own possessions at Vichy, Plombières, and elsewhere, did not obtain any such legal defenses against competition for their water sources. No attempt was made to provide them until the 1830s, when digging and drilling to capture mineral water sources, often at the expense of existing establishments, came to be seen as a serious problem: Cauterets, in the Pyrenees, lost thereby half of its 12 sources in this period.[34] In 1836, the Budget

---

[31] The texts of the decisions can be found in Sabadel 1865: 89–99 and in Mallat 1915: 291–300.

[32] *Lasaigne*, Conseil du Roi, Inventaire des Arrêts 1730–6, no. 22702.

[33] Rotureau 1859: 810.

[34] Astruc 1933: 22.

Commission of the Chamber of Deputies, the lower house of the legislature established under the constitution of the so-called July Monarchy of Louis-Philippe, recommended the enactment of general legislation to protect existing mineral water sources, and the following year a proposal in this sense was introduced into the upper house, the Chamber of Peers.

This bill was both brief and vague. It contained only four short articles. The first provided that a spring might be declared *d'utilité publique* (of public utility), the test imposed by the Civil Code (article 545) as a prerequisite (along with just and prior compensation) for any act of expropriation. The proposal went on to empower the prefect to prohibit any activity that might suppress, deviate, or pollute such a source. It required the owner of a spring declared to be of public utility, if he or she had requested prefectoral intervention, to compensate the person whose activity was thus restricted at a figure to be reached by agreement, and provided for the amount to be settled by the ordinary courts if the parties failed to agree. That was all. The Chamber of Peers passed the law by an impressive majority of 90 votes to 2, with only a couple of minor amendments.[35]

The Chamber of Deputies, to which the proposal was then submitted, was not so easily satisfied.[36] In plenary debate, criticisms rained in from all sides. The most general complaint was of the infringement of the rights of property of neighboring owners. The prefect's power was wide enough to prevent a wide range of works, including the digging of foundations for building, and was not restrained either by a statutory definition of which springs were worthy of classification as being of public utility or by any indication of a zone of protection in which the power might be exercised. The negative impact on competition was also noted: existing establishments would be protected and new ones discouraged. One deputy, Monsieur Hennequin, offered what we would now recognize as a public choice analysis, seeing the measure as a piece of administrative empire building by prefects, who favored bathing establishments because of the visitors they attracted and the expenditures they engendered, adding darkly that "it is not always easy to find anyone who is ill in these establishments."

Even those who favored protection were not satisfied with the proposal. Monsieur Colomes, with a constituency in the Pyrenees, which at that time had been the area most affected by competitive development, noted that without the power to require works to be declared in advance to the prefecture, the damage would almost always be done before the prefect had an opportunity to intervene. In consequence, he favored an amendment allowing the declaration of public

---

[35] *Moniteur Universel* 1837: 169–70, 330, 351–2.
[36] *Ibid.* 816–17, 862–6.

utility to stipulate a zone of protection within which such prior notice would be required.

It was the concern of the government and the commission to minimize effects on property rights that was their undoing. Though they clearly had in view that a very small number of spas would win the declaration of public utility qualification—perhaps as few as six—they would not prejudge this issue by a statutory stipulation of what was to be protected and what not. Nor would they contemplate making provision for a zone of protection. The primary reason was the same as that which led English and American judges, in *Acton v. Blundell* and the cases that followed it, to apply the rule of capture to underground water: not enough was known about the subterranean courses of the relevant mineral waters.[37] Another factor, however, was the belief that creating a zone of protection, where excavation and drilling would require prior permission, would be seen as an unacceptable infringement of property rights. The result was that they failed to satisfy those who wanted effective protection for existing sources, while giving ammunition to the vociferous defenders of private property—most of whom, we should notice, belonged to the ranks of the center-left opposition.

At all events, the Chamber of Deputies rejected the proposal—which may have been no great loss, given its obvious defects. Matters might have rested there for some considerable time had an unfortunate dispute not broken out at Vichy, certainly the most important of the state-owned spas at this time.[38] In 1833, the lease and management of the springs and baths at Vichy had been granted to two brothers, the Brossons. They came from Volvic, a minor spa town, and after success in the business of operating quarries there, they sought new opportunities in the running of spas like Vichy. Their hopes of a renewal of their lease on its expiration were dashed by the arrival in Vichy, as inspecting physician, of Clément-Victor-François-Gabriel Prunelle, a man of considerable standing and political influence—he was a deputy and also mayor of Lyon—who was firmly convinced that the right way to run a spa like Vichy was not through leasing it out, but through direct state management: *en régie* is the French term. The Brossons had in fact tried to ward off this danger by working to secure the appointment of Prunelle's rival for the post, the existing deputy inspector, Petit, and their failure in this earned them Prunelle's abiding enmity and his irksomely intrusive supervision of their operations.

After their lease terminated in 1841 with no prospect of renewal, they therefore chose the alternative path of competition. In 1843, they obtained drilling

---

[37] Above, Ch. 2, at 36–7.

[38] On this dispute, see generally Mallat and Cornillon 1909: 239–65; Mallat 1915: 887–914; Chambriard 1999: 33–6.

equipment from a Paris firm that had previously drilled several artesian wells in the area and set to work on property about 100 meters away from the main Vichy spring, the Puits Carré. They drilled to 54 meters and obtained a supply of mineral water, later confirmed as seriously affecting the flow at the Puits Carré. Adding insult to injury, they also hired their equipment to other local explorers, notably the mayor of the nearby town of Cusset, who opened three sources there.

The Vichy authorities reacted strongly: the mayor of Vichy issued an order forbidding the Brossons' drilling, and his deputy dispatched the local forces of order on an urgent mission out of town just as irate local crowds were descending on the Brossons' site, which they were thus able to vandalize at their leisure. A criminal prosecution was next launched against the Brossons for breach of the mayor's order, but it failed in the local court in January 1844, on the ground that the order was without legal foundation. The Brossons, however, blocked up their well the following month, when they applied for an authorization for their source under the 1823 ordinance.

Continuing obstruction from the commune of Vichy, accompanied by lengthy litigation, eventually persuaded the Brossons to sell out in 1851, but in a kind of posthumous vindication of their efforts, their enemy Prunelle was evicted two years later; the indefatigable Petit, having turned official opinion against the notion of running the spa *en régie*, took his place; and a concession to run the Vichy establishment was granted to the Lebobé and Caillou Company. Part of the payment made by the company was the transfer to the state of the Brosson sources, which the company had acquired from their 1851 purchaser.

Though this Vichy dispute—there would be others—came locally to a tidy ending, its national ramifications were much less positive. The Brossons' prosecutor, in 1844, challenged the finding that the mayor's order was unlawful through a reference to the Cour de Cassation, France's highest appeals court, arguing that the order could be sustained on the basis of the decisions of the Conseil du Roi relating to Balaruc and Barèges, and the imperial decrees that confirmed them. The court gave this argument short shrift, holding that these decisions had no operation or effect beyond the areas to which they applied, and confirming that the surface proprietor was entitled, as articles 544 and 552 of the Civil Code indicated, to dig and drill as he wished on his land, and that the proximity of established mineral water sources gave the mayor no power to stop him.[39]

Prunelle and the Vichy authorities were now compelled to carry the fight to the legislature. A petition to the Chamber of Deputies by the citizens of Vichy appears to have been one of the forces prompting the introduction in 1845 of a new bill to

---

[39] *Brosson*, Cass. crim. April 13, 1844, S. 1844.I.664.

protect key mineral water springs.[40] This fared no better than its predecessor 10 years earlier. Its form was very similar. There was still no provision to create zones of protection: it was thought too difficult to set appropriate limits. This issue took center stage in the chamber's debates. Contrary to its position in 1837, when it sided with government in resisting such an idea, the commission examining the bill inserted an amendment providing for any declaration of public utility to incorporate a zone of protection.

But the government, supported by a number of speakers, would not be moved. The hydrology of Vichy itself was cited as a reason: drillings a couple kilometers distant, on the far side of the River Allier, on which the town stands, were thought to have affected the flow of its springs. Zones might have to be impracticably large. François Arago, a prominent scientist and statesman who was perhaps the first proponent of control in 1836, reminded the chamber that the well drilled at his instigation (as a Paris councilor) to furnish water to the Grenelle abattoir there drew its water from deep strata of the Paris basin, whose surface outcrops were found in such places as Bar-sur-Aube, some 230 kilometers away. This well may have exercised an influence even on the course of English litigation on subterranean water: in *Chasemore v. Richards* (1859), where the House of Lords, as England's highest court, applied and confirmed the principle of *Acton v. Blundell*,[41] Lord Brougham, one of the members of the House hearing the case, referred to this phenomenon of long-distance percolation, and his reference was picked up by Mr. Justice Wightman, speaking on behalf of the judges called upon to advise the House in this matter, to support the idea that the paths of underground percolation were too uncertain to warrant any restriction on the right of people to take water from their own land.[42]

Fortified by science, the government carried its point, but though it eventually secured passage of the bill by the impressive majority of 247 votes to 2, it could not get the proposals through the Chamber of Peers.[43] Here discussion focused strongly on the way the bill would restrict competition and discourage the search for new sources (an activity dismissed in the Chamber of Deputies as attributable to "enterprises excited by speculation"), as well as on the effect on property rights. Despite support engendered by some horror stories as to the damage done by competitive drilling—at Le Vernet the previous winter, a noble foreign personage had nearly died because a competitor's diggings had cut off the supply of water,

---

[40] For proceedings, see *Moniteur Universel* 1845: 1665, 1921; 1846: 215, 417, 640, 664 (Chamber of Deputies).

[41] Above, Ch. 2, at 37.

[42] At 7 H.L. Cas. 349, 371, 11 Eng. Rep. 140, 149.

[43] *Moniteur Universel* 1846: 825, 842, 1342f, 1386f.

which was used not just for medicinal purposes, but also to heat the establishment and its sleeping quarters—the Chamber of Peers rejected the bill by the narrow majority of 62 votes to 57.

The Decree of 1848

With two parliamentary defeats within a decade, the prospect for modifying the Civil Code's uncompromising invitation to competition appeared remote indeed, and in fact it took a revolution to achieve it. The July Monarchy of Louis-Philippe fell on February 24, 1848. Bad harvests, widespread unemployment, and disenchantment among the political elite produced public disturbances in Paris, which turned into a full-scale uprising with barricades in the streets when a procession was fired on outside the Ministry of Foreign Affairs, with dozens killed or injured. A republican government emerged the following day in circumstances of the utmost confusion. In these tumultuous circumstances, one might have assumed that the mineral water issue would not rank terribly high on the priority list of the provisional government. But no: within a fortnight of taking office, that government turned from its projects of abolishing slavery in all French territories and establishing universal suffrage to promulgate a decree about mineral water.

This Decree of March 8–10, 1848, went far beyond the proposals twice exhaustively debated, and twice rejected, by the legislatures of the previous regime. It established a zone of protection of 1,000 meters radius around every mineral water spring that was duly authorized under the ordinance of 1823. Within that zone, no drilling or subterranean works could be undertaken without the prior authorization of the prefect. The notion of the elite group of spas that alone would enjoy the accolade of a declaration of public utility, the protection of neighboring owners deriving from the associated inquiry procedures, the obligation to provide compensation for loss of development opportunities, were all brutally swept away. Remarkably, the government that did this included people who had been persistent, under the previous regime, in seeking to protect property rights: notably Eugène Bethmont, the minister of agriculture, who had strongly criticized the compensation provisions in the 1845–1846 proposal and successfully moved an amendment to strengthen them.[44]

Antonin Mallat, the historian of Vichy, argues that one cannot attribute this coup to any proliferation of threats to the state's interests in the waters of Vichy, because there had been no competitive drilling between 1846 and 1848. (However, another new source had been drilled in 1845 by a former lawyer named Lardy, who succeeded in obtaining an authorization for its use from the Academy

---

[44] *Moniteur Universel* 1846: 644–53.

of Medicine in May 1848.)[45] For Mallat, it was the presence of François Arago as a member of the provisional government (and a signatory of the decree) that was crucial.[46] Arago was a close friend of Prunelle's, and Prunelle was at this time still inspecting physician at Vichy and still locked in legal dispute with the Brosson family.[47] But Arago was not just interested in Vichy: the origins of his campaign in 1836–1837 stemmed from concerns about his native Pyrenees, and the legislative debates in 1845–1846 had been introduced by a recital of the damage done to springs in a range of departments: Allier, Bouches du Rhone, Haute Garonne, Ardèche, Loire, Basses-Alpes, Bas-Rhin, and others.

There is ample scope for doubt about the legality of the March decree.[48] Its terms were certainly in contravention of articles 8 and 9 of the Charter of 1830, providing that properties were inviolable and could be taken only in pursuit of a legally determined public interest, and subject to an indemnity paid in advance. Not surprisingly, its life was short. Legislation to establish a permanent protective regime was brought forward yet again in 1856, this time with success, and provided for the abrogation of the 1848 decree with effect from January 1, 1857. Nonetheless, it perhaps produced a significant effect in creating a general belief, which may have survived for some years after 1857, that drilling in the proximity of the state sources had been made illegal.

The Second Empire and the Law of 1856

In the few years between 1848 and 1856, France had once more been the scene of more general upheavals: a bloody uprising in June 1848; the proclamation of a republican constitution in November of that year; the election of Napoleon Bonaparte's nephew, Louis-Napoleon, to the executive presidency under that constitution in December; his coup d'état three years later when he and his supporters were unable to secure the two-thirds legislative majority that would have permitted him a second term as prince-president; and his promulgation, in January 1852, of a new constitution, which quickly became, in November of that year, the constitution of the Second Empire then established. Under that constitution, the Legislative Body, consisting of only 261 deputies (of whom the great majority bore the label of "official" candidates), had the right only to

---

[45] Mallat and Cornillon 1909: 283–92.

[46] Mallat 1915: 274–5, criticizing suggestions by Nadault de Buffon 1870 and de Benazé 1893: 36 that the decree responded to new competitive drilling in Vichy following the February revolution.

[47] Above, at 101–2.

[48] Astruc 1933: 28 claims that the decree was endorsed by decisions of the Cour de Cassation and Conseil d'Etat, but the references he provides are to cases on quite different subjects.

"discuss" bills and taxation, the emperor having the exclusive power to initiate legislation.

This was a much more promising framework in which to organize the long-delayed protection of the springs feeding the most important watering places, and the proposed Law on the Conservation and Improvement of Sources of Mineral Water, introduced in the name of the emperor in August 1855, was duly approved by the Legislative Body on May 22, 1856, by 231 votes to 6. It seems probable that the state's ownership interest in a number of important spas was at the root of its persistence in this policy through three different constitutional regimes, none of which can be accurately characterized as marking a turn to a consistently activist state role in economic development generally.[49]

This 1856 law, which still provides the basis for the physical protection of sources from disturbance, was a much more sophisticated document than its predecessors. The official presentation of the reasons for the proposal acknowledged clearly, for the first time, the need to balance the protection of important sources against the property rights of adjoining owners and the contribution they could make, by further drilling, to the enlargement of the supply of mineral waters.[50] Government finally abandoned its stubborn opposition to the notion of zones of protection, which were now seen as a way of ensuring this balance in appropriate circumstances.

As amended by the commission of the Legislative Body, the law provided for an authorized spring to be declared *d'intérêt public* (of public interest, a term lacking the expropriatory connotations of public utility) by imperial decree after a local inquiry (article 1). This would examine such matters as the flow of the spring, its mineral composition, the characteristics of the associated facilities, the number of *curistes*, and criteria demonstrating its importance.[51] This same decree could create and delimit a zone of protection, which might be modified later if circumstances changed; or a zone could be decreed later, and separately, for a source already declared to be of public interest (article 2).

Within such a zone, the basic rule was that there could be no drilling or subterranean works without prior authorization (article 3), and works could also be provisionally suspended by the prefect for six months even if previously authorized (article 4), or outside such a zone (article 5) or where no zone had been declared (article 6), if the prefect judged them likely to damage or diminish a spring declared of public interest under article 1. Owners of springs could also come onto the land of others to undertake works necessary for the conservation

---

[49] See Gueslin 2003: 69–89.
[50] Reproduced in Rotureau 1859: 907–14.
[51] See the implementing decree of September 8–20, 1856.

and distribution of their spring waters, if approved by the relevant minister after hearing the owner of the land (article 7); such occupation required the authorization of the prefect and could give rise to a right in the landowner, in some circumstances, to require that the spring owner purchase the land (article 9). Landowners also had a right to compensation for costs incurred as a result of suspensions under articles 4 to 6 and works on their land under article 7, but not for the loss of their right, under the Civil Code, to exploit their land as they wished.

In this respect, the 1856 law was far less respectful of general rights of property than were its predecessors, which had provided for compensation payable by the spring owner for any prevention of development. The issue was clearly still sensitive, however: the sole dissenting voice in the brief plenary debate, that of Monsieur Millet, argued for general compensation for neighboring proprietors; Monsieur Lelut, on behalf of the commission examining the bill, suggested that subsurface property, especially in mineral waters, was somehow not of the same nature as other property by reason of the long-standing authorization requirements; and the government's representative, Monsieur Vuillefroy, reminded potential complainants of their good fortune in owning land in proximity to a prosperous watering place.[52]

The report of the commission shows that it gave careful attention to property right issues in the light of knowledge (or, more accurately, ignorance) about the behavior of subterranean waters. Rejecting what seems to have been the majority scientific opinion at the time—that mineral water was not of surface origin, but was produced from the very bowels of the earth[53]—the commission described mineral water as being produced by the long presence of rainwater in mineralized rocks or soils, manifesting itself as infiltrations, deposits of water trapped in the rock, or veins rising to the surface.

This understanding was apparently enough to justify provision for zones of protection, but still too uncertain to make it appropriate to apply to mineral water the regime for hard rock minerals. By way of exception to article 552 of the Civil Code, control over such minerals was reserved to the state, which could deal with them by way of the grant of a mining concession under the terms of the Law of April 21, 1810. This stipulated that the concession would make provision for the payment of a royalty—in kind, or of a fixed sum or one proportional to the value of the product—to the owner or owners of the surface under which the concession lay. The language used by Monsieur Lelut to reject the possibility of compensating neighboring surface proprietors in this way

---

[52] *Moniteur Universel* 1856: 365–6.
[53] Lecocq 1836: 75; Bouquet 1855: 267, cited in Chambriard 1999: 17.

closely echoes that of the American courts when first faced with issues relating to rights in subsurface water:[54] "nothing is more uncertain at present, and probably for a long time to come, than the deposits feeding the majority of these springs, or, rather than the deposit, the link, the course, in a word the movement, of the layers of water, of the veins or liquid seams, of which they [the springs] form a sort of escape pipe."[55] Consequently, it was impossible to adopt a concession regime or to allocate to overlying proprietors any of the value from products of these springs. The information needed for such an allocation was simply not available.

This uncertainty, however, had not prevented the adoption a few years earlier of a concession system for saltwater wells. After a judicial decision (*Parmentier*, 1832) holding that such wells did not fall within the Mining Code,[56] they were subjected by the Law of June 17, 1840, to a rule providing that they could be exploited only under a concession, subject to a payment to the surface owner.[57] What provoked this law (which was introduced six times into the legislature before it finally passed) was the attempts by private entrepreneurs in a number of eastern departments, legitimized by the *Parmentier* decision, to tap saltwater sources in which the state enjoyed a valuable monopoly, by drilling close by and setting up a processing plant. The uncertain nature of the flows of underground water carrying the salt from subterranean deposits was again acknowledged in debate, but in this case, the state's priority appears to have been to bring these competitive drilling operations under sufficient control to be able to tax them efficiently and put them on a footing of equality with other salt production operations. Accordingly, it chose the concession route but fixed the maximum area of a saltwater well concession at only one square kilometer. It might well be that all or some of the product of such a concession came from under land outside its area. The surface owner of such land got no compensation but was free to seek a concession and drill competitively for the salt.[58] With mineral water, by contrast, the key priority was clearly to protect the integrity of the existing spring; we shall see that creating concessions that would have achieved this object would have been extremely costly for their owners.

---

[54] Above, Ch. 2, at 37–9.

[55] Rapport Lelut, *Moniteur Universel* 1856, Annexe H, 32; reprinted in Rotureau 1859: 912–30, at 920.

[56] Cass. crim., September 8, 1832, *Parmentier*, S. 1832.1.643.

[57] *Moniteur Universel* 1840: 1569; reprinted in Michel 1896: 583–96.

[58] See *Moniteur Universel* 1840: 763–4, 1393–6, 1412–15.

Law and Practice since 1856

From the standpoint of property rights, the effect of the 1856 law was to set up a threefold classification of mineral water sources in France. Those not declared to be of public interest—which were expected to represent the great majority of sources—continued to be subject to the general rules of the Civil Code. Neighboring owners thus could take advantage of article 552 to drill in their own land and capture any flows of mineral water passing beneath, even if this damaged the existing spring. Any limitations of this right of capture would need to be imposed by judicial interpretation and restriction.

A second group would consist of sources that had been declared of public interest under article 1 of the 1856 law, but without the simultaneous provision of a zone of protection. Here a modified version of the rule of capture applied, in that a neighbor's drilling or excavation, though requiring no prior declaration or authorization, might be suspended by the prefect if it had the result of diminishing or damaging the flow of the source (articles 5 and 6). The neighbor's rights were thus defeasible by administrative intervention, which might be rendered permanent by the subsequent declaration of a zone of protection; in the interim, compensation would be payable.

Finally, springs that were of public interest and enjoyed the benefit of a zone of protection were effectively removed from the regime of capture and placed instead, by official decree, under a regime of prior appropriation. For the application of this regime, it was not enough, as was the case under the law of surface streams being developed in the American West at that time, simply to show a legitimate established use:[59] the claimant had to meet tests of quantity, quality, and therapeutic and economic importance applied to the source.

In 1998, the Ministries of Employment and of Industry jointly published, in the semiofficial periodical *Réalités Industrielles,* an inventory of mineral water sources compiled from returns from the different departments.[60] This listed 701 springs in metropolitan France. Of these, 158, distributed across 58 communes, have been the subject of a declaration of public interest. And among these 158, 100 have been the object of a decree declaring a zone of protection. While the actual number of zones is lower, as certain zones will embrace a number of closely grouped springs, their economic significance is rather greater than the raw figures would suggest. Bertrand de l'Epinois and Eugène Papciak, who were among the compilers of the inventory, have pointed out that only some 400 springs, clustered on 150 sites, are exploited "industrially," for bathing establishments or bottling of

---

[59] See above, Ch. 2, at 48–9.

[60] France. Ministère de l'Emploi et de la Solidarité, Secrétariat de l'Etat à l'Industrie 1998.

mineral water; of these sites, 49 enjoy a zone of protection.[61] Nonetheless, it is clear that, as constantly promised by the proponents of a specialized regime, the great majority of springs remain subject to the general rules of the Civil Code. Protection has been extended only selectively.

What also appears from the inventory is that, particularly in the first decades of the law's operation, years sometimes passed between the declaration of public interest and the provision of a zone of protection—if indeed such a zone were provided at all. Taking a few examples at random, the Puits César (Caesar Well) at Néris-les-Bains, declared of public interest in 1878, received a zone of protection only in 1925; the first group of springs to be declared at Le Mont-Dore, in 1860, was not protected until 1874; and most striking, the state springs at Plombières, first to be declared in July 1857, obtained a zone of protection only in 1928 and 1929. More than 40 other springs declared to be of public interest before 1900 never received protection.

One reason for this delay or abstention may be that the onerous procedures needed for the creation of a zone were set in motion only when some threat to the source appeared on the horizon.[62] Such a threat need not necessarily be from competitive drilling for water; mining operations, for coal or other resources, could have even more serious consequences. But given the government's long-held skepticism about zones of protection, suddenly abandoned between 1848 and 1856, it would be surprising if part of the delay were not due to the difficulty of delimiting an appropriate zone in the light of the uncertainties freely acknowledged even as the law was being passed. For evidence of this, we have only to look to what happened in Vichy after 1856.

While the grant of the 1853 concession may have ended the Brosson affair,[63] it simultaneously triggered a new threat.[64] Nicolas and Charles-Amable Larbaud were chemists in Vichy who did a nice trade in the manufacture of barley sugar, using mineral water, and in the retail sale of mineral water. A side effect of the grant of the concession was to cut off their source of supply, and the Larbauds began an energetic search for sources of their own, Charles drilling for and finding a source in Vichy in 1853 and Nicolas drilling in nearby Saint-Yorre, where he found a number of springs between 1853 and 1858.[65]

---

[61] L'Epinois and Papciak 1998: 39–40.

[62] Indeed, de Benazé suggests that even the *déclaration d'intéret public* would be sought only in such circumstances: de Benazé 1893: 126.

[63] Above, at 101–2.

[64] Material on Vichy in the following paragraphs is based on the accounts given in Mallat and Cornillon 1909 and Mallat 1915 save where otherwise indicated.

[65] Chambriard 1999: 41, 54–5.

These activities rang alarm bells in Paris as well as in Vichy, and the Ministry of Agriculture instructed the prefect of the Allier to begin work on a zone of protection even before the law was approved. After various delays and misunderstandings, experts from the Service des Mines (Bureau of Mines) produced proposals in early 1858, and a statutory inquiry was launched in March of that year, but the engineers' report proved inadequate and the inquiry stalled. At this point, another member of the Service des Mines, Monsieur de Gouvernain, outlined what he claimed was the zone necessary to protect the springs of Vichy from damage or diversion. His zone extended to 13,358 hectares, taking in almost the whole area of the communes of Vichy and Cusset, with substantial extensions to the south and west across the river Allier. A circle with this area would have a diameter of 13 kilometers. De Gouvernain qualified his proposal by suggesting that the rule of prior authorization for works should apply only within 150 meters of each spring to be protected; nonetheless, as Antonin Mallat delicately put it in his exhaustive treatise on the Vichy waters, "the boldness of the project ... alarmed the government somewhat."[66] Not the least of the difficulties associated with de Gouvernain's proposal was providing the map of it required by the implementing decree of September 8, 1856. This had to be on the generous scale of 1/1000, so the proposal would have demanded a map measuring ... 18 by 12 meters.

The authorities threw up their hands at this point and decided merely to issue, in January 1861, declarations of public interest for the most important springs in and near Vichy. This meant that they could intervene only after the event if it appeared that drilling for new sources was having deleterious effects. By 1873, after a pause which Mallat attributes to public misunderstanding of the legal position, the situation had again become disturbing, with works being undertaken to open up new sources in Vichy itself by several entrepreneurs, among whom were the Larbauds and, most persistent, one Pierre Dubois, who worked in a law office and was perhaps better informed than others about the limits of the restrictions imposed by the 1861 decree. The prefect responded by securing, in 1874, the creation of small zones of protection—for Vichy, Cusset, and Hauterive—extending only to 1,000 meters around each source.

Though his works were well within the Vichy zone, Dubois carried on regardless, despite a decision of the Conseil d'Etat that the fact that his works had started before the decree of May 1874 was passed did not exempt them from authorization under article 3 of the law[67]—an authorization he might have found it difficult to obtain. Nor was he deterred by a prefectoral order to cease work

---

[66] Mallat 1915: 770.

[67] Conseil d'Etat, December 13, 1876, *Dubois*, Rec. Lebon 899.

accordingly. He continued, was duly prosecuted before the criminal court, sitting in Riom near Clermont-Ferrand, and enjoyed the satisfaction of being acquitted.

The Riom court seemed to show some of that tenderness for traditional property rights that the Conseil du Roi had guarded against in its Balaruc decision of 1783.[68] It disagreed with the Conseil d'Etat's view as to the effect of declaring a zone of protection on works already commenced within it, and it also held that authorization had to be given under article 3 if the relevant works were harmless to existing sources. This finding, if allowed to stand, would have robbed the zone of protection provisions of the 1856 law of most of their effect, forcing the authorities to wait to ascertain the effect of drilling or digging within the zone before they granted or withheld an authorization. Not surprisingly, therefore, the prosecutor appealed to the Criminal Chamber of the Cour de Cassation, the highest legal authority, with a view to quashing the decision of the Riom court as wrong in law. Dubois' acquittal was not affected, but it was important, as the prosecutor put it, that others tempted to operate within the zone of protection should not enjoy the same impunity. The chamber duly quashed both holdings of the Riom court, and the efficacy of the 1856 regime was preserved.[69]

Legally speaking, however, Monsieur Dubois had the last word—or at least, his family did. Dubois himself was bankrupted in 1875 by the costs of his struggle with the state and it was his brother-in-law who repurchased his furniture for him when it was sold at auction by his creditors in 1877 and who at the same time took over the Source Dubois. Work on the source was completed and application made for authorization to exploit it under the 1823 ordinance. This was refused by the minister of agriculture, notwithstanding a positive opinion as to its quality from the Academy of Medicine, and the still-unbowed Dubois must in 1886 have derived a special pleasure in again seeing his official opponents wrong-footed in court, the Conseil d'Etat holding judicially, and contrary to the advisory opinion given by its public works section to the minister, that in deciding on applications under the 1823 ordinance, the minister could take into account only public health considerations. Using this power to secure the protection against competitive drilling provided by the law of 1856 was to proceed on irrelevant considerations, and the refusal was therefore quashed.[70] The authorization was finally awarded in 1887.

The subsequent history of Vichy has been one of regular attacks on the monopoly position of the concessionaire company by explorers looking for new sources. In the early 1890s, again in 1900, 1906, and in the 1920s, drilling outside

---

[68] Above, at 98–9.
[69] Cass. crim., March 12, 1880, *Dubois*, D.P. 1880.1.282.
[70] Conseil d'Etat, July 16, 1886, *Dubois*, Rec. Lebon 631.

the Vichy zone of protection produced new and substantial sources that led the Vichy authorities to fear for the future quality and quantity of the established springs and to secure the extension of the zone of protection on four occasions: in 1895, 1901, 1907, and 1930.[71] This last extension, giving the zone its current limits, brought its area to some 15,600 hectares. Fortunately, the mapping requirements that had so inconvenienced Monsieur de Gouvernain in 1860 had by then long been amended to the more reasonable scale of 1/10,000.[72]

While the situation of Vichy is unique by reason of the extent of the area through which the waters reach the surface, the degree of interference among wells located at significant distances, and long-standing uncertainty about the nature of the underlying hydrological mechanism,[73] its history since 1861 reflects a fact common to France as a whole: that the protection afforded by the 1856 law did not stifle competition for new mineral water sources, but merely shaped its geographical occurrence. "Thermal fever" accelerated, as we have seen, throughout the later decades of the nineteenth century, with the business of promoting and financing new bathing establishments—which normally required new sources—closely resembling the contemporaneous "railway mania" that gripped the United Kingdom or the dot-com boom of more recent memory. The well-publicized visits of the Emperor Louis-Napoleon to spas like Vichy and Plombières for treatment and recreation can only have increased fashionable enthusiasm and the appetite of promoters. In protected areas like Vichy, hopefuls drilled on the borders of the zone of protection.

Such areas were however few. By 1890, a date when applications for new authorizations under the 1823 ordinance were at an early peak,[74] only 13 communes across the whole of France enjoyed zones of protection. Everywhere else, the Civil Code principles opened the way to competition. The dramatic results of the vigorous rivalry of old and new proprietors at Vernet-les-Bains in the Pyrenees, which had failed to impress the Chamber of Peers in 1846, likewise left unmoved the Civil Chamber of the Cour de Cassation. Called upon in 1849 to rule in a suit brought by the proprietors of the baths against their new rival, the chamber confirmed the holding of their criminal brethren in *Brosson*[75] that article 552 of the Civil Code gave the defendant unrestricted rights to explore for and develop sources of mineral water that might run under his property.[76]

---

[71] Chambriard 1999: 62–7.

[72] Astruc 1933: 45.

[73] Chambriard 1999: 16–19.

[74] See statistics for some major basins in Chambriard 1998: 24.

[75] Above, n. 39.

[76] Cass. civ. December 4, 1849, *Mercador c. Couderc et Lacvivier*, D.P. 1849.1.305. The facts of the dispute antedate the promulgation of the 1848 decree.

An additional problem for the exploitation of sources owned by the state and other public bodies was created by a decision of the Conseil d'Etat in 1868.[77] Work to improve the flow of water in the state baths at Plombières had had the effect of drying up a neighboring spring owned by a Monsieur Dangé, who sued for damages. One would have assumed that the Civil Code principles would have operated as a complete defense for the state, but the Conseil held that these were *travaux publics* (public works), and that under the regime of strict liability applying to damage occasioned to third parties by such works, Dangé could indeed recover. The fact that Plombières enjoyed the status conferred by a declaration of public interest may actually have worked against its interests by emphasizing the public character of the service it provided and strengthening the case for applying the special rules of French public law and not the principles of the Civil Code. The decision must have been a source of anxiety for other public bodies that owned and ran spas, such as communes and departments, but in 1883, the Tribunal des Conflits (Disputes Tribunal, the court that determines whether a case is subject to public law principles and to the jurisdiction of the public law courts headed by the Conseil d'Etat) decided that where a similar effect had been produced by work on a communally owned spring (which happened not to be the subject of a declaration), the ordinary courts were competent and the general law applied.[78] The commune was assumed to be undertaking the work in its private interest in order to exploit its property more profitably.

Numerous local histories record examples of rivalrous behavior in exploring and exploiting the commune's resources, sometimes taking the form of decades-long wars of attrition from which only a single operator emerged unscathed.[79] Two of these merit special attention. The first is the case of Saint-Galmier, in the department of the Loire near Saint-Étienne.[80] Here and in surrounding communes, a long-standing and gratuitous local usage of the waters (some inhabitants apparently drank up to 15 to 20 liters a day), defended by local mayors, discouraged investment in thermal establishments, which left a clear field for the development by Monsieur Auguste Badoit of a substantial enterprise in the bottling of the water that still bears his name. His success in this attracted numerous rivals in the 1850s, 1860s, and 1870s. These were eventually driven off, and by 1880, Badoit had a de facto monopoly; but on the way, the tactics of one of

---

[77] Conseil d'Etat, December 19, 1868, *Dangé*, Rec. Lebon 1071.

[78] Tribunal des Conflits, November 25, 1883, *Cazeaux c. Ville de Bagnères*, D.P. 1884.3.50. The complainant actually won the case on other grounds. For commentary, see de Benazé 1893: 124–9.

[79] See, for examples, Chambriard 1999: 33–59 (Vichy, Cusset, Saint-Yorre); Faure 1985 (Saint-Galmier and district); Penez 1994: 21–46 (Châtel-Guyon); Roux 1975: 75–134 (La Bourboule); Sarazin 2000 (Châteldon).

[80] Faure 1985.

his rivals, Monsieur André, another enterprising pharmacist, gave rise to the first judicial qualification of the rule of article 552.

André and Badoit possessed sources within a few meters of each other and of the local spring at Saint-Galmier. André installed a pump at his source, whose effect was to cut the flow in Badoit's source by two-thirds and limit the flow in the Saint-Galmier spring as well. Instead of using the water he got, however, André allowed it to run off into the River Coise. The court in Lyon found that this behavior evidenced a desire simply to damage the neighboring sources and held that while one had the right to abuse one's own property, that right "finds a necessary limit in the obligation to allow one's neighbor the enjoyment of his own property," and it could not excuse what, by reason of the intercommunication between the sources, was "an activity aimed at the neighboring landholding, to affect its substance and destroy or diminish a natural good that provides its principal value." André was thus held liable in damages.[81]

The interest of this decision was immediately perceived, the annotator of the report remarking that the court was recognizing an exception to the general principle declared by the Cour de Cassation in the *Brosson* and *Mercador* cases.[82] With the passage of time, it has even attracted attention in other jurisdictions, on the ground that it is one of the earliest decisions on which one might found the doctrine of "abuse of right" in French law—that is to say, the doctrine that the exercise of an admitted right may be wrongful, and give rise to liability in damages, if it represents an "abuse," commonly equated with a malicious exercise of the right, designed purely to harm another.[83] Whatever the merits or demerits of this contested concept, early American cases such as *Hague v. Wheeler*[84] and *Ohio Oil Co. v. Indiana*[85] will suggest to those with an interest in the rule of capture that a notion of correlative rights, rather than abuse of right, was what the court was groping toward in the *Badoit* case.

Of particular interest is the emphasis placed by the court on an official report to the effect that the relevant sources were intercommunicating, either through infiltration or by reason of deriving from a common reservoir. It is this fact that a *common* property was involved that demanded the restriction of the landowner's ordinary right to abuse his own property. Forty years later, the reasoning of the Lyon court was confirmed at the highest level by the decision of the Cour de Cassation in *Forissier c. Chaverol*, a case on rather similar facts also from Saint-

---

[81] Cour imp.de Lyon, April 15, 1856, *Badoit c. André*, D.P. 1856.2.199 (my translation).
[82] Above, nn. 39, 75.
[83] Gutteridge 1933: 33; Cueto-Rua 1975: 965; Taggart 2002: 147.
[84] Above, Ch. 2, at 26–7, 40–1.
[85] Below, Ch. 7, at 181–4.

Galmier, but between different parties.[86] This case, too, has been cited as a milestone in the development of the "abuse of right" doctrine,[87] but like *Badoit*, it can be explained as one where the court was unwilling to tolerate a purely destructive operation on a common resource.

Our second example is the one with which this chapter opened. It concerns the village of La Bourboule, in the Puy-de-Dôme, the department centered on Clermont-Ferrand.[88] La Bourboule, a close neighbor of Le Mont-Dore, had been in use as a watering place even in Roman times, but in the middle of the nineteenth century, it was apparently a hamlet composed of 15 or so "wretched dwellings," in a state of almost complete neglect, whose bathing house was "in ruins,"[89] though it was still managing to attract a couple hundred *curistes* each year.

Pierre Choussy, its inspecting physician and manager, was less interested in development than making the waters available to the poor of the region.[90] In 1854, however, the chemist Louis-Jacques Thénard demonstrated that the waters of La Bourboule contained high concentrations of arsenic, valued for its beneficial effects in the treatment of allergies and other conditions. Access to the village, previously reachable only on horseback, improved dramatically with the opening of a road in 1856, the same year that the railway line from Paris reached Clermont-Ferrand, 50 kilometers away. Though the number of *curistes* doubled in the next three years, and the receipts at the baths increased by 50 percent, the council of the commune of Murat-le-Quaire, of which La Bourboule then formed part, was dissatisfied with the progress made by the Choussy family in developing the bathing establishment and increasing the rather feeble flow of the springs. This led them into a bitter struggle with the Choussys for the waters of La Bourboule, which was to last until 1879.

The commune opened hostilities in 1863 by granting a 50-year lease of one of the springs claimed by them to the Vicomte de Sédaiges, along with the right to explore for and capture the mineral water resources belonging to the commune and to defend them against "usurpations." Other rivals were the Mabru family, neighbors of the Choussys, who failed in litigation in 1864 laying claim to the Choussy lands and sources. In 1865, the Mabrus joined forces with de Sédaiges and a mason named Perrière in a program of digging and drilling, which, two years later, found a substantial source on their own land. They thereby succeeded in

---

[86] Cass. req. June 10, 1902, D.P. 1902.1.454.

[87] Cueto-Rua 1975: 989.

[88] The sources for this account, unless otherwise indicated, are Nivet 1879; Eudel 1911 [2007]; Roux 1975: 75–134; Verdier 1993: 1–51. They are frequently contradictory.

[89] Rotureau 1859: 553.

[90] On Pierre Choussy, see also above, text above n. 17.

effectively drying up two existing springs of the Choussys, whose works ran to the boundary of the Mabru lands. On the strength of this, the Mabrus converted their hotel into a bathing establishment competing with that of the Choussy family.

Meanwhile, Léonce Choussy, now the owner of the Choussy properties, had sought to protect his family's interests by trying, for a second time, to obtain a declaration of public interest and a zone of protection for his springs. On the first attempt, in 1858, the application had been refused because of the insufficient development of the bathing establishment. In 1866, a second refusal was motivated by the fact that in granting the concession of 1863, the commune had deliberately opted for competition in the supply of mineral water. Taking the hint, Choussy initiated, with the drilling of the Choussy no. 1 and 2 wells, a battle of drilling and counterdrilling against the Mabru, Perrière, and de Sédaiges partnership, each side drilling or deepening wells in close proximity to the other's. One of these wells was dug by Perrière under the commune's concession in the roadway just 2 meters from the Choussys' garden wall, a provocation that led Léonce Choussy to supplement self-help with a further attempt at legal action, attacking the commune before the courts in 1869–1870 for allowing illegal excavations, but without success.

Between 1870 and 1875, some kind of accommodation appears to have been reached between the rival interests, who were managing to obtain, from the same underground sources, enough water from their wells for their respective needs. They even cooperated in 1873 in organizing the construction of a chapel for the use of *curistes* (a "primitive" casino had already been erected in 1871 to address their more worldly needs). On the municipal front, however, La Bourboule, after a vote of its inhabitants, was in 1875 erected into a commune independent of Murat-le-Quaire, and the new council took forward a proposal under which the de Sédaiges concession, now in the hands of the well-capitalized Compagnie des Eaux Minérales de la Bourboule (Mineral Water Company of La Bourboule), was enlarged and extended for a further 20 years, in return for various payments and an undertaking to construct a major new establishment by 1880.

This was the signal for renewed hostilities. Louis Choussy, successor to his brother Léonce, installed pumps that dried out the Perrière well; the Compagnie des Eaux responded in kind. The contest affected the quality and quantity of water in both establishments; drew protests from hoteliers, doctors, and *curistes*; and led the public authorities to consider closing down both establishments on the ground that, remarkably, neither had obtained the authorization required under the ordinance of 1823.

The year 1878 was a fatal one for the Choussy interests. On February 25, the Court of Appeal at Riom dismissed the family's claim to the ownership of the land on which the principal wells dug by de Sédaiges and Perrière were situated.

Simultaneously, the deepening of one of the Choussy wells with the "scarcely disguised aim of drying up the Perrière well yet again"[91] backfired spectacularly by damaging it rather than its rival. Choussy sold out to the Compagnie des Eaux Minérales de la Bourboule in January 1879 and died six months later.

The struggle at La Bourboule offers a number of interesting lessons of relevance to the oil industry. First, it is clear that though the multiple drillings for new sources had their dangers, the end result was a much better understanding of the hydrology of La Bourboule[92] and a much increased flow of water, from 35 liters per minute in 1855 to at least 632 liters per minute in 1877.[93] Left to themselves, it seems unlikely that the Choussy family would have obtained these results.[94] Second, the inability of the Choussys to obtain a declaration of public interest shows that, contrary to the fears of opponents of the 1857 law, the protective powers it conferred were not mechanically applied and did not necessarily act as a restraint on competition. Things might have turned out very differently had the Choussys been able to assert any kind of legal right of first appropriation of the sources in and around their property. Even without owning the land adjoining their wells, they would have been able to demonstrate the interconnection of the sources and hence their priority stemming from their original acquisition of the sources in 1828. Finally, it is striking that though the parties involved were certainly not averse to litigation, and though their behavior on several occasions, hovering on the borderline between malice and self-protection, produced situations closely resembling those in the *Badoit* and *Forissier* cases, neither side appears at any point to have contested the legality of the other party's competitive drilling.

CONCLUSION

The history of the French mineral water industry serves as a useful illustration of the fact that oil is not the only subterranean fluid to be considered a worthwhile subject of costly competition and hence to pose difficult property right problems. The discussion here has, however, been designed to highlight some more specific contrasts and parallels between the two industries.

---

[91] Roux 1975: 133.

[92] See 1 Daubrée 1887: 120–2 for a description and diagrammatic representation of the strata reached by the different wells.

[93] Penez 2005: 14, citing Verdier 1993: 15, 49.

[94] Compare Pogue 1938 and Frankel 1969, above, Ch. 1, at 11.

One important contrast is to be found in the much more vertically integrated nature of the mineral water industry than of its petroleum counterpart. John D. Rockefeller and others showed, as we shall see, how you could make the most money out of the oil industry by concentrating on refining and transport, while leaving producers to compete themselves into bankruptcy through competitive drilling without regard for market demand.[95] In mineral water, the profits were likewise perceived to lie downstream—in retail sales of water; in the operation of the casinos, hotels, and other facilities that provided the spending opportunities for *curistes*; indeed, also in real estate speculation that might accompany the creation of a spa, the subject of Jules Romains' novel *Les Superbes*[96]—but as a side effect of the public health controls over mineral water, these profits were indissolubly linked to acquiring proprietary rights over the sources themselves. Those who sought to build their fortunes on water in nineteenth-century France had therefore either to buy an existing thermal operation, to identify a hitherto unexploited one (and convince the world of the curative properties of its water), or to seek to capture water from a source of proven reputation so as to compete with its existing operator.

This made for a very different competitive environment from the one prevailing in the first years of the U.S. oil industry in Pennsylvania and elsewhere in the Northeast. Instead of the frantic rush of hundreds of hopefuls for petroleum, all with access to the same information (or, more exactly, misinformation) and the same land, with no one in a position to claim some anterior, preemptive rights, competition for mineral water sources in France was more in the nature of an attempt to win away a specific set of advantages enjoyed by an established incumbent. The results of such an attempt might well be positive, as with the growth at La Bourboule resulting from the ferocious struggles between Choussy and the commune-sponsored competition. But they might also appear simply as a zero- or even negative-sum game, where the division of an existing flow of water— and clientele of *curistes*—between rival establishments might damage the physical and technical capacity of both. When contrasting the readiness of the French state to engage in legislative adjustments of property rights, in contrast with the profound silence of its American counterparts, we should bear in mind this substantial difference of competitive context, along with the difference in the degrees of familiarity felt by legislators on either side of the Atlantic with the industries they were called upon to deal with.

Notwithstanding these differences, it is striking to notice the resemblance between the kinds of arguments that were deployed in both countries in favor of the application of the competitive principle—arguments that, as we have seen,

---

[95] Below, Ch. 7, at 172–4.
[96] Romains 1933.

were in practice more successful in France than might be suggested by the existence of the administrative prior appropriation regime, and by the well-known but isolated abuse of right cases. In France and the United States alike, it was the principle of being able to do as one wished on one's own land, as a legitimate application of the rights of property sanctified by the French Civil Code and the Fifth and Fourteenth Amendments to the U.S. Constitution, that carried the most conviction both with state courts (notably in *Hague v. Wheeler* and *Kelley v. Ohio Oil Co.*)[97] and with French parliamentarians. Both in American judicial reasoning and in French legislative debate, the rule of capture thus appears as an expression of a right to the free use and disposition of property, to be defended on the one hand against litigious neighbors and on the other against an officious state protective of established privilege.

We may suspect that these arguments were eventually defeated in the French legislature not so much because they did not correspond to the convictions of its members as by virtue of the political and personal interests of the vast majority of members of the 1857 Chamber of Deputies, committed, as "official" candidates, to support the regime of Louis-Napoleon. Outside the legislature, as is evidenced by the rarity and snail-like slowness with which the administration exercised its power to declare zones of protection even for sources long recognized as being of public interest (*d'intérêt public*), the invocation by neighbors of their rights to free use of their property appears to have carried much more weight. The strength manifested by the capture principle in France in the face of official desires to protect a group of established mineral water operations should be a powerful corrective to the idea that acknowledgment of this right somehow expressed a peculiarly American notion of free access to natural resources, for which the courts strained to find expression in an artificial wild animal analogy.

At the same time, the French experience offers us, in the shape of the arrangements for zones of protection, an application of a principle alternative to the rule of capture for the purpose of determining property rights in a subterranean fluid: the principle of prior appropriation, whereby the person who first exploits a given source, flow, or pool acquires an exclusive right to the whole. We have seen that the concept of a zone of protection was not unknown in early American petroleum practice, but that operators never succeeded in establishing it as a normal feature of a petroleum lease.[98] Nor was the idea of prior appropriation of an oil or gas reservoir ever presented to nineteenth-century American courts as a plausible alternative to the rule of capture.[99] But in the light of French practice

---

[97] Discussed above, Ch. 2, at 26–9, 40–1.

[98] Above, Ch. 3, at 75.

[99] Above, Ch. 2, at 48–9.

(not forgetting the practical difficulties sometimes experienced in defining such zones), it seems worth considering whether the idea could have offered a basis for legislative developments, and later chapters will show that it has indeed figured in legislative discussions in a variety of times and places and has been influential in shaping some petroleum regimes.[100]

---

[100] Below, Ch. 9, at 269, n. 133, Ch. 10, at 314–5.

CHAPTER 5

ASPHALT IN TRINIDAD: DIGGING YOUR NEIGHBOR'S PITCH

THE TRINIDAD ASPHALT INDUSTRY

The first hydrocarbon compound of which man made systematic use was asphalt, a heavy, sticky material that manifests itself in ground seepages and is also found in asphaltic rocks. In early Mesopotamia—now Iraq—from some three millennia before the Christian era, the Sumerians, Assyrians, and Babylonians coped with their lack of local supplies of stone and timber by developing a range of uses for this product. They mixed it with sand and fibers to form a construction material; used it in building roads; applied it as a waterproofing for baskets, mats, and the keels of ships; refined and blended it for medicinal purposes; and even employed it punitively: under Assyrian law, certain categories of delinquent were forced to submit to having jars of molten bitumen poured over their heads.[1]

This versatile technology was lost with the conquest of the neo-Babylonian kingdom around 600 BC by the Persians, who preferred their own methods of construction (and perhaps of punishment also). Greeks and Romans alike had

---

[1] Williamson and Daum 1959: 4, citing research by R. J. Forbes.

convenient alternative building materials, and asphalt was relegated to scattered and sporadic local usages. Among these, the caulking of ships probably remained the most important, but even here, the inhabitants of a then thickly forested Europe had a ready alternative in pitch of vegetable origin produced as a by-product of charcoal burning.

The European discovery of the Americas, however, brought reports of large deposits of asphalt, notably in and around the Caribbean, which were soon being applied by Europeans venturing there for the repair of their ships. Among those to write home about this new resource was the English adventurer and courtier Sir Walter Raleigh. He made voyages to the West Indies in 1595 and 1617, on both occasions visiting a spot on the Trinidad coast "called Tierra del Brea or Piche [where] there is that abundance of stone pitch that all the shippes of the world may be therewith laden from thence, and wee made triall of it trimming our shippes to be most excellent good, and melteth not with the sunne as pitch of Norway, and therefore for shippes trading south portes very profitable."[2] From Raleigh's later account, which speaks of the pitch as covering a plain some two leagues by one in area (about 6 by 3 miles), he may have visited what is now known as the Great Pitch Lake of La Brea. This is a remarkable natural deposit of asphalt, which after more than 100 years of industrial exploitation was recently estimated still to contain about 10 million tons of pitch in a basin some 100 acres in area and with a depth at the center of 250 feet.[3]

Pitch did not win the immediate acceptance accorded in Europe to Raleigh's other transatlantic discovery, tobacco, and until the latter part of the nineteenth century, attempts made to apply pitch from the lake and the surrounding lands at La Brea to various industrial and agricultural purposes met with little commercial success. Large-scale exploitation and export of pitch from La Brea really got going only after a Belgian chemist named de Smedt, who had emigrated to the United States, invented a process for blending Trinidad asphalt with siliceous sand or carbonate of lime to form a paving material equal in quality to the natural rock asphalt found in parts of Switzerland and France. Successful trials of this material in Jersey City, Newark, New York, and Washington, DC, created a strong American interest in Trinidad pitch from around 1880 and placed the industry on a new commercial footing. Trinidad pitch gained a firm place in American and European paving and road-building markets and held it for some decades, with a late peak created by motorway construction. Handling difficulties and transport costs, however, always left Trinidad pitch exposed to competition from local substitutes, and in more recent years, it has been largely confined to specialized uses

---

[2] Quoted in Higgins 1996: 4.

[3] See the Trinidad Lake Asphalt Company website, www.trinidadlakeasphalt.com/.

such as bridge decking. The last of the private companies that had exploited the pitch under a series of concessions and leases went into receivership in 1977, and the lake is now operated by the government-owned Trinidad and Tobago Oil Company (Trintoc).[4]

In its heyday at the end of the nineteenth century and the beginning of the twentieth, and at just about the time that U.S. courts issued their crucial series of decisions touching on the principle of capture of oil and gas, the working of pitch from the lake and the adjacent land at La Brea became the subject of acute legal controversy. No less than 83 lawsuits were filed on this issue between 1891 and 1902; two of them were appealed as far as the highest court of the British Empire, the Judicial Committee of the Privy Council in London. The ferment was stilled only by the dispatch from London of a Royal Commission, the most solemn form of government inquiry, and the enactment of local legislation based on its report.[5]

The reason for taking an interest here in this long-forgotten quarrel in a now marginal industry is that it shows what may happen when courts take a different line from that followed in the United States and France and reject the rule of capture as the principle for dealing with the exploitation of fugacious minerals. That was the gist of the decision of the Privy Council in *Trinidad Asphalt Co. v. Ambard* in 1899.[6] To understand the decision and its effects, we need to know something about the location and physical characteristics of the pitch at La Brea, as well as the system of property rights obtaining in Trinidad at that time.

THE PITCH OF LA BREA

The pitch at La Brea is found in two distinct locations. The Great Pitch Lake, described above, was, at the time of the litigation, 140 acres in area, lying some 130 feet above sea level. Originally the surface of the lake projected above the surrounding land, but by the end of the nineteenth century, excavation had lowered the surface so as to leave an overlying rim of land around it. From the lake, the land slopes down northward for a mile or so to the sea, and within this land lies a belt of pitch about 450 feet wide, on which there stands, at its northern end, the village of La Brea. This latter belt is known as the "pitch lands," in contradistinction to the lake.

---

[4] See generally Higgins 1996: Ch. 3.

[5] This was published as the *Report of the Asphalt Industry Commission*, submitted to the secretary of state for the colonies in January 1903 by the two commissioners, J. W. Gordon, a London barrister with strong scientific qualifications (he later wrote a number of learned papers on optics), and Henry Louis, a professor at the Royal School of Mines.

[6] [1899] A.C. 594.

The Royal Commission, for reasons that will become apparent, inquired at some length into the nature, if any, of the connection between the asphalt in the lake and that in the pitch lands and concluded that the latter was in the nature of an overflow from the lake that had occurred in the past, when the asphalt levels were higher, and that the two deposits were not traceable to a common subterranean source.[7] It also found that because of the viscous nature of the asphalt and the slope on which it lay in the pitch lands, there was, even in the absence of any excavation, a very gradual downward creep of the asphalt toward the sea where, because of lower and more stable underwater temperatures, a shelf or talus of subterranean asphalt had been established over the centuries, forming a terminus for this natural flow.[8] Even before pitch began to be dug in large quantities, the instability of the pitch lands was not hard to see. An official surveyor's report in 1824 referred to the fact that "the houses in the village of La Brea on the sea shore … are sometimes raised a foot or two more at one end than the other, continue so for a year, then sink and perhaps rise at the other end, and … the road … is annually made from the lake to the village by cutting out the watercourses with hatchets, which are filled again with pitch before the return of the period."[9]

This is in fact the first mention of any settlement at La Brea, though "Negro houses" are referred to in an earlier report made by a Mr. Nugent in 1809. Until the late eighteenth century, the population of Trinidad, composed of South and Central American Indians who had traveled from the mainland, was tiny. Trinidad was at that time a Spanish possession, and in 1783, the Spanish king issued a Royal Cedula (Decree) of Population, designed to encourage immigration for agricultural purposes.[10] The cedula granted 30 acres of land to any Roman Catholic who settled on the island, with an additional 15 acres for every slave the newcomer brought along. This produced a considerable influx from other Caribbean territories, mostly of whites and "free coloureds" from neighboring French colonies. According to George E. Higgins's *History of Trinidad Oil*, these Spanish titles gave the owners both surface and mineral rights[11]—which is a little surprising in view of the fact that the Spanish Mining Ordinance, also of 1783, asserted the king's ownership of all minerals, even where the surface had been granted to private individuals.[12] The pitch lands, however, can hardly have been attractive for such settlement.

---

[7] Trinidad. Asphalt Industry Commission 1903: 12–15.

[8] *Ibid.* 16–17.

[9] Edmistone Hodgkinson, cited *ibid.* 17.

[10] Reprinted in Carmichael 1961: 363–9.

[11] Higgins 1996: 99.

[12] Reprinted in Rockwell 1851: 4–111. See further below, Ch. 8, at 217–21, for the importance of the ordinance in relation to Texas.

The British seized Trinidad from the Spanish in 1797. They recognized valid Spanish land titles but were slow to make formal grants of other land, preferring first to issue informal permissions to occupy land and then—in the interests of maintaining a substantial pool of nonlandowning labor—adopting a highly restrictive policy of making no grants smaller than 680 acres. This set the bar so high as to choke off any agricultural settlement, and in the 1850s and 1860s, various exceptions were made. The Asphalt Commission records the allotment of lands in the village only in 1851 by the warden of the district, though it is clear that some inhabitants claimed to hold pitch land under earlier Spanish titles,[13] while others were doubtless among the large class of squatters who had been unable to obtain land titles under the restrictive British rules. Such squatters were given the chance to regularize their position when new legislation was passed in 1869, reducing the price of land to £1 ($6.48) per acre and the minimum size of holding to 5 acres.

Under the accession system prevailing in common-law countries, minerals would ordinarily pass with a grant of land. The practice of the British government in granting or reserving mineral rights when making land grants in Trinidad varied from time to time,[14] and the Commission did not indicate whether mineral rights were included in these allotments, though it is clear from its report that the inhabitants proceeded on the basis that they had the right to dig pitch on their land. We can presume, however, that at least some of the pitch lands and the Great Pitch Lake were not allotted to individuals in 1851, as a Crown (that is, government) lease for 20 years was granted in that year to the tenth earl of Dundonald, over a tract of pitch-bearing land that included some 26 acres of the lake and also land at the seaward end of the pitch lands. Other leases over parts of the lake also appear to have been granted between 1851 and 1871.[15]

LEGAL ARRANGEMENTS FOR WINNING PITCH: MONOPOLY AND COMPETITION

In 1871, the government decided to lease out its remaining property in the Great Pitch Lake in 5-acre lots, under regulations providing for 14-year leases at a yearly rent of £2 ($12.96) per acre, to be awarded by auction for a cash premium.

---

[13] Such titles were at the root of the litigation in *Attorney-General v. Eriche* (1894), 1 Trinidad and Tobago Supreme Court Reports 19; and *Trinidad Lake Asphalt Co. v. Warner* (1894), *ibid.* 10.

[14] Higgins 1996: 99; Rampaul 2003.

[15] A note on asphalt in the *Bulletin of the Business Historical Society* for 1929 (Anon. 1929: 13) refers to the award of eight leases for 21 years, covering the entire lake, in 1869, but it seems more likely that these were the result of the leasing process undertaken in 1871 (see below).

It retained one 5-acre lot in its own possession.[16] The successful application of asphalt for paving uses in America created considerable interest in the lake, and by 1877, it had come under the control of only four lessees. Over the succeeding years, their interests were largely merged as a result of the efforts of Amzi Barber, the pioneer of asphalt paving in the United States.

In 1886, the government contemplated using its sole remaining 5-acre lot on the lake to compete with these interests, and there ensued a negotiation that led to the grant by the government, in 1888, of a concession in favor of Barber's company and its British partners. The Trinidad Lake Asphalt Company (replaced in 1897 by the New Trinidad Lake Asphalt Company) was formed to hold the concession. This was to run for 14 years, eventually extended to 42 years; it covered the whole lake and provided for an initial cash premium, export duty, and a royalty. The partners took the view that they needed a monopoly of production of Trinidad asphalt in order to protect their investment, and they sought this both by extending their holdings in the pitch lands and by securing an undertaking from the government, as part of the concession, that asphalt should not be won or carried away from lands "in the possession of the Crown" within three miles of the lake—a distance sufficient to cover all the existing pitch lands.

Though the result of the asphalt company's efforts was that a rather small area of pitch lands was left in the hands of private diggers, this did not choke off competition to the extent they had sought. The reason for this lies in the properties of pitch and the traditional method of digging it. The pitch lay at or near the surface of the land; the digger would excavate to a depth of a few feet, and then go and dig somewhere else until the excavations at this first place had filled up again, because of the tendency of the viscous material to flow from all sides toward the excavation until a condition of temporary equilibrium was reestablished, the surface of the entire mass now being lowered by an amount proportional to the amount excavated. As a result, in the words of the Commission:

> the asphalt yielding capacity of even a small plot of land, if favourably situated, may be large, out of all proportion to the area of the plot itself, since asphalt from the neighbouring land flows into replace that which is extracted. The asphalt producing power, therefore, of the private diggers and their opportunities of competition with the Company in the asphalt market are by no means limited in the same proportion as the area of their asphalt producing lands. It was most natural that out of such conditions difficulty and dissatisfaction should arise.[17]

---

[16] Henry 1910: 127–8.
[17] Trinidad. Asphalt Industry Commission 1903: 19–20.

From 1889 onward, private digging on pitch lands became steadily deeper and more efficient, leading the company to complain bitterly to the government both of loss of pitch from its own pitch land holdings into adjacent diggings, and of similar losses from unexploited Crown lands, losses it claimed the government was legally bound to prevent by reason of the clause in its concession forbidding the winning of pitch from Crown lands. Receiving no adequate satisfaction by this means, it turned to litigation and, after a series of unsuccessful attempts, finally achieved a favorable judicial result in the case of *Trinidad Asphalt Co. v. Ambard*,[18] initially before the chief justice, Sir John Goldney, in 1897, and then, after his decision was reversed by the Trinidad Court of Appeal, on further appeal to the Privy Council in London.

THE *AMBARD* DECISION

The facts here, probably typical of practice at the time, were that the defendants Ambard and François dug for pitch on their lot 15, adjacent to lot 15A, which belonged to the plaintiffs (who were the predecessors in title of the Trinidad Lake Asphalt Company). They dug right up to the boundary of lot 15A to a depth of 12 feet, so close to lot 15A that some of the boundary posts fell in. Pitch began to ooze into the excavation to replace that which had been removed; a depression shaped like a half saucer appeared in the plaintiffs' lot, cracks developed in the surface, and some buildings or sheds of no great value were more or less wrecked. A total of some 200 to 300 tons of pitch was eventually won from the excavation.

The plaintiffs did not base their action on the simple ground that the defendants had unlawfully taken their pitch. They asked rather for an injunction to prevent further digging on lot 15 on the ground that it would deprive their land of lateral support—a well-recognized civil wrong.[19] An earlier attempt to restrain digging by resort to this principle had failed in the Trinidad courts in 1889,[20] but the chief justice and the Privy Council were prepared to grant the injunction, holding that the actions of the defendants had let down the surface of the plaintiffs' land, with injurious results. In addition, they were prepared to grant the plaintiffs damages corresponding, not to the paltry value of the damaged buildings, but to the much greater value of the pitch that had flowed from lot 15A into lot 15.

In reaching this result, the Privy Council was effectively denying that the rule of capture applied to pitch in the pitch lands. Though the plaintiffs based their action

---

[18] [1899] A.C. 594 (Privy Council).

[19] Wylie 1986: 126 and above, Ch. 2, at 45–7.

[20] Henry 1910: 129.

exclusively on the right of support, the defendants sought to rely on the rule of capture by analogizing pitch to water and claiming that by reason of its semifluid character, it did not become the plaintiffs' property until they had reduced it to possession by abstracting it from their land. They also used the water analogy to address the support issue, claiming that there was no right in English law to support from underground water.

The Privy Council, and the chief justice, found it easy to dismiss the analogy with water. "Asphaltum," said the chief justice, "is a mineral, not water."[21] It may seem surprising that the defendants made no reference to the American case law on capture of petroleum, until we consider that those cases were of recent date and mostly involved natural gas (only the *Kelley* case, decided in 1897, dealt with capture of oil),[22] and that citation of foreign authorities even in the highest UK courts was at this time virtually nonexistent. In rejecting a rule of capture, the Privy Council was—as it effectively acknowledged—making any exploitation of the pitch lands difficult, if not impossible, since any excavation, even if not conducted with the bravura of Mr. Ambard's, would be liable to lower the level of adjoining lands by reason of the subterranean flows of pitch that would eventually fill the excavation. For the Privy Council, the answer to this problem was either some agreement between the different parties or legislative intervention. As Lord Macnaghten put it, speaking on behalf of the Council:

> If the inhabitants of La Brea cannot dig their own pitch without invading their neighbours' rights, it is quite possible that the hope of reciprocal advantage and the apprehension of mutual liability may lead to some arrangement for their common benefit, or the difficulties of the case may induce the Legislature to step in and regulate the digging of pitch and the management of the pitch lands.[23]

This was not in fact the first thing that happened. As might have been expected, the immediate consequence of the case was a rash of injunctions through which proprietors in the pitch lands, notably but not exclusively the Trinidad Lake Asphalt Company, sought to restrain digging by their neighbors. These injunctions were granted on a temporary basis on the simple application of the affected party, but they effectively became permanent unless the defendant could show good cause why they should be lifted: a well nigh impossible task, given the generality of the language in which the Privy Council declared the right of support to be applicable.

The local courts interpreted the judgment as meaning that any risk of letting down the surface gave grounds for an injunction, even if there was evidence that

---

[21] Quoted by the Privy Council at [1899] A.C. 594, at 602.

[22] Above, Ch 2, at 28–9, 45–7.

[23] [1899] A.C. 594 at 603.

that surface had previously been let down or modified by digging by the plaintiff or by the natural creeping of the pitch. As the commissioners pointed out, this was inconsistent with the key authority on which the Privy Council had relied, the case of *Humphries v. Brogden*,[24] which laid down the rule that the landowner was entitled to such support as "would protect the surface from subsidence and keep it securely at its ancient and natural level." In the light of the nature of the pitch lands and the history of their exploitation, the commissioners arrived at the view that "the [*Ambard*] case obviously has no application to a district such as we have described in which the ancient and natural level has already been disturbed."[25] Given that the *Ambard* case arose in that very district, this can only be taken to mean that the decision was wrong; but with exemplary tact, dictated perhaps by the fact that their legal member was a junior barrister in practice in London, the commissioners, while opining that *Ambard* was argued and decided upon "a highly artificial view of the facts of the case,"[26] cast responsibility for the local situation firmly upon an "error of inadvertence" by the local courts in the application of the *Ambard* judgment.[27]

The effect of the *Ambard* decision, as the Privy Council had been warned, was to impose a virtual freeze on private digging in the pitch lands, thus reinforcing the company's monopoly. Rather than the negotiation and agreement piously hoped for by the Privy Council, the mood in the region was reflected in the 23 outstanding injunctions noted by the commissioners; the memorial to the Commission by 676 laborers of La Brea,[28] stating that the injunctions had "entailed much suffering" for them; and the continuing discontent of the company, rooted in the fact that the government refused to take legal action to assert its supposed right to lateral support for unexploited Crown lands within the pitch lands except where serious substantial damage was threatened, thus enabling some continued winning of pitch. As already noted, the company claimed this was a breach of a clause in its 1888 concession.

SUBSEQUENT DEVELOPMENTS

The path out of this unhappy situation chosen by the colonial government was the appointment of the Royal Commission, whose findings I have already quoted on

---

[24] (1850) 12 Q.B. 739, 116 Eng. Rep. 1048.
[25] Trinidad. Asphalt Industry Commission 1903: 24.
[26] *Ibid.*
[27] *Ibid.* 4.
[28] *Ibid.* App. XIV-A.

several points. The Commission had a broad and demanding mandate.[29] The government wanted it to find out what had been the effect of the *Ambard* decision; whether fresh legislation was necessary for the proper administration of the district (the commissioners were specifically asked to comment on a draft ordinance already prepared in Trinidad); and if so, whether this could be enacted without undue interference with private rights, especially the concession rights of the New Trinidad Lake Asphalt Company. It also asked the commissioners to take a view on the exact obligations imposed by the contested clause in the concession regarding winning of pitch from lands in its possession, as well as on proposals by the company to extend the reach of the concession. Beside these rulings on legal issues, it also wanted the commissioners to pronounce on "the nature of the physical laws to which pitch is subject."

Some of the commissioners' answers to these questions have already been indicated. Elsewhere in their report, whose tone was generally rather critical of the company (and unfavorable to its proposals for the extension of the concession), they took a narrow view of the government's concession obligation to prevent the winning of pitch from its land, holding that this did not extend to enjoining adjacent diggings.[30] Their general attitude on this point was confirmed by the Privy Council a couple of years later in the case of *New Trinidad Lake Asphalt Co. v. Attorney-General*, adopting a narrow definition of the concession term "in the possession of the Crown."[31]

The commissioners also felt that the company's concession rights should form no obstacle to the enactment of a legislative scheme to regulate digging. An important element of their reasoning toward this conclusion was that at the time the concession was granted, there was already an "established practice, amounting perhaps to a custom, of pitch diggers to draw asphalt to a certain extent from a common stock. This practice can be traced back for a considerable period— certainly exceeding thirty years—and to a date probably anterior to that at which the subsisting titles to land in this neighborhood take their rise in Crown grants."[32]

The courts had been in error in failing to take account of this custom, whose existence negated the possibility, for pitch lands, of any absolute right of lateral support that might be an obstacle to the enactment of regulatory legislation. As to such regulation, the commissioners reviewed the government's draft proposal and

---

[29] *Ibid.* 3–7.

[30] *Ibid.* 5–6, 30–2.

[31] [1904] A.C. 415, reversing the decision of the Supreme Court of Trinidad and Tobago, (1900) 1 Trinidad and Tobago Supreme Court Reports 83.

[32] Trinidad. Asphalt Industry Commission 1903: 26. On the evidence and legal requirements for such a custom, see in detail 33–36 and App. F.

proposed a range of modifications. Their essential purpose was to provide for a control of digging, to be provided for in regulations or in a "digger's license," such as would "allow the owner of pitch lands to win as nearly as possible all the Asphalt that may be from time to time within his land, without at the same time unduly depleting the lands of his neighbours."[33] This would involve restriction of the amount of asphalt that might be removed from an excavation of any given size (or of the size of the depression in neighboring lands that it might produce) along with stipulation of periods that must be allowed to elapse between diggings, provision for notice of diggings, and so on. An inspector of mines for the colony would need to be appointed for the expert determination of the relevant measures and quantities and to furnish continuing supervision of the activities of the industry.[34]

It took until 1906 for the necessary regulations to be promulgated, in the form of the Asphalt Industry Regulation Ordinance.[35] The ordinance created the recommended inspectorate and entrusted it with the operation of a dual system of control applicable to any "asphalt-bearing land," as determined by the governor. Any digging for pitch on such land was illegal unless preceded by a notice in writing to the inspector in terms prescribed by the ordinance. Landowners could then proceed to dig without further formality, but if they did so, they might be liable to neighbors for taking their pitch under the principle of the *Ambard* decision, subjecting themselves to irksome proceedings for injunction and damages.

To avoid this, a landowner could in addition apply for a *permit* to dig pitch on his or her land, in which case regulations annexed to the ordinance would apply. These prohibited digging within 2 feet of one's boundaries or at an angle steeper than 85 degrees to the horizontal; required the depth and proposed yield of the excavation to be specified; and provided for publicity for permit applications, the opportunity to oppose them, and the possibility of a hearing by the inspector in case of opposition. In return for submitting to such regulation, the digger obtained protection from litigation. Actions by way of injunction and damages were ruled out: any complaint by a neighbor that pitch had passed from his or her land into the diggings had to be made to the inspector, who would arrange for the land to be inspected and, if necessary, hold a hearing. If satisfied that the diggings had *unduly* depleted any asphalt-bearing land, the inspector would issue a certificate indicating the quantity of material lost by the undue depletion. Possessed of such a certificate, the complainant could obtain restitution of an equivalent quantity of asphalt or its value, unless the High Court ordered payment of damages instead. Frivolous

---

[33] *Ibid.* 42.

[34] *Ibid.* 42–3.

[35] No. 10 of 1906, now the Asphalt Industry Regulation Act.

claims were deterred by requiring that the complaint be stamped, the cost of the stamps being unrecoverable unless the complaint was sustained in relation to a quantity of asphalt with a value greater than this cost. This procedure by way of complaint to the inspector was also available, as a convenient alternative to litigation, in cases where pitch had been dug after notice rather than under permit.

These rules followed the essence of the Commission's recommendations, with the interesting refinement of making the regulatory regime an essentially voluntary one, offering legal security in return for submission to control. They appear to have dealt satisfactorily with the problems of exploiting the pitch lands (the Great Pitch Lake continued to be covered by the terms of the 1888 concession); at least, we hear of no further litigation or controversy.

CAPTURE OF PITCH, CAPTURE OF OIL, CAPTURE OF WATER

On the spectrum of liquids, pitch must be about as far away from water as one can get, with crude oil, in its various manifestations from heavy to light, occupying different points of the space in between. Yet the short and turbulent story of pitch in Trinidad shows how the same kinds of issues arise, and same kinds of concepts come forward, whatever the blackness and stickiness, or purity and transparency, of the subterranean fluids involved.

Correlative Rights

At the very core of the Asphalt Commission's findings lay the notion that, regardless of the pattern of surface landholdings, there existed a "common stock" of pitch in the pitch lands of La Brea, and that by the time disputes broke out at the beginning of the 1890s, there had developed a customary method of working, summarized as "cut and come again," that was consistent with the collective use of this common stock. The Commission's central proposal was to give this customary notion regulatory expression and support. Freedom to dig one's holding in the pitch lands (the lake being subject to the quite different regime of the 1888 concession) had therefore to be limited by reference to this collective interest. This is the same idea as underlies the development of the notion of "correlative rights," in both oil and gas and in underground water, by American courts in the same period, most notably by the U.S. Supreme Court in *Ohio Oil Co. v. Indiana.*[36]

The approach taken by the Commission and, later, the Trinidad legislator to the issue of concretizing these correlative rights offers a telling demonstration of

---

[36] 177 U.S. 190 (1900), below Ch. 7, at 181–4.

the limitations of this notion as a basis for a judicially elaborated policy for the equitable and efficient exploitation of oil and gas. Though the pitch of Trinidad was far more accessible, and its physical location and characteristics were far more easily determined, and though the commissioners' own terms of reference and evidentiary resources were of far broader scope than would ordinarily be offered by litigation, they still felt it beyond their capacity to offer anything more than a general principle upon which, with suitable expert quantification, a set of working rules could be erected. Later, the drafters of the ordinance, whose regulations descend into considerable detail, as noted above, still felt it necessary to confer certain additional discretions on the inspector in settling the terms of permits. We shall see in Chapter 7 that American courts were never able to put much flesh on the bones of the correlative rights concept in its application to oil and gas; instead, the concept served, as in Trinidad, as a springboard for legislative development. At least one of the lines of approach followed in Trinidad, addressing the physical characteristics of excavations, provides a kind of pre-echo of the notion of regulating the spacing of wells, which was one of the first protections of correlative rights offered by U.S. legislatures.

Zones of Protection

Another idea that assumed importance in the Trinidad inquiry was that of the zone of protection—as we have seen, the key device adopted in France for the control of competitive drilling for mineral water sources in the vicinity of major establishments. At the center of the lengthy debate between company and government from 1890 until 1905 or thereabouts was the issue of the extent of the government's obligation to use its rights so as to prevent any capture by private diggers of pitch that might compete with the company's production. In effect, the 1888 concession, in imposing this obligation in respect of all "lands in the possession of the Crown" within 3 miles of the lake, created a zone of protection that embraced all the asphalt resources of La Brea. Obviously it did not and could not affect the rights of existing private diggers on their own land in this area— expropriatory legislation would have been necessary for that—and in that respect, it was less sweeping than its French counterparts. Had it been interpreted in the way the company demanded, however, digging anywhere in the vicinity of retained Crown land would have become impossible.

Despite the company's vigorous arguments, on the familiar lines of "what is good for Trinidad Lake Asphalt must be good for Trinidad," no one outside it— most notably the Trinidad colonial administration—seems to have been convinced that such a generous interpretation would represent good or fair policy. French governments, as we have seen, showed remarkable perseverance, in the face of legislators' doubts and hostility, in seeking protection for owners of sources, but we should not assume that this represents an ideological difference or reflects a greater sympathy for capitalistic enterprise. Those protected in France were at least first on the scene as owners of the established sources, and French administrations did not have to deal with the colonial factor or with the very real danger the company's position represented for the traditional livelihood of the La Brea population.

Custom

The notion of a mining custom that modifies the general law was a familiar one to British judges at the beginning of the twentieth century. Lead mining in Derbyshire and tin mining in Cornwall and Devon alike had their specialized legal regimes grounded on custom.[37] In the light of the evidence given to their own inquiry, the commissioners found it surprising that diggers like Ambard and François had never raised the argument of local mining custom against the claims for lateral support that rained in on them from the mid-1890s.[38] It may be that the commissioners, with their emphasis on the collective interest in the common stock, took a more benign and balanced view of the "custom" than did the inhabitants themselves. One of the company's witnesses stated that the working belief was simply that "all within my boundaries is mine,"[39] and in the *Ambard* case, the Privy Council was clearly more struck by the capture aspect of local practice than by the collective sense of the community, quoting a witness who described it as follows: "Pitch bulges out and they shave it off each morning. That is the plan adopted when you want to dig your neighbour's pitch."[40]

However weak the regulatory capacity of this custom may have been, the invocation of the notion in Trinidad makes one ask what its relevance might have been for the development of the American oil industry. We have seen how quickly there developed, in Pennsylvania, practices of leasing and subleasing land for oil development which were inconsistent with any idea that a landholder had a legal right to demand that subterranean fluids in his or her subsoil were left undisturbed.[41] It is possible that had courts started to take a line protective of such landholders, they might have been faced with claims of an industry custom permitting—indeed grounded upon—the legitimacy of capture. As things turned out, no such argument was necessary. Only in the cases opposing Mr. Kelley and

---

[37] Bainbridge 1878: 138–60.
[38] Trinidad. Asphalt Industry Commission 1903: 26.
[39] *Ibid.* 34 (McCarthy).
[40] [1899] A.C. 594 at 598.
[41] Above, Ch. 2, at 62–4.

the Ohio Oil Company in the 1890s[42] do we find references to oil industry custom. There the judicial recognition of the drilling of offset wells as a customary rule of the industry—clearly, a rule reflecting the legitimacy of capture—gives some support to that notion. Kelley's assertion of a contrary industry custom, as to the placing of wells, that would limit capture appeared to carry so little conviction in the court below that his counsel did not even mention it in appellate argument.

Rights of Support

We have already seen that one of the challenges for those who would resist the application of the rule of capture to oil and gas in nineteenth-century America, a challenge never successfully met in that period, was to identify the wrong that was committed by landowners who, through the exploitation of their own land, caused the diversion or abstraction of oil and gas originally under that of their neighbors. Only with the conception and working out of the idea of correlative rights did it become possible to draw a line between the exploiter's legitimate conduct and behavior that was illegitimate in that it went beyond the scope of the rights all shared in common and breached duties owed to others having such rights in the common pool.[43] The Trinidad experience again points to a road not taken in the United States. The claim that the digging of pitch on the land of A breached the right of lateral support owed by A to the land of B provided, as we have seen, the key that opened to the Trinidad Lake Asphalt Company the path of suppression of competition through litigation.

The extent of the right recognized by the Privy Council should be noticed. The Council declined to measure the company's damages flowing from the breach by reference to the loss resulting from the letting down of the surface. This was the position taken by one of the judges in the Trinidad Court of Appeal, who would have awarded just £10 ($48) in damages and refused an injunction. Instead, following the chief justice, the Privy Council measured the damages by the value of the pitch abstracted from the company's lot, at £100 ($480).[44] The implications of this mode of valuation were never really worked out by the Privy Council, but in practice, it suggests that it is to the stratum of pitch that the right of support attaches, as much as to the (essentially worthless) surface of the land. This implication was brought out in the commissioners' inquiry. They reported that "the Attorney-General argued for the position that the decision [in *Ambard*] involves the right of a landowner to claim lateral support for the purpose of

---

[42] Above, Ch. 2, at 28–9.

[43] See generally below, Ch. 7, at 181–94.

[44] [1899] A.C. 594, at 599–600.

maintaining not only the surface but also all the contents of his land at their ancient and natural level."[45]

The relevance of this claim to the oil and gas industry is not hard to see. Once the concept of the stable and contained oil and gas reservoir had obtained general acceptance, the application of this version of the rule of support would indeed have entitled a landholder to restrain operations by neighbors on the ground that the support for the oil and gas sitting quietly under his or her land was being withdrawn. We have seen that this precise point was raised by the plaintiff's counsel in *Kelley v. Ohio Oil Co.*,[46] but that the court dismissed his case without even deigning to discuss it. The commissioners' assessment of the Attorney-General's position supplied the argument that the Ohio court might have made: "It may be admitted ... that support for the surface implies support for the underlying material by which the surface is in its turn supported. ... But if the right of lateral support be claimed for underlying strata quite apart from any relation to the exposed surface, then we can find no ground for such a claim either in principle or authority."[47]

Even where the surface of adjoining lands has been adversely affected, American courts have paid little attention to the notion of lateral support. In the well-known case of *Elliff v. Texon Drilling*,[48] the defendants' negligence in drilling a gas well caused an explosion that killed many of the neighboring plaintiffs' cattle, led to the cratering of their land, and started fires that burned for years and drained enormous quantities of gas from the common reservoir. The plaintiffs obtained damages; but only on proof of negligence.

CONCLUSION

The two decades of controversy traversed by the asphalt industry in Trinidad coincided with a period of important developments in U.S. oil and gas law. They also involved significant American financial interests, through the asphalt paving industry, which was the chief Trinidad market. Yet there is little evidence of American awareness of or interest in the Trinidad developments, at least from the legal point of view. The *Ambard* case was, however, briefly noted in the *Harvard Law Review*.[49] The writer was critical of the decision, suggesting that the Privy

---

[45] Trinidad. Asphalt Industry Commission 1902: 37–8.

[46] Above, Ch. 2, at 45–7.

[47] *Ibid.* 38.

[48] 146 Tex. 575, 210 S.W. 2d 558 (1948).

[49] Anon. 1899b: 299.

Council should not have put to one side the earlier decisions denying any right of support for underground water, because asphalt shared with water the key quality of instability. No direct reference was made to the case of oil and gas, though one may find a veiled allusion in the writer's comment that "[w]hat the court would hold if the supporting substance had a density less than asphalt and greater than water does not appear, since they declined to discuss the question of degree."

There are certainly no grounds for suspecting this writer of a predisposition toward a wider application of the right of lateral support in U.S. jurisdictions, but the note may be seen nonetheless as hinting at a possible defense against capture. The *Kelley* case, however, had already indicated how one American jurisdiction would treat such an argument—with contempt—and it does not appear that anyone had the temerity to try it again. North of the border, an ingenious litigant did confront a later Judicial Committee of the Privy Council with its predecessors' thoughts about lateral support. The idea that where the free gas in a reservoir belongs to one party and the oil to another, the obligation to provide support for the gas might prevent the latter from drilling for its oil, was raised in *Borys v. Canadian Pacific Railway*.[50] But it won no sympathy from the judges, who were unwilling to see Imperial, the company with rights to the oil, effectively prevented from exercising them by this means and sought instead to console the gas owner, in terms reminiscent of Judge McIlvaine's "go and do likewise,"[51] with the thought that "[i]t may well be that the appellant can recover his own substance by any usual and customary method but cannot prevent the respondents from following a similar course."[52] Though they took some pains to make no explicit endorsement of the rule of capture, it seems plain that this is the direction in which the Privy Council was headed.

---

[50] [1953] 2 A.C. 217 (Privy Council).
[51] See above, Ch. 1, at 15.
[52] [1953] 2 A.C. 217 (Privy Council) at 230.

CHAPTER 6

AMERICA'S EARLY OIL RIVALS: PETROLEUM AND PROPERTY RIGHTS IN GALICIA, ROMANIA, AND RUSSIA

INTRODUCTION

Ivan Franko was a nineteenth-century Ukrainian poet and patriot who also wrote short stories, often set in and around the village of Boryslaw, now in western Ukraine but then part of Galicia, a province of the Austro-Hungarian Empire. One of his stories, *Poluika* (The Bonus), set in the early 1870s,[1] describes how workers who are digging an oil well for their greedy and much-loathed employer, Yonya, close to the border of his property, get their revenge by removing the oil under cover of night and selling it to his kindlier neighbor. When this well quickly runs dry while those on the neighbor's land remain productive, madness seizes Yonya, and he dies by falling into a newly dug well that he is trying to protect with his own body against further thefts. Franko's story, which includes plenty of circumstantial detail about the appearance of the oil, the usual ways and depths of digging, and even some elements of oilfield regulation, serves as a reminder that

---

[1] Franko 1899: 3–29.

while the United States was the dominant oil power of the nineteenth century, it was certainly not the only one.

When the Drake Well was drilled in 1859, small-scale commercial oil production was already under way in a number of places as far apart as Alsace on the Franco-German border, Yenangyaung on the Irrawaddy River in Burma, and southern Ontario in Canada, across Lake Erie from the Pennsylvania fields. The first major oil province to be identified in Europe was in fact found in the sandstones of the Carpathian mountains and their foothills, in territory which forms an arc descending from what is now southern Poland, through western Ukraine, and down through eastern Romania to the area north and east of Bucharest. Production from pits in this region, on an occasional basis, can be dated back to 1810,[2] and it was the desire to find new uses for the substantial supplies of crude which appeared to be available that led first to successful, if still imperfect, processes for the refining of crude oil, and then to the development of lamps in which it could be burned without the appalling odors and risks of conflagration that had previously been associated with it. Both achievements were the work of staff at a leading pharmacy in Lviv called Pod Gwiazda (Under the Star) and resulted, in the 1850s, in the use of petroleum-burning lamps in the Lviv Hospital and on the stations of the Emperor Ferdinand Northern Railway, which ran from Vienna to the salt mines of Galicia, and in the lighting of Bucharest with oil from a refinery at Ploesti by 1859[3]—all this at a time when coal-oil distillation was the leading-edge technology of choice for domestic lighting in the United States.[4]

The explosive growth of its production, however, quickly made the United States the dominant oil power and leading exporter of petroleum, a position unchallenged until the development of effective infrastructure and transport links brought to European and world markets, from the 1880s onward, oil from the enormous and free-flowing fields at Baku, in the Russian Caucasus. In 1882, the Baku fields produced only 4.5 million barrels compared with the American total of 30 million, but by 1888, their output had expanded to 23 million barrels, and in 1898, Russia outstripped the United States as the world's leading producer of crude, producing 50 million barrels to the United States' 45, with the American share of world production further reduced by the rapid development of the industry in the Dutch East Indies, now Indonesia, and in Burma.[5]

This long period of American dominance makes it easy to forget that a simultaneous process of oil industry development was occurring in a number of

---

[2] Forbes 1959: 93.

[3] Frank 2005: 56–8; 2 Gerretson 1955: 287.

[4] Williamson and Daum 1959: Chs. 2, 3.

[5] *Ibid.* 630–2; Longmuir 2001: 236.

Year	Romania	Galicia	Russia	Canada	U.S.
1860	1,188	n/a	9,179	n/a	68,774
1870	11,649	n/a	27,948	34,250	720,757
1880	15,900	31,373	411,137	47,950	3,601,182
1890	53,300	90,289	3,930,667	108,911	6,277,888

Table 6-1. Comparative Oil Production, 1860–1890 (in metric tonnes)
Source: Pizanty 1931: 8
Note: 1 metric tonne = about 7.4 barrels

countries in the nineteenth century. Early production statistics for some of these areas are unlikely to be very reliable, but a rough idea of orders of magnitude of the relevant national production in the nineteenth century can be collected from a table offered by the Romanian author Mihail Pizanty in 1931[6] (Table 6.1). Daniel Yergin offered an estimate of 36,000 barrels of European production in 1859, equivalent to about 4,864 tonnes, "primarily from Rumania and Galicia,"[7] a figure that, if correct, gives an idea of Galician production at this time.

Although growth continued into the twentieth century in all these countries, it is clear from the table that with the exception of Russia, there was no repetition of the explosive early growth witnessed in the United States. Why was this? The characteristics of the deposits, the technology available locally for exploiting them, the entrepreneurial spirit (or lack of it) in the local population, and the availability of markets all suggest themselves as possible factors. But another tempting explanation for this is to look at the issue of property rights. Did private ownership of petroleum resources in the United States, in association with the rule of capture, create a competitive drive for development that was missing elsewhere because the property right system was different? In particular, was the competitive spur of the rule of capture lacking in these jurisdictions?

This chapter briefly reviews the early history of oil exploration and production in the significant nineteenth-century oil provinces—Galicia, Romania, and Russia—against the background of the legal rules on property in oil and gas and control of their exploitation. It will show that despite sometimes significant differences of political, economic, and social context, the experiences in these places repeat, with remarkable fidelity, what was happening in the northeastern United States.

---

[6] Pizanty 1931: 8. Georgescu (1991: 126), using different sources, gives similar figures for Romania.

[7] Yergin 1991: 25.

GALICIA[8]

Galicia became part of Austria-Hungary as a result of the first partition of Poland in 1772 and returned to Polish control after the First World War. The history of the growth of the industry is entirely framed by the politics and law of the Austro-Hungarian Empire, whose end was marked by the withdrawal of its governing dynasty from power after World War I, in November 1918. Galician oil production suffered a steep decline after its peak in 1909, when its output of 15.36 million barrels represented more than 5 percent of world oil production,[9] and it never thereafter regained the levels of the first decade of the 1900s. Galicia was the easternmost province of the empire, the most remote from Vienna. The Galician Provincial Diet (legislature) was dominated by Polish nobles with vast landholdings who felt little sympathy either for imperial desires for development or for the mass of the Ukrainian-speaking peasant population who might have benefited from it. Tension between the diet and the imperial government and legislature in Vienna was an important factor in shaping the development of the oil industry.

That development got under way years before Drake drilled his well. Peasants were recorded as collecting oil from seepages for agricultural use in the early eighteenth century; by 1853, oil wells had been dug in no less than 151 villages, and the numbers of shafts, and their depth, steadily increased over the years, with more than 2,400 in the main oil district around Boryslaw in 1865. In the 1850s, shafts might be 10 to 12 meters deep and produce some 3 to 4 barrels a week; by the mid-1860s, as the deposits nearest the surface were exhausted, wells were down to 25 to 45 meters and might be producing 5 to 15 barrels weekly.[10] This looks minuscule compared with American figures for flowing wells, but at this time the Galicians had no steam engines to power their drilling. Their wells were hand dug, and the capital equipment of an oil explorer could be limited to "a ladder, a windlass, a pickaxe, a shovel, a rope and a pail."[11] This was a more primitive technology even than the spring pole drilling rigs, powered by human muscle, that were used by some hopeful prospectors in the Oil Creek region of Pennsylvania, but in both cases the equipment was within the means of a large class of energetic and adventurous men. As in Pennsylvania, then, we find a high level of demand for oil exploration opportunities.

---

[8] Information on the Galician industry is drawn, save where otherwise noted, from Alison Fleig Frank's impressive study, *Oil Empire: Visions of Prosperity in Austrian Galicia* (2005).

[9] Lender 1934: 15.

[10] Forbes 1959: 95–6. Franko's story, however, set in the late 1860s, refers to a well producing 20 barrels a day: Franko 1899.

[11] Frank 2005: 60.

What is perhaps more surprising, in the light of assumptions about the uniqueness of the American property rights system, is that we also find a land-holding system that was well adapted—indeed, in terms of the long-term health of the industry, too well adapted—to meet that demand. The equivalent of the Oil Creek farmer—of the Rynds, McClintocks, Bloods, Tarrs, and McElhenys who grew rich on Oil Creek sales and royalties—was the Galician peasant and small landholder, blessed or cursed since the emancipation decree of 1848 with a plot, often of poor land, that may well have been insufficient to support a family. Much of the land in Galicia was held in this way, despite the presence of the great Polish-owned estates, which accounted for some 40 percent of the land. This division of land into small and uneconomic lots would have been quite irrelevant to the development of the Galician industry if the oil rights had been under the unified ownership or control of the state. The peasant would have had to go on bitterly scratching a living from the surface while the state's concessionaires drew the petroleum wealth from beneath it.

One might have expected this to be the system in force at the time when interest in oil production began to grow in the 1850s. The mining law of Austria put the disposition of mines and mining rights in the hands of the emperor.[12] This prerogative right was extended by imperial patent to Galicia in 1804. Between that time and 1854, however, the imperial authorities twice removed liquid petroleum from within the ambit of the prerogative and twice—as soon as they noticed that interest in the product was growing—restored it. The general rules for mining were restated in considerable detail in the General Mining Law of 1854, providing for mining under governmental concession in return for an area fee and a royalty: the surface proprietor had no right to prevent mining on the land or to mine it otherwise than under a concession. An interpretation of the law by the Imperial Ministry of Finance affirmed that it covered solid and liquid bitumens, and was followed by a distribution of concessions for their exploration, and an explicit holding in 1860 that liquid petroleum was covered.

In the face of determined opposition from the Galician Provincial Diet, however, the imperial government changed its mind yet again and in 1862 legislated to remove the reservation of liquid petroleum in Galicia.[13] In the absence of such a reservation, petroleum was subject to the general principles of land law applicable there. That law, the Allgemeines Bürgerliches Gesetzbuch (General Austrian Civil Code) of June 1811, was less explicit than the French Civil Code on the rights of landowners to recover whatever they might find under the surface of

---

[12] 1 Cancrin 1825: 4, 13–14.
[13] Aguillon 1890: 73.

their land,[14] simply recognizing the right of an owner of property to do as he or she wished with it, subject to certain limitations such as the avoidance of nuisance to neighbors (articles 362–364).

The result was a muddy and chaotic struggle for resources. The techniques may have been more primitive than those in use in Pennsylvania at the time, but the oil behaved in the same way, and the imperatives of ownership and production were therefore similar: if you own oil-bearing land, divide it into the smallest lots possible and get the biggest royalty you can. If you want to get oil, dig as close as you can to your boundary and to your neighbor's well; and dig deeper. Alison Fleig Frank, in her book *Oil Empire*, cites an 1870 text as recording that 6,000 square meters of land (about 1.5 acres) might be shared among 30 to 40 different operators;[15] her calculations for the Boryslaw area in 1881 show a scarcely improved picture, with an average density of wells (save on one large holding) of one for every 336 square meters.[16]

This sort of concentration was not reached in the United States until the twentieth century, at places like Spindletop.[17] One factor present in the United States was, however, crucially absent in Galicia: secure property rights, not in the oil, but in the land itself. Peasant-owned land was not normally included in land title registers, which made a secure title all but impossible to obtain and gave rise to enormous amounts of litigation. And if land were leased for oil production purposes—the usual system, with leases resembling the American model and providing for an annual rental replaced, on achieving production, by a royalty—the lease would not be recorded in the land title register, which meant that a future purchaser of the land might plausibly deny that the lessee had any rights surviving the sale.

The consequence of this legal insecurity was the inability of Galicia to attract the investment to support a general move away from spade and bucket production methods toward the machine-powered drilling that was driving the American industry steadily forward. Local and foreign capitalists found it impossible to assemble the landholdings they needed to justify substantial investments enjoying reasonable protection against risks of drainage of the oil they had found by innumerable small-scale operations on their perimeters. The arrested state of development of the industry, coupled with the grave environmental and social consequences of this pattern of exploitation—widespread pollution, collapse of land surfaces, sinking of streets and houses, grossly unsafe working conditions—led to

---

[14] Art. 552, discussed above, Ch. 4, at 96–8.
[15] Frank 2005: 62, citing Lipp 1870: 101–2.
[16] *Ibid.* 67.
[17] Below, Ch. 7, at 198.

regular attempts by imperial ministries and their inspectors to achieve reform and regulation. After much debate and discussion among a complex and shifting set of interest coalitions—traditionalist landowners, small proprietors, development-minded landowners, small capitalists, large (mostly foreign) investors—revolving mostly around the question of whether the Imperial Mining Prerogative should be restored in relation to petroleum, a new Imperial Petroleum Law was eventually passed in 1884, shortly followed by a law of the Galician Provincial Diet that recapitulated its key provisions and added more detailed rules for petroleum operations.

Frank has suggested that these laws might seem "modest in scope,"[18] but they represent a substantial advance over anything that oil-producing states in America had achieved by this date. While the legislation left the property rights in petroleum in the hands of surface landowners, it tried to tackle legal insecurity by establishing a distinct new property right, that of exploiting an oilfield, and providing for the creation of oil registers in which these rights could be recorded. The 1884 legislation addressed the other ills of the industry by providing for the supervision of oil production activities by the Imperial Mining Authority, setting up a mining police and regulating working conditions, though it devolved the power to make subsequent regulations to the diet, an important victory for local autonomy. It also incorporated the first attempt anywhere to address the evils flowing from overintensive exploitation. The stimulus for this may have been provided by a *Gesetzentwurf* (draft law) presented in 1881 to the diet by the Verein zur Hebung der Naphtaindustrie (Galician Petroleum Industry Improvement Society). The society had proposed that oil leases should cover not less than 1 hectare, to inhibit drainage and overdigging or overdrilling, nor more than 36, to restrain speculation via the purchase of rights to large tracts of land for subletting.[19] This direct attack on the contractual freedom of landowners found no reflection in the 1884 legislation; instead, the Galician law stipulated (in article 15) that the Mining Authority was to prohibit the commencement of operations if the shape or size of the area notified to it for exploitation "does not permit of its rational development."

The passage of the petroleum law followed closely upon 1881 legislation enabling foreign joint-stock companies to run mining operations in Austria and the construction in 1883 of a railway line linking the oil-producing region with the rest of the empire. Together these developments opened the way for the investment and technological advance that the Galician oil industry had hitherto lacked. Among the leaders of the drive toward a more modern industry were the partners

---

[18] Frank 2005: 74.
[19] *Ibid.* 72–3.

William MacGarvey, a Canadian driller, and the English entrepreneur John Simeon Bergheim, who together introduced Canadian cable tool drilling methods to Galicia and thereby immediately opened up numerous oil basins lying below the reach of hand-dug wells; and the Polish-born man of all parts Stanislaw Szczepanowski, whose entry into the Galician oil industry in 1880 was preceded by nearly a decade's work in economics and statistics in the British India Office.

The precocious success of Szczepanowski, a man without experience or expertise in the industry, in striking large oil deposits with his first, hand-dug wells (his 1881 Wanda Well, which made him famous, was dug to a depth of between 90 and 150 meters) led to a local oil boom and a major inflow of financial capital to his and his competitors' operations. Yet because of the operation of the rule of capture in Galicia, Szczepanowski was drawn into a spiral of investment—in wells, storage, transport, and refining—and borrowing to meet its cost, which nearly bankrupted him in 1893 and eventually led to his financial collapse, prosecution, and disgrace in 1899. As he put it in a book published in 1886:

> My God, your neighbors are so greedy for this oil that you cannot sell, leaking out of thousands of barrels, that every day, every hour, you hear about new intentions to sink ever more wells close to your "Eldorado" and take away your treasure. So then you have to sink new wells yourself under the worst conditions, quickly, quickest! Spend more money! Spend money on engines, tools, fuel and people. Spend money to build roads, for rail transport ... [20]

These unfortunate results occurred despite the general provision of article 15 of the 1884 law (above) and the fact that Galicia had already equipped itself, under the 1884 legislation, with regulations stipulating minimum distances between wells (30 meters) and between any well and the boundary of a property (10 meters).[21] While this originated as a fire prevention measure, a commission that reviewed the rules in 1903 noted that excessively close drilling, provoked by the desire to capture oil from neighboring land and encouraged by a tendency to value a petroleum property according to the number of wells on it, was economically disadvantageous because it artificially inflated production costs.[22]

Exactly the same problems existed in the United States, but as we shall see, no well-spacing rules were adopted there until 1915.[23] Maybe this was not such a bad

---

[20] Szczepanowski 1886, cited and translated in Frank 2005: 86.

[21] Lipp 1870: 101–2 states that in 1870, a rule was already in force setting a minimum distance of 10 klafter (18.9 meters) between wells, but his figures on actual well densities (above, text at n. 16) indicate that if this indeed were the case, the rule was ignored.

[22] Austria-Hungary. Kommission zur Untersuchung der Betriebsverhältnisse des Erdölbergbaues in Galizien 1904: 17–18.

[23] Below, Ch. 9, at 259–60.

thing, as in fact the Galician requirements had a highly perverse effect. On bigger tracts, which were usually in the hands of larger and more experienced operators, wider spacings (50 to 70 meters) were adopted anyway. Where plots were small, however, if you let your neighbor get a well down first, 10 meters from the boundary, your own well would need (by reason of the 30-meter rule) to be at least 20 meters from the boundary, which gave your neighbor a clear drainage advantage and might, on a small plot, make it hard to find anywhere to drill a well at all. Spacing requirements thus gave an added incentive to drill as quickly and as close to property lines as possible.[24] Having duly noted all this, however, the commission did no more than recommend that in future, spacings be enlarged to 40 and 20 meters, with a power in mining officials to grant "essential" exceptions on the basis of "legitimate requests."[25] There is a strange pre-echo here of the way the Texas Railroad Commission, 20 years later, eviscerated its own well-spacing rules by the openhanded granting of exceptions for small tracts.[26]

The more experienced MacGarvey and Bergheim partnership coped better with these problems. Their deep drilling techniques gave them first access to fields others could not reach. They pursued mineral rights with great vigor, protected them forcefully through litigation, bought out smaller competitors, and created a vertically integrated operation extending not only to refining and storage, but also to the manufacture of drilling and other equipment.[27] MacGarvey remained a leading figure in the Galician oil industry throughout the period of its greatest growth, from 1895, when the Jakôb gusher was struck at Schodnica, until the outbreak of World War I. The period was one of considerable overproduction, which by 1908 had driven the price of Galician crude down to 5 to 7 crowns a tonne (around 14 to 19 cents a barrel), from nearly 40 crowns ($1.08 a barrel) immediately after the Schodnica find.[28]

Galician crude was expensive to get, and its products had difficulty in competing with American imports even in nearby markets like Germany. Storage capacity was woefully inadequate. The tendency of local producers (including MacGarvey, who by this time identified himself wholly with Galicia) was to blame a flood of foreign speculative capital for this crisis, but what may have been most important was not the source of the capital, but the fact that the majority of investors, whether from within or outside Galicia, had small stakes, small parcels,

---

[24] Anon. 1903: 5; Anon. 1908a: 139, 182, 199, 227.

[25] Austria-Hungary. Kommission zur Untersuchung der Betriebsverhältnisse des Erdölbergbaues in Galizien 1904: 22.

[26] Hardwicke 1952, and below, Ch. 9, at 260–2.

[27] Frank 2005: 90–4; Morritt 1993: 126–32.

[28] Lender 1934: 69.

and sought quick returns. As in Pennsylvania in the early years, collective attempts to organize production had no discernible effect. The Galician Provincial Petroleum Association, in which both Szczepanowski and MacGarvey at one time played important roles, never seems to have attempted this task. Later initiatives taken in 1908—a company to provide collective storage facilities, make agreements with refiners, and organize sales, and a government-sponsored consortium to provide fuel for the state railway system—had some positive effect but tackled the consequences rather than the causes of overproduction.[29]

In the same year, however, the Galician Provincial Diet, in its revised Petroleum Law of March 22, 1908, did offer a robust response to these long-standing problems of overintensive operations, though it came too late to save the industry from decline. Putting to one side the timorous proposals of the 1903 commission, the diet opted for a prohibition of oil production activity on holdings less than 12,000 square meters (2.97 acres) in area, with a spacing rule requiring any well to be not less than 30 meters from a boundary (article 31). This prohibition must have operated as a severe deterrent to the subdivision of property that had earlier been so damaging and was to continue to impair rational development in the United States. To avoid the effective confiscation of oil underlying tracts below the minimum size, the law went on (in article 31a) to provide that where such land was surrounded by oil properties, its owner could demand a decision from the Mining Authority compelling the neighboring proprietors to acquire the land, dividing it up in proportion to the lengths of their respective boundaries. If they failed to act or to agree on a price, a judicial settlement could be imposed.

That the Galician oilfields had given of their best was really not appreciated until after the end of the First World War—a war that, in Galician territory, claimed by both the reestablished state of Poland and by a would-be Western Ukrainian republic, did not end until the two sides concluded an armistice in September 1919, under which the oil-bearing areas of Galicia became part of Poland. The prize was a disappointing one. Continuing foreign investment—notably French—was unable to discover new fields and stem the sharp fall of production. The Petroleum Law of 1908, which had maintained the principle that petroleum rights belonged to the surface landowner, remained in effect. Despite its provisions on the minimum size of exploitable holdings, it appears that development continued to be hampered by the division of petroleum rights into small parcels and the resistance, "sometimes malicious," of some landowners and producers to attempts to create rational exploitation areas.[30]

---

[29] Frank 2005: 150, 167–8; Lender 1934: 70.
[30] Schaetzel 1938: 155–6.

The Galician oil era was roughly contemporaneous with the Pennsylvanian one and shows some remarkable parallels: the importance of low-cost operations on small parcels of land, the way production was unrestrained by the lack of market opportunities, the rapid working out of fields with considerable waste, and the inability of producers to combine effectively. A key difference was the ability of government to secure regulation—through the Imperial and Galician Petroleum Laws of 1884 and the more comprehensive Galician Law of 1908—at a relatively early stage. This legislative achievement should not be underrated. It represented the first comprehensive attempt to provide a rational legal structure for an oil industry operating on the basis of private ownership, by defining the property rights of the landowner and the oil producer, regulating oil operations in the interests of safety and good oilfield practice, and incorporating rules designed to address the small-tract problem and moderate the negative effects of the rule of capture. It is unfortunate that early errors in the framing of such rules were corrected only when the industry was about to decline from its peak. Nevertheless, timely attention to the Galician experiments could have spared the U.S. industry considerable damage and loss.

ROMANIA

Romanian oil development shows many similar features to that of Galicia. The industry was slower to get under way, but production reached higher levels—1.848 million tonnes in 1913, of which 57.2 percent was exported[31]—and Romania continued to be a significant producing country until the middle of the twentieth century. As in Galicia, national oil policy in the key period of development, between about 1890 and 1930, was strongly shaped by the tension between two goals that have come to characterize policy in new oil states worldwide: the need to attract foreign investment for effective exploitation by reason of lack of domestic technical and financial capacity, and the nationalistic desire to keep the control of, and the benefit from, this natural resource firmly in domestic hands. This latter factor operated with special importance in Romania by reason of the fact that the period of oil development followed closely upon the achievement of independence and unified statehood.

Romania was formed from the two principalities of Wallachia and Moldavia, which trace their history to the fourteenth century but were, over most of their history, formally subjects of the Ottoman Empire.[32] Through treaties with the

---

[31] Georgescu 1991: 126. Pizanty's figure is 1.886 million: Pizanty 1931: 18.
[32] See generally Georgescu 1991: Chs. 3, 4; Hitchins 1994: Introduction.

sultan, they preserved a greater degree of political, social, and religious autonomy than countries south of the Danube, and when Ottoman power in southeast Europe began to weaken in the nineteenth century, Romanians were effective in soliciting the great powers (notably France, particularly sympathetic as another "Latin" country) to support their ambitions for both independence and unity. The latter goal was achieved first: after the Crimean War, and in accordance with the Treaty and then the Convention of Paris (1856, 1858), the principalities recovered the right to elect their own princes and chose the same man, Alexandru Cuza. By 1861, Cuza had completed the administrative unification of the principalities, but the erection of Romania into a single and independent state was achieved only in 1866, following a coup against Cuza, the installation of Prince Charles of Hohenzollern-Sigmaringen as king, and the promulgation of a new constitution. Independence gave a boost to hitherto undeveloped industrial activities, including oil search and production; perhaps in consequence of this, the oil industry was always a focus of nationalist sentiment. Foreign capital was sought and admitted from time to time but always stood upon a rather precarious footing.

Oil production in Romania began, as in Galicia and elsewhere in Europe, with the collection of oil from seepages or the digging of shafts and is recorded in legal documents dating back to the seventeenth century.[33] In 1857 there were apparently 250 pits in operation; by 1865, production by this method had reached 5,426 tonnes (around 40,000 barrels), and the first—though unsuccessful— attempts at methodical exploitation were getting under way.[34] Pizanty's figures, already cited, suggest that growth in production by this method was slow, increasing by only about 1,000 tonnes a year over the whole period between 1860 and 1880. Production in this period was still from large numbers of hand-dug pits, normally about 50 to 70 meters deep, though depths of more than 200 meters were sometimes attained.[35]

It took the arrival of North American investors and drilling techniques after 1880 to lay the foundation for a new phase in the development of the industry. As in Galicia, such investors faced formidable uncertainties and legal risks. Their source was, again, the basic legal provisions relating to landholding and in particular to mineral rights.[36] Until the adoption of the Romanian Civil Code in 1865, the property law of the principality of Moldavia was derived from the Codul

---

[33] Forbes 1959: 99.

[34] Serdaru 1921: 21.

[35] Forbes 1959: 105; Bennett 1897: 12; 2 Gerretson 1955: 287. By reason of the gases encountered at such depths, such workings depended on the miners' having a piped supply of fresh air: Sutherland 1899: 98. In the hand-dug wells in Burma, the technology of the air helmet was not introduced until 1896; wells could then be deepened to about 120 meters: Longmuir 2001: 158–9.

[36] Buzatu 1998: 41.

Callimachi of 1817 and that of Wallachia from the Leguirea Caragea of 1818. Whereas the Codul Callimachi reserved rights in minerals to the ruling prince, the Leguirea Caragea gave mining rights to the first occupant of the subsoil. A later law common to both principalities, the Règlement Organique des Principautés Roumaines of 1831, granted surface owners the right of free exploitation of the minerals beneath their land, subject to the payment of a 10 percent royalty to the prince (article 178), who retained the right to grant a mineral concession to a third party, with indemnity to the surface owners, if they did not want to exploit their land themselves (article 179).

The state's abrogation of its mineral rights was completed with the promulgation of the Romanian Civil Code, whose articles 489 and 491 imported the basic principle of French law, already examined,[37] under which the surface proprietor owned the subsoil and was free to exploit it subject to respect for any special provisions of mining laws. It has been suggested that this proviso had the effect of preserving the mineral rights of the state under the 1831 regulation and the old codes until such mining laws should be passed,[38] but the better opinion is that its effect was purely prospective, so that for the next 30 years, until the 1895 Mining Law was enacted, landowners could treat the minerals under their land as their own. Certainly Romanians behaved in this period as if this was their belief.

From the point of view of the successful development of the Romanian petroleum industry, this was unfortunate, as about a quarter of the land in Romania was held in small parcels whose ownership had been transferred to peasants from large landowners in 1864, and which subsequently had been further broken up by the operation of the succession laws. Another quarter was in the hands of the state, and the rest was held by some 12,000 to 15,000 absentee landowners.[39] Holdings transferred in 1864 averaged 4 hectares in size;[40] by the end of the century, however, the average size of a plot in Wallachia was no more than an acre (0.4 hectare).[41] Oil operations were further complicated by the peasant practice of organizing their plots in extremely narrow but very long strips running from the valley up into the hills, so that each should have roughly the same conditions for their traditional vine and orchard plantings. These plots might be only 6 to 10 meters wide.[42] Thus, even though Romania did not have the kind of intensive artisanal development that had honeycombed areas like Boryslaw in

---

[37] Above, Ch. 4, at 96–8.
[38] Cohen 1926: 3–8.
[39] Bennett 1897: 3.
[40] Gioni 1984: 30; Georgescu 1994: 132–3.
[41] Pearton 1981: 17.
[42] Beeby Thompson 1961: 214; Pizanty 1931: 13.

Galicia with pits, explorers were no less exposed to risks of capture by way of competitive shafts around their boundaries sunk by neighbors exercising their rights under article 491, unless an explorer could put together a reasonably sized tract of land for exploration.

Unfortunately the foreign investors who commanded the necessary skill and capital to deal with Romanian conditions in this way could not secure a good title by straightforward purchase, as article 7 of the Constitution of 1866 forbade foreigners to hold landed property. Explorers who wanted to avoid the drainage of their discoveries by competitive drilling thus needed to build a block of territory by taking concessions of mineral rights from a large number of small proprietors. Easier said than done: until the very end of the nineteenth century, the legal basis for a lease of mineral rights was far from clear, and it was commonplace for explorers, driven by the urgency of winning access to promising territories in the face of competition, to end up with titles that might be defective in some way.[43]

Hard on the heels of a dispatch from the acting British consul general in Romania drawing attention, in 1896, to the petroleum opportunities offered by the new Romanian Mining Law,[44] discussed below, his successor felt it necessary to issue a warning against purchasing convenient bundles of leases from unscrupulous speculators, romantically styled *chevaliers de l'industrie* (knights of industry). These gentlemen operated by bringing large numbers of peasants, well primed with strong liquor, before local tribunals where they were induced to sign leases in return for small payments, regardless of the title, if any, they held over the land in question.[45] The oil company's entry on the land was thus regularly accompanied by lawsuits instigated by the true proprietors, by signatories now restored to sobriety, or by other victims of similar procedures. The peasants, whose life, despite the emancipation of 1864, was one of utter misery and degradation, exposed to repressive conduct of large landowners and their agents and to the ill-regulated use of coercive and even corporeal sanctions,[46] could hardly be blamed for taking a cynical view of property rights and deriving the maximum immediate benefit from their inadequate holdings—though most of the profit, it appears, ended up in the hands of the *chevaliers*.[47]

Beside these privately held lands, which covered most of the country, the Romanian state, unlike the Galician government, also disposed of directly held state lands, which came into its hands by way of the land reform of 1864. Once

---

[43] Durandin 1995: 186; Bennett 1897: 5.

[44] Bennett 1897.

[45] Liddell 1897.

[46] Gioni 1984; Durandin 1995: 162–4; Georgescu 1991: 132–3; Hitchins 1994: 166–9.

[47] Durandin 1995: 186; Buzatu 1998: 44.

petroleum became a matter of serious concern to Romanian governments in the 1890s, a double stream of legislation developed, with distinct arrangements for petroleum under state and private lands. Its common source was a comprehensive mining law passed in 1895, after four previous unsuccessful attempts at legislation, by a conservative government committed to the modernization and industrialization of Romania and ready to accept the contribution of foreign capital for these purposes. The law covered both hard rock minerals and petroleum and had separate provisions for state and private lands.[48]

For private land, the main problems were access and security of tenure. To encourage the exploitation of hard rock minerals such as coal and iron, the law gave the state the right to exploit minerals in private land or to concede the exploitation to a third party if, having been requested to do so, the owner failed to exploit them within a given period. In such a case, the state could grant a concession for a term of 75 years, and this concession was, as under the French Code Minier (Mining Code),[49] a piece of property that could be held independently from the surface rights and was fully transferable and mortgageable. This reform represented, for the liberal opposition and the large landowners whose interests they represented, a savage attack on rights of property.

It did not, however, apply to petroleum, asphalt, and ozokerite (a type of paraffin wax), which were left (by article 65) to the free disposition of the surface owner. Among the unconvincing reasons for making this exception offered by the government was the proposition—true at one time, maybe, but certainly not in the age of deep drilling then under way—that exploitation of petroleum, unlike other minerals, was a simple matter requiring modest capital and no advanced technology. Ghita Buzatu, in his comprehensive history of Romanian petroleum, suggests that making this exception was the price paid by the government for getting its law through at all.[50] The law imposed no restrictions on petroleum operations on private land other than to apply general rules of mining law for the protection of neighboring property and of employees. Requirements for provision to the state of regular information regarding work on private land—plans of work, notification of new wells, production and well records—were added by regulation in 1900.

The 1895 law set off a rush for oil land in Romania and produced a significant influx of foreign capital. While foreign companies generally had more efficient production methods, in general exploitation was neither rational nor economic.

---

[48] See generally on the 1895 law Pearton 1981: 18–20; Pizanty 1931: 14; Serdaru 1921: 31–2, 62–5; Buzatu 1998: 42–6.

[49] Below, Ch. 10, at 312–4.

[50] Buzatu 1998: 44.

Operators who had been able to secure only small areas of land engaged in acute competition for immediate rewards, each concessionaire trying to "steal" oil from the neighboring subsoil.[51] It also soon appeared that the 1895 law did not do enough to ensure security of tenure of petroleum interests granted by private owners: oil leases or concessions remained as purely personal contracts, and the frequent existence of conflicting concessions led to "real battles to get possession of land."[52]

Further legislation was thus enacted both in 1904 and—to the same effect but in more detail—in 1913. It treated the private concession, like the state concession granted under the 1895 law, as a registrable property right in land, with priority determined by the date of registration, and provided an elaborate procedure called "consolidation" for settling conflicts between rival concessionaires. A "consolidated" concession was valid even as against surface proprietors with valid titles who had not been able to participate in the process, a provision characterized by Virgiliu Serdaru as a fundamental attack on property rights explicable only by the need to protect foreign concessionaires.[53] These provisions appear to have worked well enough up to the time when they were rendered irrelevant for the future by the nationalization of mineral rights under article 19 of the new Romanian Constitution of 1923, as implemented by the Mining Law of 1924.[54] Production in 1913, before the Romanian oilfields began to be fought over in World War I, was more than 20 times greater than the level reached at the time of the 1895 law.[55] These later laws, however, did not in any way modify the code provisions that were at the root of competitive drilling practices, and such practices seem to have continued: we find the oil consultant Arthur Beeby Thompson, on a visit in 1925, noting the "specially favourable conditions" enjoyed by an oil lease that was "large enough to escape objectionable offsetting."[56]

With the 1924 law, the history of Romanian petroleum became one of the management of a wholly state-owned resource, raising the sorts of issues that I discuss (in relation to other countries) in Chapters 10 and 11. Here, however, it is worth looking briefly at Romania's management of state oil resources between the 1890s and 1924,[57] as this period coincides with one of great uncertainty in the United States as to how oil in federal lands would be managed, uncertainties which

---

[51] *Ibid.* The quotation marks are Buzatu's.

[52] Serdaru 1921: 35.

[53] *Ibid.* 68–76.

[54] Pearton 1981: 112–25.

[55] Pizanty 1931: 18; and see text at n. 31 above.

[56] Beeby Thompson 1961: 230.

[57] Material on this topic is drawn from Serdaru 1921: Ch. 6, save where otherwise noted.

led to considerable waste and inefficiency until brought to an end by the passage of the Mineral Leasing Act 1920.[58]

Romania's first attempt at mineral (including petroleum) regulation was contained in a regulation of 1893[59] governing exploration on such state land. Described by Serdaru as "liberal without limit," it provided for the grant on demand of concessions of 10 years' duration, covering between 3 and 10 hectares, and requiring the holder to dig to 50 meters or drill to 100, with an annual rental of 20 lei (then equivalent to approximately $4) per hectare and a royalty of 2 lei (40 cents) per tonne of crude recovered. The minimal royalty sought may certainly be described as liberal, but the other terms—notably the short duration and small extent of the concession—were not especially attractive to a serious investor. They did not survive very long: regulations under the 1895 law introduced new concession arrangements for state land, lasting 30 years, extending up to 40 hectares, and subject to a 4 percent royalty (on net, not gross, revenue). These regulations, like those already in force in Galicia, included a requirement for minimum spacing between wells (article 17), but the fact that this was set at only 10 meters, with no special provision for wells near boundaries, suggests that safety rather than drainage was the issue it sought to address. Little was achieved under these regulations: only eight concessions were granted, covering a total area of 228 hectares, which is less than a square mile.

In the face of financial crisis, notably a budget deficit of 33 percent for 1898–1899, the government swung to the other extreme and accepted a Standard Oil proposition to select and acquire 15,000 hectares of state land, with exclusive rights to lay and use a pipeline to a Black Sea port, in return for an "advance on royalties" of 10 million lei.[60] Arrangements for the remaining state land were modified by regulation in 1900 so as to enlarge the length and size of concessions to 50 years and 100 hectares, while increasing the royalty to 10 to 15 percent.

The Standard Oil deal was never carried through and contributed to the collapse of the government and its replacement by the liberals, much more suspicious of foreign involvement in the Romanian economy; the reform of concession terms produced slightly better results in that by 1905, more than 100 state concessions had been awarded. Only 16 of these, however, were actually being worked, and in 1905–1906 a new conservative government had a fourth try at securing effective exploitation, withdrawing the unworked concessions and securing the passage of a new concessions law, which sought for the first time to link proven with unproven land in a single holding. Now 50-year concessions

---

[58] This story is recounted in Ch. 8.
[59] Pearton 1981: 18 gives 1890.
[60] Durandin 1995: 186; Pearton 1981: 28–9.

covering up to 100 hectares of proven territory, associated with 10 times as much unproven territory, were offered, with the award going to the highest royalty bidder in the event of competition. Terms were demanding: one concessionaire could hold only three lots; 2 million lei ($400,000) had to be deposited as a performance guarantee; a minimum number of wells, to specified depths, had to be drilled in both proven and unproven areas; both a sliding-scale royalty and a net profit share were payable to the state; and the state could reclaim half the concession area in the event of a discovery.[61]

These provisions have a remarkably modern feel to them and could well be encountered in a contemporary state lease or license including reasonably prospective territory. In the Romania of a century ago, they held little appeal. The country's strategic position, especially in relation to the European gasoline market, made it highly attractive to major foreign interests such as Româno-Americană, a subsidiary of Standard Oil; the Telega and Buştenari Companies of the German Disconto-Gesellschaft/Bleichroder group; Royal Dutch's Astra Română; and the formerly Austro-Hungarian Steaua Română, now controlled by Deutsche Bank. But these companies, by far the largest investors in exploration and development,[62] found the state terms "prohibitive"[63] and were quite content to take leases of private land on less demanding terms. Local investors also seem to have found the terms impossible to meet; at all events, according to Pizanty not a single concession was awarded under this regime up to the outbreak of World War I. At that time, subsisting earlier concessions extended to 1,681 hectares; but petroleum rights were held over about 30,000 hectares of privately owned land.[64]

The Romanian experience in the first years of the twentieth century offered a foretaste of the difficulties many states would have in securing the effective exploitation of petroleum resources they held. Handing over large blocks of territory for monopolistic exploitation by major companies was easy, but if this were excluded for nationalistic reasons or simple fear of monopoly power, the state was faced with the problem of creating a pattern of holdings, and a set of terms, that would bring in the desired range of competing companies. The Romanian mistake of overestimating the attractiveness of one's territory and offering small parcels on unattractive terms was quickly repeated elsewhere, as we shall see in a later chapter. The Romanian approach also reintroduced the issues of capture and drainage even in relation to large-scale state holdings of petroleum rights, once these had been parceled out in small units, necessarily in ignorance of the

---

[61] On the 1906 law (and a further law of the same type passed in 1909), see also Buzatu 1998: 55–6.

[62] Pearton 1981: 21–33. Other companies are listed by Pizanty 1931: 16.

[63] 2 Gerretson 1955: 294.

[64] Pizanty 1931: 16–17.

topography of possible oil reservoirs. I explore the contemporary implications of this practice in Chapter 11.

RUSSIA

Among America's Old World oil rivals, it was Russia that came last on the scene, but Russia too that, developing its productive capacity with extraordinary speed in the last quarter of the nineteenth century, was by 1898 the world's leading producer of crude, a position it held until the Baku oilfield strikes and riots of 1903 drastically reduced production. What is most remarkable is that almost all of this production of some 50 million barrels of oil came from a few thousand wells in a small and remote region on the shores of the Caspian Sea;[65] it was not spread around a vast continent like American production of that period.

Its commercial and industrial development may have come relatively late, but Baku, on its narrow peninsula on the southwest coast of the Caspian Sea, can perhaps lay claim to a longer petroleum history than any other spot on the surface of the globe, its flaming seepages of gas making it famous even in antiquity as the "Land of the Eternal Fire"[66] and forming a focus for religious worship. Marco Polo, who visited Baku in 1272, recorded the collection of oil from the area's seeps and its export as a commodity.[67] The Khanate of Baku came into Russian possession as a result of the Treaty of Gulistan with Persia in 1813. Existing oil pits belonging to the ruler were taken over by the Russian state and until 1873 were either worked directly by the government (1834–1849) or leased to a single contractor for four-year periods, with no guarantee of renewal. Neither of these arrangements was calculated to produce significant investment or technological advance, and indeed, the system is said to have engendered among oilmen a philosophy of seeking quick returns at least cost, which persisted long after it was replaced.[68]

Almost until the end of this period, production was by the traditional method of digging pits, from which the oil was removed in skin bags, to be transported—at least locally—on the two-wheeled carts in general use in the region for centuries. The first drilled wells were completed only in 1871–1872 by the last holder of the contract monopoly, Mirzoev. Baku's distance from Russian centers of population—more than 1,000 miles—severely restricted opportunities for

---

[65] There was also some nineteenth-century production from Grozny, in what is now Chechnya: Leeuw 2000: 74–6.

[66] Marvin 1891: 161–80.

[67] Polo 1908: 36.

[68] Tolf 1976: 43.

expansion. Production figures given by authors for this early period vary greatly but near its end appear to have been around 25,000 tonnes (185,000 barrels) yearly.[69]

A new regime for the disposal of state petroleum lands was introduced in 1872, ushering in the period of Baku's extraordinary growth, in which massive gushers seem to have been discovered every other day. Yet this period is remarkably poorly documented. Baku and Batoum, the oil port on the Black Sea with which it was connected, were the areas where a generation of future Bolshevik leaders, notably the Georgian Josef Stalin, earned their spurs in organizing the strikes that led to the first Russian General Strike of 1903 and, two years later, to racial strife in Baku between the local Tatar population, armed by the government as a bulwark against the spread of industrial disorder, and the Armenians, many of whom were oil industry proprietors. Armenians were massacred in large numbers and the Baku oil installations wrecked.

After the revolution ended and the industry began to rebuild, Stalin, sent back to Baku, fomented further unrest and strikes until he was sent to northern Russia for imprisonment in 1910.[70] Stalin's aim was to inspire "unlimited distrust of the oil industrialists,"[71] and once the Bolsheviks obtained power, the achievements of the industry prior to the 1917 Russian Revolution were more or less wiped from the record. Petroleum texts of the Soviet period dismiss the entire pre-1917 period as one that saw little technological advance and make no mention of the oil industrialists—notably the Nobel family, the "Russian Rockefellers"—who brought the industry to a point where it could rival that of the United States.[72]

There was strong British interest in Baku throughout the period from 1873 up to the Russian Revolution, partly because of the strategic importance of this area and of the territories on the other side of the Caspian, in the context of the "Great Game" for the dominance of central and southern Asia between Russia and the United Kingdom, but also because of the keenness of British investors to get a foothold in Baku oil production. The most comprehensive early work on the petroleum of Baku, Arthur Beeby Thompson's *The Oil Fields of Russia and the Russian Petroleum Industry* (1904), resulted from the author's period as the manager of a British oil company's interests in Baku around 1898. The work deals mainly with geological, engineering, and other technical issues; for more detail on commercial and property questions, we need to look to the livelier accounts offered by journalists who visited the region. James Dodds Henry, editor of the newly

---

[69] Pizanty 1931: 8; Tolf 1976: 43; Marvin 1891: 205.
[70] Yergin 1991: 129–31.
[71] *Ibid.* 131.
[72] Tolf 1976: xiv.

created *Petroleum World* magazine, was there in 1904 and published his account of the development of Baku and contemporary conditions in 1905, at the height of the disturbances there.[73]

While Henry also wrote extensively on the petroleum industry in other parts of the world,[74] his predecessor Charles Marvin devoted himself principally to convincing the British public of the strategic importance of Russian petroleum and the commercial opportunities it offered. Marvin's *The Region of the Eternal Fire* went through a number of editions in the late 1880s and early 1890s and was subtitled *An Account of a Journey to the Petroleum Region of the Caspian in 1883.*[75] In the style of popular works by pioneer travelers, the book freely dispensed information to those who might follow, on subjects ranging from the quality of eastern European railway refreshment rooms (Oswiecim, "indifferent"; Volotchisk, "wretched"; Jmerinka, "fine and remarkably cheap"; Michaelova, "excellent")[76] to local sartorial conventions ("Small revolvers are invariably carried in the Caucasus"; "Visits [to the governor of Baku] should be made in the morning, and it is better that the caller should wear a dress coat").[77]

Marvin spoke excellent Russian and had spent much of his childhood in Russia. His earlier career as a clerk in the British Foreign Office had come to an abrupt and ignominious end after he memorized a secret Anglo-Russian treaty he had been given to copy and communicated its contents to the *Globe and Traveller* newspaper. In an age when the British government relied on loyalty rather than law for the protection of its secrets, its lawyers could not find any offense with which he could be charged, and he was thus released from arrest, his exploit providing the basis for one of Arthur Conan Doyle's *Sherlock Holmes* stories[78] and provoking a tightening of internal regulations that eventually led to the enactment in 1889 of the United Kingdom's first Official Secrets legislation.[79] Marvin was an acute and experienced observer of oil industry developments both in Central Asia and elsewhere[80] and provided much useful detail on what he saw in Baku at a time when the opening up of massive gushers was an almost daily experience.

Baku's quite literally explosive increase of production began with the public auction in 1872 of the state oil lands just north of the town. There are some

---

[73] Henry 1905.

[74] Henry 1910, 1914.

[75] Marvin 1891.

[76] *Ibid.* 14, 16, 18, 122.

[77] *Ibid.* 4, 138.

[78] "The Naval Treaty" in Conan Doyle 1894.

[79] Vincent 1998: 78–87.

[80] Marvin 1887; and for his campaign for the development of Burmese oil, see Longmuir 2001: 137–8.

discrepancies in different authors' accounts of this event,[81] but the core facts appear to be that a total of rather more than 6 square miles in the Balakhani plateau was offered in sections of 10 dessiatine (a measure of land equaling 2.7 acres or 1.1 hectares). Some of this land was sold outright, a number of plots being given away to local officials and military men, and sometimes passed on almost immediately for trifling sums. Other land was offered on lease for a cash premium coupled with an annual rental of 10 roubles per dessiatine, rising to 100 roubles after 10 years. (At exchange rates then prevailing, this represents a rental of about $2.50 per acre, rising to $25.)

Some of these plots attracted great interest and large premiums (fueled, no doubt, by the fact that one of Mirzoev's two drilled wells had hit a gusher earlier that year). It seems clear that the main concern of the authorities was to draw the maximum immediate profit from this discovery: they made no provision in their leases for any royalty, and though Russia already had well-established and detailed regulations for hard rock mining,[82] they did not—at least at this time—encumber their grantees with any restrictive operating regulations that might limit the perceived value of the rights granted. Nor did they put any limits on the future subdivision of the plots.

Immediately, enormous gushers were opened up by the new operators. Some plots obtained at auction were resold for massive sums: one, for which the equivalent of $5,000 had been paid, fetched $3.3 million, a sum that the new purchaser recouped on striking a gusher a month later.[83] None of the operators had thought to provide themselves with storage facilities, however; indeed, some had plots too small to permit this. With the first gushers, prices immediately plunged from 45 to 5 copecks per pood (from about $2.30 to 25 cents per barrel) and rose only gradually from these levels over the rest of the century. Nonetheless, these wells were so prolific—not only did they flow at rates undreamed of in the United States and elsewhere, but they went on flowing for months or years—that new companies and new capital continued to flow into the region.

Among them was the Nobel concern, which began by purchasing several parcels of oil land and a small refinery from the captain of the ship on which Robert Nobel had traveled to Baku in search of wood supplies for rifle stocks. Under the direction of Robert's brother Ludwig, the Nobel firm soon distinguished itself as the best-organized and most farsighted of the operators, notably in the pioneering of pipeline and tanker transportation—the oil tanker was invented by Ludwig Nobel to carry his product across the Caspian—which enabled the Nobels to move

---

[81] Marvin 1891: 206–7; Henry 1905: 51ff; Hassmann 1953: 22–3; 1 Gerretson 1953: 210.

[82] Kursky and Konoplyanik 2006.

[83] Henry 1905: 53.

their oil efficiently from Balakhani over the enormous distances to the markets of Moscow and St Petersburg.[84] In common with Rockefeller's Standard Oil,[85] though over a shorter space of time, the Nobels began in refining and only later became major producers on their own account;[86] and like Standard Oil, they became the overwhelmingly dominant force in their province.

Not all the oil land around Baku was in the hands of the Russian state. The accession system of mineral rights had been definitively adopted in Russia in 1782, so private landowners were free to exploit minerals under their land or arrange for their exploitation by others.[87] Local entrepreneurs appear to have used the same techniques as in Romania to accumulate such land and make it available for oil production: "Many stories are popularly related in Baku which describe how certain Tartar and Armenian millionaires became possessed of their lands in the Balakhany-Saboontchy-Romany oil fields by deliberately bribing the natives to swear to their ownership of certain lands, formerly valueless, when the oil craze developed."[88]

A second boom occurred in 1875 when a successful well was brought in on private land at Saboonchi, leading to a rush of small operators who took parcels measured not in dessiatine but in saghens (a saghen was the Russian fathom of 7 feet, as opposed to the 6-foot English fathom) under leases of 10 to 12 years granted for a cash premium and substantial fixed royalties. "Properties," wrote Henry, "were no longer bought by hundreds of *saghens* but by tens."[89] A plot of 25 square saghens would have measured a little less than 12 yards square. It appears that the same sort of subdivision went on in the state lands of the Balakhani plateau, where Marvin wrote of "innumerable" small plots.[90] Later, communal land south of the town at Bibi-Ebat was opened up, again proving enormously prolific.

Operating on this basis, with close-packed derricks in an area where oil was likely to manifest itself in high-pressure gushers (the local term was *fontan*, or fountain), was a recipe for disaster in terms of waste and environmental damage. The most spectacular case, which provoked the financial ruin of its operator, a small Armenian-owned company, was the notorious Droozhba gusher. Tapped in 1883 at Balakhani, this well was estimated to have flowed initially at up to 2 million gallons (more than 47,600 barrels) a day, and three months thereafter,

---

[84] Tolf 1976: Ch. 4; Marvin 1891: 282–4.

[85] Below, Ch. 7, at 174.

[86] Marvin 1891: 280–1.

[87] Kursky and Konoplyanik 2006: 232–3.

[88] Beeby Thompson 1904: 125.

[89] Henry 1905: 61.

[90] Marvin 1891: 217.

it was still uncontrolled and flowing at over 5,500 barrels a day. The loose nature of the reservoir sands at Baku meant that such gushers threw up large quantities of rock with their oil, capable of grinding away in a few days or even hours the thick boilerplate with which operators tried at this time to cap their wells. The Droozhba Well was eventually capped successfully by a neighboring well owner four months after it started flowing and after perhaps 2 million barrels of oil had been wasted, inundating neighboring properties or flowing away onto wasteland or into the Caspian through hastily cut channels. The little oil the company could save sold at rock-bottom prices, far too little to save it from bankruptcy resulting from the damages due to its neighbors, whose buildings had in many cases been completely buried by the sand thrown up with the oil and whose derricks were prevented from working.[91]

One would also assume that intensive production of this sort would necessarily involve constant drainage between the often very small plots being exploited. Marvin, however, took pains to insist upon an apparent lack of communication between reservoirs tapped by adjacent wells, offering a number of examples of producing wells being unaffected by the opening of gushers only a few yards away. Droozhba, he wrote, was one such gusher, though later he noted—without acknowledging the inconsistency—that when it was successfully capped, "a great disturbance took place in Nobels' No. 14 Well, showing a connection of both with the same reservoir."[92]

The attention Marvin paid to this point suggests that the potential British investors who must have formed an important part of his intended readership were already aware of the problem of "interference between wells," perhaps from American experience, perhaps from the developments in Galicia and Romania described earlier in this chapter. His explanation for the lack of interference between wells, borrowed from Ludwig Nobel, was that the oil-bearing strata beneath Baku had been subject to multiple violent fractures and dislocations, which had left its oil in large numbers of small pockets at greatly varying depths.[93] Later geological investigation bore out this view of the Baku reservoirs,[94] but later experience also showed that Marvin was unduly sanguine about the long-term effects of close and careless drilling. At the time he wrote, the exhaustion of a well could be easily remedied simply by drilling deeper, where a further deposit was likely to be found.

---

[91] *Ibid.* 210–13, 229–32.
[92] *Ibid.* 231.
[93] *Ibid.* 189–91.
[94] Dalton 1909.

In 1883, when Pennsylvanians were already drilling in the Bradford field down to 2,000 or 3,000 feet, the deepest well at Baku was at 825 feet, and gushers were regularly found at much shallower depths. On the basis of production to date, Marvin therefore argued that "there must be enough left in the basins below 825 feet, and in the untouched 1,197 square miles of the Apsheron Peninsula, to stock the markets of the world for ages."[95] That operators were less worried at this time about drainage than about inadequate prices was evidenced by the substantial number of flowing wells that Marvin found shut in and awaiting better times.

Within 20 years, however, drainage appears to have been perceived as a problem: when the Russian government was preparing its 1900 auction of available oil lands, the council of the Baku Oil Producers' Association submitted a memorandum suggesting, among other reforms, that lease areas should be a minimum of 37.5 dessiatine (101.25 acres or 41.25 hectares), and that the distance between their boundaries should not be less than half a verst (583 yards or 535 meters).[96] This suggestion was not taken up. The government continued with the system codified in 1893, whereunder a plot of 37.5 dessiatine could be taken up for prospecting in unproven land, but on discovery, only an area within the plot of up to 10 dessiatine could be retained, the remainder being made available for allotment through government auction. Proven oil acreage was likewise available only through auction in lots of 1 to 10 dessiatine.[97] By the time Beeby Thompson arrived in 1898, it was clear to him that competitive drilling was the norm, with operators working on small plots, each anxious "to extract the cream of prolific oil sands before his neighbour."[98]

The incentive under the leasing arrangements for intensive and competitive drilling was strongly reinforced by the financial terms of the various auctions up to 1900. The system adopted was one of royalty bidding, coupled with minimum royalty payments based on a notional production figure for each lot auctioned. Discovery of gushers had continued into the 1890s, and by 1900, royalties reached over 12 copecks per pood, a figure far higher than the sale price of Baku crude following the first gusher of 1873.[99] The fact that royalty was on a fixed rather than percentage basis left producers painfully exposed to falls in prices; in 1910, these fixed royalties were equivalent to rates of up to 70 percent.[100] This excessive

---

[95] Marvin 192.

[96] Anon. 1899a.

[97] Mining Code 1893, arts 557–66 (prospecting); 567–85 (allotment); 586–93 (Crown oil-bearing lands), incorporating Oil Field Regulation of June 3, 1892, and reproduced in translation in Beeby Thompson 1904: App. B; Mitzakis 1911: Ch. IX. See also Mitzakis 50–2.

[98] Beeby Thompson 1961: 57–8.

[99] Anon. 1900: 196; Henry 1905: 142.

[100] Anon. 1910: 174.

financial burden helps explain why, when the Baku fields were brought back into production after the devastation wrought by the strife of 1905, production recovered so slowly, reaching only 6.5 million tonnes in 1913 (say 48 million barrels in a year in which U.S. production reached nearly 250 million),[101] and never regained its 1904 peak of 10 million tonnes (74 million barrels).[102]

Just as important, however, was the legacy of the wasteful production methods of the previous 30 years. Fewer gushers were found, and producers had to drill ever deeper at higher cost but often found their wells ruined by ingress of water from higher strata, where former operators had failed to case or plug their wells adequately or indeed—shades of Pennsylvania practice—had purposely neglected water shutoff along the borders of their land out of jealousy of their neighbors.[103] Government and industry capacities to control such abuses were inadequate. Though the Baku Oil Producers' Association, founded in 1886, had some deliberative and dispute settlement powers, and also sought to authorize and control trial drilling on new land,[104] it never seems to have been able to influence the general mode of operation in the industry.

Official regulations were promulgated in 1892 and thereafter for operations on both public and private lands, covering such matters as fire prevention, controlling gushers, and preventing water flooding, but their content was sketchy and enforcement mechanisms weak.[105] Only in 1909 did the government establish a supervisory office in Baku; up to then, the industry had been administered from Tiflis (Tbilisi), 350 miles away.[106] This came much too late to save the Baku fields from the depredations of "small, unenlightened entrepreneurs, feverishly seeking to further their own ends to the exclusion of everything else."[107] The picture is a familiar one. Perhaps fortunately, Charles Marvin never witnessed the collapse of the hopes he had pinned on Caucasian oil. He had died in 1890, at only 36 years of age, in the same quiet London suburb where he was born.

---

[101] Williamson et al. 1963: 16.

[102] 3 Gerretson 1957: 140–8.

[103] Beeby Thompson 1904: 196–8; 3 Gerretson 1957: 147–8.

[104] Tolf 1976: 142.

[105] They are reproduced in detail in Beeby Thompson 1904: 456–70. See also Mitzakis 1911: 91–2; 3 Gerretson 1957: 147.

[106] Anon. 1909: 216.

[107] 3 Gerretson 1957: 147. It should not be assumed that large entrepreneurs (with the exception of the Nobels and a few others) were models of probity and responsibility. According to Essad-Bey 1932: 42 (the son of one of them), their lives left nothing to be desired "in the way of barbaric luxury, debauchery, despotism and extravagance."

CONCLUSION

These short histories of nineteenth-century oil development in the "Old World" illuminate the American experience in a number of ways. The course of development in the different regions is the first thing of which we should take notice. Exploration and production began everywhere as a small-scale enterprise using primitive methods: spade and bucket technology, as I have called it. Drilling as the normal means of operation started first in Pennsylvania and there (and in Canada) was immediately mechanized by the generalized use of steam power, enabling explorers to get access to deeper horizons as the sands nearer the surface were exhausted, though we should not forget that manual drilling methods were also in use in Pennsylvania in the early 1860s, and that the digging of oil wells remained commonplace in some areas (notably California) until the end of the century.[108] The capacity to raise local capital to sustain mechanized operations was clearly many times greater in the northeastern United States than in Galicia or Romania, where production technology could not progress until foreign capital could be attracted. In Baku, by contrast, the explosive productivity of the oilfields from the very outset of the period of intensive exploration meant that local capital could readily be raised to meet at least the investment demands of unsophisticated drilling and refining methods.[109]

One significant result of this disparity in early access to finance and technology was that uncertainties about property rights, including, though not limited to, the issue of capture or "interference between wells," were less of a brake on development in the early oil-producing states of America than in Galicia and Romania. It will have become apparent from the discussion earlier that the rule of capture was part of the law determining property in petroleum in these countries. This was clear beyond question in Romania from the time of the adoption of the Romanian Civil Code in 1865, and the same was probably true in Galicia once the imperial government abandoned in 1862 its claim to prerogative rights over petroleum, leaving the matter to be covered by ordinary land law.

The practices of the industry in Galicia and Romania—and for that matter, on private or communal land around Baku as well—in terms of subdivision of properties and intensive competitive drilling, thus closely resembled those in Pennsylvania, but the commercial insecurity they created was exacerbated by a further source of legal insecurity: the possibility that title to land, or to leases or concessions held over land, might be defective. This was a consequence of lacunae in Galician and Romanian land law that made it difficult or impossible to acquire,

---

[108] Blakey 1985: 36.
[109] Henry 1905: 61.

and hold securely, interests in oil-bearing land sufficiently ample to bring the risks created by the rule of capture down to bearable levels. Those who wished to follow this strategy in the United States, like the Phillips Brothers in Pennsylvania or the H. L. Taylor firm from Cleveland,[110] could accumulate interests without undue concern about title questions, but the growth of foreign investment in Galicia and Romania was certainly retarded (in the latter country, even into the twentieth century) by such fears about legal insecurity.

The fact that the government in Romania, and the provincial and imperial governments in Galicia, saw a potential engine of national development stalled by legal uncertainties may help explain one of the most striking differences between the early U.S. experience and that of other oil-producing countries—that is, the degree of readiness of governments to address problems of the industry through legislation. While legislative efforts in the United States were largely confined to some small-scale attempts to alleviate the worst causes of waste in production, notably water ingress from abandoned wells and the large-scale flaring of gas, we find a comprehensive petroleum law enacted for Galicia in 1884 and revised and developed in 1908, and in Romania—albeit only from the rather late date of 1895—a regular sequence of legislative dispositions for petroleum within the framework of general mining legislation. In part, this Romanian activity was triggered by the need to deal effectively with the state's own petroleum interests, but adjusting private relationships and improving legal security for lease-holding oil companies were also major legislative goals.

As for Russia, a comprehensive set of oilfield regulations was in place by 1892, covering with some elaborateness the disposal of state oil properties and, more cursorily, operational practice on both public and private lands. Russian observers of the U.S. oil industry were struck by the remarkable freedom from any kind of official regulation enjoyed by American producers.[111]

While the European legislators were concerned about security of title to oil-bearing land, only in Galicia do they seem to have made a connection between the rule of capture and the chaotic and backward nature of the industry. Even there the abandonment of the accession system and reapplication of the imperial mining prerogative to petroleum was seen as the most straightforward way to remedy the overdigging, collapsing and abandoned wells, speculation, inefficient production, and worker accidents and mortality with which the industry was plagued.[112] It was only when this proved politically impossible to achieve that legislators and regulators began to develop rules to promote the rational exploitation of privately

---

[110] 2 Boyle (*Derrick's Handbook*) 1900: 203–4. See further below, Ch. 7, at 175–6.
[111] Gulishambaroff 1902.
[112] Frank 2005: 63–72.

held oil lands. Romanian legislators and regulators, despite their ample production of norms, do not appear, at any time prior to the nationalization measures of 1924, to have treated capture as a source of the industry's problems, and some of their measures, such as the small areas (10 hectares) of the early state oil concessions seem likely to have extended the risk of capture to operations on state lands. As for Baku, the government appears for many years to have adopted a resolutely hands-off attitude despite the enormity of the waste that occurred, ignoring industry proposals that might have reduced wasteful competition. In 1904, the mining law still stated as a principle that "the system of exploiting oil is left entirely to the producer."[113]

The history of America's early oil rivals shows us clearly that the rule of capture and the frenetic competition for resources that went with it were in no way an American peculiarity or an expression of a special trait of the American economic personality. Indeed, the Russian case demonstrates that the "forest of derricks" phenomenon can occur in areas where there is unified state ownership of petroleum in the ground, no less than under an American private ownership system. Whether this was a local anomaly or points to a more general truth is a question to be explored in later chapters. The fact that competition seemed to drive development positively in the United States, but held it back in Galicia and Romania was the result of an unhappy combination in those countries of lack of local investment capacity and defects in security of land titles, problems that did not trouble the oil entrepreneurs of America's Gilded Age.

---

[113] Art. 598, reproduced in Beeby Thompson 1904: 440.

PART III

MODIFIED CAPTURE: THE UNITED STATES IN THE TWENTIETH CENTURY

CHAPTER 7

CORRELATIVE RIGHTS AND THE BEGINNINGS OF CONSERVATION

PRODUCTION AT THE TURN OF THE CENTURY

By the end of the nineteenth century oil and gas were being produced in substantial quantities in 11 states: Pennsylvania, West Virginia, Ohio, California, Kentucky, Tennessee, Colorado, Indiana, Wyoming, Texas, and Oklahoma.[1] The United States had just lost to Russia its position as the world's largest oil producer, though it was soon to regain it when the disturbances of 1905 caused damage to the prolific Baku oilfields, from which they never fully recovered.[2] Almost all American production still came from the Appalachian fields of Pennsylvania, West Virginia, Kentucky, and Tennessee (58 percent) and the Lima-Indiana fields in Ohio and Indiana (34.5 percent), a distribution that was to change radically in the space of a few years with the discovery of Spindletop and other major fields in the Texas Gulf and rapid expansion in California beyond the long-exploited Los Angeles fields.

---

[1] Myres 1973: 51–3; Williamson et al. 1963: 17–19.
[2] Above, Ch. 6, at 157–8.

By 1919, the northeastern regions' contribution had dwindled to just 9.3 percent of the total.[3] It was in these regions, however, that the key commercial practices and legal relationships of the petroleum industry were developed in its first 40 years of life, and this development continued on the same paths as the industry spread to other parts of the country. The diaspora of Pennsylvania oilmen like John Cullinan, who oversaw Texas's first substantial oil development at Corsicana in the 1890s,[4] brought competence and experience to new areas, but at the same time meant there was no felt need there for a fresh start in thinking about the industry's basic legal and commercial precepts. Only in technology was there significant change: Texas saw the first use for oil of the rotary drilling technique, which had been successfully used for water wells but had not yet displaced cable tool drilling in the Northeast.[5]

In this and the next two chapters, I trace the processes through which the law of capture has attained its present position as "a cornerstone of the oil and gas industry" in the United States.[6] This chapter, reflecting the continuities just referred to, takes up the story from the point where we left it in Chapter 3, so as to show how practice and thinking in the latter part of the nineteenth century shaped the important developments at the beginning of the twentieth—in particular, the new sense that natural resources might not be inexhaustible. This brings our story to 1920 or thereabouts, and in Chapter 8 I trace to around the same date the particular history of oil and gas resources that were found not under privately owned lands like the farms of northwestern Pennsylvania, but under public land in federal or state ownership. The way these resources were managed gives important clues to the nature of the policy measures that would later be adopted to address waste and overproduction in the industry and the effects those measures would have. Finally in this section of the book, Chapter 9 offers a brief account of oil and gas conservation policy from the time of the "naming and blaming" of the rule of capture until the present day. This is not intended as a comprehensive conservation history, but as an explanation of why capture remains such a deeply rooted principle and why, judged by global standards, the policy that would effectively displace it—unitization, whether voluntary or compulsory, of oil and gas reservoirs—has enjoyed such limited success.

In the earliest years of the industry, entry to any phase of its operations was open to anyone who could assemble a very modest capital. Production required derrick, drill, and pump and a steam engine to drive them; transportation was a matter of

---

[3] Williamson et al. 1963: 17.

[4] King 1966; King 1970: Chs. 1–4.

[5] King 1966; Brantly 1971: 216–20.

[6] *Coastal Oil and Gas Corp. v. Garza Energy Trust*, 268 S.W. 3d 1, at 13 (Tex. 2008).

boats and barrels; and refining could be undertaken (after a fashion) with equipment hardly more complicated than a pot still. Throughout its first decade, oil was an industry of small business, intensely competitive and liable to massive and disturbing swings in prices as production and demand alternately marched ahead of one another. In response to these disturbances and to technological pressures, a steady process of concentration got under way at the beginning of the 1870s. Producers and refiners now needed to rely on capital-intensive rail, and later pipeline, transport; massive overcapacity in refining led to the increasing dominance of the industry by the more technically advanced and financially astute refiners, of whom John D. Rockefeller was the exemplar.

As prices continued to seesaw in the 1870s and 1880s, producers blamed their financial woes on the monopoly being accumulated by the major refiners and conspiracies between them and the railroads. How much truth these allegations held has been a matter of popular, political, and scholarly controversy for at least 100 years.[7] There is no need to enter here into that discussion, only to remark that a crucial problem for the producers was that throughout this period, their sector of the industry continued to be one of small business, attempting to confront massive, intelligently directed, and coherently operated organizations by means of producers' associations under various titles. These associations had little success in their main tactic of trying to hold crude off the market by sales, production, and drilling embargoes: the only shut-down arrangement that enjoyed sustained success was that of November 1887–November 1888, which had the active support of Standard Oil. Here, for once, the interests of Pennsylvania producers and Rockefeller's refining and marketing combine came together, with producers seeking a remedy for high inventories and low wellhead prices, and Standard anxious to sustain long-term levels of Appalachian supply in the face of the Russian challenge.[8]

The lack of concentration, and even of substantial enterprises, on the production side of the industry at this date is striking. Harold Williamson and Arnold Daum estimated that 16,000 producing firms might have been operating, and that in 1880, the eight largest firms in the oil regions (which at that time hardly extended beyond western Pennsylvania) operated 600 wells, representing only some 3 percent of all existing wells.[9] Production remained the least demanding branch of the industry from the point of view of capital requirements: capital costs might have been expected to go up as the drill went deeper down, but capital costs

---

[7] A thorough account, designed to rehabilitate Standard Oil, appears in Olien and Olien 2000: Chs. 2–4.

[8] Williamson and Daum 1959: 562–8.

[9] *Ibid.* 374, note.

in 1874–1884 were still of the same order—$3,500 to $6,000—as they had been in the mid-1860s and could be substantially reduced if the producer could get hold of secondhand equipment. By this means, wells in the prolific Bradford field could be drilled for as little as $1,500.[10] If this helps explain why small operators maintained their place in the industry, it does not tell us why the number of large firms, and the wells and acreage they controlled, remained so small for so long.

Part of the answer doubtless lies in the fact that the people whose business acumen and drive would have enabled them to build large production enterprises realized at an early stage that more money could be made less riskily by investing in other phases of the industry's operations. One of the first to see this was Johnson Newlon Camden, a successful oil producer in West Virginia in the early 1860s, who in 1866 sold off his substantial oil properties in order to invest in refining. Camden's refining company, based in Parkersburg, West Virginia, was later one of those that entered into secret deals with John D. Rockefeller whereby they came under the control of Standard Oil, while appearing to remain independent and, indeed, to present themselves as vigorous rivals of that company.[11] As for Rockefeller, it is said that a two-month exploratory visit to the Oil Creek region in 1860 or thereabouts on behalf of a group of Cleveland businessmen convinced him that the production side of the business was far too risky and competitive.[12] This may be an industry folktale, as Rockefeller, in old age, could remember no such visit,[13] and in fact, Standard did have some production interests in the 1870s but sold out in 1878 after a legal dispute. Standard came back into production after developing the technique to refine the heavy, high-sulfur crude oil found in the Lima field in Ohio in 1885, at a time when it felt growing concern about the long-term sustainability of Appalachian oil production—or possibly about its availability to Standard, as the success of the 1887–1888 shutdown led the producers' association to launch more ambitious plans for the development of its own transportation and refining capacity.[14] In 1888, Standard's production, from properties ancillary to other purchases, amounted to only 200 barrels a day, but it then began an extensive program of acquisition of Ohio oil properties, including producing companies, new leases, and large land purchases.

Among the first of these acquisitions was a company whose name was to appear in the two most significant oil litigations around the turn of the century: the Ohio Oil Company, whose unneighborly relations with Mr. Kelley gave rise to the

---

[10] *Ibid.* 156–8, 374; Olien and Olien 2000: 28.

[11] Summers 1937: Williamson and Daum 1959: 419–21.

[12] Asbury 1942: 289.

[13] 1 Nevins 1940: 172; Chernow 1998: 80–3.

[14] Williamson and Daum 1959: 605–8; 2 Boyle [*The Derrick's Handbook*] 1900: 218–19.

definitive capture ruling, *Kelley v. Ohio Oil Co.* (1897),[15] and whose defiance of Indiana antiflaring legislation was the trigger, just three years later, for the U.S. Supreme Court's recognition of correlative rights in oil and gas reservoirs in the crucial *Ohio Oil Co. v. Indiana* decision (1900).[16] The company, formed only in 1887 by the amalgamation of a number of independent interests, was the core of Standard's production effort and disposed of over 20,000 acres of oil properties and nearly 150 wells. By 1891, Standard was producing more than half the crude from the Ohio-Indiana fields and had extended its purchase program to New York, Pennsylvania, West Virginia, and Kentucky.[17]

The other part of the explanation for the scarcity of big producing firms lies in the way landowners and other lessors sought to protect themselves from the cross-boundary drainage that was the inevitable result of carving up land into small lease areas. Their answer was to require early drilling of wells as a condition of survival of the lease. In such an environment, the obtaining and holding of substantial acreages involved massive and risky investments. High premiums and royalties had to be paid for leases in proven territory. Even those who wanted to operate on a more substantial scale by applying scientific theories of oil finding, such as the belt theory applied with success in the early 1870s by Cyrus Angell and his imitators,[18] so as to identify and reserve possible oil-bearing territory in advance of wildcat strikes, found the conventional form of lease obligation onerous because of the need for early drilling on every lease, despite the fact that the unproven nature of the territory may have enabled them to get generally easier terms. Angell mapped a belt, only 30 or so yards wide, running northeast from property he held at Belle Isle, on the Allegheny River, all the way into the proven oil region north of Oil City. He obtained leases, incorporating options to purchase, over all the land in the southern sections of the belt but was finally able to develop successfully only the southernmost six miles, the remaining leases lapsing.[19]

What finally made possible a systematic approach to petroleum exploration, involving the orderly survey and drilling of large tracts of land, was the introduction of a new element in leasing arrangements: the delay rental clause. While continuing to stipulate that operations should start within a fixed period, the lease also offered the lessee the option of paying a rental, per acre or for the whole lease, for any succeeding periods in which work had not yet been started. We

---

[15] Above, Ch. 2, at 28–9.

[16] Below, 181–4.

[17] Williamson and Daum 1959: Ch. 22. The *Derrick's Handbook* suggests that by 1900, Standard was producing 25 percent of Pennsylvania crude: 2 Boyle 1900: 219.

[18] Williamson and Daum 1959: 32–5; deGolyer 1961: 22–4.

[19] Asbury 1942: 273–8, quoting a contemporary article by C. E. Bishop in the *New York Tribune*, 1871.

find a delay rental clause in the 1872 lease that gave rise to the well-known case of *Brown v. Vandergrift* in 1875. The court construed the clause strictly, holding that it would not prevent a forfeiture of the lease if rentals were tendered late.[20] The 1900 volume of the *Derrick's Handbook of Petroleum* credits the generalized use of the clause to the activities of the firm of Phillips Brothers, which developed its holdings on the basis of a refined version of Angell's belt theory. The total area of the Phillips leases incorporating the clause and listed in the *Handbook* as concluded between 1872 and 1898 amounted to more than 23,000 acres. While a handful of small leases covered only a few acres, the great majority were for areas between 50 and 100 acres.[21] With leases of this size, Phillips Brothers was able to space its wells in a more rational pattern and ran much less risk of drainage than the traditional operator on an acre or quarter-acre lot. Thomas Phillips, who from 1884 was sole partner in a business described by the *Handbook* as that of "monopolizing desirable Butler County oil territory in a highly successful manner,"[22] was a leading figure in the Producers' Protective Association, which organized the 1887–1888 shutdown, and went on to sit in the U.S. Congress, where he promoted in 1899 the appointment of an industrial commission—one of whose main objects of attention was Standard Oil.[23]

Since the very earliest years of the industry, concerns had been raised about the damaging effects of the intensive drilling patterns engendered by small block leasing. Articles in the *Scientific American* in 1863 and 1865 referred to the loss of gas pressure resulting from drilling large numbers of wells, and complaints of wasteful production and overdrilling were reiterated in the next decades by geologists including Pennsylvanians J.P. Lesley and John Carll;[24] the West Virginian I. C. White;[25] and Indiana's S. S. Gorby.[26] The growing share of total production in Ohio, Indiana, and Pennsylvania accounted for by large-scale operations at the end of the nineteenth century certainly did not eliminate this problem. The *Kelley* litigation shows both that the generally more rational pattern of well spacing adopted by larger proprietors in the Ohio fields[27] did not wholly eliminate the practice of drilling along property lines, and that the courts there thought it a perfectly reasonable means of protecting one's interests.

---

[20] 80 Pa. 142 (1875).

[21] 2 Boyle [*The Derrick's Handbook*] 1900: 203–17.

[22] *Ibid.* 205.

[23] Williamson and Daum 1959: 563, 716; Olien and Olien 2000: 89–90.

[24] Williamson and Daum 1959: 376, 765; Olien and Olien 2000: 122–3.

[25] Thoenen 1964: 268–324; Van Hise 1910: 58–9.

[26] Rarick 1980: 23.

[27] Williamson and Daum 1959: 593.

As we shall see, most of the major new fields discovered in the first two decades of the new century were opened in circumstances that gave landowners and promoters plenty of opportunities for the creation of numerous small lease lots, and the advantages of assembling blocks of leases were greatly reduced by the way most courts interpreted the obligations of oil companies under such leases. Nonetheless, when conservationist voices finally got a hearing from the public authorities at the end of the nineteenth century, leasing practices and their implications for drilling seem to have slipped from the center of attention. It was concern about particular wasteful uses of hydrocarbons that eventually provoked further public intervention in the affairs of the oil industry in the 1890s and led to a revised legal conception of property rights in oil and gas in place.

THE FLARING OF GAS

The Context

The waste that caught the attention of legislatures of oil and gas states in the last decade of the nineteenth century was the burning of off gas in vast quantities. "Conspicuous waste" seems a feeble term to describe the practice of letting "[t]orches of gas, called 'flambeaux' burn continuously along many city streets and country roads [so that] in some areas night was hardly distinguishable from day,"[28] as was reported of Indiana at this time. The gas came from the giant Trenton field underlying east-central Indiana and much of western Ohio. When the first well to strike the formation was drilled in Findlay, Ohio, in 1884, the applications of the gas as an industrial fuel and a source of lighting for cities and townships were quickly perceived, and used as a magnet by local authorities to bring industrial development to a hitherto agricultural area.[29]

The Trenton formation, however, was also found to contain substantial amounts of oil. As a heavy, high-sulfur crude, its refining for kerosene had to await the developments undertaken by Standard Oil, but it quickly established itself as a fuel oil. By 1889, just four years after a well drilled at Lima, southwest of Findlay, first produced oil, production from the Lima-Indiana fields reached 12 million barrels.[30] Those who looked for this oil, scattered in compact deposits across the Trenton field, often found gas instead, existing either alone or in association with oil. Unwilling to invest in the transport facilities needed to get the gas to market,

---

[28] Rarick 1980: 23.

[29] *Ibid.* 10–11.

[30] Williamson and Daum 1959: 591, 595.

they would burn it off while producing the oil with which the gas was associated or while hoping that some oil might eventually appear.

Eventually the two legislatures were moved to act to stop this waste. Ohio legislated in 1889 to require gas wells to be shut in within three months, a figure it reduced to 10 days in 1893, but this restriction did not apply to any oil well, even though such wells might also be producing—and wasting—large quantities of gas.[31] Indiana legislated in 1891 and again in 1893 to control the flaring of gas, providing in section 1 of the latter act that it should be unlawful to allow gas or oil to escape from a well for more than two days after the flow started: it had to be confined within the well or in pipes "or other safe and convenient receptacles."

This legislation brought the state of Indiana into direct conflict with Standard Oil, which, as we have seen, had since 1888 moved vigorously into oil production in the Lima-Indiana fields. Standard's approach, when it drilled an oil well that produced substantial quantities of associated gas, was simply to ignore the prohibition and flare the gas. It persisted in this attitude notwithstanding the decision of the Indiana Supreme Court, in *Townsend v. State* (1897),[32] upholding the constitutionality of the 1891 act forbidding the burning of gas in flambeau lights. In May 1897, the Ohio Oil Company, by then in Standard's ownership, drilled six wells at Alexandria that produced both oil and gas, did not shut in the gas as required by the 1893 act, and apparently announced its intention of continuing to flare the gas and drilling other wells in the vicinity, which it would exploit in the same way. In fact, a total of 73 wells were drilled at Alexandria between May 1897 and March 1898, and the gas flared off.[33] Since the penalties provided by the statute were plainly insufficient to deter Standard/Ohio Oil, as indeed was any diminution in the respect or affection it might enjoy from the people of Indiana, the state authorities went to court to seek injunctions against the company's waste of gas. Penalties for breach of such an injunction would be far more severe and could indeed extend to imprisonment of the company's officers for contempt of court.

The Constitutional Context: Private Property and Due Process of Law

This was the litigation that eventually reached the U.S. Supreme Court and produced its decision in *Ohio Oil Company v. Indiana*.[34] Several actions appear to have been started by the state, producing different results in the trial courts, but on

---

[31] McAfee 1949: 360.

[32] 147 Ind. 624, 47 N.E. 19.

[33] Rarick 1980: 24–5.

[34] On the litigation in general and its background, see Veasey 1927: 592–8.

appeal, the Indiana Supreme Court adhered to its previous approach in *Townsend v. State* and granted the injunctions sought.[35] Modern readers from outside the United States may wonder at the fact that what looks like a simple enforcement action against a recalcitrant subject should go not just to the supreme court of a state, but beyond it to the U.S. Supreme Court. State constitutions had long protected their citizens against deprivation of property otherwise than in accordance with "the law of the land" or with "due process of law," and this obligation of the states was reinforced by the Fourteenth Amendment to the U.S. Constitution in 1868, which guaranteed this protection as a matter of federal, as well as of state, constitutional law. By the end of the century, these provisions were being applied so as to call into question the constitutionality of an ever-widening range of state regulatory legislation, which was being struck down with such frequency that, in the words of one commentator, "it would almost seem as though the courts held that statutes were to be deemed presumptively invalid."[36]

Two trends were working together to produce this result. One was a steady movement away from the narrow concept of property as something purely tangible and physical, whose "taking" was thus easily recognizable, to one in which property could subsume new, abstract, and intangible forms of wealth and could be described as "everything which has exchangeable value."[37] From here it was a short step to the notion that any state action that reduced that value might be construed as a "taking" of the relevant property. On this footing, any state regulation of private activity in the public interest, in the exercise of what, following continental European nomenclature, had come to be called the "police power" of the state,[38] was open to challenge under the Fourteenth Amendment and usually the state constitution also, and the courts deployed the due process requirement as a demand for substantive justification of regulation by reference to worthy public interests.

As Thomas Cooley explained in 1868, giving due process a purely formal significance would be tantamount to telling the legislature that it should do no wrong unless it chose to. Rather, "[d]ue process of law in each particular case means, such an exertion of the powers of government as the settled maxims of law sanction, and under such safeguards for the protection of individual rights as those maxims prescribe for the class of cases to which the one in question belongs."[39] What these maxims and safeguards might be at any time, and hence what public

---

[35] *State v. Ohio Oil Co.*, 150 Ind. 21, 49 N.E. 809 (1898).

[36] 1 Willoughby 1929: 44, cited by Merrill 1930: 401n.

[37] Justice Swayne in the *Slaughterhouse Cases*, 83 U.S. 36, 127 (1872); Vandevelde 1980.

[38] For definitions, see Tiedeman 1886: 1–5; Novak 1994: 1084–5.

[39] Cooley 1868: 354, 356.

interests the legislature could legitimately protect, were very much matters for judicial discretion. Protection of the physical safety of the consuming public was smiled upon by the judges; legislation with the aim or effect of protecting people's economic interests was looked on with much more suspicion.[40]

The other trend was the reflection in judicial review of a growing spirit of distrust of economic regulation and of public economic initiative generally. The oil industry developed at a time of disillusionment with the capacity of public authorities to carry through efficiently and honestly the substantial programs of infrastructure improvement with which they had earlier been entrusted, and this disillusionment was reflected in a much less confident attitude toward the regulatory capacities of the state as well.[41] It would be wrong to see such disillusionment as ushering in a period of legislative immobility, of pure laissez-faire. Indeed, those of conservative temper saw the period as one in which "governmental interference is proclaimed and demanded everywhere as a sufficient panacea for every social evil which threatens the prosperity of society."[42]

Judges, however, increasingly cast themselves in the role of defenders of private rights against legislative excess, though not in an undiscriminating way. As James Willard Hurst and other legal historians have pointed out, the courts followed the trend of continuing popular demand for state action supportive of private developmental initiative, taking a generous attitude toward a considerable expansion of eminent domain powers in support of private industrial and infrastructure development,[43] while giving particular protection, via the doctrine of due process, to venture capital: "property in motion or at risk rather than property secure and at rest."[44]

This, of course, was the sort of capital the Ohio Oil Company and other petroleum producers had in play. We have already seen how vigorously and explicitly courts in states like Pennsylvania supported mineral or industrial development over established uses of land.[45] Would they be equally firm in resisting restrictions on such developments imposed on the grounds of an alleged public interest? The company, having lost its battle to prevent the legislation from getting onto the statute book in the first place, was certainly not going to submit to it without giving the courts the chance to demonstrate such firmness and invalidate

---

[40] The classic example is *Lochner v. New York*, 198 U.S. 45 (1905) (striking down a statute limiting bakery employees' hours of work to protect their health); for many earlier examples, and contrasting cases on topics such as food safety, see 1 Tiedeman 1900: Ch. IX.

[41] See Hartz 1948 for an account of Pennsylvania development in the period to 1860.

[42] Tiedemann 1886: Preface.

[43] Scheiber 1973.

[44] Hurst 1956: 25.

[45] *Wheatley v. Baugh*, 25 Pa. 528 (1855), and above, Ch. 2, at 39.

the law on constitutional grounds. In issuing its challenge, the Ohio Oil Company appeared as the standard-bearer of an industry that has hardly ever allowed a measure of legislative regulation to operate without vigorous and in some cases repeated attempts to secure its invalidation through judicial review. In the extensive literature devoted to later U.S. conservation measures, the absence of constitutional challenge to a given law is itself a matter worthy of comment.

The Ohio Oil Decisions

The line taken by the Ohio Oil Company was that since the oil it was producing and the gas it was wasting were its property, and because the oil it wanted could not—or so it claimed—be produced without wasting the gas, a law prohibiting such waste represented a "taking" of the company's property, by preventing its profitable exploitation. The state's invocation of the need to conserve gas for the benefit of the public that relied on it for light and heat, of the industry that relied on it for fuel, of the orphans and insane, the deaf and the dumb who occupied the state institutions that it heated and lit was, said the company, but a mask for the state's desire to benefit gas manufacturers over equally worthy oil producers like itself.

The Indiana Supreme Court and the U.S. Supreme Court agreed in sustaining the injunction and the Indiana statute. But the reasons each court advanced for doing so were significantly different. The Indiana court simply held that there was no ownership of natural gas until it was reduced to possession. Ohio Oil had let the gas go free instead, and therefore the statute, whatever its nature and motives, could not be an "unwarranted interference with private property."[46] Though the court laid heavy emphasis on the damage that would be inflicted on consumers, industry, and the state budget by large-scale wastage of gas, it did not explicitly assert that this would be a sufficient and appropriate public interest to justify an interference with private property of the kind alleged by Ohio Oil, though this appears to have been the basis of its decision in the earlier case of *Townsend v. State.*[47]

Later courts in other states, as we shall see, have felt less difficulty in holding that waste of hydrocarbons justifies legislative intervention notwithstanding the protections of the Fourteenth Amendment. In reaching its "no ownership" holding, the Indiana Supreme Court explicitly refused to follow the statement of the Supreme Court of Pennsylvania in the *Westmoreland* case to the effect that "[t]hey [the water, gas, and oil] belong to the owner of the land, and are a part of it,

---

[46] 150 Ind. 21 at 32, 49 N.E. 809 at 812. A similar view, that the act was purely for the protection of the public interest, not private interests, was taken by the Federal Circuit Court of Indiana in *State v. Allegheny Oil Co.*, 85 F. 870 (1898).

[47] Above, n. 32.

so long as they are on it or in it and are subject to his control; but when they escape, and go into other land, or come under another's control, the title of the former owner is gone."[48] Treating gas as analogous to fish in a river, the Indiana court suggested that this supposed shifting ownership of oil and gas was "no less absurd ... than to say that ... fish, in their passage up or down a stream of water, become the property of each successive owner over whose land the stream passes."[49]

If the court's approach, making the constitutionality of legislation regulating hydrocarbon production dependent on the existence or otherwise of ownership rights in oil and gas in the ground, had been adopted by the U.S. Supreme Court, the way would have been open for the adoption of radically different judicial approaches to conservation legislation in different states, depending on whether their courts took an "ownership" or "no ownership" view on this question. By 1900, courts in oil-producing states were already at odds on the issue: Pennsylvania, as we have seen, had opted for the ownership rule, as had West Virginia (departing from the *Wood County* decision),[50] whereas Indiana and New York held against it.[51] A few courts did indeed treat the conclusions of the *Ohio Oil Co.* litigation as irrelevant in their state on this kind of ground,[52] but the general consensus has been that a state's concepts of oil and gas ownership should not determine the validity or otherwise of its oil and gas conservation legislation.[53] In view of the confusion that surrounds these concepts even today, that is something for which we should be profoundly grateful.

The U.S. Supreme Court took a different route to the same result. Justice White, speaking for a unanimous court, began by noting that "the power which exists in everyone who has the right to bore from the surface and tap the reservoir involves in its ultimate conception, the unrestrained license to waste the entire contents of the reservoir by allowing the gas to be drawn off and to be dispersed in the atmospheric air, and by permitting the oil to flow without use or benefit to anyone."[54] If the exercise of such a power were lawful—and the Supreme Court of Pennsylvania had already held to this effect in *Hague v. Wheeler*, involving deliberate waste of gas[55]—no owner of land overlying the reservoir could claim to

---

[48] 130 Pa. 235, at 249, 18 A. 724, at 725. See further above, Ch. 2, at 20–3.

[49] 150 Ind. at 32, 49 N.E. 809 at 812.

[50] See *Williamson v. Jones*, 39 W.Va. 231, 19 S.E. 436 (1894).

[51] See Adams 1915; Simonton 1921; Greer 1923; and above, Ch. 2, at 30–2.

[52] See, e.g. *Gas Products v. Rankin* (Montana 1922), discussed below at 190.

[53] For Texas, where the "absolute ownership" principle holds sway (above, Ch. 2, at 32), see *Henderson Inc. v. Railroad Commission*, 56 F. 2d 218 (W.D. Tex. 1932), *Brown v. Humble Oil and Refining Co.*, 126 Tex. 296, 83 S.W. 2d 935, 87 S.W. 2d 1069 (1935).

[54] 177 U.S. 190, 201.

[55] 157 Pa. 340, 27 A. 714 (1892), above, Ch. 2, at 27–8.

own any part of its contents, because the rights claimed would lack an essential element of ownership: the right to prevent any other person from taking or destroying what is asserted to be the subject of the right of property. The argument that legislation of the type in question was a taking of property without due process of law was thus the fruit of a "confusion of thought," because in the absence of some such regulation, there could be no property in oil and gas until it had been reduced to possession.

Justice White went on to draw a new kind of analogy with the law relating to wild animals. Under the doctrine of *Geer v. Connecticut*,[56] the state might regulate the taking of such animals in pursuit of its function of holding the property in such animals in trust for the public as a whole, "in order to protect them from undue destruction, so that the right of the common owners, the public, to reduce to possession, may be ultimately efficaciously enjoyed." While no such "trust" property could exist in oil and gas, because only the owners of land overlying a reservoir could have the right to drill that land to recover the hydrocarbons beneath, all those owners had the "co-equal" right to take oil and gas from the common source of supply. The legislative power might, therefore, in a similar way,

> be manifested for the purpose of protecting all the collective owners, by securing a just distribution, to arise from the enjoyment, by them, of their privilege to reduce to possession, and to reach the like end by preventing waste. ... Viewed, then, as a statute to protect or prevent the waste of the common property of the surface owners, the law of the State of Indiana ..., in substance, is a statute protecting private property and preventing it from being taken by one of the common owners without regard to the enjoyment of the others.[57]

By thus recognizing *collectively* held rights to oil and gas in the ground, the U.S. Supreme Court provided a new base for conservation legislation, in the protection and adjustment of what quickly came to be referred to as the "correlative" rights of the respective owners. The term does not appear in Justice White's opinion, but we have seen that it was already applied to describe rights to oil and gas in the ground in the opinion of Judge Noyes that the Supreme Court of Pennsylvania reversed in *Hague v. Wheeler*.[58]

Henceforward we find state legislatures and the administrative bodies they entrusted with the supervision of oil and gas production defending their laws, regulations, and rulings sometimes on the basis of the general public interest in

---

[56] 161 U.S. 519 (1896).

[57] 177 U.S. 190, 209–10.

[58] Discussed above, Ch. 2, at 40–1.

avoiding waste, sometimes on the basis of protecting correlative rights, and usually on both grounds. We pick up this regulatory story later, at the time when finds of major new fields in Texas and Oklahoma produced massive oversupply and led to quite new kinds of regulatory measure. The more immediate concern, at least of lawyers seeking to digest the implications of this ruling by the nation's highest court, was whether this notion of "co-equal" or correlative rights announced by the court might have some bearing on the position of parties at *common law*, in the absence of any regulatory legislation. The relevant common-law principles, including the rule of capture, were a matter of state, not federal, law, so the Supreme Court's remarks could be of no more than persuasive effect.

SUBSURFACE WATER AND THE CORRELATIVE RIGHT OF REASONABLE USE

In the next decade, the possibilities of common-law development of the correlative rights concept were demonstrated by the way in which certain state courts began to approach analogous issues of rights to groundwater, an approach endorsed, in 1911, by the U.S. Supreme Court itself. The first sign that American courts might move away from the doctrine that landowners might do as they wished with percolating water found under their land, whatever the detriment to neighbors who had long drawn from the same supply,[59] was given by the Superior Court of New Hampshire in 1862, when it announced that rights in percolating water were not absolute, but correlative, and must be subject to some notion of reasonable use.[60]

Not until the very end of the century did this decision find an echo in other state courts. In two cases, *Smith v. City of Brooklyn* in 1897[61] and *Forbell v. City of New York* in 1900,[62] the highest court of the state of New York found for plaintiffs complaining of drainage of water from under their land by the New York City authorities. To supply the city, the authorities had installed pumping stations and pipeline systems that drained large areas of neighboring agricultural land. The court followed (though it did not cite) the *Bassett* case in holding that the use of land that produced such drainage must be reasonable, and that to be so, it must benefit the land that was being exploited. Here there was no such benefit, because

---

[59] *Acton v. Blundell* (1843) 12 M. & W. 324, 152 Eng. Rep. 1223; *Greenleaf v. Francis*, 18 Pick. 117 (Mass. 1836); see Ch. 2, at 37–8.

[60] *Bassett v. Salisbury Manufacturing Co.*, 43 N.H. 569 (1862), above, Ch. 2, at 39–40.

[61] 18 App. Div. 340, 46 N.Y. Supp. 141, 54 N.E. 787.

[62] 160 N.Y. 357, 58 N.E. 644.

the water was being taken elsewhere and sold there. To do justice to their agricultural neighbors, the water authorities should have exercised their powers of eminent domain—that is, the forced sale of water rights, which would have involved compensating people like Mr. Smith, whose stream had dried up, and Mr. Forbell, who could no longer grow celery and watercress on his farm. *Forbell* was decided after the Supreme Court's *Ohio Oil* decision but did not refer to it and, indeed, made no reference to the common pool factor that had been an important part of the reasoning in *Bassett.*

A couple of years later, however, on the other side of the country, the Supreme Court of California faced, in *Katz v. Walkinshaw*,[63] an issue identical to that in the New York cases. Here the equities were, if anything, stronger in favor of the plaintiffs, as the pumping, transportation, and sale of water of which they complained were the work of private interests who were realizing large sums from the sale of the water to third parties, including water companies. This was a case with major policy implications, and was argued twice before the state's supreme court, with a number of water supply companies being permitted to argue, on rehearing, that a decision in favor of the established agricultural users would gravely impair the development of the state. Each time, however, the court reached the same conclusion: the defendant's use of the water was unreasonable and should be restrained. In so doing, it came closer to the reasoning in *Bassett* and *Ohio Oil* by basing its decision on the fact that "the members of the community … have a common interest in the water. It is necessary for all, and it is an anomaly in the law if one person can for his individual profit destroy the community, and make the neighborhood uninhabitable."[64]

This rapprochement may have been facilitated by the fact that the water in the *Katz* case collected in an artesian basin whose confines could be at least roughly mapped. The old ideas about the "secret, occult and concealed" habits of subterranean water[65] could thus be confidently discounted. But in addition, this factor of confinement, which had been the express basis of the decision of another state court to depart from the *Acton v. Blundell* rule in favor of a reasonable use requirement,[66] was seized on by the defendants, on rehearing, as a basis for forecasting an alarming side effect of any decision in the plaintiff's favor. If the rule of reasonable use were adopted for subsurface water, they said, "it must for the same reason be the law with regard to the extraction of petroleum from the ground,

---

[63] 141 Cal. 116, 70 P. 663 (1902); 141 Cal. 116, 74 P. 766 (1903).

[64] At 141 Cal. 141, 70 P. 665.

[65] *Frazier v. Brown*, 12 Ohio St. 294, 311 (1861).

[66] *Erickson v. Crookston Waterworks Co.*, 100 Minn. 481, 111 N.W. 391 (1907). See Hardwicke 1935: 417n; Clayberg 1915: 132–3; Huffcutt 1903.

and, if so, it would entirely destroy the oil development and production of this state, and for that reason also … is against public policy and injurious to the general welfare."[67]

The court was unimpressed by this menace. Despite the fact that property rights in oil and gas had been shaped by its colleagues elsewhere at least partly by reference to the characteristics of percolating water, it saw no reason why there should be a spillover from one substance to the other. It reasoned:

> It does not necessarily follow that a rule for the government of rights in percolating water must also be followed as to underground seepages or percolations of mineral oil. Oil is not extracted for use in agriculture, or upon the land from which it is taken, but solely for sale as an article of merchandise, and for use in commerce and manufactures. … Whether, in a contest between two oil producers concerning the drawing out by one of the oil from under the land of the other, we should follow the rule adopted by the courts of other oil-producing states, or apply a rule better calculated to protect oil not actually developed, is a question not before us, and which need not be considered.[68]

As the Texas oil and gas law authority Robert Hardwicke was to point out some years later, the fact that petroleum was not produced for the benefit of the land overlying it put major difficulties in the way of operating a principle of "reasonable user" in relation to oil and gas operations; had the courts adopted such a principle, they would have become involved in constant and detailed supervision for which they were in no way equipped.[69] The quite detailed regulatory arrangements required in Trinidad to support a principle of reasonable user of the pitch lands there reinforce the point.[70] Texas itself, we should notice, was never troubled by the need to explain the adoption of different common-law rules for groundwater and for oil: its supreme court, in *Houston and Texas Central Railroad Co. v. East*,[71] a year after the *Katz* decisions, stuck firmly to the *Acton v. Blundell* rule for water, and continues to do so to this day.[72] Even in relation to water wells, the application of the reasonable user rule proved to be far from simple. It was one thing to sustain, by reference to a concept that extraction of water may not exceed what "may be necessary for some useful purpose in connection with the land from which it is taken," the constitutionality of a statute regulating the characteristics and use of

---

[67] *Katz v. Walkinshaw*, at 141 Cal. 122, 74 P. 767.

[68] At 141 Cal. 137, 74 P. 772–3.

[69] Hardwicke 1935: 410.

[70] Above, Ch. 5, at 131–3.

[71] 98 Tex. 146, 81 S.W. 279 (1904).

[72] *Sipriano v. Great Spring Waters of America, Inc.* (1999) 1 S.W. 3d 75 (Tex.). See generally Drummond et al. 2004; Mullican and Schwartz 2004.

artesian wells,[73] but quite another to determine, in a situation of scarcity, just what amount might be reasonable on this basis, and whether all parties who have, for a variety of uses, been taking water from an artesian basin have the same rights.[74]

If the *Ohio Oil* decision hovered discreetly in the wings in the *Katz v. Walkinshaw* case, it took center stage in a legislative and judicial drama that developed around the usage of the celebrated Saratoga mineral springs in New York State. Americans may not have the same special reverence as the French for the curative properties of mineral water, but the United States has long had its own small spa and mineral water industry. Arguably the first piece of conservation legislation passed by the U.S. Congress was an act of 1832 creating a federal reservation, 4 square miles in area, to protect hot mineral springs in Arkansas at what is now the town of Hot Springs, where President Bill Clinton grew up.

At Saratoga, the use of the lightly carbonated water has been traced back to 1774, with the bottling of water starting in the 1820s, dates that parallel the chronology of French spa and mineral water development.[75] At the height of the French "thermal fever," Saratoga was likewise in its prime as a spa: a town of 9,000 people had developed there and received some 20,000 visitors each summer. Like its major French counterparts, it offered large luxury hotels and a wide range of amusements, including horse racing and casinos. All this activity was thrown into jeopardy when, at the end of the century, the striking of pockets of "free" carbonic acid gas in the vicinity of the springs led a number of companies to acquire land, drill wells, and pump vast quantities of gas, and of mineral water from which gas was extracted, to supply a large commercial demand for gas to produce fizzy drinks and use in refrigeration applications. The Ohio Oil Company had used gas as a propellant to bring to the surface the oil they wanted, and had then thrown it away; companies like the Natural Carbonic Gas Company and the New York Carbonic Acid Gas Company did the opposite, wasting the water that contained the gas they sought.

The critics of the early judicial analogies between water and oil liked to remind their readers that while oil and gas deposits were both confined and nonreplaceable, water percolated freely and renewed itself through rainfall; but as we saw from French examples, mineral water tends to be confined in deep basins

---

[73] As in, for example, *Ex parte Elam*, 6 Cal. App. 233, 91 P. 811 (1911). Compare *Huber v. Merkel*, 117 Wis. 355, 74 N.W. 354 (1903), holding a similar Wisconsin statute unconstitutional.

[74] See Barraqué 2002, and compare *City of Barstow v. Mohave Water Agency*, 23 Cal. 4th 1224, 5 P. 3d 853 (2000), with *City of Pasadena v. City of Alhambra*, 33 Cal. 2d 908, 207 P. 2d 17 (1949), for different methods of allocation in situations of scarcity.

[75] Lund 1993, whose account is largely based on Swanner 1988, and from which material here on the history of Saratoga is drawn save where otherwise noted; compare Ch. 4, at 94–6.

and to have long—sometimes incredibly long—replenishment cycles.[76] Certainly the pumping by the gas companies quickly had a devastating effect: a number of the springs dried up, and others lost their mineralized character.

The spring owners initially failed in attempts to restrain this pumping by litigation, which may seem a little surprising, given that the *Smith* and *Forbell* cases, establishing the principle of reasonable user, had already been decided. Having failed, they, with other interested parties like the hotel owners and the town authorities, turned to the legislature. The gas companies protested vigorously, claiming that the deterioration of the water antedated their activities and painting a lurid picture of spa owners' "employment of chemicals and their secret conveyance at night to ... private rooms, where solutions have been prepared for mixture with the waters of the springs of Saratoga."[77] The legislature, unimpressed, passed a statute forbidding any pumping that modified the natural flow of mineral water springs, both generally and when this impaired the flow or quality of springs belonging to others.

Challenges to this legislation were raised twice before the New York Court of Appeals and once before the U.S. Supreme Court. The New York court affirmed a preliminary injunction granted against the gas companies, on the grounds both that the spring owners did have a right at common law to restrain an unreasonable use of the spring water, and that the statute was constitutional if the pumping prohibition were confined to cases where the flow and quality of other springs were impaired.[78] But the companies went on pumping, and when the state came to court to enforce its act, it was met by the companies with the argument that the pumping did not in fact cause the damage that had been alleged, which was said to arise from quite independent causes. The lower court having refused to admit the companies' evidence on this point, the case had to be returned for further hearing.[79]

A definitive victory by the spring owners was achieved only when the issue was considered by the Supreme Court, this time in the form of a stockholder suit against the Natural Carbonic Gas Company. In a unanimous opinion, the court signaled a possible convergence between petroleum and subterranean water jurisprudence. To sustain the constitutionality of the legislative prohibition—as confined to cases of unreasonable and damaging abstraction of mineral water from a common supply—it relied upon a long citation from its *Ohio Oil* decision, recognizing the symmetry of the factual circumstances of the two cases.[80]

---

[76] Above, Ch. 4, at 89–90.

[77] Anon. 1908b.

[78] *Hathorn v. Natural Carbonic Gas Co.*, 194 N.Y. 326, 87 N.E. 504 (1909).

[79] *People v. New York Carbonic Acid Gas Co.*, 196 N.Y. 421, 90 N.E. 441 (1909).

[80] *Lindsley v. Natural Carbonic Gas Co.*, 220 U.S. 61 (1911).

There was a Pyrrhic element to this victory: the companies' skillful management of the litigation had enabled them to go on pumping until the end, and in total they abstracted at least 10 times the natural flow of all the springs in Saratoga put together. Relief came only in 1911, when the state bought out the two major companies under legislation passed during the judicial marathon and began to rebuild the much reduced water supply, shutting in many springs and protecting them by acquiring land, or water and mineral rights, over a total of 672 acres. It took more than a decade for the mineral water in all the springs to return to normal concentrations of minerals and carbon dioxide.

Though its subject was water, the Saratoga Springs litigation offered a number of pointers to the future of the rule of capture and correlative rights as they applied to all fugacious resources in the United States: the *Lindsley* opinion was relied upon in a number of key oil and gas cases on the constitutionality of conservation measures.[81] In the light of the French approach to analogous problems, one is struck by the great difficulties under which legislators labored in attempting to protect publicly prized uses of common-pool property. In France, a spa and mineral water resource as well-established and prestigious as Saratoga, if not already protected by a public interest declaration and the drawing of a zone of protection, certainly would have received such protection once the menace of large-scale abstraction of gas presented itself.[82] This involved a far more sweeping restriction of activity by neighbors on their own lands—albeit over a more limited area—than did the New York statute and could be accorded by administrative decision after appropriate hearings, without the need to wait for the feared damage to begin.

In New York, by contrast, the judicial review powers of courts suspicious of any and every impairment of rights of property effectively confined the legislature to enacting what the courts declared to be the common law anyway, and created the additional problem—which occupied a good part of the opinion of the Supreme Court in *Lindsley*—of limiting the scope of its prohibition on drilling for and pumping mineral water in such a way as to avoid any alleged arbitrary discrimination in contravention of the "equal protection of the laws" provision of the Fourteenth Amendment.

Again, the French had no difficulty in speaking of their spa industry as invested with a quite general public interest, which it was incumbent upon the state to protect by legislative and administrative means in the absence of protection under the general law. In New York, however, the chief justice went out of his way to assert, by means of a separate concurring opinion in the case of *People v. New York*

---

[81] E.g., *Julian Oil and Royalties Co. v Capshaw*, below, Ch. 9, at 109–13.
[82] See generally Ch. 4, at 254–5 *passim*.

Carbonic Acid Gas Co., that the legislation under review could be justified only on the ground that it protected correlative private rights, and *not* on that of a public interest in the health of the mineral water industry.[83] Once regulation of oil and gas production began in earnest in the 1920s and 1930s, it remained for a while far from clear that courts would accept a pure public interest justification for legislative control of waste.

One arguably wasteful use of natural gas is in the manufacture of carbon black, a substance with various industrial applications, notably the processing of rubber. The methods used in this period, and indeed for decades thereafter, required very large volumes of natural gas (1,000 cubic feet of gas per pound of carbon black produced), which was burned in an atmosphere with inadequate oxygen so as to produce a carbon-rich soot.[84] Both Wyoming and Montana passed, in 1919 and 1921, respectively, statutes forbidding the use of natural gas for this purpose. In the former case, but not the latter, the prohibition was limited to situations in which the gas wells were within 10 miles of an incorporated town or industrial plant—in other words, where there might be a market for lighting or fuel uses. While the Montana Supreme Court struck down the Montana statute, saying that if the state were allowed to forbid the use of gas to make carbon black, it might prohibit any use,[85] the U.S. Supreme Court sustained the Wyoming one,[86] but only over a dissent by three members including (then Chief) Justice White, who had delivered the *Ohio Oil* opinion, and Justice Van Devanter, who had delivered the opinion in the *Lindsley* case. No opinion accompanied their dissent, but it is at least plausible to suggest that while they would accept a correlative rights justification for regulation, they drew the line at a pure public interest rationale.

CORRELATIVE OIL AND GAS RIGHTS IN COMMON LAW: A CONSERVATION CUL-DE-SAC

These first cases suggested that while legislating to control the wasteful effects of the rule of capture in the oil industry was going to be difficult, there was hope for continuing development of the common law on oil and gas in this sense on the basis of the *Ohio Oil* decision. Such hopes were to be disappointed, though some early judicial developments looked quite promising. The Indiana Supreme Court decided within three months after the *Ohio Oil* decision that the operation of the

---

[83] 196 N.Y. 421, 440, 90 N.E. 441, 448 (1909).

[84] Moses 1945.

[85] *Gas Products v. Rankin*, 63 Mont. 372, 207 P. 993 (1922).

[86] *Walls v. Midland Carbon Co.*, 254 U.S. 300 (1920).

rule of capture was limited *at common law* by the correlative rights of property holders in a common reservoir. Quoting at length from the *Ohio Oil* opinion, it held in *Manufacturers' Gas and Oil Co. v. Indiana Natural Gas & Oil Co.*[87] that

> while each [owner] has the right to bore or mine for [natural gas] on his own land, and to use such portion of it as, when left to the natural laws of flowage, may rise in the wells of such owner and into his pipes, no one of the owners of such lands has the right, without the consent of all the other owners, to induce an unnatural flow into or through his own wells, or to do any act with reference to the common reservoir, and the body of gas therein, injurious to, or calculated to destroy, it. ... [T]he manner of taking must be reasonable.[88]

Professors Bruce Kramer and Owen Anderson have pointed out that this decision imposed no fewer than four restrictions on the principle of capture: only "natural flowage" could be captured; reasonable means must be used; and the common source of supply must be neither injured nor destroyed.[89]

Again, in the case of *Louisville Gas Co. v. Kentucky Heating Co.*, in 1903,[90] the Kentucky Court of Appeals invoked the correlative rights principle to affirm an injunction granted to a gas company to close down a carbon black factory operated by the defendants. Although, as we have seen, you get a very small amount of carbon black out of a very large amount of natural gas, the defendants' production was, even by such standards, suspiciously slender. Over a period of five months, they burned some 90 million cubic feet of gas to produce 300 pounds of carbon black with a total value of $12. The fact that the plant was run by only two employees, one a 16-year-old boy and neither of whom had any knowledge of the production of carbon black, may have contributed to this meager result, but it appeared from the evidence that the essential purpose of the defendants in acquiring gas leases, drilling wells, and employing the gas thus obtained was simple revenge on the plaintiffs—who had successfully challenged their monopoly of gas supply in Louisville—exacted by deliberately running down the pressure in the field from which the plaintiffs drew their gas. Some of the language used by the court suggests that it viewed the principle of *Ohio Oil Co. v. Indiana* as requiring that the use made of a common-pool resource like gas should be "reasonable,"[91]

---

[87] 155 Ind. 461, 57 N.E. 912 (1900).

[88] *Ibid.* at 469–70, 915. To the same effect, see *Richmond Natural Gas Co. v. Enterprise Natural Gas Co.*, 66 N.E. 782 (Ind. App. 1903).

[89] Kramer and Anderson 2005: 916.

[90] 117 Ky. 71, 77 S.W. 368.

[91] *Ibid.* at 78, 370.

but it also referred more than once in the same paragraph to waste and to wanton injury or destruction.

In other states, the idea that the common law might impose restrictions on capture was viewed with much greater reserve. In particular, the idea, implicit in the first two restrictions mentioned in *Manufacturers' Gas*, that the courts might police the techniques of petroleum production never obtained support outside Indiana. Perhaps it was the large-scale reliance on natural gas in that state, and an awareness of the special characteristics of the giant Trenton gas field, that made its courts unusually sensitive on this point. The Supreme Court of Pennsylvania had decided in the contrary sense just before the *Ohio Oil* decision was handed down, affirming without opinion a lower court decision sustaining the use of a gas pump which was improving the yield of the defendant's wells at the expense of that of his neighbor's: *Jones v. Forest Oil* (1900).[92] Similar decisions were reached after the *Ohio Oil* case in Kentucky (*United Carbon Co. v. Campbellsville Gas Co.*)[93] and in Louisiana (below).

So far as the *Louisville Gas Co.* case is concerned, the difficulties in assessing reasonableness of uses of oil and gas, hinted at in *Katz v. Walkinshaw*, make it unsurprising that the Kentucky court's references to reasonable use found no echo elsewhere. Much more telling is the almost complete absence, so far as I have been able to discover, of any subsequent cases in which the deliberate flaring of gas, or other deliberate wastage of petroleum, was even invoked by a plaintiff as a common-law wrong, still less restrained by a court on this ground. The nearest the case law came to this was in the 1919 Louisiana case of *Higgins Oil and Fuel Co. v. Guaranty Oil Co.*,[94] which is of particular interest here because Louisiana's code, closely modeled on the French Civil Code, furnished the basic property right principles to be applied by the court, including the rule (article 505) that a landowner "may construct below the soil all manner of works, digging as deep as he deems convenient, and draw from them all the benefits which may accrue, under the modifications as may result from the laws and regulations concerning mines and the laws and regulations of the police."[95]

After a detailed analysis of French commentaries on the related provisions of the French Civil Code, including reference to the decision in *Badoit c. Andre*,[96] the court ruled that a deliberate refusal to plug an abandoned well would be unlawful if motivated not by the defendant's desire to protect his own land from drainage, but

---

[92] 194 Pa. 379, 44 A. 1074.
[93] 18 S.W. 2d 1110 (Ky. App. 1929).
[94] 145 La. 233, 82 So. 206.
[95] Cf. French Civil Code, art. 552, above, Ch. 4, at 96–8.
[96] Above, Ch. 4, at 114–6.

to impair the plaintiff's recovery from his own land. The refusal appears to have been in the nature of self-help by a defendant who objected to the plaintiff's use of a vacuum pump on his land as an "artificial" means of increasing recovery. The judges, following their Pennsylvania rather than their Indiana brethren, saw nothing illegal in the use of the pump itself. There was nothing more artificial in using a pump, they said, than in drilling a well in the first place.

Later cases like *Elliff v. Texon Drilling Co.*,[97] where neighboring oil lessors or lessees successfully sued for damages consequent on badly performed production operations, are often cited as examples of the common-law application of the correlative rights doctrine.[98] The cases are few in number, however, and it is not easy to see what real effect the correlative rights doctrine has produced, in that the courts have consistently demanded evidence of negligence. The duty of care that is central to negligence liability could easily be found in pure considerations of proximity, without any need to resort to a specific concept of interrelated property rights.

When the few oil and gas cases in which the correlative rights doctrine had a real effect at common law are brought together, one can see that, rather like *Kelley v. Ohio Oil Co.*, a sequel to earlier litigation, they all had some element that heightened the intensity of conflict between the parties: the special sensitivity to pressure conditions in the Trenton gas field in the *Manufacturer's Gas* case, against the background of the earlier irruption on the scene of Standard Oil;[99] a long-standing feud between rival gas companies in the *Louisville* case (one of a series between the parties that extended over a decade);[100] a game of tit-for-tat in *Higgins.* Where such exacerbating circumstances were absent, oilmen seem to have taken the view that no good would be served by attacking their neighbors for practices—notably the flaring of enormous quantities of gas—that they might well find convenient to engage in themselves. Indeed, unless they were actively engaged in gas supply, they were probably united in regarding the gas shut-in laws that states began to enact in the 1890s as an infernal nuisance. In the absence of concerted industry pressure, it is hard to understand why, to take but one example, the West Virginia legislature should have refused no fewer than five times to take up the governor's urgent plea for the enactment of a law to prevent the wastage of natural gas.[101] If this were the general industry attitude, we should not be surprised

---

[97] 210 S.W. 2d 588 (Tex. 1948).

[98] Kellam 1960; Kramer and Anderson 2005.

[99] Epstein 1997: 256 explains the results of the *Ohio Oil Co.* litigation as a decision in favor of in-staters as against out-of-staters, though simply on the basis of the company's Ohio provenance; he does not register its ownership by Standard Oil.

[100] Kramer and Anderson 2005: 918.

[101] White 1909: 29.

at the absence of litigation based on correlative rights, which, if successful, would have made such restriction a matter of common law.

JUDICIAL READJUSTMENT OF THE LESSOR–LESSEE RELATIONSHIP

So far as more straightforward issues of capture were concerned, nothing had happened in the industry to call into question the expectations and practices formed in its earliest years. People had a better idea of who was draining what, but a resort to litigation must have seemed to an energetic oil operator an ineffective and even effete measure as compared with the hallowed practice of getting in first with the best leases and the biggest wells. Even some geologists gave their blessing to this approach. Dorsey Hager, in his book *Practical Geology* (the adjective designed no doubt to sell it to that "75% of the prosperous oil operators who began as drill hands and [whose] limited education [did] not usually enable them to understand or appreciate geological reports"[102]) offered five precepts for those who would engage in what he called "offensive drilling" tactics: to sink wells before neighboring companies drilled; to drill holes of larger diameter than those of the neighboring company; to drain sands unknown to the neighbors; to place the wells so as to be sure of draining as much territory as possible; and to speed the wells as fast as possible.[103]

A factor in industry thinking easily forgotten today is that in the earliest years of the industry, the average life of an oil well was only about 18 months.[104] While it had risen to 3 years in Pennsylvania by 1871 and 11 years in the Appalachian Region by 1900, the duration of wells in new regions, as they were opened up, was significantly lower, ranging between 3 and 5 years.[105] With timescales like this, it made little sense for operators to divert resources to defending uncertain rights in existing wells from the crucial tasks of obtaining acreage and drilling new ones.

The position appeared rather different, of course, to the landowner. One can imagine the feelings of farmers and ranchers as they looked out over their land to their boundaries just beyond which their neighbors' derricks were flowing or pumping enviable quantities of oil, while their own property, though leased, remained undrilled or yielded but a trickle of oil and a drip of royalty. Most, though not all, courts were sympathetic to landowners who found themselves in such a position after they had signed leases with delay rental clauses, and then

---

[102] Williamson et al. 1963: 45, citing a contemporary source.
[103] Hager 1915: Ch. VIII, especially at 140.
[104] Williamson and Daum 1959: 159.
[105] *Ibid.* 375; Williamson et al. 1963: 44.

found that their lessee, though unwilling to drill, was not prepared to relinquish. Courts had from an early date reasoned that the fugitive nature of oil and gas entitled lessors to insist on prompt and precise performance of lease obligations,[106] but only in the last years of the century did they begin to suggest that the nature of the lessor–lessee relationship, in which the lessor might rely entirely on royalty payments—and hence on development efforts by the lessee—for compensation, might lead them to imply development obligations in the lease in supplementation of those expressed. The claim by lessees that the payment of delay rentals according to the lease absolved them from any development effort, even where drainage was occurring from neighboring properties, was viewed with increasing distaste by courts in several jurisdictions from the mid-1890s onward.[107]

To protect lessors, courts began to read into the lease terms for reasonable development of the lease, and the drilling of offset wells to prevent drainage, usually taking effect—regardless of delay rental provisions—once the initial stipulations of the lease as to the drilling of wells had been fulfilled. In particular, courts were vigilant to protect lessors against drainage by their own lessees' drilling on adjoining land. There were variations in the approach of different courts, but Maurice Merrill, whose book *Covenants Implied in Oil and Gas Leases*[108] is the standard reference on the subject, considered that the notion of such implied covenants was generally accepted by 1903, citing decisions from Ohio, Indiana, California, and Texas.[109]

Some of the language in the opinions indicates strong judicial disapproval of attempts by companies to accumulate substantial lease acreages within which exploration and production could be efficiently managed by reference to the delay rental clause. The Supreme Court of West Virginia referred in 1896 to "the patent facts—that those engaged in the production of oil send agents armed with printed leases to solicit leases, and they take leases for great areas, and they are forms already prepared, and the people in many instances know little of them, are inexperienced in oil operations, and are without legal advice."[110] Courts that used such language appear to have paid little heed to the fact that the revenue of whose loss the landowner was complaining was wholly unearned, a pure windfall profit. They focused instead on the comparative disadvantage of the landowner with an inactive lessee, the loss of the opportunity for windfall profit that neighbors were enjoying. Such profit might well be enhanced by royalties of oil or gas drained

---

[106] *Brown v. Vandergrift*, 89 Pa. 142 (1875); *Munroe v. Armstrong*, 96 Pa. 307 (1880).

[107] E.g., *Bettman v. Harness* (1896), 42 W.Va, 433, 26 S.E. 271 (1896); *Harris v. Ohio Oil Co.*, 57 Ohio St. 118, 48 N.E. 502 (1897), *Huggins v. Daley*, 99 F. 606 (4th Cir. 1900).

[108] 1926, 2nd ed. 1940.

[109] Merrill 1940: 47.

[110] *Bettman v. Harness*, 42 W.Va. 433, at 448; 26 S.E. 271, at 276 (1896).

from under the unfortunate one's land. Recognition of the fact of capture doubtless sharpened the sense of unfairness as between landowners that drove these decisions. Nor did courts in places like Indiana and West Virginia treat as relevant the fact that they had held that the landowner had no property in oil and gas until it had actually been reduced to possession;[111] like their counterparts in "ownership" states, they restricted their inquiry to the nature of the lessor's expectations under the contract.[112]

In thus seeking to do justice to the landowner as the presumed weaker party to the deal, the courts substantially diminished the benefits of large-scale operations by compelling lessees, whatever the express terms of their leases, to drill offset wells along surface property lines, wells that would not have been drilled at all had they been able to follow a rational well spacing policy based on factors such as the degree of porosity of the oil-bearing sands. They did not remove those benefits altogether, because it was accepted that the lessee was not obliged to drill an offset well in every case where there might be drainage. Only if drainage was proven and a well would, in prevailing market and reservoir conditions, prove profitable was the drilling of an offset well an implied obligation under the lease. As it was put in the leading case: "Whatever, in the circumstances, would be reasonably expected of operators of ordinary prudence, having regard to the interests of both lessor and lessee, is what is required."[113]

Some courts, it should be said, were less sympathetic to lessors and were content if the lessee, in a case of drainage, had exercised in good faith its business judgment as to whether it was worth drilling.[114] In particular, the Pennsylvania courts manifested, until well into the twentieth century, a marked reluctance to offer lessors rights beyond the express terms of their lease. Perhaps this owed something to the fact that the Pennsylvania judges had the longest experience of the industry, an experience that encompassed periods when the balance of bargaining power over leases was not necessarily in favor of the lessee.

At all events, the only nineteenth-century decision implying terms in favor of the lessor[115] was quickly explained away on the ground of "fraud" by the lessee,[116]

---

[111] *Wood County Petroleum Co. v. West Virginia Transportation Co.*, above, Ch. 2, at 23–5; *State v. Ohio Oil Co.*, above, n. 35.

[112] *Bettman v. Harness*, above; *Gadbury v. Ohio and Indiana Consolidated Natural and Illuminating Gas Co.*, 162 Ind. 9, 67 N.E. 259 (1903).

[113] *Brewster v. Lanyon Zinc Co.*, 140 F. 801, at 814 (8th Cir. 1905).

[114] Merrill 1940: Ch. VIII. For an example, *Ammons v. South Penn Oil Co.*, 47 W.Va. 610, 35 S.E. 1004 (1900).

[115] *Kleppner v. Lemon*, 176 Pa. 502 (1896).

[116] *Colgan v. Forest Oil Co.*, 194 Pa. 234 (1899); *Young v. Forest Oil Co.*, 194 Pa. 243 (1899).

and in the well-known case of *Barnard v. Monongahela Natural Gas Co.* in 1907,[117] a lessee of two adjoining properties was held to have no duty to drill an offset to its own well drilled only 35 feet from the common boundary and probably taking three-quarters of its production by drainage from the plaintiffs' land. This was on the ground that when the plaintiffs, unsurprisingly, had complained, the company had drilled a dry hole on the plaintiffs' tract and near their boundary— but 1,350 feet away from the successful well. The court did not refer expressly to the business judgment of the lessees, but it felt that "a well on each farm, and [the neighbor's] farm twice as large as that of the plaintiffs', does not show partiality toward [the neighbor]," so as to ground a finding of "fraud."[118] In such situations, the lessee's remedy was to "go and do likewise." In the circumstances, the unfortunate plaintiffs were able neither to "go and do likewise" themselves, because they had leased away this right, nor could they compel their lessees to do so.

With a decision of 1915, however, the Pennsylvania courts seem finally to have fallen in line with the general trend, and lessees, wherever they might be operating and whatever might be the terms of their leases, needed to weigh the risks of legal action if they failed to develop each lease—or at least, each lease that they wished to retain—rapidly and continuously, offsetting any wells drilled close to their property lines. With hindsight, it is clear that these risks led to the drilling of very large numbers of unnecessary wells, with greatly inflated capital expenditures and suboptimal recoveries by reason of loss of reservoir pressure.[119] The first of these consequences would have been clear enough to operators from the moment these obligations were first imposed, but was presumably suffered as a necessary evil. The second, however, took much longer to be fully understood: a deep-rooted belief in the industry that if you drilled more wells, you must necessarily get more oil, was not finally extirpated until the 1930s.[120]

BOOM, BUST, AND THE BEGINNINGS OF COMPREHENSIVE CONSERVATION LEGISLATION

Though leasing arrangements were thus rebalanced in favor of lessors around the turn of the century, they remained effective in ensuring both a continuing supply of land for leasing and a continuing effort of exploration and production. Indeed, the scope, pace, and style of oil industry development in this period were such as to

---

[117] 216 Pa. 362, 65 A. 801.
[118] 216 Pa. 362 at 365–6, 65 A. 801 at 803.
[119] Merrill 1930: 397; Hardwicke 1935.
[120] Below, Ch. 9, at 242, 262, 268.

raise new concerns. From 1900 to 1919, one new oil province after another was opened up, the process almost invariably involving the reproduction of the boom phenomenon witnessed in Pennsylvania in the industry's earliest days. Spindletop, near the Texas Gulf Coast, and its nearby successors at Balson, Saratoga, and Sour Lake;[121] the Oklahoma discoveries in the Glenn Pool and the Cushing and Healdton fields;[122] and the extension of California's production from Los Angeles city into the Kern and Fresno counties in the San Joaquin Valley[123] all followed the same inexorable pattern.

The first wildcat strike provoked a frenzied search for leases, satisfied by a process of division and subdivision of surface or mineral interests that led to the erection of the same forests of derricks the first observers of the industry had wondered at, the same explosion of production beyond the capacity of markets or of secure surface storage. Waste of capital was colossal; reservoir damage was immediate. At Spindletop, the inexperienced Hogg-Swayne syndicate—led by a former governor of Texas and mostly composed of Texas attorneys—contributed heavily to the early collapse of field production (and plunged themselves into financial peril) by subdividing a 15-acre lease for which they had paid handsomely ($310,000) into lots as small as 12 by 12 yards (often further divided by their grantees), relying on percentage royalties rather than lease bonuses for their return. When the overproduction thus stimulated drove prices down to a few cents a barrel, the improvidence of this behavior became evident to the syndicate; but it was too late.[124]

Where nature arranged that a substantial reservoir should be found under an established town or city, the existing layout of small town lots ensured the same results, without the need for the legal effort and expense of subdivision. The Los Angeles city field, where development began around 1893, was perhaps the first example.[125] Others included Corsicana, the first significant Texas discovery;[126] Burkburnett, in northern Texas, where by 1920 there were 1,200 wells on 1,500 acres, prompting the new metaphor of derricks being as thick as "bristles on a hair brush";[127] and in the next decade, the giant Oklahoma City pool.[128]

While landowners in these boom areas joyously reaped the harvest of land sales and lease bonuses and royalties, oil operators focused their energies on getting what

[121] King 1970: 92–101; Olien and Olien 2002: Ch. 3; Clark and Halbouty 1952.

[122] Franks 1980: 40–3; German 1938: 111–12.

[123] Rintoul 1976: Ch. 1.

[124] Clark and Halbouty 1952: 108–10; King 1970: 97–100.

[125] Rintoul 1976: Ch. 5; Testa 2005.

[126] King 1966; King 1970: 15–22; Olien and Olien 2002: 4–9.

[127] Olien and Olien 2002: 83–4.

[128] German 1938: 157–96.

acreage they could. We should notice that the arrival of an increasing number of substantial firms on the production side of the industry had certainly not progressed far enough in this period to change the conditions under which new areas would be exploited. With some exceptions, like the Ranger field in north-central Texas, where the Texas Pacific Coal Company was lucky enough to acquire 23,000 acres from the town authorities on land close to a previously successful wildcat well,[129] major lease accumulations seldom seemed to correspond with the profiles of oilfields. As for town lot areas, the problems substantial operators experienced in putting together significant acreage were nicely captured by Upton Sinclair in his novel *Oil!* in which an early chapter, probably based on the Signal Hill development in Long Beach, described the frustrations of trying to get small lot holders in the Los Angeles suburbs to agree on a community lease, big enough to allow the operator to protect its borders from drainage and under which the lot holders would share a single stream of royalties. Strenuous, even violent discussions among them as to the sharing principle broke down on the insignificant question of whether, for the purpose of dividing up the royalties, the surface of the streets in the area would be treated as common or attributed according to each lot holder's street frontage.[130]

We have seen that the traditional response of oil producers, when flush production from large new pools drove prices down below bearable levels, was to attempt a temporary consensual shut-in of production, possibly coupled with a campaign for legislation to control the activities of railroads or pipelines, convenient scapegoats for producers' inability to find a market for their product. This response was taken a step further by Oklahoma producers in 1914, after the opening up of the prolific Cushing (1912) and Healdton (1913) fields caused a total collapse of prices.[131]

At this time, Oklahoma was already equipped with a wider range of regulatory measures than any other state. A statute regulating the casing and plugging of wells and prohibiting the flaring of gas in certain situations had been passed in 1905, when Oklahoma was still a territory. Experience on the opening of the massive Glenn Pool on Indian lands in 1905, notably large-scale drainage by operators with pipelines at the expense of neighbors whose oil they refused to carry, led in 1909 to the passage of a ratable taking law for oil, under which producers had to divest themselves of their crude oil pipelines, and those pipelines were compelled,

---

[129] Olien and Olien 2002: 79–83.

[130] Sinclair 1927 [2008]: Ch. 2, and see Rintoul 1976: 152–3 for an account of a successful Signal Hill community lease.

[131] Material in this and the following paragraphs is drawn, save where otherwise indicated, from German 1938: 113–34; Franks 1980: 139–41; MacDonald 2003: 305–7.

in case of excess of supply, to take the same proportion of the amount offered from each supplier.

This principle was extended to gas supply in 1913, and a second gas conservation act of that year restricted gas wells to 25 percent of their natural flow (to preserve field gas pressures) and provided that within this limit, producers could take from a common field only the amount of gas corresponding to the share of their wells in the total natural flow of the field, which meant that if others had to shut in their wells for lack of pipeline connections, those lucky enough to possess them could not increase their take. This was a vigorous legislative application of the notion, advanced by the Supreme Court in *Ohio Oil Co. v. Indiana*, of correlative rights as implying a "just distribution"[132] of the privilege to reduce to possession natural gas in a common reservoir, and it is worth noticing that it has never been subject to constitutional challenge.

These measures, however, were powerless against the great flood of oil from the Cushing and Healdton fields: the pipelines took ratably as the law demanded, but at ever-decreasing prices as the market was glutted. After unsuccessful voluntary curtailment action, a large number of independent producers formed an association—the Independent Producers' League—and turned to the Oklahoma Corporation Commission, the state agency entrusted with the operation of the 1913 acts, with a view to obtaining by diktat what they could not achieve by agreement.

Casting around for a legal basis on which to act, the commission lighted upon Oklahoma's antitrust law, and in September 1914, it issued several orders based on an opinion in which it argued that as the pipeline companies still possessed a monopoly of marketing opportunities, the state's power to prevent waste, recognized in *Ohio Oil*, could be exercised by fixing a minimum price for crude oil and forbidding any production in excess of what might be sold at this price. Though the commission, in which two of the three members were lawyers, supported its conclusions with some strenuous rhetoric, picturing producers as "carried along in a whirlpool of production, as helpless as a child in mid-stream," invoking the danger of destruction of what might be "the last great oil field on this continent," and claiming that regulation of monopoly had been "the law since Moses descended Mount Sinai," the links in its chain of reasoning were fragile and the legality of its orders was doubtful.

The orders were initially accepted by producers, but these doubts, together with difficulties in their application, greatly limited their effectiveness. Standard Oil subsidiaries soon lowered their buying prices, contrary to the order, to 55 cents a barrel, which the commission was forced to endorse, and challenged the

---

[132] 177 U.S. 190, at 210.

price-fixing order in court when a further reduction was not accepted by the commission. Eventually producers were forced onto the market, selling regardless of commission prices.[133]

The fact that this curtailment effort ended in the usual way is much less important than its significance as the first enlistment of the state in the business of controlling production. The experience was quickly followed by the enactment in 1915 by the Oklahoma legislature of the country's first *general* petroleum conservation statutes—one for oil, one for gas—which prohibited any production constituting "waste." The oil statute defined "waste" in the broadest terms to include, "in addition to the ordinary meaning, ... economic waste, underground waste, surface waste, and waste incident to the production of oil or petroleum in excess of transportation or market facilities or reasonable market demands." In addition, where full production of oil from a common pool would involve waste in any of these senses, the production of each person's wells drawing on such a pool was to be limited to the same proportion of their total capacity as that capacity bore to the total productive capacity of the pool.[134] In this provision, the principle of "just distribution" enunciated by the Supreme Court in the *Ohio Oil Co.* case, already applied to gas by the 1913 law, was for the first time given legislative expression in relation to oil.

The Oklahoma laws represented the first legislative authority for what the industry has always called prorationing of production. We shall see in Chapter 9 that the relationship between techniques of prorationing and the demands of the rule of capture has been, to say the least, a troubled one.

THE CONSERVATION MOVEMENT AND DRAINAGE FROM PUBLIC LANDS

In deploying the concept of waste as part of a scheme whereby production might be limited in the future so as to sustain prices, the Oklahoma initiative identified a point of common interest between oil industry operators and a movement with an increasingly powerful voice in national politics: the conservation movement. The late nineteenth century saw the steady growth, among the middle class in cities like Chicago, of a sense that the Social Darwinism of the Gilded Age had produced socially inhumane results, and in particular that an increasing proportion of the natural, commercial, and financial wealth of the United States had accumulated in

---

[133] Ise 1926: 129–32.

[134] The text of the provisions is reprinted in Williamson et al. 1963: 321–2. See also MacDonald 2002: 306–7, and Ely 1933b: 279–80, 289–90, reprinting the provisions, applying to gas and oil, respectively, as codified in 1931.

the hands of large-scale enterprises or monopolies and was being ruthlessly exploited by them. In the same period, the federal government took the first steps toward natural resource conservation, notably through the addition to the General Revision Act of 1891 of a section providing for the creation of public forest reserves, and the creation of Yellowstone National Park by an act of Congress in 1872.[135]

With the accession of Theodore Roosevelt to the presidency, on the assassination of William McKinley in 1901, these ideas were linked as part of the cluster of "progressive" causes he sought to advance (the adjective achieved the dignity of a capital "P" only with the creation of his Progressive Party in 1912). Prominent among these were the breakup of industrial trusts (of which Standard Oil was the prime example), regulation of railroads, improvement of conditions of labor, and regulation of the quality and purity of food and drugs.[136]

Roosevelt in 1907 appointed an Inland Waterways Commission to take an integrated view of the use of the nation's waterways, and in 1908 was persuaded by Gifford Pinchot, by then head of the U.S. Forest Service and a passionate advocate of conservation,[137] to summon a conference of state governors to discuss issues of natural resource conservation. Attended by 34 governors along with representatives of all other states, cabinet members, heads of bureaus in Washington, representatives of scientific and industrial societies, and others, the conference ranged over all natural resources. Forest conservation and coal mining were the key concerns. Only one paper was presented on fuel minerals, by Dr. I. C. White, the state geologist of West Virginia, and that paper dealt largely with coal, while devoting a few pages to waste through the flaring and blowing of natural gas.[138]

The absence of concern about petroleum conservation in the "new" producing states, which had already outstripped the production of the northeastern fields, is suggested by the fact that the governors of California, Oklahoma, and Texas all stayed away from the conference. It was not surprising, therefore, that its brief concluding declaration said little that was specific about oil and gas, confining itself to a vague recommendation for "the enactment of laws looking to the prevention of waste in the mining and extraction of coal, oil, gas and other minerals with a view to their wise conservation for the use of the people."[139]

Much more important to the future of oil and gas conservation was the decision of the conference to establish a National Conservation Commission, which

---

[135] Gates 1968: 563–8.
[136] Gould 2001: 676–7.
[137] On Pinchot, see Bates 1957: 33.
[138] Blanchard 1909: 26–37.
[139] *Ibid.* 194.

promptly set on foot a survey of national oil resources, undertaken by David Day.[140] The results of this survey—Day projected exhaustion of domestic supplies by 1935[141]—were immediately enlisted by the conservationist movement in support of their arguments for withdrawing oil-bearing public land from disposal, controlling the flaring and blowing of natural gas, prohibiting or restricting petroleum exports, and reducing production so as to conserve fragile oil supplies for more valuable future uses. These arguments are all to be found in the brief section devoted to petroleum in a pioneering book on conservation published in 1910 by Charles Van Hise, president of the University of Wisconsin, a participant in the conference and member of the commission.[142]

What one notices about this work is that while it acknowledged the fugacious character of petroleum, it did not identify the rule of capture, nor the practice of offset drilling and other lease requirements for immediate production, as contributing to conservation problems.[143] A part of the reason for this omission was that at the time of the conference, there was little appreciation of how the overdrilling of oilfields resulting from the rule of capture was likely to damage reservoirs and leave massive quantities of oil in the ground.

While the function of natural gas in pressurizing the reservoir was well understood, its role in reducing the viscosity of the oil in which it was held in solution, and hence helping it move freely to the wellbore, was not. The focus of the work by people like Van Hise and Day was thus more on how overproduction artificially lowered the price of oil and led to its application to nonpremium uses than on how producers were leaving large quantities of oil in the ground that might never be economically recoverable. It was only in the next decade that scientific papers began to be published demonstrating just how damaging, in terms both of loss of field pressure and increased viscosity of remaining oil, was the waste of gas through uncontrolled drilling.[144] The significance of such papers was in any event slow to penetrate the consciousness of an industry that remained committed to a popular belief that more wells—no matter when and where they were drilled— meant more oil.[145]

Quite apart from the state of scientific understanding, capture and offset drilling requirements presented a conundrum within the political context for the

---

[140] Day 1909a, 1909b.

[141] For criticism of Day's methodology, see Olien and Olien 2000: 124–6.

[142] Van Hise 1910: 47–65.

[143] Compare Havemeyer 1930: 49–51, a re-edition and updating of Van Hise, identifying competitive drilling as the main cause of contemporary overproduction but dismissing earlier fears of exhaustion of reserves.

[144] Huntley 1913, and see other references collected in Hardwicke 1961: 4–5, fn. 8.

[145] See further below, Ch. 9, at 242.

conservation movement furnished by "progressive" thinking. Antimonopoly sentiment was a driving force for the movement. This, remember, was the decade preceding the judicial breakup of Standard Oil in 1911.[146] The geologist W. J. McGee delivered in 1910 an address that served as a kind of manifesto for the newly formed National Conservation Association, formed as a private body to carry Roosevelt's ideas forward after his successor, William Howard Taft, agreed with Congress that executive commissions like the National Conservation Commission could have no constitutional standing. McGee associated waste with a policy of "free giving" of land with its appurtenant valuable resources like minerals and timber, as a result of which "resources passed under monopolistic control with a rapidity never before seen in all the world's history; and it is hardly too much to say that the Nation has become one of the Captains of Industry first, and one of the People and their chosen Representatives only second."[147]

A similar line of thought appeared in I. C. White's governors' conference paper, where the thwarting of successive governors' attempts to secure legislation to stop the waste of natural gas in West Virginia was attributed to "some unseen power greater than Governor or Legislature," later unmasked as "the forces of greed and selfishness...entrenched behind corporate power and influence."[148] But if the capture rule benefited anyone in particular, it was not the Standard Oil–type monolith that McGee and White seem to have had in mind. By reading early development and offset well obligations into leases, the courts had already done much to protect from monopolistic exploitation at least that fraction of McGee's "People" represented by small farmers and other surface owners: as we have seen, large companies that painstakingly assembled substantial acreages for "rational" exploitation were then obliged to drill large numbers of otherwise unnecessary wells around their lease borders both to protect from external capture and to meet their lease obligations to the different owners within their block of leases.

The rule encouraged and protected the wildcat drillers who aimed to get into an area first and obtain as much flush production as possible before others followed in their wake, but its key beneficiaries were those who had the luck and good judgment to follow directly on the wildcatters' heels, and the foresight and capital to provide their own pipeline transportation to get their oil or gas to market. If you could do that you did not—even if you were a substantial company—need large lease blocks. You could cheerfully drain your neighbors' oil or gas by operating a pocket handkerchief lease, while adjoining lessees, for want of means to get their product to market, were forced to run their oil into pond storage or even shut in

---

[146] See *United States v. Standard Oil*, 221 U.S. 1 (1911).

[147] McGee 1910: 367.

[148] White 1909: 29, 36.

their wells. We shall see in Chapter 9 that the most determined opponents of proration and other conservation devices were the small, integrated operators of this type, who had understood how to make the law of capture work to their fullest advantage.

CONCLUSION

The decade that commenced in 1910 was sprinkled with events that would shape and change perceptions of the oil industry among those most closely concerned with its development, paving the way for the regulatory upheavals of the 1920s and 1930s: the dramatic breakup of the Standard Oil trust; the first experience of prorationing in Oklahoma and the beginnings of a wide regulatory competence to deal with waste; the start of a real debate on the long-term sustainability of the burgeoning oil economy, sharpened by the lessons of the First World War on strategic supplies and on government–industry cooperation; and the advancement of scientific understanding of processes of oil and gas production.

Still, while these developments certainly provided the springboard for change, they did not immediately lead even those committed to conservationist policies to look critically at the rule of capture. Max Ball, perhaps the best-informed official of his time—he was chairman of the Oil Land Classification Board of the U.S. Geological Survey, and then legal adviser to the Bureau of Mines—laid out, in a 1917 lecture, the damaging consequences of competitive drilling in the most vivid detail, in terms suggesting a close acquaintance with the latest technical evidence.[149] Yet he took the existence—and, it might appear, the inevitability—of the (as yet unnamed) law of capture entirely for granted, arguing that the crucial problem to be addressed (he did not say how) was the small tracts on which drilling was conducted. In fact, it was the combination of the holding of small tracts with the principle of capture that was fatal to the rational and economic development of American oil resources. I shall argue later that when we take foreign experience into account, it is clear that capture can produce positive effects when the small-tract problem is eliminated.

Nonetheless, it is surprising that Ball should have made no mention of capture at a time when officials and policymakers in the federal government were being confronted by evidence of the damage the rule was doing to important national interests, in the shape of the significant losses by drainage being suffered by the United States from the oil reserves it was trying to maintain for strategic purposes. To understand how this situation came about, we need to make a brief

---

[149] Ball 1917.

examination of the methods by which the public lands were disposed of and managed up to this time, and in particular, of how rights to minerals in such lands were treated. That process culminated in the Mineral Leasing Act of 1920, a landmark in the history of U.S. oil and gas law and a measure that was to have an important influence on developments elsewhere in the world. The act, as we shall see, nicely exemplifies the tensions set up within the conservation movement by its double repugnance for monopoly and for waste.

CHAPTER 8

OIL AND GAS IN THE PUBLIC LANDS

THE PUBLIC DOMAIN IN 1859

Americans entrusted to their federal government the management of the enormous areas of unsettled land to the west and south of the original 13 colonies.[1] Between independence and federation, most of the new states agreed, at the Continental Congress in 1785, to place their often conflicting western territorial claims under national administration. After federation, the lands contained in the Louisiana Purchase from France in 1803 likewise became national property, subject to disposition and regulation by the U.S. Congress. Subsequently treaties with Spain, Mexico, and the United Kingdom added the territories that now constitute Florida (1819), Oregon, Washington and Idaho (1846), California and parts of other western states (1848), and the remainder of the Southwest (1850, 1853) to that vast area. Texas was an exception, as it had already attained independent statehood when it joined the Union in 1845, and it retained title to all

---

[1] See generally Gates 1968, especially Chs. IV, VII–XI, XII–XIV; Hibbard 1939, especially Ch. II.

the public lands within the present boundaries of the state while in 1850 selling extensive lands outside those borders to the federal government. By the time Drake drilled his well near Titusville in 1859, the United States had amassed a public domain extending to 1.31 billion acres (2.19 million square miles).[2]

Of course not all of this land was at that date still unappropriated in the hands of the government. Since its creation, the federal government had practiced an energetic though erratic policy of land disposals, at first favoring sales of undeveloped land, at the best prices obtainable, as a source of revenue, later emphasizing sales at low prices in order to encourage settlement and development; initially trying to deter squatting by heavy penalties, later recognizing the value of squatters' development contributions by legislation enabling them to make preemptive claims for the purchase at minimal prices of the land they occupied. The most general, and generous, of these acts was the Preemption Act of 1841. Sales between 1820 and 1859 disposed of some 312,000 square miles, and sales under the credit sale regime previously in force under the act of 1796, which put the Land Ordinance of 1785 on a legislative footing, of at least an additional 30,000 square miles.

As new states were created from the territories, substantial amounts of public land within their borders were granted to them to support the development of public infrastructure, notably in education. Commonly one-eighteenth of the land (two sections each of a square mile in each "township" of 36 square miles) was granted for the use and support of schools, and various other parcels for other purposes. With 20 new states (apart from Texas) created between independence and 1859, a very rough calculation suggests that some 100,000 square miles may have passed into state administration by 1859. Extensive grants were also made, either to the states or to public utility companies, for public works such as swamp clearance, river improvements, and the construction of turnpike roads, canals, and railroads,[3] and it became commonplace for Congress to grant developers half of the undeveloped land on either side of the proposed route in a belt generally extending to 12 miles before 1866 and 20 miles thereafter; proceeds from the sale of these lands would assist in financing the project. By around 1860, 43,560 square miles had been promised by Congress in this way for railroad development. Summing these totals, we might guess that perhaps a quarter of the federal public domain had passed into state or private hands by 1859, leaving an estate of some 1.66 million square miles in federal hands.[4]

---

[2] Hibbard 1939: 31.

[3] Gates 1968: Chs. XIII, XIV.

[4] This figure tallies reasonably well with Leshy's estimate (Leshy 1987: 50) of 1 billion acres (1.56 million square miles) in federal hands in 1872.

THE MANAGEMENT OF MINERAL LANDS

When its oil industry began, therefore, the United States was the owner of an estate more than half the size of Australia—and infinitely richer in petroleum resources. Within 50 years, it found itself in a position where it was struggling to create out of this estate a petroleum reserve for its navy that would be secure against depredation by drainage from drilling on adjacent private land. To achieve this sort of shrinkage requires very bad luck, bad management, or a remarkable indifference to (or lack of foresight of) public needs. All of these causes in fact contributed to the evolution of a system (if we can dignify it with that term) for the disposition of petroleum in public lands that succeeded in reproducing the worst features of the private ownership arrangements without the aid of significant judicial intervention.

I should start by saying that the federal government and Congress were certainly not unaware of the potential mineral wealth that might be stored up under the public domain. From the beginning, mineral lands received special treatment under disposal policies. The Land Ordinance of 1785 reserved one-third of all gold, silver, lead, and copper mines in any land disposed of, a slight expansion of the general approach of English common law and similar provisions in colonial charters, where royal rights and reservations were normally limited to gold, silver, and perhaps precious stones.[5] When the ordinance expired, however, on the dissolution of the Continental Congress, no comparable provision was enacted in the land disposal laws of the U.S. Congress. Instead, these acts generally withheld "mineral lands" from disposal.[6] In cases where there was ambiguity on this point, the U.S. Supreme Court was consistent in holding that such lands had been reserved—for example, from the grants of township sections made by Congress on admissions to statehood.[7] The problem, of course, was how to find out, in advance of disposal, whether lands were "mineral lands" or not—a particular problem in relation to petroleum, as only expensive and time-consuming drilling could reliably determine whether oil was present far beneath.

Why, one is now inclined to ask, did Congress impose on the officials of the General Land Office such a delicate and often impossible task, instead of separating the rights to the minerals beneath the surface from those to the enjoyment of the land itself, granting out the latter while reserving the former? Doing this would have made more land available for settlement while preserving a potential stream of

---

[5] *Case of Mines* (1568) 1 Plowden 310, 75 Eng. Rep. 472; Charter for the Province of Pennsylvania 1681.

[6] See the listing of such acts in *United States v. Sweet,* 245 U.S. 563, at 568–70 (1918).

[7] *United States v. Sweet,* 245 U.S. 563 (1918) and authorities there cited, notably *Mining Co. v. Consolidated Mining Co.,* 102 U.S. 167 (1880) (California school sections).

revenue for government from any mineral wealth that might subsequently appear. And though officials could not know this for many decades, it would also, as applied to petroleum lands, have avoided the fragmentation of ownership and access rights that provoked the practice and law of capture.

One possible reason may have been doubts about the legal security of separate grants of minerals and surface. The fact that the colonial charters generally made explicit reference to the fact that mines and minerals were granted with the land suggests that a reservation in favor of the Crown was at least viewed as a possibility, and after independence this possibility was noted in a Georgia case of 1843, though with the comment that the reservation must be express.[8] Nonetheless, this approach could possibly have been thought productive of difficulties by reason of the older English requirement of a (symbolic) physical delivery of land to effect its legal transfer from one person to another, known as livery of seisin. In the sixteenth and seventeenth centuries, this procedure was replaced by the delivery of the deeds by which it had come to be evidenced, but doubts may have lingered, and drifted across the Atlantic, about the effectiveness of a deed to convey something like a deposit of minerals, which, at least if undeveloped, and thus unknown and invisible, could not be the subject of a livery of seisin. Only in 1858 did the Supreme Court of Pennsylvania, in what is now regarded as the leading case on the issue, expressly announce the irrelevance of this ancient notion to an age of written conveyances and hold (having noted that in Pennsylvania coal country, "nothing [was] more common than that the surface right should be in one man and the mineral right in another") that, given an appropriate conveyance, such minerals could be held as a separate piece of landed property and not as a mere right of exploitation.[9]

In any event, leasing of minerals was viewed by the middle of the century as an impracticable and "un-American" expedient.[10] A public land act passed in 1807 reserved known lead mines and contiguous lands in the Upper Mississippi Valley and provided for them to be leased by the president. Though the act totally lacked detail as to administration, royalties, and other key matters, the lead mines in Missouri were successfully leased, but the program was short-lived. It lacked any mechanism for enforcement, and miners strongly resented having to take leases when neighbors who held preexisting French and Spanish land grants were able to mine their land freely.[11] The mines were sold when Missouri became a state in

---

[8] Kerr 1894: 253–4.

[9] *Caldwell v. Fulton*, 31 Pa. 475 (1858).

[10] This paragraph draws on Wright 1966; Swenson 1968: 702–6; Hibbard 1939: 513–15. See also Scott 2008: 205–6.

[11] These grants were extensive: Gates 1968: 97–108.

1829. In the so-called Galena lead district in parts of what are now Illinois and Wisconsin, however, a leasing program under the act was operated until the 1840s, at first with success, thanks to an energetic and committed administrator who filled by regulation the gaps in the statute, but later with rapidly increasing laxity and corruption. Although the miners themselves were generally content with the leasing system, pressure from speculators and settlers led to the unlawful disposal of enormous amounts of mineral land from 1834 onward by the newly appointed land registrar with the connivance of the superintendent of mines, an avowed opponent of leasing.

By 1840, the lease arrangements had little land on which to operate, and it was clear that the government was incapable of providing any security of tenure to its mining lessees. Competition for land in the lead district was fueled by the fact that the leases were not for a severed mineral estate, but for the land as a whole, thus ruling out any possibility of agricultural settlement even where this was compatible with mining beneath—though tensions between miners and agriculturists might have been even more acute had they had to coexist on the same landholdings under a split tenure system. The reaction of Congress was to provide in 1847 for the outright sale of land containing valuable minerals in Illinois and Wisconsin, while the government decided to permit, on the basis of an 1850 ruling by the attorney general, the disposal as agricultural land, at low prices, of lands containing "only" iron ore.[12] While other mineral leasing initiatives had certainly occurred in the first half of the nineteenth century—the act that reserved land around the thermal springs at Hot Springs, Arkansas, also reserved large areas of land around salt springs in the territory and authorized the governor to lease out the springs—and may well have been more successful, the Galena experience led to a rejection at federal level of the idea of leasing retained mineral lands, and this was not reversed until 1920. While the aim was always to dispose separately of mineral lands at higher prices, federal grants of land under the numerous homesteading, preemption, and right-of-way acts included, until that time, rights to any minerals that might be discovered, as well as to the surface.

CALIFORNIA, 1848–1866: SELF-REGULATION BY MINERS AND PETROLEUM OPERATORS

Leasing under the 1807 act also exposed a problem that was to assume much more dramatic proportions with the discovery of gold in California in 1848. The act failed in part because the federal government would not or could not make

---

[12] Swenson 1968: 706–7.

available the resources to police the leasing system and test the genuineness of claims to land patents. The much greater difficulty of exercising any public control over miners rushing to remote places in search of immediate wealth was exemplified by the situation of the military governor of California in 1848, once news of the gold find at Sutter's Mill became widespread. At this time, California was not yet a U.S. state and was a region virtually without laws so far as property was concerned. The treaty under which California was ceded by Mexico on February 2, 1848, maintained in force all Mexican laws not in conflict with the U.S. constitution, and those laws made mineral lands government property and provided mechanisms for the acquisition of mining rights. Ten days after its signature, however, California's military governor, Richard Mason, who was possibly ignorant of the treaty's contents or even its existence, proclaimed the abolition of Mexican laws and customs relative to mining rights on public lands.[13] According to John Umbeck, the general laws of the United States did not take effect officially in California until September 1850, shortly after California was admitted to the Union as a state, and thus a legal vacuum existed for the first two years of the California gold rush.[14]

As Governor Mason was clearly aware, he had no legal basis on which to impose fees or royalties, issue licenses, or otherwise regulate gold mining, and even after 1850, when the miners' formal legal position became that of trespassers on public land, no legal basis for any action other than eviction was available. But eviction, or any other kind of enforcement action, was all but impossible: the governor commanded insufficient force to impose his will on the more than 4,000 miners then at work, having lost most of his troops to desertion and having been unsuccessful in the only campaign he could mount, a series of newspaper advertisements offering rewards for the capture and return of his own troops. Though he personally favored either the licensing of mining activity or the sale of the land,[15] discretion appeared the better part of valor. He thus reported in August 1848, "[U]pon considering the large extent of country, the character of the people engaged, and the small scattered force at my command, I resolved not to interfere, but permit all to work freely, unless crimes and broils should call for interference. I was surprised to learn that crime of any kind was very unfrequent. ... "[16]

This hands-off attitude was maintained by the federal authorities until the enactment of the first general mining law in 1866, notwithstanding occasional

---

[13] Umbeck 1981: 69, 137 n. 6.

[14] *Ibid.*

[15] Ellison 1968: 71–2.

[16] Report of August 17, 1848, printed in Public Land Commission 1880: 312–17, at 314. See also Umbeck 1981: 71–2.

attempts, such as John C. Fremont's bill introduced to Congress immediately after statehood in 1850, to provide some legal framework for mining. The main argument of the principal opponent of the bill, Senator Alphaeus Felch, was that it would have installed a leasing system of the type that had failed to work on the Upper Mississippi.[17] Fremont's bill was shelved and the mineral land question remained in limbo, though it should be noted that such lands were not open for acquisition by the ordinary methods applied to agricultural land, including preemption.[18]

As is well known, the regulatory void in California, and later in Nevada also, was filled by the development, by the miners themselves, of mining camp rules.[19] From 1851, by virtue of section 621 of the California Civil Practice Act, such rules could be admitted as evidence in mining litigation and were to govern the court's decision when not in conflict with the U.S. Constitution and laws of the state.[20] Key features of such rules were the establishment of a general legal jurisdiction over the area occupied by the camp; provision of a system for recording claims; the determination of the size and defining features of each claim (for example, along a lode or a length of streambank, or an area of land); restrictions on the number of claims that might be held; and fixing of the work obligations required to preserve the claim—if these were not respected, the claim would be forfeited.[21] The laws of January 1850 for the Jacksonville Camp, for example, established both a civil and a criminal jurisdiction and announced that practice in applying the laws was to be as near as possible to that of the United States.[22] The camp's penal arrangements, however, reflected the special features of the miner's life. Theft of a mule or other beast of burden was punishable by hanging; smaller thefts attracted a sanction of cruelly deceptive mildness: the offender was to have his head and eyebrows close-shaved and leave the encampment within 24 hours. To wander the desolate mining regions wearing the insignia of a thief cannot have been a comfortable experience.

The chief interest for us of these mining camp laws is that they provided a precedent for some of the earliest arrangements for organizing oil exploration in California. In 1864, Professor Benjamin Silliman of Yale, whose report nine years earlier on the excellent illuminant qualities of Pennsylvania rock oil had set on foot the enterprise that led to the drilling of the Drake Well, wrote in the most glowing terms of the potential of Los Angeles as an oil region. Unfortunately, the samples

---

[17] Ellison 1968: 74–5.

[18] Hibbard 1939: 515–16.

[19] Umbeck 1981; Shinn 1885; Libecap 1979: 368–9; Libecap 1993: Ch. 3.

[20] On the Civil Practice Act, the forerunner of the Code of Civil Procedure, see Miller 1955.

[21] Umbeck 1981: 94–6.

[22] The rules are reproduced in Public Land Commission 1880: 317–18. For Nevada rules, see Libecap 1979: 384–5.

of "seepages" that he was given to analyze had been cut by the promoters with high-quality kerosene imported from the East. No commercially producible oil was found (at least in this period), and Silliman lost his reputation and eventually his chair at Yale.[23] In the excitement, however, "petroleum mining districts" were formed to provide some kind of framework for oil exploration on unpatented public lands.

The first such districts were established even before the Los Angeles boom got under way, in 1864 in Humboldt County, northern California, where oil seeps had attracted attention three years earlier. Their rules were very simple. Those of the first to be formed, Mattole District, provided only for the size of a claim—one quarter section, or 160 acres—"to be taken in one square body"; for its recording; for the limiting of the number of claims that could be held by occupancy to one; for the work obligation needed to maintain it (one day's work every three months); for the exclusion from claim of any farm occupied for agricultural purposes; and for the revision of the rules by a duly notified miners' meeting. Numerous other districts were created in the region in the next few months, but the first season's results were disappointing, and by 1866, despite enthusiastic reporting of oil shows by the *Humboldt Times* (whose editor happened to hold shares in several local exploration companies), activity had ceased.[24]

In 1865, similar districts were created for the county of Los Angeles and in San Fernando, the latter covering the canyons of the Santa Susana Mountains, in which there had already been activity. Perhaps reflecting the greater level of interest, the laws of these districts limited the size of a claim to "one thousand feet square upon any Petroleum, Naphtha or Asphaltum bearing lead"—that is, about 23 acres, though the discoverer of a lead was entitled also to a second such claim on it. Any number of existing claims could be purchased, however, and the laws provided for the recording of the conveyances. Claims might also be held jointly and severally, which would enable a group to acquire several claims and work them together, though as in Humboldt County, the work obligations were hardly onerous: one day's work each month, and once $100 had been spent, the claimant was entitled to "an absolute deed of conveyance" from the mining recorder elected under the laws and was not exposed to forfeiture.[25] Results of work in these districts were not quite as disappointing as in the north, and claims continued to be recorded in the San Fernando district into 1867.[26] But the small production obtained, often by tunneling into the sides of the Santa Susana canyons rather than by drilling, could

---

[23] Swenson 1968: 730–1.
[24] Coy 1929: 229–37.
[25] Mining Laws of Los Angeles Mining District 1865, Los Angeles County Records, Misc. R., vol. 1.
[26] White 1976: 28–31.

not compete with the imports from Pennsylvania, which gradually resumed after the end of the Civil War,[27] and there was little further activity until Edward Doheny's discovery of the Los Angeles City oilfield in 1892.

By the time of this discovery, on private land recently subdivided into residential lots,[28] the amount of unappropriated public land in California had diminished substantially, and the federal hard rock mining legislation was believed—wrongly, I shall suggest—to furnish an appropriate means by which an oil operator might obtain title to such land. The cooperative self-government approach to oil exploration and production in the United States was thus stillborn, something one may regret in light of the fact that it might have offered a more rational system of exploitation than that developed under the regime of private property in Pennsylvania and its neighbors. Assigned acreages corresponded more closely to the needs of efficient drilling and production than the minuscule lots into which Pennsylvania farmers and their head lessees divided their land; the Los Angeles double-claim reward for discovery encouraged exploration;[29] and the absence of a royalty-hungry surface proprietor eliminated one source of pressure for production at any price. Elinor Ostrom has reported on experimental studies which suggest that under certain circumstances it may be easier to create and sustain cooperative exploitation of common pool resources than established economic theory would suggest, thus avoiding wasteful competition to appropriate them; homogeneity of expectations and capacities among producers registers as a particularly important factor.[30]

Ostrom also noted that such cooperative systems could be disrupted or destroyed by external shocks, and one may wonder whether the organization of the oil districts would have survived the pressures created by truly substantial discoveries. It seems doubtful that miners' meetings, or mining recorders as their executive officers, would have had the capacity, even if they had the desire, to prohibit the intensive competitive drilling near the lines dividing claims that surely would have followed such discoveries. Possibly they might have been more successful in preventing the subdivision of claims, by the simple expedient of refusing to record them. And it is not impossible, in the light of later cooperative efforts by operators to control production,[31] to imagine such a self-governing organization developing field regulations and settling disputes, particularly if it had

---

[27] Henderson 2001: 2–3.

[28] Testa 2005.

[29] It was to be imitated in the Mineral Leasing Act of 1920 and in the early petroleum legislation of several Australian states: below, at 234–5, and in Ch. 10 at 328–33.

[30] Ostrom 1999.

[31] Below, Ch. 9, at 252–3.

come to enjoy the sort of legal support given to miners by the California Civil Practice Act.

In this field of investigation as elsewhere, cross-country and cross-cultural comparisons should be treated with caution, but it is worth mentioning the only other cooperative system for oil and gas production of which I am aware, whose roughly contemporaneous fate tends to reinforce these doubts. In Upper Burma, 24 families of hereditary well owners, the *twinzayo*, had for centuries produced, without serious dispute, substantial quantities of oil from the Yenangyaung fields near the Irrawaddy River.[32] The wells were hand dug, but until the European and American developments of the mid-nineteenth century, this was the only place where oil was produced on an industrial scale, with transport down the Irrawaddy to meet Burmese and export demand for oil for lighting and other uses. Location of wells, and transfer of rights relating to them, was regulated on behalf of the corporation of *twinzayo* by an elected head, the *twingymin*.

Within 20 years after the British annexation of Upper Burma in 1886, however, the *twinzayo* system had largely broken down. Although the British authorities went to considerable lengths to protect the *twinzayo* and their traditional methods of production, the arrival of competing commercial interests led traditional owners and diggers to sell or lease sites within the *twinzayo* reserve to companies using deep-drilling techniques. As competition among such companies intensified at the beginning of the twentieth century, the price bid for an existing well site increased dramatically, from £7 (about $34) in 1895 to £4,000 ($19,464) in 1908. The usual consequences followed: competitive drilling, drainage and waste (in 1908, the average distance between wells, still mostly hand dug, was only 60 feet), and serious oilfield fires.[33] Thereafter, the *twinzayo* system was effectively replaced by British administration of conventional state oil concessions.

Throughout the 1850s and onward into the 1860s and later, miners in the Far West took gold and then silver worth hundreds of millions of dollars out of federal public lands, paying nothing for the privilege and submitting to no public regulation. Not even the outbreak of the Civil War, and the consequent need of the Union for financial resources with which to fight it, could change this situation. Plans for both taxation and sale of the mines were advanced at this time by members of the federal government, and in 1865, a bill providing for sale of the gold and silver mines in small tracts was introduced into Congress but made no progress in the face of western opposition.[34] Even at the level of the federal government, however, there was strenuous opposition to the idea that the United

---

[32] See generally Longmuir 2001.

[33] *Ibid.* Chs. 3, 12.

[34] Ellison 1968: 83–5.

States might retain title to its minerals and draw a continuing profit from their working. A plan by the commissioner of the General Land Office to require miners to obtain a license on payment of a small fee, plus an area rental and a percentage royalty on production (on the model of a scheme being successfully operated in neighboring British Columbia), was denounced by the secretary of the treasury as impracticable, un-American, and unconstitutional.[35] That this was a common, though perhaps unconscious, sentiment was confirmed by what happened when Texas, restored to the Union after taking the Confederate side in the Civil War, came to draft its Reconstruction Constitution in 1866.

THE TEXAS GIVEAWAY

Texas had entered the Union in 1845 as an independent state. Originally part of the Spanish colony, and from 1821 of the state, of Mexico, it achieved independence through its successful revolution of 1836, at a time when a majority of the population were immigrants who had come from the United States at the invitation of the Mexican government. In its independence constitution of 1836, however, it maintained in force "all laws now in force in Texas and not inconsistent with this constitution," leading its second president, Mirabeau Lamar, to complain that Texans were the only people "to have adopted a system of laws of which the great body of the people are entirely ignorant [and which] are written in a foreign tongue. ... "[36] Nonetheless, it is clear that by this measure, Texas was adopting Mexican land law, which incorporated the Spanish Mining Ordinance of 1783, applicable to all of Spain's American possessions save Peru, and under which title to minerals was retained by the Crown even after the surface had passed into private ownership. The list of minerals in the ordinance was comprehensive and not confined to precious metals, even extending to "bitumen and liquids of the earth."[37]

While the Republic of Texas legislated on the footing of state ownership of minerals, in 1842 authorizing landowners to open gold, silver, and lead mines on their own land subject to a 5 percent royalty to the state, it is not clear that ordinary Texans, probably more familiar with the U.S. system of disposing of all rights in land, including minerals, would have been aware of this restriction on their rights. There being a general law to this effect, no explicit reservation of minerals would

---

[35] *Ibid.* 84.

[36] Quoted in Hawkins 1947: 12. Material in this and the next two paragraphs is drawn from Hawkins save where otherwise stated.

[37] Ch. VI, s. 22. A translation of the ordinance appears in Rockwell 1851: 4–111.

have appeared on their title documents (which, if Spanish or Mexican grants, they probably could not read anyway). Oil leases were being granted by surface owners in Texas from at least 1859, and the first under which production was achieved, the Skillern lease in Nacogdoches County, though concluded in 1865 under the regime of the ordinance—the Statehood Constitution of 1845 and the Confederate State Constitution of 1861 had both maintained rights of property and current laws in force—was in typical Pennsylvania form and purported to be a disposition of petroleum rights by the surface owner; it was recorded, without objection, by the chief justice of the county.[38] By this date, the Supreme Court of Texas had already decided, in *Cowan v. Hardeman*, a long, drawn-out case on title to a salt spring in central Texas, that a patent to one of the litigants under which the state relinquished "forever all right and title in and to said lands" did not operate to convey the mineral estate, so the state was still the owner of the salt.[39] The basis of the decision was, however, the legislative confirmation by the independent Texas legislature in 1837 of the prohibition of grants of salt and minerals, and thus the continuing operation of the 1783 ordinance may have been obscured. In any event, the case was decided in 1862 amid the confusion and stress of the Civil War and not reported until 1867, so news of it had perhaps not reached Chief Justice Johnson in Nacogdoches.

Oil, however, was the least of the concerns of the constitutional convention that met in Austin in February 1866 and set out to draft a constitution for Texas as a readmitted state of the Union. That constitution, as published, expressly incorporated a provision (article VII, section 39) terminating the effect of the 1783 ordinance in Texas. It stated "[t]hat the State of Texas hereby releases to the owners of the soil all mines and mineral substances, that may be on the same, subject to such uniform rate of taxation, as the Legislature may impose."[40]

What brought about this radical change remains mysterious. Certainly there were delegates at the convention who felt that the general reservation of minerals was a brake on development, or that California's position of private ownership coupled with free access on public lands was preferable, but not everyone was of this view, and some were more concerned simply with quieting title to land after the disturbances of the Civil War. At all events, the origin of the provision was an

---

[38] Warner 1939: 22–5, 309–11.

[39] 26 Tex. 217 (1862). The opposite conclusion was reached in relation to gold deposits in California, held in *Moore v. Smaw*, 17 Cal. 199 (1861), and other decisions, to have been conveyed by U.S. grant of the lands that included them. Here, however, Mexican lands passed directly, by the Treaty of Guadeloupe Hidalgo, into the hands of the U.S. government, and the 1783 ordinance could thereafter have no effect.

[40] The provision became article XIV (7) of the current (1876) constitution but was removed as "dead wood" under article III (42) in 1969.

amendment introduced in a directly contrary sense, seeking to confirm the state's title to the great salt lake of Hidalgo County, El Sal del Rey, the subject of a highly politicized three-way litigation that had continued for nearly two decades.

During the Civil War, this salt was seen as a crucial state asset, and operation of the saltworks had been taken over by the government to assure Confederate supplies. When, however, the committee to which this amendment was submitted reported to the convention as a whole, it substituted the text above, which was adopted on the last day of the convention. Personal preferences and rivalries may not have been irrelevant to a step that was to have momentous consequences for the oil industry in Texas—the chair of the committee had been the attorney for the party whose patent was defeated in *Cowan v. Hardeman*—but that there was a more policy-driven sentiment in favor of change is suggested by the approval by a different convention committee of a proposed ordinance of an even more radical character, which would have denied to the state even the right to make reservations of mineral rights when granting land in the future. This ordinance was never brought before the convention as a whole. In any case, the possibility of unified ownership of petroleum rights throughout Texas, and with it the chance of avoiding the waste engendered by the rule of capture, evaporated like the moisture from the salt lake itself.

Very large areas of land were still in state ownership after 1866, however, and these were divided under legislation of 1883 between the University of Texas and public schools and asylums, though the State Land Office retained management of the land until 1895 and of mineral rights until 1929. In *Cox v. Robison* in 1912,[41] the Supreme Court of Texas made an exhaustive examination of the circumstances in which article VII, section 39 of the 1866 constitution came to be passed, concluding that it had not in truth been passed as a part of the constitution at all, but only as an associated ordinance, and in consequence—and in light of its particular association with El Sal del Rey—ruling that it, and the provisions of subsequent constitutions that repeated it, should not have prospective effect so as to prevent state lands being granted thereafter subject to a reservation of minerals. Further cancellations of mineral reservations were however made by statute in 1879 and 1895. Nonetheless, much public land remained on which there was a separation of surface and mineral rights, either because the surface was leased for ranching or farming purposes or because it was sold after 1895 with a reservation of mineral rights. Apparently it was the practice of the commissioner of the Land Office up to 1919 to classify all public school land as mineral, without reference to evidence or information as to mineral-bearing qualities or possibility, with the result that any purchasers got only the surface rights.

---

[41] 105 Tex. 426, 150 S.W. 1149.

This was a recipe for future strife, because the rule in Texas, traceable to the supreme court's decision in *Cowan v. Hardeman*, was that the mineral estate was "dominant"—that is to say, "the right to the minerals ... carries with it the right to enter [the land overlying the minerals], dig and carry them away, and all other such incidents thereto as are necessary to be used for getting and enjoying them."[42]

This notion of the dominant mineral estate derives from English common law and denies to the surface owner any compensation for the damage or disturbance produced by mineral operations or drilling for oil and gas. Surface owners who themselves carve out an oil and gas lease can hardly complain if they fail to protect themselves, by the terms of the lease, from damage and inconvenience; those who purchase or lease land already subject to a severed, and dominant, mineral estate are in a less happy position, even if they may be presumed to know the risk to which they are exposed. In 1917, the first Texas legislation leasing the oil and gas rights the state had retained under former public school lands did provide for a payment to surface owners or lessees to compensate for disturbance from oil exploration and production operations, but this proved insufficient to ensure their cooperation,[43] and since noncooperation in Texas tended to be expressed by "a show of dogs and shotguns,"[44] the legislature attempted to sweeten the pill by enacting the Relinquishment Act of 1919. This act made surface owners of public school lands (university lands were not covered) its "agents," charged with leasing out the oil and gas in the land, and "relinquishing" to them fifteen-sixteenths of oil and gas in the land as compensation for this service and for any disturbance or damage to the land. The effect of this provision was to give the surface landowner half of the normal one-eighth royalty (and of other payments such as signature bonuses) and entire discretion as to whether and when the land would be leased.

By a breathtaking display of intellectual acrobatics, the supreme court managed to hold, in *Green v. Robison*,[45] that this statute was constitutional despite diverting to surface owners money and assets reserved by the constitution to the Permanent School Fund. The words used by the statute, "[t]he State ... relinquishes and vests in the owner of the soil an undivided fifteen-sixteenths of all oil and gas which has been undeveloped ... that may be upon and within the ... land" were, said the court, "confusing and uncertain of meaning, and perhaps not of importance. ... There is no vesting of title or interest in the oil and gas in the owner of the soil."

---

[42] *Cowan v. Hardeman*, above, text at n. 39, cited in *Empire Gas & Fuel Co. v. State*, 121 Tex. 138, 47 S.W. 2d 265 (1932).

[43] See Freeman 1975: 64.

[44] Olien and Olien 2002: 162.

[45] 117 Tex. 516, 8 S.W. 2d 655 (1928). For comment, see Walker 1928, *Empire Gas & Fuel Co. v. State*, 121 Tex. 138, 47 S.W. 2d 265 (1932), and *Norman v. Giles*, 148 Tex. 21, 219 S.W. 2d 678 (1949).

The Relinquishment Act was replaced in 1931 by legislation that treated subsequent grantees with even greater generosity,[46] but it has remained in force in relation to grants made between 1919 and 1931 and still covers more than 7 million acres of land. Surface owners and lessees whose land is burdened by operations under severed oil and gas interests that have been created in other ways—as by private dealings in lease and royalty interests—are far less fortunate. Unlike a number of other states, Texas has never enacted a damage compensation statute for the benefit of surface owners, who, in the absence of effective lease restrictions, can therefore recover for damage and disturbance only in cases of negligence or in certain other, very restricted, circumstances.[47]

The consistent pattern in Texas, therefore, has been one of giving away the state's rights in minerals inherited from its Spanish and Mexican predecessors, either directly, by way of regular cancellations of the mineral reservations in grants, or indirectly, by way of the richly remunerated status of "agent." In neither case has the state made any attempt to retain any rights of management of the relevant oil and gas deposits or shown any interest in the possibilities of using its rights in oil and gas over often extended areas as a means of securing more effective conservation of these resources. The policy is an eloquent expression of a preference for private enrichment over public welfare and a signal that even had the effect of the 1783 ordinance continued after 1866, it would not have long survived the arrival of large-scale oil production in Texas.

OIL AND GAS UNDER THE MINING LAW OF 1872

Between 1866 and 1872, Congress finally got around to passing three statutes that together supplied the long-missing legal regime for the mineral lands in the public domain. An act of 1866 dealt with lode claims, which were for certain specified minerals running along an identified lode or seam, and a second act of 1870 added provision for placer claims—that is, claims to any minerals in a particular area of land. The two acts were combined, amended, and replaced by the law of 1872, though the distinction between the two forms of claims was maintained for clarity and simplicity of operation. The principle of the acts was that of free mining: any miner could come onto unclaimed and ungranted federal public land and look for valuable minerals. If a discovery was made, the miner could stake, or "locate," a claim to its minerals and, by properly marking the claim and doing a defined amount of work on it, could, in the absence of adverse claims, obtain as of right a

---

[46] Freeman 1975: 76.
[47] Miller 2004; Smith 2008.

patent granting absolute ownership of the land—the surface as well as the mineral rights—on payment of a modest fee: $5 per acre for lode mines, $2.50 per acre for placer mines. Lode claims were limited in size to 1,500 feet along the vein or lode and 600 feet wide, placer claims to 20 acres.

Proponents of low-price, small-tract sales for mineral lands had thus won out against both opponents of any interference with the activities of miners and those who favored some form of leasing and continuing returns to the federal purse. The difficulty of achieving *any* result in the face of these contending forces is evidenced by the fact that the 1866 act had as its full title "An Act Granting the Right of Way to Ditch and Canal Owners over the Public Lands, and for Other Purposes," having been passed by the expedient of substituting it for the original content of the act with this title. This move, undertaken by its promoters in the Senate, had the purpose and result that when it arrived in the House of Representatives, it went for consideration to a committee favorable to its provisions, and not to the House Public Lands Committee, which had previously approved a significantly different proposal, anathema to the miners and their congressional supporters, under which mining lands would be sold in small tracts by auction.[48]

Despite its doubtfully legitimate birth, its many defects of drafting that have often required correction by Herculean feats of judicial interpretation, and its most uneasy relationship with modern concerns for both resource conservation and environmental protection,[49] the Mining Law of 1872 remains in force today and is still argued by some to represent the most appropriate and efficient mechanism for disposing of mineral lands.[50] And though the Congress that passed it certainly did not have oil and gas exploration in mind—indeed, John Leshy, in his major study of the law, has suggested that it did not have up-to-date methods of hard rock mining in mind either[51]—the law furnished the only regulation of oil and gas exploration and production on federal lands until the passage of the Mineral Leasing Act of 1920.

A less appropriate framework for such activity can scarcely be imagined. Placer claims were limited under the Mining Law to 20 acres (though an association of eight persons could obtain 160), and crucially, a claim could not be located until a discovery had been made,[52] so that operators had no security of possession of their chosen site until they struck oil. Mere indications of the possible presence of oil

---

[48] On this episode, see Ellison 1968: 84–6; Leshy 1987: 14–16; Swenson 1968: 715–19.

[49] See Leshy, *passim.*

[50] Morriss et al. 2006.

[51] Leshy 1987: 96–7.

[52] See the provisions now printed at 30 U.S.C. §§ 23, 35.

were not enough.[53] Early drillers seeking to rely on the act were thus confronted with a scenario where

> as soon as there were rumors of oil prospecting, there converged on the scene countless "professional" entrymen whose nuisance value had to be reckoned with. Holders of military bounty warrants, railroad indemnity rights, and forest lieu rights [all bases for claiming land for agricultural settlement] could not be prevented from harassing prospectors because no one could demonstrate that the land was actually valuable for minerals at that time.[54]

But while the law did not grant the possessory protection the driller might have hoped for against such a nuisance, to hold that petroleum fell outside it would leave the driller equally defenseless. Because the wording of the placer provisions of the law, referring to "all forms of deposit" except veins of quartz or other rock in place, was certainly wide enough to include petroleum, the Department of the Interior, under Land Office circulars dating from the 1870s, acted on the basis that placer claims could be made, until the secretary suddenly announced a reversal of position in 1896. This decision was in its turn quickly disowned by his successor, but the resulting confusion led to the rapid passage by Congress of a brief act stating simply "that any person authorized to enter lands under the mining laws of the United States may enter and obtain patent to lands containing petroleum or other mineral oils and chiefly valuable therefor under the provisions of the laws relating to placer mineral claims."[55] In presenting this provision as a bill, the House Public Lands Committee solemnly averred that "[i]t has never been held by any authority that the provisions of the placer acts were not adequate to meet the conditions surrounding the development of mineral oils."[56]

The scene over which these authorities were unseeingly presiding was, however, not a pretty one. The small size of the claim acreage, along with the initial insecurity and the immediate work required to protect it, meant that the placer system reproduced the features of haste, waste, and competitive drilling engendered by capture in the private ownership system. In 1897, in a decade without major petroleum discoveries, this may not have been seen as a problem—indeed, many defended the arrangements on the grounds of the energetic activity that resulted—but the placer system had the additional vice of institutionalizing fraud in oil operations. Even responsible operators might need to assert falsely that they had found some mineral other than oil, in order to satisfy the discovery

---

[53] *Nevada Sierra Oil Co. v. Home Oil Co.*, 98 F. 673, at 675 (S.D. Cal., 1899).
[54] Swenson 1968: 732.
[55] Oil Placer Act 1897.
[56] United States. House of Representatives, Committee on the Public Lands 1897.

requirement for location pending the slow and costly process of drilling, or might need to use nominees in order to assemble a block of claims sufficient to permit efficient operations. Tolerance of this latter practice was signaled by the remark of Representative Sylvester Smith of California that "a man with a reasonable supply of relatives" could get about all the land he wanted.[57] The less responsible operator or speculator could easily find complaisant Land Office officials who would approve the patenting of oil claims on the basis of developments linking a number of public and private parcels where no work had actually been done on the public land included.[58]

For the least scrupulous, the successors of William Wright's "experienced men,"[59] the wide variety of bases for agricultural entry offered by the public land laws provided ample opportunities for fraudulent acquisition of oil lands and vexatious litigation against legitimate occupants. An example is *Cosmos Exploration Co. v. Gray Eagle Oil Co.* in 1900,[60] where the complainants attempted to oust oil producers who had located under the Oil Placer Act, on the basis of fraudulent claims to the land as agricultural under certificates granted in return for relinquishment of forest lands. Some of the affidavits in the case, reproduced at length in the judgment, give a sense of the brazenness with which these frauds were perpetrated. Purported homesteading, under the Homestead Act of 1862, was another popular method of getting access to land for what was in reality oil exploration: put up your shack, wait a decent while, then drill your hole.[61]

WITHDRAWALS AND RESERVES: THE ROAD TO TEAPOT DOME

Within a decade of the passage of the Oil Placer Act, its effects on the oil-bearing lands in the public domain were giving grounds for serious official concern. With the award of a patent, the act effected a once-and-for-all transfer of all rights in the land from public to private hands. The shrinking of the public domain as a result of such transfers, and the corresponding shrinking of the oil reserves that might still be owned by the nation, proceeded in California and Wyoming at a spanking pace, aided by the withdrawal of much of this land from agricultural settlement from 1900 onward in order to protect genuine oil operators from the nuisances I have described.[62] Conservationist interests grew alarmed; already in 1906,

---

[57] Quoted in Ise 1926: 302.

[58] Bates 1963: 63–77.

[59] Above, Ch. 3, at 68.

[60] 104 F. 20 (S.D. Cal. 1900).

[61] On these devices, see generally Ise 1926: 296–306.

[62] Ball 1916: 20–3, and on the operation of the 1897 act generally, 27–59.

Progressive Senator Robert La Follette, from Wisconsin, one of their earliest and loudest voices in the theater of politics, suggested the adoption of a leasing system for the remaining public petroleum resources.[63] What eventually pushed the government to action, however, was the strategic concern of ensuring an adequate oil supply for the U.S. Navy, which was gradually moving—though with less conviction than its British counterpart[64]—toward a definitive switch from coal to oil fueling. George Otis Smith, the head of the U.S. Geological Survey, on this basis convinced Secretary Richard Ballinger, and through him President William Howard Taft, that if something were not done quickly, "the government will be obliged to repurchase the very oil that it has practically given away."[65]

Taft's response was to issue, with no advance warning to the industry, his proclamation of September 27, 1909, temporarily withdrawing "from all forms of location, settlement, selection, filing, entry, or disposal under the mineral or non-mineral public-land laws" some 2.87 million acres in California and 170,000 acres in Wyoming.[66] Although the proclamation promised that existing and valid claims as of September 27 might proceed to entry in the usual manner, it threw the industry in California and Wyoming into total confusion by reason of doubts as to its constitutionality (already expressed in relation to extensive earlier executive withdrawals of coal and forest lands effected by President Roosevelt)[67] and of the uncertainty surrounding locations under the 1897 act.

This uncertainty was not dissipated, but compounded, by the Pickett Act of 1910, under which Congress gave the president express power to make withdrawals of certain classes of unpatented lands, including oil lands. Under this act, Taft subsequently renewed and reaffirmed his original withdrawals of oil lands. Section 2 of the act, however, offered protection to anyone "who, at the date of any order of withdrawal, is a bona fide occupant of oil or gas bearing lands and who, at such date, is in the diligent prosecution of work leading to the discovery of oil and gas." The term "bona fide" was not one of easy application in the western oilfields at this time, not only because of the institutionalized fraud that I have described, but also because the Supreme Court, in a hard rock case in 1904,[68] had endorsed an existing but legally unwarranted practice of allowing location of claims in advance of discovery. Large numbers of petroleum claims, on which little activity

---

[63] Bates 1963: 19.

[64] Below, Ch. 10, at 319.

[65] Quoted in Swenson 1968: 732.

[66] Bates 1963: 21–3; Olien and Olien 2000: 129–30; Swenson 1968: 732–3.

[67] Swenson 1968: 725–30.

[68] *Creede and Cripple Creek Mining and Milling Co. v. Uinta Tunnel Mining Transportation Co.*, 196 U.S. 337 (1904).

and no discovery had taken place, had been located in this way and had received possessory protection from Californian and Wyoming courts.[69]

Analyses of industry behavior in the next few years split cleanly down the middle according to whether they are offered by oil industry sympathizers or historians[70] or by conservationists and chroniclers of the conservation movement.[71] The former show us perplexed western oilmen looking for ways of protecting existing drilling investments, and anxiously consulting their lawyers as to the constitutionality of the president's actions, before proceeding with drilling and production on lands withdrawn in 1909 or 1910 or both. The latter offer a picture of illegal defiance of an administration with limited enforcement capabilities and the deliberate acquisition of "masses of protected unworked claims by pioneers [who] drove through the sagebrush in fast runabouts. Though they carried guns, their principal weapon was the checkbook,"[72] which they used to buy out prior occupants, notably in the Salt Creek field in Wyoming. Many of these Wyoming claims ended up in the hands of the Midwest Oil Company, and it was in litigation relating to one of these claims that the Supreme Court, in 1915, eventually declared the constitutionality of the 1909 proclamation.[73] That, however, did nothing to settle the proper application, case by case, of the protection clause of the Pickett Act, and congressional attempts for a decade after that act to find a suitable permanent basis for the development of the remaining unappropriated oil-bearing land in the public domain were stymied time after time by disagreements about how to deal with the reiterated demands by California oil operators for blanket relief from the effects of the withdrawals.[74]

The effect of this stalemate was that while the erosion of the public lands was slowed, any oil under them continued to disappear almost as fast as before. This was in part a result of the fact that, as Roger and Diana Olien put it, some operators dealt with the uncertainty of their position on the public lands by "develop[ing] what they had at an all-out rate, cheerfully draining the tracts of those who had opted to be law-abiding."[75] But the losses also reflected a fact not so far adverted to, which was that the remaining public lands were often held in a checkerboard pattern, with retained sections alternating with others that had been the subject of grants: originally even-numbered sections, later odd-numbered ones, a slightly more generous arrangement because sections 16 and 36 in any 36-section

---

[69] See cases cited by Colby 1915: 274.

[70] Olien and Olien 2000: 129–30; White 1976: 439–59.

[71] Bates 1963: 24–44; Ise 1926: 309–23.

[72] Bates 1963: 29.

[73] *United States v. Midwest Oil Co.*, 236 U.S. 459 (1915).

[74] Swenson 1968: 738–41; Ise 1926: Chs. XXII, XXIII.

[75] Olien and Olien 2000: 130.

township were ordinarily reserved for the state for school and governmental purposes. This was the usual system adopted with the railroad grants already mentioned, subject to an overriding rule that the railroad could not take any of these alternate sections that were mineral lands, but must select other sections in lieu from a wider belt outside the principal one.[76]

One implication of this was that Taft's withdrawal orders affected far less public land than the crude measurements of the described areas suggested, as there was much checkerboarded private land within those areas, perhaps half of the total acreage. Second, with most of these railroad grants being made before anyone could know whether the relevant lands might be valuable as oil-bearing, ample opportunities appeared for purchase or leasing of railroad land, and companies fortunate enough to find oil under such lands were free, under the rule of capture, to drain oil in large quantities from under the now withdrawn adjoining sections of public land. And of course they did.

The problem was especially severe in the San Joaquin Valley in California, where the Southern Pacific Railroad held very large areas of land selected in 1903 and 1904 in lieu of land in their original railroad grants. In 1910, the Justice Department began a campaign to invalidate these selections over large areas on the ground that they had been obtained by fraud, because the railroad must have been aware that oilfields would be developed in the region. In litigation commenced in 1913 and not concluded until 1919, the department eventually recovered little more than a quarter of the land it had sought.[77] At the same time, President Taft sought to improve the security of supplies for the navy by using the powers he now undoubtedly possessed under the Pickett Act to create two adjacent naval petroleum reserves in the area, No. 1 at Elk Hills and No. 2 at Buena Vista, covering a total of some 68,000 acres. A third reserve was established in 1915 on undeveloped land at Teapot Dome in Wyoming, south of the heavily exploited Salt Creek field.

Given what we know about drainage and capture, the description of Elk Hills and Buena Vista as "reserves" needs to be taken with a large pinch of salt. Gary Libecap has summarized the property right position there:

> Of the 30,080 acres of the Buena Vista Hills reserve, 20,320 acres were private land in 640-acre blocks, checkerboarded across the reserve because of past railroad and state school land grants. Of the remaining 9,760 acres, 7,520 were contested by private claimants. Hence, there was little land in Buena Vista Hills that could be considered a true naval reserve. Elk Hills and Teapot Dome were more viable storage

---

[76] Gates 1968: 356–69.

[77] *United States v. Southern Pacific Co.*, 251 U.S. 1 (1919) (selections invalidated); *United States v. Southern Pacific Co.*, 260 F. 511 (S.D. Cal. 1919) (selections sustained).

sites because they had fewer private claims. The Elk Hills reserve of 37,760 acres had less checkerboarded land because of a U.S. Supreme Court ruling ... canceling much of the Southern Pacific Railroad land grant in the area. Nevertheless, there were 6,760 acres of patented land checkerboarded in the reserve and outstanding private claims under the placer law. Within Teapot Dome, there was no patented land, though Pioneer Oil claimed all but 400 acres of the 9,481-acre reserve.[78]

The vulnerability of the reserves to drainage, even if all outstanding claims on the public lands could be canceled, can be appreciated from an illustration originally offered by J. Leonard Bates (see Figure 8-1).

[B]y 1920 Elk Hills was being drained by Standard Oil production from fifty wells on sections 35 and 36 (which the company owned within the reserve), and twenty-nine wells directly along the reserve's boundary in sections 27, 35, and 36. Additionally, private wells operated by other companies were scattered within the reserve. Buena Vista Hills, more seriously checkerboarded, was subject to drainage from 599 wells on private land in the reserve and 183 wells on adjacent lands.[79]

The navy thus found itself in the position familiar to private landowners, wanting to hold on to oil in the ground but having to watch helplessly while others drained it away. Although the secretary to the navy since 1913, Josephus Daniels, had been an ardent defender of the naval reserve idea and a vigorous proponent of a policy of naval independence of private suppliers, favoring government ownership of armorplate factories, for example, he had not gone so far as to take the navy into the oil business; its only response to the drainage problem until 1921 was to grant a few small leases to private operators so that offset wells could be drilled to allay the most serious drainage at Buena Vista and Elk Hills.

When the Warren G. Harding administration replaced Woodrow Wilson's in 1921, however, the new secretary to the navy, Edwin Denby, agreed to the transfer of the reserves from his department to that of the interior. Harding's secretary of the interior was Senator Albert Fall, a New Mexico rancher and miner of whom Gifford Pinchot was reported as saying, "It would have been possible to pick a worse man for Secretary of the Interior, but not altogether easy."[80] Fall took the view that the best way to secure the navy's strategic needs was to provide large quantities of secure surface storage and to produce the reserves fully under lease, exchanging the navy's royalty oil for fuel oil to fill the tanks. He accordingly granted multiple leases for the navy's scattered acreage in Buena Vista. He then

---

[78] Libecap 1984: 386.

[79] *Ibid.* 388.

[80] Yergin 1991: 212; Stratton 1998: 211. On Pinchot, see further above, Ch. 7, at 202.

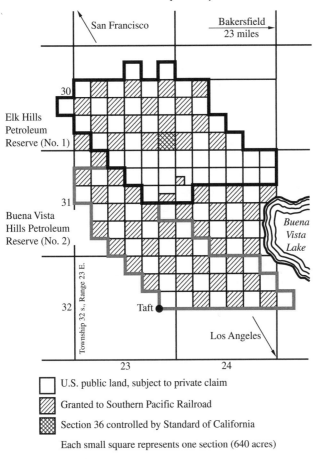

San Joaquin Valley

San Francisco

Bakersfield
23 miles

30

Elk Hills
Petroleum
Reserve (No. 1)

31

Buena Vista
Hills Petroleum
Reserve (No. 2)

Buena
Vista
Lake

Township 32 s., Range 23 E.

32   Taft

Los Angeles

23   24

U.S. public land, subject to private claim

Granted to Southern Pacific Railroad

Section 36 controlled by Standard of California

Each small square represents one section (640 acres)

Figure 8-1. The Naval Petroleum Reserves
Source: Bates 1963: 26

awarded large-scale leases to *all* the navy's lands in Elk Hills and Teapot Dome, respectively, to the Pan-American Petroleum and Transport Company controlled by Edward Doheny, the pioneer of the Los Angeles City oilfield, and to Harry Sinclair's Mammoth Oil. Under these leases, Doheny and Sinclair were to pay substantial royalties, from 12.5 to 35 percent in Elk Hills and 12 to 50 percent at Teapot Dome, though the department agreed to commit these in priority to defraying the costs of constructing extensive fuel oil tankage for the navy at Pearl Harbor and in California and a pipeline from Teapot Dome into the Midwest, which the oil companies would thus get free of charge. From the public interest standpoint, the leases have been defended as providing both the best means of ensuring security of supply for the navy at a time when there were serious fears of

Japanese aggression in the Pacific and the most rational use of the reserves from the conservation point of view.[81] Effectively, they permitted unit operation of the naval acreage in Elk Hills and Teapot Dome in the very earliest days of discussion of the unitization concept.[82]

It was a pity, then, that these possibly defensible transactions should have been carried out in secret, with no competition for the leases, and with the assistance of a loan of $100,000 in cash delivered to Fall's office in a "little black bag" by Doheny's son Edward Jr. and cash, bonds, and pedigree livestock provided by Sinclair, all for the development of Fall's New Mexico ranch. Press rumors and political pressure accelerated Fall's resignation and led to a full-scale Senate investigation in 1923–1924 and, after the death of Harding and his succession by Calvin Coolidge, to the appointment of special prosecutors and criminal proceedings against Fall, who was convicted, and Doheny and Sinclair, who were not.[83]

THE MINERAL LEASING ACT OF 1920: COMPETITION VERSUS CONSERVATION

One of the hotly debated issues at the outset of the Teapot Dome scandal was the true extent of the risk of drainage of the contents of the naval reserves through borderline drilling: the greater the risk, the more reasonable were Fall's leases. For the first time, probably, the drainage issue was brought to the attention of a public broader than those professionally involved with the oil and gas industry, and as already noted, the coinage of the term "capture" to describe drainage of oil and gas dates from this period.[84] Some have suggested that it was the political need for the new Coolidge administration to be seen to be doing something about an apparently corrupt (and corrupting) industry with some players powerful enough to buy politicians at the highest level that led in 1924 to the creation of the Federal Oil Conservation Board, whose activities are discussed in the next chapter.[85] Teapot Dome may also be seen as a dramatic epilogue to a weary struggle over the management of federal oil and gas lands waged throughout the period following the Taft land withdrawals, a long-fused bomb whose explosion occurred only after most of the participants had staggered from the scene of their inconclusive combat.

---

[81] Libecap 1984; Trabish 2005.

[82] Stratton 1998: 345. See below, Ch. 9, at 276–80.

[83] Noggle 1962; Bates 1963; Stratton 1998: Chs. 7, 8; Trabish 2005.

[84] Above, Ch. 1, at 10–11.

[85] Libecap 1984: 391; Noggle 1962: 179; Nash 1968: Ch. 4.

After 10 years of legislative initiatives and battles over the treatment to be afforded to oil placer claimants, Congress had finally passed, in 1920, the Mineral Leasing Act, abstracting oil operations on federal lands from the perverse incentives of the 1872 Mining Law. The act also provided for the leasing of coal and certain other minerals, and given the heat generated by the petroleum debate, it is worth recalling at this point that the extent of coal land withdrawals greatly exceeded those related to oil.[86] Even before the act was passed, Congress had breached a decades-old taboo by agreeing in a range of enactments to separate the surface from the mineral estate, a move already urged in 1907 by Secretary of the Interior James Garfield and endorsed by the National Conservation Commission.[87] Acts of 1909 and 1910 allowed limited agricultural entries on coal lands, an approach extended by an act of 1912 to oil, gas, and phosphate land, but only in Utah. This state had apparently been selected as unimportant enough to be the *locus* of an experiment that was generally unappealing to western interests in Congress, who therefore decided "to try it first on the dog."[88] The dog survived, and after a second experiment under 1913 legislation applying only to Idaho, nonmineral patents were in 1914 generally authorized on withdrawn lands containing phosphate, nitrate, potash, oil, gas, or asphaltic deposits, with a reservation to the United States of such deposits.[89]

A further large extension of the principle of the severance of surface and mineral estates was effected in 1916 by the Stock-Raising Homestead Act, under which large areas of federal land hitherto thought unsuitable for homesteading were made available for purchase, but with the mineral rights reserved to the federal government. Some 70 million acres of land have been transferred to private ownership under this act, and much of it is now occupied not by cattle, but by residential property following subdivision.[90] An innovation in the act was provision for compensation to the surface owner in the event of mineral development. The notion thus finally gained acceptance that the title to minerals might be safely and properly separated from the surface and retained for public management.

How was this newfound capacity for continuing management of the nation's remaining public oil and gas resources to be used? Establishing a leasing regime for a petroleum estate that need not be fragmented by the accidents of surface

---

[86] Libecap 1984: 382.

[87] Hibbard 1939: 523–4; National Conservation Commission 1909.

[88] Swenson 1968: 740.

[89] Colby 1915: 288n.

[90] See www.earthworksaction.org/SRHA.cfm (visited August 26, 2009). For strong criticism of the act, with statistics up to 1942, see Gates 1968: 512–23.

boundaries offered an opportunity for an escape from the law of capture. And the time seemed ripe for such an escape: the general problem of drainage from small tracts, leading to competitive drilling and overproduction of a resource now feared to be approaching exhaustion, was of increasing concern to officials in the U.S. Geological Survey,[91] and drainage represented an immediate threat to the navy's prized reserves. Such considerations suggested a leasing policy that would keep to a minimum the number of operators on any given petroleum structure, so that each could explore and produce in a rational manner and cooperation among them, if necessary, could be facilitated. Honestly and competitively awarded, Fall's Teapot Dome lease might not have been far off the mark.

To approach leasing in this way, however, was to collide with a deeply rooted sentiment that was at least as old as the first western mining discoveries and, indeed, can be traced farther back in other controversies about the public lands. This was the profound suspicion of any legal or policy arrangements that might do anything to promote monopoly or the concentration of economic power through property rights in land, or might favor the interests of those already possessing such power ("eastern" capitalists, for example) over the needs of individuals seeking to acquire property through their own effort and labor. That such a sentiment might be acutely felt in relation to oil lands at a time when the Standard Oil monolith had just been broken up by the Supreme Court after 30 years of campaigning by its enemies is hardly surprising, but it would be wrong to assume that it was Standard's methods and success that brought it to life.

The very earliest discussions of what was to be done about the California goldfields, such as the 1850 report to President Zachary Taylor by his California agent Thomas Butler King, a Georgia congressman and former cotton planter and lawyer, evoked the conflict of interest between the worthy but penurious individual miner and the wealthy capitalist acting through paid agents, and generally favored the permitting, leasing, or sale of the mineral lands in tracts small enough to be accessible to individual miners. The desire to erect barriers against any monopolization of mineral lands is apparent in all the proposals for legislation that came forward, both from the federal government and from western interests, up to the passage of the Mining Law (which was shaped by the same concern), and the adequacy of protection against monopolization often seems to have been the key test for critics of such proposals.[92] In this the miners and their champions were doing no more than reflecting the by then well-established national conviction that the only proper end of public land policy was to promote individual settlement and exploitation, and that the law should thus support the industrious squatter

---

[91] Ball 1916: 20; Ball 1917.
[92] Ellison 1968.

against the moneyed purchaser by all reasonable means. Hence the retreat from the early policies of large-scale sales of land to capitalists (which had often been tainted by fraud or bribery),[93] the righteous tones adopted by squatters in announcing the formation of the claims associations designed to defeat purchase by others of "their" land at government sales, and the legislative recognition of such claims in a series of preemption statutes culminating in the general Preemption Act of 1841.[94]

While some of the early efforts at oil exploration in the Appalachians may not have required skills or capital of a different order of magnitude from those needed to travel west, erect a log cabin, and clear and cultivate some acres of land, by 1920 oil exploration and production was a sophisticated and capital-intensive business. Most of the pressure for relief for claims under the placer laws, that supposed bastion of individual enterprise, was coming from large companies such as Union Oil or Standard of California.[95] Yet the old rhetoric of the honest individual toiler versus the monopolizing capitalist could still be voiced—or at least evoked—by participants in the debates on the Mineral Leasing Act and the various unsuccessful proposals that preceded it, and it is clear that on the conservationist side, the trust-busting instinct of politicians like Senator Robert La Follette and campaigners like Gifford Pinchot got the better of the preferences of technicians like the U.S. Geological Survey's Max Ball.[96]

The act that finally emerged in 1920, like some earlier proposals,[97] made a distinction between proven and unproven oil lands, and on proven lands, "situated within the known geologic structure of a producing oil or gas field," it empowered the secretary of the interior to grant leases of 20 years' duration, renewable, by competitive bonus bidding for areas of up to 640 acres, at a royalty of not less than 12.5 percent (section 17). No one could be in any doubt by this time that oilfields might extend to much more than 640 acres—indeed, the section of the act enabling a placer claimant to convert to a lease made explicit provision, by way of exception to the 640-acre limitation, for a lease of up to one-half of the area within the geological oil or gas structure of a producing oil or gas field, subject to a maximum of 3,200 acres (section 18). Competitive development on the same oilfield was thus an essential feature of the act. Its antimonopoly credentials were

---

[93] The most egregious example—though not one involving federal authorities—was perhaps the so-called Yazoo land fraud in Georgia in 1795, in which speculators obtained massive areas of land at 1.25 cents an acre by bribing all save one of the members of the Georgia legislature. A further Georgia act the next year, annulling the sale, was held unconstitutional by the U.S. Supreme Court in *Fletcher v. Peck*, 6 Cranch (10 U.S.) 87 (1810). See Magrath 1966.

[94] Gates 1968: Chs. VII–X; Hurst 1956: 3–7, 35; McGowen 1956: 1–8.

[95] Ise 1926: 346–7.

[96] Above, Ch. 7, text at n. 149.

[97] Colby 1915: 287.

reinforced by limiting the number of leases that might be held by any individual, association, or corporation to one in each producing oil or gas field and three in any one state (section 27).[98]

Apart from the placer conversion provision, the only element of the act that operated in favor of an approach to operations that might be more respectful of reservoir mechanics was the provision for the grant of prospecting permits for unproven land, defined as any land outside the known geological structure of a producing field. Such permits were valid for two years and could cover up to 2,560 acres; at least one well had to be drilled to 2,000 feet within a year (section 13). A permittee who discovered "valuable deposits of oil or gas" was entitled to a lease on favorable terms (5 percent royalty) for a quarter of the permit area and to a "preference right" to a lease for the remainder of the permit land, but for this the permittee might have to compete in a royalty auction with other potential applicants (section 14). Would-be permittees were left to determine for themselves the acreage for which they wished to apply, subject to a broad obligation of "compactness," so a lucky and well-prepared permittee might wind up possessing much or even all of a small oil or gas accumulation.[99]

Another small protection against drainage provided by the act for all permittees and lessees was a prohibition on drilling any well within 200 feet of the boundary unless the adjoining lands were in private hands.[100] Permits and leases were also to be subject "to the further condition that the permittee or lessee will, in conducting his explorations and mining operations, use all reasonable precautions to prevent waste of oil or gas developed in the land, or the entrance of water through wells drilled by him to the oil sands or oil-bearing strata, to the destruction or injury of the oil deposits" (section 16).

Such provisions kept the federal system in line with what, as we shall see in Chapter 9, was emerging as the best current regulatory practice for operations on private land in some of the leading oil states, notably Oklahoma; but as a whole, the scheme of the act represented an almost immediate abandonment of the possibilities for conservation through rational production afforded by unified mineral ownership in the hands of the federal government. As was noted by the

---

[98] This limitation was relaxed as early as 1926 to allow for 2,560 acres to be held within a single field and 7,680 acres in one state: Act of April 30, 1926. Today there is no field-by-field limit; limits per state are 300,000 acres for each of northern and southern Alaska, and 246,080 acres in any other state: 30 U.S.C. §184 (d)(1).

[99] The operation of these provisions was terminated in 1935, however, and unproven lands were thenceforward disposed of—until 1987—in the form of 640-acre leases under a first come, first served system: Act of August 21, 1935.

[100] Section 16. For an earlier federal regulation to similar effect, see below, Ch. 9, at 259 (Indian lands).

conservationist oil industry commentator John Ise, the smallness of the leases under the act was the feature that contrasted most decisively with the laws of most foreign oil-producing countries, such as Persia, India, the East Indies, and much closer neighbors like Mexico and Venezuela, where "at least a degree of monopoly is taken for granted."[101]

It would take another decade of wasteful production, on private as well as public land, before the mainstream of industry opinion, as well as political opinion, could be brought by campaigners for unitization to accept that a monopoly of production from a given field could be balanced by competition between fields. The Federal Oil Conservation Board, in its report of 1930, argued this point at some length in an attempt to convince its readers that unitization was not a first step on the broad road to monopoly.[102] Roger and Diana Olien, in their review of the impact of the conservation movement on the oil industry in this period, quote a 1918 statement from the magazine *Outlook* that the "superlative danger" to oil resources was "not the danger of monopoly [but] the danger of waste." Their general conclusion was that antimonopoly discourse, while important, was distinctly secondary to conservationist discourse.[103] This may be true of discourse, but in terms of action, on the only major change in oil property rights since the beginning of the century, it was antimonopoly sentiment that won out over conservation imperatives. Within 10 years, it would become painfully clear that the need for a solution to the capture problem was just as urgent on federal leases as on private land.

---

[101] Ise 1926: 352. Compare the position in Romania under the 1905–1906 law for leasing of state petroleum lands on a small-tract system: above, Ch. 6, at 155–6.

[102] United States. Federal Oil Conservation Board 1930: 170–1. See also, for a foreign observer's view, Woolnough 1931: 77.

[103] Olien and Olien 2000: 144.

CHAPTER 9

CONSERVATION REGULATION AND THE INSTITUTIONALIZATION OF CAPTURE

INTRODUCTION

Generalizations about the behavior and attitudes of the U.S. oil industry are almost certain to be wrong: the range of companies within the industry, in terms of size, strength, interests, and participation in its varied phases of activity, has been and remains immense, and its dynamism and the pace of external change have been such as to produce constantly shifting constellations of interests. Even the categories commonly used to sort out the players in industry have had an uncertain and shifting content. The term "independent," for example, began life as a means of describing companies that were not affiliated with the Standard Oil empire but later was appropriated by those who wanted to distance themselves from any large companies with overseas operations (and thus plead for protection of domestic production against imports) and now is likely to be used about any producer outside the ranks of the largest 20 or so integrated corporations—the "majors." Thousands of producers, from one-man operations to substantial companies, today fall within this definition.[1] A wildcatter—somebody who is willing to go into unproven territory to drill a well—is not necessarily going to be an independent in this sense, but in fact independents, in the decade from 1969 to 1978, drilled 89.5 percent of new field wildcat wells. "Integrated" has sometimes been used as an antonym for "independent,"[2] but there have at all times been smaller producing companies with integrated operations extending from the wellhead through to the refinery.

In the twentieth-century history of the American oil industry, there have certainly been moments when opinion on a major issue divided rather neatly between large integrated companies and independent domestic producers. The campaign for an oil import tariff mounted in 1929–1930 by the newly formed Independent Petroleum Association of America offers a good example.[3] More often, though, producing interests resisted such neat categorization, and this was particularly true of industry attitudes to conservation and conservation legislation.

In 1927, James Veasey, then chief counsel to the Carter Oil Company, an Oklahoma subsidiary of Standard Oil of New Jersey, suggested that oilmen could be divided into three classes: the ultraconservative individualists, who saw no need either for cooperation with their fellows or for regulation, whatever the circumstances; those ready to undertake intelligent and possibly unselfish cooperation; and those who, despairing of cooperation, were ready to invoke state or federal regulation in order to replace or reinforce it.[4] He tactfully avoided naming names, but while we can now see that independents were far likelier than major companies to be found in the first of these classes, with the opposite result for the second and third, there certainly were plenty of smaller companies that, for one reason or another, favored cooperation or regulation, and at least one major—Gulf—could be fairly classed at that time among the "individualists." Independents in some organizations, such as the Texas Oil and Gas Conservation Association and the Mid-Continent Oil and Gas Association, were rather supportive of conservation policies, while those in the Independent Petroleum Association of Texas and the Independent Oil Operators of Oklahoma were vigorous opponents of prorationing.[5] Within a few years, the obvious inability of the industry to cope by itself with the disturbances caused by the discovery of vast new fields drove ever larger numbers of companies into the third class, but their varying situations meant that the regulatory remedies they sought might point in

---

[1] Olien and Olien 1984: 3–11.
[2] As in Kokxhoorn 1977.
[3] Nordhauser 1979: Ch. IV.
[4] Veasey 1927: 581.
[5] Olien and Olien 2000: 182.

radically different directions; indeed—and this was particularly the case with the major companies—they might at different times prefer different remedies or combinations of remedies.

It is this division of opinion as to the kind of regulatory solutions that should be adopted that is crucial to my story here. At no time has it been possible to identify a single consensus approach to dealing with the "produce at all costs" mentality engendered or at least supported by the rule of capture. As petroleum conservation became a public issue in the 1910s and early 1920s, we can see developing two contrasting lines of thought about the issue, giving rise to different strategies, involving different instruments, and representing profoundly different attitudes to the rule of capture.

The first approach may be called conservative realism. Its proponents began from the position that everything was basically all right. There was no reason to believe that oil resources were subject to early exhaustion; after all, great new fields were being discovered all the time. Cheap oil was thus an unmitigated good; intensive production methods produced more oil overall, not less; no more gas was being flared than was needed to produce the oil that came up with it; waste was not a great problem. But it could be desirable to stabilize the market when flush production from big new fields sent prices plummeting and to clamp down on particular dangerous or undesirable oil field practices. On this view, the key control instrument, for the avoidance of both market instability and the associated waste (notably through losses from surface storage), was the setting of production limits and the allocation of the permitted production among the different producers: prorationing. The need for controls such as those demanding proper casing and plugging of wells was admitted, as indeed was some measure of control over flaring and other wasteful uses of gas, and experiences of town lot drilling also led to support, even among conservative realists, for regulation of the spacing of wells for reasons of safety and amenity. This program treated the rule of capture as a given, possibly even a boon for its effect in stimulating drilling, and certainly not something to be called into question; but as we shall see, capture was a reef on which the policies of adequate spacing of wells, and efficient allocation of production among wells, ran constantly aground.

The other approach may be labeled revolutionary and idealist. The concerns it reflected were principally about waste. Its tenants were a sometimes uneasy coalition of conservationists, federal officials, industry radicals (especially petroleum engineers), and some specialist lawyers. They were far less sanguine than industry leaders about the future of U.S. oil production and were convinced that enormous volumes of oil and gas were being left in the ground by overdrilling. This group laid the blame for waste and disorder in the industry squarely at the door of the principle of capture. It was they indeed who, by reiterated use of the term led us all to talk about capture instead of drainage. For them, the solution to the whole problem lay in one simple measure: unitization. They aimed to make capture irrelevant by securing that each oilfield was developed as a single unit, regardless of the property lines that crossed its surface. Landowners and leaseholders should pool their interests—under legislative compulsion if necessary—so that a single field operator could locate wells regardless of surface boundaries, produce efficiently, and remunerate each interest holder with a share of production and royalties appropriate to that person's share of the resource in place.

In this chapter, I trace the progress of each of these two sets of ideas, against the background of the economic shocks caused by major field discoveries, the growth of scientific and technical knowledge, and not least, the barriers to regulation set up by the U.S. Constitution and state constitutions, as well as the barriers even to private agreement thought to derive from federal and state antitrust laws. Unlike many of the other matters covered in this book, this phase of U.S. oil history has been the subject of an extensive literature that addresses rather directly the issues of petroleum property rights and their effects, which are my core concern. Conservation and capture questions were regularly the subject of articles in the legal and engineering journals of the period and of conference discussions of bodies such as the American Bar Association (ABA) and the American Institute of Mining and Metallurgical Engineers; they also received a number of book-length treatments, notably in a regularly revised and reedited series of studies under the auspices of the ABA titled *Legal History of Conservation of Oil and Gas.*[6] Other significant and influential studies were produced by economists: the early works by George Stocking[7] and John Ise[8] and later reviews and analyses by Erich Zimmermann[9] and Stephen McDonald.[10]

With this wealth of secondary material available, I shall not try to give a comprehensive history of developments in this period, but shall concentrate on those moments and issues that most strongly illuminate the state of thought, practice, and law relevant to the capture principle. I shall thus pass rapidly over certain matters that were highly controversial at the time, notably the issue of federal, as opposed to state, competence to regulate production, which absorbed an enormous amount of industry energy and emotion during the 1930s. Forming an important part of the New Deal politics of the time as well as of oil industry history, the dispute led to the almost inextricable interlacing of arguments about

---

[6] American Bar Association 1938; Murphy 1949; Sullivan 1960.
[7] Stocking 1925.
[8] Ise 1926.
[9] Zimmerman 1957.
[10] McDonald 1971.

states' rights with those about policy for the industry. Its chief importance for the argument and narrative here stems from the fact that the first proponents of unitization promoted federal control of production as a necessary adjunct of a successful unitization plan; when federal control was definitively rejected in 1935, the cause of unitization may likewise have been set back.

THE FEDERAL OIL CONSERVATION BOARD HEARINGS OF 1926 AND THEIR AFTERMATH

The theater for the first public confrontation between these rival approaches was the 1926 hearings of the Federal Oil Conservation Board (FOCB). The board comprised four cabinet officers—the secretaries of the interior, war, navy, and commerce—under the chairmanship of Interior Secretary Hubert Work. President Coolidge announced its establishment in a letter of December 10, 1924, "to study the Government's responsibilities [in relation to the conservation of oil and gas] and to enlist the full cooperation of representatives of the oil industry in the investigation."[11]

The creation of the board has been attributed to Coolidge's desire, as a Republican president, to be seen as doing something about the oil industry in the aftermath of the Teapot Dome scandal.[12] Certainly such a move requires some explanation in light of the reputation of Coolidge's administration as "the most conservative ... in modern American history,"[13] but there were genuine grounds for concern. America had just come through a major war that demonstrated the crucial strategic importance of oil. Production, although it had nearly doubled since the war's end, had just fallen back for the first time since 1906, while consumption had massively increased as a result of a range of factors, notably ever-expanding automobile possession and use (numbers of vehicles had more than doubled, and mileage covered tripled, between 1919 and 1924).[14] What is significant for our purpose is the degree to which Coolidge's announcement "that the present methods of capturing our oil deposits is [sic] wasteful to an alarming degree in that it becomes impossible to conserve oil in the ground under our present leasing and royalty practices if a neighboring owner or lessee desires to gain possession of his deposits"[15] reflected the concerns set out in a letter addressed to

---

[11] The text of the letter is reproduced in Williamson et al. 1963: 311–12.

[12] See above, Ch. 8, at 229–30, and Williamson et al. 1963: 310; Olien and Olien 2000: 157.

[13] Burner 2001: 161.

[14] Williamson et al. 1963: 37, 302, 305, 446–7.

[15] Letter of December 10, 1924, above, n. 11.

him just three months earlier by the oil industry's loudest proponent of a radically changed approach to production and conservation, Henry Doherty.[16]

Doherty was at that time the head of the third-largest integrated oil company in the United States, Cities Service. His preoccupation was with waste of oil through overdrilling, and his proffered solution was unitization. Having seen his ideas summarily rejected in 1923 within the American Petroleum Institute (API), which had been established in 1919 as the industry's representative and research body, he wrote at length to Coolidge in September 1924,[17] pointing to the dangers of premature exhaustion of the nation's oil reserves, and hence of danger to its security interests, by reason of its wasteful methods of oil production. These ills he laid firmly at the door of the common law.

[U]nder our present unfortunate laws each pool as discovered must be immediately devastated. No other property, or product from property, is subject to similar laws except wild birds and animals—and what has happened to our wild birds and animals is rapidly happening to our oil.

Practically every evil of the oil business, and everything about which the public complain, is due to the fact that oil does not follow the usual law of property rights but belongs to the man who can capture it. ... The discovery of an oil pool means that every landowner or lessee can take as much from this common pool as he can get, and there is always a frenzied scramble to bring the oil to the surface before somebody else can get it regardless of whether the market needs it or not.

In consequence, "the first step in conservation must be to provide that ownership shall be determined otherwise than by capture." This was to be achieved, according to Doherty, by making the unitization of oilfields compulsory under federal law. Neither he nor Coolidge, we should notice, made any reference to the small-tract problem to which Max Ball had drawn attention some years earlier,[18] and which made the effects of the rule of capture so noxious.

The FOCB did not hold public hearings until February 1926, but in the meantime, it sent out questionnaires to more than 300 oil companies and industry associations. Doherty and the API were no less active, Doherty presenting his plan for federally imposed compulsory unitization to meetings of a range of national bodies such as the Petroleum Division of the American Association of Mining and Metallurgical Engineers, perhaps the key association of the industry's technical personnel.[19] The API's effort produced a remarkable document entitled *American*

---

[16] See above, Ch. 1, at 9–10.

[17] The text of his letter is reproduced in Hardwicke 1961: 179–90.

[18] Above, Ch. 7, text at n. 149.

[19] Doherty 1925.

Petroleum: Supply and Demand, nicely published as a book in 1925 by the McGraw-Hill Book Company and sometimes known as the Committee of Eleven report. All of the members of this committee were top executives of large oil companies. This report's message, to the board and to the public, was that there was absolutely nothing to worry about. Enormous quantities of oil remained to be discovered in regions as yet unexplored that possessed oil potential or in deeper, still unpenetrated sands in established oil regions. While it was accepted that large quantities of oil had been left in the ground by the production methods used to date, more advanced technology would succeed in recovering a "considerable proportion" of this oil, albeit at higher cost than hitherto. Even if oil reservoirs were drained dry, there would be plenty of oil recoverable from oil shales and, if need be, coal.[20]

So far as the accusations of waste framed by Doherty and earlier conservationist voices were concerned, the committee adopted a pose of injured innocence. Proclaiming that "[w]aste in the production, transportation, refining and distribution of petroleum and its products is negligible,"[21] the committee vaunted the industry's "ceaseless watchfulness" and explained that though the "mad rush" for production within a newly proven field might create an "appearance of confusion" and "an impression of disorganization and consequent inefficiency and loss," this was pure illusion, in that all the oil recovered was safely sent to storage. Moreover, it took the view, in direct opposition to the industry's critics, that the more wells were drilled simultaneously on a given field, the greater the ultimate recovery would be.[22] This, it said, was the majority view among industry experts, and case studies said to support it were discussed in some detail, though curiously this section of the report concluded with a lengthy extract from a technical paper that tended to show the exact opposite: that "if the withdrawal of oil from the structure is rapid ... much greater energy loss [i.e., of gas pressure] will be occasioned per barrel, than if the structure is drained slowly and the differential pressure kept to a minimum."[23] While spreading its evidence and arguments over more than 250 pages, the committee dismissed Doherty's specific proposal of unitization as the solution to most of the industry's problems with a single word: "unattainable."[24]

It may have been the ridicule to which the report of the Committee of Eleven was exposed in some professional quarters[25] that led API's representatives to offer a

---

[20] American Petroleum Institute 1925: 3–5, 7–15.

[21] *Ibid.* 5.

[22] *Ibid.* 24–5.

[23] *Ibid.* 85.

[24] *Ibid.* 24.

[25] Parodies by the geologists L. C. Snider and Everette DeGolyer, at first circulated privately, were later published in the weekly *National Petroleum News* and are reprinted in Hardwicke 1961: 193–201.

rather more nuanced industry view on conservation at the main hearings before the board in February 1926. Its main spokesman on this occasion was Amos Beaty, a lawyer by training and president of the Texas Company. Beaty, entrusted by the API with the review of Doherty's unitization proposals in 1923, had described them in correspondence as "contrary to the spirit of our institutions" and "vicious in principle" and had asserted an "absolute" right of capture.[26] In his presentation to the board, however, he acknowledged that intensive town lot drilling *did* in fact lead to waste, at least in capital investment, and to flooding of markets, and that many more wells were being drilled than was warranted by good practice. Indeed, he disclosed that the API had over the previous three years been trying to develop a legislative proposal for submission to state legislatures that would have empowered state regulatory commissions to limit ex ante the number of wells that could be placed on a declared drilling site and would have enabled surface owners or lessees who were thereby prevented from drilling, and so lost oil to drainage, to obtain compensation.

The proposal had foundered on the drafters' inability to devise means by which such owners and lessees could be prevented from opportunistically subdividing lots so as to increase the rewards they might obtain without incurring the risks and costs of exploration. Whether this was conceived as a milder version of Doherty's proposals is unclear, but it can certainly be seen as the forerunner of the compulsory pooling laws that are now a feature of the laws of almost all oil-producing states.[27] API also favored official support, by way of guarantees of immunity from antitrust proceedings, for agreements to avoid competitive drilling—though at this stage it almost certainly had in mind not unitization, but voluntary production restrictions.[28]

What might be called the "hard" API line was represented at these hearings by E. W. Marland, an oil company president from Oklahoma and member of the Committee of Eleven. Though he had taken the opposite position only three years earlier,[29] Marland vigorously defended intensive drilling as productive of the highest ultimate oil recovery, and painted an idyllic picture of the social benefits of the low-priced oil that was the result and the access to motoring it permitted:

---

[26] Nordhauser 1979: 14–15.

[27] See further below, at 268–75.

[28] United States. Federal Oil Conservation Board 1926a: 10–18.

[29] Marland 1923, and above, Ch. 1, at 10. Marland's enormous drilling programs in West Texas brought his company to the brink of collapse in 1928 and led to his ejection from its management: Myres 1973: 585–8. He later became a Democratic congressman for Oklahoma and then its governor—and a moving spirit behind the creation of the Interstate Oil Compact Commission, below, Ch. 12, at 375–6.

Driving in their flivvers, with their tent and ax, their sack of flour and side of bacon, their fishing rod and frying pan, they are in this day of enervating influence of steam heat and kindred comforts, returning to the hardy manner of life of their pioneer ancestors, gaining health and knowledge and love of country, such as no man ever gains within city walls. ... [As for] city people, who cannot enjoy these long holidays, ... [m]illions of our tired workers and their families get into the country on holidays and Sundays.[30]

Apparently automobiles were used by a quite different class of people in Oklahoma from those in Kansas, the home state of John Ise, author of the strongly conservationist *The United States Oil Policy*, also published in 1926. His motorists were

fat-bellied bankers and *bourgeoisie* riding back and forth, to and from their business, when they need nothing so much as a walk; ... gay boys and girls in questionable joy rides, when they most need a little more companionship with their parents and contact with their homes; ... youthful and ... mature smart Alecks, who find here an exceptionally flashy and effective way of flaunting their wealth before those not so fortunate as themselves; and ... all manner of men and women, who ride about upon our roads and streets in stupid, thoughtless, aimless, pointless diversion, ... when they might be improving their minds with good books or with anything that might tend to mental enlightenment.[31]

Clearly it could only be for such people's own good to keep petroleum in the ground and out of their reach.

Arguments for unitization were presented to the board not only by Henry Doherty, who repeated the points in his letter to Coolidge, but also by Earl Oliver, an executive of Marland's company (where free speech clearly reigned) and scourge of the Pennsylvania judges,[32] and by James Lewis who, as a geologist with the federal Bureau of Mines, had been the coauthor of the first technical paper to propose compulsory unitization as a necessary remedy for oilfield waste.[33] The state of industry feeling about unitization at this time was nicely captured in a remark by Lewis that since entering private practice as a petroleum engineering consultant, he had not publicly advanced any unitization proposals "for fear of harming our reputation as practical operators."[34]

---

[30] United States. Federal Oil Conservation Board 1926a: 81. "Flivver" was a term used to describe a cheap elderly automobile and was particularly attached to Ford's Model T, first produced in 1908.

[31] Ise 1926: 168.

[32] United States. Federal Oil Conservation Board 1926a: 92–108, and see above, Ch. 1, at 13–14. For further papers by Oliver, see Oliver 1930; 1931; 1935; 1937.

[33] United States. Federal Oil Conservation Board 1926a: 49–65; McMurray and Lewis 1916.

[34] United States. Federal Oil Conservation Board 1926a: 65.

When the FOCB issued its first annual report, late in 1926, the API might have congratulated itself that it had won the battle with the reformers. The board saw cooperation as the key to dealing with the industry's problems. It urged the industry to regulate itself, and not to treat antitrust law as any kind of barrier to cooperative action, and invited the states to enact legislation that would cause the orderly development of the oil resources within their borders. It also suggested that Congress put aside any thoughts of legislating for national control of oil production as Doherty had proposed.[35] At the same time, however, the report largely rejected the industry's sunny picture of limitless oil prospects and profound devotion to best practice: *something* had to be done to control production and combat waste. Perhaps for this reason, the editors of the industry's periodical mouthpiece, the *Oil and Gas Journal*, called it a "dangerous report" with "disturbing" suggestions.[36] Henry Doherty had anticipated this kind of reaction, telling Coolidge that oilmen, like bankers, would prefer to work under irrational and damaging laws rather than risk inviting the attention of legislators they viewed as irresponsible.[37]

THE PRORATIONING SOLUTION

In the years following the FOCB's report, the tide of opinion in the industry began to turn, and turn fast. The complacency of the Committee of Eleven vanished with the substantial reductions in rates of profit and dramatic falls in the value of oil company stocks[38] that followed the massive 1926–1927 production increase attributable to the Greater Seminole and West Texas fields. Larger companies and federal officials began to explore together means by which domestic production could be brought under control. The major companies' preferred approach was to secure nationally coordinated agreements to restrict production, and to obtain immunity for such agreements from prosecution under federal or state antitrust law. There is a pleasant irony in the fact that in taking this route, they were espousing one of the original oil conservation proposals in the much maligned 1909 report of David Day on U.S. petroleum resources:[39] Day had suggested—albeit as a conservation rather than price stabilization measure—"limiting by statute the amount that each producer shall extract per acre within a specified time."[40]

---

[35] United States. Federal Oil Conservation Board 1926b.

[36] September 16, 1926: 40, cited in Olien and Olien 2000: 170.

[37] See Hardwicke 1961: 188–9.

[38] Wiliamson et al. 1963: 332–6; Veasey 1927: 579; Work 1927: 567.

[39] Above, Ch. 7, at 203.

[40] Day 1909a: 459.

The FOCB lent a hand by seeking the cooperation of the American Bar Association, which created a nine-member Committee on Conservation of Mineral Resources to study this and other conservation issues. This committee in turn delegated three of its members to serve on another "Committee of Nine," established by the FOCB itself, on which they were joined by three API representatives and three more nominated directly by FOCB. These two committees considered what changes ought to be made in federal and state law to encourage or enforce agreements for "cooperative development," a point I explore later,[41] and to enable prorationing schemes to operate free from the threat of antitrust prosecution. The FOCB Committee of Nine, in early 1928, produced a draft federal law designed to lift this threat from prorationing agreements among producers, if and for as long as the FOCB had declared the existence of a "period of overproduction," and subject to the possibility that the FOCB might declare a particular agreement to be not in the public interest.[42]

For its part, the ABA committee drafted two pieces of model legislation for adoption by states.[43] The first of these gave a broadly similar antitrust immunity both to "cooperative development" agreements (including unitization agreements) and to prorationing agreements entered into during periods of actual or threatened overproduction. This proposal attempted an objective definition of "over-production" and excluded any discretion such as that granted to the FOCB by the Committee of Nine draft. Neither the federal nor the state draft ever achieved enactment, however. So far as prorationing was concerned, the ABA draft had by 1929 already been overtaken in some states by the assumption of explicit state powers to order or approve prorationing schemes, and others would soon follow.[44]

Meanwhile, the API was busy developing plans for a worldwide and permanent production policy that called for the restriction of U.S. production, over the coming years, to 1928 levels. To achieve this aim, the API proposed setting up regional committees across the United States (together with one for Mexico and the northern part of South America) to administer the program, investigate what might be appropriate state regulatory legislation, and look into the suitability of unitization schemes.[45] Members of the API committee that devised this plan were apparently shocked to be told, at a meeting with the FOCB in April 1929, that according to advice received from the attorney general, FOCB endorsement of the

---

[41] Below, at 281–2.

[42] United States. Federal Oil Conservation Board 1929: 18–19.

[43] *Ibid.* 26–49.

[44] Below, at 257–8.

[45] See generally Williamson et al. 1963: 530–2; Yergin 260–9; United States. Federal Trade Commission 1952: 199–218.

plan would do nothing to provide antitrust protection: the board lacked any legal competence of this kind.[46] It is not clear why this should have come as such a shock, as the FOCB Committee of Nine had already indicated that legislation would be needed for this purpose, and no action had been taken on its proposed bill. Whether any informal assurances of antitrust immunity were later given to the industry we do not know; at all events, prorationing schemes were never challenged in the federal courts on this ground.

Another concern driving the larger companies to seek "stabilization" through restriction of domestic production was their desire to protect their position in international crude and product markets in the face of ever-increasing competition fueled by the growth of oil supplies elsewhere—notably in Venezuela, but also in Russia, Romania, and Persia (today's Iran). September 1928 saw the conclusion of an informal agreement drafted by the heads of Standard Oil of New Jersey (apparently acting on behalf of a number of major American companies), the British company Anglo-Persian, and Standard's great rival Royal Dutch Shell to stabilize their shares of world markets—the so-called Achnacarry, or "as is," agreement. The fact that the Achnacarry agreement explicitly excluded the imposition of obligations affecting U.S. imports or its domestic market, out of concern to avoid the sanction of American antitrust law, while the API sought to impose such obligations and to obtain antitrust exemption for its policy, later led the Federal Trade Commission to characterize the U.S. conservation program, as it developed during the 1930s, as the link that needed to be forged to fit the domestic U.S. industry into the cartelized arrangements of the international oil industry.[47]

Whatever the importance of international factors in shaping the attitudes of major companies at this time, it was clear that the Hoover administration, though sympathetic to the industry's woes, was unwilling to act. To the extent that official intervention was needed, the answer would have to be found at the state level. Efforts to orchestrate state action by organizing a conference of governors at Colorado Springs in May 1929 were counterproductive.[48] Western interests used the conference as a platform to complain about the federal government's recent closure of its oil lands and cancellation of permits; independents, who found a powerful voice in Oklahoma oilman Wirt Franklin, denounced the API's plan and the interstate coordination measures that had been proposed in support of it as a monopolistic conspiracy, designed to enable the majors to increase imports at the expense of small domestic producers. The conference broke up without agreement:

---

[46] Nordhauser 1979: 38–42.

[47] United States. Federal Trade Commission 1952: 217, citing Frankel 1969: 116–17 (in 1st ed. 1946); Blair 1977: 156–64.

[48] On the conference, see generally Nordhauser 1979: 42–6; Olien and Olien 2000: 178–9.

for the time being, at least, stabilization efforts would have to depend on the willingness of individual states to support the policy and on the mechanisms each might have available for this purpose.

CONSERVATION IN THE STATES: AGENCIES AND POWERS

By 1929, several of the leading oil-producing states had significantly advanced their petroleum conservation policy beyond the sparse and rudimentary regulations in force in the first years of the century. At the time of the 1909 governors' conference, for example,[49] the only regulations one could confidently expect to find in all oil-producing states were those designed to prevent damage to reservoirs by water ingress, by way of requirements as to the casing and plugging of wells. A few states, led by Indiana, had also legislated—not always effectively—to prevent wastage in the form of flaring or venting of unwanted natural gas. But in the next decade or so, Oklahoma, where the disturbance created by the discovery of large new pools was greatest, led the way toward a much more comprehensive and effective approach to oil and gas regulation. Two key elements were involved: a general obligation on the industry to avoid conduct productive of "waste"; and the conferment, on a state regulatory agency, of a real capacity to promote and enforce such conduct by framing and implementing more detailed rules with this objective.

As we have seen,[50] Oklahoma in 1915 adopted statutes relating, respectively, to conservation of oil and of gas, each of which adopted a broad definition of waste. That for oil encompassed "in addition to the ordinary meaning, ... economic waste, underground waste, surface waste, and waste incident to the production of oil or petroleum in excess of transportation or market facilities or reasonable market demands"; that for gas included venting, flaring, water flooding of gas strata, underground waste, and "wasteful utilization."[51] By 1920, two other leading oil states had adopted comparably broad—but not identical—definitions of waste, Texas in 1919, Louisiana in 1918 for gas and 1920 for oil. The fourth major producer, California, had prohibited, by an act of 1911, the "unnecessary or

---

[49] Above, Ch. 7, at 202.

[50] *Ibid.* at 201.

[51] Texts of conservation statutes up to the end of 1932 are conveniently collected in Ely 1933b, though the incorporation of the statutes into codified compilations of legislative provisions sometimes obscures the date of enactment of a specific legislative change. See under "Principal Laws, Regulations, and Treaties Cited" in the References section (below, at 477–9) for detailed references to the state conservation laws mentioned in these paragraphs. The relevant provisions of the Oklahoma oil statute are also reproduced in Williamson et al. 1963: 321–2.

wasteful escape of gas" but failed to develop any general definition of waste during this time.

So far as enforcement agencies were concerned, the states followed contrasting paths. Although California was slow to develop a substantive law of conservation, it did equip itself in 1915 with a specialized administrative structure to deal with oil and gas regulation, establishing an appointive office of state oil and gas supervisor within its Department of Natural Resources. The supervisor worked in association with a board of commissioners for each of five districts, elected by industry interests and empowered to enforce and hear appeals from orders of the supervisor. Louisiana followed a similar path. The state already had an office of conservation, established in 1908 with responsibility for all of its natural resources, and it was natural that this agency, which in 1916 became the Department of Conservation, headed by an appointed commissioner, should assume control of oil and gas matters when Louisiana's first legislation was enacted in 1912.

Oklahoma and Texas approached the issue of a conservation agency from a different direction. In each of these states, early interventions in the industry took the form of a control on the activity of pipeline companies in the form of a ratable taking law, compelling pipelines to take from each producer the same proportion of the oil or gas being offered for carriage. Against this background, it was natural, if the state already possessed an agency entrusted with the regulation of monopolistic public utilities, to charge it with the enforcement of such a law. This was how the Oklahoma Corporation Commission, established in 1907 by article 9 of the new state's constitution to regulate public utility corporations such as railroads and telegraphs, got its foothold in oil and gas regulation, at the time of enactment of the state's ratable taking law of 1909. Its jurisdiction in the field rapidly expanded thereafter as the problems of the Cushing and Healdton fields showed the need for broad regulatory powers.[52] For the last century, the oil and gas industry has doubtless been the commission's most important field of activity, but it continues to regulate public utilities like electricity, gas distribution, telecommunications, and transport.

Texas likewise looked to its public utility agency when it passed its first comprehensive petroleum conservation act in 1919. Earlier legislation to prevent water intrusion passed in 1899 and 1905 had made no provision for continuing supervision and appears to have had little positive effect.[53] In 1917, however, the Texas legislature had passed an act to impose common carrier status on oil pipelines in the state, the legal consequence being that the pipelines would thereby be bound to accept consignments, on nondiscriminatory terms, from any producer

---

[52] Above, Ch. 7, at 199–201.
[53] King 1970: 71–2; Warner 1939: 58–9.

who offered them. Not unnaturally, the responsibility for administering the act was placed on the body already concerned with public transportation utilities, the Texas Railroad Commission. But the act also treated as an emergency the level of waste that was being recorded in Texas oilfields and empowered the commission to promulgate rules to prevent such waste and dangerous practices in the oilfields.[54] Further, more wide-ranging legislation was enacted in 1919, prohibiting waste of oil and gas in general terms and giving the commission large rulemaking and enforcement powers.[55]

Both the Oklahoma Corporation Commission and the Texas Railroad Commission are elected bodies, with three commissioners serving staggered six-year terms and competing in statewide popular elections. This may seem an odd way to recruit a body charged with a task of expert and continuous administrative supervision, and David Prindle, in his detailed study of the Texas Railroad Commission, has noted how the commission's lack of a competent and sufficiently numerous specialist staff during the crisis period of Texas overproduction in the 1930s gravely impaired the efficacy of its response. But his description of it as being, up to that time, "largely a sinecure for over-the-hill Texas politicians"[56] does it scant justice. Its members when it received its new responsibilities in 1919 had been first elected or appointed to it at an average age of 38, and whatever hills they may previously have descended, they were vigorous enough to produce draft conservation rules, hold a hearing of operators, and promulgate the rules, all within 100 days of the passage of the 1919 act.[57]

In addition, popular election may well have acted as a brake on the oft-documented tendency of regulatory bodies to become identified, sooner or later, with the interests of the industry they are supposed to regulate rather than with those of the general public. Analysts of this phenomenon have likewise appropriated the useful metaphor of capture and refer to it as "regulatory capture."[58] In the oil industry in Texas, the notion that underlies this literature, of an opposition between public and private interest, was hardly appropriate. That state's position, over most of the twentieth century, as by far the largest oil producer in the United States meant that the interests of the general public in Texas, and those of the oil industry, were largely identical; the weight of consumer interest was spread across the rest of the United States. The true cleavage, hinted at

---

[54] Warner 1939: 64–5; Hardwicke 1938: 217–18. See also Prindle 1981: 20, and Olien and Olien 2002: 55–6, who view the act as part of a compromise between independent producers and integrated companies.

[55] Warner 1939: 67.

[56] Prindle 1981: 32.

[57] Warner 1939: 67–8.

[58] For recent surveys of a voluminous literature, see Dal Bo 2006; Levine 1999.

in an address by Commissioner Olin Culberson in 1941, was between the interests of the people of Texas and the independent, homegrown, and state-capitalized sector of the oil industry on the one hand, and the consuming public of the United States and the major oil companies, controlled by out-of-state capital, on the other.[59]

Given this lineup, it is not surprising that the commission, over the vital decades since 1930, should have consistently favored the independent operators and small landowners over the interests of larger companies, even when, as we shall see, this choice ran counter to an effective conservation policy. The election process must have reinforced this orientation, but it was not a prerequisite for it. Even appointed commissioners loyal to their states probably would have acted in the same way, and indeed, the great majority of commissioners between 1930 and 1980 were initially appointed by the governor because of the tendency of existing commissioners to retire or die in midterm. Oklahoma commissioners, one might note, have seemed to be more likely to depart, whether by defeat or retirement, at election time, so that state has had far fewer gubernatorial appointments. Prindle's study of Texas appointments makes it clear that while a candidate to whom the industry was hostile would not be appointed, the positive preferences of the industry, as expressed in consultations, were seldom followed.[60]

PRORATIONING OF PRODUCTION

This was the framework within which a divided industry approached its problems of dealing with excessive production and declining demand as the Great Depression overcame the country in 1929. That the industry's attitudes at such a time should have been driven by a desire to preserve activity and profits rather than protect future generations through improved oilfield practice is hardly surprising, but they are important in explaining the form assumed by conservation measures in the crucial decade of the thirties. Capture was at the root of the problems these measures were trying to address, but the need for quick-acting solutions meant that the approach chosen was one in which the symptoms of the malaise were forcibly suppressed while the underlying sickness went untreated.

That approach was state-by-state restriction of production, and the legal basis on which the industry sought to rest it was the prevention of waste. Oklahoma's 1915 oil conservation statute conveniently included in its definition "waste incident to the production of crude oil or petroleum in excess of transportation or

---

[59] Prindle 1981: 49.
[60] *Ibid.* 156–9.

marketing facilities or reasonable market demands."[61] Schemes permitting control on this latter basis have been generally referred to as "market-demand prorationing." Not every oil-producing state was prepared to accept market demand as an appropriate basis for production restrictions. The association of the two notions was uncomfortably suggestive of official endorsement of monopolistic price fixing. The Texas statute of 1919 had omitted this basis for control, Louisiana explicitly admitted it only for gas, and California never succeeded in passing any kind of prorationing statute, though it is said to have achieved prorationing "to a limited extent" by voluntary agreement through the Conservation Committee of California Oil and Gas Producers.[62]

Whether based on production in excess of market demand or on the risk of some other form of waste, either physical or economic, prorationing involved dividing up the permissible production among producers from a common source. Proration orders were drafted after hearings by the relevant commission, were elaborately reasoned, and reflected considerable input by producers. Indeed, producers—where they could agree—effectively designed the structures employed. In the first proration order, No. 920 of June 5, 1915, made by the Oklahoma Corporation Commission in relation to the Healdton field, the restrictions were applied by gauging the potential production of each well and reducing its output to the same fraction of that potential as was being applied to the field as a whole.[63] Assessing well potentials took time, and some large new fields, like Oklahoma City and later East Texas, were initially prorated simply by dividing the permitted production by the number of wells. Thus, the order for the Oklahoma City field, issued after imposing an initial 30-day shutdown, provided for proration on a "time basis," with each well allowed to run wide open for a proportion of a given period—initially a week—corresponding to the permitted fraction of fieldwide potential. This was initially 40 percent, allowing wells to be run 2.8 days a week; within a year, it was down to 2.75 percent, so that an operator could run its wells for only 8 hours in any 12-day period.[64] This must at least have helped reduce labor costs.

The first experiences with prorationing in Texas did not occur until 1927, when operators on the isolated Yates field in West Texas, under the leadership of William Farish of Humble Oil, agreed a voluntary prorationing scheme for the field. Originally based solely on well potentials, it was almost immediately modified so as to allocate only 75 percent of the total allowable to wells, the remainder being

---

[61] Ely 1933b: 288–91.
[62] Williams 1952: 1160.
[63] German 1928: 129–33.
[64] *Ibid.* 153, 158, 170.

allocated on an acreage basis by reference to 100-acre "units" into which the field was divided. This was done because operators had immediately started drilling extra wells to increase their allowable production.[65] The logic of this is easily grasped. Assume you are a producer in a 100,000-barrel-a-day field where there are 100 wells, and that the allowable total production has been limited to 20,000 barrels (20 percent). You have one well producing 1,000 barrels a day. With your one well, you are allowed to produce 20 percent of its potential: 200 barrels. If you drill a second well likewise capable of producing 1,000 barrels, the overall allowable will decline to 19.8 percent (because the field is now a 101,000-barrel-a-day field), but if no one else does as you did, you can now produce 396 barrels (2 × 198). Of course, in the absence of any official power to control the drilling of new wells, everyone is likely to do as you did until the per-well allowable has come down to a point where drilling costs can no longer be recovered over a reasonable period. An acreage element dampens this tendency by making part of each producer's allowable dependent on the acreage held rather than the number of wells drilled.

Adjusted for this acreage element, and with administration placed in the hands of the Railroad Commission, the Yates field arrangement appears to have worked well. That there were only 20 operators on a field extending to some 20,000 acres and having a potential production of up to 500,000 barrels a day must have helped.[66] A very different story attached to the Hendrick field in the far west of Texas, discovered at about the same time, which promoters had split into 5-acre tracts that they sold by mail order and to which a large number of operators had been attracted by a promising wildcat in totally unexpected territory. Extensive competitive drilling went on in the 18 months after the field was opened in July 1926. A serious problem of water intrusion on the edges of the field, coupled with the general slide in oil prices, led operators to seek the help of the Railroad Commission in early 1928. In May, the commission issued its first formal proration order, basing allowable production principally on the potential of each well, with some adjustment for acreage. But the allowables were set too high, and initially the commission did not control the number of wells that could be drilled, with the result that the number steadily increased according to the logic I have just described.[67] The reasons for this failure of control will become clear when we examine the use of well spacing regulations in Texas.

---

[65] Myres 1973: 459–60; Olien and Olien 2002: 156.

[66] Myres 1973: 460–3.

[67] *Ibid.* 487–504; Warner 1939: 295–6; Olien and Olien 2002: 158–61. For other local prorationing attempts at this time, see Myres 1973: 419 (Howard-Glasscock field); Warner 1939: 240–1 (Panhandle), 264–5 (Darst Creek).

The Oklahoma Corporation Commission made its first statewide proration order in September 1928. Texas followed in August 1930, but in the intervening two years, and notwithstanding the need for control manifested by the local prorationing initiatives just mentioned, the Texas legislature had actually restricted the conservation powers of the Railroad Commission, qualifying the very general reference to waste in the 1919 act with a 1929 amendment providing that waste should not be construed to include "economic waste." This may seem a bizarre thing to have done at a time of obvious overproduction and falling prices, but there was deep suspicion in Texas, as there had always been, of the large out-of-state oil companies like the various Standard companies and their subsidiaries, and the idea that such companies might be promoting a national, indeed worldwide, monopolistic scheme to raise oil prices was fueled by the API's control plan for U.S. oil production.[68] It may be no coincidence that this rejection of the notion of "economic waste" came just two weeks after the API's plan was unveiled at a meeting in Houston in March 1929.[69]

In the following year, the legislature took a step in the opposite direction, however, by passing a "common purchaser" act, under which purchasers who were common carriers or affiliated with such carriers (e.g., pipeline companies) must purchase oil ratably from producers without discrimination. It was against this confused legal background that the Railroad Commission made its 1930 order to restrict production in the state to 750,000 barrels a day—a cut of only 50,000 barrels from the previous year's average. The order recited that limitation of production to levels of reasonable market demand was necessary to prevent waste, in such forms as wastage of oil in surface storage, through evaporation and leakage, and underground waste as by loss of gas pressure and water invasion.[70]

It took only a few days for a producer to mount a challenge against the legality and constitutionality of this order.[71] The plaintiff was the Danciger Oil and Refining Company, which held oil leases in the panhandle. Here, by late 1930, the commission's order, as renewed and revised, permitted production of 64,616 barrels a day out of a state total of 680,238. In terms of the profile of the plaintiff, a small producer with its own refining capacity, the suit was a precise echo of two earlier Oklahoma cases in which the same kind of company had challenged, unsuccessfully, the Oklahoma City field proration orders: *Julian Oil and Royalties*

---

[68] Above, at 271–2.

[69] Olien and Olien 2002: 181–2; United States. Federal Trade Commission 1952: 211–13.

[70] Hardwicke 1938: 222–3.

[71] *Danciger Oil & Refining Co. v. Railroad Commission of Texas*, 49 S.W. 2d 837 (Tex. Civ. App. 1932).

Co. v. Capshaw (1930)[72] and *Champlin Refining Co. v. Corporation Commission of Oklahoma* (1932).[73] One writer indeed suggested in 1938 that "almost without exception, it has been concerns ... owning both production and a refinery in reach of their production, that have sought in recent years to defeat conservation movements."[74]

The Supreme Court of Oklahoma in the first of these cases, and the U.S. Supreme Court in the second, had sustained the orders as a reasonable use of the police power to prevent waste of petroleum and had rejected suggestions that they constituted disguised price-fixing measures. In *Champlin*, moreover, the Supreme Court's opinion expressly rejected the company's argument that its investment in a pipeline and refinery, which put it in a position to produce oil when others, for want of offtake facilities, could not, entitled it to any special consideration:

> Plaintiff insists that it has a vested right to drill wells upon the lands covered by its leases and to take all the natural flow of oil and gas therefrom so long as it does so without physical waste and devotes the production to commercial uses. But if plaintiff should take all the flow of its wells, there would inevitably result great physical waste, even if its entire production should be devoted to useful purposes. The improvident use of natural gas pressure inevitably attending such operations would cause great diminution in the quantity of crude oil ultimately to be recovered from the pool. Other lessees and owners of land above the pool would be compelled, for self-protection against plaintiff's taking, also to draw from the common source and so to add to the wasteful use of lifting pressure. And because of the lack, especially on the part of the non-integrated operators, of means of transportation or appropriate storage and of market demand, the contest would, as is made plain by the evidence and findings, result in surface waste of large quantities of crude oil.[75]

In relation to capture, this was a crucial finding by the nation's highest court, insofar as it confirmed that prorationing schemes could properly nullify the ability of producers with outlets for their oil to drain the holdings of those less fortunate. This was the situation in the Cushing field that had set Oklahoma on the path to prorationing in the first place.

In the *Danciger* case, however, the Texas commission faced a more formidable challenge than its Oklahoma counterpart, by reason of the express Texas exclusion of economic waste from the commission's purview. In fact, this did not prevent either the district court or the Texas Court of Civil Appeals from finding in favor of the commission, holding that the order was directed to reducing the physical

---

[72] 145 Okla. 237, 292 P. 841.
[73] 286 U.S. 210.
[74] German 1938: 166.
[75] 286 U.S. 210, at 233.

waste that was taking place in the field, and that to use market demand as an "economic standard … bear[ing] a direct or reasonable relationship to physical waste" for the purpose of determining by how much production should be restricted was a legitimate choice among possible methods and did not amount to attacking economic waste.[76] The victory, however, was a completely hollow one. By the time the decision was handed down, the biggest field of all, East Texas, had been opened up in October 1930 by the wildcatter "Dad" Joiner, and the events that followed had reduced the commission to a state of utter helplessness.[77]

This field was a regulator's nightmare. The biggest ever discovered in the United States, it was easily accessible to markets and transportation, situated in an area where tracts of land were relatively small, and because the Woodbine sand that underlay the area had proved disappointing elsewhere, it was of little initial interest to large companies, so that very large numbers of independent operators came into the field in its first months. It also was most unusual in being a water drive field, where the pressure driving the oil to the surface came mainly from water held in the sands to the west of the field. The limited scientific understanding of this type of action in 1930 added further to the problem of finding an adequate technical and legal basis for control.

When the commission eventually got around to issuing a proration order for the field in April 1931, operators reacted angrily, with many simply ignoring the order and many others going to law to get the courts to quash it—not, however, to the state district court, which had already sustained proration in the *Danciger* case, then under appeal, but to the federal district court for the Western District of Texas, at Austin. Here the operators dealt a heavy blow to proration and the commission by obtaining from the three-judge court, in *Macmillan v. Railroad Commission of Texas* in July 1931,[78] a finding directly contrary to the one in *Danciger*, to the effect that such orders had no reasonable relation to physical waste, and dismissing the extensive scientific and practical evidence relating to water intrusion and loss of pressure as "theory and speculation." Not only did competitive drilling on the field run out of control after this decision, but the legislature, which had been discussing in a special session a more comprehensive petroleum conservation bill incorporating express powers of market demand proration, was persuaded by the governor, and by what had been a minority opposing proration as a monopolizing device of the big companies, to pass what became known as the Anti-Market Demand Act of 1931, expressly forbidding the

---

[76] Above n. 71, at 843.

[77] See generally Smith 2008; Olien and Olien 2002: 166–92, and for the legal details, Hardwicke 1938: 228–47.

[78] 51 F. 2d 400 (W.D. Tex. 1931).

commission to consider market demand in any prorationing scheme. By the time this act was passed on August 12, the East Texas field was producing a million barrels a day, one-third of the entire demand of the United States.[79]

There is no need to retell here the violent and muddled story of the next few months, in which commission orders were routinely overturned by the federal district court, competitive drilling went ahead at suicidal rates, and control was secured—but only temporarily, as that same court struck it down—by a declaration of martial law that sent troops into the field. Things improved a little after the legislature reversed itself in November 1932 and passed the Market Demand Act, under which economic waste could be taken into account and proration by reference to market demand was expressly authorized. The commission's subsequent proration orders for the field continued, however, to be the subject of successful challenge in the federal district court, principally on the ground that the method of allocation of the field total under these orders was unreasonable and arbitrary. Perhaps because of the uncontrolled proliferation of wells in the field, the commission's first prorationing order after martial law was declared, that of September 1931, simply divided the field allowable, set at around 400,000 barrels a day, by the number of wells, regardless of their potential. This was considered grossly unfair by those with the better wells, but the commission persisted in this method even after the 1932 act eliminated the market demand problem that had been the main basis for the suits against it up to that date. Only in April 1933 did it recognize differing well potentials, assessing allowables for what by then amounted to 10,000 wells on the field on the basis of measurements taken from a few hundred sample wells.

It was on the basis of this method of proration, and a field allowable of some 450,000 barrels, that the commission finally succeeded in early 1934 in obtaining, from the federal district court for the Eastern District, an endorsement of a prorationing order, in the case of *Amazon Petroleum Co. v. Railroad Commission of Texas*, where the opinion of Judge Hutcheson contained a useful summary of the court's earlier negative decisions.[80] Hutcheson, a former mayor of Houston, was a progressive Democrat firmly convinced of the monopolizing tendencies of "big oil," which he saw as using scientific evidence to obfuscate its projects of price maintenance and market control. A consistent and acerbic critic of the commission since his opinion in the *Macmillan* case, he could not resist a parting swipe at it: "[T]he record of their proceedings exhibits more of supplicativeness and wavering and less of firmness and administrative vigor than might well be expected of them in the discharge of their great function as statutory agents of Texas for the

---

[79] Hardwicke 1938: 229–32.
[80] 5 F. Supp. 633 (E.D. Tex. 1934).

conservation and protection, in the private and public interest, of the state's natural resources of oil and gas."[81]

But he sustained the commission's order as being within the limits of its administrative discretion, his decision was not appealed, and the commission's control, with a reasonable level of protection against waste, could be reasserted over the East Texas field. How effective that control was on the ground was another matter. The confusion of the three preceding years had been such that many operators thought it quite natural to produce without regard for their allowables, and they continued with such practices, adopting an extraordinary variety of expedients, such as pipelines dug and laid in the middle of the night, to defeat production inspections and get their "hot oil"[82] to market. Despite these maneuvers, many of them retained an unimpaired sense of righteous justification. In the course of the House of Representatives' Cole Committee's nationwide inquiry into the oil business in 1934—an inquiry whose failure to subject the evidence submitted to rigorous testing by cross-examination led Robert Hardwicke to characterize it as no more than "a travelling Wailing Wall"[83]—it received at one stop in East Texas a submission from a lawyer who claimed to represent "the legitimate violators of the law": the Texas hot oil producers.[84]

Considerable success in reducing hot oil running was achieved in the brief period of federal regulation of oil production, which lasted from the promulgation in September 1933 of the Code of Fair Competition for the Petroleum Industry (known as the Petroleum Code) under the National Industrial Recovery Act of 1933 until May 1935, when the Supreme Court, in *Schechter Poultry Co. v. United States*,[85] held the 1933 act and its code system invalid and effectively ended federal power over production. The Cole Committee had already shelved the suggestion of a more permanent and specialized system of federal control for the industry,[86] so that until the Second World War, federal intervention was limited to controlling the movement of hot oil in interstate commerce under the Connally Act, passed in 1935 in substitution for earlier powers invalidated by the Supreme Court in *Panama Refining Co. v. Ryan*.[87] In the absence of federal competence, the producing states established their own advisory mechanism for coordination of production restrictions in the shape of the Interstate Oil Compact Commission, on which I shall have more to say in Chapter 12.

---

[81] *Ibid.* at 637.
[82] This refers to oil produced in contravention of applicable regulations.
[83] Hardwicke 1938: 248.
[84] Pettengill 1936: 6.
[85] 295 U.S. 495 (1935).
[86] Extracts from its report appear in Pettengill 1936: 287–300.
[87] 293 U.S. 388 (1935).

WELL SPACING

Prorationing was to remain the key weapon in the regulator's armory until, in the face of declining production and the increasing need for imports, most of the Texas fields were allowed to run wide open from March 1971. Even today, the argument continues as to whether it was really a conservation measure or simply a lightly disguised system of protection and price maintenance for the American oil industry in general and small Texas producers in particular.[88] My concern here is less with this question than with the relationship between the prorationing policy and the rule of capture, and to understand this properly, it is necessary to show how prorationing was linked to another control device available to at least some regulatory authorities in the 1920s and 1930s, that of the spacing of wells.

In Europe, as I have shown, the idea that a minimum spacing between oil wells should be imposed by regulation goes back at least to the late 1880s and perhaps even functioned earlier.[89] In the United States, despite (or perhaps because of) familiarity with the sight of derricks jammed together in flush fields, and despite the often realized risks of destruction by fire, the first spacing regulations did not appear until November 1915. They formed part of a set of regulations made by the secretary of the interior to govern operations by the lessees of Indian lands in Oklahoma.[90] The regulations were largely modeled on the Oklahoma Corporation Commission's conservation rules, promulgated as Order 937 a couple of months earlier, but those rules made no provision for well spacing. (There was in fact no provision for the control of spacing on private land in Oklahoma until close spacing appeared in the Oklahoma City field in 1930, when control was imposed by way of a city ordinance.)[91] This spacing rule, which prohibited drilling within 300 feet of a property line and hence allowed a maximum of one well on every 8.25 acres, appears—like West Virginia's pioneer 1871 well plugging legislation[92]—to have been forgotten. By reason of the enormous amount of controversy and litigation it was later to produce, all attention has instead been focused on the next spacing rule to appear, Rule 37 of the Texas Railroad Commission, promulgated in November 1919 as part of an addition to its first set of rules. In its initial formulation, it read:

---

[88] See 1 Bradley 1996: Ch. 3, and for earlier discussions, authorities cited in Williams 1952: 1163, n. 31.

[89] Above, Ch. 6, at 146–8.

[90] German 1938: 146.

[91] *Ibid.* 161; Franks 1980: 147.

[92] Most commentators (e.g. Summers 1938: 1) erroneously identify the Pennsylvania statute of 1878 as the first to impose casing and plugging requirements and, therefore, the first conservation statute.

No well for oil or gas shall hereafter be commenced nearer than ... 300 feet to any other completed or drilling well on the same or adjoining tract or farm; and no well shall be drilled nearer than ... 150 feet to any property line; provided, that the Commission, on petition filed, showing good cause, and provided that no injustice will be done, may after hearing had, upon notice to adjoining tract owners or lessees, allow drilling within shorter distances than as above described. Rule 37 shall not for the present be enforced within the developed and defined oil fields known as the Gulf Coast fields.[93]

The promulgation of this rule at this time may owe much to the chaotic and intense drilling that had occurred with the discovery in July 1918 of a substantial oilfield extending under the North Texas town of Burkburnett. By the beginning of 1920, 1,200 wells had been drilled on 1,500 acres, sometimes at the density of five or six wells to the acre. What this sort of town lot drilling entailed for the inhabitants emerges from the case of *Grimes v. Goodman Drilling Co.* in 1919, an attempt by a Burkburnett resident to secure the removal of a well drilled in his front yard. Among the inconveniences of which he complained was that the noise of the engine driving the drill was so loud that he and his family could converse only by shouting, and that the engine's boiler had been placed so close to an outer door giving access to his bedroom that he could not open it. The court denied relief because he had known that the land was subject to an oil lease when he bought it; had the defendants not drilled where they did, oil under the lot might have been lost to neighbors.[94] U.S. Bureau of Mines engineers have estimated that one well for every 5 acres would have been sufficient to drain the Burkburnett field.[95] (A little calculation will show that Rule 37, in its original form, provided for one well on every 2 acres, four times the density under the earlier Indian lands rule.) The early exhaustion of the field was accompanied by four fires in 1919 alone. Whether or not the rule was actually suggested by producers, it received support almost immediately from a committee of the Mid-Continent Oil and Gas Association, a producer body, which in 1920 recommended the rule's application to two specific districts in order to prevent water incursion and fire risk from closely spaced wells.

The first reported litigation on Rule 37 occurred in 1927, when the lessee of a narrow strip of land rather more than 3 acres in area, on which the rule would have prohibited the drilling of any wells, sought damages from the federal courts in Texas on the ground that Rule 37 infringed its property right to drill wells on its land, contrary to the Fourteenth Amendment. The lessee had in fact been

---

[93] Printed in Harrison 1970: 361, who identifies it as the first U.S. spacing rule.
[94] 216 S.W. 202 (Tex. Civ. App. 1919).
[95] Stocking 1925: 157–8.

successful in obtaining from the commission an exception from Rule 37 enabling the drilling of four wells but claimed that in the time required for this procedure, the oil under its land had been largely drained by its neighbor. In rejecting the complaint on appeal, the Circuit Court of Appeals viewed the rule as being based on the power of the commission to make rules "to require wells to be drilled and operated in such manner as to prevent injury to adjoining property"[96] and cited the *Ohio Oil Co.* and *Lindsley v. Natural Carbonic Gas Co.*[97] cases as providing constitutional justification, a choice that clearly evokes a "correlative rights" rationale for the rule.[98] The decision of the court below had been even more explicit in referring to the drainage of oil from under neighboring properties that would result from the placing of wells on this narrow strip.[99] When, however, state as opposed to federal courts in Texas came to review the rule and its application, as occurred in relation to this same order in *Railroad Commission of Texas v. Bass*,[100] they preferred to rest the justification of the rule on protection against such physical waste and damage as might arise from fire or water incursion, a rationale which, though somewhat forced, had the practical merit of not requiring the court to think about the awkward relationship between spacing and capture.

That the rule was from the beginning seen by the commission as having a broad conservation purpose is indicated by its first decision, in December 1919, on an application for a Rule 37 exception. On an application to drill a specific offset well, the commission, with the parties' agreement, took into account the situation of three abutting lease properties and, "in accordance with the most approved development practices and the best interests of all concerned in the economic development of their respective leases," settled the number of permitted additional wells and minimum well distances on all three.[101] It seems clear that the commission was aiming to achieve an equitable distribution of the parties' chances to capture the oil in that part of the field through the wells on their respective leases, in a case where one party with a relatively narrow strip of land was in danger of being drained by its neighbors, the reverse of the position in the *Oxford Oil Co. v. Atlantic Oil Producing Co.*

Within two years of the promulgation of the rule, its wording had been changed so as to be distinctly more favorable to the applicant for an exception: whereas the power of the commission to grant an exception had been discretionary ("the

---

[96] Ely 1933: 340.

[97] Discussed above, Ch. 7, at 181–4, 188–90.

[98] *Oxford Oil Co. v. Atlantic Oil Producing Co.*, 22 F. 2d 597 (5th Cir. 1927).

[99] 16 F. 2d 639 (N.D. Tex. 1926); and see an anonymous comment, Anon. 1927: 328.

[100] 10 S.W. 2d 586 (Texas Civ. App. 1928). For later cases, see Brin 1934: 120.

[101] Warner 1939: 68, and 315–17, where the decision is printed in full.

Commission ... *may* ... allow drilling within shorter distances"), and the criterion of "injustice" was presented as a constraint on that power ("provided that no injustice will be done"), the 1921 wording had a quite different structure, stating that "the Commission *will* grant exceptions ... to permit drilling within shorter distance ... whenever the Commission shall determine that such exceptions are necessary either to prevent waste or to protect vested rights" (emphasis added).

Here there is no discretion once the determination as to waste or protection of rights has been reached and no balancing consideration for the position of neighbors of the applicant. I have found nothing to indicate why the commission made this early and rather substantial change in its rule, but it seems likely, in view of the consistent tenderness it later showed to small-tract owners in prorationing as well as spacing decisions, that it came under considerable early pressure from owners and lessees with existing tracts of a size and shape that made drilling an offset well, or sometimes any well, impossible without an exception. Stocking reported that by 1925, 2,250 applications for exceptions had been submitted, of which 9 in every 10 had been granted.[102]

CAPTURE AS A CONSTITUTIONALLY PROTECTED PROPERTY RIGHT

One can readily see the legal and constitutional difficulties faced by the commission in refusing a Rule 37 exception in a case where no well could be drilled on a tract without one. The result would certainly be that the oil under the tract would be drained by operations on neighboring land. Although Texas courts had followed the national trend and recognized the law of capture in 1911,[103] and by implication the notion that offset drilling was the only protection against it, they had also held that oil while in place was the property of the surface owner.[104] Forbidding drilling that would protect against drainage thus clearly amounted to a taking of property, and while it was already established that such a taking of petroleum property might be justified by considerations of public safety,[105] and perhaps for other public purposes also, there had been no sign that courts would be prepared to sustain such action purely on grounds of waste.

At this time, in fact, the majority of oilmen and, as we have seen, some technical specialists were still to be found in the "more wells, more oil" camp. Indeed, in 1927, we find James Veasey, who as general counsel to a Standard Oil subsidiary

---

[102] Stocking 1925: 158–9.
[103] *Hermann v. Thomas*, 143 S.W. 2d 195 (Tex. Civ. App. 1911).
[104] *Texas Co. v. Daugherty*, 107 Tex. 226, 176 S.W. 717 (1915).
[105] *Winkler v. Anderson*, 104 Kan. 1, 177 P. 171 (1919).

was hardly assignable to the "ultra-conservative individualist" group that he had just spoken of,[106] arguing that spacing regulations as a whole were innately bad because they interfered with what he described as "a property right of the highest sanctity": that by which an operator "may locate his wells anywhere on the lease premises, even though his wells are so located as to drain much or the greater part of their production from adjacent lands."[107]

Against this background of law and opinion, it does not seem so surprising that the commission should have modified its rule in such a way as to recognize the fact that in a large number of cases involving small tracts, a decision in favor of an exception would be all but automatic. However, Veasey's protest points to an inevitable consequence of routinely allowing wells, or more wells than would ordinarily be permitted, on small tracts: that the owners and operators of such tracts were likely to be placed in a position where they had special advantages in capturing their neighbors' oil, because their wells could be spaced closer to property lines than was the norm.

This raises a question about capture that we have not previously needed to confront—that is to say, what *kind* of legal rule it is. In the very few nineteenth-century drainage cases examined in Chapter 2, it was enough, for disposition of the issue, to say that a person suffering drainage of oil and gas from under his or her land had no legal remedy. This meant, of course, that the party doing the draining was free to do so, but it did not carry any necessary implication that that party had a *right* to draw oil from under the neighbor's land. If the neighbor could find a legal way of stopping the drainage—excluding, therefore, such maneuvers as setting fire to the derricks or pouring cement down the wellbore—he or she was equally free to do so; and the familiar, and judicially recognized, method was by offset drilling. In terms, therefore, of the classification that legal analysts have commonly used to describe different kinds of legal relationships among people, drainage or capture could not properly be called a *right*, because there was no corresponding *duty* on anybody else not to prevent it. At best, capture was a *liberty*, the term used to describe actions that one has no duty to others to refrain from, but that others, at the same time, have no duty to permit.[108]

Veasey's 1927 language, however, marked an insidious shift, one perhaps helped along by the language of "vested rights" adopted by the commission in 1921, toward treating capture as a genuine right—indeed, one of the "highest sanctity"—so as to throw a constitutional shadow over the competence of the commission to control the phenomenon. Strong condemnation of this view as

---

[106] Above, at 237–8.

[107] Veasey 1927: 615–17.

[108] Hohfeld 1923.

being "utterly inconsistent with the ownership theory" operating in Texas was uttered some years later by another leading legal authority, Professor A. W. Walker Jr., and we should notice that he ascribed it to the "unfortunate" introduction into judicial opinions of the term "law of capture": he thought the idea that there was a positive right of capture was "a dangerous and ... unjustified inference ... from the use of this expression."[109]

Whatever the origin of the idea (and we should notice that Veasey and other critics of spacing rules wrote well before judges started talking about capture), the practice of the Railroad Commission in freely granting small-tract exceptions can only have comforted their owners' belief that they had a God-given—or at the least, judge-given—right to take their neighbors' oil. The penalties this practice could impose on large-tract operators were severe. When the East Texas field was opened up, a local spacing rule was adopted providing for a well on every 10 acres.[110] A 40-acre lease would thus be entitled to 4 wells, but it might be surrounded—and could easily be drained—by acre or half-acre leases, each almost certain to receive from the commission a spacing exception allowing for a well. The holder of the 40-acre lease could easily thus wind up with 40 to 50 wells around its perimeter. Drainage on a large-scale was inevitable, so to be "fair," the commission would allow the 40-acre leaseholder, by way of further Rule 37 exceptions, to offset the surrounding wells. To secure the oil that might have been obtained with 4 wells, therefore, the leaseholder might have to drill up to 50, thereby incurring massive capital costs and slashing profits. And as we have seen, failure to do this would result in reduction of allowable production, and a possible forfeiture of the lease.[111]

By the end of 1937, in fact, no less than 24,629 wells had been drilled on the East Texas field's 140,000 acres, a density of 1 well for every 5.7 acres. Of these wells, more than 17,000 were drilled under Rule 37 exceptions.[112] The commission's openhanded exceptions policy operated not just to promote the drilling of unnecessary wells, but also to give an extra boost to landowners' penchant to subdivide tracts in pursuit of increased royalties (and more energetic exploration and development). Such subdivision naturally multiplied the opportunities for obtaining exception wells and thereby for capturing oil from neighbors.

---

[109] Walker 1939: 375.

[110] Hardwicke 1952: 103.

[111] Above, Ch. 7, at 194–7.

[112] Ely 1938: 1230. For comparable 1935 figures, see Prindle 1981: 49–50.

This loophole was largely blocked when the Supreme Court of Texas, in *Brown v. Humble Oil and Refining Co.*,[113] quashed a Rule 37 exception granted for a well on the second of two 1.5-acre tracts that had been carved out of a larger property subsequent to the application of spacing rule to the field. The court below had found that the well, far from preventing waste (the first ground of exception under the rule), would cause it, and would also drain and damage the Humble Oil Company's adjoining land. Accordingly, the supreme court held that there could be no claim as of right to a well after a voluntary subdivision of land under the "vested right" arm of the exception invoked by the commission. The commission, however, retained a discretion in such cases, but

> where it would be proper, right, and just to permit tracts to be subdivided and such subdivisions drilled after the adoption of the rule ... it is the duty of the Commission to give to the owner of such smaller tract only his just proportion of the oil and gas. By this method each person will be entitled to recover a quantity of oil and gas substantially equivalent in amount to the recoverable oil and gas under his land.[114]

This was an admirable statement of principle and of respect for the concept of correlative rights—the court cited the *Ohio Oil Co.* case at length in its opinion—but the possibility of its realization in Texas has been gravely impaired both by the Railroad Commission's general approach to prorationing and by a constraint on prorationing imposed by the Texas legislature in 1931 and subsequently renewed, the so-called Marginal Well Statute. This act provided that wells it defined as marginal could not have their production restricted by the commission under prorationing orders if such artificial curtailment would cause damage, loss of ultimately recoverable production, or premature abandonment. At the time *Brown* was decided, these were pumping wells of depths of up to 2,000 feet producing up to 10 barrels a day, with increments of 5 to 10 barrels according to depth down to 8,000 feet, after which the limit was 35 barrels a day. Producers quickly came to appreciate the advantages of marginal well status and worked hard to achieve it by such devices as using undersize tubing, employing small pumps with short strokes, and keeping the well and tubing dirty.[115] While other states, including Kansas, New Mexico, and Louisiana, also passed marginal well statutes, it was the number of these wells in the East Texas field that produced the most remarkable results in terms of large-scale capture of oil by small leases from large ones.

---

[113] 126 Tex. 296, 83 S.W. 2d 935; on rehearing, 126 Tex. 314, 87 S.W. 2d 1069 (1935).

[114] 126 Tex. 312, 83 S.W. 2d 944.

[115] 1 Bradley 1996: 180.

In *Railroad Commission of Texas v. Rowan and Nichols Oil Co.*, the U.S. Supreme Court sustained proration orders for the East Texas field made in 1938 and 1939.[116] The first order, setting a field allowable of 522,000 barrels, was based purely on well potentials, which would mean that assuming a field potential of 1 million barrels, each of the 25,408 wells might, other things being equal, have expected an allowable of 52.2 percent of its potential. This, however, was to reckon without the Marginal Well Statute and massive overdrilling on parts of the field covered by small tracts. Having given 451 marginal wells their full 20 barrels a day according to the statute, the commission then applied a working principle under which no more productive well could get a percentage allowable that would reduce its permitted production below the 20 barrels awarded to marginal wells. Given the temperament of the people likely to be operating such small but not technically marginal wells, one can see that this was a politically prudent move and perhaps also a good defensive legal strategy. But it meant giving 20 barrels each to another 19,032 wells, leaving only 136,610 barrels for the remaining 6,325 wells, the most productive. These wells "enjoyed" a percentage allowable of 2.32 percent, as against figures of up to 100 percent for many others. Unfortunately for the plaintiff oil company, by the time this case came to trial, the Supreme Court, unlike the lower federal courts in Texas at the beginning of the decade, had decided to adopt a deferential attitude to the expert evaluations of the commission, and the order, along with its successor (which readjusted the calculation slightly in favor of more productive wells), was sustained.

There was an alternative approach: to adopt a basis for prorationing that corresponded more closely with the correlative rights principle by using not wells, but acreage, and the potential of the sands underlying the acreage, as the unit of distribution in conjunction with an appropriate spacing rule, and dealing with the small-tract problem by inviting—or requiring—owners of tracts too small to justify a well to pool their tracts with others so as to form a drilling unit of the appropriate size. We saw in Chapter 6 that Galicia had adopted a variant of this approach as early as 1908,[117] and the next section will show how most states eventually applied the pooling solution. The Texas Railroad Commission, however, with judicial support, stuck to policies favoring the independence of the small-tract owner and small producer. Instead of promoting voluntary pooling by tightening its policy on Rule 37 exceptions, it introduced a series of increasingly complex working rules that were designed to provide some compensation to owners of larger tracts, but whose cumulative effect was to increase well densities even further. Over several decades, it continued to grant almost every spacing

---

[116] 311 U.S. 570 (1941).
[117] Above, at 148.

exception requested (1,519 out of 1,538 requested in 1956, for example)[118] and to use as its standard bases for proration 50 percent well potential and 50 percent acreage for oil, and (because of its tendency to flow more easily and further underground) 33.3 percent well potential and 66.6 percent acreage for gas. These ratios imposed substantial drainage losses on large tracts, discouraged voluntary pooling, and pushed up field costs overall by encouraging unnecessary drilling.

Until the 1960s, the commission's policies were regularly endorsed by judicial decisions sustaining Rule 37 exceptions "to prevent confiscation" whenever there was a risk of drainage from a small tract[119] and even suggesting that the rule of capture might encompass a right of property in the oil and gas under other people's land. Sustaining a proration order that was alleged to be productive of substantial drainage in favor of small-tract holders over the life of the field, the Texas Court of Civil Appeals, while invoking the principle of *Brown* that "the rules and regulations adopted must, as far as practical, and within reasonable limitations, afford the several property owners a fair opportunity to produce the recoverable oil underlying their lands or its equivalent," went on to deduce that

> [a]s a corollary ... the owner of an "involuntarily"[120] segregated tract cannot be denied the right to drill at least one well on his tract however small it may be. From which it would seem that his allowable cannot be cut down to the point where his well would no longer produce, ... nor below the point where it could not be drilled and operated at a reasonable profit.

> There are certain natural advantages which the small tracts have over large tracts in unrestricted production; and we think these natural advantages may properly be taken into consideration in administering the conservation laws.

These "natural advantages" appeared to be the ability of such tracts to capture their neighbors' oil: the court in fact adopted Veasey's "heretical" 1927 view[121] in saying, in so many words, that the "unlimited right of capture" was "a property right" that could not be infringed except in proper administration of conservation laws.[122]

---

[118] Prindle 1981: 74. This paragraph is largely based on Prindle's account at 73–81.

[119] E.g., *Magnolia Petroleum Co. v. Railroad Commission of Texas*, 120 S.W. 2d 553 (Texas Civ. App. 1938). On the dozens of Rule 37 judicial decisions, see generally Hardwicke 1952.

[120] I.e., one that was already a separate tract when the spacing rule was first applied to the field in question.

[121] Above, at 262–3.

[122] *Railroad Commission of Texas v. Humble Oil and Refining Co.*, 193 S.W. 2d 824, at 832 (Tex. Civ. App. 1946).

Though this decision was locally condemned as "unsound,"[123] and large operators in Texas scored occasional victories in spacing cases in succeeding years,[124] we shall see that it was not until the 1960s that a change in the position of the state's supreme court led to a grudging acceptance by the legislature and the Railroad Commission of the policy, by then almost universal elsewhere, of protecting small-tract owners through compulsory pooling arrangements. In explaining the distinctive conservation policies of the Texas Railroad Commission over the decades between 1930 and 1960, commentators have sometimes stressed its sensitivity to the opinions and demands of the independents in Texas[125] or suggested that it was in thrall to outdated opinions such as the "more wells, more oil" theory, which, if official industry belief in the 1920s, had steadily lost both intellectual and industry support in the succeeding years.[126]

Despite its harshness to larger operators and its uncertain effects in conservation terms, we should not assume that the commission's policy was in any way irrational. It provoked the drilling of enormous numbers of unnecessary wells, but so long as Texas dominated the domestic petroleum market—in 1937, for example, it produced 40 percent of the country's oil and held half of its reserves[127]—the commission was able to restrict overall production, through prorationing, to levels that would sustain prices high enough to make those wells economically viable. The prices were paid by consumers, largely outside Texas; the employment and manufacturing benefits of all this overinvestment would be largely enjoyed by Texans and within Texas. The commission was not shy about its concern for the economic well-being of Texans. In 1938, its then chairman said in so many words that Rule 37 exceptions were in part granted in order to increase employment and to add to the taxable properties in the state.[128]

POOLING: AN ALTERNATIVE ANSWER TO THE SMALL-TRACT PROBLEM

The radical alternative to cosseting the small-tract owners and small independent operators at the expense of everyone outside Texas was Henry Doherty's scheme to make small tracts irrelevant by unitizing the operation of each field and distributing royalties in proportion to tract owners' interests in its resources. While

---

[123] Hardwicke 1952: 117.

[124] E.g., *Hawkins v. Texas Co.*, 146 Tex. 511, 209 S.W. 2d 338 (1948).

[125] Prindle 1981, especially Ch. 8.

[126] Ely 1938: 1231.

[127] *Ibid.* 1211.

[128] Hardwicke 1938: 256: "one wonders where the Commission gets its authority for granting exceptions for such purposes."

Doherty probably drew on the work of William McMurray and James Lewis,[129] their paper was not the first to propose this kind of solution. As explained in Chapter 6, the European oilfields were likewise bedeviled by small tracts and competitive drilling, and the man with the best claim to be the "father" of unitization was one Claudius Angermann, a petroleum engineer and geologist with experience in Galicia.

Angermann's geological work was noted with respect in Edgar Owen's massive compendium of the history of petroleum exploration,[130] and in 1905, in a paper given at the Second International Petroleum Congress at Liège, in Belgium, and reprinted in the *Petroleum World*,[131] he sought to apply its lessons to shape legal development. Noting that drilling was discouraged and exploration costs increased by the "mutual taking away of production"—"no sooner is a well brought in than the flow is tapped by an adjacent well"—he proposed that once an explorer had identified a spot where he wished to drill, the authorities should have the property carefully investigated by a practical geologist—ideally, perhaps, by Herr Angermann—at the expense of the operator, "so as to ascertain the lay of the supposed oil beds as well as their probable width." They should then define a drilling site extending 250 meters in each direction from the well site and of appropriate width. The applicant would have the exclusive right to drill in this parallelogram, and any other future drill site must be at least 500 meters distant from its boundary. Each operator would thus enjoy a "zone of protection." A similar notion of leaving space between leased areas had been unsuccessfully proposed at Baku a few years earlier.[132]

Angermann's belief that an oilfield could be delineated by drilling—or perhaps even before drilling—a single exploratory well might have been plausible in Galician conditions but would doubtless have raised a hollow laugh from any American wildcatter who happened to read the *Petroleum World*. If, however, we leave aside the practicality of his scheme, it can be seen to embody an idea akin to the "first appropriation" principle operative in western water law and in the French mineral water regime: the first operator on the scene enjoys a protected position.[133] Angermann, however, also needed to deal with the surface owner's interest (recall that in Galicia, and also Romania, oil in place was at this time the property of the landowner), and the solution he offered to avoid the effective

---

[129] Above, n. 33.

[130] Owen 1975: 148–9.

[131] Angermann 1905.

[132] Above, Ch. 6, at 163.

[133] A variant of Angermann's scheme, involving a much larger—but temporary—area of protection ("say 9 square miles"), was offered by a witness representing the wildcatter interest at the FOCB hearings in 1926: United States. Federal Oil Conservation Board 1926a: 84–90.

expropriation of neighboring landowners entitles him to be regarded as the first prophet of unitization. All the owners of properties within the drilling site, said Angermann, should form a company, each to receive a share of the royalty corresponding to the areas of his or her property. As he correctly pointed out, this would avoid one landowner's profiting, through drainage, at the expense of another and would release producers from the compulsion to drill wells according to the configuration of the surface plots, leaving them free to carry out rational drilling programs.

Angermann assumed, one imagines, that surface owners would be led to form their company by the threat of loss of royalties if they did not join in. Under Galician conditions, he did not have to worry about the Fourteenth Amendment. In the United States, however, though your right to the oil under your land might be precarious in that your neighbor could take it away by capture, it was constitutionally protected against any legislation that purported to deny you the opportunity to exercise it—as by forbidding drilling—unless that law could be sustained under the police power by some overriding public interest. For any scheme like this to make headway in the United States, some such public interest would have to be found. While Henry Doherty and his cohorts were prepared to tackle this challenge head-on, by invoking the danger of waste, others, like Doherty's fellow directors at the API, clearly regarded this sort of proposal as too radical to be sustained even by the broad definitions of waste that key states had adopted by 1920. It was therefore fortunate that a quite different kind of public interest could be found to support this kind of approach, at least in the case where lack of control was likely to do most damage to reservoirs: town lot drilling (Figure 9-1).

Town and city dwellers initially showed considerable tolerance of invasions by oil producers seeking to ply their smelly, noisy, and dangerous trade. When, in 1892, Edward Doheny struck oil close to the center of Los Angeles, "in a elite area occupied by elegant Victorian mansions,"[134] prospective royalties must have outweighed present amenity for many of their owners, as 300 wells were drilled in the area within the next three years.[135] Not until the 1920s were Los Angeles city authorities prepared to allow amenity to trump oil development in some areas by imposing restrictive zoning ordinances, one of which withstood judicial scrutiny in *Marblehead Land Co. v. City of Los Angeles* in 1931.[136] Many city authorities, though, did not want to ban drilling outright. They wanted the prosperity oil might

---

[134] Testa 2005: 82–3.

[135] *Ibid.* 83 says they were on an area of less than 4,000 square feet, but at one well for every 1.5 square yards, this is hardly plausible.

[136] 47 F. 2d 528 (9th Cir., 1931).

Figure 9-1. Town Lot Drilling, Court Street, Los Angeles, 1901
Source: Huntington Library, Los Angeles

bring, but without the inconvenience, pollution, and danger of unnecessarily intensive development. The Texas experience indicated that a spacing regulation with an exception—even discretionary—for small lots was unlikely to be effective; but without exceptions, it would deprive most town lot owners of drilling rights and would be an easy target for legal attack. The passage through this Scylla and Charybdis eventually identified by city authorities (or their lawyers) was the combination of spacing regulations with a form of community lease. When a city ordinance of this type successfully withstood judicial challenge in 1929, it marked an important step on the difficult road to unitization in the United States.

POOLING ORDINANCES AND LEGISLATION

The ordinance in question was promulgated by the small town of Oxford, in southern Kansas, in June 1927, roughly on the model of one passed a few months earlier for the rather larger town of Winfield, a little to the west, where substantial oil development was starting up. Whereas the Winfield ordinance effectively made the conclusion of a community lease, of a defined minimum area, compulsory before drilling could start in any area within the city,[137] the Oxford ordinance bypassed this stage by allowing only one well per city block, allocating a one-eighth royalty interest among the landowners in the block in proportion to their acreage, and awarding the right to drill to the operator holding the majority of the acreage in the block under lease. Landowners could also participate in the working interest by contributing to the cost of the well, again in proportion to acreage.[138]

In light of the nuisances occasioned by oil development in residential and business areas, the U.S. Court of Appeals had no difficulty, in the case of *Marrs v. City of Oxford*, in sustaining the ordinance as being an effective protection of the public welfare and, indeed, commended it as a desirable protection of correlative rights and protection against capture.[139] With this endorsement, this ingenious attempt to avoid the necessity for landowners to reach agreement seems to have enjoyed deserved success: Oxford may today be a typical small town of around 1,200 inhabitants, with its two banks, four restaurants, and 10 churches, but in the 1930s, it enjoyed an oil boom that produced enough wealth to permit a variety of town improvements including an opera house, doubtless an expression of that aspirational cast of mind that led the town's founders to call it Oxford in the first place.

Oxford's immediate significance was that its ordinance demonstrated the workability of pooling acreage as a means of getting around the particularly dangerous and wasteful practices represented by competitive drilling on town lot tracts. Whereas California chose to follow the Winfield precedent, adopting in 1931 a state law requiring wells to be at least 100 feet from property boundaries or roads (thus allowing a maximum density of one well per acre) but allowing owners of smaller tracts to get the benefit of the act by having them produced under a single lease or as a single operating unit, the Oxford ordinance found application in Oklahoma and Texas. The Oklahoma City authorities applied the principle of the ordinance to restrain competitive drilling within the part of the giant Oklahoma City field lying within its jurisdiction, a measure sustained in *Gant v. Oklahoma City*.[140]

In Texas in 1935, the city of South Houston adopted a very similar ordinance, which was sustained by a federal bench chaired by Judge Hutcheson. The court also sustained special spacing rules for the area, replicating the ordinance that had been adopted by the Texas Railroad Commission.[141] Though the commission was

---

[137] Harris 1938: 55–6.

[138] *Marrs v. City of Oxford*, 24 F. 2d 541 (D.C. Kan. 1927).

[139] *Marrs v. City of Oxford*, 32 F. 2d 134 (8th Cir. 1929). The word "capture" was used by the court, perhaps for the first time in a reported decision on oil and gas law.

[140] 150 Okla. 86, 6 P. 2d 1081 (1931).

[141] *Tysco Oil Co. v. Railroad Commission of Texas*, 12 F. Supp. 195 and 202 (S.D. Tex. 1935).

here assisting in the operation of a compulsory pooling scheme, it consistently denied, until the passage of the Texas pooling legislation in 1965, that it had any general power to enforce pooling,[142] a position perhaps linked with the Texas legislature's express stipulation, in its Anti-Market Demand Act of 1931, that it was "not the intent of this Act to require ... that the separately owned properties in any pool be unitized under one management, control or ownership."[143] Given that pooling, like unitization, necessarily involves, for smaller tract owners and their lessees, loss of independent decisionmaking power over how the tract is to be exploited, one can see why the commission took a broad and cautious view of this constraint.

The significance of the *Marrs* case was quickly perceived by proponents of unitization.[144] It furnished a judicial endorsement of the particular kind of restriction of property rights inherent in unitization: having to entrust the development of one's petroleum resources to someone else if they were to be developed at all. As it turned out, however, the decision stimulated their campaign less than they might have hoped. Instead, it facilitated the adoption by states of compulsory pooling of acreage as a means of avoiding the fatal weakening of the effect of field spacing rules by way of small-tract exemptions. Prorationing schemes that included an acreage element commonly attached an allowable to each "drilling unit," whose size was determined in function of the relevant field spacing rule adopted by the state regulatory commission. The required spacing would tend to vary with the characteristics of the field: wide spacing and large units for gas fields, close spacing and small units for reservoirs of low porosity or permeability. Instead of providing exceptions on the Texas pattern for tracts smaller than the relevant drilling unit, *Marrs* indicated that states might be able to protect small-tract owners by requiring others interested in the drilling unit to pool their interests with such owners, so that despite the absence of wells on the small tracts, their owners could share appropriately in the royalties attributable to production from the well on the unit.

Between 1935 and 1945, Oklahoma and New Mexico (1935), Arkansas and Michigan (1939), Louisiana (1940), and Alabama, Florida, Georgia, and North Carolina (1945) all passed statutes empowering the relevant state agency to establish drilling units for prorationing purposes and entitling any owner within a drilling unit whose tract did not have a well to share in royalties; provision was also made, in certain circumstances, for small-tract owners to drill on their own

---

[142] Chairman's statement in 1937 quoted in Ely 1938: 1236n.

[143] Ely 1933b: 331.

[144] Witness the use made of the case in early pro-unitization articles like Oliver 1930; German 1931: 395–6.

tracts, but subject to a reduced allowable corresponding to their acreage.[145] The Oklahoma and Louisiana statutes were duly challenged as unconstitutional deprivations of property, but were sustained by the respective state supreme courts,[146] and appeals to the U.S. Supreme Court were dismissed for want of a substantial federal question—that is to say, that court took the view that its earlier case law on state oil and gas conservation legislation put the constitutionality of these statutes beyond argument.[147]

By the mid-1960s, all states except California, Kansas, and Texas had legislation of this type. Texas finally enacted compulsory pooling in 1965 in the shape of its Mineral Interest Pooling Act, though it framed the statute in terms so restrictive that it is in fact seldom used to pool small tracts and has been described as "an Act to encourage voluntary pooling—rather than ... to provide compulsory state action."[148] Given the "natural advantages" that small-tract holders already enjoyed under the Railroad Commission's Rule 37 exemptions policy, it may seem surprising that it was politically feasible to pass a pooling statute in any shape or form, but the game had been radically changed by two decisions of the Supreme Court of Texas overturning commission proration orders for two gas fields in 1961 and 1962.[149] The issue in these cases was purely one of correlative rights. Over the protests of larger operators, the commission applied its one-third well potential, two-thirds acreage rule to both fields, with the likely result that small-tract wells in the first field, Normanna, would drain 400 to 500 times the amount of gas present under the tracts, while in the second, Port Acres, 20 wells under Rule 37 exceptions, with 0.65 percent of total acreage, would drain 14.6 percent of all the gas in the field. In both cases, the court, unimpressed by the attorney general's assertion that "townsite operators do have a property right in the reserves underlying the large tract owners, and that that right extends to the right to drain enough oil or gas from other tracts in the field to yield a reasonable opportunity for a profit to the operator,"[150] decided that this was unacceptable in terms of correlative rights and quashed the order, even as it recognized that the amount of gas in place under a small tract was not sufficient to make the drilling of a well an economic proposition.

---

[145] King 1948: 324–5.

[146] *Patterson v. Stanolind Oil and Gas Co.*, 182 Okla. 155, 72 P. 2d 83 (1938); *Hunter v. McHugh*, 202 La. 97, 11 So. 2d 495 (1942).

[147] *Patterson v. Stanolind Oil and Gas Co.*, 305 U.S. 376 (1939); *Hunter v. McHugh*, 320 U.S. 222 (1943).

[148] Smith 1965: 1009.

[149] *Atlantic Refining Co. v. Railroad Commission of Texas*, 346 S.W. 2d 801 (Tex. 1961); *Halbouty v. Railroad Commission of Texas*, 357 S.W. 2d 364 (Tex. 1962).

[150] *Halbouty v. Railroad Commission of Texas*, 357 S.W. 2d 369.

Texas thus rejoined, albeit reluctantly, the main stream of conservation regulation in the U.S. oil industry, where correlative rights were principally protected, and capture restrained, by the device of creating efficient spacing units within fields and ensuring that any tract, whether drilled or not, could share appropriately in the production from the unit. Attempts to provide a model for conservation regulation that might be applied in any oil-producing state had been ongoing since 1940, when the Legal Committee of the Interstate Oil Compact Commission, the body established in 1935 to facilitate interstate cooperation in oil and gas after federal withdrawal from the field, first proposed "A Comprehensive Suggested Oil and Gas Conservation Law Containing Provisions Suitable for Adoption in Any State."

This lengthy document, containing large numbers of alternative proposals, was steadily refined and recast during the next decade, and in 1950, the committee produced and the commission approved "A Form for an Oil and Gas Conservation Statute," designed to be particularly suitable for adoption by states that had not yet developed their own comprehensive conservation law.[151] At this point, the statute was presented as a consensus on best practice; alternative provisions were eliminated save in respect of arrangements for review of decisions by the state's regulatory commission.

Not all of the statute's provisions have been widely adopted in subsequent state conservation legislation; we shall see that its compulsory unitization provision was more sweeping than that in force even today in most states, and its provision for limitation of production by reference to market demand achieved very limited acceptance.[152] By contrast, the statute's provisions for the creation of spacing units and for compulsory pooling of tracts within units, which broadly followed the precedents set in Oklahoma and Louisiana, have been closely reflected in the oil and gas legislation of such states as Colorado, Utah, Montana, and North Dakota, where substantial production is a relatively recent phenomenon.[153] Kansas, however, has never introduced forced pooling, and California's powers are still restricted to the town lots covered by its 1931 law.[154]

---

[151] Interstate Oil Compact Commission 1950. For commentary, see Walker 1951, and for the current version, see Interstate Oil and Gas Compact Commission 2004.

[152] Wilson 1989: 18–13 to 18–14.

[153] *Ibid.* 18–12.

[154] Above, at 272.

THE CAMPAIGN FOR UNITIZATION

Henry Doherty, of course, was beating the drum for the much more ambitious project of compulsory unitization several years before even the earliest forced pooling provisions, in the form of the Winfield city ordinance, were promulgated.[155] By the time of his appearance at the FOCB hearings in 1926, and despite the indifference and even active hostility of his fellow oil producers, a varied coalition of supporters of unitization had begun to take shape. Among conservationists, George Stocking, who had at one time worked for Doherty, identified the oil pool as "the logical unit for exploitation."[156] Already in 1909, David Day had noted that "a combination of all the interests" in a field was a way of avoiding premature exhaustion through competitive drilling.[157] Federal officials such as George Otis Smith, the director of the U.S. Geological Survey, also reacted sympathetically.[158] Support also came from petroleum engineers, including some working for substantial oil companies. At the 1926 board hearings, as I have noted, presentations favorable to unitization were given by James Lewis, coauthor of the original 1916 paper recommending unitization, and by Earl Oliver.[159]

Despite their 1925 dismissal of the objective of unit development of fields as "unattainable," and the fact that the FOCB, in its first report, had set aside the notion of compulsory unitization,[160] the American Petroleum Institute turned almost immediately to further study of the subject. Doubtless the Seminole and Oklahoma City booms, and the enormous amount of unnecessary drilling they entailed for large leaseholders, operated more strongly on the minds of oil company executives than anything Henry Doherty might have said. This was also the period when the scientific approach to oil exploration and production really began to come into its own—E. W. Marland had one of the largest company geological departments in the industry—and the work of the scientists and technicians on topics like the importance of preservation of gas pressure to ultimate oil recovery[161] led quickly to an acknowledgment within API, at least at a technical level, of the value of unitization.[162]

---

[155] Olien and Olien 2000: 151–5.
[156] Stocking 1925: 141.
[157] Day 1909a: 459.
[158] Olien and Olien 2000: 158.
[159] Above, at 244.
[160] Above, at 242, 245.
[161] Notably, Miller 1929.
[162] Oliver 1930: 725–6. Oliver chaired the Technical Subcommittee of API's Gas Committee in 1927.

The same thing was happening in some of the larger companies. Humble Oil, the largest Texas producer and a subsidiary of Standard Oil of New Jersey, was an excellent example.[163] William Farish, its chairman, who had served on the Committee of Eleven that produced the API's 1925 report, had by the following year been convinced by his company's scientists and by the press of events of the merits of unitization. He caused it to be adopted as an element of company policy, in association with the strategy of obtaining large blocks of leases covering entire fields and securing their orderly development through the payment of advance royalties to lessors in exchange for the right to delay drilling beyond what the leases would ordinarily permit. Where this was not possible, he tried to achieve unit development through agreement with other operators, succeeding in this in the Van field in Texas in 1929. This field, discovered in Van Zandt County in East Texas by Pure Oil, was one in which only five major companies—Pure, Sun, Shell, Texas, and Humble—were interested.[164] It was thus relatively easy for them to agree on how to produce the field, but the agreement, though said to be based on a form agreement for unitization at the exploration stage, was not a unitization agreement in the full sense of that term: it provided for unified management by way of a merger of the lessees' interests and the appointment of a single operator, but the location of wells was still determined to a considerable extent by surface boundary lines and conflicting royalty interests rather than by reservoir structure and content.[165]

The difficulties encountered by Humble's lawyers in drafting even this limited agreement so as to minimize the risks of attack under the state's stringent antitrust laws (of which more later), coupled with other likely difficulties in securing agreements of royalty owners on a purely voluntary basis, led Humble to give vigorous support to the bill that became Texas's 1929 oil conservation statute. The bill originally contained a provision authorizing the majority of producers in a field, with the permission of the Railroad Commission, "to make and enforce orders for orderly development of separate tracts," forced unitization in fact if not in name. Humble even attempted a public education campaign on the benefits of unitization through two widely distributed pamphlets.[166]

The enthusiasm of recent converts is often an embarrassment to long-term practitioners of a religion, and Doherty and his followers might well have preferred to see the seeds of unitization policy being scattered on less stony ground than that of Texas and by a less controversial prophet than Humble, widely reviled by politicians and independents there—whether justly or not was, in the

---

[163] Material in this paragraph is drawn from Weaver 1986: 51–60 unless otherwise indicated.
[164] Warner 1939: 162.
[165] Marshall and Meyers 1931: 60.
[166] Larson and Porter 1959: 312–16.

circumstances, unimportant—as the worst kind of oil industry monopolist. The assessment of Jacqueline Weaver, author of the definitive work on the legal history of unitization in Texas, is that the association of the policy with Humble dealt it a body blow from which it never recovered.[167] The immediate response to Humble's campaign was to avoid any reference to unitization in the 1929 act and to underline this by the express exclusion of "economic waste" from the kinds of waste the Railroad Commission might seek to prevent. The legislature followed this up in 1931 with the denial, already noted, of any pooling or unitization power by the Anti-Market Demand Act.

Texas still has no compulsory unitization statute. The nearest it has approached to enforced unitization has been the policy initiated by Commissioner William Murray, on his arrival at the commission in 1947, of shutting down entire fields whose uncoordinated operation was leading to unacceptable waste. This drastic measure was first applied in 1947 to the Seeligson oilfield to prevent the massive waste of casinghead gas through flaring, by pressuring producers to cooperate in building and operating a processing plant for the gas so that it could be pipelined to market.[168] Once this measure was judicially sustained, the commission administered this cure to 17 further fields and went on to apply the same sanction to fields suffering damaging declines in gas pressure. While putting casinghead gas to use did not necessarily involve any measure of unitization, gas recycling and repressurization could seldom be effective without it, and a number of major voluntary fieldwide and partial unitizations were achieved in this way. Out of concern for the sensibilities of independents and his fellow commissioners, Murray was at pains to maintain that the commission did "not require or even suggest that unit operations be followed."[169] This pretense enabled Texans to maintain their hostility to enforced unitization unimpaired while enjoying some of its benefits.

On the national scene, although some major companies, such as the Texas Company and Gulf Oil, were strongly opposed to unitization—Gulf, indeed, was resistant to regulation of any kind—the pro-unitization faction made steady progress within the industry. The engineers devoted a substantial part of their Petroleum Division meeting in 1929 to discussion of the benefits of unit operations.[170] The API's World Production Plan of 1929 focused on production restrictions but suggested that its proposed regional committees study the issue of unitization, and in December of that year, API's board of directors formally

---

[167] Weaver 1986: Ch. 3.

[168] Prindle 1981: 62–69; Weaver 1986: 143–51. Casinghead gas is gas produced as solution or associated gas from an oil well.

[169] Quoted in Weaver 1986: 148.

[170] Olien and Olien 2000: 174.

endorsed unitization on a voluntary basis.[171] Strong official support also came from the FOCB. In its fourth report, published in 1930, it made a forceful plea for cooperative development through unit operation, describing surface property lines as "a checkerboard for title-searchers and lease-lawyers to play on," identifying the oil reservoir as "the natural unit of property ownership in oil," and going so far as to say that "affirmative action by either court or legislature, whereby the co-equal rights of all the owners may be recognized and protected, is sorely needed."[172]

Unitization had the great advantage of offering different things to different people. For the engineers, it gave the satisfaction of securing a far greater recovery of oil from any given sands than did existing competitive methods; for the larger producing companies, it held out the prospects of producing oil at much lower cost by eliminating the need to drill unnecessary wells and of being able to control the rate of recovery from the reservoir so as to keep production in line with market demand. American executives no doubt listened enviously to Sir John (later Lord) Cadman, chairman of their British rival Anglo-Persian, as he described at an API meeting in 1929 his company's operation, as a single unit, of the giant Masjid-i-Suleiman field in Persia, still in flush production after 17 years of operation and at that time widely regarded as "probably the most efficiently developed oil pool in the world."[173] Cadman explained that at Masjid-i-Suleiman, whose wells were a mile apart, "all that has to be done now is to open the necessary valves by means of which the production of crude can from day to day or from hour to hour be regulated to our requirements to a nicety, just as regularly and as accurately as when one turns on the water for one's bath."[174] A few years later, one East Texas hot oil producer may have taken this beguiling metaphor too literally: he sought to conceal his production by rigging the flow controls for his well in the privacy of his bathroom.[175]

Another attraction of the unitization platform was its incidental but not insignificant merit of transferring the responsibility for the misdeeds with which the industry was so forcefully being belabored by its critics—waste, improvidence, economic irrationality, even the sapping of American moral fiber through the effete pursuits made possible by cheap gasoline—to someone else: the hapless Pennsylvania judges who were supposed to have invented the rule of capture, which unitization would finally cast into outer darkness. By laying the blame on dead judges, unitization campaigners offered the senior oil executives of the 1920s

---

[171] Hardwicke 1961: 48.

[172] United States. Federal Oil Conservation Board 1930: 17–24.

[173] Owen 1975: 1207.

[174] Cited in Marshall and Meyers 61–2.

[175] Olien and Olien 2002: 188.

and 1930s, who doubtless saw themselves as good and responsible people, the role of innocent victims in the toils of the law, rather than villains. This absolution echoes the "helplessness" of the oil industry to resist ruinous competitive drilling, evoked by the Oklahoma Corporation Commission in 1914 (though without assigning the blame explicitly to the rule of capture) to justify its intervention in the Cushing and Healdton fields.[176] Unjust and error-ridden as was the criticism of the judges, it clearly appealed to industry opinion at the time, and by dint of repetition[177] and wide dissemination in the popularizing works of Samuel Pettengill,[178] it achieved the status of a received truth.[179]

LEGAL ISSUES AND LAWYERS' VIEWS

Despite these advantages, it was clear from the outset that the success of plans for unitization, and indeed, plans for reinforcing control of production by other means, would depend very heavily on the ability of their framers to steer around a formidable set of legal and constitutional obstacles: the protection of property offered by the Fourteenth Amendment of the U.S. Constitution, guaranteeing the equal protection of the law and that property would not be taken without due process of law; the antitrust laws of the United States and of individual states, imposing severe restrictions on agreements between competitors in the same business; and the obligations of oil and gas lessees, whether express or implied by judicial decision, to develop and protect the leased property, if necessary by drilling offset wells. Unitization was thus included within the remit of the two Committees of Nine set up by the ABA and FOCB in 1928. While both committees, as we have seen, recommended antitrust exemption for "cooperative development," a term wide enough to include voluntary unitization, they balked at any notion that unitization might be imposed by compulsion.

Although the FOCB's committee was prepared to accept that cooperative development of the entire field was essential to avoid leaving excessive quantities of oil in the ground and provoking overproduction, it thought the imposition of any kind of development scheme by state law, on the model of laws establishing irrigation districts, was unacceptable. Even if constitutional difficulties were left to one side, the widely varying characteristics of oilfields created too great a risk of getting the scheme wrong and thereby perhaps inflicting great injustice on some of

---

[176] German 1938: 120–3, and above, Ch. 7, at 200–1.
[177] Oliver 1930; 1935; 1937.
[178] Pettengill 1940: 96. See also Pettengill 1936: Ch. 9.
[179] Above, Ch. 1, at 16–17.

those holding interests in the field. Voluntary agreement, supported by antitrust exemption, was thus the only way.[180]

The ABA's committee, however, thought that such voluntary action "was improbable if not impossible," and it therefore put forward a draft bill for adoption by state legislatures under which "cooperative development" of new oil pools might be made compulsory by the relevant state agency if a majority of operators in the pool so requested. It defined "cooperative development" widely enough to include, besides limitation and spacing of wells, more demanding projects such as gas reinjection programs and "any other method or methods ... for ... effecting economies in development and operation, bringing about orderly production, conserving ... gas energy ..., and enlarging the ultimate recovery of oil and gas,"[181] but it was careful to distinguish such cooperative development from compulsory unitization, involving the merger of the holdings of operators. Though this was the ideal solution, compulsion to obtain it was out of reach, because a forced merger of interests would constitute a taking and not a regulation of property.[182] In general, the committee showed much more tender consideration for the property rights of those with interests in an oilfield, and much more circumspection about constitutional restrictions on conservation, than did the state legislatures that had already faced these issues or were to do so in the near future. Thus, the committee not only dismissed compulsory unitization, but also thought that the general system of collective control it was proposing could be applied only to new fields. Even this was too much for one of its members. Reflecting the policy of Gulf Oil Corporation, of which he was general counsel, one member, Frederick C. Proctor—"a dyed-in-the-wool individualist of the old school"[183]—rejected any form of compulsion and refused to concur in the report.

Today the report appears unduly cautious, and even pessimistic, but we need to remember that it was drawn up by a group of lawyers, whose natural and indeed necessary bent was to identify legal difficulties that might stand in the path of even the most desirable policies. The other fact to remember is that the report would have been drafted before there had been any litigation on the constitutional validity of the kinds of schemes the committee was discussing, with the sole exception of the Texas cases sustaining the validity of the spacing rules there.[184] The significance of the *Marrs* case, decided in March of the same year, had perhaps not

---

[180] United States. Federal Oil Conservation Board 1929: 13.

[181] American Bar Association 1929: 762–77 (text), 752–7 (commentary). See also comments in Merrill 1930: 398–9; Marshall and Meyers 1931: 62–3.

[182] American Bar Association 1929: 744–6, 750–1.

[183] Larson and Porter 1959: 315.

[184] Above, at 260–1.

been assimilated (though at least two members of the committee, Chester Long and James Veasey, must have been well aware of it: they argued the city of Oxford's case before the Circuit Court of Appeals), and the key Oklahoma decisions in *Julian* and *Champlin* were yet to come.[185] Effectively, these cases, in legitimating production control arrangements that lacked the formal consensual basis insisted on by the committee, and that indeed were imposed on production from existing fields, quickly reduced this part of the report to the status of a historical curiosity.

THE ANTITRUST ISSUE

The ABA committee's discussion of the antitrust issue as it might affect voluntary agreements, including full-scale unitization agreements, was of longer-term interest. While providing a model state statute to give such agreements antitrust exemption in unambiguous terms, it expressed doubt as to whether the antitrust laws of any important oil-producing state, save perhaps California and Texas, would operate to condemn an agreement among operators for unit or cooperative development. Nonetheless, it accepted that as a practical matter, it was wise to remove what the industry claimed to see as an obstacle to making such agreements.[186] Two states in fact legislated in 1929 in the sense suggested by the committee, one of them being California, which inserted a new section 8 C in its principal 1911 conservation act permitting agreements for unit or cooperative development (defined in terms very similar to the ABA model), subject to the approval of the state oil and gas supervisor.[187]

If the other state had been Texas (it was in fact New Mexico), the antitrust shadow might have been largely lifted even in 1929, but Humble's actions and propaganda at that time only stoked the suspicion of monopoly—always associated with out-of-state capital—that had shaped Texas oil policy from its earliest days.[188] Accordingly, the Texas legislature not only ruled out compulsory unitization in 1931, but also reasserted, even while passing the Market Demand Prorationing Act of 1932, its fervent commitment to antitrust policy, stating not once but twice in section 13 of the act that nothing in the act should be construed as being in conflict with antitrust law, and that if it were so construed, antitrust law should prevail.[189] We do not now need to puzzle over how prorationing was

---

[185] Above, at 254–5.

[186] American Bar Association 1929: 746–8.

[187] See Ely 1933: 59–60.

[188] Olien and Olien 2002: 20–3, 53–7.

[189] Ely 1933: 376; Weaver 1986: 62.

supposed to operate in Texas when subordinate to an antitrust act (that of 1889) that prohibited any combination created for the following purposes, among others:

> to limit or reduce the production, or increase or reduce the price of merchandise or commodities;
>
> to prevent competition ...;
>
> to make or enter into ... any contract ... by which they shall agree to pool, combine or unite any interest they may have in connection with the sale or transportation of any such article or commodity that its price might in any manner be affected.

Somehow it did operate despite these strictures. Where voluntary unitization was concerned, however, it was certainly possible that a reluctant participant might argue that such an agreement was as bad as limiting or reducing production, at least in the short term; and who was to say that no judge would agree? Whether such a suit, or indeed a prosecution, was at all likely is another matter. A 1936 article in the *Texas Law Review* pronounced the state's antitrust law "dead": a survey of the previous 10 years' law reports produced only 34 cases, of which 31 were civil cases where the act was pleaded as a defense to contractual liability. None involved a production restriction.[190]

Even if Texas antitrust law was moribund, federal antitrust law remained very much alive, as evidenced by its application in 1971 in a long-running dispute between the owners of 90 percent of a Texas gas field and a competitor who had acquired a few town lot leases, representing less than 0.5 percent of the acreage. With 9 or 10 wells on these leases, he was in a position to produce disproportionate quantities under the field's one-third well potential, two-thirds acreage prorationing formula, which remained in place in this particular field despite the general condemnation of such a formula in the *Atlantic Refining* and *Halbouty* cases.[191]

The parties were unable to agree on terms for unitizing the field, and after the majority owners refused their competitor access to their pipeline and made it difficult for him to build his own, they found themselves the object of a charge of "monopolization" contrary to section 2 of the Sherman Act of 1890. Overruling the opinion of the trial judge, a federal court of appeals held that the elaborate Texas regulatory regime did not displace antitrust law, and that the jury could properly find that the actions of the majority, including "refusal to unitize," constituted "monopolization" and gave rise to liability in damages. The court insisted that it was "not saying that pooling, unitization, and joint operating

---

[190] Nutting 1936.
[191] Above, at 274.

agreements are in themselves maligned under the Sherman Act," but immediately added that "even if we consider that the act impliedly immunizes these collective activities as benign in themselves, they cannot be the instruments of economic predation or oppression."[192]

Despite this limited assurance, the decision can hardly have done other than make voluntary unitization more difficult, especially in Texas. Small operators with a highly advantageous allowable position were thereby encouraged to adopt an inflexible stance in unitization discussions, confident in the knowledge that if the majority did not cave in and meet their demands, they could make an antitrust complaint of its "refusal to deal" if things later got difficult. Annual approvals of voluntary unitization agreements by the Texas Railroad Commission dropped significantly in the 1970s from the level of the previous decade, from an average of 62.8 (1960–1969) to one of 18.1 (1970–1978).[193] It has been suggested that "pervasive government intervention in oil production," or the fact that remaining fields were technically more difficult to unitize, produced this result,[194] but a more difficult negotiating environment seems just as likely a cause.

AFTER 1930: CONSENSUS VERSUS COMPULSION

Despite the signal provided by the *Marrs* decision, the practical proposals of the two Committees of Nine, and the continued proselytizing of engineers like Earl Oliver, the campaign for unitization as the ideal remedy for the ills of capture lost much of its impetus during the 1930s. One part of the reason was the pre-occupation of everybody connected with the industry with the prorationing wars. Then, as prorationing gradually achieved acceptance and the period of federal control, though short, left behind a coherent multistate system for production control,[195] the sentiment developed that the essence of what was needed to tackle the industry's worst problems had now been done. Another factor was the near impossibility of concluding voluntary unitization agreements that would cover all the interests in a field.

A list of factors offered in 1986 to explain why parties might hesitate to enter such an agreement would certainly have been valid in the 1930s, when the state of

---

[192] *Woods Exploration and Producing Co. v. Aluminum Co. of America*, 438 F. 2d 1286 (5th Cir. 1971).

[193] Figures calculated from Weaver 1986: App. IV; 1 Bradley 1996: 209.

[194] Bradley 1996: 208; Weaver 1986: 317.

[195] Discussed below, Ch. 12, at 374–6.

technical knowledge was far more limited, and the variation in the performance of oil operators perhaps much greater, than was the case half a century later. These factors included differences in natural endowments of particular tracts; uncertainties; changes in the manner and timing of production that might have differentiated effects among tracts; pride of ownership and the desire to retain operational control; mistrust among operators and among royalty owners; the possibly very large numbers of parties involved; fear, real or pretended, of violating antitrust laws; and fear of increased legal problems.[196] One might add to this list the fact that in the 1930s, few if any leases would have given the lessee a right to unitize, as is common today, so that failure to get the lessor's consent might imperil the lease. And when one reflects that the trading and division of royalty interests had by 1930 produced a situation where it was not unknown for royalty fractions to have denominators running to five figures,[197] the task of bringing the hundreds or thousands of people involved to agree might alone have been enough to cause an operator to desist. For all these reasons, when voluntary agreements *were* achieved, there might well be tracts in the field that were not included, creating additional risks for the unitizing parties that the unrestricted operation of such tracts might provoke drainage and limit the benefits of the agreement.

All this was very dispiriting for the supporters of unitization, and the stalling of the movement is suggested by the fact that over the decade, only three additional states— Arkansas, Kansas, and Mississippi—enacted antitrust exemptions for unitization agreements, despite the fact that this excuse for inaction was still being widely deployed.[198] It was only in the next decade that the position improved significantly: by 1952, 22 states were reported to have such legislation on their statute books. This may perhaps reflect the provision of an additional stimulus to agreement: the fact that impatience with the progress of the voluntary approach began to lead legislators at both state and federal levels, under pressure from the relevant specialized agencies, to give serious consideration to the previously unthinkable option of compulsion.

It was the federal government that showed the way. As the owner of the oil and gas interest under all federal lands, the government could use its leasing power under the Mineral Leasing Act of 1920 to impose an obligation to unitize, when appropriate, as part of the terms of the lease itself. So too could any state that had retained the power to lease out the oil and gas interest in its public lands. Texas, as we have seen, had abandoned this power to the surface owners and lessees of its public school lands, though it was retained for the still extensive lands held and

---

[196] Weaver 1986: 29–33. For a similar list, see McDonald 1971: 213–16.

[197] Marshall and Meyers 1931: 62. On the general difficulties and costs produced by this phenomenon of "fractionalization," see Anderson and Smith 1999: 2-4–2-26.

[198] Moses 1943: 765.

administered by the Texas university system.[199] The familiar constitutional hurdle of the due process of law clause was no obstacle where all the mineral interests involved remained, prior to leasing, in public hands; in such cases, there was but a single lessor interest, and the property rights of the lessees derived exclusively from the lease that incorporated the unitization requirement.

It was the discovery of the major Kettleman Hills field in southern California in 1928 that led the federal government to implement an active unitization policy for its lands. Kettleman Hills extended across a large tract of territory checkerboarded between public and private lands according to the system of land grants for railroad development that I have already described.[200] The discovery led immediately to a competitive drilling program and the wastage of enormous quantities of gas. The Hoover administration reacted to this development, and the contemporaneous glutting of the market by oil from the Oklahoma and West Texas discoveries, by closing the public domain, suspending the issue of oil and gas permits and leases (save as required by legislation), and canceling a very large number of inactive permits. At the same time, the secretary of the interior negotiated a shut-in agreement for Kettleman Hills suspending drilling until January 31, 1931, pending federal legislation to authorize a unitization program. A temporary act for this purpose was passed in July 1930, and the rapid success of the arrangements then adopted for Kettleman Hills led to permanent provision for unitization of federal public lands in the act of March 4, 1931.[201]

According to Hardwicke, the purpose of the 1930 and 1931 acts was to eliminate the antitrust law risk that might otherwise attach to unitizations involving federal land—unitizations that, by reason of the frequency of checkerboarding, might frequently involve privately owned land as well.[202] While they certainly served this purpose by explicitly authorizing unit agreements between permittees and lessees, they also offered additional security by providing that any lease operated under a plan for cooperative or unit development approved by the secretary of the interior should continue automatically until the termination of the plan, and not expire and require renewal after 20 years. They also exempted unitized leases from the overall acreage limitations imposed by the 1920 act: at that time, 2,560 acres within a single field and 7,680 acres in one state.[203] More

---

[199] Above, Ch. 8, at 220–1. For current rules on leasing of state oil and gas rights, see Texas Natural Resources Code, §§ 52.151–52.154. Although these rules impose an obligation on lessees to drill offset wells to prevent drainage, they still contain no provision enabling the state to incorporate a unitization obligation in its leases.

[200] Above, Ch. 8, at 226–7.

[201] Ely 1949: 602–5.

[202] Hardwicke 1951: 38.

[203] § 27, as amended by act of April 30, 1926.

remarkably, the 1931 act also "authorized the Secretary to require unit operations whenever needed for efficient operation of a pool or field"—at least, this was the view of Northcutt Ely, one of the leading resource lawyers in the United States, who was at the time executive assistant to the secretary of the interior.[204]

In fact, the 1931 act, in amending section 27 of the 1920 act, said nothing about how a unit agreement might come into being, simply authorizing such agreements if they were "for the purpose for [*sic*] more properly conserving the natural resources of any single oil or gas pool or field [and] whenever determined and certified by the Secretary of the Interior to be necessary or advisable in the public interest" and providing for their consequences. Nonetheless, when the public domain was reopened in April 1932, it was on the basis of new regulations issued by the secretary of the interior under which every applicant for a permit accepted an obligation to submit a plan, agreed upon with any other interested parties, for unit development of any pool affected by the permit within two years; failing such agreement, the secretary could prescribe a plan "which shall adequately protect the correlative rights of all permittees and other parties in interest, including the United States." Applicants were also required to agree that they would not produce any oil or gas in commercial quantities other than pursuant to such a plan and would comply with any operating methods laid down by the secretary, as well as with state and federal conservation laws, including prorationing.[205]

No legal challenges to these regulations appear to have reached the courts, but in 1935, compulsory unitization was put on a firmer footing by further amendment of section 17 of the Mineral Leasing Act so as to give explicit expression to the secretary's power to require it by way of lease stipulations.[206] This amendment also prospectively eliminated the system of prospecting permits for unproven land, replacing them with noncompetitive leases, available on a "first come, first served" basis, subject to an initial term of 5 years and continuing thereafter only for as long as oil or gas was produced "in paying quantities"; competitively awarded leases for proven oil lands had an initial term of 10 years with the same condition for continuance. Unitized leases, however, continued in force for as long as the unit operated.

In subsequent years, several states—Arizona, Florida, Illinois, Indiana, and Washington—followed the federal example by taking powers to impose unitization of operations under leases of their own public lands, but none of

---

[204] Ely 1949: 603.

[205] The text of the regulations appears in Ely 1933b: 21–3.

[206] Act of August 21, 1935, amending section 17, Mineral Leasing Act 1920.

these was at that time a significant oil producer from such lands.[207] Federal lands were much more productive, and the vigor and effectiveness with which the unitization requirements of federal regulations and leases were employed is indicated by statistics for 1947–1948: some 8 million acres of public domain was covered by some 11,000 oil and gas leases, but about half of the production for 1947, some 70.36 million barrels, was derived from leases within 148 unitization agreements covering 2.12 million acres of land.[208]

The success of the federal program seems to have made little initial impression on state legislators, faced with the prickly constitutional problems attaching to the unitization of oil and gas fields under private lands. Until the end of the Second World War, only one state, Louisiana, grasped this nettle, enacting in 1940 a statute providing for both compulsory pooling and compulsory unitization where this was needed for recycling gas in certain fields.[209] Two other states, Alabama and Georgia, followed in 1945 with statutes similarly restricted to facilitating secondary recovery operations such as gas recycling, pressure maintenance, or waterflooding (injecting water into existing or new wells around producing wells to sweep the oil toward them). In the same year, Oklahoma, always the pioneer, went a decisive step further with a unitization law that empowered the Corporation Commission to impose a scheme of unit development for secondary recovery purposes or where "reasonably necessary in order to effectively carry on ... any other forms of joint effort calculated to substantially increase the ultimate recovery of oil and gas from the common source of supply."

There were some early but unsuccessful attempts to get the legislature to repeal the statute, and its constitutionality was challenged in the 1951 case of *Palmer Oil Corp. v. Phillips Petroleum Co.*[210] and was sustained by a bare majority of a nine-judge state supreme court bench. Under the law, unitization had to be requested by lessees of at least 50 percent of the proposed unit area, giving rise to notices, commission hearings, and an eventual commission decision; but on objection by lessees of 15 percent or more of the proposed or declared unit area, the commission was bound to abandon the plan.

These elements of industry initiative and control had respectable antecedents. As we have seen, it was groups of producers who, from the first beginnings of production control in Oklahoma, demanded, and often shaped in detail, the measures applied by state conservation agencies, and detailed decisions on matters like well potentials were

---

[207] Material in this paragraph is drawn from Hardwicke 1951: 41, and Hardwicke 1961: 166–7.

[208] Ely 1949: 613.

[209] Act 157 of 1940.

[210] 204 Okla. 543, 231 P. 2d 997 (1951). The decision was confirmed on appeal to the U.S. Supreme Court, which found that it raised no substantive federal question.

often delegated to field umpires drawn from the industry. Indeed, the ABA's Committee of Nine, which drafted its model compulsory cooperative development law (while balking at compulsory unitization on the grounds that it must be unconstitutional), thought it crucial to provide expressly for this kind of initiative by operators if state-backed regulation efforts were to succeed.[211]

The plaintiffs argued, however, that these provisions represented an unconstitutional delegation to private parties of the state's police power, a contention that the majority of the court disposed of without difficulty by pointing out that the effective decision was that of the commission, not the proponents. In the lead dissenting opinion, Justice Welch put things another way, saying that it was hard to understand how, once a compulsory unitization proposal had been solemnly held after inquiry to be "reasonably necessary," the statute could contemplate that the mere written protest of holders of 15 percent of the lease rights affected should nullify the whole scheme.[212]

One can see some force in Welch's analysis, and the Oklahoma legislature took the hint and rewrote its law in 1951 so as to merge the "popular approval" provisions by stipulating that a compulsory unit operation order of the commission could become effective only if approved by 63 percent of both operating and royalty interests in the unit area.[213] The omission of royalty interests from the decisionmaking process had been another ground of attack on the 1945 law. The Interstate Oil Compact Commission's Model Conservation Statute, adopted at about the same time, also provided for a vote on a proposal by operating and royalty interests, but it left considerable discretion to the State Conservation Commission as to the course to be followed in the event of a failure to assemble whatever majority the enacting legislature had thought fit to provide for.[214]

THE FATE OF UNITIZATION IN THE UNITED STATES

Given that the entire history of twentieth century petroleum regulation had been one of state-supplied coercion solicited by producers incapable of self-regulation, Welch's objection to producer initiatives and vetoes in decisionmaking on unitization looks like either willful blindness to the historical facts or an unusual degree of hypocrisy. Nonetheless, it did crystallize the suspicion that seemed to hang then, and in places like Texas still hangs now, over every cooperative development proposal: that the benefits, or at least some of the benefits, expected

---

[211] Above, 281.
[212] 204 Okla. 562, 231 P. 2d 1016–17.
[213] Walker 1951: 294–5.
[214] *Ibid.* 295–6.

by those who put it forward are going to be obtained at the expense of other participants in the field. The idea that unitization can be a positive-sum game for all seems a very hard one for some people in the industry to accept. A sense of the feeling of many industry participants about unitization can be gathered from the language that an oil company executive felt he had to use when addressing a group of Texas oil and gas lawyers in 1949:

> In approaching the problem of unit operation along that line of thought, there is no preachment for monopoly, no call for the elimination of the system of free enterprise, no advancement of an un-American doctrine. Unit operation of an oil pool is consistent with the American system of free enterprise, with the American system of law, and with the American concept of the rights of individuals. It is not un-American to produce twice to three times as much mineral wealth as might otherwise be obtained. It is not un-American to obtain the maximum recovery from an oil and gas pool. It is not un-American to conserve a vital national resource.[215]

At the same time, it would require another kind of blindness or naïveté to maintain that the framing of conservation schemes, whether in the nature of prorationing, well spacing, pooling, or unitization, has always been a process in which all parties acted disinterestedly in support of securing maximum efficient recovery from a given field. A paper by Sheldon Graham, an Exxon staff lawyer, listed a remarkable range of factors adduced at Texas Railroad Commission hearings as relevant to setting prorationing allowables under field rules: excess water, offers to pool, pressure, production costs, drilling costs, penalties for large tracts, effect on the state's economy, time of depletion, location of the structure, natural advantages, depth, density, and permeability. He concluded with the thought that "[i]t is coincident almost to the point of miraculous how often the proposed formula would work out to the largest possible allowable for the proponent."[216]

The calculations going into the apportionment of production among leases under a unitization scheme are essentially of the same type, in that they may involve a choice among variables (what measure of reserves to adopt, for example) whose application could produce different distributions of benefits. Moreover, they lead to a situation where the individual lessee (unless the unit operator) and lessor lose all possibility of independent action, a much more dramatic loss of autonomy than under any other form of conservation scheme. Among the opportunities thus definitively lost is that of obtaining more oil or gas by means of independent operation than any objective apportionment formula would ascribe

---

[215] Kaveler 1949: 333.
[216] Graham 1975: 63–4.

to one's tract, by exploiting the opportunities that continue to be afforded, even today, by the operation of the rule of capture.[217] Small wonder, then, that commentators continue to lament the difficulties of achieving voluntary unitization and to urge broader compulsory powers.[218] Small wonder, too, that in the face of continuing suspicion, state legislatures continue, half a century after the *Palmer* case, to approach with the utmost reserve the issue of compulsory unitization. Gary Libecap and Steven Wiggins demonstrated in 1985 how these same factors that inhibit voluntary unitization by contract operate to block legislative change that would make compulsion easier.[219]

Neither the first (Pennsylvania) nor the mightiest (Texas) among the oil and gas producing states has a compulsory unitization statute.[220] In Texas, the latest of a number of attempts to secure passage of such a statute failed in 1999.[221] Unfortunately for the cause of efficient production, Texas is still by far the largest U.S. oil and gas producer, providing one and a half times as much oil and three times as much gas as its nearest rivals among the states.[222] Data on the next 15 states on the production ladder indicate that the majority, in their legislation, specifically associate compulsory unitization with secondary recovery operations, though usually with an additional general power in their commission or other regulatory body to require unitization for "any other form of joint effort calculated to substantially increase the ultimate recovery of oil and gas from the common source of supply."[223] Arguably, this formula does not exclude a compulsory unitization at the exploratory stage, if a convincing case that unitization will increase recovery can be made at that time.

An attempt to create a large exploratory unit in Utah in 2007, where the oil and gas unitization provision is broadly of this type,[224] failed on the ground that the seismic data—there had been no drilling—did not provide sufficiently convincing evidence of the existence of a reservoir, a prerequisite for the exercise of jurisdiction by the Utah Board of Oil, Gas and Mining. The board, although finding "many of the policy

---

[217] See generally below, at 295–302.

[218] For recent examples, see Libecap and Smith 2002; Kramer and Martin 1999: Ch. 17.01; Anderson and Smith 1999; 2004.

[219] Libecap and Wiggins 1985: 706–12.

[220] Documents of the Pennsylvania Department of Environmental Protection, the responsible agency, refer to unitization orders under Pennsylvania statutes, Title 58, Ch. 7 (the Oil and Gas Conservation Act of 1961) § 408, as does Carr 2003: App. A, but this provision refers only to compulsory pooling of interests in a spacing unit.

[221] Weaver 2004: 190–1. The bill was reintroduced in 2001, again without success.

[222] United States. Energy Information Administration 2007b.

[223] Interstate Oil and Gas Conservation Compact Commission 1999: 9, 20–23; 1 Bradley 1996: 206–7; Carr 2003: App. A.

[224] Utah Code, Title 40 § 6.7.

arguments in favor of early unitization persuasive," also held that the applicants had provided insufficient evidence to support a claim of increased recovery.[225] Only Louisiana (for reservoirs at depths of 15,000 feet of more)[226] and Arkansas[227] do not impose any limitation tending to restrict compulsory unitization to periods subsequent to the initial development of the field. In addition, all the states with compulsory powers save Alaska require approval by mineral interest owners representing a statutory minimum percentage of acreage in the field before unitization can be imposed on the remainder. Unless the commission, the courts of the state, and the requisite majority of interest holders are prepared to accept and act on the general proposition that a sound scheme of unitization will result in greater recovery of oil and gas than drilling and production regulated by the state's spacing and pooling rules, these requirements mean that unitization will never be imposed until substantial development has already taken place.

A 1973 experiment seeking to correlate the outline of a hypothetical, randomly situated, substantial oilfield (1 by 1.5 miles in extent) with lease boundaries in southern New Mexico suggested that the chances that such a field would be contained within the bounds of a single lease were negligible, and that an average of more than 7 leases would be needed to cover such a field.[228] Given that southern New Mexico is a dry area with unusually large landholdings, this suggests that most if not all substantial fields in the United States will involve multiple leases and should thus be produced under unitization arrangements. Is this likely to happen? The chances are very closely correlated with the nature of ownership of the oil interests. We have already seen that even before 1950, a very substantial proportion of federal production came from unitized fields, thanks to the power to require unitization at the exploration stage.[229] In Alaska, where in 2008 around 98 percent of oil and gas was produced from either state or federal lands, oil production from unitized fields represented over 99 percent of total production in that year; the figure for gas was about 93 percent. Such proportions have been maintained since 1977.[230]

The comparative advantage of public ownership is borne out by the only systematic study of the extent of unitized production ever undertaken. This was the

---

[225] *In re the Request for Agency Action of Petro-Hunt, LLC, for an Order Establishing the Wales Exploratory Unit*, Finding of Facts, Conclusions of Law, and Order, Docket No. 2006-015, Cause No. 176-04 (January 12, 2007). I am grateful to Professor Owen Anderson for drawing my attention to this application.

[226] Louisiana Revised Statutes, Title 30 § 5.1.

[227] Arkansas Code Title 15, Ch. 72 § 309(2)(3).

[228] Miller 1973: 417–18.

[229] Above, text at n. 205.

[230] Figures kindly supplied by the Alaska Oil and Gas Conservation Commission.

work of Libecap and Wiggins, indefatigable students of the unitization phenomenon, who painstakingly compared lists of fully unitized fields held at state oil and gas regulatory commissions with privately published field production data.[231] Although their comparisons were subject to some uncertainties arising from difficulties in matching field names from one source with unit names from another, they were able to compile a comparative list of percentages of production from unitized fields in three states, Wyoming, Oklahoma, and Texas, for each year from 1948 to 1975. In all three states, this percentage steadily rose over these 27 years, but to remarkably different levels. In Wyoming, with a very large percentage of federal land, the range was from 58 percent in 1948 to 82 percent in 1975; in Oklahoma, which may be regarded as having a typical compulsory unitization statute in terms of purpose and percentage threshold, from 9 to 38 percent, with little increase between 1967 and 1975; and in Texas, lacking any powers to compel unitization, from 0 to 20 percent. These figures were from fully unitized fields; if we also include partially unitized fields, the percentages were certainly higher—48 percent of Texas crude oil production in 1979, 64 percent of Oklahoma crude oil production in 1982[232]—but these fields continue to be subject to competitive drilling across boundaries between unitized and nonunitized areas and between the subunits into which large fields are often divided.

There is no way of knowing for sure how far, if at all, whole-field unitization has advanced since 1975 because, of the five leading oil and gas producing states, only Alaska, highly atypical with almost all production coming from state-owned resources, was able to provide me with any indication of the percentage of state production deriving from unitized fields. It is hard, however, to identify any particular change since 1975 that would modify the fundamental lessons of the Libecap–Wiggins study: that publicly owned petroleum resources are far more likely to be exploited in a rational manner than privately owned resources, and that the extent of unitization of such privately owned resources is far lower than the widespread existence of compulsory unitization statutes might lead one to assume.

The favored current path for reform is thus to persuade states to relax their daunting requirements for compulsory unitization, notably by adopting the express provisions for compulsory unitization at the exploratory stage contained in the current version of the Interstate Oil and Gas Compact Commission's Model Oil and Gas Conservation Act of 2004.[233] The act requires only that the costs of operating the exploratory unit be reasonable in light of the possible risks and rewards and that "[e]xploratory unit operation for that area or portion thereof is

---

[231] Libecap and Wiggins 1985: 701–3.
[232] Weaver 1986: 316.
[233] See Part VII, §§ 22–8.

reasonably necessary to prevent waste, to encourage reasonable, orderly, effective, and efficient exploration and potential development, to avoid the drilling of potentially unnecessary wells, and to protect correlative rights."[234]

The insertion of this provision in the act may be seen as evidence of a further step along the stony road of unitization reform, as may the fact that the Texas Independent Producers and Royalty Owners Association supported the unsuccessful 1999 attempt to pass a state compulsory unitization statute.[235] State regulatory commissions may sometimes be ready to exert pressure in favor of unitization by issuing shut-in orders to prevent waste that might otherwise result from nonunitized secondary recovery. Wyoming offers some strong examples of this type,[236] which echo the Texas campaign in the 1940s led by Commissioner Murray.[237] But the distance still to be traveled to reach Henry Doherty's goal of a regulatory regime that would replace other mechanisms and render the rule of capture irrelevant can be measured by the simple fact that four of the five leading oil and gas producing states—Texas, Oklahoma, Louisiana, and California— collect no data on unitized production. Stephen McDonald's complaint of 40 years ago still rings true: "[T]here seems nowhere to be an understanding that unitization is a *fundamental* solution of the conservation problem at the reservoir level; that private pursuit of profit under unitization *substitutes* for regulation in all respects except that pertaining to external damages."[238]

HOW CAPTURE SURVIVES

Meanwhile, the law of capture survives and thrives in the fertile soil of the American private ownership system. It may seem hard to believe, but in Pennsylvania today, one of the largest remaining U.S. gas resources, the Marcellus Shale, is being developed under a law of capture unmodified by any of the regulatory arrangements analyzed in this chapter. By the time the movement for conservation regulation got going in the 1910s, Pennsylvania's hydrocarbon production had declined so far from its peak in 1891 that the enactment of elaborate legislation was thought unnecessary. Not until 1961 did the state enact an Oil and Gas Conservation Act incorporating controls such as spacing and

---

[234] § 22(1). For commentary, see Anderson and Smith 2004.

[235] Smith and Weaver 1998: § 11.8(C).

[236] See, e.g., *Majority of the Working Interest Owners in the Buck Draw Field Area v. Wyoming Oil and Gas Conservation Commission*, 721 P. 2d 1070 (Wyo. 1986).

[237] See text above, at n. 168.

[238] McDonald 1971: 226 (emphasis in original).

pooling, and even then existing productive strata, defined as those lying above the Onondaga horizon, were by its section 3(b) excluded on the ground that their "uninterrupted exploration and development ... have been carried on exhaustively since the discovery of oil in the Drake Well in 1850 [*sic*] without regulatory restriction or control to such an extent that at the present stage of development it would be impractical and detrimental to the operation of such shallow horizons to impose regulations under this act."[239]

Although the Marcellus Shale is encountered at depths of up to 2 miles, it lies above the Onondaga horizon and can thus be exploited without regard to the conservation requirements of the 1961 act.[240] Successful exploitation of the shale calls for advanced techniques of horizontal drilling and hydraulic fracturing (which I discuss below in connection with the exploitation of the Barnett Shale in Texas), but although the feasibility of large-scale production was demonstrated in 2005, starting a new Pennsylvania hydrocarbon boom, the state legislature has not yet (as of April 2010) gotten around to bringing it within the Oil and Gas Conservation Act.

In other states, where time has not stood still, a sense of when and how the rule of capture may matter, despite regulatory attempts at control, can be gleaned from one or two of the individual stories that appear in the guise of litigation in state and federal courts. The facts in *Cowling v. Board of Oil, Gas and Mining*, decided by the Supreme Court of Utah in 1991,[241] were simple. Mrs. Cowling and the other plaintiffs were heirs of Adra Baird, who had granted to a company called Celsius a lease of her lands. Celsius discovered a new gas field with a well drilled on the lease but thought the field might extend into adjoining federal land it also held on lease from the federal Bureau of Land Management (BLM). Pursuant to Utah's Oil and Gas Conservation Act, Celsius promptly applied to the board for a spacing order, which would determine the area that might be drained by a single well on the field and could be followed by a pooling order under which an owner of other acreage within the field (in this case, the BLM) would be entitled to a share of the royalties on production from the field corresponding to its share of the acreage in the spacing unit. An order was initially refused because the board thought Celsius had provided insufficient information to determine how large an area its well would drain. By the time an order was made, on the basis of a second application two years later, showing that the Baird family lease overlay 110.14 acres of the field and the BLM lease the remaining 90, Celsius had been producing the field for two

---

[239] Oil and Gas Conservation Act 1961, Declaration of Policy.

[240] Operations are, however, subject to other legislation regulating the drilling of wells for the protection of environmental and coal-mining interests: Oil and Gas Act 1984.

[241] 830 P. 2d 220. For criticism, see Richards et al. 1994.

years and had paid all the royalties, some $230,000, to the Baird family. The board therefore made the associated pooling order retroactive and told the Bairds to repay to the BLM the royalties Celsius had paid on gas that had in fact been drawn from under the federal lease.

The Conservation Act gave the board power to make an order that would be "just and reasonable," and it might at first sight look as if it would be only just and reasonable for the Bairds to pay back money they had received in respect of oil from their neighbor's land, especially since the Conservation Act recognized and purported to protect the correlative rights of landowners in oil and gas, defining these as "the opportunity of each owner in a pool to produce his just and equitable share of the oil and gas in a pool without waste." This conclusion seemed to be reinforced by the fact that Utah also had a general spacing rule, Rule C-3(b), akin to Rule 37 in Texas, preventing the drilling of a well within a given distance of another well and of a property boundary. The effect of that rule, unless the board granted an exception, would be to prevent the drilling of a second well on the BLM lease so as to protect it from drainage.

These puny obstacles could not withstand the battering ram of the rule of capture, as wielded by the Utah Supreme Court. The Conservation Act, it said in a unanimous opinion, might have modified the rule of capture, but it had not wholly displaced it. Before a spacing order was entered, the statutory correlative right was nothing more than "a right to an undifferentiated and unquantifiable interest in an oil or gas pool beneath one's land," and it was therefore wrong to make the pooling order retroactive to a time before the spacing order here was made, because this "would give adjoining interest owners correlative rights before those rights are definable."[242] The rule of capture, in other words, held unfettered sway until the regulatory regime was activated by the making of a spacing order for the field. And Rule C-3(b)? Nothing more than a "minor restriction of a landowner's right to drill under the law of capture [which] does not mean, however, that the law of correlative rights attaches." The court went so far as to suggest that the bureau should have protected its position by applying to the board for permission under the rule to drill a totally unnecessary second well.[243]

Cowling was not an unusual decision, save perhaps in that the court was overturning a decision by the conservation authority. Other authorities, such as the Oklahoma Corporation Commission and the Louisiana Commissioner of Conservation, have operated on the principle that their oil conservation regulation comes into effect only when a field spacing order is made, and that production

---

[242] 830 P. 2d 226–7.
[243] *Ibid.* at 228.

prior to that moment is subject to the rule of capture, and this position has been affirmed by their state courts.[244]

There are, however, cases where a court has sustained retroactive pooling. A similar story unfolded in the Nebraska case of *Farmers Irrigation District v. Schumacher*,[245] and a majority of the court, holding that the producing party was guilty of "delaying tactics," found that the commission was entitled to make pooling effective from the date of first production, but only over a strong dissent from a three-judge minority. Both opinion and dissent stressed the danger that allowing parties who had not developed their land to share from the beginning in the fruits of drilling and investment on neighboring leases would encourage free riding and leave the drilling party with an unfair allocation of risk. One suspects that it is this policy consideration, reflecting a strong and continuing American preference for enterprise and self-help, that underpins continuing judicial attachment to the rule of capture.

The Utah court's embrace of the rule remains, in any event, relatively cool and calm compared with that of its Texas brethren. In *Cowling*, the court found the board guilty of nothing more than misreading the conservation statute. But when the Texas Railroad Commission attempted in 1981 to backdate a pooling order under the state's Mineral Interest Pooling Act, the court of appeals qualified this action as "an unconstitutional retroactive interference with vested property rights"[246]—that is, with the right to capture. Despite the Texas Supreme Court's decisions in the *Atlantic Refining* and *Halbouty* cases,[247] the status of capture as a constitutionally protected right to take other people's property (remember that Texas has subscribed for the last hundred years to the notion of the absolute ownership of oil and gas in place) seems to remain as strong in Texas as ever.

As oil gets more difficult to find and recover, capture seems to be conquering new areas of operation. Since the earliest days of the oil industry, there has been an issue over whether the use of particular methods of recovering oil and gas was or was not covered by the general principle of capture. With very few exceptions, such as the Indiana doctrine that correlative rights principles limited any producer to taking the "natural flow" from its wells,[248] courts have consistently favored the use of efficient

---

[244] *Wood Oil Co. v. Corporation Commission*, 205 Okl. 537, 239 P.2d 1023 (1950); *Desormeaux v. Inexco Oil Co.*, 298 So.2d 897 (La.App. 3rd Cir. 1974). For general discussion of these and other cases on the issue, see Anderson 1982b.

[245] 187 Neb. 825, 194 N.W. 2d 788 (1972).

[246] *Buttes Resources Co v. Railroad Commission of Texas*, 732 S.W. 2d 675, at 682 (Texas Ct App 1987).

[247] *Atlantic Refining Co. v. Railroad Commission of Texas*, 346 S.W. 2d 801 (1961); *Halbouty v. Railroad Commission of Texas*, 163 Tex. 417, 357 S.W. 364 (1962).

[248] Above, Ch. 7, at 190–1.

production technology and refused to draw artificial lines between "natural" and "unnatural" production methods. As the Supreme Court of Louisiana once put it, there is nothing "natural" about drilling a well in the first place.[249]

This acceptance of technological advance became less easy with the generalization of methods of secondary recovery from oilfields whose natural flow was exhausted, often by overintensive initial drilling. As was well understood as early as the 1920s, to get more out of such fields, one needed to restore gas pressures by reinjection of gas or to recover remaining oil from the most favorably sited wells by waterflooding. Frequently such operations, involving costly plants or new drilling, could not be attempted with any chance of success unless a group of lessors or lessees with contiguous leases could agree on at least a partial unitization of the field for this purpose, and this, as we have seen, was the main driver for state promotion of voluntary and compulsory unitization. Such unitizations provided a contractual solution for what, in their absence, appeared as a new kind of capture problem. If, for example, lessee A planted a row of water injection wells on the edge of its lease in order to drive the remaining oil toward its producing wells, lessee B might find that its own nearby wells, on the same accumulation of oil, were now producing nothing but A's injected water.

Unsurprisingly, people in the position of lessee B were quick to complain when this happened, and the cases they brought confronted the courts with an awkward problem of classification, not dissimilar to those they had evaded by silence in the nineteenth century. Was A guilty of some kind of civil wrong in affecting B's land in this way? Making someone's land less valuable by bringing onto it (or here, into it) a substance like water immediately evokes, for a lawyer, the wrong of nuisance, and the facts of the leading British nineteenth-century case of *Rylands v. Fletcher*,[250] where a landowner was found liable in nuisance when water he had accumulated in a reservoir on his land escaped and inundated the land of his neighbor, even though he had been in no way negligent. Alternatively, the act of waterflooding could be seen as a trespass, an actual invasion of lessee B's land by the introduction of water under pressure. Either of these characterizations, though, could be countered by the claim that A was doing no more than apply the most advanced techniques to get its own oil, and that any disadvantage this produced for B, by the displacement of its oil and gas, was just another manifestation of the familiar principle of capture: a "negative rule of capture," as it was termed by the authors of one of the leading oil and gas legal texts. As they put it: "Just as under the rule of capture a landowner may capture such oil or gas as will migrate from

---

[249] In *Higgins Fuel and Oil Co. v. Guaranty Oil Co.*, 145 La 233, 82 So. 206 (1919), discussed above, Ch. 7, at 192–3.

[250] (1868) L.R. 3 H.L. 330.

adjoining premises to a well bottomed on his own land, so also may he inject into a formation substances which may migrate through the structure to the land of others, even if this results in the displacement under such land of more valuable with less valuable substances."[251]

The choices courts have made between the alternatives thus offered have sometimes been obscured by the fact that such secondary recovery operations have usually been authorized by the relevant state regulatory commission in the exercise of its conservation powers, thus setting up a further conflict between regulatory authorization and possible common-law liability. Generally, however, they have refrained from giving any explicit endorsement to the notion of a "negative rule of capture"—probably wisely, given the stubborn resistance to control exhibited by its "positive" elder brother.

The nearest a court has come to such endorsement was in the Texas case of *Railroad Commission of Texas v. Manziel*,[252] where the Supreme Court of Texas referred with apparent approval to the notion of "negative capture" and held that the waterflooding activities complained of by Manziel, which had been approved by an order of the Railroad Commission in pursuit of express statutory authority, did not constitute a subsurface trespass. Courts in other states have generally taken a similar view on the trespass issue but have been reluctant to deny recovery to adversely affected parties altogether, even in cases where the secondary recovery program involved has regulatory sanction; instead, they have used concepts like nuisance or applied the principle in *Rylands v. Fletcher*, or the notion of the "unnatural flow" occasioned by the activity, as the basis of liability.[253] In some of these cases, we find the court stating explicitly that the rule of capture is not applicable in such circumstances.[254]

The latest capture drama relates not to the effects of secondary recovery, but to a primary recovery procedure that, though in use for many years, has existed in a kind of legal limbo. This is the technique of hydraulic fracturing, usually called "fracing," which permits the extraction of gas from "tight" reservoir formations with low permeability, through which the gas will not flow naturally to the wellhead. Today it is of crucial economic importance because of the enormous amounts of gas contained in shale formations like the Marcellus Shale in Pennsylvania and New York State and the Barnett Shale in the Dallas–Fort Worth area of Texas. Such gas can only be recovered by this means. "Fracing," in the

---

[251] Williams and Meyers 2003: para. 204.5.

[252] 361 S.W. 2d 580 (Tex. 1962).

[253] See authorities cited in Thibault et al. 2008: 24-11–24-13, and also *Tidewater Oil Co. v. Jackson*, 320 F. 2d 157 (10th Cir. 1963).

[254] E.g., *Jameson v. Ethyl Corp.*, 271 Ark. 621, 609 S.W. 2d 346 (1980), a brine pumping case.

words of the majority opinion of the Texas Supreme Court in *Coastal Oil and Gas Corp. v. Garza Energy Trust* (2008),[255] involves

> pumping fluid down a well at high pressure so that it is forced out into the formation. The pressure creates cracks in the rock that propagate along the azimuth of natural fault lines in an elongated elliptical pattern in opposite directions from the well. Behind the fluid comes a slurry containing small granules called proppants— sand, ceramic beads, or bauxite are used—that lodge themselves in the cracks, propping them open against the enormous subsurface pressure that would force them shut as soon as the fluid was gone. The fluid is then drained, leaving the cracks open for gas or oil to flow to the wellbore.[256]

A legal question mark has hung over fracing, because the cracks it creates may well extend several thousand feet and pass beyond the boundary of the property on which the well is drilled. Arguably, therefore, fracing could constitute a subsurface trespass, so that any drainage from the adjoining property would be the consequence of an unlawful act and would not be excused by the rule of capture. Perhaps judging that it was best to let sleeping dogs lie, the Texas Railroad Commission has never taken a position on the issue, while the state's courts have skirted it nervously: language used by the supreme court in *Gregg v. Delhi-Taylor Oil Co.*[257] suggested that there might be a trespass when fracing fluid moved beyond the lease line, but having held to this effect in an opinion in *Geo-Viking Inc. v. Tex-Lee Operating Co.* in 1992, the court withdrew the opinion on rehearing as having been "improvidently granted" and said it did not need to decide the issue.[258]

Given the potential clash between production expediency and presumptive illegality, the decision of the court was keenly awaited when the issue was squarely raised in 2008 in the *Coastal* case. Here the plaintiff landowners sought damages from Coastal, which was both their lessee and the mineral owner on adjoining land, for subsurface trespass occasioned by the "massive" fracing of a well on Coastal's own land not far from the property line between the parties, which the Garza Trust claimed had produced extensive drainage from its land. The Railroad Commission, the land commissioner, the royalty owners, and the independents all piled into this dispute on the side of the fracing oil company by submitting amicus curiae briefs—arguments offered as "friends of the court"—offering dire warnings

---

[255] 268 S.W. 3d 1.

[256] *Ibid.* at 6–7.

[257] 162 Tex. 26, 344 S.W. 2d 411 (1961).

[258] 839 S.W. 2d 897 (Tex. 1992).

as what to would happen to production, employment, tax revenues, and exploration in Texas if the court made the wrong decision.

The court listened and dismissed this part of the plaintiffs' claim, but the reasoning of the majority opinion was so convoluted as to seem almost deliberately calculated to muddy the issue. Clear positions *were* articulated in dissenting and concurring opinions. A three-judge dissent took the view that fracing was indeed a subsurface trespass, and that the rule of capture could not apply to justify the consequent drainage of gas, because that rule protected only *lawful* drainage. A concurring opinion held that the court ought, with the public interest in view, to adjust notions like trespass to the circumstances in which the action complained of occurred, and that causing cracks in the ground and invasions of fluid and ceramic beads 2 miles down (the depth of the well in question) should simply not be regarded as trespass.

The five-judge majority could not bring itself to adopt either of these clear positions. It began by asserting that though the plaintiffs were lessors, and therefore not in possession of the oil interest in their land (which they had passed to Coastal as their lessee), they could still maintain an action of trespass, but only on the basis of actual injury to their residual, nonpossessory interests—that is, their royalty interest. Because, however, the only injury alleged by the Garza Trust was the loss of gas occasioned by the fracing operation, it could not recover because such a claim was "precluded by the law of capture. ... The gas he claims to have lost simply does not belong to him."[259] The court rejected the idea, advanced by the plaintiffs and accepted in the dissenting opinion, that there was no substantive difference between recovery from under neighboring property by creating subterranean fissures and by drilling a directional well bottomed on the neighbor's property, a common, indeed almost customary, practice in the East Texas field at one time but one judicially condemned as subsurface trespass.[260] It went on to offer four reasons why the rule of capture should not be "changed": the person suffering drainage had other remedies (offset drilling, suing the lessee for breach of covenant, forced pooling); this would represent judicial interference with the capacity of the Railroad Commission to protect correlative rights ("[w]ithout the rule of capture, drainage would amount to a taking of a mineral owner's property—*the* oil and gas below the surface of the property—thereby limiting the Commission's power to regulate production to assure a fair recovery by each owner"); the question whether propped fractures actually crossed property lines would raise evidentiary difficulties for courts, which were also ill equipped to take into account social policies, industry operations, and the greater good, all

---

[259] 268 S.W. 3d, at 13.
[260] *Hastings Oil Co. v. Texas Co.*, 149 Tex. 416, 234 S.W.2d 389 (1950); Prindle 1981: 81–91.

"tremendously important" in evaluating a practice in use for 60 years; and finally, everybody who was anybody in the industry, from royalty owners to drilling contractors, had put in briefs saying so.[261]

Fracing is really nothing more than today's high-tech version of the nineteenth-century technique of "improving" wells by dropping a container of nitroglycerin down them and standing well back. This, it will be recalled, was held in 1892 to be a legitimate operation that did not make unlawful the drainage of oil or gas from neighboring land, drainage that would ordinarily—it was so conceded by the plaintiff—be justified by the law of capture.[262] It is extraordinary how this 2008 opinion on fracing takes us back to the issues that surrounded the first capture cases. Effectively, the opinion spells out, as compelling in the operation of capture today, the same considerations, then largely unspoken, that earned capture judicial recognition in the first place. People had been doing it for years. Intervening would upset established relationships. Evidence was difficult to obtain. A self-help solution (offset drilling) was available.

It seems abundantly clear, from *Coastal Oil and Gas Corp. v. Garza* and from the other examples cited here, which could be multiplied several times over, that the rule of capture retains its century-old grip on the mind of the American judge, despite more than 100 years of legislation and regulation aimed at mastering its unfortunate consequences. *Coastal* demonstrates the extraordinary difficulty of eradicating, or even modifying, a common-law rule of property in a country that gives constitutional protection to property rights. It also reflects, in its references to the protection of correlative rights by the Texas Railroad Commission, the paradox that the rule of capture has actually been strengthened by the creation of the massive regulatory apparatus it engendered, because that regulation has been constructed on a property right foundation of which capture forms part.[263] If capture were not the rule, for example, spacing rules would commonly represent an uncompensated taking of property, because regulatory spacing units of a standard 40, 160, or even 640 acres are highly unlikely to coincide with the areas actually drained by the wells drilled on them. Such drainage is in practice tolerated as being generally compensated on a "swings and roundabouts" principle, but in the absence of a law of capture, it could be restrained by injunction at the suit of an uncooperative interest owner. To adopt, at this stage, an alternative common-law rule to that of capture would involve bringing down the entire edifice of oil and gas conservation regulation.

---

[261] 268 S.W. 3d, at 14–17.

[262] *People's Gas Co. v. Tyner*, 131 Ind. 408, 31 N.E. 61 (1892), above, Ch. 2, at 27.

[263] See, in this sense, Kuntz 1957: 408–9; Kramer and Anderson 2005: 951–4, and also 933–49, where the relevance of the rule of capture to other recent cases is examined.

PART IV
EVADING CAPTURE?

CHAPTER 10

SECURING UNIFIED NATIONAL
CONTROL OF PETROLEUM RESOURCES

PATHS TO UNIFIED STATE OWNERSHIP AND CONTROL

The history of unitization in the United States, and the extent to which production derives from unitized fields in different states and on federal lands, demonstrates that it is much easier to achieve rational and economic oil and gas production when rights to petroleum are disconnected from the ownership of the land than when they follow the patterns of surface ownership. Put the rights in one pair of hands, those of the state, and it can pursue the development of its petroleum resource while avoiding the many varieties of wasteful behavior—overdrilling, overinvestment, over-production—engendered by the rule of capture. Such disconnection and unification today operate in virtually every country outside the United States, though there continue to be a few private lessors in Canada and Trinidad. This chapter aims to explain how this has come about, and to determine how—if at all—this global choice is linked with the problems that the United States, as the world's first great petroleum power, experienced in dealing with the results of the rule of capture.

There are three main routes to the state ownership or control of petroleum in the ground. First, state sovereign rights are now recognized to extend to substantial areas over which no surface rights can exist because the areas are underwater—that is, in the seabed of the state's territorial sea and continental shelf. Second, the general property law of the state may separate mineral rights from surface rights and grant the state the ownership, or at least the exclusive control, of these rights. And third, of those countries that, like the United States, subscribe to the accession theory of mineral ownership—and this is true of the entire common-law world as well as a number of other countries—most have taken measures to ensure that petroleum rights, along with other valuable mineral rights, remain in or revert to state ownership. Such countries have often taken specific legislative measures relating to petroleum, and in the latter part of this chapter, I examine in some detail the processes through which petroleum was brought into state ownership in three such jurisdictions: the United Kingdom and, within Australia, the states of Queensland and Western Australia. How far were such nationalization measures inspired by a desire to avoid reproducing in the local oil industry the problems experienced in the United States? The analysis will suggest that while the unfortunate side effects of the rule of capture were indeed among the justifications for these moves, states were as likely as not to adopt policies that reintroduced capture as a potential problem.

SUBSEA RESOURCES

A substantial proportion of the world's petroleum production and reserves is today to be found in the seabed of maritime areas under coastal state control and jurisdiction, where no privately held surface rights can exist. Under article 77 of the 1982 United Nations Convention on the Law of the Sea (UNCLOS), "the coastal State exercises ... sovereign rights over the continental shelf for the purpose of exploring it and exploiting its natural resources [which] are exclusive in the sense that if the coastal State does not explore the continental shelf or exploit its natural resources, no one may undertake these activities without the express consent of the coastal State."[1]

These exclusive coastal state rights have been widely recognized since the first state claims to continental shelf were made in the aftermath of the Second World War, and are now an incontestable feature of international law. The United States was the first country to make an unequivocal claim to continental shelf, by the Truman Proclamation of September 1945, but as of April 2010, it remains one of only a handful of states that have refused to ratify the UNCLOS. Signatory or nonsignatory to the convention, no state denies the principle of state sovereign

---

[1] UNCLOS 1982, art. 77(1), (2).

rights over the natural resources of the shelf, nor the related, much older notion of state sovereignty over the seabed of the territorial seas that lie in immediate proximity to state coasts.[2] Most state claims to territorial sea extend to 12 nautical miles, though the fact that international law permits that width to be measured not necessarily from the coastline itself, but from "baselines" that may be drawn across the mouths of certain bays and between closely spaced offshore islands, means that the maritime area under such state sovereignty may be substantial. Again, the notion of the continental shelf, in law, is much more ample than its geographical definition.

The first national claims to continental shelf were made on the basis that the shelf was a natural prolongation of the land mass of the state, sloping gently into the sea for a distance before declining at a steeper angle until it met the deep seabed. The distribution of such continental shelves is, however, far from even. Not every coastal state possesses a shelf in this sense; quite often, the slope of the land mass extends only a short distance underwater before plunging abruptly to the deep seabed, or to a trough that intersects what might otherwise be a continuous area of shelf. States disfavored by geography in this way, such as those on the west coast of South America, were unwilling to accept a purely geographical definition of the shelf and sought to repair their position by claiming territorial seas of up to 200 nautical miles, so as to ensure their sovereignty over the seabed. The compromise eventually worked out at the United Nations Conference on the Law of the Sea was designed to meet the concerns of such states by granting all coastal states sovereign rights in the seabed up to 200 nautical miles from the baselines of the territorial sea, and indeed beyond that, where it can be shown that the state's geographical continental margin, as defined in the 1982 convention, extends beyond the 200-mile limit.[3] The convention also provided for a 200-mile exclusive economic zone (EEZ) in which states enjoy rights of fishery and environmental control.[4] Taking the continental shelf and EEZ provisions of the convention together, the International Court of Justice has held that a state enjoys a continental shelf of 200 miles even if the profile of the seabed is such that its geographical continental shelf terminates much nearer to its coast.[5]

Over a substantial part of the earth's surface, therefore—estimated at 24.3 million square kilometers[6]—there has never been any possibility of private ownership of subsoil resources such as petroleum. This represents not only a

---

[2] 3 Gidel 1934: 329–30.

[3] UNCLOS 1982, art. 76.

[4] Pt. V, arts. 55–75.

[5] *Libya v. Malta* [1985], I.C.J. Rep. 13.

[6] See earthtrends.wri.org (visited March 2008), presenting data from Pruett and Cimino (2000).

substantial addition to the earth's land area of 148.9 million square kilometers, over most of which states enjoy territorial sovereignty, but also, by reason of the thickness of sedimentary rocks on the continental shelf, a disproportionately important source of hydrocarbons. For Australia, for example, which has the world's fourth-largest continental shelf, after Russia, Canada, and the United States, the major part of its hydrocarbon production has come from offshore. The industry's own figures for 2007 suggest that offshore operations accounted for some 95 percent of production of oil and condensate (liquids that were in gaseous form in the reservoir) and 89 percent of gas production.[7]

States can manage these resources as they wish, subject only to the general—and not very constraining—rules of UNCLOS and customary international law. These rules are designed to preserve traditional freedoms of passage above and upon the continental shelf, such as for the laying of submarine cables and pipelines, and have caused little difficulty.[8] A much more delicate topic is that of how the continental shelf should be divided up among states with adjacent or opposite coastlines, a question intimately connected with that of how to deal with cross-border deposits of oil and gas, and which I discuss in Chapter 12. The way that certain states have managed their continental shelf petroleum resources, and the relevance of the law of capture to that management, is explored in detail in the next chapter.

DOMANIAL AND REGALIAN LEGAL SYSTEMS

The accession system, whereby mineral rights, like airspace rights, are seen as "accessory" to rights in the surface, traces directly back to Roman law texts of the republic and early empire.[9] But as Northcutt Ely, one of America's most prominent oil and gas lawyers of the last century, has explained:

> [T]he legacy of the Roman Empire for mining systems in the modern world was not the accession system, but rather the regalian system. This situation resulted from the fact that a great majority of mines and known mineral deposits outside Italy were acquired by conquest, and hence became the property of the Republic, and later the Empire. Due to this extensive state ownership of mines, the underlying theory became accepted that the state held the primary control over all mineral resources.[10]

---

[7] Australian Petroleum Production and Exploration Association 2008.
[8] UNCLOS 1982, arts. 78–80.
[9] Campbell 1956.
[10] Ely 1975: 7.

Like some other authors, Ely applies the term "regalian" to any system in which rights to some or all minerals are either the *property* of the ruler—or of the state, as we would now say—or under the ruler's exclusive *control*, so that only he or she could grant permission to exploit them, with surface landowners being restricted at best to a right to a royalty or some other financial compensation for the use of their land. I prefer to reserve the word "regalian" for this latter type of system and to use a different term, "domanial," for legal regimes that recognize a right of *property* in the ruler.[11] Although the many feudal lords who ruled and squabbled over European territory in the centuries following the fall of the western Roman Empire generally claimed to control the minerals on their lands, their hold on them was far from secure, was often displaced or qualified by local mining custom, and was seldom asserted for anything beyond precious metals and gemstones. But from the seventeenth century, the growing power of national rulers in Europe enabled them to enforce and, in some cases, extend these rights.

Spain and Latin America

Don Francisco Xavier de Gamboa's *Commentaries on the Mining Ordinances of Spain*, first published in 1761, show how surface owners' rights to precious metals in their land, subject to the payment of a royalty to the Crown, had been steadily cut away, making the prince the absolute owner;[12] and in 1783, Charles III of Spain by ordinance declared all mines, of whatever material and wherever located, to be royal property.[13] The domanial system was thus introduced into the Spanish colonies of South and Central America and has subsequently formed an important component of the legal regime for hydrocarbons there, supporting the notion that hydrocarbon resources form part of the inalienable riches of the nation and sometimes being translated into severe constitutional restrictions on the admission of private, especially foreign, capital to the search for oil and gas.[14] The annexation of Texas in 1845 gave the United States a taste of a domanial system of mineral tenure, as Texas brought into the Union the land law that Mexico had inherited from its Spanish rulers. That system, as we saw earlier,[15] was largely dismantled before the major Texas oil finds brought to the Southwest the anarchy of northern leasing and drilling practice.

---

[11] As do, e.g., Blinn et al. 1986: 24–7.

[12] Gamboa 1830: 15.

[13] For an English translation of the ordinance, see Rockwell 1851: 4–111.

[14] E.g., Constitution of Mexico 1917, art. 27: see Abramowski 1995; Constitution of Brazil 1988, art. 177: see Borromeu de Andrade 1989.

[15] Above, Ch. 8, at 217–9.

It might seem strange that a state should voluntarily give up mineral rights of this kind, but in fact this is not an isolated example. The same thing happened in Mexico itself in 1884, when the government of President Porfirio Diaz handed ownership of subsoil mineral resources to farmers, ranchers, and other surface owners—a step that was to lead to foreign control of 90 percent of oil properties and eventually to the renationalization of Mexican oil reserves under its 1917 constitution.[16] Nor were Texas and Mexico the only states to have hesitated between a domanial and an accession system. In Galicia, the imperial Austro-Hungarian government dithered for years over whether it should exercise domanial rights over oil and gas, finally deciding not to.[17] And as recently as 1991, the Australian Industry Commission gave serious consideration to the notion of handing back mineral rights—which state governments had generally reserved to themselves since the late nineteenth century—to surface owners, inquiring as to whether this would increase the efficiency with which they were managed.[18] Its findings were negative and it did not take the specifics of oil and gas into account, but the inquiry reminds us that it is not axiomatic that states will believe themselves to be the best managers of their mineral resources.

Among Latin American states, Venezuela offers a particularly interesting contrast with Mexico.[19] Venezuela has always been a highly successful oil power. A small producer in the early years of the twentieth century, it was by 1929 second only to the United States in total production, and by 1932 the chief source of Britain's imported oil. With Saudi Arabia, it organized the creation of Organization of the Petroleum Exporting Countries (OPEC) in 1959–1960. It carried through a successful "soft" nationalization of concession rights in the early 1970s, keeping the major companies involved as service contractors.[20] Recent relations between the government and oil companies (including Venezuela's own state company) have been turbulent, but in 2007, Venezuela still accounted for 3.4 percent of world oil production and was estimated to have the largest oil reserves outside the Middle East.[21] Throughout its oil history, Venezuela has never wavered from the domanial principle, but it is clear that this has been no obstacle so far as the oil companies were concerned; indeed, rather the reverse.

Venezuela's Federal Constitution of 1864 affirmed state property in all petroleum and combustibles, and ushered in a practice of granting hydrocarbon

---

[16] Yergin 1991: 232, 271–2; Murphy 1984: 92.

[17] Above, Ch. 6, at 143–4.

[18] Australia. Industry Commission 1991.

[19] For a chronology of Venezuelan oil development, see Martinez 1989.

[20] Yergin 1991: 233–7, 510–23, 648–50.

[21] BP 2008: 6, 8.

concessions—the main early interest was in mining asphalt, as in neighboring Trinidad[22]—which steadily increased in importance and sophistication, and started bearing fruit with significant petroleum discoveries at the beginning of the First World War. But the early concessions, on the pattern which was to become familiar in the Middle East, covered enormous areas for long periods, and the work obligations, which had been designed in the context of mining for solids, were quite inappropriate for petroleum.[23] In 1918, therefore, the Venezuelan government began development of a petroleum law, a process that soon took on the character of a negotiation between the government and oil company interests, in which companies used the threat of withholding investment to secure favorable terms. The resulting Petroleum Law of 1922, fiscally very generous, provided for the grant of 10,000-hectare exploration permits valid for three years, during which time the concessionaire could select for exploitation alternate rectangular parcels of 500 hectares each covering half the permit area; the rest had to be handed back to form part of the national petroleum reserve. There was no limit to the amount of land any one company could hold, and no power to regulate the drilling and production activities of the oil companies.[24]

The principle that only the president could grant concessions, with no right of intervention by the legislature, had already been established by the end of the nineteenth century, and created a common interest of president and companies in concessions as a source of mutual enrichment. Started by President Cipriano Castro (1899–1908), the practice of granting concessions to friends and acquaintances, who immediately sought to sell them on to an oil company with a percentage return to the president, was brought to the level of high art by President Juan Vicente Gomez (1908–1935), whose ever-widening circle of family, friends, and favored acquaintances, known locally as the *gomecistas*, dealt in concessions as a kind of private currency, greatly enlarging the president's wealth and influence in the process.[25] Gomez thus had unusually specific incentives to make concessions attractive to oil companies, and they recognized this by hailing the 1922 law as the best in Latin America and a model of fair dealing between government and industry.[26]

This appreciation is revealing of oil company attitudes—in particular, American oil company attitudes—toward capture and conservation in the 1920s, in that the system of the 1922 law, with its checkerboarding of production areas of

---

[22] Above, Ch. 5.

[23] Lieuwen 1954: Ch. II.

[24] *Ibid.* 24–9; McBeth 1983: Ch. 2.

[25] McBeth 1983: Ch. 3

[26] Lieuwen 1954: 29; McBeth 1983: 66.

moderate size, was highly likely to create problems of drainage between adjacent lots in the hands of different concessionaires. Subdivision of large pre-1922 concessions could produce similar results, and there was no requirement of maintaining a certain distance between wells and concession boundaries to restrain offset drilling. Thus, on the eastern side of Lake Maracaibo, three companies— Shell onshore, Gulf in the shallows, and Standard of Indiana out in the lake—each drilled numerous offset wells to protect its production from the common reservoir, a practice later repeated in the La Rosa, Ambrosio, and Punta Benitez fields.[27] The companies did, however, make joint agreements from time to time on well spacing and other drilling and production problems.[28]

France and the Netherlands

Perhaps the most important European legislation affirming state rights to mineral resources, largely to the exclusion of the surface owner, was the French Mining Law of 1810.[29] We have already seen[30] that the Civil Code, promulgated only a few years earlier, consecrated accession as its key property principle in its article 552. This had indeed been the established position under the civil law of the Ancien Régime. The code itself, however, made that principle subject to the laws and regulations relating to mines, and landowners had already been forced, by the Law of 12–29 July, 1791, to renounce, in favor of the state, any rights to minerals at a depth of more than 100 feet beneath their land. This decision was based on arguments directly pertinent to our theme. The Compagnie des Mines de Charbon d'Anzin (Coal Mining Company of Anzin), at that time the largest French coal-mining company, complained to the revolutionary government of the impossibility of rational exploitation of mines in which dozens of surface owners might have an interest.

Mirabeau (Honore-Gabriel Riqueti), one of the leaders of the revolution, took up their cause before the National Assembly. The surface, he said, was divisible but the mine was not; the mine was never coextensive with the surface divisions; the accession system was destined to lead to confusion over the ownership and exploitation of the mine; an individual surface owner seldom had the resources to develop the mines.[31] Some of Mirabeau's remarks could easily have been uttered in the context of American petroleum conservation debates a century and more later.

---

[27] Lieuwen 1954: 39, 44–5.
[28] Hill and Estabrook 1930: 19.
[29] See generally Aguillon 1912.
[30] Above, Ch. 4, at 96–8.
[31] Mirabeau 1973: 352–71. See Bouvet 1995: 677–81; Campbell 1956: 306.

He anticipated both the need for a system of correlative rights—"Nothing is to be gained from declaring mines private property, because it will almost always be necessary that all the owners of a large land area should agree to cooperate, without which this property of each individual will in reality be that of nobody"—and that wasteful competitive exploitation was a corollary of small-tract ownership: "Two thousand owners will dig two thousand pits for a mining operation that a company would have effected with four."[32]

The right to regulate mineral exploration and production was thus reserved in principle to the state, a task completed by Napoleon's Mining Law. This law subjected the operation of mines to the grant of a state mining concession, confining the surface owner to a limited right to compensation, the *redevance tréfoncière* (subsurface charge), in respect of the use of his land. Thanks to Napoleon's European conquests, the Mining Law was a highly influential document, adopted as such in some territories like the Netherlands and used as a basis for local development elsewhere. Although in France, boring for groundwater, even highly mineralized groundwater, never came within the ambit of the Mining Law, boring for salt was brought within the scope of the concessionary regime in 1840,[33] and the fact that the law referred to "bitumens" was thought sufficient to bring liquid petroleum within its scope as well.

The French mining law expert Louis Aguillon pointed out that Antoine-François de Fourcroy, the person responsible for presenting the draft Mining Law to the Conseil d'Etat (which acts as an adviser on legislation as well as an administrative court) was also an eminent chemist whose classification of bitumens distinguished several different forms of liquid petroleum.[34] For Aguillon, this piece of legislative history was ample rebuttal for arguments that the Mining Law regime was inappropriate because the fluid nature of petroleum meant that the subject matter of a petroleum concession could not be defined with sufficient precision. This argument had been deployed with success to defeat suggestions that landowners near protected mineral water springs should enjoy a *redevance tréfoncière* to compensate them for the loss of development opportunities.[35] Aguillon pointed out that the concession did not give ownership of either the relevant part of the subsoil or the petroleum within it, but only the right to exploit that petroleum and dispose freely of it once recovered.

---

[32] Mirabeau 1973: 359, 369 (my translations).
[33] Law of June 17, 1840: see above, Ch. 4, at 108.
[34] Aguillon 1890.
[35] Above, Ch. 4, at 107–8.

What appears as a matter of defining common-law rights in the United States, in terms of "absolute ownership," "qualified ownership," or "no ownership" solutions,[36] thus appears in France as a matter of identifying the precise rights granted by a state concession; and we shall see that it is exactly this question that determines whether there is scope for the rule of capture to operate within the context of regimes for the management of state petroleum resources in countries such as the United Kingdom, Australia, and indeed, the United States.[37] In taking the position he did, Aguillon seems to have been fully aware that this characteristic of petroleum could lead to competitive drilling between adjoining concession holders—and quite unconcerned about it. "Two neighbouring petroleum concession-holders will thus be able to exercise their rights freely and to the fullest extent, and one need not be concerned about the original location, within the subsoil area, of the petroleum that the one or the other brings to the surface."[38] This might have been true enough, if "one" were the conceding authority; but neither the concessionaires themselves nor, still less, the surface proprietors whose *redevance* was calculated by reference to the value of the mineral recovered from under their land were likely to be as relaxed about the matter.

The Mining Law also contained a lacuna that, though insignificant in relation to hard rock minerals, was likely, if American experience was any guide, to cause real difficulties in relation to oil and gas. Napoleon was reluctant to be seen to be expropriating private property, and thus while the law recognized the concession, once granted by the state, as a form of property quite independent from that in the surface of the land, it left open the question of who owned the minerals before the concession was granted. With the landowner free at this stage to grant access rights to the land, the system, as applied to petroleum, could easily have produced the disorder that followed the application of the placer mining system on federal lands in the United States, with any successful drilling site immediately attracting a swarm of rivals boring in the closest possible proximity.[39] A rational surface landowner might well wish to encourage, rather than prevent, such competition.

The French authorities saw no virtue in this sort of disorderly competition,[40] and so in 1922 they followed the precedent established by the British a few years earlier[41] and established a specialized regime for petroleum,[42] with exploration regulated by the need to obtain the so-called *permis H*, a permit awarded on a

---

[36] Above, Ch. 2, at 29–32.

[37] Below, Ch. 11, at 359–67.

[38] Aguillon 1890: 72.

[39] Above, Ch. 8, at 222–4.

[40] Fehr 1939: 50–1.

[41] Below, at 321–3.

[42] Devaux-Charbonnel 1987: 47–9.

discretionary and exclusive basis by the state. The holder of the permit had a right to a concession in the event of making a discovery. The impact of the rule of capture was limited by the large permit areas that could be granted (5,000 hectares under the Law of 16 December 1922, increased to 50,000 hectares in 1938 and made unlimited by the Law of 4 February 1943).

The 1943 law also removed earlier limits on the size of concessions, so that since then, it has been possible to grant a concession to correspond with the areal extent of the field, and the concession is open to revision by the government, at its discretion, if the field is subsequently shown to extend into land, not subject to mineral occupation, beyond the original concession limits. If such land is already subject to a mineral title, the concession requires the two parties to proceed by agreement, subject to the imposition of working rules by the prefect if they fail to do so.[43] These arrangements could produce unitization but need not do so; the neighboring title might not even relate to petroleum. France has turned out to hold little in the way of hydrocarbon deposits, so these issues have remained largely academic, but it is clear that the rule of capture now has little space in which to operate. It is worth noting, though, that the French approach favors the "first appropriator" both of petroleum, by way of the fieldwide concession, and of sources of mineral water, by the device of the zone of protection.

The Netherlands, where the discovery of the vast Groningen gasfield in 1959 was the trigger for the opening up of the North Sea petroleum province, has effectively arrived at a domanial system for petroleum ownership along similar paths to those taken by France.[44] As in the French Civil Code, the basic principle is that of accession, qualified by the concession arrangements of the 1810 Mining Act, which is simply Napoleon's Mining Law as applied in the Netherlands. As in France, petroleum was regarded as falling under the act, and state control was at first incomplete because exploration for petroleum—as opposed to its production—was unregulated, being a matter for agreement between landowner and explorer. Once discoveries began to be made, however—the first in 1924— exploration was gradually brought under control by a succession of licensing requirements, which under the Mining Exploration Act of 1967, passed after the discovery of the massive Groningen field in 1959, extended throughout the country.

Meanwhile, the Continental Shelf Act of 1965 had also formally claimed for the state the ownership of mineral resources in the Dutch continental shelf, into which the Groningen reservoir extended. From 1967, therefore, state control was effectively complete. Astonishingly, though, it was not until 2003 that the Dutch

---

[43] Décret 81-374 of April 15, 1981.
[44] See generally Roggenkamp 1991: Ch. 1; Roggenkamp 2001: 637–44.

managed to bring into force a replacement, in the form of the Mining Law of that year, for Napoleon's Mining Code, which thus lasted much longer in the Netherlands than in his own country. This new Mining Law, which applies both onshore and offshore, is unequivocal: "Minerals are the property of the State" (article 3(1)).

Islamic Law in the Middle East

Middle Eastern and other nations in the Islamic law tradition, which have met and continue to meet such an enormous proportion of the world's petroleum needs, have, since the discovery of petroleum in their territories, likewise operated what is in effect a domanial system. Today it is possible, in all these jurisdictions, to point to legislative provisions declaring hydrocarbons and other natural resources to be part of the patrimony of the nation and hence under the control of the state. Early and massive petroleum concessions, like that granted by the shah of Persia in 1901 to William Knox d'Arcy over 500,000 square miles of Persia—the whole country save for several northern provinces where Russian influence was strong—were doubtless justified by the same principle, though it appears that there was considerable controversy among the different schools of Islamic law as to where title to minerals lay.

According to an analysis by Walied El-Malik in 1993,[45] only the Maliki school took the position that all kinds of natural resources were state-owned; the Hanafi school took the opposite view and held that mineral ownership followed surface ownership, while the other two schools, Shafie and Hanbali, drew a distinction between "hidden" and "unhidden" minerals. This distinction related *not* to the location of the mineral, underground or visible on the surface, but to its nature: "unhidden" minerals were those that could be clearly distinguished and used once found (e.g., salt, tar, naphtha, and other hydrocarbons) whereas "hidden" minerals (e.g., gold, silver, iron, and copper) needed to be extracted from the ores in which they were held. For these schools, hidden minerals were the property of the surface owner, whereas unhidden minerals were not subject to private ownership. Rulers did not allow these differences to stand in the way of their claims to deal with hydrocarbons, through concessions, without regard for any possible rights of surface owners, though the extent to which the gains from the grant of the early concessions were distributed or held in trust as part of the national patrimony is open to some doubt.

In these and other domanial and regalian systems, the basic property right notions in relation to minerals were clearly formed long before the problems that

---

[45] El-Malik 1993: 50–6.

might be posed by the risk of underground drainage of petroleum were perceived. In principle, the unity of control of minerals that they conferred should have meant that this risk could be eliminated without difficulty. In practice, the risk was simply transmuted from one inherent in the property right system, as in the United States, to one contingent upon the mode of exercise of the state's power over petroleum.

STATE RESERVATION AND ACQUISITION OF PETROLEUM DEPOSITS IN ACCESSION-BASED SYSTEMS

Curiously, the United Kingdom seems to have adhered more faithfully to the accession system of mineral ownership established in Roman law than did its civil law neighbors on the continent of Europe. It certainly emerged from the feudal period without any general disposition to recognize a broad right to minerals in feudal lords or in the monarch as the highest among these. An attempt by Queen Elizabeth in the sixteenth century to expand the royal prerogative in this area met with only limited and temporary success. Elizabeth claimed the right to work and take copper from private land, as an extension of a claimed royal prerogative in mines of gold and silver. The royal argument was that mines of copper or lead frequently contained some gold or silver and should therefore be regarded as "royal mines."

A challenge to the queen by a landowner, the earl of Northumberland, led to a decision of all the judges recognizing her rights to all mines in which gold and silver might be mixed with other ores, but there was no sign of any judicial willingness to extend those rights any further,[46] and in the late eighteenth century, the decision was reversed by a statute limiting the monarch to a right of preemption of the product of copper, tin, lead, or iron mines.[47] In the absence of any such royal prerogative or any local mining custom recognized as law, such as the customs of the tin miners of Cornwall or the lead miners of Derbyshire,[48] the freehold owner of land would hold the mineral rights also. In some—but probably very rare—cases, such rights might figure explicitly in the original grant of lands from the Crown. In the vast majority of cases, that grant would have been lost, or be silent on the matter, and the attachment of the mineral rights to the surface would follow as a presumption on the basis of the accession principle.

---

[46] *Case of Mines* (1568), 1 Plowden 310 at 336–7, 75 Eng. Rep. 472 at 510–11.
[47] Bainbridge 1878: 117–34.
[48] *Ibid.* 138–60.

In territories conquered or colonized by the British, the matter took on a different aspect. Through the acquisition of lands by treaty from the original inhabitants, or the application of the convenient theory of "discovery" or its Australian counterpart of *terra nullius*, making their enjoyment of their lands subject to the pleasure of the government,[49] the British Crown acquired the right to dispose of enormous areas of land. The process of granting land to individuals in the new territories thus offered the Crown, if it wished, the opportunity of reserving mineral rights. Practice on this matter has varied from time to time and from place to place. In the North American colonies, minerals generally passed with the original Crown grants: Charles II's 1681 grant to William Penn, for example, expressly included all minerals, including gold, silver, and precious stones, though with a 20 percent royalty on gold and silver ore.[50] As we saw in Chapter 8, general postindependence practice in the United States, by or under congressional legislation, also tended to leave mineral ownership with the proprietor of the surface. The same approach, normally subject to a reservation of gold and silver to the Crown, was taken in the Australian states for up to a century after the first British settlement in 1788. At various dates between 1884 and 1909, however, all of the states changed their policies and enacted legislation under which subsequent freehold grants were to be made subject to a reservation of minerals. Mineral rights in land previously granted were left in private hands.[51] By the early decades of the twentieth century, therefore, some minerals in Australia were privately owned, some that underlay privately owned land were still in state ownership through reservation, and the rest, likewise in state ownership, were under land that either had never been alienated by the state or was the subject of pastoral leases granted over large tracts of land for running cattle and sheep.

Because the system of private ownership of minerals worked well in the United Kingdom, providing efficient access to the resources of coal and iron needed to drive the Industrial Revolution, the idea of legislating to take minerals in the ground into state ownership was absent from British political discourse right up to the time when finding petroleum became a matter of practical concern in the first years of the twentieth century. The same was true of lands in the British Empire that had been alienated by way of grants including mineral rights. From that time onward, however, the question of state ownership and control of petroleum took

---

[49] See *Johnson v. McIntosh*, 21 U.S. (8 Wheat.) 543 (1823); *St. Catherine's Milling and Lumber Co. v. Attorney-General for Ontario* (1887) 13 S.C.R. 577 (Canada); *Mabo v. Queensland (No. 2)* (1992) 175 C.L.R. 1 (Australia).

[50] Text available at www.yale.edu/lawweb/avalon/states/pa01.pdf.

[51] For details and dates for each state, see Forbes and Lang 1987: 17–26.

shape as a question of British, or better, imperial, oil policy, which involved colonies like Trinidad and dominions like Australia, as well as the mother country.

IMPERIAL PETROLEUM POLICY

In the period leading up to the First World War, the British government became convinced of the value of converting its navy to burning oil, not coal, and acutely concerned about its dependence upon foreign sources—then principally the United States and Russia—to secure that oil, as well as the extent to which such supplies could be controlled by companies like Standard Oil and Royal Dutch Shell.[52] Britain's policy to address this problem was twofold.[53] One element was a vigorous search for oil rights in undeveloped territories beyond the bounds of Britain's imperial possessions, expressed notably in support for the Anglo-Persian Oil Company's takeover of the enormous D'Arcy oil concession in Persia. This went as far as the taking of a majority government shareholding in the capital of Anglo-Persian, in order to provide financial support for the company's exploration efforts.[54]

The other—the thread we shall follow here—was a determined effort to find adequate oil resources within the bounds of the empire, while at the same time preventing any such resources from falling into the hands of "trusts" and "monopolies" like Standard Oil and even Royal Dutch Shell (which, despite being 40 percent British-owned, was never regarded by British governments as a truly British company). The government's fear, which had some basis in the light of the behavior of both companies up to that time, was that they might use their market power to restrict supply or raise prices, and that they could not be relied upon to put British interests first—or indeed anywhere—in time of national need. Keeping these leviathans out of promising oil territories within the empire, such as Burma, where native miners were already producing at least 45,000 barrels of oil a year when the country was annexed to the Indian Empire in 1886,[55] or Trinidad, where a promising find was made in 1903, had somehow to be reconciled with finding enough capital from other sources for oil development, including pipelining, refining, and marketing.

Britain's answer, first developed by an interdepartmental committee that examined the situation in Trinidad in 1904, and subsequently applied in relation

---

[52] Jones 1981: Ch. 1.
[53] See generally Jones 1981; McBeth 1985.
[54] Yergin 1991: Ch. 8.
[55] Longmuir 2001: 23, 94 (giving different figures); Jones 1981: 88.

to other colonies and possessions, notably Burma, was a policy that closed access to concessions in these territories to any but British companies, while simultaneously attempting to engender interest in exploration among such companies and to promote joint ventures and other associations if necessary to secure this end.[56] This "closed door" policy was never very successful, as the colonies in which it was applied—including, besides Burma and Trinidad, British Guiana, Nigeria, the Gold Coast (now Ghana), Brunei, and Papua—were not able, in this period, to make significant contributions to British oil needs, but it aroused much American resentment and was eventually abandoned in favor of a qualified "open door" policy in 1930.[57] By that time, Britain found itself still dependent on oil from the United States and Venezuela, with the supply of the latter controlled by Standard Oil and Shell. Fear of the United States' adopting an "unfriendly neutral" posture in this respect in the event of war, and experience of the damage done to British interests in the United States by the requirement of reciprocal access imposed by the Mineral Leasing Act of 1920—foreign-owned companies could get permits or leases only if their home state offered the same facility to U.S. companies[58]—convinced the British petroleum authorities, and the cabinet, of the merits of a change in position.

While the "closed door" policy lasted, however, it certainly had some impact on the way in which petroleum regimes developed in the empire. One obvious prerequisite for the operation of the policy was that the relevant colonial government should have control over its petroleum resources, or a substantial part of them. This was the case in both Burma and Trinidad, where the government was in a position to grant concessions over very large tracts of territory. The reservation in Burma of some areas of the established Yenangyaung (Burmese for Stinking River) oilfields for operation by the native miners who had traditionally worked them, and the existence of some small oil operations on private lands in Trinidad, did not significantly detract from the Crown's extensive proprietary rights, obtained through annexation. Although the policy was originally conceived in relation to colonies like these, it was not surprising that attempts should be made to apply the same notions in other places colored pink on the world map, including the United Kingdom itself and the self-governing dominions like Australia and Canada. Here, however, the fact that rights to petroleum (or at least, rights to control access to the surface above it) would often—indeed, in the United Kingdom itself, almost invariably—be in private hands meant that the acquisition of ownership or control required difficult political decisions.

---

[56] Jones 1981: 107–8; McBeth 1985: 1–2.
[57] McBeth 1985: 121–7.
[58] On the act in general see above, Ch. 8, at 234–5.

ESTABLISHING PUBLIC CONTROL OF PETROLEUM IN THE UNITED KINGDOM

Bringing oil exploration and development under public control in the United Kingdom thus necessitated either a comprehensive scheme that would enable the state, rather than landowners, to dictate the place and pace of petroleum exploitation or one that would transfer the landowners' property rights in petroleum to the state—effectively, a scheme of nationalization of petroleum property rights. Between 1917 and 1934, Britain adopted both of these schemes, one after the other. Its initial objective was to reinforce its access to oil supplies during the First World War by promoting the search for oil within the United Kingdom.

Lord Cowdray, the principal of the firm of S. Pearson and Sons, which had been successful in developing substantial oil resources in Mexico, believed that oil could be found at home, and the Admiralty was keen that he should look for it, though preferably not at their expense. Cowdray, however, had had difficulty in negotiating leases with landowners and was willing to invest in a large-scale search only if he could obtain better security of tenure than he thought was currently offered by the law. As he explained in a letter to the press, he had been struck by the wastage caused by competitive drilling in the United States[59] and saw nothing in UK law that would prevent the repetition of that experience there. He assumed, in other words, that the law of capture would apply. It is not clear on what legal advice, if any, he based this belief, but it seems unlikely that he got much help from the government. When questioned in Parliament on this point in 1919, the Attorney-General, as the government's legal adviser, responded in terms of nicely calculated ambiguity. Asked whether the surface owner had any property in the oil beneath his land, Sir Gordon Hewart responded: "This is a difficult question, upon which opinions may easily differ. Personally I incline to the view that the surface owner is the owner of the oil beneath his land in the sense that he alone has the right on his land to search and bore for oil and becomes the owner of the oil if and when he gets it."[60]

While this answer appears to reflect a notion of ownership that incorporates the principle of capture, it does not explicitly exclude the opposite view. One sympathizes with the Attorney-General, faced as he was with the conflicting, but not directly applicable, precedents of *Trinidad Asphalt Co. v. Ambard*[61] on the one hand and the *Acton v. Blundell* line of percolating water cases on the other,[62] especially since the Lord Chief Justice had quite recently ruled that neither line of

---

[59] Reprinted in United Kingdom. Ministry of Munitions 1918: 6.

[60] 119 House of Commons Debates col. 1128 (August 12, 1919).

[61] Above, Ch. 5, *passim.*

[62] Above, Ch. 2, at 36–7.

cases provided an obvious solution to a dispute between two companies competing in pumping brine from a common reservoir formed by the flooding of old salt mines, where each was capturing, in the brine, salt that might originally have been under the land of the other.[63]

Faced with this legal uncertainty, Cowdray pressed for the passage of legislation that would facilitate his access to land and protect him against future competitive drilling in the event of success. Using its war powers, the government introduced a regulation in early 1917 forbidding drilling for petroleum without an official license and granting itself powers to enter on land for this purpose, but this was not enough for Cowdray, as such provisions would lapse with the cessation of hostilities. The first bill introduced for this purpose, in August 1917, accordingly reserved to the government the sole right to explore for and exploit petroleum, with power to issues licenses to companies to undertake these activities. While avoiding all mention of the tricky issue of ownership of petroleum in the ground, and providing no powers of entry on private land beyond those granted for war purposes, it recognized landowners' rights to the extent of providing for the payment to them a royalty of 9 pence per ton (about 2.5 cents per barrel at prevailing exchange rates) for petroleum produced from under their land. This met vigorous objection, on both sides of the House of Commons, from members who argued that landowners should not be rewarded for the extraction of resources that they had done nothing to discover or develop.[64] The government was defeated on the royalty provisions, application of which would have required some kind of administrative pooling scheme, and withdrew the bill.

Successful passage of the legislation was achieved only the next year, just after the war ended, by stripping out the royalty provisions and ensuring that

> all vexed questions [were] postponed until after the war ... whether there is property in oil, and if there is property in oil whether it belongs to the owner of the land on which the bore happens to have gone down or whether the adjoining owners have any claim, or whether the discoverer of the oil is the person entitled to it—all these questions are reserved until after the war. ... The main object is to protect oil pools by preventing indiscriminate and wasteful borings.[65]

This permitted the conclusion of an agreement between the Minister of Munitions and S. Pearson and Sons under which the company, acting as the government's agent but without charging any fee, would obtain entry to 15 already

---

[63] *Salt Union Ltd v. Brunner, Mond & Co.* [1906] 2 K.B. 822 (High Ct.), and compare the circumstances that led the French legislature to control salt well drilling: above, Ch. 4, at 108.

[64] 98 House of Commons Debates cols. 615–37 (October 22, 1917).

[65] Petroleum (Production) Act 1918; 109 House of Commons Debates 620–1 (August 1, 1918).

selected sites and start exploration there, financed by the ministry up to the agreed sum of £1 million ($4.76 million).[66] Other persons might search for petroleum under licenses to be granted under the act, but still needed to negotiate access and royalty or other compensation with the relevant landowner. The act had little effect: the wartime emergency had already ended, and quite soon after its passage, and after only three licenses had been granted, the government abandoned as fruitless its arrangement with Pearson to search for oil within the United Kingdom, a step that could only discourage private venturers in the field. It also put aside its idea of following up the 1918 act with further legislation to create a comprehensive peacetime petroleum regime. Nonetheless, the act opened the door to further change by instituting a regalian regime for petroleum and putting it on a different footing from other minerals.

This difference was dramatically reinforced when, in 1934, the government decided upon the further step of taking all petroleum in the ground (with the exception of any that might be covered by 1918 act licenses) into public ownership,[67] thus bringing the United Kingdom into the large and growing class of countries where the ownership of subsoil petroleum was concentrated in state hands. It is not at all clear, from the parliamentary debates, why the government should have brought forward this measure at this time. Certainly the 1918 act, requiring any venturer to obtain both an official license and a private lease, had done nothing to encourage petroleum exploration. Five licenses appear to have been granted between 1918 and 1924,[68] but in the next 10 years, up to 1934, only 10 licenses had been applied for under the act, of which only two had been granted. The license holders had, among them, drilled a total of only four or five wells.[69] It may be significant, however, that shortly before the Petroleum (Production) Bill was introduced into Parliament, five license applications (out of the 10 just mentioned) were pending.[70] As an oil rush, this was not on the scale of Oil Creek or Spindletop, but it may have persuaded the government that there was something to be gained from lowering the barriers to exploration. When he introduced the bill into the House of Commons, the responsible minister, Walter Runciman, stressed the need to remove obstacles to petroleum operations, citing in particular the continuing uncertainty about the ownership of oil in the ground and the possibility of multiple claims by adjoining landowners.[71]

---

[66] United Kingdom. Ministry of Munitions 1918.

[67] Petroleum (Production) Act 1934.

[68] 91 House of Lords Debates col. 664 (April 19, 1934).

[69] Great Britain Petroleum Department 1938: 129.

[70] 288 House of Commons Debates cols. 17–18 (written answers) (April 9, 1934).

[71] 291 House of Commons Debates cols. 215–17 (June 19, 1934).

The government's solution was simply to strip surface owners of any rights they might have had in petroleum in place, and to do so without compensation, on the ground that because no petroleum had been discovered (other than small quantities under 1918 act licenses), there was no reason to pay people for losing what they never knew they had—an argument that, as we shall see, had already been deployed in Queensland some 20 years before. It did not, however, go so far as to compel landowners to give petroleum license holders free access to their land for exploration and production purposes. Licensees first had to try to negotiate access, but if they failed—for example, because the landowner unreasonably refused to grant it or demanded terms that were unreasonable in the circumstances—the matter could be referred to the court, which could order access subject to appropriate compensation. A recent attempt to argue that the statutory principles for assessing compensation allowed the landowner to attach the equivalent of a royalty to the grant of the access right was rejected by the Court of Appeal.[72]

The other key change introduced by the act was the creation of a more orderly system for the design and award of licenses to search for and get petroleum. While the act, in section 2, gave the relevant minister very broad discretion as to who should receive licenses and as to the royalty payments to be made to the state, it required that licenses, save in special circumstances, should incorporate model clauses as set out in regulations to be made under the act (section 6). This system, which ensures publicity, consistency, and a measure of parliamentary control and is still in operation today, onshore and offshore, under the consolidating Petroleum Act of 1998, was initiated by the promulgation of the Petroleum (Production) Regulations of 1935. The regulations provided for the grant of both prospecting and mining licenses, with the former valid for a maximum of five years and giving the right to the grant of a mining license on expiration; discovery of petroleum was not a prerequisite. Lord Cowdray's concerns that competitive drilling would be encouraged by the licensing of small areas were reflected in the provision of minimum as well as maximum areas for licenses: 8 to 200 square miles for prospecting licenses, 4 to 100 for mining licenses. Competitive drilling was further restrained by a prohibition on locating wells within 400 feet of the boundaries of the license area without the written consent of the ministry. In addition, the license was to contain a compulsory unitization clause.[73]

---

[72] *Bocardo SA v. Star Energy UK Onshore Ltd* [2010] Ch. 100 (Ct. of Appeal).
[73] Below, Ch. 11, at 348–51.

ESTABLISHING PUBLIC CONTROL OF PETROLEUM IN AUSTRALIA

At the Imperial War Conference of 1918, dominion governments such as those of Australia and Canada were urged to promote the search for oil in their territories. The British government also offered some direct provision of funds for oil search in the colonies, notably Papua, which, with New Guinea, came under Australian administration respectively during and shortly after the First World War.[74] Though the "closed door" policy never applied explicitly in the self-governing dominions, the same concerns about the need for protection from powerful foreign oil interests were pressed on dominion governments in the first decades of the century and canvassed at the conference and elsewhere. Legislation securing the reservation of any oil to the Crown (that is, to the state) was identified by the conference as a first step essential to the protection of imperial interests.[75] Certainly we find that when in this period Australian governments, abandoning their earlier approach of treating "mineral oil" as one among a number of subjects of general mining law, started to enact specialized petroleum legislation, worries about infiltration by interests such as Standard Oil figured prominently in public discussion of the laws proposed. These concerns also seem to have contributed to shaping the content of the legislation in what can, from this distance, be seen to have been highly unfortunate ways.

The Search for Petroleum

That the Australian states should have legislated at all for petroleum exploration at any time before the Second World War may in itself seem surprising. Although the search for oil in Australia was pursued sporadically in the nineteenth century and more or less continuously in the twentieth, the first commercial oil find did not occur until the 1960s.[76] Australians seemed, however, to have formed the view, early in the century, that their continent *ought* to be as prolific as North America in its provision of oil and gas. The basis for this conviction long remained little more than speculation based on slender and usually misconceived grounds. Australia had nothing like the persistent surface indications of oil that led people to the rich fields of Pennsylvania and Baku. Bitumen was observed in 1839 by the crew of

---

[74] Payton-Smith 1971: 17. The UK government published a selective and abbreviated account of proceedings at the conference, which tells us that the delegates talked about petroleum, but not what they concluded.

[75] See the speech by the West Australian minister of mines introducing the Mining Act Amendment Bill in 1920, Western Australia Parliamentary Debates 1920: 1308.

[76] See generally Wilkinson 1988: 4–16; Conybeare 1980: 1–16; Di Stefano 1973.

Charles Darwin's ship HMS *Beagle* at the mouth of the Victoria River as it flowed into the Bonaparte Gulf, in the remote wilderness of Australia's northern coast. The Gulf overlies what has only recently been recognized as the highly productive Bonaparte Basin. Regular reports were later made of bitumen finds on the Australian south coast. Speculators refused to be deterred by the unpromising geology of the area, but no oil was ever found. Inquiries eventually suggested that the likeliest source of the material was seepage from barrels of bitumen buried on the beaches by the crews of whalers active in the Australian Bight in the nineteenth century and maybe earlier; the bitumen would enable them to recaulk their ships on coming ashore.[77]

A few years after news of Drake's Well had reached Australia, it was a similarly sticky, flammable, apparently bituminous substance that caught the Australian imagination: deposits of what came to be called coorongite, covering flat salty land in the district of Coorong on South Australia's southeast coast. Local interests thought this might be the product of seepage and dug Australia's first oil well at Coorong in 1866, abandoning it—one might feel somewhat faintheartedly— when it reached 8 meters without finding oil. A further unsuccessful attempt, drilled to 110 meters, was made in 1880. The only heat coorongite generated was in the vigorous, indeed sometimes vicious, controversy over its nature and origins that ensued over the following decades. Eventually shown to be the product of accumulated airborne algae, coorongite is possibly more interesting now, in the era of the search for alternative hydrocarbon resources, than it ever was before.[78]

1866 was also the year when a police constable Edwards journeyed several days from the small Western Australian town of York in the company of two aborigines to inspect a supposed oil spring emerging, somewhat improbably, high up on a granite rock face. The intrepid constable, mounting to the source of the seepage by means of an upturned dead tree, succeeded in bringing back a sample, which was forwarded to the governor along with his report and a recommendation from his superior that he and his native companions be given a small reward. After due consideration, the find was followed up, and a specialist was sent out with Edwards to inspect this and perhaps other sites ... in February 1871.[79] We do not know the result of this expedition, but it is possible that the substance was the "pseudo-bitumen" referred to in later correspondence between the Western Australia Government Geologist A. Gibb Maitland and his counterpart in Tasmania.

---

[77] According to a 1925 report by the geologist Arthur Wade: see Western Australia, State Records Office, cons. 3172, Petroleum—General Vol. III (1923–1953), item 1923/040. See also Wade 1915.

[78] A Google search (March 2008) showed 1,450 references, almost all to scientific articles.

[79] Western Australia, State Records Office, cons. 129, items 09/297 (1866), 16/059 (1871).

In a letter of February 1919, Maitland complained that "material of this kind has continually been brought to me as 'proof positive' of the occurrence of petroleum, even when obtained from *granite* country, etc." Indeed, the files of the Geological Survey, from the turn of the century until the 1930s, are full of correspondence between excited providers of "oil" samples and a weary Maitland and his successor, who explain again and again that the geological characteristics requisite for petroleum deposits are not present in the region of the supposed find. Small wonder, perhaps, that just before his letter of February 1919, Maitland had spent nine months in the Blue Mountains west of Sydney, recovering from "a complete breakdown."[80]

Hydrocarbons were eventually struck by drilling not in Western Australia, generally considered the most "prospective" state, but in Queensland.[81] In this case, elation was quickly followed by acute disappointment. In 1900, gas was discovered accidentally at Hospital Hill, near Roma, when a well was being drilled for water for that town. The town authorities, who at first considered the gas a nuisance, got around in 1906 to erecting a gasholder and piping it around the town, which thus enjoyed the novelty of brightly gas-lit streets—but only for 15 days, after which the well ran dry. The Roma district was the site of persistent exploration efforts but did not produce another significant find until 1927, when the drilling of a successful condensate well started a minor boom. Companies were floated, promoters prospered, locals lost money, but none of the further wells drilled was successful, and the original well gave out in 1931. Meanwhile, some low-level production was achieved at Lakes Entrance, in East Gippsland near the southeast Victoria coast, where a field was discovered in 1924 that yielded very small quantities of oil for some 30 years. Throughout the first half of the twentieth century, nothing else was found remotely resembling a commercial field, whether of oil or gas.

In the 1960s, however, no less than four oil or gas finds followed one another in quick succession in widely distant parts of Australia: oil at Moonie in southeastern Queensland in 1961; gas in the Cooper Basin, linking northeastern South Australia and southwestern Queensland, in 1963; oil at Barrow Island, just off the northwest Australian coast, in 1964; and gas and later oil in the Bass Strait, dividing Victoria from Tasmania, in 1965. These last three finds represented the opening up of major, highly productive basins. Barrow Island, though it now has

---

[80] Western Australia, State Records Office, cons. 3712, Petroleum—General (1901–1919), item 1902/116.

[81] See generally, on material in this paragraph, Conybeare 1980, Wilkinson 1988, Di Stefano 1973.

little oil left, is about to become a center for the transshipment and processing of gas from some of the world's largest fields, in deep water far off the northwest Australian coast.

The Development of Specialized Petroleum Law in Queensland and Western Australia

Australia's petroleum age can thus be seen to have begun in earnest in the 1960s. Australia's petroleum law age, however, started half a century earlier. In those 50 years, Australian governments, at both state and federal levels, displayed far more energy than did the occasional reservoirs penetrated by exploratory drilling. Reading the debates in state and commonwealth parliaments, one gets the impression that their members honestly believed they could legislate the oil out of the ground. Four of the six Australian states had specialist petroleum legislation on their statute books before the Second World War. In Queensland, no less than six acts to regulate petroleum exploration and production were passed between 1912 and 1939,[82] a period during which it had no sustainable petroleum production, while Western Australia and Victoria each passed two.

It does not take a rabid advocate of free markets and laissez-faire to conclude, on reviewing the record, that most of this legislative effort was remarkably ill judged and must have played a significant role in retarding petroleum search in Australia. The earliest Queensland legislators—and their counterparts in other states as well—seem to have made two assumptions, both false. The first was that the existing law of hard rock mining could, with some minor adaptations, be made to work satisfactorily as a basis for petroleum operations; the second was that one petroleum find, of dubious sustainability, at Roma meant that it was more important to guard against the risks associated with a petroleum mining boom than to attract capital and know-how to the search for oil and gas. These, they seemed to believe, would flow in naturally once any regulatory structure for petroleum exploration was established.

Accordingly, though the find at Roma suggested the presence of what was then called "free" petroleum, to be obtained by drilling, the Queensland Coal and Mineral Oil Act of 1912 followed the precedent established by the South Australian Mining Act of 1893, which identified "coal and mineral oil leases" as one of several classes of mineral leases on public lands (gold leases being the most important class) and established the same rules for both substances: a "miner's right" authorizing prospecting and the pegging of claims of up to 640 acres (1 square mile) and a lease of up to the same area that would authorize production.

---

[82] Di Stefano 1973.

The identical treatment of coal and mineral oil suggest that what the South Australia legislature had in mind was not free petroleum, but oil shale, which had been used as a source of kerosene in Australia since 1865.

The 1912 act applied only to state-owned land, but given the large areas of undeveloped land in the state and the large tracts held under pastoral leases from the state, it probably covered a very substantial area.[83] It substituted for the miner's right a "license to search" whose grant and renewal were subject to the discretion of the minister but was still valid for only a year, over an area—both for coal and mineral oil—of 2,560 acres (4 square miles) (section 5). The act, however, drastically cut back the permissible area of an oil mining lease to 30 acres (as opposed to 640 acres for coal). The government originally proposed 60 acres but accepted 30 in the face of objections from the Labour Opposition to any measure that would admit private capital to the search for petroleum. The search area was said to correspond to that common in U.S. practice at the time, where the standard lease area was said to be 160 acres. In fact, this figure was that fixed by the Mining Law of 1872 for placer claims by a body of individuals on federal land, a law that many thought totally unsuited to govern oil and gas operations but whose application to them had been confirmed by Congress in the Oil Placer Act of 1897. As noted already,[84] this provoked such insecurity, so much competitive drilling, and so many contested claims that the federal government adopted a policy of withdrawing potential oil lands from entry under the act and eventually secured the substitution of a quite different access system under the Mineral Leasing Act of 1920.

The Queensland government does not seem to have been aware of any of this. The Labour Opposition in fact argued that the act was premature: it would have preferred that the task of exploration be placed directly in the hands of the government, to avoid the risk that Standard Oil would come in, take the acreage, and then shut in any well that was not a gusher. When that notion was rejected, its spokesman argued for securing the greatest degree of competition possible, in terms that make it clear that he assumed the rule of capture to be part of the law of Queensland.[85] For him, 160 acres was the maximum appropriate size for a license to search, because "one well would serve to drain all the pools in the neighbourhood, so there was no need for such a large area to be held by one company." This seems a clear anticipation of drainage, confirmed by his approving reference to American oilfields with "derricks about as thick as peas in a bottle":

---

[83] For parliamentary discussion of the act, see Di Stefano 1973: 15–20; 111 Queensland Parliamentary Debates 1912: 519–31, 555–61, 574–94.

[84] Above, Ch. 8, at 221–4.

[85] 111 Queensland Parliamentary Debates 1912: 583.

"[t]he closer the proprietors get to one another the better." He even revived the underground water analogy: "When boring for water also, if the owner of one run found artesian water near his boundary, the owner of the adjoining holding would not bore in the centre of his paddock, but would go as near to his boundary as possible so as to tap the same flow." This was the thinking that led the opposition to propose and secure the reduction of the lease area to 30 acres.

There was no immediate rush to take up licenses under the 1912 terms, but the Labour government that took power in June 1915 was still worried enough about the monopoly power of Standard Oil and the risks of "wild, feverish speculation" in the event of an oil find to pass new legislation, the Petroleum Act of 1915, asserting that all petroleum in the ground, whether under land that was still in the ownership of the state or land it had granted to individuals, was and always had been the property of the state, and reserving to the state the function of searching for it. [86] The act thus made no provision for petroleum licenses or leases. It clearly represented an expropriation of the petroleum rights of the holders of any land that had been granted by the Crown without a reservation of minerals. As such, it appears to have been the first such expropriation operated by a government within the British Empire—as against its own landholders, that is; expropriation of all the land interests of indigenous populations had been commonplace as an incident of conquest and settlement. Like subsequent expropriations of this type, no compensation was offered for the acquisition of these oil rights, on the ground that in the absence of any successful exploration hitherto, "[we] are not taking anything from anyone, because no one knows at present that his property has any oil in it."[87]

Fear of capture seems to have played a part in shaping this policy. The secretary for mines referred to the position at Roma: "If [the bill] excluded land which was already alienated, and the government put down a bore at Roma, then the whole of the people owning land around that bore, land which was cut up into small allotments, would have a right to put down a bore and participate in the advantage arising from the discovery of oil."[88] In the absence of a rule of capture, such a right, if any, would have been highly circumscribed.

The Western Australian government, the second to present specialized petroleum legislation in the form of the Mining Act Amendment Act of 1920, presented similar arguments, including the suggestion that such a provision was necessary in order to prevent adjoining private landowners draining oil from state-granted leases, in an attempt to justify the inclusion of a clause proclaiming that

---

[86] See generally Di Stefano 1973: 27–8; 122 Queensland Parliamentary Debates 1915: 2171–9, 2390–2, 2560–3, 2621–7, 2669–76.

[87] *Ibid.* 2622.

[88] *Ibid.* 2669.

petroleum was and had always been the property of the state. It failed, however, to convince the legislature to accept what was (correctly) perceived as an expropriatory provision, and the clause was dropped.[89]

Accused elsewhere in Australia of doing "incalculable harm" to the country's image among British investors,[90] the Queensland Labour government quite quickly abandoned its monopoly of oil exploration and production, restoring the previous licensing and leasing system in 1920,[91] and then introducing comprehensive new legislation, the Petroleum Act of 1923 (which, albeit with major amendments, remained the source of Queensland petroleum law until 2004 and still governs many areas licensed before its replacement[92] came into force). Introduced into Parliament by the secretary for mines, the Hon. A. J. Jones, widely known as "optimistic Alf" for his ability to believe that any oil show presaged immense hydrocarbon riches, the act finally demonstrated some understanding of the sorts of conditions that were needed to attract overseas capital to the search for oil in Queensland.[93] The act did not modify the domanial principle introduced in 1915—wisely so, for as we have seen, the need to negotiate with numerous landholders had just been cited by Lord Cowdray as a significant potential barrier to oil search in the United Kingdom. But it addressed concerns about security of tenure by providing that an explorer could hold two prospecting permits valid for up to four years, for areas of up to 10,000 acres each, coupled with a right to a lease or leases within the permit area of up to the same extent if petroleum in payable quantities were found. The act had elaborate provisions reserving access to permits and leases to British subjects (which at this time included Australians) and to British- or Australian-registered companies that were British-owned. The specter of Standard Oil still loomed large over the Queensland horizon. The act was also explicit on development obligations, requiring the drilling of one well for every 100 acres of the lease, unless the minister agreed to fewer (article 34(1)).

The parliamentary debates again make it clear that the government believed that the rule of capture would apply in relation to petroleum in the subsoil and took this into account in the design of the legislation. But in contrast to the belief expressed in 1912 in competition and close spacing as a motor for development, Labour now wanted to protect the first discoverer by offering a sufficiently large lease area to protect from capture. In rejecting an amendment to reduce this area to

---

[89] 63 Western Australia Parliamentary Debates 1920: 1954.

[90] Gardiner, in 63 Western Australia Parliamentary Debates 1920: 1868.

[91] By the Petroleum Act 1920.

[92] Petroleum and Gas (Production and Safety) Act 2004.

[93] See generally Di Stefano 1973 52–6; 142 Queensland Parliamentary Debates 1923: 1510–38, 1541–74, 1728–30.

1,000 acres, Jones remarked: "The honourable gentleman would not be very pleased if he spent his money on an oil lease and then someone came out and pegged alongside him and drained the oil that he had discovered."[94] The government was not, however, prepared to carry the "first appropriation" principle thus hinted at to its logical conclusion, and grant the first discoverer the whole of the oilfield he might eventually delineate, as opposed to a fixed (though for the period generous) allotment of acreage.

Elsewhere, the lesson that excessively small exploration and production areas in unproved territory have a chilling effect on investment still had not been learned. In Western Australia, despite a propaganda campaign conducted on behalf of Anglo-Persian, which indicated its readiness to sink substantial sums into exploration if it could expect to receive a lease area of 100,000 acres, government and legislature could not bring themselves, in their 1920 legislation, to do anything that might cause an "oil monopoly" to arise in the state, and restricted lease acreages to 736 acres for a first discovery of an "oil basin" on state land and 48 acres for all subsequent leases. Part of the reasoning behind this appears to have been a belief that it was "usual for an oil basin to be confined within an area of a square mile."[95] Curiously, this parsimonious attitude toward leases was coupled with a provision enabling areas of any size to be made the subject of a prospecting license, conferring the exclusive right to bore and search for mineral oil in the area granted. No specific obligations beyond "reasonable endeavours to search" were imposed in return for this privilege, and in consequence, it is not surprising to find that within little over a year from the passage of the act, the government geologist was writing to an American inquirer that the whole of the state had already been parceled out into oil concessions. These "concessions"—in fact, prospecting license areas—ranged in size from 100 square miles on the south coast, where the appetite for whalers' bitumen was still keen, to 98,000 square miles in the eastern central part of the state, which was mostly an area of trackless desert. Like its Queensland predecessors, the act could hardly have been better designed to stifle serious investment, and though some systematic surveys and drilling work took place over an extended period in the Kimberleys in the far north of the state, efforts were generally sporadic and poorly financed, and were totally unsuccessful.

The government came back to the legislature in 1936 with new proposals but, despite acknowledging that "[w]e have never succeeded in securing one penny-piece from Great Britain or any outside country for the purpose of prospecting for oil within the Commonwealth,"[96] insisted on repeating several of the mistakes of

---

[94] *Ibid.* 1568–9.

[95] 63 Western Australia Parliamentary Debates 1920: 2756.

[96] Munsie, in 97 Western Australia Parliamentary Debates 1936: 414.

the past in slightly different form. This time, however, it did obtain acceptance for an assertion of state ownership of all petroleum in the ground;[97] the recent UK legislation to the same effect, and the fact that there still had been no commercial discoveries, must both have helped. While effective exploration requirements, including drilling, were now imposed in relation to substantial but realistic prospecting license areas (up to 225 square miles, or 144,000 acres), a petroleum lease still could not normally exceed 160 acres (section 55(2)). The act included elaborate "incentive" provisions making larger lease areas available to the first discoverers of petroleum in any particular region, but fear of monopoly led the minister—apparently with legislative support—to reject the notion urged on him by a member (and supported by the commonwealth's geological adviser)[98] that any discoverer should be able to get a lease corresponding to the extent of the field discovered.[99] The act recognized this "first appropriation" principle (which, as we have seen, was already incorporated in French petroleum law)[100] only for the first discovery in the state, for which a "whole of field" lease of up to 225 square miles could be awarded (section 17).

Legislative Protection against Capture

Despite this insistence on restricting grants to small areas of land, with the accompanying risk of dividing oilfields among different titleholders, it is clear that Australian authorities saw capture as something more than an excuse for taking unexploited petroleum into public ownership. The Queensland Act of 1923 made direct reference to the main American response to capture in requiring the lessee to "drill all necessary wells fairly to offset the wells of others on adjoining land on petroleum deposits" (section 34(2)). The sense of such a provision when it appears in a U.S. petroleum lease is to protect the landowner against loss of royalties as a result of drainage from drilling on neighboring land.[101] Under the domanial regime in Queensland, however, drilling—unless already accomplished on private land before the act came into force—could be lawful only under a license or lease granted under the act, and any production from such drilling would ordinarily produce the same royalty returns to the state as that under the original lease.

---

[97] Petroleum Act 1936, § 9.
[98] See further below, Chapter 11, at 351.
[99] 97 Western Australia Parliamentary Debates 1936: 1265–7, 1666–8.
[100] Above, 314–5.
[101] Above, Ch. 7, at 194–7.

The parliamentary debates give no clue as to why the government felt it had to force its lessees to protect their interests by competitive drilling, when its own returns were not affected. Nor do legislators appear to have noticed that they were at the same time approving another clause that would ordinarily forbid the drilling of the very offset wells they were demanding, or at least seriously restrict the efficacy of those wells: section 48 of the act forbade the drilling of wells within 200 feet of the outer boundaries of the permit or lease unless the adjoining land had *not* been allocated for oil exploration purposes. By definition, an offset well could not fall within this exception.

The offset well provision remained in the Queensland law for many decades and was copied into other Australian legislation. It figured as section 33(2) of Victoria's Mines (Petroleum) Act of 1935, the first venture of the Victorian legislature into this field. It also appeared in the commonwealth's petroleum legislation for Papua and New Guinea[102] until an industry source pointed out that the wording of the section did not accurately express its presumed intention to prevent a lessee from interfering with the drilling operations of the holder of a neighboring lease, and that it would involve operators in unnecessary and often pointless expenditure without any advantage to the Crown.[103] In the next revision of the Papua–New Guinea ordinances, the provision was accordingly replaced by a distance criterion like that in section 48 of the Queensland act. It would have been too much to expect that the distance stipulated should be the same as in the Queensland act; apparently the safe distance in Papua and New Guinea was 325 feet,[104] whereas in Victoria, where the 1935 act, on first presentation, adopted the Queensland distance, the government, in the course of the act's passage, amended it to 150 feet, offering no explanation save that 200 feet was "too far."[105] Meanwhile, the Western Australian Act of 1936 had adopted the figure of 330 feet prevailing in Papua from 1936 to 1938.[106] Unsurprisingly, the feeling developed within the commonwealth government that some measure of standardization of petroleum law across the country might be desirable, and we shall see in the next chapter that significant progress in this direction was made over the next few years.

---

[102] See, e.g., Papua Ordinance no. 10, 1934, § 55(3).

[103] National Archives of Australia, A518 A846/1/59 Part 2, letter from managing director, Commonwealth Oil Refineries Ltd., dated February 13, 1936.

[104] Papua Petroleum (Prospecting and Mining) Ordinances 1938–1939, § 62.

[105] 197 Victoria Parliamentary Debates 1935: 5139; see generally 3414–25, 4170–4200, 4906–7, 5122–45, 5271–8.

[106] Petroleum Act 1936, § 77(1); see 97 Western Australia Parliamentary Debates 1936: 1661–2. The figure of 330 feet was also adopted in 1939 in the Canadian province of Alberta in place of the 300 feet previously provided for: Harrison 1970: 369.

CONCLUSION

Between 1899 and 1939, the second 40-year span after the drilling of the Drake Well, world oil production increased from about 125 million to nearly 2,100 million barrels annually; within these totals, annual non-U.S. production went up from 67 million to 821 million barrels.[107] Almost all this extra production came from countries in which—in contrast to the United States—the accession system of mineral property had either never operated, or had long been discarded, or had been deemed inappropriate for application to petroleum resources. But despite the absence of this crucial feature of American property law, U.S. experience and practice, shaped by the capture principle to which that law gave rise, had considerable influence on the ways in which these countries' petroleum regimes developed.

To suggest that foreign petroleum regimes took the form they did simply by way of reaction to the defects of the American system would be grossly exaggerated—indeed, in many cases, simply untrue. Yet there exist multiple causal links between the American experience and the design of other systems, at least from the beginning of the twentieth century onward. The relationship between capture and monopolization is a complex one. Obviously, any oil company entering new territory will seek as large an exclusive exploration area as it can obtain, so long as the price of holding the land is not too high. Quite aside from any issues of capture, more acreage means more flexibility as to both when and where to explore, more chances to find oil, and more freedom to develop only the best and most profitable prospects. Attainment of such company objectives was greatly facilitated by the unification of oil holdings in the hands of the state or the ruler under a regalian or domanial system, and one may wonder how much the opening up of the Middle East or South America as an oil region would have been delayed if the desired acreages had to be assembled by negotiations with individual landowners (or soi-disant landowners), as happened in Romania.

Indeed, the desire to exploit large concession areas in a way that was rational in terms of their overall production strategies, free from the domestic risks of capture and the related artificial constraints imposed by production controls, may have accelerated overseas ventures by American oil companies in Latin America and, later, the Middle East.[108] In accession systems, too, we find oil companies actively pressing for moves toward regalian or domanial regimes, as did Pearson in Britain in 1917 and Anglo-Persian in Western Australia a few years later; though as the Mexican example shows, the enthusiasm for state control and ownership was

---

[107] Williamson and Daum 1959: 631–3; Williamson et al. 1963: 726–8.
[108] Kokxhoorn 1977: 44.

unlikely to be as strong where it was imposed on a region already being actively exploited under accession-type arrangements.[109]

Part of the company case, put most explicitly by Lord Cowdray in his statement of March 1918,[110] was the need to adopt such a system to avoid the anarchic competition and waste experienced in the United States as the result of combining the rule of capture with the accession principle. Governments seem to have been ready to accept this argument as a basis for taking over or recovering oil rights, but when it came to allocating those rights, most of them—Venezuela and the United Kingdom were exceptions—discounted the risks of capture that had justified that takeover and preferred the conflicting logic of avoiding monopolization by granting small exploration and production areas, much as had the framers of the Mineral Leasing Act of 1920. The Australian governments whose professed fears of the Standard Oil companies explained their resistance to monopolization never appear to have reflected on the fact that what made the old Standard Oil such a dominant player was Rockefeller's precocious appreciation of the enormous power conferred on owners of transport and refining assets by irrational competition in production driven by the rule of capture. These governments were either ignorant of the risks of property right uncertainty that their allocation policy created or confident of their ability to manage them. If the latter was the case, it is surprising that they did not have equal confidence in their administrative capacities to ensure that operators of large lease areas developed them in the public interest.

In fact, it was not until well after the Second World War that states began to move much beyond suspicion of monopolization (or dissatisfaction with its results where, as in Saudi Arabia, the Emirates, Iraq, and Iran, it had been accepted) and toward a type of petroleum policy in which competition for petroleum acreage came to be used, in conjunction with a range of other control elements, as a positive tool designed to promote the comprehensive early exploration and effective development of the state's petroleum territory. The emergence of this sort of policy among petroleum-producing states generally, its implications for the rule of capture, and the way those implications have been addressed are the subjects of the next chapter.

---

[109] Yergin 1991: 232–3.
[110] Ministry of Munitions 1918: 6–7.

CHAPTER 11

CAPTURE REVIVIFIED? COMPETITIVE ACREAGE ALLOCATION BY GOVERNMENTS

MODERN PETROLEUM LICENSING REGIMES

Some oil-rich states today want nothing to do with international oil companies; they prefer to exploit their petroleum resources through a national oil company, which is the sole recipient of the exploitation rights and feels no need to enlist other enterprises as risk-sharing partners. Such companies, and their governments, can confidently put concerns relating to capture of petroleum to one side (so long, that is, as they do not suspect the presence of oil or gas pools underlying their borders with other countries).[1]

This is not necessarily the case for the large number of other countries that continue to rely, in some measure or other, on the capital and know-how of international oil companies to develop and exploit national oil and gas resources. Many of these countries, we should notice, have also created a national oil company that may be the grantee of all their petroleum rights but will exploit them through a variety of agreements with such international oil companies, notably the

---

[1] This is the issue discussed below, in Ch. 12.

increasingly popular production sharing contract (PSC). Others continue to use a concession or lease system as the framework for a direct relationship between government and international oil company. This chapter aims to explain the relationship between these different arrangements and the rule of capture. The particular attention given in the chapter, as in the last, to developments in the United Kingdom and Australia means that my detailed examples are drawn from concession-type regimes, but in a final section, I consider briefly the nature of the PSC and the question of whether the choice of this vehicle for company participation in petroleum exploration and production is likely to affect the significance of the rule of capture. In reviewing this material, it is useful to keep in mind that in one way or another, national oil companies now control some 80 percent of the world's oil reserves.[2]

It was the unsatisfactory experience—in terms of fiscal returns and development effort—of the countries that had granted the large and long-running "traditional" concessions of the 1920s that both led to the creation of the Organization of Petroleum Exporting Countries (OPEC) and demonstrated to the governments of the new oil provinces that began to be opened up in the 1950s and 1960s the need for a significantly different approach to the granting of oil and gas acreage if a national objective of rapid and thorough exploration, leading to early production and enhanced energy security, was to be achieved. Today one might identify the key elements of such an approach as including regular acreage releases, backed by appropriate public geological information, organized in such a way as to promote competition for the most prospective areas, and incorporating incentives for early exploration by such means as requirements for regular relinquishment of territory, binding exploration or exploration expenditure commitments, brevity of exploration period, or some combination of these.[3]

Only gradually have these different elements come together to furnish a rational petroleum licensing regime. The idea of competitive allocation of acreage goes back to the Russian auctions of the state-held territory in the prolific Baku fields, from 1872 onward. From the point of view of rational exploitation, these were disastrous: the drilling of uncontrolled gushers, by operators who had made no provision for storage, soaked the soil for miles around; the small size of the tracts (27 acres) and the absence of provision for continuing supervision, or of restraints on subleasing, opened the way for mutually destructive competitive production.[4] From the fiscal point of view, however, the auctions were an enormous success, as

---

[2] Jaffe 2007: 2. At the end of 2007, the U.S. share of proven world oil reserves was only 2.4 percent: BP 2008: 6.

[3] See generally Bunter 2002b.

[4] Above, Ch. 6, at 159–64.

there was widespread knowledge of the potential of the fields. Competitive allocation of small blocks of proven territory likewise appeared to give satisfactory results in the United States from the time of enactment of the Mineral Leasing Act of 1920. The act introduced in section 17 the notion of organized competition to obtain leases over defined parcels of land, through the regular release by the Bureau of Land Management of unappropriated acreage "within the known geologic structure of a producing oil or gas field," while making unproven territory subject to a system of prospecting permits available on demand (section 13). This approach clearly did not eliminate the possibility of drainage—indeed, by providing for the possibility of several leases on the same structure, it almost guaranteed it—but it was calculated to produce more orderly competition than had occurred under placer mining law as applied to oil and gas, and an influential precedent was thus established for the normal modern practice of periodic acreage releases, though the act's arrangements for noncompetitive leasing of lands outside "known geologic structures" gave rise to fraud and to windfall profits in lease trading, and were radically modified in 1987.[5]

Where, however, governments attempted to dispose of small parcels in circumstances where industry was not convinced of the attractiveness of the offer, whether because of its terms or of the uncertain prospectivity of the territory, grave disappointment followed. I chronicled in the last chapter the disproportion between the efforts devoted by the Australian states before World War II to the design of petroleum regimes and the results obtained in terms of production, or even exploration, a disproportion reflecting that between the size of the areas on offer and their prospectivity. The Australians had their eyes fixed on the United States; they would have done better to look at Romania, where in 1905–1906, as already noted, a competitive release of state territory on demanding terms and in small parcels (so far as proven territory was concerned) resulted in not a single award.[6]

One lesson that more farsighted governments began to learn in the 1920s and 1930s was that unless they had territory that was clearly attractive—as, say, in Venezuela—they might need to take the initiative in securing the geological information that would persuade oil companies to invest in drilling. Britain moved in this direction in 1918 with the state-supported program of test drillings by the Pearson company, which unfortunately pointed to the absence, rather than the presence, of any substantial onshore petroleum deposits.[7] The National Socialist regime in Germany accompanied its 1934 nationalization of petroleum deposits

---

[5] Federal Onshore Oil and Gas Leasing Reform Act of 1987, analyzed in Sansonetti and Murray 1990.

[6] Above, Ch. 6, at 155–6.

[7] Above, Ch. 10, at 322–3.

with vigorous programs of centralization of geological information and state-sponsored exploratory drilling.[8] Australia, by contrast, relied for many years on ineffective financial incentives for private exploration: a commonwealth reward scheme for a successful find was in operation from 1920 to 1925, when it was replaced with a pound-for-pound subsidy for exploration in approved areas.[9] Official attempts to show the prospectivity of areas within Australia began only with the creation in 1946 of the Commonwealth Bureau of Mineral Resources, which started a comprehensive program of geological mapping.[10] State-supplied geological information is today a basic element of petroleum acreage releases.

Another significant development was the standardization of acreage offers made under such releases, by the use of lines of latitude (parallels) and longitude (meridians) to define the areas to be offered. Such lines can be seen as the basic elements of a grid superimposed on the earth's surface in which areas can be identified by measurements in degrees and minutes (60 minutes = 1 degree) so as to produce a wide range of standardized sizes and shapes ranging from 1 minute by 1 minute to 1 degree by 1 degree. At the equator, a 1-by-1-degree area covers just over 12,300 square kilometers (4,749 square miles); a 1-by-1-minute area, 3.43 square kilometers (848 acres). As we move closer to the poles and lines of longitude converge, these areas become smaller and more rectangular in shape. A first use of this approach, sometimes referred to as "graticulation," has been traced to the Libyan Petroleum Law of 1955, passed shortly after the country obtained its independence, under which contract areas, limited to 35,000 square kilometers in most of Libya, were required to consist of a number of whole 5-by-5-minute blocks. Companies were, however, allowed to define their own areas, subject to this limitation and to avoiding overlap with anyone else.[11]

The Libyan law was also an early example of a further key element of modern regimes: provision for progressive relinquishment of fractions of the licensed area at specific dates within the period of the concession, as an encouragement to early and thorough exploration. Relinquishment was not at that time a new idea. It has a natural place in any system that, like those in Australia, France, or the Netherlands, offers separate titles for the exploration and production phases, restricting the grant of the latter to the discovery area. But the device also made an early appearance in systems in which all activities, from exploration through to production, were covered by a single title. The earliest example may be in the abortive 1905 Romanian regulations already referred to, which called for the

---

[8] Bentz 1938: 95; Fehr 1939: 159–65.
[9] Commonwealth of Australia *Gazette*, January 2, 1920; *Daily News* (WA), August 15, 1925.
[10] Blainey 2003: 342.
[11] Bunter 2002b: 162–5.

return to the state, on the making of a discovery, of half the original concession area. More successful were the Venezuelans, whose 1922 Petroleum Law provided for subdividing exploration areas of up to 10,000 hectares into 500-hectare lots, of which alternate lots could be selected for production, on a checkerboard pattern and over up to half the exploration area, after three years' exploration.[12] The remainder would return to form a state petroleum reserve. This system appears to have operated successfully over the lifetime of the petroleum law. Such relinquishment—not now usually on a checkerboard pattern—is today an almost universal practice, U.S. federal onshore and offshore leasing law furnishing a rare exception, but one that is natural given the very small initial size of the areas granted there: 2,560 acres onshore and (normally) 5,760 offshore.[13] The Libyan law provided, against the background of a concession of 50 years' duration, for relinquishment of 25 percent of the concession area after 5 years, a further 25 percent after 8 years, and a final 16.66 percent after 10. Use of the 5-by-5-minute grid facilitated requirements to hand back at these times regularly shaped areas that could be easily regranted later.

Gradually, the combination of these elements—releases of defined acreage for competitive bidding, publicly provided geological information, graticulation, and relinquishment obligations—became the most common system in use by states for securing the exploration for and development of their petroleum resources by oil companies. This is not to say that they have become universal. A number of states admit in varying degrees the notion of "over-the-counter" grants of acreage, in which the selection may be made by the grantee (though the award is not necessarily made without competition). An example is Denmark, where a part of the country's onshore and offshore areas is open for applications each year between January and September as a means of offering incentives to companies to explore in virgin territory. Denmark was also distinctive, until 1981, in allocating its entire territory—onshore, territorial seabed, and continental shelf—to a single licensee, the A. P. Møller shipping company, with no relinquishment requirements.[14] All the other countries that participated in the opening up of the North Sea continental shelf in the 1960s adopted some variant of the common system, though with differing graticulation methods: the United Kingdom, for example, used 10-by-12-minute blocks with an area of about 250 square kilometers, Norwegian blocks were twice this size, and the Netherlands and Germany used blocks of about 400 square kilometers.

---

[12] Lieuwen 1954: 24–9.

[13] 30 U.S.C. § 226(b)(1)(A) (but 5,760 acres in Alaska); 43 U.S.C. § 1337(b)(1): the secretary may grant a larger lease if "necessary to comprise a reasonable economic production unit."

[14] Rønne 2001: 340–5.

RE-CREATING THE CONDITIONS FOR CAPTURE

The United States is a place of which it is commonly believed that things—the economy, automobiles, ranches, freeways, meals, people—are larger than the equivalent things elsewhere, so instances where the reverse is true are worthy of some attention. One example is the relatively small size of the leases of federal land available for oil and gas exploration and production, as compared with the indications offered for countries like the United Kingdom and Norway from the block sizes mentioned above. As we have already noticed in relation to onshore leases, and as is the case also with offshore leases, these limited dimensions mean that it is quite common for a lease boundary to intersect an oil or gas reservoir. Situations frequently arise, therefore, in which one lessee may be in a position to drain oil or gas from under the lease area of its neighbor. Other modern regimes for the disposition of state-owned petroleum rights seldom contemplate such small lease areas. Alberta, where 90 percent of the petroleum rights were reserved to the province, offers a rare exception, with lease areas ordinarily ranging from 160 acres to 9 square miles. Alberta petroleum law and practice have in many respects followed those of its southern neighbor, and its regulatory regime has a distinctly American appearance, incorporating as it does disciplines such as well spacing, pooling, and even prorationing.[15]

The general disparity between the size of American and other lease, concession, or contract areas has led some in the United States to conclude that capture must therefore now be a peculiarly American problem. As Ernest Smith and his colleagues put it:

> There are several reasons why the rule of capture is rarely an issue under modern development arrangements. First, governmental agencies in some countries use information obtained from initial geological surveys to avoid splitting geological structures between different licensed areas. Second, unlike onshore oil and gas leases in the United States, licenses, concessions and production-sharing agreements typically cover very large areas, such as the 50,000 hectares (123,500 acres) authorized by the Turkish petroleum code. … Third, if a reservoir underlies areas licensed to different companies, the licensees may be required to enter into a plan of coordinated development. If a reservoir crosses national boundaries, such plans, which are referred to as unitization agreements in the United States, may also be mandated by treaty.[16]

Each of these reasons has some truth to it, yet to say that capture is "rarely an issue" may be misleading. It does not arise as an issue associated with the

---

[15] Crommelin 1975.
[16] Smith et al. 2000: 262.

exploitation of virtually every oil and gas accumulation, as is the case in the United States, but it is still a matter of frequent and serious concern even under domanial and regalian regimes. A pointer to the realities of the current situation is the fact that the Association of International Petroleum Negotiators, a worldwide body but created in the United States and still predominantly reflecting American preoccupations, has recently added to its valuable stock of model form petroleum agreements an "international unitization agreement"—that is to say, an agreement for use in countries outside the United States by companies that wish to exploit an oil or gas field, subject to two or more different license, lease, or concession interests, as a single, fieldwide unit.[17] As we have seen, such unitization agreements, whether voluntary or compulsory, are generally viewed in the United States as the only truly effective means of wholly eliminating the risks of wasteful and inefficient development engendered by the rule of capture.[18] A survey by two leading Texas oil and gas lawyers of 12 significant oil-producing countries around the world shows that almost all of them make legal provision, by one means or another, for compulsory unitization of interests where two or more parties have rights in a single field.[19] Clearly there is the perception of an important problem for which such unitization is seen as the solution; that problem is, in almost all cases, the operator behavior induced by fear of drainage and capture.

In the next section of this chapter, I show from Australian and British offshore licensing history how this problem arises in relation to state-owned or state-controlled oil and gas deposits despite often very generous initial allocations of territory. I go on to look at how unitization provisions have been developed in several states over the same period, paying particular attention to the rules for exploitation of offshore regions in the United States, Australia, and the United Kingdom. Other regulatory powers retained by the state in its petroleum regime may also be relevant to situations where reservoirs are shared between licensees. Drainage as between the areas of adjoining licensees has in fact been a regular problem in these jurisdictions. Why should this be the case, notwithstanding the presence of unitization provisions? For an explanation we must look beyond unitization and consider the more fundamental question of whether the production rights that the state grants to its lessees or licensees themselves incorporate or assume a rule of capture. In a final section, I explore the different bases on which these production rights may be granted in modern petroleum regimes, with a view to seeing whether particular types of regime—notably the production-sharing contract regime, now almost universally adopted among

---

[17] Association of International Petroleum Negotiators 2006.

[18] Above, Ch. 9, at 276–94.

[19] Weaver and Asmus 2006.

developing states—may be better adapted to eliminating the problem of capture than are others.

STATE ALLOCATION PRACTICE AND THE DIVISION OF RESERVOIRS: AUSTRALIAN AND BRITISH EXPERIENCES

A system for the exploitation of Australian offshore petroleum resources was jointly adopted by the Australian Commonwealth and the Australian states in 1967 and incorporated in the commonwealth's Petroleum (Submerged Lands) Act of 1967 and corresponding state legislation.[20] It represented a compromise of conflicting state and commonwealth claims to offshore jurisdiction and property rights, which I examine in the next chapter.

The 1967 act—now replaced, with the addition of extensive provisions on carbon sequestration, by the Offshore Petroleum and Greenhouse Gas Storage Act of 2006—was more complicated than some contemporary regimes in that it continued the practice, inherited from state legislation, of separate authorizations for exploration (permits) and production (licenses),[21] but it generally conformed to the common style of petroleum regime described above. It provided for the allocation of exploration permits through regular acreage releases, based on a graticulation system with 5-by-5-minute blocks, and with a relinquishment requirement of half the area of the permit at the end of its six-year term, at which time the permit was renewable as of right (unless the holder was in breach of legal requirements, in which case renewal was discretionary) in respect of the remaining territory for a further five years. This process could continue until the permit was reduced to four blocks or less, after which further renewals, which could go on indefinitely, could take place without further relinquishment. (Permits granted since 2003, however, can be renewed only once.) The competitive factor in bidding for permits was not a cash premium, as in the United States, but the size and quality of the work program (acquisition of data, seismic surveys, and exploration drilling) proposed by the applicant.

This is the sort of regime that led Professor Smith and his colleagues to think that capture problems were unlikely to arise. The act allowed for permits covering up to 400 blocks. The area of blocks ranges from about 83 square kilometers in the northerly latitudes of Australia (such as the prolific northwest shelf off the north coast of Western Australia) to 67 square kilometers in the south (such as Bass

---

[20] See generally Daintith 2006.

[21] To which was added, from 1985, a "retention lease," enabling a find such as a gas field to be held without development pending the establishment of a market for the gas.

Strait). A permit could thus cover anything up to 33,200 square kilometers, and early awards sometimes approached this size. Some such permits, including the one within which the northwest shelf consortium led by the Australian company Woodside found the prolific Rankin gas fields, simply represented adoption under the new regime of permits previously granted by states. In determining what acreage to offer in any release, and how to divide it among a number of discrete permit areas on offer, the offering authority (initially each separate state under the 1967 regime as originally enacted, and from 1987 a commonwealth–state joint authority) doubtless would have liked to "use information obtained from initial geological surveys to avoid splitting geological structures between different licensed areas",[22] but given that there had been no offshore exploration drilling outside the Bass Strait off southeastern Australia, and little if any seismic survey, the information that might have enabled them to do this was nonexistent. Gravity and aeromagnetic surveys were capable of identifying sedimentary basins and indicating the possible attractiveness of subbasins within them, but short of granting an entire subbasin to a single explorer, the risk of splitting a structure could not be diminished in this way.

As time went on, the level of knowledge increased through the seismic work and drilling done on permit acreage, but such acreage was ex hypothesi unavailable for release unless relinquished, and organizing access to as yet unexplored areas faced the same uncertainties. Relinquished acreage might or might not have been the subject of detailed exploration; in either case, the process of relinquishment itself produced a pattern of available acreage, and acreage under permit or license, of increasing complexity. With regular licensing rounds, relinquishments occurred every year. Relinquished acreage might well be reoffered, if the government's technical adviser—the agency that now goes under the name of Geoscience Australia, the successor of the Commonwealth Bureau of Mineral Resources—was more sanguine than the previous permittee about the chances for discovery there. As the process of discovery went on, successful wells, whether themselves commercial or not, might indicate the existence of highly prospective areas nearby that either had never been offered or had been relinquished at some time previously. It is today accepted practice to offer much smaller parcels of acreage in areas such as these than in what are now called "frontier" areas, in which little or no exploration has been done, and Australia has followed this practice. Current policy stipulates maximum areas ranging from 8 blocks in mature regions to 80 blocks in frontier regions.[23]

---

[22] Smith et al. 2000: 262.

[23] Australia. Department of Industry, Science and Resources 1999, quoted in ACIL Consulting 2000: para. 4.2.1.

Other typical offshore offerings are even smaller. The average size of a UK block, it will be remembered, is about 250 square kilometers. After the first three licensing rounds between 1964 and 1970, and save in a few exceptional later cases where a deliberate attempt was made to open up virgin territory, such as the Thirteenth ("Frontier") Round in 1990–1991, when six licenses covered 66 blocks, the normal size of a license has been between one and two blocks. Moreover, most early multiblock licenses covered several discrete areas, not one large one. Later license awards might well be for an area less than an entire block, as UK law, in contrast to Australian law, envisages the relinquishment of areas smaller than a block; relinquishment obligations have varied from time to time.[24]

These policies and procedures tend to mean that a mature and vigorously managed offshore petroleum province, like that of Australia or the United Kingdom, will present a picture of permit and license holdings totally at odds with the notion of spacious and geologically tidy allocations. The point can best be made with an illustration. The map in Figure 11-1 shows a segment of the UK continental shelf, a group of blocks off northeast Scotland abutting the line of delimitation between the United Kingdom and Norway.[25] Exploration and development in this area have now extended over a period of some 40 years.

Shaded blocks and part-blocks were under license when Figure 11-1 was produced; the others have at one time been licensed but have since been relinquished. Note how the regular block pattern has been broken up by partial relinquishments, the frequency with which fields overrun the boundaries of blocks or subblocks, and the fact that in this area alone there are two fields—Boa and the giant Frigg field—that underlie the line of delimitation between British and Norwegian waters, an issue that I discuss in the next chapter.

UNITIZATION: AN ADEQUATE RESPONSE?

The Australian and UK examples demonstrate that the desire to boost exploration and production investment through mechanisms of competition for and relinquishment of acreage has consistently won out over fears of the difficulties that might be engendered by the creation of multiple interests in reservoirs. They, rather than the old-style "whole-of-territory" concession, now typify the geography of national awards of oil and gas exploration and production rights. Since the 1930s, the general assumption has been that there existed adequate prophylactics

---

[24] See generally Daintith et al. 2008: Part 1, Ch. 3.
[25] Based on the map visible at www.og.berr.gov.uk/information/BB_updates/maps/Q9.pdf.

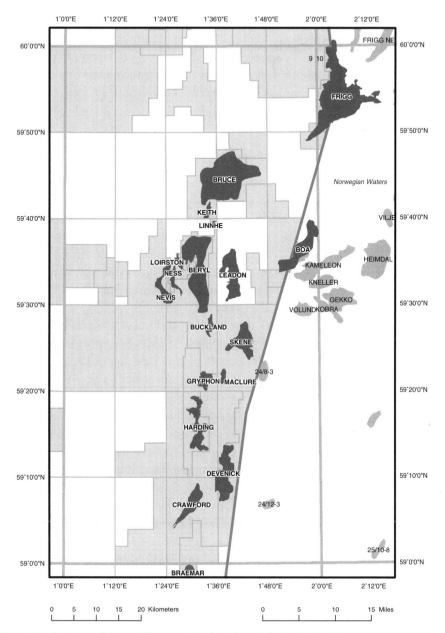

Figure 11-1. Petroleum Fields and License and National Boundaries in the North Sea

Source: Map kindly supplied by the UK Department of Energy and Climate Change, which assumes no responsibility for errors or omissions

Note: Shaded areas of the UK grid represent areas under license in June 2009

against, or at least palliatives for, these difficulties. Chief among these has been unitization. Countries like the United Kingdom, Australia, or Norway, which came relatively late to the discovery and exploitation of important petroleum reserves, were able to avoid the painful experiments and missteps by which the United States had groped its way toward conservation of petroleum and stabilization of its production.

Compulsory Unitization: The United Kingdom

One of the petroleum engineers heavily involved in U.S. unitization discussions in the 1920s and 1930s, Dr. J. B. Umpleby, delivered a paper on the subject at the first World Petroleum Congress, held in London in 1933. In it, he argued strongly for unitization of fields at the earliest possible stage or, better, for permitting the drilling of new acreage only where a plan for the unitization of any eventual discovery was in place.[26] Only through unitized production, he maintained, could one hope for the efficient preservation of reservoir pressures, most notably through avoiding the dissipation of dissolved gas.

As we have seen, Umpleby's arguments have even today achieved only limited acceptance on privately held lands in the United States,[27] but early unitization was adopted for federal lands in the 1935 amendments to the Mineral Leasing Act.[28] In the same year, the United Kingdom also adopted the idea of making development conditional upon fieldwide unitization when the field appeared to be shared between two or more leaseholders (license holders, in British and Australian parlance). Its 1935 Petroleum (Production) Regulations included a compulsory unitization clause as one of the model clauses to be incorporated in all petroleum mining licenses.[29] With minimal modification, this clause was carried over into the regime for offshore petroleum exploitation created by the Continental Shelf Act of 1964; it has figured in the various sets of regulations providing model clauses for incorporation in offshore licenses (now called petroleum production licenses)[30] and has thus applied to all operations on the UK continental shelf. The clause empowers the minister to require the preparation by licensees, and submission for

---

[26] Umpleby 1933: 303. See also Umpleby 1930; Oliver and Umpleby 1930.

[27] Above, Ch. 9, at 289–94.

[28] Above, Ch. 9, at 285–8.

[29] Petroleum (Production) Regulations 1935, Schedule 2, Part III.

[30] The clauses issued up to 1999 are collected in the Petroleum (Current Model Clauses) Order 1999.

his or her approval, of a unit development scheme for a field (or to impose one if they fail to do so):

> If at any time during the term hereby granted or any renewal thereof the [minister] shall be satisfied that the licensed area or any part thereof forms part of a single geological petroleum structure or petroleum field (hereinafter referred to as "an oil field") in respect of other parts of which licences granted in pursuance of the Act are then in force and the [minister] shall consider that it is in the national interest in order to secure the maximum ultimate recovery of petroleum and to avoid unnecessary competitive drilling that the oil field should be worked and developed as a unit in co-operation by all the persons, including the Licensee, whose licences extend to or include any part thereof . . .

Probably not until the end of the 1960s, or even later, when intensive development of the North Sea was fully under way and fields were being discovered that extended across the borderlines between adjacent license blocks, did it become apparent that this carefully drafted clause might not serve to render capture issues irrelevant to North Sea operations. Where such a field turns out to extend into two or more license areas, the licensees involved may make their own agreement as to how to develop the field, and such agreements—which may include the field's development as a unit or a variety of other devices, such as the sale of one party's entire interest to the other or the coordination of the respective parties' development plans—have been common, though they have on occasion given rise to subsequent controversy, and indeed litigation, between the parties.[31] Parties may, however, find it difficult or impossible to agree, and one of the situations where this outcome is most likely is where a field covered by one license has a relatively small extension into the area of another. Several such extensions are visible in Figure 11-1.

In the high-cost environment of offshore petroleum operations, possibly in deep and difficult waters and with long pipeline runs to shore, a licensee might be forced to the conclusion that the quantity of oil in place in such an extension could not justify the drilling of a well. At the same time, the licensee with the majority of the field area might calculate that appropriately placed wells in its license area could efficiently drain the extension as well as the body of the field. In such circumstances, not only is agreement going to be difficult, but also the criteria for the enforcement of compulsory unitization cannot be satisfied. The minister can only exercise this power "in order to secure the maximum ultimate recovery of petroleum and in order to avoid unnecessary competitive drilling." If, however, the reservoir can be efficiently drained by drilling on only one of the two blocks, unitization will not increase ultimate recovery; and if it is uneconomic for one of the parties to drill anyway, there can be no risk of competitive

---

[31] Polkinghorne 2008: 314–18.

drilling, "unnecessary" or otherwise. The unitization clause, in consequence, does not serve to regulate the exploitation of fields like these.

Unless, therefore, the operations of the licensee undertaking development breach other protective provisions of the license, as by drilling within the prohibited distance from the license boundary (set in 1935 at 400 feet, now 125 meters),[32] the licensee of the extension will be able to resist drainage only if it is able to show that the licensee undertaking development would breach the terms of its license by draining an area beyond the license boundary—in other words, that the rule of capture does not form part of the UK petroleum licensing regime. This is a question not of English (or more likely Scots)[33] common law, whose operation in relation to petroleum has never been tested, but of the interpretation of the rights granted by the license.

In a later section, I examine the nature of UK license rights along with those from other jurisdictions. Here I would add only that unless those rights, properly construed, exclude the possibility of lawfully recovering oil drained from another license area, the existence of other, more general control powers conferred on the minister by the license cannot be of help to the licensee threatened by drainage. Although the powers of the minister to grant a consent for the development of a field,[34] and to consent or refuse consent to the drilling of any well,[35] are on their face unqualified, their exercise to negate a right—that of capture—granted by the license would represent an unlawful misuse of power, a conclusion strengthened by the presence in the license of the compulsory unitization clause, which is explicitly directed at some, but not all, of the circumstances in which capture might occur.[36] This now appears to be the official view in the United Kingdom.

At one time, on the basis of the interpretation just mentioned, the responsible department refused to grant development consent for a field that was thought to extend into other license areas unless all interested licensees had concluded a unitization agreement or licensees in those other areas had unconditionally or provisionally waived their rights to the petroleum underlying those areas. It abandoned that position in 1997, apparently because of a change of official view on the extent of the rights granted by the license, and now "does not consider that

---

[32] Petroleum Licensing (Production) (Seaward Areas) Regulations 2008, Schedule, cl. 20. The unitization clause in the schedule appears as cl. 27.

[33] Most UK offshore fields have been found in waters to which Scots law is applied under Continental Shelf Act 1964, § 3.

[34] Petroleum Licensing (Production) (Seaward Areas) Regulations 2008, Schedule, cl. 17(1).

[35] Ibid. cl. 19.

[36] Daintith et al. 2010: para. 5-2758; Daintith 2006: para. 5408.

powers to require unitisation extend to issues of fairness and equity between groups of Licensees."[37] It thus judges field development plans purely on the basis of whether they will maximize the economic recovery of oil and gas.

Compulsory Unitization: Australia

In countries where petroleum development was only at its first beginnings, the possibility seemed to exist of avoiding the capture problem altogether by the provision of adequately large areas for exploration and the grant of exploitation rights over the whole of any field that might have been delineated after discovery. This was the message brought back to Australia from an extended visit to the United States in 1930 by Dr. Walter Woolnough, the commonwealth's geological adviser. After citing the usual examples of waste deriving from competitive drilling, he stated that as long as there were in place stringent conditions compelling active operations on a field, "[t]here was absolute unanimity of opinion on the question of monopoly. In a nutshell, this opinion is that the highest degree of efficiency is obtained by granting, as nearly as possible, monopoly for each particular field, but maintaining competition between different fields."[38]

One does wonder whom Dr. Woolnough talked to in Texas. At all events, he recommended that prospecting areas be sized between 10,000 acres and 100 square miles, and that areas around discoveries be reserved for long enough to enable evaluation—say at least 1 square mile for at least a year.[39] As we have seen,[40] state laws passed before 1930 made provision for much smaller areas at both exploration and production stages, an approach strongly criticized by Woolnough in intragovernmental communications.[41] He made no explicit recommendation, however, that any kind of compulsory unitization clause be written into the law. Five years later, a well-informed opposition member read extensive extracts from the Umpleby paper into the Western Australian legislative record in an attempt to get larger lease areas written into the state's 1936 Petroleum Act[42] but had to acknowledge that "the feeling of the House was against" his idea "that each person

---

[37] United Kingdom. Department of Trade and Industry 2000: para. 2.5.1, reproduced in Daintith et al. 2010: para. 7-215, and in Weaver and Asmus 2006: 191–2. For the earlier practice, see Daintith et al. 2010: para. 5-2732.

[38] Woolnough 1931: 77.

[39] *Ibid.*

[40] Above, Ch. 10, at 332.

[41] Woolnough 1933[?].

[42] Western Australia Parliamentary Debates 1936: 1266 (Legislative Council).

discovering oil should have a right to the structure," because "it would be too much in the direction of a monopoly."[43] Lease areas remained small, and the debates— and the act—made no reference to compulsory unitization. The same was true of Victoria's Mines (Petroleum) Act of 1935. Australian state governments seemed to assume that the requirement to place wells a certain distance from permit or lease boundaries would achieve all that was necessary.

From 1939 onward, however, we find states with hopes of oil production inserting compulsory unitization provisions into their statutes. The stimulus for this move was an attempt by the commonwealth government to promote petroleum exploration and production in the administered territories of Papua and New Guinea. These were considered highly promising as oil provinces, but the amount of exploration under existing ordinances had been very limited, and companies pressed the commonwealth government, during the 1930s, for a more favorable regime under which much more extensive areas would be available for exploitation under lease, to permit the eventual recovery of the very large sums that needed to be expended in exploration and development.[44] Advisers like Woolnough were generally sympathetic to such demands but were still fearful of creating conditions where there could be monopolization of the resource by large companies, possibly acting in concert, or of permitting the kind of "blanketing" of areas that had occurred, for example, under the Western Australian Act of 1920.[45]

A significant liberalization of terms was effected by two Petroleum (Prospecting and Mining) Ordinances of 1938, one for Papua, the other for New Guinea, which were largely identical.[46] Each of these ordinances contained, in its section 75, a compulsory unitization provision. In discussions prior to the making of the ordinances, the need for such a section had been pointed out by a representative of Anglo-Iranian Oil (formerly Anglo-Persian), who provided a copy of the provision in the United Kingdom's 1935 Petroleum (Production) Regulations as a precedent,[47] and by another company active in Papua, which feared drilling

---

[43] *Ibid.* at 1267.

[44] See, e.g. National Archives of Australia, A A518/1 B846/4/48 and Y834/1 Part I (letters and meetings with Anglo-Iranian Oil Company and Vacuum Oil Company).

[45] Above, Ch. 10, at 332.

[46] Papua Petroleum (Prospecting and Mining) Ordinance 1938 (No. 13 of 1938); New Guinea Petroleum (Prospecting and Mining) Ordinance 1938 (No. 43 of 1938).

[47] National Archives of Australia, A518, Y834/1 Part I, doc. JRH/JO (discussion of March 2, 1938, between Southwell, Woolnough, and Wade).

on its permit boundaries by rival companies if its exploration showed favorable prospects.[48] These representations appear to have convinced advisers like Woolnough that a unitization provision would be a useful element in the government's control apparatus.

The section that appeared in the ordinances bore a family resemblance to the British clause in empowering the minister to demand the preparation of a unit development scheme in appropriate circumstances, with a reserve power to impose a scheme on recalcitrants. It went further, however, in enabling the minister to extend the area of the license or lease if a field within that area were found to extend into adjoining vacant land. The test it imposed as a precondition for compelling unit development was also more broadly worded. The point on which the minister had to be satisfied was that "it is desirable, for the purpose of securing economy and efficiency and of avoiding wasteful and harmful development and practices, that the oilfield should be worked as one unit."[49] Though less precise than the British wording, this formulation still required that there be some net economic gain from unitization, whether in terms of quantities ultimately recovered or of savings in drilling and other investments in the field. It did not entitle the minister to consider issues of equity, as by imposing unitization purely to protect the interests of a lessee holding acreage overlying an extension of the type discussed in the UK context above.

In November 1939, the Australian Prime Minister Robert Menzies told the Commonwealth Parliament that the 1938 Papua and New Guinea ordinances "conform[ed] to modern requirements and good oil-field practice throughout the world."[50] Tactfully, he refrained from adding that his advisers were of the view that state legislation did not meet this standard,[51] but instead moved to press the states to adopt a uniform petroleum law reflecting the improvements enacted for Papua and New Guinea.[52] By the standards of a federation, this approach bore rapid fruit. Victoria[53] and Queensland[54] enacted amending legislation in 1939, South Australia[55] and Western Australia[56] in 1940, in each case amending existing

---

[48] National Archives of Australia, A518/1 B846/4/48 (letter from C. A. le M. Walker, May 19, 1938).

[49] Papua Petroleum (Prospecting and Mining) Ordinances 1938–1939, § 75(1).

[50] Commonwealth of Australia, 162 Parliamentary Debates 1576 (November 23, 1939).

[51] Woolnough 1933 [?].

[52] Di Stefano 1973: 123; Minister of Mines, in Victoria Parliamentary Debates 1939: 2046–7.

[53] Mines (Petroleum) Act (Vic.) 1939.

[54] Petroleum Acts Amendment Act (Qld.) 1939.

[55] Mining (Petroleum) Act (SA) 1940.

[56] Petroleum Act Amendment Act 1940 (WA).

legislation in the sense of offering enlarged exploration and production areas, identical to those provided for under the UK regulations of 1935: a prospecting license covering between 8 and 200 square miles, a production lease covering between 4 and 100 square miles.

The states were more reticent about the adoption of the unitization clause incorporated in the commonwealth's draft statute. Only South Australia and Victoria included it in their amending legislation just referred to,[57] in Victoria on the specific ground that the production of the small Lakes Entrance field could be restarted by secondary recovery operations, notably the repressuring of the field, for which the cooperation of all the interested licensees and lessees would be required.[58] Queensland waited until 1958 to enact such a provision,[59] and Western Australia until 1967.[60]

This Western Australian legislation was modeled on the commonwealth's Petroleum (Submerged Lands) Act of 1967. For some reason, the drafters of the latter act clearly felt that the 1938 model for the clause could do with improvement. Accordingly, they further modified the criterion for compulsory unitization, providing that the Joint Authority could direct unitization "for the purpose of securing the more effective recovery of petroleum from the petroleum pool."[61] Though the language has been made still more general, the test continues to address only questions of how petroleum can best be recovered and says nothing about issues of equity between adjoining licensees. It may be that the responsible minister thought otherwise, as the Explanatory Memorandum for the Bill, having referred to the importance of ensuring "that the most effective recovery of petroleum is made in the most economic manner possible," continued by stating that "unless there is some provision enabling the recovery from [a shared] petroleum pool to be co-ordinated, severe injustices may be inflicted on a licensee having rights in respect of the pool by the actions of another person having rights in respect of the same pool and who unfairly, or improperly, draws petroleum from the pool."[62]

Perhaps it was assumed that recovery from *any* shared reservoir would be made "more effective" through a unitization scheme. We have already seen that this is not the case. The point was conceded by the commonwealth government in the

---

[57] Mining (Petroleum) Act (SA) 1940 § 72; Mines (Petroleum) Act (Vic.) 1939 § 16.

[58] Victoria Parliamentary Debates 1939: 2046, 2251.

[59] Petroleum Act 1923 (Qld.), § 61B(4), introduced by amendment in 1958.

[60] Petroleum Act 1967 (WA), § 69.

[61] Petroleum (Submerged Lands) Act 1967, § 59, now reenacted as Offshore Petroleum and Greenhouse Gas Storage Act 2006, § 191.

[62] Department of National Development 1967: 51–2.

late 1990s, when it refused to direct unitization of a reservoir that could be fully drained by one party, notwithstanding the launching of judicial review proceedings by the licensee holding the extension acreage. These proceedings were abandoned after the parties reached an alternative form of agreement providing some compensation to the complainants for the gas produced from the extension.[63]

In consequence, Australian legislation, like that of the United Kingdom, continues to leave a number of shared reservoirs uncovered by compulsory unitization powers, and thus the question of whether production rights include capture remains a live issue—indeed, a highly controversial one. Two recent attempts by the commonwealth government to reshape the unitization provision have foundered on divisions in the industry between those who calculated they might gain from any change and those who feared they might lose. The situation has been so sensitive that this is the only provision of the Petroleum (Submerged Lands) Act that has not been rewritten, in what is thought by Australian legislative draftsmen to be "plain English," in the Offshore Petroleum and Greenhouse Gas Storage Act of 2006. Section 191 of this act reproduces almost word for word section 59 of the 1967 act, which it replaces. The lacuna in the Australian regime is especially glaring in that the unitization power applies only when a reservoir is shared between two holders of production licenses, or such a holder and a person enjoying rights to recover petroleum under some other legal regime.[64]

The introduction of this restriction, which was not to be found in the 1938 model, was perhaps a result of the notion that unitization was particularly associated with secondary recovery, as in the Lakes Entrance field in Victoria and as has been commonplace in U.S. practice.[65] This might also explain the reference to *more effective* recovery as the key criterion, which implies that recovery is already under way.[66] At any event, if the government wanted to promote equity among holders of titles, this change in legislation for offshore application was singularly ill judged. The high costs of offshore operations mean that holders of exploration permits will not commit to production, and hence apply for a production license, unless they can be assured of returns high enough to cover these costs. The need to operate on a shared field greatly increases these commercial uncertainties, but until a permittee is in actual possession of a production license, it cannot protect its interest in that field by seeking compulsory unitization. This creates a further class of cases in which it is the application—or nonapplication—of the rule of capture that will determine the respective rights of the titleholders in a shared field.

---

[63] Daintith 2006: para. 5418.

[64] Offshore Petroleum and Greenhouse Gas Storage Act 2006, § 191(1).

[65] Above, Ch. 8, at 291–2.

[66] Craig 1991: 483–4.

Compulsory Unitization: Other Countries

The argument so far might seem to suggest that the continuing relevance of the rule of capture in systems of state ownership or control was a result of arrangements for compulsory unitization that failed to cover every case where drainage might occur. Capture could thus be swept entirely from the scene by laws, regulations, or contract terms between the state and the operator envisaging unitization in every case where a reservoir was found to extend into blocks licensed or leased to different parties. (A complementary rule, to eliminate drainage of which the state itself might be the victim, would require that where a field was found to extend into unlicensed acreage, the licensee would be required to obtain an additional license or an extension of the existing one. Of course, if payments to the state were wholly based on the amount of petroleum recovered, it should be indifferent to the location of production so long as full recovery from the whole reservoir was being achieved.)

All-embracing unitization provisions are in fact not uncommon. Generally they provide that the parties must unitize wherever there is a shared reservoir and the relevant authority (usually the minister) so requests. The survey to which I referred earlier in this chapter examined unitization provisions in 12 countries, including the United Kingdom, already discussed here. Another country covered, Indonesia, has new provisions, and these I mention below. Among the remainder, a "comprehensive" unitization clause of this type can be found in Angola, Brazil, China, Colombia, and Egypt, usually in the model contracts to be concluded with oil companies.[67] Elsewhere, the draft Azerbaijan Petroleum Law of 2000, article 13, appears to contemplate only a voluntary unitization;[68] clauses in the laws, rules, and contracts applicable in Ecuador and Nigeria refer to "improved efficiency" or "maximum ultimate recovery" as criteria for the exercise of unitization powers;[69] and Russia and Yemen have no specific unitization clauses.

Compulsory unitization of shared reservoirs at the discretion of either the responsible ministry or the state oil company, without other preconditions, thus appears on the basis of this small survey to be a common, perhaps the commonest, approach. Difficult questions about maximum or improved recovery therefore do not need to be answered, and even very small extensions create the conditions for unitization. But unless the competent authorities receive immediate access to all operational data—which is likely only where a state oil company is involved, most

---

[67] Weaver and Asmus 2006: 103, 111, 123, 125, 172.

[68] *Ibid.* 106.

[69] *Ibid.* 128–30, 179–81.

probably as a PSC partner[70]—the efficacy of this approach depends on timely and accurate reporting by the titleholder doing the drilling that suggests the presence of a reservoir extension beyond its boundary. Where, as is quite likely, there is doubt about the interpretation of drilling data, the understandable decision of the titleholder may well be to continue drilling and start producing, steps that may be necessary in any event to prove the size of an extension and the amount of flow from it. Drainage is thus taking place, and the issue of whether the relevant petroleum law permits or forbids capture is again ineluctably posed.

It can also happen that the state authority declines or fails, for one reason or another, to exercise its discretion to require unitization even where the presence of a shared reservoir is demonstrated, and if this happens, it will again be necessary to consider the capture issue. This source of uncertainty can be avoided by eliminating the need for a discretionary decision. Such simplification may, however, carry a cost. One of the clearest "automatic" clauses was contained in the Petroleum Mining Code promulgated under a treaty between Australia and Indonesia, establishing a zone of cooperation in an area where they were unable to agree on an appropriate line of delimitation between their continental shelves.[71] The code provided, in article 21, that

[w]here a petroleum pool is partly within a contract area and partly within another contract area, ... the Joint Authority shall require the contractors to enter into a unitisation agreement with each other within a reasonable time as determined by the Joint Authority, for the purpose of securing the more effective and optimized production of petroleum from the pool. ... The Joint Authority shall approve the unitisation agreement before approvals under Article 17 of this Petroleum Mining Code are given.

Note that there was no discretion left to the Joint Authority (the body that represented both Australian and Indonesian interests in the zone), and that the effect of the reference to article 17 was to make development and production impossible in the absence of an agreement, since that article forbade the construction of production structures without the approval of the authority. The reference to the purpose of "securing more effective and optimized recovery" seems here to have been transformed into a criterion for the content of the agreement rather than—as in domestic Australian law[72]—a precondition for the power to demand it. These provisions perhaps reflected the very stringent Indonesian

---

[70] See further below, at 367–9.

[71] For the text of the treaty, see Petroleum (Australia–Indonesia Zone of Co-operation) Act 1990 (Cth), Schedule. The code appears as an annex to the treaty.

[72] Above, at 354–5.

approach to unitization. This is now to be found in its Government Regulation No. 35 of 2004 on upstream oil and gas business activities, whose article 41.1 simply states that "[a] Contractor is required to conduct unitization if it is proven that its reservoir extends into another Contractor's Work Area."

Making production conditional on the conclusion of an agreement means that the timing of production may be dictated by the interests of the party that is less far forward in its program of exploration and appraisal. Such parties may have a variety of reasons for not wanting to move quickly. Investment in this particular field may not be high on their list of priorities; if the field is a gas field, they may not have identified any markets for the gas or may be looking toward markets that may develop at some time in the future; the process of concluding a unitization agreement is costly; and given that the field information they possess is likely to be inferior to that of the party that is ready to produce, they may be doubtful as to whether rapid agreement will adequately recognize their interests in the reservoir.

In light of these considerations, it may be significant that, following the independence of East Timor from Indonesia and the consequent replacement of the zone of cooperation treaty with a new Australia–East Timor agreement, the Timor Sea Treaty of May 2002, a new Petroleum Mining Code[73] for what is now called the Joint Petroleum Development Area relaxed the earlier approach by providing, in article 10.1(a), that

> [w]here a Reservoir is partly within a Contract Area and partly within another Contract Area, but wholly within the JPDA, the Designated Authority may require by written notice the Contractors to enter into a unitisation agreement for the purpose of securing the more effective recovery of Petroleum from the Reservoir.

Where an agreement is required, the same prohibition on development or production approvals before the conclusion of the agreement applies as before (article 10.2), but the provision of discretion for the Designated Authority (which replaces the former Joint Authority) as to whether or not to require unitization is, at the least, a powerful instrument for securing rapid agreement from the holder of a minority stake in the reservoir, and may enable that stake to be ignored altogether if effective recovery is not prejudiced.

---

[73] The code is promulgated under article 7 of the treaty.

THE NATURE AND EXTENT OF EXPLOITATION RIGHTS UNDER STATE REGIMES

Modern petroleum legislators may have assumed that by providing for compulsory unitization, they were eliminating the capture issue, but if they did, they were wrong. In any regime that does not have a watertight unitization clause, it may be necessary to determine whether the rule of capture applies. The key to this determination lies in the nature and extent of the production rights that the country's legal scheme grants to those who hold the appropriate production title, be it called a concession, lease, or license. A granting clause that made it clear that the titleholder could produce only the petroleum that, at the time of grant, lay beneath the area of land or sea referred to in the grant would effectively displace the rule of capture. Conversely, a clause that, following the principle of article 552 of the French Civil Code, stipulated that the grantee would obtain ownership of any petroleum it might recover within the area of its title, without making reference to the original location of that petroleum, might be taken to indicate that the rule would apply, at least if there were indications that the rule formed part of the general property law of the country relating to underground fluids like water. Such an interpretation would be reinforced by the presence among the applicable legal rules of clauses protecting against the ordinary consequences of the rule, as by imposing minimum distances of wells from the title area boundary or, indeed, imposing compulsory unitization.[74]

Despite the fundamental importance of the granting clause in determining relationships both between the titleholder and the state and among different titleholders, it does not appear that those drafting such clauses have given much thought to their relationship with the rule of capture. This is true whether the clause appears as part of petroleum legislation (as in Australia) or as part of a model contract between state and titleholder (as in the United States, United Kingdom, and most other countries). Exceptionally, the U.S. regulatory draftsman has been clear as to the intentions behind the regulations, stating in the preamble to the unitization regulations for the outer continental shelf (OCS) that "[a] lease does not grant lessees the ownership of minerals in place, and the Law of Capture applies to the development and production of OCS minerals."[75]

The granting clause of the relevant lease form provides in its section 2 that "[t]he Lessor grants and leases to the Lessee the exclusive right and privilege to drill for, develop and produce oil and gas resources, except helium gas, in the submerged

---

[74] Forbes and Lang 1987: 328.

[75] 30 C.F.R. § 250.50, cited in *Alabama v. Department of Interior*, 84 F. 3d 410, 413 (11th Cir., 1996). The preamble does not appear in the current version of the regulation.

lands of the Outer Continental Shelf comprising [] acres or [] hectares (hereinafter referred to as 'the leased area') ... "[76] The intention of the draftsman is thus that the words determining the geographical location of the lease should be taken to fix the area within which the *activities* of drilling, developing, and producing oil and gas are to be carried on, and not to identify a specific body of oil and gas in place. In the absence of the evidence of intention, the latter reading would be a possible but, in my opinion, implausible one. Were the rights of the lessee restricted to recovering a specific body of hydrocarbons underlying the lease area, one would have expected at least the provision of the definite article—"*the* oil and gas resources ... in the submerged lands"—to signal this intention.

Similar granting formulas are to be found both in the UK seaward production license—"exclusive licence and liberty during the continuance of this licence and subject to the provisions hereof to search and bore for, and get, Petroleum in the sea bed and subsoil under the seaward area more particularly described in Schedule 1 to this licence"[77]—and in the petroleum production license under the Australian offshore legislation: "[a] production licence authorises the licensee, in accordance with the conditions (if any) to which the licence is subject: (a) to recover petroleum in the licence area."[78] The Australian legislation also makes it clear that if "petroleum is recovered by a production licensee in the licence area [it] becomes the property of the ... Licensee [and] ... is not subject to any rights of other persons (other than a person to whom the ... licensee transfers, assigns or otherwise disposes of the petroleum or an interest in the petroleum)."[79]

Elsewhere, I have argued that each of these granting clauses should be construed in the same way as the U.S. lease clause. This means that each clause, read in light of other provisions of the applicable law, notably the well spacing requirement and reference to competitive drilling in the United Kingdom and the property transfer and unitization provisions in Australia, has the effect of instituting a "statutory" rule of capture, so that drainage of hydrocarbons from an adjacent block by operations that are in compliance with all relevant rules affecting the title is perfectly legitimate.[80] For a number of years, however, the view of the responsible UK government department was that the rule of capture was not part of the UK regime. This position was based on the reasoning that the presence of a well spacing clause and a unitization clause among the model clauses signified a *rejection*

---

[76] United States. Department of Interior, Minerals Management Service 1986.

[77] Petroleum Licensing (Production) (Seaward Areas) Regulations 2008, Schedule, cl. 2. This has been the form of the clause since 1935.

[78] Offshore Petroleum and Greenhouse Gas Storage Act 2006, § 161(1).

[79] *Ibid.* § 285.

[80] For the United Kingdom: Daintith 1978; Daintith et al. 2010: para. 5-2732; for Australia: Daintith 2000: 103–7.

of the rule of capture,[81] the exact opposite of the argument here that it is the *recognition* of the rule of capture as the basic operational principle under the Petroleum Act that makes these clauses necessary. As noted earlier, a legal review of the department's practice in 1997 resulted in a change of view, and the department now accepts the legitimacy of drainage that does not impair maximum ultimate recovery or provoke competitive drilling.[82]

In Australia, we have seen that there is ample evidence from the legislative record that the early state legislators all assumed that the rule of capture would apply: the risk of capture and drainage under proposed leasing arrangements was frequently pointed out to state ministers, and they used it as an excuse to assert state rights to subsurface petroleum.[83] Yet while the disorder and wastefulness of the American system were held up on all sides in the legislative debates as something to be avoided, drainage from one lease or license area to another seems to have been accepted by governments as an unavoidable incident of production, which might possibly be forestalled or limited by boundary spacing rules or countered by offset drilling but could not be legally excluded. Once the state had brought those resources into unified ownership, however, as happened in 1915 in Queensland, 1935 in Victoria, and 1936 in Western Australia, there was no reason at all why legislation should have had to reproduce the effects of the rule in the arrangements made for managing subsurface petroleum resources. Still, governments and legislators never seem to have given any thought to whether they could so design the rights they were granting to oil operators under their leases as to eliminate the problem of capture.

The legislation paid little attention to the way the granting clause of the oil lease was to be expressed. The 1912 Queensland act and 1920 Western Australian act simply referred to leases "for mining for mineral oil" (sections 7(1) and 11(1), respectively), and the 1936 Western Australian act was in analogous terms (section 55). The wording of some clauses under other legislation, however, gave some basis for thinking that the rule of capture was *not* intended to apply. Queensland, in 1923, and Victoria, in 1935, provided that the lease should "confer upon the lessee the exclusive right to drill for, mine, extract, recover, remove and dispose of all petroleum in or under the land demised."[84] "[A]ll petroleum in or under the land demised" could be construed as referring only to the oil in place at the time of grant, in which case the lessee could not lawfully recover petroleum that was under other land at that time. In the same legislation, however, we find not only a

---

[81] Hughes 1991.
[82] Daintith et al. 2010: para. 5-2732.
[83] Above, Ch. 10, at 329–30, 331–2.
[84] Petroleum Act 1923 (Qld.), § 31(2); Mines (Petroleum) Act 1935 (Vic.), § 30.

boundary spacing requirement, but also an offset well obligation, which suggests that the legislator thought the rule would apply and wanted to protect against its operation. Whether a court, forbidden at that time to look at legislative debate on the act it was invited to construe, and coming uninstructed to the issue, would have taken the same view is far from certain.

Continuing lack of exploration success in Australia barred that particular potential fork in the capture road, and it was not until the much more successful years of operation in the waters of the northwest shelf that the issue arose again in Australia, under the rather different wording of the 1967 offshore legislation, reenacted in 2006, discussed above.[85] The view I expressed there has received support from some, though not all,[86] commentators on the issue. The fact that the commonwealth government has refused to impose unitization or exercise its other powers over development and production in a case where drainage from a neighboring block did not impair effective recovery[87] suggests that its advisers support a similar interpretation of the act.

I suspect that in many other state petroleum regimes, the issue of whether the rule of capture will apply when a compulsory unitization provision (if there is one) does not is one of considerable difficulty on which it is impossible to find clear rulings. In one country, however, we can now state definitely, on the basis of a judicial decision of the highest authority, that the petroleum licensing arrangements do not incorporate the rule of capture, and thus production of petroleum by way of drainage from an adjoining licensed block is, in certain circumstances at least, unlawful and will give rise to a duty of compensation. This is the Netherlands, where the case of *Unocal Netherlands B.V. v. Continental Netherlands Oil Co.* ("Conoco"), which in 2005 reached the Hoge Raad (Supreme Court),[88] showed how drainage issues could slip past unitization requirements and confront a court squarely with this question. The actions giving rise to the dispute began in 1985, and litigation was still continuing in 2010 on how to apply the Supreme Court's ruling.

Conoco and Unocal held production licenses for adjoining blocks on the shelf, L16a and Q1. It appears that Conoco drilled in L16a at some time before 1985, and that in 1984 and 1985 the parties exchanged information, on the basis of which they concluded that the oil structure of which the Logger field in L16a was

---

[85] See text at n. 79, and n. 80, above.

[86] Agree: Forbes and Lang 1987: 328; Keen 1998; doubtful: Crommelin 1986.

[87] See above, at 354–5.

[88] Case C04/127HR, October 14, 2005. Details of this dispute are drawn, save where otherwise noted, from the conclusions presented to the court by Advocate General Spier on May 27, 2005 (Spier 2005). My thanks to Adrian Hill and Dagfin Nygard for supplying English translations of the decisions and the advocate general's conclusions.

part also extended below Q1. In 1985, Conoco started producing from the Logger field through two wells, one of which was very close (88 meters) to the field boundary. The relevant Dutch laws in force at the time were the Continental Shelf Mining Act of September 23, 1965, and the Decree of January 27, 1967.[89] The act provided (in article 11.2.b) for the attachment to production licenses of regulations dealing with unitization, among other things, and the decree, containing such regulations, stipulated (in article 28):

> If, in the licence area, an economically exploitable quantity of oil or natural gas is demonstrated in a deposit which, at the discretion of the Minister is deemed to go beyond the boundary of the licence area, the licensee, in accordance with a request thereto by the Minister, is required to co-operate in reaching an agreement between the licensee and the party entitled to produce oil or gas in the adjoining area, in pursuance of which the production will be carried out in mutual consultation.[90]

The drafting of this clause is far from clear, but a lower court appears to have decided that grounds for unitization do not exist unless the "economically exploitable quantity" is contained in the extension, though it is not necessary that exploitation should be through the extension block. If exploitation is economic by way, for example, of recovery via a well or wells in the block covering the main area of the field, under a unitization agreement, then the test is satisfied.[91]

At all events, and whatever was its own interpretation of the powers under article 28, Unocal did not refer the matter to the minister until December 1992. An initial decision by the minister to require an agreement was reversed in May 1994 after objection by Conoco, on the ground that there no longer existed any economically recoverable oil under block Q1: it had all been produced by Conoco through its wells in block L16a. The minister took the view that a decision under article 28 could not be retrospective, so any dispute between the parties about rights to oil already produced would need to be settled through private law proceedings. These duly ensued in 1998, around the key issue of whether Conoco was entitled to the oil it had taken, by reason of the application of ... the rule of capture.

Judgments of Dutch courts tend to be economically worded, and this one, in relation to capture, was no exception:

---

[89] The act and decree have been repealed and replaced, with effect from January 1, 2003, by the Dutch Mining Act, applying both to the continental shelf and onshore: see below, 366–7.

[90] Translation in Roggenkamp 1991: 289 of the article as reenacted in the Decree of February 6, 1976.

[91] Hague Court of Appeal, case 98/854, ruling of December 18, 2003, para. 1.3(d).

According to Conoco ... the Rule of Capture implies that the licence holder is authorized to produce oil in its licence area without any restriction derived from the (mere) provenance of the oil. ... The Rule of Capture in [this] sense ... is not applicable as a valid rule of Dutch law to the production licence granted pursuant to the Mining Act Continental Shelf.

The appellate court correctly considered that the production licence gives the licence holder the exclusive right to produce oil in its licence area and that the removal of oil from another licence area, for which another party is the holder of a production licence, constitutes an infringement of the subjective right of that other party, provided the oil removed would have been economically extractable in some way for the other licence holder. This legal interpretation tallies with the system and the purport of the Mining Act Continental Shelf and the Royal Decree of 27 January 1967 based on it, as is shown (among others) by the parliamentary history of the act as stated in sections 8.44–8.54.1 of the conclusion of the Advocate General.[92]

That was all the Supreme Court had to say about the matter. In its initial ruling, the court below did not offer any authority—or indeed, reasoning—to support its characterization of the production license right as a subjective right (that is, a legal right directly enforceable against third parties in litigation by the right holder). It treated the drainage of oil from a production license area as an infringement of that right on the ground that this affected the occurrence of oil in that area and consequently the value of the party's exclusive right to produce oil. The Court of Appeal refused to treat capture as any kind of industry norm or custom, saying that it "did not find any starting points for assuming that this infringement would be acceptable between holders of production licences according to generally accepted standards." But its only specific ground for interpreting the license in this way was that "the explanatory memorandum to section III: 28 of the Royal Decree dated 27 January 1967 (Bulletin of acts, orders and decrees 1967, 24)—providing that the parties, if overlapping structures are involved in case of a unitization agreement, as a rule first of all will determine to which reserves each of the parties is entitled—points out that each of the parties is entitled to the oil reserves occurring in its area."[93] The royal decree itself, however, did not say anything about the determination of reserves, and the memorandum, in anticipating such a determination, necessary in any unitization agreement whether against a rule of capture background or not, carried no implication as to the *preexisting* rights of the parties.

Throughout the conclusions of Advocate General Spier before the Supreme Court on the capture issue, one sees a similar tendency to find evidence of an intention not to incorporate the rule of capture into the system of the act and

---

[92] Case C04/127HR, October 14, 2005, at paras. 8.2.1, 8.2.2.

[93] Court of Appeal, The Hague, case 98/854, October 16, 2000, para. 7.3.

decree of 1967, even in what might appear to be noncommittal or irrelevant statements.[94] These conclusions (which under Dutch procedures form a kind of official opinion on the merits of the case, though one that the court is free to accept or reject on any point) offered a lengthy analysis of the structure of the legislation and of elements of the legislative proceedings. One example of Spier's approach, from paragraph 8.42 of the conclusions, must suffice.

> Article II.3 of the 1967 Royal Decree provides a rule in case a license also applies to an area to which a licensee applies for a mineral other than the mineral to which the first license applies. In that case, the Minister can order the license holder "that the holder of this other license (. . .) exercises his rights resulting from the license." If the rule of capture would apply, I believe that this provision would have been unnecessary.

A rule designed to enable two licensees of different minerals to operate in the same area is not obviously relevant to a problem involving the recovery of the same mineral, petroleum, from two different areas by way of operations in one of them. Because, however, the advocate general started with what can fairly be called a strong prejudice against the applicability of the rule of capture—he began by hinting that it legitimized theft[95]—such silences and ambiguities tended in his view to show the absence of the "valid arguments" he demanded to justify applying the rule in the Netherlands.[96]

His next step was to provide background to the domestic issue by examining first the position in international law, as to which he concluded—and we shall see in the next chapter whether he was correct—that the rule did not apply as between states where petroleum deposits underlay their land or maritime borders,[97] and then in "foreign legal systems." His discussion here was confined to the United States. It was not difficult for him to find a citation indicating the tendency of the rule of capture, unless restricted and moderated in its application, to produce the range of evils—physical and economic waste, environmental damage—with which we are familiar,[98] but it was unfortunate that he should have been led, by relying on careless phraseology in one of the only three American cases he cited, *Alabama v. Department of Interior* (1996),[99] to conclude that every American state save

---

[94] Spier 2005: paras. 8.1–8.60.

[95] *Ibid.* para. 8.2.

[96] *Ibid.* at para. 8.36.

[97] *Ibid.* paras. 8.10–8.18.

[98] *Ibid.* especially at para. 8.30.

[99] 84 F. 3d 410.

Texas had "abandoned" the rule.[100] The court in the *Alabama* case was certainly not speaking as precisely as one might have desired when it said that "[b]ecause of its negative effects, nearly every state has abrogated the rule of capture legislatively with well-spacing rules, production regulations, and/or other conservation mechanisms."[101]A much more exact account of the general effect of conservation mechanisms had been offered by the Supreme Court of Oklahoma, when it stated in 1943 that conservation laws "do not abrogate the law of capture. They are not self-executing. They simply authorize administrative boards to issue orders that have the effect of regulating or abrogating in a measure the law of capture."[102] We have already seen that capture remains a fundamental property right principle in all states, and one that is of continuing practical significance in drainage cases.[103]

One may doubt whether this misunderstanding, or others such as the apparent belief that the American courts modeled the law of capture on English hunting law (whose principles were actually in basic opposition to those adopted in North America),[104] in fact bore very heavily on the conclusions the advocate general reached, but it is a pity that the only petroleum capture case to have emerged in the last hundred years from a civil law court should be just as unsatisfactory in its reasoning—albeit in quite different ways—as the American cases that established the rule in the first place. As to the future impact of the case in the Netherlands, all parties seemed to assume that its circumstances could not recur because of the clearer provisions of the new Dutch Mining Act, coming into effect at the beginning of 2003 and replacing the legislation analyzed in *Unocal Netherlands B.V. v. Continental Netherlands Oil Co.* Article 23.1 of the new act provides that

> [t]he holder of a production licence for hydrocarbons shall not proceed with the production from a deposit that can reasonably be assumed to straddle the border of the licence area, so long as there is no agreement in force as referred to in Article 42.2 [which describes an agreement for unitization or, at least, cooperative exploitation], unless Our Minister has granted an exemption with respect to the obligation to conclude an agreement.

This is certainly a very strong form of compulsory unitization requirement, comparable with the now abandoned arrangements in the Petroleum Mining Code for the Australia–Indonesia area of cooperation.[105] Yet it still does not make the

---

[100] Spier 2005: para. 8.20.
[101] 84 F. 3d 410 at 413.
[102] *Gruger v. Philips Petroleum Co.* 192 Okla. 259, at 262, 135 P. 2d 485, at 488 (1943).
[103] Above, Ch. 9, at 294–302.
[104] Above, Ch. 2, at 33.
[105] Above, at 357–8.

capture issue wholly irrelevant: if the minister grants an exemption that may have the effect of authorizing drainage, the party whose acreage may be drained can seek to nullify it by invoking the decision in *Unocal Netherlands B.V. v. Continental Netherlands Oil Co.*, because its rights will have been infringed by any extraction of oil that it could have recovered economically by any means, including a unitization agreement with the draining party. The case may thus significantly reinforce the position of the "extension" license holder in any future dispute.

THE IMPACT OF PRODUCTION SHARING CONTRACTS

The concession is the traditional instrument through which states have invited oil companies to contribute their capital and expertise to the search for oil, in return for the right to treat any oil they can find and recover as their own. The right will ordinarily be limited by the obligation to deliver to the state a proportion of the oil recovered—or its cash value—as a royalty and perhaps by other constraints, such as reserving a quantity of hydrocarbons for the domestic market; special taxes, like the petroleum revenue tax in the United Kingdom, the petroleum resource rent tax in Australia, and Norway's special hydrocarbons tax, additional to ordinary profits or corporation taxes, may also be imposed and form a major element of so-called "government take" from oil operations. Concessions, which go under a variety of names—leases in the United States and Canada; licenses in the United Kingdom, the Netherlands, Norway, and Australia; concessions in civil law countries and some others inspired by civil law concepts, such as Thailand—remain the favored instrument of "First World" countries for oil development, but elsewhere they have been largely replaced by a different form of agreement: the production sharing contract (PSC).[106]

It is possible to design concession regimes and production sharing contract regimes so that, given the realization of relevant modeling assumptions (size of reservoir, production costs schedules, and so on), they produce identical financial rewards for operating companies, and thus it may be suggested that from the negotiation point of view, it is irrelevant whether the company is confronted by a concession or a PSC regime. The essential nature of each of the two contracts is, however, very different.

The PSC may properly be regarded as a type of *service* contract, in that the oil company's essential role is to provide exploration and production services for the state, which usually acts through its national oil company or some other specialized agency. Because it provides these services, and the heavy investments that go with them, at its

---

[106] Johnston 1993; Blinn et al. 1986: 69–81.

own risk, the company is rewarded in the event of success by both a share of the recovered oil or gas that covers its vouched costs incurred in exploration and production and an additional share designed to represent the proportion of the profits of the operation to which it is entitled under the agreement. There is enormous variation in the ways different agreements may provide for the coverage of costs and the allocation of profits, but what they all have in common is the fact that, in contrast to the concession, the oil that ends up in the hands of the contracting company is acquired, at a moment determined by the agreement, as the result of a payment by the state contracting partner for the services rendered, and not as an incident of the grant of exploration and production rights. Under the production sharing contract (as with other forms of service agreement), all rights to the oil produced or to be produced remain with the state or the entity through which it concludes the PSC, until the moment of transfer fixed by the contract.

Although, in conceptual terms, this represents a basic difference from the concession system, it does not bear directly on the issue of capture, as is evidenced by the fact that most PSCs (or the regulations under which they are written) incorporate a compulsory unitization clause.[107] The effects are more subtle but nonetheless significant. The first is that the PSC system rules out any claim on the part of the oil company contractor to property rights to petroleum in the ground. What property rights, if any, are conferred on a concessionaire, licensee, or lessee must be a matter of interpretation of the instrument in light of general principles of the national law, though we should note that some sort of claim to oil in place is necessarily involved in any attempt to resist capture under such regimes: we have seen that the Hague Court of Appeal thought that the Dutch production license created a subjective right in its holder to the recovery of a specific body of hydrocarbons.[108] In a PSC system, however, it would appear that the best the victim of drainage can do is to sue its contractual partner for allowing the drainage to occur within the framework of its contract with the capturing neighbor. Within that contractual framework, however, a second, preemptive, effect may occur.

One of the attractions for states that decide to adopt the PSC approach is that it implies a greater involvement by the state contracting party in the management of exploration and production operations. Again, there is great variation in what PSCs, whether presented as model forms or as actually concluded, may stipulate. Some PSCs may, save in their clauses dealing with compensation and fiscal issues and with the disposition of petroleum, look remarkably like their concession counterparts, but it is certainly not uncommon for a PSC to establish a management committee comprising representatives of the company and the state

---

[107] Weaver and Asmus 2006.
[108] Above, 364.

contracting party, with a broad competence to review and approve essential activities under the contract.[109] Either thanks to such an arrangement or by other means, the state oil company or other agency may be closely involved in operations on both sides of the line dividing two PSC areas and hence in a position to ensure, even before a unitization power is invoked, that no development occurs that could have the effect of provoking significant uncompensated drainage between contract areas. The same capability, we should notice, can be created under a concession system, if it is a condition of all concessions that the state should enjoy a significant level of participation through the agency of the national oil company. Although there can be no guarantee that this capability will be deployed to the satisfaction of operators in both segments of the shared reservoir, it represents an alternative, and in principle effective, means of ensuring that capture issues do not arise.

---

[109] For an example, see Timor Sea Authority 2006: article 14; the authority has been replaced since July 2008 by the East Timorese Autoridade Nacional do Petróleo (ANP).

CHAPTER 12

THE CROSS-BOUNDARY PETROLEUM DEPOSIT AS A FEDERAL AND INTERNATIONAL ISSUE

WAR IN KUWAIT

When Saddam Hussein sent his army into Kuwait in 1990 with the aim of annexing it to Iraq, two of the justifications he offered had to do with oil. The first was that Kuwait was the leader of a conspiracy among some member states of OPEC to produce in excess of their national quotas, with the purpose and effect of driving down prices and crippling Iraq's effort to earn its way out of the economic crisis brought on by the recently terminated eight-year war with Iran. The second was the accusation that some of Kuwait's production was effectively of oil stolen from Iraq. One poorly defined and contested segment of Kuwait's border with Iraq passed between Iraq's giant Rumaila oilfield and Kuwait's Ratqa field. Tariq Aziz, Iraq's foreign minister, claimed in a memorandum to the secretary general of the Arab League in July 1990 that for at least the previous 10 years, Kuwait had been attempting to advance its border in the area, engaging in slant-hole drilling into Iraqi subsoil, and adversely affecting the pressures in the Rumaila field by heavy production from Ratqa, which Iraq claimed was no more than a southerly extension of Rumaila. The issue was discussed, without agreement, at the last meeting between envoys of the Iraqi and Kuwaiti rulers before the invasion took place in August 1990.[1]

The general opinion among experts appears to be that Rumaila and Ratqa do form a single field, and it is thus likely that the Kuwaitis had indeed been capturing Iraqi oil over a period of years, particularly during the period when Iraq mined its Rumaila wells to prevent their falling into Iranian hands—though the Iraqi claim of loss of oil worth \$2.4 billion has been considered exaggerated.[2] The case thus looks like a projection onto the international level of the familiar domestic phenomenon of drainage between adjoining oil properties, and the question it naturally provokes is whether the rules of national laws governing oil and gas property rights can be transposed onto the international plane. More particularly, can we or should we assume that the rule of capture, which I have argued is widely adopted as a basic property rule even if subsequently overlain or displaced by restrictive regulation, will, in the absence of any contrary dispositions of international law, regulate such shared resource situations?

Claims of improper drainage are not usually settled by invasion (though sending a gunboat is a common reaction to alleged maritime trespass, as we shall see), and the subsequent drama of the two Iraq wars has perhaps obscured a significant feature of the dispute: the apparent need felt by the Iraqis to allege that Kuwait had not simply drained oil from Rumaila by operations in its own part of the reservoir, but had bottomed its wells under Iraqi land by slant drilling across the frontier. These accusations were renewed by the post-Saddam Iraqi government in 2003 and 2005. Its claims that the Kuwait Oil Company was capturing Rumaila oil through horizontal wells were denied by the company, which admitted to drilling such wells but maintained that they ran along the border, not across it.[3] The repetition of this claim of subsurface trespass may suggest that the Iraqi authorities are not confident that simple drainage would involve any wrongdoing by Kuwait; in other words, they may fear that the rule of capture applies in international law. Are they right?

This chapter aims to address this issue as it arises in international contexts, normally offshore but occasionally, as between Iraq and Kuwait, on land, but I want to look first at the analogous situation that can arise within a state that is organized on the federal principle, so that competing claims between component units of the state can arise where a boundary between them is found to overlie a valuable petroleum deposit. Two such countries are the United States and Australia. In the first, the rule of capture is part of the common law as it is applied

---

[1] Lauterpacht 1991: 73–7; Schofield 1993: 134–6; Khadduri 1997: 106–7, 115–17.

[2] Finnie 1992: 173.

[3] Anon. 2003, 2005.

in all oil-producing states; in the second, though the issue has never been definitively tested, I have argued that capture has been assumed, by state and commonwealth legislators, to be part of the common law.[4] It should not be too readily assumed, however, that the rule should or will be carried over so as to determine rights as between entities that can properly claim, in accordance with federal principles, to enjoy sovereign rights within the bounds allotted by the federal constitution. Within this federal context, it is also worth touching briefly on another question, one that was of major importance in the United States of the 1930s and had an unexpected echo in the Iraqi claims of 1990. This is the problem of how to maintain a proper balance between the production ambitions of sovereign entities that are committed to a common policy of production control. Kuwaiti disrespect for such a policy, incorporated in the OPEC agreement since the 1960s, was another of Iraq's pretexts for war; the problem of ensuring that states did not beggar each other's oil producers by slacking on production control was one of the most difficult and delicate of the prorationing decade in 1930s America.

INTERSTATE ISSUES IN THE CONTINENTAL UNITED STATES

An oil or gas field that underlies a border between two of the Lower 48 states is not likely to be perceived as creating a special problem, so long as the petroleum rights are in private hands and both states do no more than let the rule of capture do its work. The fact that the giant Bradford field, developed in the 1870s, extended from northern Pennsylvania into southwestern New York State appeared to trouble nobody. Producers drilled their leases in the normal way, draining and counterdraining through borderline wells, and the fact that some of these borders may have coincided with the state line seems to have been of little concern to the state authorities: private, not public, property was in play. In a regime of unregulated private ownership of oil and gas resources, the only cross-border situation likely to involve a substantial state interest would be one of significant one-way drainage from a state imposing an oil and gas severance or production tax. Such a tax was first imposed by Texas in 1905, and exists today in one form or another in almost all oil-producing states, sometimes furnishing a significant share of the state's revenue, but I am not aware of any severance tax issues arising at any time from exploitation of cross-border oil and gas reservoirs.

---

[4] Above, Ch. 10, at 329–34.

More difficult issues were raised by the discovery of oil in the Rodessa field in July 1935, in the extreme northwestern corner of Louisiana.[5] The field, up to 4.5 miles wide and 32 miles long, was eventually found to extend from Marion County, Texas, through Louisiana, with a small extension of about 4 square miles into southwestern Arkansas. Production in the Texas portion started at the end of 1936 and in Arkansas in mid-1937. This was, again, private land, but the new factor was prorationing. Control over the massive East Texas field, less than 100 miles away from Rodessa, had only recently been imposed, with wells at that time being held to a daily allowable of 25 barrels. In the words of Louisiana lawyer Yandell Boatner, letting Rodessa production go uncontrolled "would not only outrage public opinion but would demoralize markets." "With apparently prophetic discernment," he continued, the Louisiana legislature passed, the day after the Rodessa discovery, a new oil conservation law authorizing market demand prorationing, and the commissioner of conservation limited production by a series of orders imposing steadily shrinking per-well allowables, reduced by May 1936 to 350 barrels per day. For some reason, however, wells on a 120-acre lease in the center of the field were permitted, for a couple of months in 1936, to run at 20,000 barrels a day before being cut back to the common figure, and it is a measure of the sensitivity of production control at this time that this anomaly received front-page coverage in the *Wall Street Journal*, which recorded that it had had "a depressing effect on oil securities."

In Arkansas, though a prorationing order was made in 1937, it was not implemented until the beginning of 1938, by which time many more wells than necessary had been drilled on this small extension. While this certainly contributed to a rapid loss of reservoir pressure, it is doubtful whether it caused much drainage from Louisiana to Arkansas; "hundreds" of wells were drilled in the Louisiana section in 1936,[6] doubtless stimulated by the fact that prorationing there was on a per-well basis; and there was massive waste of natural gas, the daily figure "approaching ... an amount equal to one-half the daily domestic consumption of natural gas in the United States."[7] These wasteful arrangements were not terminated until the Louisiana commissioner of conservation issued, at the beginning of 1937, an order creating a quite new basis for prorationing of the field, based 50 percent on acreage and 50 percent on bottom hole pressure, subject to a gas–oil ratio of 2,000 cubic feet of gas to a barrel of oil. This original combination of factors was effective in eliminating five-sixths of the gas wastage from the field and was quickly adopted by the Texas Railroad Commission in its own

---

[5] Material in this paragraph is drawn from Boatner 1938: 68–73, save where otherwise indicated.

[6] Arkansas Oil and Gas Commission [n.d.]: 75.

[7] Boatner 1938: 69

prorationing order shortly thereafter. In terms of cross-border drainage, Texas was probably the main loser: peak production from the field (19.2 million barrels) was in 1936, at a time when almost all activity was in Louisiana.[8]

Northcutt Ely, writing in 1938, saw the Rodessa case as "dramatizing" a more general problem resulting indirectly from the rule of capture. "A state which voluntarily imposes restrictions from its own flush pools has no recourse (in the absence of an interstate agreement) against a neighboring state which permits its flush pools to produce at an excessive rate."[9]

The industry was well aware of this difficulty from the earliest days of its post-Seminole search for "stabilization" of oil production: it will be recalled that the American Petroleum Institute's ill-fated 1929 plan for voluntary production restrictions of 1929 envisaged a voluntary system of regional controls supported by federal antitrust immunity.[10] When that failed, officials—including Ely, then an assistant to the secretary of the interior—put together, in consultation with members of the industry (among whom the lawyer James Veasey played a major behind-the-scenes role), a draft interstate oil agreement under which the leading states, Texas, Oklahoma, and California, would set up a committee with wide-ranging authority to control output to prevent waste, including economic waste. This ambitious idea did not survive the ill-fated Colorado Springs conference,[11] and the oil industry entered its most turbulent decade with no mechanism for coordination of state efforts of control.

The period of federally mandated control under the National Recovery Act and the Petroleum Code, from 1933 to 1935, marked a hiatus in efforts at interstate coordination, but by 1933, one element of the eventual structure was already in place in the shape of a Committee on Petroleum Economics of the Federal Oil Conservation Board, established in 1930 and presided over by an economist from the Bureau of Mines, which in the next three years issued six surveys of national petroleum demand for crude oil.[12] The national figure was then broken down into amounts in barrels for the three large states and for the remainder, with the idea that these figures might be treated as authoritative and impartially determined targets for production ceilings in each of the main oil-producing states. Quite how demand, and consequent production ceilings, could be determined without any reference to price was obscure, but everybody save some obtuse and obstructionist independents united in saying that this was purely a scheme for avoiding waste and

---

[8] Arkansas Oil and Gas Commission [n.d.]: 75.
[9] Ely 1938: 1221.
[10] Above, Ch. 9, at 246–7.
[11] Above, Ch. 9, at 247–8.
[12] See generally Nordhauser 1979: 58–62.

had nothing whatever to do with price fixing. Until 1933, some coordination in applying the committee's numbers was achieved through an Oil States Advisory Committee created by the governors of seven oil-producing states. Besides the big three, Arkansas, Kansas, Louisiana, and Wyoming were also represented. The committee promoted the passage of more effective conservation laws in its member states and even brought about a one-page agreement by which, in September 1931, the governors of Oklahoma, Kansas, and Texas agreed on production quotas for each state.[13]

After the Supreme Court found the National Recovery Act and Petroleum Code to be unconstitutional in 1935,[14] the states and the oil industry successfully resisted pressure for the imposition of a new system of federal control and, in effect, returned to a refined and developed version of the pre-1933 arrangements for the purpose of assuring a fair allocation of production opportunities among states, within the framework of a continuing "stabilization" policy. Over a period between December 1934 and August 1935, state representatives, led by E. W. Marland, then governor-elect of Oklahoma, formulated an Interstate Compact to Conserve Oil and Gas.[15] The announced purpose of this compact was "to conserve oil and gas by the prevention of physical waste thereof from any cause" (article II). Member states committed themselves to enact legislation adequate to this purpose within a reasonable time (articles III and IV) and set up an Interstate Oil Compact Commission (now Interstate Oil and Gas Compact Commission) to keep conservation methods and practices under review, report findings and recommendations to the states, "recommend the coordination of the exercise of the police powers of the several States within their several jurisdictions to promote the maximum ultimate recovery from the petroleum reserves of said States, and ... recommend measures for the maximum ultimate recovery of oil and gas" (article VI). The compact was of course not designed as a price-fixing measure—or so it said. "It is not the purpose of this compact to authorize the states joining herein to limit the production of oil or gas for the purpose of stabilizing or fixing the price thereof, or create or perpetuate monopoly, or to promote regimentation, but is limited to the purpose of conserving oil and gas and preventing the avoidable waste thereof within reasonable limitations" (article V).

Under section 10(3) of the U.S. Constitution, congressional authority is required for the authorization of interstate compacts of this kind, and since important elements within Congress still saw federal control as the only appropriate national solution, this was not obtained without difficulty. Passage of

---

[13] Ely 1959: 50.

[14] Above, Ch. 9, at 258.

[15] Text available at iogcc.state.ok.us/charter.

the necessary act was, however, secured on August 27, 1935, when the compact, initially ratified by New Mexico, Texas, Oklahoma, Kansas, and Colorado, went into effect. Although the compact established quite elaborate voting rules for the taking of any "action" by the commission (both a majority of the member states present and a majority measured in terms of the percentage shares of total production represented by those states), the strongest action it can take is to make a recommendation. Nonetheless, during the period of prorationing, the commission, though it never exercised any overt control, was an effective and doubtless necessary mechanism for supervising and adjusting the procedure whereby the federal Bureau of Mines made forecasts of demand, and of crude oil production needed to meet it, and proposed the allocation of that production among the different states.

The ability of the commission to produce results without the possession of any coercive power was demonstrated in 1939, at a time when uncontrolled production from Illinois was inflating stocks. An announcement by a major company of a reduction in its crude purchase price was followed, after a meeting of the commission (at which it simply passed a resolution that each state should handle its production problem as it saw fit), by the imposition of a coordinated shutdown of production by the relevant state commissions, led by Texas. After a fortnight, prices duly went back up.[16] Not for nothing, perhaps, did the Interstate Oil and Gas Compact Commission's general counsel describe it in 1960 as "the most powerful powerless organization in the world."

Bilateral cooperation—or the lack of it—still seems, however, to have been the crucial factor in the specific case of cross-border fields, and the Rodessa experience established no clear precedent in this area. Whereas the Texas Railroad Commission and its New Mexico counterpart dealt with the exploitation of the shared Bronco field by way of joint hearings and a joint order in 1954, 13 years later the Oklahoma Corporation Commission had to make unilateral adjustments of well allowables when it found that Texas and Kansas had set higher allowables—apparently without consultation—for wells on their portions of shared fields extending into Oklahoma.[17]

STATE-FEDERAL OFFSHORE BORDERS

It may be less easy to settle things by consultation if a border transects a reservoir where ownership rights are in public hands. The interests in tax revenues and in

---

[16] Williams 1952: 1161–3; Zimmermann 1957: 232–3.
[17] Morris 1967: 213–14.

markets that might make states protective of privately owned resources on their territory are then supplemented by the powerful sentiment of concern for one's own property. When oil and gas were discovered under a section of the bed of the Red River bordering Oklahoma and Texas, which was claimed by the states and also by the federal government, the Supreme Court was called upon to decide the claims and recorded

> that many persons were proceeding to drill for, extract and appropriate these minerals with uncertain regard for the dispute over the title and for the true ownership; that possession of parts of the bed was being taken and held by intimidation and force; that in suits for injunction the courts of both states were assuming jurisdiction over the same areas; that armed conflicts between rival aspirants for the oil and gas had been but narrowly averted and still were imminent; that the militia of Texas had been called to support the orders of its courts, and an effort was being made to have the militia of Oklahoma called for a like purpose.[18]

With this dramatic exception, however, the important divide here has not been state lines on the mainland, but the line drawn between the regions of state and federal jurisdiction in the offshore area constituted by the "marginal" or "territorial" sea[19] and continental shelf of the United States.[20] A similar divide may be of importance to offshore petroleum development in any federal state.

The United States

The discovery in the United States that there was petroleum offshore, and the development of the means to exploit it, led quite quickly to conflict between state and federal governments. California, Louisiana, and Texas had all granted offshore leases before the Second World War, and successful drilling had been undertaken a mile off the Louisiana coast in 1938.[21] The federal government had not objected; indeed, Harold Ickes, Roosevelt's secretary of the interior and the man most closely associated with the drive for permanent federal control of oil production in the 1930s,[22] in 1933 signed (though he later claimed he did not necessarily agree with) a letter explaining that he could not issue a license for offshore lands under the Mineral Leasing Act of 1920 because "the title to the shore and lands under water in front of the lands so granted inures to the

---

[18] *Oklahoma v. Texas*, 258 U.S. 574, at 579–80 (1922).

[19] "Territorial" is the preferred term in the law of commonwealth countries, "marginal" in the United States.

[20] On the definition of the continental shelf, see above, Ch. 10, at 306.

[21] Gramling 1995: 7.

[22] Yergin 1991: 252–6.

State in which they are situated. ... Such title to the shore and lands under the water is regarded as incidental to the sovereignty of the State ... and cannot be retained or granted out to individuals by the United States."[23]

Whatever Ickes really thought in 1933, in a few years, growing fears about the long-term adequacy of U.S. supplies in a period of increasing international tension, and worries about waste if offshore resources were left in state hands—California still had no comprehensive oil and gas conservation law and had not adhered to the Interstate Oil Compact—enabled him to persuade the administration to change position and assert ownership of the resources of the offshore seabed. This provoked a great deal of congressional pushing and shoving, with numerous bills and resolutions being introduced seeking to affirm the federal position or confirm state property claims, but these hostilities were stilled by America's entry into the Second World War in 1941.

In September 1945, however, President Harry Truman made a formal claim on behalf of the United States to the natural resources of the continental shelf contiguous to its coasts,[24] asserting that they "appertained" to the United States and were "subject to its jurisdiction and control," the first national claim of this nature. Truman's executive order referred only to the continental shelf beneath the high seas, beyond general U.S. territorial jurisdiction, and thus did not affect the marginal sea in whose bed the states claimed rights, but it was swiftly followed by litigation in which the federal government claimed that the states had no rights in the seabed beyond low-water mark. The first of these cases, known collectively as the "Tidelands cases" (though erroneously, "tidelands" being areas between high- and low-water marks), was brought against California, with later cases against Louisiana and Texas.[25] In each of these suits, the U.S. Supreme Court, in the face of a substantial body of contrary historical evidence and prior case law, held that the original colonies had established no rights in the seabed of the marginal sea prior to independence, and that states subsequently entering the Union, like California and Louisiana, did so on an "equal footing" with the original states and could therefore have no greater rights. The court applied this reasoning even to Texas, an independent state when it entered the Union in 1845. Arguing from the international aspect of maritime claims, the court discerned in the United States "paramount rights in

---

[23] Quoted in Metcalfe 1953: 41.

[24] By Proclamation 2677 and Executive Order 9633, 10 Fed. Reg. 12303 (1945).

[25] *United States v. California*, 332 U.S. 19 (1947); *United States v. Louisiana*, 339 U.S. 699 (1950); *United States v. Texas*, 339 U.S. 707 (1950). These cases engendered a large literature: see, for example, Metcalfe 1953; Dubner et al. 1980; Fitzgerald 1988b.

and power over [the 3-mile] belt, an incident to which is full dominion over the resources of the soil under that water area, including oil."[26]

Federal-state relations regarding offshore oil and gas appear never to have quite recovered from what seemed at the time to the states to be a judicially authorized smash-and-grab raid on their offshore resources. Even allowing for the greater readiness of Americans to resort to courts to settle their differences, the amount of state-federal litigation over issues in this area between then and now has been striking in comparison with the position in Canada and Australia, and the degree of cooperation in offshore oil and gas policy much lower. Within a few months of the California decision, a conference of all state governors had demanded legislation to confirm the coastal states' clams and, in effect, overturn the Supreme Court decision, but it was not until 1952, with the arrival of a new Republican administration sympathetic to the states' position, that legislation was passed to settle the respective rights of state and federal governments in the offshore areas.

Two acts were passed by Congress in 1953. Under the Submerged Lands Act (SLA), the United States relinquished to the states all federal interest in lands beneath navigable waters within state boundaries, recognizing that within the Gulf states, those lands might extend to distances beyond 3 miles from the coast. Texas and Florida were subsequently recognized as having an entitlement to lands up to 3 marine leagues (9 nautical miles or 10.5 land miles) from their coasts. It also allowed any state to extend its coastal boundaries 3 miles from the coastline. The way was thus reopened for each coastal state to operate its own leasing system for the disposal of oil and gas interests (and other mineral interests) in these offshore lands. At the same time, the United States reserved constitutional powers of control over such lands for purposes of commerce, navigation, national defense, and international affairs. Shortly thereafter, Congress also passed the Outer Continental Shelf Lands Act (OCSLA) reasserting federal rights, as to both property and jurisdiction, over all submerged lands lying seaward of state submerged lands defined by the SLA and creating a regime for their management by the secretary of the interior, distinct from that of the Mineral Leasing Act of 1920 and contrasting with that regime in a number of respects.

With state leasing systems for the resources up to 3 or more miles from the coast and a federal system for resources farther out, there was obviously a potential for the relevant boundaries to transect valuable oil and gas deposits. Such deposits might be of interest to two adjacent states, like Louisiana and Florida, where the boundary line was between the areas they, respectively, claimed under the SLA, or between a state (or possibly two adjacent states) and the federal government, where the boundary was between SLA and OCSLA territory. The pattern of federal-state

---

[26] *United States v. California*, 332 U.S. 19, at 38 (1947).

disputing established in the 1930s continued even into the 1980s, with arguments about where these boundary lines were, as the SLA had left a number of vital questions in suspense—notably, the points from which the width of the coastal states' marginal sea was to be measured.[27] Moreover, the vagueness of the SLA's provisions as to historical claims by states in excess of 3 miles left the door open to the assertion of such larger claims at any time; thus the federal government had to go back to the Supreme Court in 1960 to defeat a Louisiana claim to a 10.5-mile marginal sea[28] and again in 1975 to meet claims by Maine, supported by other states on the seaboard, to be entitled on the basis of its colonial inheritance to lease for energy exploration lands 88 miles offshore.[29]

Perhaps because of this preoccupation with establishing where boundary lines actually were, it was not until the OCSLA was substantially amended in 1978 that the question of how to deal with cross-border reservoirs received express legislative attention. The amendments represented a comprehensive attempt to deal with a wide range of state discontents, rooted in the system of management adopted for the continental shelf by the 1953 act. This placed almost complete discretion in the secretary of the interior and gave the states no voice in whether and where leasing should take place off their coasts, possibly as close as only 3 miles from shore. Nor did it make any provision for compensation to the states either for damage, as by pollution, that might occur as a result of oil exploration and production operations or for the costs associated with onshore development and disturbance related to this activity. Congressional legislation in the late 1960s, notably the Coastal Zone Management Act, sought to repair these omissions, but it was not until 1978 that OCSLA was radically revised to place the secretary of the interior's leasing powers within a detailed legislative framework, calling notably for leasing to be based only on five-year programs developed in consultation with state governors.

In association with this reform, Congress inserted into OCSLA a new provision, known as section 8(g), dealing with the situation in which a proposed federal lease sale might involve tracts within a 3-mile belt starting at the outer edge of a state's offshore zone. This required the secretary to consult with the state governor on any tracts that might be leased in the sale and might underlie the boundary and, if so requested, to enter into negotiations for an agreement for the fair and equitable distribution of the revenues from such a lease. Failing agreement, the lease sale could still go ahead, but the distribution was to be decided by the U.S. district

---

[27] For the numerous post-1950 "Tidelands" cases, see generally Fitzgerald 1988b. Whether or not the Supreme Court consistently got these decisions wrong, as Fitzgerald claims, I do not pretend to judge.

[28] *United States v. Louisiana*, 363 U.S. 1 (1960).

[29] *United States v. Maine*, 420 U.S. 515 (1975).

court. Within a year, Texas and Louisiana were in court seeking to prevent federal lease sales that included territory in the "8(g) belt" adjacent to their offshore lands in the Gulf of Mexico, on the ground that the secretary was not respecting the procedural requirements of the section.[30]

Looking at the general course of federal-state discussions on offshore issues up to that time, there is nothing surprising about this rapid rush to judgment. What does need explaining, against the background of the Tidelands cases, is the fact that up to 1979, there was no attempt by states to attack the federal government on the ground of drainage from state offshore lands occasioned by drilling on contiguous federal leases. It has been suggested that there was not much development of the outer continental shelf (OCS) between 1953 and the time when the United States suddenly became painfully aware of its energy import dependence and enlarged and accelerated its offshore leasing program starting in 1971.[31] But while the rate of leasing certainly increased significantly in the 1970s, acreage under lease and production from that acreage were already substantial in 1971. By that time, 11,280 square miles of the shelf was under oil and gas leases, over 80 percent of which was in the Gulf of Mexico.[32] In 1971, production from this acreage already represented 11.78 percent of total U.S. oil production and 12.46 percent of natural gas production.[33] Unless the department had deliberately refrained from leasing up to the federal-state boundaries, one would expect this policy, coupled with an active leasing policy on the part of the states, to have produced at least some cases of cross-boundary fields, and in fact, Interior Secretary Cecil Andrus acknowledged in a communication to Congress in 1977 that "there are instances in which a part of [OCS lease revenues] may have been derived from oil and gas drained from State land."[34]

The key states were already well aware of the problem. A Louisiana submission to a House committee in 1972 anticipated "a multiplication of drainage, offset and unitization problems" now that the federal-state boundary had been fixed after a further Supreme Court decision and suggested that the way to avoid repeating the "forest of derricks" problems of the early days of the industry was to establish some form of joint federal-state commission to deal with cross-border issues.[35]

---

[30] *Texas v. Secretary of Interior*, 580 F. Supp. 1179, at 1205 (E.D. Texas 1984).

[31] Fitzgerald 1988a: 255–6.

[32] Calculated from United States. Department of the Interior, Minerals Management Service 2009: Table 1.

[33] United States. Department of the Interior, Minerals Management Service 2008. The latest percentages (2007) were oil, 26.8; natural gas, 14.2.

[34] Quoted in Fitzgerald 1988a: 269.

[35] *Ibid.* 264. This approach has been adopted to address a number of international delimitation issues: below, at 397–8.

Three years later, a California submission sounded a more plaintive note, pointing out that a substantial part of that state's 3-mile belt comprised sanctuaries reserved from oil operations for environmental reasons and asking if the State Land Commission could get prior notice of federal leasing intentions, so that "[i]f a small pool, say, underlies mostly the state sanctuary and 1 or 2 or 3 miles into the federal zone, perhaps we could convince you people not to drill."[36]

What clearly underlies all these remarks, and also goes to explain the lack of litigation on the matter, is a generally shared assumption that the law of capture applies as between the states and the United States as the respective holders of the rights in the subsea reservoirs in question. Congress certainly shared that assumption when it enacted section 8(g), as did the state and federal parties to the case of *Texas v. Secretary of the Interior*,[37] as well as the district court called upon to interpret section 8(g) in that case. It was common ground between them that the section was designed to compensate the state for drainage from its lands; the specific question at issue was whether it also entitled the state to share in "bonus enhancement"—that is, the part of a successful bonus bid reflecting knowledge of the potential of the federal lease on offer derived from previous lease activity on neighboring state blocks. There was, however, no reason why it should follow, as a matter of law, that a rule determining the property rights in oil and gas of private surface owners was necessarily applicable to determine the legal relationship of public entities possessing rights of government and property within the framework of the U.S. constitution.

The special character of offshore rights was emphasized by the initial finding of the Supreme Court, in the first of the Tidelands cases, *United States v. California*, that the federal government derived a paramount power over offshore resources from its position as the entity responsible for the external relations of the United States. That power, the court later held in *United States v. Maine*, enabled it to determine the allocation of rights to the resources in the offshore areas claimed by the United States, and that allocation was effected by Congress's enactment of the SLA relinquishing any federal claims in resources within 3 miles of the coastline (or a state's recognized or traditional maritime boundaries, if more extensive), vesting "title and ownership" in the relevant states, and confirming that resources beyond those limits "appertained" to the United States.[38] The titles thus created were not identical with the private property rights in land recognized by the common law of the several states. The key distinction is that these titles were and remain subject to a variety of limitations under international conventions that have

---

[36] Quoted in Fitzgerald 1988a: 265.
[37] 580 F. Supp. 1179 (E.D. Tex. 1984).
[38] 43 U.S.C. § 1311(a), (b), 1302.

been accepted by the United States (notably the 1958 Geneva Conventions on the Territorial Sea and Contiguous Zone and on the Continental Shelf), limitations that are inconsistent with the basic common-law property principle that rights to the surface of land include, in the absence of contrary disposition, rights to everything that lies above and beneath that surface.[39] The United States does not own the high seas above the continental shelf, and rights over the marginal sea are limited by such obligations as that of allowing innocent passage to foreign ships.[40]

In principle, it would have been perfectly plausible to argue that the definition of the rights of property held by the states and the United States in the offshore seabed presented original legal issues not controlled by the private law of petroleum property rights. The law might, for example, have recognized that as between the central and local powers in a federation, each endowed with governmental competences and sovereign within its constitutionally allotted sphere, there should be a presumption of noninterference with each other's property, such as to displace the operation of the rule of capture. As we shall see, this is the position that has been taken by some international law scholars in relation to national sovereigns and their maritime property. In practice, an idea like this never seems to have entered anyone's head. The legitimacy of drainage was assumed by all parties to the discussion of the 1978 amendments to OCSLA, including section 8(g).

Following criticisms by the *Texas v. Secretary of the Interior* court of the practicability of the original arrangements,[41] a revised version of 8(g) was enacted in 1986,[42] and when this came before the courts again the following year, the Court of Appeals for the Fifth Circuit disposed of the issue with the same casual ease as its Pennsylvania counterpart a century earlier: "Because oil and gas reserves can straddle the jurisdictional boundary, it is possible for the lessee of one government to drain the reserves located on the other government's territory. Under the common law rule of capture, which we apply to the OCS, the owner of land has the right to capture oil and gas underlying his property, including that which migrates to his property from another's land."[43] The court gave the authority for the application of the rule to the outer continental shelf in a footnote, which referred to nothing more compelling than the preamble to the unitization provisions of the regulations then in force under OCSLA: "[a] lease does not grant

---

[39] Above, Ch. 3, at 56.

[40] See *Commonwealth v. Yarmirr* (2001) 208 C. L. R. 1, at 59, [2001] HCA 56, at para. 70, making the same point in an analogous Australian context.

[41] 580 F. Supp., at 1223–4 (E.D. Texas 1984).

[42] 43 U.S.C. § 1337(g).

[43] *Louisiana v. United States*, 832 F. 2d 935, at 938 (5th Cir. 1987).

lessees the ownership of minerals in place, and the Law of Capture applies to the development and production of OCS minerals."[44] Leaving aside the question of whether a U.S. Court of Appeals should take its law from an anonymously drafted preamble, the sentence quoted clearly referred to the rights of lessees, not to those of the federal government or the state as the granting property holder; and the issue was not simply one of OCS rights, but involved state rights in the marginal sea as well.

More telling, but perhaps too obvious in the court's view to merit a mention, was the fact that a legislative mechanism for compensation would hardly have been needed if it were unlawful for federal lessees to drain petroleum from state lands in the first place. Section 8(g) can be seen as a legislative endorsement of the application of the rule of capture as an element of the property rights of state and federal governments. The 1986 revision of section 8(g) arguably reinforced this endorsement, insofar as it sought to resolve the drainage compensation problem once and for all by giving the states 27 percent of all revenues derived by the federal government from the "8(g) zone" of 3 miles bordering the state's marginal sea. Confusingly, however, Congress did not remove the possibility of specific agreements between a state governor and the secretary of the interior, providing, in the new section 8(g)(3), that if the secretary had leased or intended to lease a cross-border field, a unitization or royalty sharing agreement could be negotiated between secretary and governor. If, however, the negotiations failed, the secretary could go ahead with the lease anyway. In its 1987 litigation, Louisiana invoked this provision in aid of an argument that the general 27 percent federal payment was aimed at compensating the state for all costs related to development in the 3- to 6-mile belt, that drainage compensation was still to be dealt with by agreement under section 8(g)(3), and that there could be no development on the federal side of a shared reservoir without agreement. All of these contentions were dismissed by the court.

A further muddying of the waters on state-federal boundary rights resulted from congressional action in 1990, when, by the Oil Pollution Act of 1990, it inserted a new section 5(j) into the OCSLA.[45] Having recited that competitive drilling on cross-border tracts could produce a range of harmful effects—unnecessary wells, physical waste, and impairment of correlative rights—Congress simply provided that "[t]he Secretary shall prevent, through the cooperative development of an area, the harmful effects of unrestrained competitive production of hydrocarbons from a common hydrocarbon-bearing area underlying the Federal and State boundary." The task of explaining what Congress might have meant by this Delphic utterance

---

[44] This preamble does not appear in the current version of the unitization regulations at 30 C.F.R. § 250.1300ff. See further above, Ch. 11, at 359–60.

[45] 43 U.S.C. § 1334(j).

fell this time to the Court of Appeals for the Eleventh Circuit, in the case of *Alabama v. United States* in 1996.[46] The court was not helped by the fact that the legislative record was minimal, with no committee proceedings and little floor debate, though there had been significant change in the provision between its introduction and its enactment. One might indeed speak of emasculation rather than mere change:

> As originally offered in the Senate, section 5(j) required the Secretary to "prevent the harmful effects of unrestrained competitive production of hydrocarbons from a common hydrocarbon-bearing area underlying the Federal and State boundary *by protecting against drainage* through the cooperative development of such area." *See* 135 Cong. Rec. S8488-03, S8500-S8501 (1990) (emphasis added). Section 5(j) further provided both the federal government and the affected coastal state with the authority to seek an injunction in district court "*in order to prevent the drainage of federal oil and gas resources*" until the parties could agree on a "*fair and equitable apportionment* of the oil and gas resources involved," or until the district court entered final judgment in favor of one party or the other.[47]

It appears that what the promoters of the provision were seeking was a compulsory unitization provision for cross-border fields akin to the sort commonly found in national laws regulating offshore petroleum operations[48] and, indeed, in the relevant regulations made for the outer continental shelf by the secretary of the interior.[49] One can see a number of reasons why this might have encountered opposition: state interests would not have favored a provision that only applied to protect federal resources, and both sides might have feared that a compulsory provision would hamper development. Nonetheless, while the court held that Congress had successfully stripped out anything that might give Alabama a new source of rights to drainage compensation, it took the view that section 5(j) required the secretary of the interior to negotiate with the state in good faith with a view to reaching a cooperative development agreement. But in the absence of the deleted provision dealing with the consequences of failure to agree, such a failure did not entail the blocking of a unilateral development decision by the secretary. Were that the case, the state, unburdened by any obligation equivalent to the secretary's under section 5(j), would be able to refuse to agree until its demands were met, safe in the knowledge that it could allow its lessees to continue to operate on its side of the boundary. "This consequence would give Alabama effective veto power over the DOI's [Department of the Interior's] lawful authorization of oil

---

[46] 84 F. 3d 410 (11th Cir., 1996).

[47] *Ibid.* at 416 (emphasis in original).

[48] Above, Ch. 11, at 348–58.

[49] These are now to be found at 30 C.F.R. § 250.1300 and following.

and gas production," and this Congress cannot have intended.[50] Looking at the facts, the court found that the secretary had negotiated in good faith, while Alabama had not.

Effectively, section 5(j), as interpreted in the *Alabama* case, has added a requirement for good-faith negotiation of a cooperative development agreement to the existing drainage compensation arrangements under the OCSLA, and in so doing, it has, as we shall see, brought the U.S. management of its federal-state relations just a little bit closer to the rules and practices that are commonly thought to govern these sorts of issues when they arise on the strictly international plane. The law, however, remains peculiarly skewed, in that the states acknowledge no comparable obligation and appear never to have departed from the principle that their lessees are free to drain any oil or gas they can get from the federal side of the boundary. Given that it appeared from evidence in the *Alabama* case that there were in 1996 no less than 150 cross-border reservoirs under American waters, this suggests the existence of a continuing problem and may explain the attempt at protection of federal resources when section 5(j) was first introduced.

Australia

There are better ways of doing things. If U.S. federal-state relations on offshore issues had not been bedeviled for years by state resentment over the Tidelands decisions, and if federal authorities had had the wit to make early provision for meeting state costs (both financial and environmental) associated with outer continental shelf development, it might have been possible for the two levels of government to exploit offshore oil and gas in the sort of cooperative spirit evident in Australia. There, the initial prospects for harmonious development were hardly more promising than in the United States.

When, in the 1960s, the long-cherished Australian hopes for oil discoveries finally bore fruit, notably in the Marlin and Barracouta discoveries in the Bass Strait between Victoria and Tasmania, resolution of the issue of offshore rights within the federation became urgent: the companies wanted the reassurance of security of title before they would invest on a large scale. The different states had quickly claimed offshore rights after Australia made a formal claim to continental shelf rights in 1953, extending their existing petroleum or minerals legislation so as to allow them to grant permits and leases in offshore areas.[51] Over the next 10 years, extensive state grants of exploration rights over continental shelf territory were made: in Victoria, over areas that proved to cover the Marlin and Barracouta

---

[50] 84 F. 3d, at 418–19.
[51] Merralls 1979: 54.

fields, and in Western Australia, over areas extending to some 470 kilometers from the coast and including a grant of exploration rights over more than 740,000 square kilometers onshore and offshore to a joint venture between local explorer AMPOL and two American majors, Texaco and Standard Oil of California. The commonwealth government had never accepted these territorial claims.

A complex state-commonwealth agreement was hammered out over the years from 1964 to 1967, instituting a system whereby exploration permits and production licenses for the offshore area would be granted and administered by states both in their own behalf and as delegates of the commonwealth, under legislation to be passed in identical terms by the commonwealth and by each state.[52] The idea was to provide legal security for oil companies without compromising the territorial claims of either level of government. The commonwealth and each state accordingly passed, in 1967, a Petroleum (Submerged Lands) Act, whose main component was a "Common Mining Code" regulating all aspects of the grant and administration of petroleum titles.

The compromise did not last long: a new commonwealth government of a different political stripe passed legislation in 1973, the Seas and Submerged Lands Act, asserting commonwealth sovereignty or sovereign rights in both Australia's territorial sea and its continental shelf. After the Australian High Court came down on the side of the commonwealth's claim in 1975, confirming the constitutionality of the 1973 act in a case brought by all the states,[53] a new constitutional settlement was necessary, and in 1980, by legislation bearing a strong resemblance to the U.S. Submerged Lands Act, the commonwealth ceded to the states property rights in and control of offshore resources out to 3 miles from the baseline of the territorial sea but retained control of the continental shelf. Nonetheless, the Australian regime remained indelibly marked by the spirit of the initial 1967 compromise, since in the 1980 settlement the Petroleum (Submerged Lands) Act was merely amended, not replaced, and each state continued to act as the "Designated Authority" under the commonwealth legislation in respect to that part of the continental shelf facing its coastline. Since 1980, the relevant commonwealth minister participates with his or her state counterpart in joint decisionmaking on the more important matters (such as the award of permits and licenses), and can overrule the state minister in the event of disagreement. In practice, such disagreement is very rare, and the states, besides playing the lead role in day-to-day

---

[52] See generally Hunt 1989.

[53] *Attorney-General for New South Wales v. Attorney-General for the Commonwealth* (1975) 135 C.L.R. 337; and see commentary in Dubner et al. 1980.

administration of the system,[54] are collectively highly influential in the development of policy.

No less important than this system of joint management is the fact that at all times since the first enactment of the Petroleum (Submerged Lands) Act, the returns to the public purse from petroleum production from areas beyond the 3-mile limit have been shared between the commonwealth and the states.[55] Returns were initially in the form of royalties, of which 60 to 68 percent went to the state, with the remainder going to the commonwealth. This system still applies to the most productive gas fields on the Australian North West Shelf, but since 1987, other fields have been subject to a commonwealth petroleum resource rent tax (PRRT), replacing royalties, whose proceeds help (in a small way) to fund a general system of revenue redistribution among the states. As a result of these arrangements, there has been far less of the sort of conflict over oil and gas exploration and production policy that has long marked federal-state relations in the United States.

Nonetheless, there remain potential issues of drainage between jurisdictions by reason of the existence of legal borders between state and commonwealth offshore territory (at a distance of 3 miles seaward from the baselines of the Australian territorial sea) and between the areas of commonwealth territory administered under the relevant legislation (now reenacted as the Offshore Petroleum and Greenhouse Gas Storage Act of 2006) by the different states. Deposits crossing this latter type of border raise questions of regulatory competence that are dealt with by consultation provisions in the act and should not be difficult to resolve. Those crossing a state-commonwealth border raise the more delicate issue of revenue entitlements, as the state stands to gain all the royalties from production within its coastal waters, but at most (and only in certain areas offshore Western Australia) a share of royalties in respect to production from outside those waters. Though such cross-border fields are found off the north coast of Western Australia, the issue has so far been regulated only by a provision for the apportionment to each of the two areas of "such proportion of all petroleum so recovered as may reasonably be treated as being derived from that area, having regard to the nature and probable extent of the pool," if both areas are in the hands of the same licensee, or if different parties hold the licenses for each area, of the proportion provided for by an operative unitization agreement concluded between those parties.[56]

---

[54] A recent exception is offshore health and safety, since 2005 administered by the National Offshore Petroleum Safety Authority.

[55] Crommelin 2008.

[56] Offshore Petroleum and Greenhouse Gas Storage Act 2006, §§ 54, 55.

The legislation is, however, silent on the situation that would arise if those licensees (or other titleholders) had not concluded a unitization agreement, so that there was a risk of drainage from state to commonwealth waters or vice versa. The fact that the rights granted by the 2006 act (the corresponding state acts are in the same terms) to a commonwealth production licensee are broad enough to permit, in the absence of a unitization requirement, drainage of oil or gas from an adjoining license or permit area[57] can say nothing about the reciprocal rights of the commonwealth and the states to the oil and gas in place in a shared field. In the absence of direct statutory provision, this is an issue that a court would need to decide by reference to common-law principles. In light of the dislike of the rule of capture expressed by authoritative modern commentators,[58] it seems probable—despite the contrary assumption shared by all earlier Australian legislators[59]—that a court would decide that the common law in Australia did not incorporate the rule. There are no direct precedents. Even if a court took a different view on capture in the common law there is, as I have argued earlier in relation to the United States, no compelling reason why a rule determining rights of private ownership should be applied to regulate relationships between the component parts of a federation. The question has never been directly presented in practice, but if it were, a "no capture" approach might be reinforced by the above-mentioned statutory provision apportioning production between commonwealth and state waters where the same titleholder is operating in both.

OIL FIELDS ACROSS INTERNATIONAL BORDERS

Delimitation of the North Sea

When the world's maritime nations met in Geneva in the mid-1950s, with the aim of concluding a series of multilateral treaties that would provide common rules for the international law of the sea in the rapidly changing circumstances of the time, the United Kingdom was one of the countries most eager for an early and clear decision on the principle that should govern the division of an area of continental shelf abutting the territorial seas of a number of different states. This was the position in the North Sea, whose coastline was shared among the United Kingdom, Norway, Denmark, Germany, the Netherlands, and Belgium, and where the seabed was, with the exception of a deep trough just off the southern coasts of

---

[57] § 161, discussed above, Ch. 11, at 360–1.
[58] Crommelin 1986; Keen 1998.
[59] Above, Ch. 10, at 329–34.

Norway, at a depth less than the 200 meters generally accepted at that time as marking the maximum depth of the continental shelf below sea level. The United Kingdom pressed for the adoption, as the means of division of such a "shared" area of shelf, of the principle of equidistance, under which lines of delimitation are drawn so that, so far as possible, each point of any such line is equidistant from the nearest points on the baselines of the territorial sea[60] of the states whose coastlines are opposite or adjacent. The principle was incorporated into article 6 of the Geneva Convention on the Continental Shelf, for application, subject to "special circumstances" that might justify an alternative line, in any case where parties could not reach agreement.

This was not an attractive rule for countries whose coastlines were generally concave in form, as it tended to leave them with a shelf that was cut off not far from the coast by the convergence of the equidistance lines projected from the points where their land boundaries with their more fortunate neighbors met the sea. Germany, squeezed between the Netherlands and Denmark, suffered gravely from this effect (though not as gravely as Iraq, whose coastline of about 11.5 miles at the head of the Persian/Arabian Gulf gives it almost no shelf at all) and accordingly refused to ratify the convention, eventually succeeding in securing a rather larger shelf area by negotiations following an International Court of Justice decision in its favor in the *North Sea Continental Shelf Case*.[61] Norway also did not ratify until 1971, perhaps fearing that the convention's requirement that a country's shelf be "adjacent" to its coast[62] might prevent it from claiming any rights seaward of the Norwegian Trough, a chasm in the seabed just off the south Norwegian coast that at some points descends to depths far greater than 200 meters.

Nonetheless, the United Kingdom, following the signature of the convention in 1958, pressed ahead in negotiations with its neighbors for the fixing of equidistance lines of delimitation. Undoubtedly the discovery of the giant Groningen gas field in 1959, in the Netherlands but thought to extend under the North Sea, was a major stimulus to the rapid development by the relevant coastal states of legal regimes for offshore oil and gas exploration. Negotiations proceeded most quickly with Norway, with which the United Kingdom concluded its first

---

[60] Under the Geneva Convention on the Territorial Sea and Contiguous Zone (1958), articles 3 and 4, the baseline is the low-water line along the coast, except where indentations in the coastline justify the drawing of a straight baseline, e.g., between the heads of a bay or between a nearshore island and a point on the shore.

[61] [1969] I.C.J. 3; see further below.

[62] Art. 1(a) defined the shelf as "[t]he seabed and subsoil of the submarine areas adjacent to the coast but outside the limit of the territorial sea, to a depth of 200 metres or, beyond that limit, to where the depth of the superjacent waters admits of the exploitation of the natural resources of the said areas."

bilateral delimitation agreement in June 1965.[63] In the interests of early settlement, the United Kingdom (and also Denmark) refrained from suggesting any departure from the equidistance principle because of the existence of the Norwegian Trough.[64] The UK government dismissed objections based on the depth of the Norwegian waters—as one member of Parliament put it, "it is no good trying to paddle off the coast of Norway"—maintaining that the trough was "not deep enough to preclude Norway from operating on the subsoil of the shallower waters beyond."[65]

When intensive exploration began in the northern half of the North Sea after the Phillips Petroleum Company's discovery of the Ekofisk field in 1969, it quickly appeared that the equidistance line drawn in 1965 cut across no fewer than three major fields: Statfjord (the largest of all North Sea fields), the Frigg gas field, and the Murchison field. Additional, smaller cross-border deposits have been discovered more recently. Possibly these discoveries found British officials privately kicking themselves for their unseemly haste; but a more aggressive British approach would certainly have sterilized development in the northern North Sea for a considerable length of time. An additional benefit of this alacrity of the North Sea countries, enjoyed around the world, was the early creation of precedents both for dealing with the possibility of cross-border deposits when drawing lines of delimitation and for the actual exploitation of such deposits once discovered.

"Unity of Deposit"

The possibility that a valuable mineral deposit might underlie a political boundary was appreciated long before 1965. In what must be one of the most comprehensive studies of the subject, Jean-Pierre Bouvet identified an agreement concluded in 1449 between the archbishopric of Salzburg and the priory of Berchtesgaden, components of the Holy Roman Empire whose border straddled the salt deposits of Duerrnberg, as the earliest known to deal with the problem.[66] The experience of subsequent centuries makes clear that even for hard rock minerals like coal, which in principle can be mined from either side of a frontier and up to the frontier as extended downward through the earth, it was frequently found necessary or useful to conclude a bilateral international agreement to deal with such issues as lateral support, convenience of exploitation, risks of flooding, and the actual delimitation of the subterranean frontier.

---

[63] United Kingdom–Norway Agreement, March 10, 1965.

[64] Bruce 1966.

[65] 688 House of Commons Debates, cols. 269, 276 (January 28, 1964).

[66] Bouvet 1997: 23.

In 1929, Professor Walter Schönborn drew the attention of the international law community to the special transfrontier problem presented by substances like mineral water and petroleum. Here one state might enjoy considerable geological advantages over the other and might even be able to abstract, on its territory, the whole product of the common source. Such a result, he thought, would be "iniquitous" and should be prevented by the application of the developing international law principles of "good neighbourliness."[67] He had to acknowledge, however, that in the absence as yet of any principles of general and unchallenged validity to regulate such situations, reliance would have to be placed on specific agreements to reconcile the divergent interests of the states involved.[68] International lawyers appear to have been pessimistic about the capacity of states to achieve such compromises: when the exploitability of petroleum deposits on the continental shelf began to look like a practical proposition, leading experts on the law of the sea suggested that any delimitation rule should be such as to ensure that no deposit was divided between states. Problems of capture were clearly present in their minds. As Admiral M.W. Mouton put it in a lecture in 1954, "[N]ever two straws in one glass."[69]

This may be a simple remedy, but it has seldom been applied. The Geneva Convention on the Continental Shelf made no explicit reference to common deposits but focused on the drawing of delimitation lines; the only foothold in the convention for the idea of "unity of deposit" was the possibility of treating a deposit as a "special circumstance" that could justify the deviation of an equidistance line (article 6). But in the first major case on continental shelf delimitation before the International Court of Justice in 1969,[70] the court refused to regard "unity of deposit" as "anything more than a factual element which it is reasonable to take into consideration in the course of the negotiations for a delimitation. The Parties are fully aware of the existence of the problem as also of the possible ways of solving it."[71]

As examples of such solutions, the court cited the "common deposit" clauses in the United Kingdom's 1965 agreements with Norway and the Netherlands, which I look at below. The court was here writing in the context not of article 6, but of customary international law, because Germany, as already noted, had not acceded to the convention. This gives its remarks continuing relevance, as the

---

[67] See Huber 1907, proposing the operation of such a principle (*Völkerrechtliches Nachbarrecht*) in relation to fisheries and hydroelectric power in shared rivers.

[68] Schönborn 1929: 147.

[69] Mouton 1954: 421. See also United Nations Secretariat 1950: 112.

[70] *North Sea Continental Shelf Case, Judgment*, [1969] I.C.J. Reports 3.

[71] *Ibid.* at 52.

United Nations Convention on the Law of the Sea of 1982 (UNCLOS), which succeeded the Geneva Conventions and has been ratified by more than 150 states (but not, as of April 2010, the United States), substitutes for the equidistance test a requirement that delimitation "be effected by agreement on the basis of international law ... in order to achieve an equitable solution,"[72] an approach consonant with the court's prescription of "agreement in accordance with equitable principles, and taking account of all the relevant circumstances."[73]

A number of agreements can be identified as establishing a line of delimitation that deviates so as to leave a known deposit in the sole possession of one party or the other, but the abstract idea of "unity of deposit" appears to have been far less important in these cases than the utility of such deviations for facilitating trade-offs between the parties or avoiding disturbance of established arrangements, as where concessions have been awarded by one or perhaps both parties, or productive oil wells drilled.[74] Thus, when Denmark and Germany agreed on a line of delimitation in the North Sea in pursuance of the court's judgment in the *North Sea Continental Shelf Case*, they drew it so as to pass south of an area already subject to a Danish license where promising oil shows had occurred, which might otherwise have ended up on the enlarged German shelf.[75]

We should notice that while delimitation agreements between states may in this way occasionally reflect what might be called past oil practice, the International Court of Justice and the *ad hoc* arbitral tribunals to which delimitation disputes have from time to time been referred have been reluctant to give much weight to past actions such as the grant of concessions or the drilling of wells unless there is convincing evidence of express or tacit agreement between the states concerned.[76] Treating nonagreed practice as relevant obviously may create an incentive for unilateral action in disputed areas, and there has been a strong preference among international lawyers for consultation and negotiation as the appropriate means of dealing with conflicting claims in connection with offshore resources.

---

[72] UNCLOS, art. 83(1).

[73] [1969] I.C.J. Reports 3, at 53.

[74] See, for examples, Kwiatkowska 1993: 90–5; Bouvet 1997: 197–221; Kwiatkowska 2005: 3229–31.

[75] Germany–Denmark Agreement of January 28, 1971.

[76] Kwiatkowska 2005: 3230–1, and for recent judicial views in this sense, *Case concerning Maritime Delimitation in the Black Sea (Romania v. Ukraine)*, at www.icj-cij.org/docket/files/132/14987.pdf (February 3, 2009), para. 198, where the court noted that state activities relating to resources had generally been treated "cautiously" as a factor in delimitation, and *Guyana v. Suriname*, arbitral tribunal award of September 17, 2007, at www.pca-cpa.org/upload/files/Guyana-Suriname%20Award.pdf, paras. 378–90, where the tribunal reviewed previous cases and awards.

Disputed Areas of Continental Shelf

It is helpful to distinguish two stages at which such conflicts may arise. In the first, the states involved (sometimes two but often more, especially in "semi-enclosed seas" like the North Sea or South China Sea) have not reached any agreement on how the continental shelf is to be divided up between them. Claims they make to areas of the shelf are quite likely to overlap, as each state chooses an approach to delimitation that is most favorable to it, in much the same way as do lessors and lessees entering negotiations on unitization formulas in the United States and indeed elsewhere. Factors—historical, economic, geographical—adduced as crucial by one side will be dismissed as irrelevant or unfounded by the other, and it will be as important and difficult for any third party called upon to settle the matter to decide upon which factors should operate as to determine just what effect each should have. The fact that UNCLOS offers no guidance beyond demanding an "equitable" solution does nothing to make this task easier. At this stage, states may see themselves as having three options: to achieve a delimitation agreement or agreements, so that the overlaps disappear; to agree that overlaps (or the most sensitive parts of them, probably those likely to contain substantial hydrocarbon resources) be left undelimited, but subject to some kind of joint development regime; or to proceed with unilateral exploitation of the whole area claimed, including overlapping areas.

This last course has obvious affinities with the rule of capture: they share a common parentage in "the good old rule, the simple plan, that he should take who have the power, and he should keep who can,"[77] but it might appear that this type of unilateral action lacks the quality of lawful competitive exploitation of a common resource that is the hallmark of capture. There *is*, however, a common resource here, because the International Court of Justice has made it clear from the beginning that the area of continental shelf "appertaining"—the word used in the Truman declaration—to a state, as the "natural prolongation" of its territory under the sea, may overlap with the area appertaining to another.[78] Delimitation is the exercise required to divide such areas of overlap, but until it is effected, both states enjoy there the "sovereign rights for the purpose of exploring it and exploiting its natural resources" recognized alike by the Geneva convention (article 2(1)), UNCLOS as its successor (article 77(1)), and customary international law. The convention texts also refer to the fact that these rights are "exclusive," but the implication of the general law is that in overlapping areas, both states enjoy such

---

[77] Cited in relation to capture in *Meeker v. City of East Orange*, 79 N.J.L. 623, 638, 74 A. 379, 385 (1909); and in Summers 1919: 179; Pettengill 1940: 96.

[78] *North Sea Continental Shelf Case*, [1969] I.C.J. 3, 22, 53.

exclusive rights. Clearly this creates the kind of dilemma that bedevils the exploitation of fugacious materials like oil, gas, and water under domestic law: the choice between recognizing a right to act unilaterally, on one hand, and an obligation to refrain pending agreement on a boundary or on joint development of the area, on the other, effectively means either imposing on one party the possible loss of a resource that it desires to conserve or sterilizing the development desired by the other until the first is pleased to reach agreement.

The nearest thing we have to an authoritative judicial ruling relating to this choice is the decision of the International Court of Justice that actions by Turkey in granting petroleum exploration permits and allowing seismic surveys in areas of the Aegean Sea claimed by Greece as part of its continental shelf did not create such a risk of irreparable prejudice to the rights in issue as might require the exercise of its power to indicate interim measures of protection.[79] The court recognized that if, in a future substantive decision on the delimitation of the shelf, exploration rights in the area were held to belong to Greece, then Turkey's seismic surveys might possibly be found to be prejudicial to those rights, but "since neither concessions unilaterally granted nor exploration unilaterally undertaken by either of the interested States with reference to the disputed areas can be creative of new rights or deprive the other State of any rights to which in law it may be entitled," and since any such prejudice, once found, could be the subject of appropriate reparation, no action by the court was needed to preserve the parties' legal position in future litigation on the merits.[80]

This decision gives some comfort both to would-be developers and to nondevelopers, assuring the latter that unilateral "oil practice" will not affect future delimitation decisions (as later case law has confirmed)[81] nor affect their rights in other ways, while giving developers some leeway to act independently subject to the risk of needing to make future compensation. One distinguished group of international lawyers has thus concluded that "a disputant State may carry out unilateral prospecting in the disputed area" without any need to consult or negotiate with its rival.[82] We should also notice that an Irish proposal in the course of UNCLOS negotiations to require the consent of the other state for such action in areas of bona fide dispute was not taken up in the convention.[83]

---

[79] *Aegean Continental Shelf Case (Greece v. Turkey) Interim Protection*, [1976] I.C.J. 3.

[80] *Ibid.* at 10, 11.

[81] See cases cited at n. 76, above.

[82] 1 British Institute of International and Comparative Law 1998: 35. Ong 1999: 802–3 says the opposite.

[83] See Ong 1999: 773.

Unilateral action without consultation, however, exposes a state to allegations of breach of the delimitation article (article 83) of UNCLOS, which, while very vague as to criteria, does impose specific procedural obligations: to effect delimitation by agreement, to invoke third-party dispute settlement if this cannot be done within a reasonable time, and, pending agreement and "in a spirit of understanding and co-operation," to make "every effort" to conclude provisional arrangements and "not to jeopardize or hamper the reaching of the final agreement."

This point was raised directly in the 2007 arbitration between Guyana and Suriname.[84] Suriname alleged that Guyana had "jeopardized agreement" by allowing its concession holder, CGX, to undertake exploratory drilling in disputed waters. In its award, the tribunal stated that it would be guided in its approach to article 83 by a distinction, based on the *Aegean Continental Shelf Case*, between "activities having a permanent physical impact on the marine environment and those that do not" and went on to find that there was "a substantive legal difference" between oil exploration activities like seismic testing, and exploratory drilling. Seismic activity, it thought, should be permissible in a disputed area, but Guyana had breached its obligations under article 83(3) in authorizing exploratory drilling without notice to or consultation with Suriname. Whether, assuming such consultation, Guyana would have been within its rights in continuing with such exploration over a peaceful protest by Suriname the tribunal did not say, though its remark that "[s]ome exploratory drilling might cause permanent damage to the marine environment" suggests that this would be a course of dubious legality. In the event, Suriname did not just protest through diplomatic channels, but also sent a gunboat to threaten the drilling rig with unspecified "consequences" if it failed to leave the disputed area as soon as possible, behavior also characterized by the tribunal as a breach of article 83(3).

The position of a state that finds its plans for offshore development clouded by a rival claim to the area by one or more of its neighbors is thus a difficult one, and that of companies to which it may have granted oil concessions or other rights may be even more so. Disputes frequently engender high levels of tension, sometimes necessitating the intervention of the UN Security Council; operating companies may, like CGX, find themselves the recipients of unfriendly visits from armed naval craft, but may at the same time be told by their host government that any suspension of activity would constitute a breach of their obligations to it. As Rodman Bundy, a lawyer practicing in this field, has put it, "[T]he host country has to decide how far to hold its concessionaires' feet to the fire."[85]

---

[84] *Guyana v. Suriname*, September 17, 2007, at www.pca-cpa.org/upload/files/Guyana-Suriname%20Award.pdf. Quotations that follow are drawn from paras. 471–84 of the award. See further Roughton 2008.

[85] Bundy 1995: 27.

In light of the emphasis in recent international case law, notably *Guyana v. Suriname*, on the obligation to seek, and not to hinder, agreement, more imaginative legal advisers have concentrated on steps that a would-be developer state can take to get a negotiating process moving and ensure that if it stalls or fails, the state will be in a better position to act unilaterally, rather than being "mesmerised" into inaction by uncertainties connected with a supposed rule of capture and by possible political and legal consequences.[86] Although the actual appropriation of resources in a disputed area of continental shelf would risk the incurring of international legal liability in most circumstances, with the possible exception of a persistent and total refusal of negotiations by the nondeveloping party, such a strategy may make it possible to move toward development without adverse long-term consequences. It is clear from the *Guyana v. Suriname* award that the tribunal was swayed in Guyana's favor by its positive attitude to negotiations on delimitation and Suriname's lack of cooperation in this task.

In practice, states have behaved in a highly pragmatic way in concluding agreements, whether for delimitation, joint development areas, or a combination of both. The experience in the North Sea in the 1960s and early 1970s, and in the Persian/Arabian Gulf over a more extended period from the late 1950s to the 1970s, suggests that the discovery or indication of substantial hydrocarbon resources is a powerful stimulus to agreement, even if progress toward it may involve a detour through international litigation. It may not always be a strong enough stimulus to overcome adverse elements, such as the multiplicity of claims, the unresolved issues of sovereignty over numerous small islands, and the cool interstate relations (to say nothing of Chinese readiness to wait "a thousand years" for others to accept Chinese views) that have so far prevented the delimitation of the South China Sea, but in general, "it is no accident that the majority of ocean boundaries in the world today involve important petroleum producing countries."[87]

Joint Development Agreements

A second way of resolving the problem of overlapping claims is to conclude an agreement for the joint development of the area in question. Such agreements remain relatively rare. They usually result from the inability of states to reach agreement on a mutually satisfactory line of delimitation. States may negotiate in good faith and have a shared desire for development, but if they start from wholly inconsistent principles, agreement on a single line may be impossible.

---

[86] Kendall Freeman 2003: 15, 21–4.
[87] Townsend-Gault and Stormont 1995: 58, 61.

The agreement between Australia and Indonesia establishing a zone of cooperation south of East Timor, now replaced by a modified agreement between Australia and independent East Timor, is an excellent example. Australia claimed that the two countries had no common continental shelf, because the very deep Timor Trough lay not far south of the East Timor coastline, so that the line of its continental shelf boundary followed the southern edge of the trough; Indonesia denied the relevance of this factor and proposed delimitation by means of an equidistance line. What is now called the Australia–East Timor Joint Petroleum Development Area, jointly administered by the two countries, lies between these two lines.[88]

Because of the variety of forms they have assumed, the good advertisement for international cooperation over natural resources they offer, and the way they preempt issues over cross-border deposits (save where the border is that of the joint development area itself), such agreements have attracted a great deal of attention from international lawyers.[89] I say no more about them here, because it is precisely the problem they preempt—that of exploiting a petroleum deposit transected by an agreed maritime border—that most directly raises the issue of the applicability of the rule of capture in international law.

Cross-Border Deposits under Delimitation Agreements

When the North Sea states started negotiating the delimitation of their common continental shelf in the early 1960s, they were well aware of the risk that the lines they would draw might cross as yet undiscovered reservoirs of oil and gas. Offshore precedents for dealing with this situation were almost nonexistent: only a 1962 protocol to the Ems-Dollard agreement between the Netherlands and Germany, dealing with an area of uncertain boundaries at the mouth of the Ems River, made provision for sharing of oil and gas production between concessionaires of the two countries operating on either side of a line dividing the area, but this was too closely tailored to the particular local circumstances to be of much use as a model.[90] The few earlier delimitation agreements in existence that might affect the continental shelf, such as the United Kingdom–Venezuela agreement on the submarine areas of the Gulf of Paria of February 26, 1942, were silent on the issue.

---

[88] There is an extensive literature. On the original Australia–Indonesia Treaty ("Timor Gap Treaty"), see Livesley 1990, and for a brief account of the current Australia–East Timor Treaty ("Timor Sea Treaty"), see Bastida et al. 2007: 411–13.

[89] See, for examples and further references, British Institute of International and Comparative Law 1990; Townsend-Gault and Stormont 1995; Ong 1999; Bastida et al. 2007: 370–2, 399–414.

[90] Supplementary Agreement to the Treaty concerning Arrangements for Co-operation in the Ems Estuary (Ems–Dollard Treaty).

The solution adopted by the negotiators of the United Kingdom and Norway, who made the fastest progress, was to incorporate in their delimitation agreement a clause recognizing the problem and committing their countries to find a solution. Given its considerable influence on the many agreements that were to follow, it is worth quoting in full:

> If any single geological petroleum structure or petroleum field, or any single geological structure or field of any other mineral deposit, including sand or gravel, extends across the dividing line and the part of such structure or field which is situated on one side of the dividing line is exploitable, wholly or in part, from the other side of the dividing line, the Contracting Parties shall, in consultation with the licensees, if any, seek to reach agreement as to the manner in which the structure or field shall be most effectively exploited and the manner in which the proceeds deriving therefrom shall be apportioned.[91]

A few months later, the United Kingdom and the Netherlands adopted a slightly different approach, concluding, simultaneously with their delimitation agreement, a separate agreement on the exploitation of "single geological structures," initially confined to petroleum structures. The terms were similar, save that this agreement also provided for resort to arbitration in case of failure to agree.[92]

Dozens of continental shelf delimitation agreements have since been concluded by countries in all parts of the world. Alberto Szekely, in 1987, was able to count 58; Jean-Pierre Bouvet, in 1997, listed more than 100 delimiting areas beyond the territorial sea.[93] A substantial proportion of these (70 percent, according to Szekely) make some provision along the lines of the early North Sea agreements. This has led international lawyers to speculate as to whether the incidence of such clauses is not now such as to evidence the consistency of practice and sense of obligation (the technical term is *opinio juris*) necessary to create a customary law rule requiring cooperation in the exploitation of cross-border deposits, rather than unilateral development. Some commentators have asserted that such an obligation now exists;[94] others are more guarded. David Ong, for example, went no further than to suggest, in 1999, that cooperation might "soon be regarded as obligatory" only in semienclosed seas like the North Sea, Persian/Arabian Gulf, and the

---

[91] United Kingdom–Norway Delimitation Agreement, March 10, 1965, art. 4.

[92] United Kingdom–Netherlands Agreement on the exploitation of single geological structures, October 6, 1965.

[93] Szekely 1987: 278; Bouvet 1997: Repertoire des clauses-types.

[94] Notably, Onorato 1968, 1977; Lagoni 1979.

South China Sea, where the most intensive use has been made of delimitation or joint development agreements.[95]

A regional approach receives considerable support from the analysis of delimitation agreements by Bouvet,[96] which makes it clear that whereas countries bordering the North Sea and in the Middle East, South and Southeast Asia, and Australasia usually include common deposit clauses demanding such cooperation in their delimitation agreements, the practice is unusual in the Americas despite the existence of a substantial number of agreements. Bouvet also identified some notable individual countries that either have never incorporated such a clause in an agreement—the former Soviet Union and China—or have hardly ever done so: France (in respect to both its metropolitan and its overseas territory)[97] and the United States. These are states of considerable significance, and Bouvet accordingly doubted the existence of an enforceable cooperation obligation based on treaty practice, referring also to the considerable variation of detail in the many concluded agreements.[98] Agreements in fact cover a spectrum ranging from a pure "agreement to agree"[99] to quite complicated arrangements stipulating the basis on which resources are to be apportioned, the mode of operation, the treatment of resources recovered by one party or the other before agreement is reached, and methods of dispute settlement.[100]

The implementation of these common deposit clauses has been no less varied. Once the evidence for the existence of such a deposit has been established, one might expect the state parties to aim for the complete unitization of the field, already understood by the 1960s to be the only approach likely to secure the maximum ultimate recovery of the hydrocarbons it contains. This has indeed been the approach of the United Kingdom and its neighbors in respect of the surprisingly large numbers of fields that straddle the United Kingdom–Norway and United Kingdom–Netherlands median lines: state-to-state unitization agreements have thus been concluded for the Frigg, Statfjord, Murchison, and Markham fields, each forming the counterpart to a separate agreement in the same sense concluded between the countries' respective licensees.[101] As between the

---

[95] Ong 1999: 798.

[96] Above, n. 93.

[97] France, however, concluded with Canada a "single geological structure" agreement in 2005 following the determination (by an arbitral tribunal) of a line of delimitation between Canada and France's territory of Saint-Pierre et Miquelon. The agreement is not yet in force (or published), but its substance is reported in United Nations. International Law Commission 2009a.

[98] Bouvet 1997: 629–32.

[99] E.g., United Kingdom and Ireland, November 7, 1988, art. 3.

[100] See the analyses in Szekely 1987: 278–85; Lagoni 1979: 229–33, 236–7.

[101] See generally Bastida et al. 2007: 393–6.

United Kingdom and Norway, indeed, the practice has become so well established that in 2005, the countries concluded a framework agreement enabling future cross-border unitizations to take place without the need for field-by-field agreements, and two further cross-border fields—Enoch and Blaine—have been unitized by this means.[102] Elsewhere in the world, state-to-state unitization agreements have been concluded between Nigeria and Equatorial Guinea and between Venezuela and Trinidad and Tobago. Australia and East Timor have agreed to unitize the Greater Sunrise field, which lies across the border between the Australia–East Timor Joint Development Zone and the Australian continental shelf.[103]

At the state-to-state level, however, unitization is a demanding option. The fact that installations on one country's continental shelf may be employed to produce oil and gas appertaining to both countries entails complex arrangements for assigning legal jurisdiction, for applying tax rules and safety and labor legislation, and for the delicate task of apportioning production between the states and their licensees. Some states have therefore preferred to exploit cross-border fields in a more rough-and-ready way, following early precedents established for cross-border fields on land, such as the Zwerndorf–Vysoka field between Austria and what was then Czechoslovakia, for which the two states established in 1960 a joint commission to oversee and ensure the coordination of the operations of their two separate concessionaires.[104] The Safaniyah–Kahfji fields, shared between Saudi Arabia and Kuwait, have been exploited in this way, as have the Marjan–Fereidoon fields, shared between Saudi Arabia and Iran. The latter agreement in fact hardly goes beyond providing continuing machinery to ensure that the two parties respect a "no drilling" zone extending 500 meters on either side of the border.[105]

A more radical attempt at achieving independence of activities on a cross-border deposit can be found in the Abu Al Bu Khoosh (ABK)–Sassan field, shared by the United Arab Emirates and Iran. Although the relevant common deposit clause, in the usual Iranian style, envisaged an obligation to "endeavour to reach agreement as to the manner in which the operations on both sides of the boundary could be co-ordinated or unitized," the parties preferred to try to separate the resources by a program of borderline waterflooding.[106] This did not prevent large-scale drainage

---

[102] United Kingdom–Norway Framework Agreement concerning Cross-Boundary Petroleum Co-operation, April 4, 2005, reprinted and annotated in Daintith et al. paras. 2-324–2-372.

[103] Bastida et al. 2007: 396–8.

[104] Czechoslovakia–Austria Agreement concerning the Working of Common Deposits of Natural Gas and Petroleum, January 23, 1960.

[105] Bouvet 1997: 334–5.

[106] Agreement between the United Arab Emirates and Iran, August 13, 1974, Churchill et al. 1977: 242; Bouvet 1997: 535–6, 564 (based on information from one of the operating companies).

to the Abu Dhabi side when Iranian installations were destroyed by the United States in 1988.[107] More generally, it should be noted that even effective cooperation arrangements short of unitization may result in some cross-border drainage in one direction or the other.

The argument among international lawyers about the significance of the common deposit clauses revolves around the possible existence of a *procedural* obligation—to inform, consult, and seek agreement—but it is intimately linked with the substantive question of whether a state has a right to exploit a cross-border petroleum deposit without the consent of its neighbor: whether, in other words, the rule of capture applies as part of the international law of continental shelf petroleum resources. The first observation to be made is that the greater the number of states that bind themselves bilaterally to develop fields crossing their maritime borders only in cooperation, the less room there is for the rule of capture—if a rule of international law—to operate. They shrink its importance in the same way that compulsory unitization requirements shrink it in domestic law. They do not, however, make the issue of the rule's application irrelevant. For one reason or another, the hoped-for cooperation may not materialize. What then? The same thing may happen in a case where there is no applicable "Anglo-Norwegian" common deposit clause, so that even if one accepts the argument that there is now a customary law rule imposing an obligation to cooperate, the need to find a rule relating to unilateral action consequent upon failure to respect it still remains. An obligation to cooperate—or to try to—is thus not inconsistent with the operation of the rule.

This leads directly to a second comment. The widespread insertion of common deposit clauses in delimitation agreements does not of itself tell us anything about whether the signatory states believed the rule of capture to be part of international law. Perhaps they did, and undertook in advance to cooperate because they wished to avoid the waste, tensions, and disputes that might follow from competitive drilling, as is suggested by the appearance in some agreements, notably those concluded by Iran with its Gulf neighbors in the 1970s, of boundary spacing rules—no wells within 125 meters of the line save with agreement of the other party.[108] Or perhaps one party, less confident than the other of its technical ability to exploit any borderline resources, wanted to ensure that it had the means to resist the prejudicial exercise of its neighbor's technical superiority. This may be why the recent U.S.–Mexico treaty drawing a line of delimitation in the deep waters of the

---

[107] Below, at 403–4.

[108] The agreements are printed in Churchill et al. 1977: 226–46. See also the Iran–Saudi Arabia Agreement, January 29, 1961, *ibid.* 216–25, which has no common deposit clause but forbids drilling within 500 meters of the boundary.

"Western Gap" in the Gulf of Mexico contains an unusual clause imposing a "no drilling" rule within 1.4 nautical miles on either side of the line for a period of 10 years—long enough, perhaps, for Mexico to catch up on deep-water production technology.[109] The fact that the great majority of agreements, following the Anglo-Norwegian precedent, refer only to those common deposits that are exploitable from across the line of delimitation, and not to any common deposit, might be thought to be an acknowledgment of the principle of capture, but in fact, the limitation was inserted at a late stage in the Anglo-Norwegian negotiations, simply in order to reduce the number of occasions on which the cooperation procedure would need to be initiated.[110]

Quite possibly, though, the reasoning behind the insertion of these clauses was exactly the opposite: that because the rule of capture might *not* apply, a recalcitrant state would be able to block its neighbor's legitimate desire for development unless the delimitation treaty imposed an obligation to try to agree on development proposals. Given that delimitation treaties tend to get signed earlier where there are hydrocarbon prospects than where there are not, this second explanation may be somewhat more plausible than the first, but we can hardly exclude that some parties, to some treaties, may have had the other scenario in mind.

With perhaps two-thirds of all potential maritime boundaries remaining to be negotiated,[111] many delimitation agreements containing no common deposit clause, and the threat of impasse always hanging over an attempt to implement common deposit clauses, the question of the applicability of the capture rule to ascertained or probable cross-border fields cannot be evaded. More than in most areas of law, the answer one gets depends on whom one asks. Ask an American legal practitioner, and the answer is a confident yes. Ask anyone else, and the answer is a rather less confident no. In neither case is it accompanied by much in the way of convincing reasoning.

A recent practitioner statement on the international law position, from Rodman Bundy in 1995, is reminiscent of some of the early American cases in its assumption that the proposition is too obvious to need argument. As he put it, "[T]he exploitation of international oil and gas reserves is still based largely on the rule of capture. This means that, in the absence of an agreement to the contrary, a State or international oil company is free to maximise its production from its side of the boundary line notwithstanding the policies of neighbouring States which share the same field."[112] On this basis, he argued that when Iran ceased—as a result

---

[109] United States–Mexico Agreement, June 9, 2000, arts. 5 and 6; see Holmes 2002.
[110] United Kingdom National Archives, FO 371/181319, Doc. GW 41/5 (January 11, 1965).
[111] Blake and Swarbrick 1998: 11.
[112] Bundy 1995: 24.

of U.S. military action—to be able to produce from the ABK–Sassan field shared with Abu Dhabi in 1988, it was quite legitimate for Abu Dhabi to increase its own production (and to add insult to injury by excluding it from an OPEC-mandated quota reduction) despite the fact that, as already noted, the parties had agreed to a common deposit clause envisaging agreement on the coordination or unitization of field operations—though they had never moved very far in this direction.[113] Bundy adduced no authorities to support either the general statement or its application in this instance.

Other practitioners have tried to offer a little more, either suggesting that because capture is an element of both Anglo-American and civil law, it must be a principle of international law,[114] or claiming that the general principle, if not the precise rule as understood in the United States, is recognized by "leading writers" on international law.[115] When one comes to look at the work of these writers, however, it is a hesitant negative consensus that emerges. The level of confidence is suggested by this remark of David Ong's:

> Miyoshi notes that a group of lawyers specializing in the international law of the sea and energy at the Third Workshop on Joint Exploration and Development of Offshore Hydrocarbons Resources in Southeast Asia, held in Bangkok from February 5 to March 1, 1985 broadly agreed that no international rule of capture exists, citing a handwritten memorandum entitled "Summary Thoughts" by Jon Van Dyke, Chairman of the Final Session.[116]

The word "broadly" perhaps reflects the fact that the reasons that have been adduced for this opinion are far from consistent. One idea, which appears to draw on the "good neighbor" principle, is that the common deposit is in essence shared property, like the resources of international rivers, so that the sharing parties have such duties to one another as avoidance of damage, equitable and reasonable use of the resource, information exchange, and an obligation to negotiate.[117] Its linkage with the ideas of correlative rights developed in U.S. water law and oil and gas law is clear, but we have seen that the correlative rights concept was never developed by the courts to the point where it would either demand equitable apportionment of the resource or inhibit unilateral action.[118] Moreover, there are no grounds for

---

[113] Above, at 401–2.

[114] Morris 1967: 205–8.

[115] Cogan and Culotta 1992: 620.

[116] Ong 1999: 778, citing Miyoshi 1988: 6, 18.

[117] Ruiz Moreno 1959; Onorato 1968.

[118] Above, Ch. 7, at 190–4. Onorato 1968: 91–2 and 1977: 328 appears unaware of this limitation.

assuming that any activity by one state in its part of the common deposit will cause the sorts of damage—blowouts, water ingress, losses through negligent "shooting of wells"—that American courts have been prepared to sanction.[119]

A different, and essentially inconsistent, idea is that the exploiting state must act cooperatively "in order to comply with international law on the inviolability of foreign territorial sovereignty and sovereign rights."[120] The thinking here appears to be that any penetration of the reservoir, by modifying pressure conditions, even slightly, produces an alteration in the condition of the neighboring state's territory. The notion of territorial sovereignty has, however, also been deployed to exactly the opposite effect, as a basis for asserting the application of the rule of capture.[121] The issue here, in relation to sovereignty, or "sovereign rights," is the same as the one that tormented early-nineteenth-century courts as they tried to adjust their ideas about property to the new pressures for development of land: whether the maxim *Sic utere tuo ut alienum non laedas* (Use what is yours in such a way as not to damage others) should yield to the idea that the right of property implied the freedom to use and develop one's property just as one liked.[122]

The international community is perhaps inching closer to a reconciliation of these conflicting positions and rationales. The International Law Commission, the United Nations' expert international law body, has adopted draft articles on the law of transboundary aquifers, as a basis for a possible international convention.[123] The articles recognize the sovereignty of each aquifer state over the portion of a transboundary aquifer or aquifer system located within its territory (article 3) but subject the exercise of that sovereignty to the principle of "equitable and reasonable utilization" (article 4). This principle implies "the equitable and reasonable accrual of benefits to the aquifer states" and involves considerations both of equity (not equality) in use and of conservation. They also impose an obligation to seek to avoid harm to other aquifer states (article 6), to cooperate together through appropriate joint mechanisms to secure equitable and reasonable utilization and protection of transboundary aquifers (article 7), and to undertake regular exchanges of data and information (article 8). These principles, it will be appreciated, would be readily applicable to transboundary oil and gas reservoirs, and in fact, both groundwater and oil and gas were included in a program of work on shared natural resources adopted by the commission in 2002.

---

[119] Onorato 1997: 328; see above, Ch. 7, at 193.

[120] Lagoni 1979: 235. See also Bouvet 1995: 649.

[121] Lagoni 1979: 220, citing Andrassy 1951: 127; see also Ong 1999: 777.

[122] Horwitz 1977: Ch. 2.

[123] United Nations. International Law Commission 2008.

The commission, however, subsequently decided, with the support of a large majority of governments, to develop its work on aquifers independently, and it must be doubtful whether it will pursue a similar project of codifying the law relating to shared oil and gas reservoirs: a number of states have expressed the view that universal rules are unnecessary, and that a case-by-case approach is best for what are delicate, technical, and bilateral issues, while others feel that caution and further study are needed before embarking on such a course.[124] Because these two groups include some very powerful states (China, Russia, and the United States) and some major oil and gas producers (Venezuela, Iran, and Norway), early progress toward general rules on shared oil and gas reservoirs seems unlikely.

Meanwhile, however, a rule of international law that is not mentioned in these debates in my view provides a surer, straighter path to the conclusion that the rule of capture does not apply in the commonest situation where two states share a common deposit: that is, on the continental shelf. In both the Geneva Convention of 1958 (article 2) and the UNCLOS Convention of 1982 (article 77), it is provided that "[t]he coastal State exercises over the continental shelf sovereign rights for the purpose of exploring it and exploiting its natural resources," and that "the[se] rights ... are exclusive in the sense that if the coastal State does not explore the continental shelf or exploit its natural resources, no one may undertake these activities without the express consent of the coastal State." This was described by the International Court of Justice as "the most fundamental of all the rules of law relating to the continental shelf" and "as reflecting, or as crystallizing, received or at least emergent rules of customary international law relative to the continental shelf."[125] We can assume that it binds even countries like the United States that have not yet ratified UNCLOS. Once the continental shelf has been delimited, the oil and gas in place in a common deposit on each side of the dividing line is subject to the exclusive sovereign rights of the state of whose shelf it forms part. No one but that state may exploit that oil and gas, so any activity on the other side of the line that could constitute exploration for it or exploitation of it must be a breach of these sovereign rights.

In practice, seismic surveys and even exploration drilling seem capable of being carried on without such breach: their primary target will be the resources in the operating state's own area, and drilling will, in any event, probably be necessary to achieve reasonably accurate appraisal of the field and of the likelihood that it extends across the boundary. At just what point thereafter unlawful exploitation of the neighboring state's resources starts occurring must be a question of fact. If the pressure drive in the field comes from across the boundary line, it might be argued

---

[124] United Nations. International Law Commission 2009b.
[125] *North Sea Continental Shelf Case*, [1969] I.C.J. 3, 22, 39.

that this happens at the moment production starts. Whatever the specific circumstances, though, it is clear that this is a property rule diametrically opposed to the rule of capture: what a state can never do, consistently with article 77(2), is (to paraphrase Hardwicke's classic definition) to "acquire title to the oil and gas which [it] produces from wells drilled [on its continental shelf], although it may be proved that part of such oil and gas migrated from [the continental shelf of its neighbor]."[126]

The current tendency among international lawyers appears to be one of putting arguments about property rights in cross-border resources to one side and focusing instead on the practice and case law developing around the relevant provisions of UNCLOS. As the tribunal in *Guyana v. Suriname* showed, article 83, in particular, provides rather comprehensive procedural guidance, adherence to which may in the end be more important than taking a position on the capture–no capture argument. Admittedly, the procedural approach does not provide an automatic answer to the problems that arise either in the case of rival claims to hydrocarbon-rich areas of continental shelf or where boundaries, established under agreements making no provision for common deposits, cut across petroleum reservoirs. The lawyers meeting in Bangkok in 1985 did not fail to notice that even if there might be no international rule of capture, "as a practical matter nations will aggressively pursue resources and conflicts may arise."[127] In this connection, it bears remembering that of the world's three most powerful nations, the United States, Russia, and China, only the first has ever accepted a common deposit clause, and that was for only a 10-year period and in respect of a *very* narrow buffer zone.[128] Remember, too, that the country most wedded to the law of capture, the United States, remained in 2010 one of the few still refusing to ratify UNCLOS and thus arguably not subject to the constraints of article 83. It may be premature, therefore, to assume that arguments based on the rule of capture can have no further place in international law disputes.

---

[126] Hardwicke 1935: 393.
[127] Miyoshi 1988: 18.
[128] United States–Mexico Agreement, June 9, 2000, arts. 5 and 6; see Holmes 2002.

PART V
CONCLUSION

CHAPTER 13

THE LEAST WORST PROPERTY RULE?

THE FORKING PATH

The "law of capture" entered the vocabulary of the U.S. oil industry as a pathological expression, a way of describing an unnatural growth that, like a cancer, rotted the body of the industry by stimulating its cells to frenetic and self-destructive (re)production. It provided a convenient means by which the ills of the industry in the 1920s and 1930s could be laid at the door of conveniently dead nineteenth-century judges, while its participants selflessly struggled to cure themselves, and at the same time to fend off the invasive and dangerous attentions of the medicine men in Congress and the state legislatures. It did not take long before a rather profound split appeared within the industry between those who insisted that capture described a fatal illness that must at all costs be eradicated and those who had come to view its admittedly serious discomforts as side effects of an essentially natural and healthy process—side effects to be treated, but not at the cost of giving up the enjoyments that provoked them. But even while this latter group was getting the upper hand and administering its preferred remedy of prorationing, the term "law of capture," or more commonly "rule of capture," continued to be employed largely as an explanation or excuse for the malfunctioning of the industry, especially in relation to the many kinds of waste it engendered. Lawyers, engineers, and conservationists were especially inclined to talk in these terms; rare was the voice that would suggest that capture had worked for the public good, as opposed to serving the interests of particular lessors or lessees.[1]

In later decades, the domestic U.S. industry, cushioned for as long as was necessary by prorationing and other protective devices, learned to live with this handicap and even to feel that, with its symptoms of wasteful production largely suppressed, it could be turned to good use. Today's lawyers and judges point to the flexibility it offers in the regulation of oil and gas production and the way it facilitates the use of advanced technologies of petroleum recovery.[2] Indeed, at least one commentator has been prepared to argue that if the damaging symptoms associated with the rule—notably, the collapse of prices—had been left untreated in the 1930s, the disease of wasteful overdrilling would have cured itself. The industry might have lost a few minor extremities in the shape of high-cost producers, but would have emerged leaner, fitter, and readier to face foreign competition.[3]

These comfortable views have not been shared outside the United States. Producers elsewhere, such as Szczepanowski in Galicia and Lord Cowdray in the United Kingdom, were complaining of the perverse effects of competitive drilling and pressing for measures to eliminate them well before Henry Doherty wrote his letter to the president in 1924,[4] and other countries' oil regimes have been designed with a view to either making the rule of capture irrelevant or closely controlling its effects. And since the beginning of the twentieth century, international law doctrine and state practice have emphasized cooperation rather than capture in the handling of fluid resources crossing international borders. In consequence, although few regimes have explicitly adopted an alternative property right rule, commentators outside the United States today tend to treat capture as a peculiarly American concept, and one that is not just crude and redolent of a less civilized age, but also morally questionable: something "iniquitous," a "law of the jungle," an invitation to "theft."[5]

---

[1] An example is Pogue 1938: 236.

[2] Kramer and Anderson 2005: 951–3; *Coastal Oil and Gas Corp. v. Garza Energy Trust*, 268 S.W. 3d 1 (Tex. 2008).

[3] 1 Bradley 1996: 115–16.

[4] Above, Ch. 9, at 240–1.

[5] Schönborn 1929: 147; Keen 1998: 438; Spier 2005: para. 8.2.

It is possible to trace, through the local histories that are the subject of earlier chapters, both a phase of parallel development largely shared in the United States and elsewhere and a phase of marked divergence. The first led to a widespread common understanding that the property right concepts on which the industry had been built during the nineteenth century, in North America, Romania, Galicia, and to a large extent Russia, were—at least from the point of view of participants in the industry—profoundly inefficient. The full extent of this inefficiency was not apparent until an adequate understanding of reservoir mechanics—in particular, the importance to recovery of maintaining the solution gas drive of the reservoir—was achieved and sufficiently disseminated, but other forms of inefficiency and waste were well understood from a much earlier date: fire damage, losses in storage, and above all, excessive investment. By the end of World War I, in 1918, the dysfunctional character of oil property rights was widely perceived. This is the starting point of a phase of divergence between the United States and almost everywhere else, which continues to this day. Countries that had conferred petroleum rights on surface proprietors under the accession system replaced it, for oil and gas, with state ownership or control; countries that had already separated mineral rights, including oil and gas rights, from surface ownership adjusted their regimes to secure more effective management of these resources. They acted, in other words, not to modify the rule of capture, but to eliminate the accession principle that was its raison d'être. The accession principle survived only here and there: in Canada and Trinidad, in the fast-declining oil province of Galicia, part of Poland from 1919 to 1947, and in the United States. Alone among the major oil powers, the United States chose instead to superimpose a system of regulation of production behavior on the existing property right framework, including the rule of capture, and indeed to regulate production, for the most part, in a way that did not neutralize the competitive pressures created by the underlying rights, but relied upon and indeed institutionalized them.

In this concluding chapter, I shall try to answer three questions that this short summary of the historical narrative brings into relief. Each of these two phases of world petroleum development, before and after 1918, presents us with a puzzle. As to the first, we have to ask why such an inefficient rule was adopted in the first place—not just in one country, but in several simultaneously. Was it, despite its defects, the best rule available—or the least worst? As to the second, we must obviously ask why, once adopted, it remained in place in the United States, despite the major difficulties it was perceived to create, while other countries were managing to create more rational and efficient systems. And third, it is certainly worth considering whether it would be useful—and if useful, feasible—to try to remove or diminish the major role the rule of capture plays in the United States and to eradicate the little that remains of it in other systems.

PHASE 1: THE LEAST INEFFICIENT RULE?

Why Was the Rule Adopted?

The standard economic explanation for the adoption of the rule of capture is to see it as a response to the "common pool" problem. Oil and gas, like fish and the water they swim in, are fluid resources, capable of moving from place to place without regard for property boundaries; thus ordinary property rules cannot work, and a right to the ownership of what one can capture is the simplest rule that can be offered.

A recent and sophisticated version of this theory has been offered by Dean Lueck, who seeks to provide a comprehensive economic analysis and explanation of the legal rules granting ownership not just of oil and gas, but also of land, personal property, intellectual property, water, and other goods. Lueck posits a basic distinction between ownership of the *flow* of output from a given *stock*, such as the contents of an oil reservoir or the whole of a herd of bison, and ownership of the stock itself.[6] Where it is possible to secure ownership of a stock, he argues that the tendency of the law will be to grant this by way of "first possession" when this is the most efficient means of disposal, and to do so at a time that limits the possibility of wasteful races between claimants. For example, by providing for the grant of title as soon as a discovery can be shown, the Mining Law of 1872 prevents the unnecessary investment by rival claimants that would occur if, say, title vested only on proving a commercial deposit. Oil and gas, however, are identified by Lueck as presenting a likeness to a type of stock—the herd of bison is the common example—whose mobile nature means that the costs of enforcing possession of the whole stock would be prohibitive. In such cases, he argues, the law falls back on the rule of capture, allowing people to capture, and thereby obtain ownership of, some part of the flow of output: the individual animal. To avoid wasteful exploitation of stocks subject in this way to the rule of capture, Lueck argues that the law will tend to restrict rights of access to the stock and forbid or limit their transfer. In the case of oil and gas, Lueck's proposition is that "[t]he fluidity of oil and gas ... can make it prohibitively costly for surface owners to establish rights to 'their' stocks as against those of neighboring drillers."[7] Hence the rule of capture is the most practicable rule.

There is a nice irony here. Academic lawyers, followed by engineers, spent decades lambasting the judges who first recognized the capture principle for the ignorance they betrayed in analogizing the behavior of oil and gas to that of wild animals. It was, they said, the judges' failure to understand that oil and gas did not roam free beneath the

---

[6] Lueck 1995. See also Lueck 1999, where the content is similar but the tone slightly less optimistic.

[7] Lueck 1995: 425.

ground, but were confined in reservoir rocks, that set the industry on its path of wasteful competition.[8] Now we have an economist reviving the old wild animal analogy: could the judges have been right all along? There are two features of Lueck's elegantly simple analysis that it will be useful to unpack and examine before taking a view on this.

The Surface Owner

The first element we should explore is the assumption, evident in Lueck's reference to "surface owners," of the existence of the accession system of property, under which the minerals and everything else in and under land ordinarily belong to the owner of the surface. As I have shown, this is but one way of dealing with property rights in minerals. Historically, the reservation of rights in minerals—particularly precious minerals—to the state or the ruler, who can thereby both profit from them and ensure their orderly exploitation, has been no less common. The accession system, however, puts that control in the hands of the surface owner.

As applied to oil and gas, it has thereby produced, from the very beginnings of the oil industry in the United States, a class of participants whose interests were and remain structurally opposed to the efficient exploitation of oil reservoirs. Surface owners, or the persons to whom they have transferred all or part of their royalty interests, naturally have an overriding interest in the rewards that can be obtained from oil operations on land in which they hold rights. This interest has operated to the detriment of the rational exploitation of oil reservoirs as a whole. The unquestioned right of landowners to dispose as they wished of the oil and gas resources to which they had, or might have, access first arose for exercise at a moment when traditional constraints on property use were falling away in favor of meeting the needs of development, and when the notion of freedom of contract was reaching its fullest expansion. In the absence of any control or restriction, its exuberant and unrestricted exercise permanently shaped the legal landscape of the American industry. The speculative pursuit of profit can be seen to have commenced on the very first day after Drake's 1859 discovery, with Jonathan Watson's attempt to lease as much Oil Creek land as he could, and continued thereafter in the crescendo of leasing, subleasing, and sales and subdivisions of royalty interests that I have previously described and that reproduced themselves on almost every occasion when new oil territory was opened up.

It is this process that is the real root of the American problem of waste in oil production. It has produced damaging effects at each stage of the development of the U.S. oil industry. From the earliest years, the frenetic subdivision of land

---

[8] Veasey 1920a: 453–5; Oliver, in United States. Federal Oil Conservation Board 1926a: 93–5.

enormously exacerbated the negative effects of the rule of capture. The smaller the area of land one controlled, the greater the risk that a neighbor would drain its oil first, and hence the greater the pressure to develop hastily and wastefully. The apparent offsetting benefit of securing increased flows of capital into the industry was greatly reduced by the fact that that so much of that capital was employed in drilling unnecessary wells. Max Ball, in 1917, related the problem of waste directly to the predominance of small tracts—he did not mention capture—and suggested that the effect in some fields had been to increase costs by over 300 percent: costs that were being borne by the consumer.[9]

Next, the landowner interest directly contradicted the efforts of lessees to produce oil and gas in a rational manner. We have seen that from the quite early days of the industry, it was the policy of more enlightened producers to acquire blocks of leases that might permit the unified, or at least more unified, operation of an oilfield. This might involve preferring production from some leases over that from others, while keeping the latter alive by way of contractual techniques such as delay rentals. Landowners, however, naturally demanded production from their leases and persuaded the courts to rewrite those leases in their favor: to read delay rental clauses out of leases, and prompt development and offset drilling obligations into them.[10] If people like Earl Oliver were looking for a stick to beat the courts with, they would have done far better—as Robert Hardwicke pointed out in 1935[11]—to castigate this judicial policy, which hobbled the attempt of producers to secure rational production and effectively made competitive drilling a common-law obligation. The courts clearly found the small farmer a sympathetic figure, at least when contrasted with the smart oilman and his devious lease agent. Doubtless the Oil Creek farmers were worthy people. Their life had been hard, and one does not begrudge the likes of farmer John Blood the life of ease that the windfall of oil provided for him and his family.[12] Yet the landowner's interest was and remains just that: a windfall, which the holders have done nothing to earn, which derives from a product that they are incapable themselves of exploiting, and which inures to them only by reason of an unthinking legal attachment to a slogan of dubious provenance: *Cujus est solum, ejus est usque ad coelum et ad inferos* (Whoever owns the land also owns to the sky above and the depths beneath).[13]

---

[9] Ball 1917.

[10] Merrill 1940.

[11] Hardwicke 1935.

[12] Above, Ch. 3, at 59.

[13] Sprankling 2008: 982–91 shows how this maxim entered American law from civil law, by way of adoption into common law (but with reference only to "the sky," not "the depths") by the seventeenth-century English judge Lord Coke, and with a little downward expansion from Sir William Blackstone (1765–1769) along the way.

The most recent effect of the subdivision of interests, among both royalty holders and working interest holders, has been to make the rectification of the underlying problems of wasteful competition immensely more difficult. I have already referred to the inherent obstacles standing in the way of attempts to secure voluntary unitization of oil reservoirs subject to a number of separate leases.[14] The more parties are involved, the greater these obstacles become, especially since numerous parties with small or minimal interests may be reluctant to agree to complex arrangements of which they have little understanding. The difficulty has been amplified by other processes of "fractionalization" that have occurred over the years, notably the subdivision of surface estates as America becomes increasingly urbanized, and the cumulative effects of division of property by inheritance.[15] I take up this point again below.

As I have tried to demonstrate, problems of capture of oil and gas are capable of arising even under domanial or regalian mineral property systems, if and as soon as the state, as holder of the rights in a reservoir, divides them among a number of concessionaires, lessees, or contractors. In such cases, however, the absence of rival royalty owners both removes a demand for irrational exploitation (by reference to surface lines) and greatly facilitates the management of the reservoir as a whole—if the grantor cares to exercise it for conservation purposes. Indeed, in the absence of the irritant of landowner competition for rewards, it might have been possible for producers in the United States to work cooperatively in a way that reduced waste. With hindsight, it may seem a colossal misfortune that the first oil strikes should have occurred on settled lands in the Appalachians rather than in the unsettled lands of the West. The cooperative approach of the oil prospectors in northern and southern California at the time of the short-lived 1860s boom gives some grounds for a cautious belief that in the absence of individual surface owners, the industry might have been able to evolve more sustainable working practices, within the framework of the sort of oil district self-regulation briefly practiced near Los Angeles. In particular, the subdivision of holdings that made capture so damaging might well have been avoided.

Earlier chapters have shown that the scenario of intensive trading in and exploitation of oil property rights was not peculiar to the United States. Galicia and Romania managed to reproduce the phenomenon of subdivision of oil lands and intensive competitive drilling despite the fact that the traditional position, both in Austria-Hungary and in the Romanian principalities, had been one in which mineral rights were reserved to the state, which was thereby enabled to control exploitation. Where oil was concerned, both countries, after a period in

---

[14] Above, Ch. 9, at 284–5.
[15] Anderson and Smith 1999.

which the accession system operated de facto for oil and gas, deliberately abandoned this prerogative as part of a political deal with powerful landed interests, Austria in its Petroleum Law of 1884, Romania in its Mining Law of 1895. For Galicia, the accession system was confirmed for petroleum by its 1908 Petroleum Law and continued until the Second World War. The Romanian state's act of self-abnegation is particularly remarkable if we remember that at the same time it retained its control, via the concession system, over hard rock minerals— which pose few of the property problems presented by petroleum. We have also seen that at the time the Baku oil development got under way, the accession system operated on privately owned lands in Russia with similar effects on property rights in oil lands and the manner of their exploitation. There, despite the existence of voluminous regulation of many aspects of production operations, no serious attempt to correct the wasteful effects of the accession principle and its accompanying rule of capture by any legislative means was made before the Bolshevik Revolution eliminated the private property right issue altogether.

These identical patterns of development on either side of the Atlantic took place against different backgrounds of political theory and action. Whereas American land policies and popular beliefs manifested an almost religious devotion to the accession principle, in Europe the question of who should hold property rights in minerals was a political issue whose resolution was likely to reflect the balance of power between landed interests and mineral entrepreneurs at different places and times. In France, accession had been the principle of the preindustrial Ancien Régime. The Revolutionary Assembly of 1791 (which, it should be remembered, was bourgeois, not proletarian, in composition) legislated to give the state control of deep-lying minerals, but it was not until Napoleon's Mining Law of 1810 that the mining concession system was established for the exercise of this control. Meanwhile the Civil Code, in its article 552, had confirmed the general principle of accession—subject to whatever such specialized mining laws might say. When it came to addressing difficult cases on the fringes of the Mining Law, the strength of the private property interest is indicated by the difficulty experienced by successive French governments in securing control. We have seen that it took four legislative attempts to control the activities of capture of mineral water springs, and legislation to subject salt wells to the mineral concession system had to be introduced no less than seven times before eventual success in 1840. The absence of consensus on the status of liquid petroleum, as late as 1890, suggests that similar battles would have occurred if France had benefited from any nineteenth-century petroleum discoveries.

Generally speaking, we may say of countries outside the United States that it was the accession principle itself, which might be seen as the conceptual substrate of the rule of capture, that operated on sufferance throughout the nineteenth century. Where it operated, the law of capture operated too, but the antiquity in civil law systems of the notion of state ownership, or at least control, of mineral resources meant that the adoption or readoption of that principle was always a possible solution to perceived problems—especially the perception of foreign dominance—in the petroleum industry.

Despite these differing European and American attitudes to mineral property, the story of the oil industry everywhere in the nineteenth century was one of vigorous, even frenetic, trading and division of rights of access to oil resources. This presents a problem for Lueck's hypothesis that the law tends to protect "capturable" resources by restrictions on rights access and transfer—represented in the United States, for example, by legislatively imposed closed seasons for game and outlawing of certain game markets. But while oil and gas access is naturally limited by landownership, transfer of access rights is certainly not. Lueck argues that production controls like well spacing and prorationing provided a substitute for transfer restrictions, and that this exceptional case can be explained by "the tremendous gains from specialization in surface (agriculture, residential) and subsurface (oil) uses of land."[16] Such gains may well explain why farmers lease their land to oil producers rather than try to develop it themselves; they do not explain why in the United States we find no legal rules tending even to restrain, let alone forbid, the multiplication of oil access rights until the adoption of compulsory pooling legislation in the 1930s and the contemporaneous adoption in Texas of the "voluntary subdivision" rule.[17]

Only in Galicia does there seem to have been some industry awareness, from its early days, that such multiplication was a factor making for waste, unproductive investment, and problems of control, and a legislative readiness to provide a legal deterrent. Over the same period, some American oil producers were also trying to find ways of avoiding the inconveniences of small-tract leasing, but there is no sign that asking for a similar legislative rule ever entered their minds. We owe to a disgruntled lessor, in dispute with corporate associates, the only attempt to enlist the common law in aid of restricting subdivision of oil lands, by invoking the old English "one stock" doctrine.[18] Under this rule, mineral interest owners could subdivide their rights only if they required their grantees to work the land cooperatively, as a single stock or with a common workforce. Honeycombing the land with scattered individual workings would unduly limit the rights of surface

---

[16] Lueck 1995: 426n.

[17] In *Brown v. Humble Oil and Refining Co.*, above, Ch. 9, at 265; see also above, at 273–4.

[18] *Chandler v. Hart*, 161 Cal. 405, 119 P. 516 (1911). On the "one stock" rule, see further Kramer and Anderson 2005: 950–1.

owners. The court, however, thought the doctrine could have no bearing on oil production, on the assumptions—later exploded—that a well would drain only about 4 to 5 acres, and the land would be sprinkled with derricks whether production was cooperative or individual. More typical lessors were, in any event, happy to see subleasing if it increased the size of their royalty checks. Amid this legal silence, when Max Ball documented the wasteful effects of such leasing in 1917, he offered little in the way of a policy prescription beyond asking his audience at the American Mining Congress to "do your part in creating a public sentiment in favour of adequate acreage."[19]

The Prohibitive Costs of Protection

The second element of Lueck's characterization that needs unpacking is the idea of the prohibitive costliness, for surface owners, of protecting "their" oil stocks. Like the familiar critiques of the judges' "formalist" analogies for oil and gas,[20] this remark ignores the remarkable lapse of time between the beginnings of the industry and the first judicial recognition of the operation of the capture principle within it. Participants in the industry operated from the very first days on the footing that there could be no constraint on getting oil from land to which one had access as owner or lessee; the consensus on this point was so strong that no one was reported as challenging it directly over the first 38 years of the industry's existence. People could hardly behave otherwise at a time when oil was thought to be tapped from crevices in the rock through which it might run long distances from whatever accumulations existed. In the absence of any notion that oil might have a stable existence in a stratum of reservoir rock covering a certain area, contesting a neighbor's actions in drilling a well close to one's own made no sense. Nor did the idea of protecting one's own "stock" of oil. Only as the understanding of reservoir geology developed in the 1880s did any basis for a possible legal attack on drainage appear. When, at this time, lessors began to sue their lessees for permitting such drainage to occur by reason of inadequate development of the lease, courts, in some cases at least, showed themselves able to identify an appropriate measure of damages for loss of oil by drainage. Lueck's assumption that defending the rights to one's "own" oil would necessarily be prohibitively costly thus no longer obtained. Yet no one challenged the *legality* of drainage until the 1890s, and of the cases decided then, only *Kelley v. Ohio Oil Co.* in 1897[21] was an attack on capture as such. Why was there not more litigation?

---

[19] Ball 1917: 16.

[20] Smith 2004: 1028–9.

[21] 57 Ohio St 317, 49 N.E. 399 (1897).

A general answer to this question is suggested by the economic analysis offered by Anthony Scott in his major study of how resource property rights have evolved over time.[22] Scott argues that development occurs only in response to a clear demand for modifications and refinements that might be supplied by courts, legislatures, or perhaps by the development of custom, and suggests in very general terms that "more demanders typically opposed than favoured individual rights to common-access resources."[23] In the case of oil and gas, individual rights—in landowners and their lessees—certainly existed; the problem was one of their imperfection by reason of the fugaciousness of the resource. To have tried, through litigation, to improve them, however, must have appeared to most active participants in the industry in the 1880s and 1890s as a negative-sum game. Success by a lessee in challenging drainage by a neighbor would immediately affect the drainage opportunities the lessee might possess under this or other leases. Leases smaller than the area thought to be capable of drainage from a single well— and we have seen how numerous these were in the industry's early days[24]—would immediately become unworkable without the consent of neighbors. In general, the value and attractiveness of the entire portfolio of leases would be restricted by the need to drill at a significant distance from border lines, even though the most promising locations for wells might be found there. Production could be expected to shrink significantly, and the consequent loss of profit might have greatly exceeded the costs of drilling unnecessary offset wells.

When these consequences are taken into account, the odds against any *lessee's* embarking on the task of persuading a court to adopt a strict property rule for oil and gas seem long indeed. The few people we do find attempting litigation on this subject are those who have a limited range of operations and a heavy stake in a specific field; the larger producers are conspicuously absent from the lists. *Lessors* of course were far less concerned with such general production and leasing strategies. They would certainly have wished to sue to restrain drainage, but having assigned their oil and gas rights to their lessees, they could not proceed directly against their neighbors. Accordingly, from the 1880s onward, they sought the aid of the courts to force their lessees to protect the leases against drainage by rapid development and the drilling of offset wells. Their success, as I have already noted, was a major factor in reinforcing the wasteful impact of oil and gas law.[25]

---

[22] Scott 2008. Scott offers a penetrating economic analysis of the development of oil property rights (see his Chs. 2 and 9) but needs to be read with caution on matters of history and law.

[23] *Ibid.* 59.

[24] Above, Ch. 3, at 62–4.

[25] Above, Ch. 7, at 194–7, and Merrill 1940: Ch. 5.

If we view the matter from the perspective of the judiciary as suppliers of property right development, the picture does not change much. Alternative property right rules for oil and gas were certainly available late in the nineteenth century. Justice Woodward's opinion in *Kier v. Peterson*[26] had already provided a basis for an argument that a producer, though not acting illegally, could be required to account to a neighbor for any oil shown to be drained from under the neighbor's land, and the ability to provide evidence of such drainage that a court might accept appears to have been established by the time the first capture case was decided. This avenue was never followed, and it was a different alternative rule, and one that would have made drainage illegal, that was offered for judicial consideration in the only direct challenge to the capture principle, in *Kelley v. Ohio Oil Co.* in 1897.[27] That was the claim that owners of rights to oil in the reservoir owed each other a duty of lateral support for the oil, so that neither could remove the oil at the boundary that was providing support for the neighbor's and preventing it from flowing away from under the neighbor's land. Although, in contrast to the other capture cases, well-grounded geological evidence was offered to the Ohio courts, they dismissed Kelley's claim without even deigning to mention this at least plausible argument. One suspects that the Ohio Supreme Court glimpsed in its mind's eye the chaos that might ensue if it turned oil property rights upside down in this way, and resolved to say absolutely nothing that could give the faintest encouragement to such an outcome.

A question that needs a little more consideration is why arguments like that based on lateral support were never raised in other states, where Ohio or Pennsylvania precedents were not binding and significant oil developments came much later. When *Kelley*'s case was decided in 1897, the United States' very substantial production came almost entirely from Pennsylvania, West Virginia, Ohio, and Indiana; the first significant production in Texas dates only from 1899, that in California from 1892. In 1899, these and other "new" oil states accounted for only 7.2 percent of crude oil produced.[28] Courts in these states thus had a relatively clean slate to work on; but courts can work only if litigants ask them to do so, and we have seen that oilmen in this phase of the industry's development apparently had little interest in litigating against one another. When relevant litigation did occur, normally between landowners rather than rival operators, and usually years after oil development began in a state, courts of these newer oil lands, without exception, embraced the rule of capture as part of the legal environment for oil exploration and production. Walter Summers, one of the earliest legal critics

---

[26] 41 Pa. 357 (1862).

[27] Above, n. 21.

[28] Williamson et al. 1963: 17.

of the rule, pictured such courts as justifying their decisions with the argument that oil development would otherwise be made impossible, by reason of the ability of landowners to stop their neighbors from drilling.[29] In fact, we do not find judges explicitly relying on this rationale, but it is impossible to believe that it exercised no influence on their decisions.

In principle, a court of a "new" oil state, in a case of first impression, might have chosen to adopt a different property rule than that applying elsewhere. Even if it based its decision rigidly on formal and doctrinal grounds alone, however, the chances that it might have taken such a course seem slim. Although by 1899 there was a not-too-distant precedent for applying the lateral support concept, the *Ambard* decision on pitch in Trinidad,[30] the rule of capture had a much better judicial pedigree: the existing American authorities may have been weak on reasoning, but they were unanimous; the principle had been recognized in relation to water at least since *Greenleaf v. Francis* in 1836; and the civil law, in the shape of the French Civil Code, spoke with the same voice as the common-law judges. Just as important, any political and economic considerations that might have entered the minds (or the unconscious) of the judges pointed in the same direction. The general trend of judicial decisionmaking on land use issues throughout most of the nineteenth century had been strongly in favor of facilitating agricultural, industrial, and mineral development,[31] but to rule against capture would have meant that whenever tracts were relatively small, landowners would be able to prevent or at least legally obstruct their neighbors' drilling for oil until they were ready to do so themselves, making the state's property law appear unfriendly to oil development. Given the tax revenues and economic prosperity that such development would bring, this was not a politically attractive position; and we should keep in mind that American judges, by reason of their backgrounds, their pathways to the bench (often by popular election or politically influenced appointment), and sometimes also their ambitions, were likely to be closely integrated into their state's political life. Certainly they would feel the heat of a politically embarrassing decision far more acutely than would the judges of the Privy Council who decided the *Ambard* case, issuing in London their rulings on appeals from remote colonies, uninformed by any direct experience of the conditions of life, or the political pressures, there prevailing.[32]

There was a further factor that the Privy Council judges did not need to trouble themselves with but would have weighed heavily on the mind of an American

---

[29] Summers 1919: 174.

[30] *Trinidad Asphalt Co. v. Ambard*, [1899] A.C. 594, above, Ch. 5.

[31] Hurst 1956; Scheiber 1973; Horwitz 1977: Chs. 2 and 3.

[32] Consider what actually happened in Trinidad after the *Ambard* decision, above, Ch. 5, at 130–3.

judge. Deciding against capture, and throwing the problem back to the legislature to fix, might not have worked at all. To make many existing and future oil and gas operations practicable, in the face of an *Ambard*-type finding, the legislator would have needed to force landowners into a scheme whereby oil and gas could be drawn by drainage from under their land even though they were unwilling to consent to such production. Even if such schemes were required to make provision for full compensation, they would constitute a deprivation of property in the sense of the Fifth and Fourteenth Amendments by the very fact of their taking away the landowner's right to decide whether to develop the land and, if so, when. It is therefore not at all surprising that the Federal Oil Conservation Board's Committee of Nine should in 1929 have summarily dismissed the possibility of replacing the rule of capture with a prohibition of cross-boundary drainage both as wholly impracticable, by reason of the "extensive and interminable litigation" it would provoke, and as subject to "serious constitutional objections."[33] What seems much more surprising is that someone (we do not know whom) was prepared to argue at this late date for the overturning of the industry's most basic legal rule. In the same year, the country's most experienced oil and gas lawyers, assembled in the American Bar Association's own Committee of Nine, opined that even compulsory pooling and unitization schemes, imposing similar constraints in the interests of eliminating competitive overdrilling, could not be constitutional.[34] They were eventually proved wrong, but a judge ruling against the application of the law of capture in a "new" oil state might well have condemned it to decades of exclusion from the benefits of oil and gas production.

What the early American legal development evidences, therefore, is not the innate rationality of the capture principle, but its emergence as the least worst solution in an environment shaped by accidents of time and place and by cultural and technological factors. The place of first discovery, coupled with American traditions and convictions regarding the acquisition and holding of property, led inexorably, and immediately, to landowner control of access and the identification of the activity of producing oil and gas with the sacred right to do as one wished with one's land. Initial ignorance of the underground behavior of oil and gas at first made "get what you can" the only practicable policy, and by the time it was realized that oil and gas, in their natural state, were in fact stable enough to be the subject of judicial protection, the immense structure of legal rights and obligations in oil and gas, erected on the basis of earlier ignorance, had closed off the path of property right reform and channeled the dissatisfaction of those who realized they were suffering prejudice through drainage into the alternative path of lease contract

---

[33] United States. Federal Oil Conservation Board 1929: 12.
[34] American Bar Association 1929: 751.

modification. Judicial choices had been preempted by a mass of individual decisions that began to be taken the day after Drake hit oil in Titusville.

PHASE 2: DIVERGENT DEVELOPMENT

Why Was the Rule Maintained in the United States?

If a simple reversal or denial of the capture principle seemed to be beyond judicial reach by 1900, its emasculation by other means remained a possibility. This was demonstrated by the U.S. Supreme Court in *Ohio Oil Co. v. Indiana*[35] within three years of the *Kelley* decision. By arguing from the position that an unrestrained law of capture meant that there could be no secure property rights in a common oil and gas reservoir, the court created a constitutional space for legislative intervention by states to control the practice of those exploring for and exploiting oil and gas, for the protection of the owners of interests in the reservoir, and perhaps for the prevention of waste in the interests of the general public also. The decision was thus of considerable importance in supporting the hitherto limited attempts of the original oil- and gas-producing states to enforce some basic conservation rules, and in providing a platform for the more general prohibitions of waste that began to appear in legislation from 1915 onward.

But in addition, an Indiana Supreme Court opinion handed down a few months later showed that the *Ohio Oil* decision could serve as a basis for recharacterizing the *common-law* rights in the oil and gas reservoir as necessarily incorporating interdependence among the different right holders, and thus as having that character of correlative rights that had already been recognized in relation to water resources.[36] This idea might have enabled the courts to anticipate the much later recognition by legislatures that the most important "correlative right" of the owner of oil lands is the opportunity to obtain one's just and equitable share of production from the reservoir.[37] The U.S. Supreme Court had provided the basis for such a judicial development in its *Ohio Oil* opinion, when it referred to behavior that "may result in an *undue proportion* being attributed to one of the possessors of the right, to the detriment of the others," and to the legislative purpose "of protecting all the collective owners, by securing a *just distribution*, to

---

[35] 177 U.S. 190 (1900), above, Ch. 7, at 181–4.

[36] *Manufacturers' Gas and Oil Co. v. Indiana Natural Gas and Oil Co.*, 155 Ind. 461, 57 N.E. 912 (1900).

[37] See statutes cited in Kellam 1960: 30–5.

arise from the enjoyment by them, of their privilege to reduce to possession, and to reach the like end by preventing waste."[38]

This development never happened. Few cases came before the courts, and no plaintiff ever tried to resist capture on the basis of the "just distribution" argument. In the cases that did arise, other courts moved away from the Indiana notion that correlative rights implied restrictions on production methods, and refused to impose liability for damage in the absence of proof of negligence. The stillbirth of common-law management of production through correlative rights may have owed something to judicial deference to industry practice, but it was also linked to a change of judicial mood and the reaction of oil companies to that change. The decades around the turn of the century were the time when, thanks largely though not exclusively to the power of the Standard Oil trust, popular suspicion of large resource corporations developed apace. Courts followed the trend: it is in this period, from around 1895 onward, that we start to find them vigorously reconstructing lease agreements so as to protect lessors from oil companies that tried to assemble blocks of leases and drill within these blocks only where it seemed efficient to do so. In the face of implied lease obligations of prompt and diligent development and offset drilling, it is not hard to see why even the larger companies, with systematic policies of acreage acquisition and development aimed at low-cost production, would resign themselves to drilling unnecessary offset wells rather than seek to resist capture by judicial means.

The platform for litigation offered by the *Ohio Oil* decision was a fragile and uncertain one; the penalties for failure might be the loss not only of oil to one's neighbor, but of the lease as well, so it seemed better just to drill. It also became apparent to percipient industry observers that even if courts had been offered, and had accepted, an invitation to put flesh on the bones of the Supreme Court's "just distribution" idea, the resulting body of rules and instances might have had less of the allure of Venus and more of the ill-stitched horrors of Frankenstein's monster.[39] Given the struggles of state regulatory commissions to formulate acceptable and efficient field rules even with the benefit of expert staff, open hearings, and quasi-legislative powers, it is hard to believe that courts, addressing individual disputes on the basis of adversarial evidence, could have achieved justice, efficiency, or predictability through the application of such a general principle.

With the path of common-law development away from capture effectively blocked, any correction of the rule's ill effects needed to come from legislators. In Galicia, Romania, and Russia, the legislator, not the judge, was already established

---

[38] 177 U.S. 190, at 210 (emphasis added).

[39] Smith 2004: 1033–7, and compare Hardwicke 1935: 410, discussing the cognate principle of "reasonable user," above, Ch. 7, at 186–7.

as the key agent for the development of the legal regime of the industry, with extensive legislative provision being made in Galicia in 1884, with further development in 1908; in Russia in 1892; and in Romania in 1895. These were countries of civil law inspiration, but a common-law system did not necessarily entail legislative inaction; we have noticed, in the early years of the twentieth century, the frenetic activity of Australian legislators and the early, if experimental, legislative interventions in the United Kingdom. The path of legislative reform in the United States was much more arduous, though this is hard to detect from Dean Lueck's assertion that statutory production controls like well spacing, prorationing, and compulsory unitization "emerged" as an adequate substitute for access restrictions and voluntary formation of units.[40] Their delivery was far more protracted and painful than this anodyne term suggests.

One key element that was missing until the 1910s was any specialized administrative machinery through which reform proposals might be generated and promoted. In Galicia, as a part of Austria-Hungary, a long history of state interest in and control of mining had produced a nineteenth-century mining administration capable of framing and implementing policies for rational and safe oil exploitation, but such capacities were totally absent at this time in the United States. Early regulations such as those relating to well plugging stemmed from isolated industry initiatives and were not seen to require any specialized administrative personnel to make them work. Official pressure for better oilfield practice in the early years of the industry came only from people like state geologists who enjoyed no powers beyond those of persuasion.

Industry participants, however, were not very amenable to persuasion. Passive in relation to their litigation opportunities, they were highly cautious, and sometimes aggressively hostile, in their approach to legislative reform. Pursuing with greater specificity the line of argument offered in general terms by Anthony Scott, Gary Libecap has argued, in relation to nineteenth-century silver mining in Nevada, that mine owners would push for greater precision in the legal rights structure only as long as they could see "private net gains" from doing so.[41] It seems clear that long after the absorption of the technical advantages offered by the better scientific understanding of reservoir behavior achieved before 1920, most oil operators failed to see that there was any "private net gain" to be obtained from pushing for legislative improvement of the rights structure for oil and gas, as opposed to temporary assistance in restricting production. They mistrusted their state legislators, feared federal intervention like the plague, and were convinced, until prices dived in the wake of the Seminole and Oklahoma City discoveries, that they

---

[40] Lueck 1995: 426n.
[41] Libecap 1978: 341.

could somehow work around the legal insecurity created by the rule of capture. Henry Doherty and later William Farish and E. W. Marland were among the few who were percipient enough to realize they could not, but the prorationing tide quickly drowned out their calls for a better rights structure, and the eventual success of prorationing in stabilizing oil prices gave unitization the appearance of a costly luxury rather than a natural and necessary arrangement.

As I argued in Chapter 9, the direct attack on capture by way of the attempt to impose compulsory unitization can hardly be termed a success. The requirement of high consent percentages among interest owners; the restriction of compulsory powers to secondary or tertiary operations, with no state yet ready to impose a general requirement to unitize exploration or primary development; and the fact that the largest-producing state continues to reject the notion altogether indicate the limited progress made over more than eight decades. Gary Libecap and Steven Wiggins have convincingly argued that this is at least in part because the same factors that prevent voluntary agreement to cooperate among interest holders also induce powerful opposition to appropriate corrective legislation.[42] Again, it is the private ownership system that both creates the problem of irrational and competitive development of reservoirs and provides the greatest obstacle to its solution. At the same time, it should be acknowledged that despite this blockage, the policy of more rational exploitation of oil and gas made steady if laborious progress in the first half of the twentieth century, through the action of state legislators and regulatory agencies in deploying "second-best" tools such as well spacing, gas–oil ratios, flaring constraints, and pooling. Indeed, as time went on, an ever-increasing number of oil states identified, as the general legal basis for these interventions, not only the need to reduce waste so far as possible, but also the principle, sketched in the *Ohio Oil* case, of recognizing and protecting the correlative rights of the owners of oil interests, notably "the opportunity afforded the owner of each property in a pool to produce, so far as it is reasonably practical to do so without waste, his just and equitable share of the oil or gas, or both, in the pool."[43] This is one formulation of a principle now expressed in various ways in the legislation of most oil states, often accompanied by more detailed stipulations to guide the state conservation agency in the protection of such rights.[44]

The development of a detailed and complex regulatory regime for oil and gas production, based on the twin principles of avoiding waste and protecting correlative rights (in some states, breach of correlative rights was treated as waste), eventually encouraged some people to think that maybe the rule of capture had

---

[42] Libecap and Wiggins 1985.
[43] Wyoming Statutes Annotated § 30-5-101 (a)(ix).
[44] Kellam 1960: 30–5.

been effectively abrogated. A Mr. and Mrs. Gruger, owners of a couple of small lots in an Oklahoma City suburb where oil production was restricted not just by state conservation laws, but also by a city zoning ordinance, tried without success to convince the Oklahoma Supreme Court of this in 1943. No, said the court, such laws do not abrogate the law of capture, but simply authorize administrative boards to issue orders that have the effect of regulating it or in a measure abrogating it.[45] The Dutch advocate general made the same mistake about the effects of the American regulatory regime as late as 2005.[46] Meanwhile, a number of attempts have been made by litigants to get the courts to apply the notion of "just and equitable share," in derogation of the rule of capture, by way of a generous interpretation of the reach of production regulations, notably through the backdating of pooling orders. With very rare exceptions, state courts have refused to weaken the impact of the rule of capture by this means.[47]

The Alternative: Undercutting Capture by Eliminating Private Ownership

Oil became a matter of strategic concern in the first years of the twentieth century, when Britain and the United States realized the major advantages of substituting it for coal as the fuel for their navies. Advisers to the British government, most notably Lord Cowdray, who had extensive experience with oil operations in the United States and Mexico, counseled strongly against allowing the development of American-style competitive drilling, with the waste and instability it brought in its wake. From the beginning of the century, therefore, imperial policy was to keep tight control of oil development in territories, including the mother country, that were being opened up for oil exploration.[48] It soon appeared that the most effective way of doing this was to hold the totality of property rights in oil and gas in the ground. This enabled the state to control the rate and location of exploration, promote competition among companies for acreage, and eliminate the wasteful side effects of the rule of capture through unitization where necessary.

In contrast to the United States, where the grants of enormous areas of public land made as settlement moved westward had incorporated no reservation of mineral rights (though a largely unsuccessful effort was made to identify "mineral lands" in advance and grant them out separately and at higher prices), nineteenth-century land policy in such places as Canada and Australia had involved substantial reservations of minerals, in terms broad enough to include petroleum, and these

---

[45] *Gruger v. Phillips Petroleum Co.*, 192 Okla. 259, 135 P.2d 485 (1943).

[46] Above, Ch. 11, at 365–6.

[47] Above, Ch. 9, at 295–7.

[48] Jones 1981; McBeth 1985.

reservations were largely completed by what were in effect nationalizations of any petroleum rights that remained in public hands.[49] Queensland was the first state to legislate in this sense in 1915; the United Kingdom followed in 1934. Analogous moves were made in other countries like the Netherlands and France, where rights to exploit minerals, including petroleum, had long been separated from surface ownership and held at the disposition of the state, but where exploration, anomalously, remained under the control of the surface owner.

These reforms caused little disturbance, because there was virtually no existing exploration or production activity at the time in the countries concerned, and no inconvenient constitutional protection of property rights either. Nationalizations that took place against the background of an established oil and gas industry naturally provoked a good deal more controversy, even if their effect, as in Romania in 1924, was simply to substitute a publicly granted concession for a private lease.[50] In Mexico, the constitution of 1917 announced the same kind of change in the legal basis for oil operations, a step resisted with such determination by the oil companies operating there (mostly American, but with a Royal Dutch Shell subsidiary as the biggest single producer) that it was never successfully implemented, with the consequence that the companies were totally expropriated, as to activities and assets as well as rights, by President Lazaro Cardenas in 1938.[51]

It is this displacement of private ownership, of the application of the accession principle to oil and gas, that has enabled almost all countries except the United States to escape the negative effects of the rule of capture: overinvestment and waste of oil and gas. In many cases, the change occurred for reasons that had nothing to do with the rule. The desire to eliminate existing foreign control of natural resources, or to forestall the risk that such control might appear in the future, has doubtless been the most common motivating factor. In a number of countries, however, it is clear that concerns about wasteful competition engendered by the operation of the rule have been a crucial or important consideration. The United Kingdom and Australia have been the examples analyzed in detail here, but the same concern is also evident in the Dutch and French moves to assert state control over exploration in the 1920s.

Whatever the motive for eliminating private ownership, however, it is clear that the change to a system of state control or ownership does not automatically displace the rule of capture. Everything depends upon the way in which the state administers its oil and gas estate and, notably, whether it chooses to secure development by inviting oil companies to compete for the rights to explore and

---

[49] See, for Canada, Scott 2008: 353–4; for Australia, Forbes and Lang 1987: 17–26.
[50] Pearton 1971: 112–25.
[51] Yergin 1991: 271–9.

exploit restricted parcels of onshore or offshore territory. Wherever this is done, the rule of capture may still operate. Instead of being an aspect of the surface owners' right to do whatever they like with their own land, it may become a component of the rights of exploitation that the state grants the company—by concession, lease, or contract—in respect of a given area of land or seabed. It is for the granting authority to decide whether to give its grantees rights to any petroleum they may recover by operations in their grant area or only to the petroleum that originally lay, undisturbed, beneath that area. If they choose the former course, as did the United Kingdom, United States, and Australia, the rule of capture will be retained; if the latter, as in the Netherlands, it will be eliminated.

The considerations of national pride and freedom from foreign economic domination or influence that commonly dictated major changes in public control of established—as opposed to possible future—private oil and gas rights could obviously find no place in the United States. (Nor, we should notice, were they influential in Galicia, where in the inter-war period the industry was in the hands of small, locally owned companies and property rights were not modified.)[52] The case for such radical changes to the system of property rights under which the great U.S. industry had grown to maturity would have to be based on the threat that its waste and inefficiency might pose to national strategic interests. Even at the height of concern about this issue, in the years during and after World War I, such an argument daunted even the most vigorous conservationists, whose arguments tended to stop short of recommending actual expropriation of surface owners' oil rights.[53] Among politicians, only President Woodrow Wilson's secretary of the navy, Josephus Daniels, a progressive Democrat who was already on record as favoring public ownership of armaments and munitions factories, dared to contemplate nationalization.[54] As we have seen, in the end, he achieved no more than the setting aside of some oil-bearing federal lands as a "national petroleum reserve," a half loaf that was possibly worse than no bread. Much of this federal land was checkerboarded with private holdings, whose lessees, benefiting from the rule of capture, gratefully set out to drain the reserves the navy was trying to hold.

In fact, the whole trend of American natural resource history has lain in the opposite direction: a steady movement of rights away from public and into private hands. The inconveniences of allowing surface owners even rights in hard rock minerals had been convincingly demonstrated, in the French National Assembly in

---

[52] Schaetzel 1938.

[53] Ise 1926: 496 (though favoring public ownership); Stocking 1925: 310–3 (favoring regulation, in particular to secure unitization).

[54] McBeth 1985: 57. Olien and Olien 2000: 131 say that the legislature of Minnesota (not an oil state) had the same idea.

1791, by Mirabeau, a man whose views—given his revolutionary sympathies—might have been expected to command a sympathetic hearing in the young American republic. Yet within a few decades, the idea that the government might retain and then lease the mineral interest, rather than dispose of it outright, was regarded as profoundly un-American, "foreign to the spirit of our race and the genius of our institutions,"[55] or even as derived from "the dark ages of the world, or from our Spanish neighbors, a nation that broiled Montezuma for his gold."[56] The authentic American sentiment on the matter was nowhere better demonstrated than in Texas, whose government steadily divested itself of the statewide mineral rights reserved to it under the Spanish landholding rules inherited from its former Mexican masters. Having given most of the rights away to its land grantees in the second half of the nineteenth century, in 1919 it went so far as to relinquish to the overlying surface owners or lessees the management of, and most of the revenue from, the remaining oil rights held on behalf of its public school system.

Even had there been any public demand or political will to embark on the expropriation of private oil interests, the constitution and its legal consequences would surely have provided an insurmountable obstacle. The program would have involved massive takings of property, requiring full compensation under the Fifth Amendment. The division of the property among hundreds of thousands of royalty and working interest owners, and the difficulty of placing values on partially developed or as yet undeveloped land, could have tied the industry up in a turmoil of regulation and litigation for decades to come.

A NEED FOR REFORM?

As a result of these varying historical trajectories, the rule of capture today will be found to occupy a different place in the legal scheme of oil and gas operations according to where they are conducted. In any country that has recognized state ownership of oil and gas resources, the rule, if not eliminated altogether, as in the Netherlands, functions as part of a system of conferring exploitation rights on companies by way of concessions, leases, or contracts. It is an element of the bundle of exploitation rights, to be exercised subject to a range of demanding regulatory controls, which often include an obligation to unitize production from shared fields. This is also the place occupied by capture in relation to the oil and gas resources owned by the federal government in the United States, both onshore and

---

[55] Counsel in *Moore v. Smaw*, 17 Cal. 199 (1861).
[56] Cited from an 1841 newspaper by Wright 1966: 80.

on the continental shelf. Broadly speaking, this is true of resources owned by state governments as well.[57]

Where privately owned oil and gas resources in the United States are concerned, however, the picture is very different. Capture, even if viewed only as a freedom from liability for taking one's neighbor's oil and not as a genuine right, continues to form part of the core notion of oil and gas property and determines title to any oil and gas that may be recovered unless and until its operation is displaced or restricted by decisions of state regulatory agencies, notably those imposing well spacing or pooling requirements, enforcing compulsory unitization, or otherwise restricting production. Because capture ceases to be a factor only when the operation of a field is fully unitized, the apparently limited reach of unitization— voluntary or compulsory—of privately held oil reservoirs means that the rule of capture may continue to influence the production of much, maybe most, of the oil and gas from such reservoirs.

Finally, I should mention the status of the rule in international law. The number of maritime boundaries remaining to be determined and the possibility that contested or unallocated maritime areas may be rich in hydrocarbons—a possibility dramatized by gestures like the planting of the Russian flag in the seabed under the North Pole in 2007[58]—means that we cannot write off the international context for capture as of merely marginal relevance. Here there appears to be a developing consensus, expressed alike in state practice, doctrinal opinion, and judicial and arbitral decisions (though apparently not shared by some American lawyers), that the primary rule for the exploration and exploitation of disputed or cross-border deposits is one of cooperation, and that it is only if cooperation is unreasonably refused that a party might be able to exploit such a deposit unilaterally despite the risk or likelihood of capture. In my opinion, even this limited resort to the capture principle is ruled out, if there has been a delimitation agreement, by the basic rule of international law allocating rights to seabed resources, but even if this is wrong, it is clear that capture's effective role in this area is rather as a lever in negotiations than as a primary legal rule.

This, in brief, is what the law of capture means today for the oil and gas industry. In light of the unkind things that have been said about it over the 80 years or so since the term was coined, should we be worried about the extent and manner of its continuing survival? In these first years of the twenty-first century, we are faced with concerns about the future availability of oil that echo those that gave rise to the American conservation debates of a hundred years ago. Today we certainly cannot project the future of oil supplies with the optimism displayed by the

---

[57] On the position in Texas, see above, Ch. 9, n. 199.

[58] Goozee 2009.

Committee of Eleven in 1925.[59] While there are wide variations of opinion as to when world oil production might peak, and after it peaks, how fast it might decline,[60] there can be no doubt that this century will see, sooner or later, a major shift away from our current reliance on oil. The major policy issues raised by this scenario are beyond the scope of this book, but one uncontroversial implication is the need to reduce to the minimum the possibility of waste in current and future production.

Seen in this light, it is only the role of capture in relation to onshore, privately held U.S. oil resources that gives grounds for real concern. Where resources are state-owned, in the United States just as elsewhere, the rule can be readily changed or reversed by modifying the terms on which leases, licenses, or concessions are granted. There are no legal obstacles to doing this in future grants, and depending on the degree of constitutional protection given to exploitation rights in any particular country and the way the grants regime is legally structured, it may be possible even to modify the relevant conditions of existing grants, as by extending requirements for compulsory unitization.[61] It is not obvious, though, that where the rule of capture presently functions as part of a state system, any advantage would flow from eliminating it. Capture can help promote states' goals of achieving early and thorough exploitation, as a natural incentive alongside the various detailed controls—such as minimum work program expenditures—found in most state regimes. Where a role for capture is retained—by offering blocks of acreage small enough to make cross-block reservoirs a likely occurrence, granting leases and concessions in terms that do not exclude capture, and making the exercise of compulsory unitization powers dependent on a showing that ultimate recovery will be impaired by competitive development—the first company to reach development stage on a shared cross-block reservoir can secure significant positional advantages.

Where a state regime is held to exclude capture, as was decided by the Dutch Supreme Court in its *Unocal* decision in 2005,[62] the effect is both to eliminate this natural, if marginal, incentive to vigorous exploration and to make the exploitation of the state's oil and gas estate harder to manage. A company holding a license or lease giving impregnable rights to the petroleum in place under its block would be able to prevent drilling by its neighbors until it was ready to develop itself. The weapon of unitization might then have to be employed to force rather than control

---

[59] Above, Ch. 9, at 241–3.

[60] A recent survey of the debate is offered by UK Energy Research Centre 2009.

[61] For a comparative analysis of this issue in four such systems (the federal offshore regimes of Australia, Canada, and the United States, and the UK regime), see Daintith 2006.

[62] Above, Ch. 11, at 362–7.

development, a much more awkward option. This seems to subject the state to a quite unnecessary handicap in a situation where, having already opened acreage and granted licenses, it must be presumed to desire prompt and efficient production. The switch might have less significance in the growing number of countries that manage private or foreign investment in their oil exploration and production efforts by means of production-sharing contracts or other forms of service agreements rather than through concessions or leases, by reason of the greater day-to-day control of operations that these contracts can confer, a control which makes resort to formal devices like compulsory unitization less necessary. In general, in state ownership jurisdictions a continuing possibility of capture is likely to have negative effects, such as wasteful production, only if the state regulatory authorities are lax in exercising their powers to compel unitization or otherwise control production.

In international law, too, the surviving influence, if any, of capture would appear to be relatively benign. Unless international tribunals move away from the positions announced in the recent case of *Guyana v. Suriname*,[63] a cooperative approach to oil and gas production operations will be required even in disputed boundary areas, and where boundaries have been settled, such cooperation will ordinarily be imposed by the cross-border deposit provisions of the relevant delimitation treaties. In either case, the possibility that, in the event of sustained failure to cooperate, unilateral action by the party desiring to develop might be held legitimate and cross-border capture of resources might occur should help in drawing reluctant parties to the negotiating table. Naturally, if future tribunals accept the more radical exclusion of the capture principle for which I argued in Chapter 12, this incentive may in certain cases be removed, and potential subsea oil and gas resources may go unexplored, and unexploited, for a longer time. We can console ourselves with the thought that if this flattens, even slightly, the anticipated peak in oil production, it might be no bad thing.

One cannot be so sanguine about the rule of capture's third and most important area of operation: privately owned U.S. oil and gas resources. The rule and the accession system of mineral property holding that gives it relevance and force are clearly a cause of waste in oil and gas production. The exploration and initial development of oilfields continue to be shaped not by the characteristics of the reservoirs, but by the patterns of surface property lines. Although opportunities for capture will normally be restricted by the imposition of field spacing rules or the operation of the state's general well spacing regulations, accompanied if necessary by pooling requirements,[64] they will not be wholly eliminated unless the field is

---

[63] Above, Ch. 12, at 396.

[64] For the special case of Pennsylvania, see above, Ch. 9, at 294–5.

comprehensively unitized. As we have seen, achieving this on a voluntary basis can be difficult or impossible, while possibilities of compulsory unitization are severely limited by high consent thresholds and by statutory criteria that tend to rule out its imposition at the exploration or first development stages, when it could be most useful. The evils this situation produces are rather different from those that were attributed to the capture rule back in the 1920s. Today high costs of drilling, exposure to unstable world oil prices, and the early imposition of spacing rules on newly discovered fields mean that frenetic, capture-fueled races for flush production are a thing of the past. Yet it remains as true as it was in 1930 that, as the Federal Oil Conservation Board then pointed out, "[c]odes of laws and judicial decisions relating to oil deposits [accord] to the surface checkerboard a sanctity quite beyond its deserts."[65]

The result has been that many, maybe most, oil and gas reservoirs have been and continue to be developed in a suboptimal fashion, so that something less than maximum economic recovery of oil and gas is achieved. It is, in other words, the accession system itself that is the direct cause of underrecoveries. The rule of capture, its inseparable companion, has been rendered relatively inoffensive by decades of regulation. That regulation diminishes the need to modify the rule and, at the same time, makes any such modification highly problematic because it assumes the operation of the rule, not its absence. Regular spacing patterns for wells are certain not to correspond perfectly with the highly variable well catchment areas, but they produce approximate justice by allowing reciprocal capture. At this stage, therefore, the rule of capture is best left alone, though this certainly does not mean that new applications of the rule, like that endorsed in the *Garza* case[66] so as to permit competitive fracing, should be uncritically accepted.

As for the accession system itself, there is a high road and there is a low road leading to solution of the problems it creates. To take the high road would demand the replacement of the system with one of public ownership and control of oil and gas in the ground, following the example of almost every other country. This prospect was never even thought about when problems of waste and security of supply were at their most acute and dramatic in the years just after World War I, and there is no reason to assume it could happen now. The political difficulties dwarf even the constitutional ones to which I have already referred. It is hard to see how royalty owners, now numbering in the millions thanks to the continual subdivision of interests through dealings and inheritance,[67] could fail in resisting

---

[65] United States. Federal Oil Conservation Board 1930: 19.

[66] Above, Ch. 9, at 299–302.

[67] Anderson and Smith 1999. Figures of 5 million and 8.5 million are claimed in different parts of the National Association of Royalty Owners' website, www.naro-us.org (visited October 12, 2009).

the expropriation of their rights in the service of an unquantifiable boost to domestic oil and gas production. These are people who proclaim themselves to be "the citizens who own our country's natural resources,"[68] a statement that would be perceived as an oxymoron anywhere outside the United States, and who retain a considerable attachment to their ownership rights despite the fact that for many of them, monthly royalty checks may be for no more than single-digit amounts. The need for the United States to be as efficient as possible in its exploitation of onshore resources, and thereby to limit the greatly increased risks involved in getting oil from ever more difficult deepwater locations, was resoundingly demonstrated by the Deepwater Horizon explosion and oil spill in the Gulf of Mexico in April 2010;[69] but the incident, occurring as it did in federal waters under the supervision of the Interior Department's Minerals Management Service, is hardly calculated to encourage Americans to place more of their oil and gas resources under public management.

Faced with such obstacles, one might consider the low road the obvious choice, were it not for the fact that this is the one that reformers have been struggling along for the last 80 years or so: the road of compulsory unitization. Nevertheless, because this appears to be the sole available path toward improvement, progress along it, however painful, needs to continue. Often the barriers seem too big to climb or get around, as when the Texas legislature rejected in 1999 the most recent attempt to get the state to adopt some kind of compulsory unitization law. It comes as no surprise to learn that Texas royalty owners, acting through their chapter of the National Association of Royalty Owners, were active in the coalition that successfully opposed the bill,[70] though a grain of comfort is offered by the fact that the Texas Independent Producers and Royalty Owners Association was one of its proponents. Thanks to the Marcellus Shale, Pennsylvania is about to reemerge as a major gas producer after a hundred years in the doldrums, yet there is no sign that its legislators are contemplating any change in its position as the only other state without compulsory unitization powers. Every so often, some more substantial advance is achieved, as when the Interstate Oil and Gas Compact Commission (IOGCC) for the first time included a compulsory exploratory unitization clause in the December 2004 version of its Model Oil and Gas Conservation Act.[71] No state has yet adopted the clause, but at least the idea, urged

---

[68] See the logo of the National Royalty Owners' Association, at www.naro-us.org.

[69] Documented in http://en.wikipedia.org/wik/Deepwater_Horizon_oil_spill.

[70] NARO-Texas News, February 2004 (at texas.naro-us.org).

[71] Interstate Oil and Gas Compact Commission 2004. For commentary, see Anderson and Smith 2004.

by reservoir engineers since the 1930s, now enjoys the endorsement of a body broadly representative of the public interest in oil and gas conservation.

There is a further path-clearing measure that the IOGCC might do well to consider. Part of the problem faced by the campaign for unitization is that there still appears to be no way of quantifying the advantages that have flowed from unitization, or might flow from it in the future, simply because no one knows how much of U.S. production is unitized. Among six major producing states—Texas, Alaska, California, Oklahoma, Louisiana, and Wyoming—the only regulatory authority that was able to provide a response to this question was the Alaska Oil and Gas Conservation Commission.[72] Given that virtually all of Alaska's oil and gas is owned by the federal or state governments, its very high unitization figure says nothing about what might have happened in other states. The recordkeeping systems of other state regulatory commissions may make even the identification of unitization orders difficult, and where this is possible, they may still need to be correlated with field production data, often collected only by private organizations,[73] in order to get a sense of the magnitude of unitized production. This was the laborious process that Libecap and Wiggins had to undertake in preparing their 1985 study, which still stands as the only quantitative indicator of progress in unitization, and that in only three states.[74]

A project under the auspices of IOGCC to link unitization decisions with production data at the field level could provide some much-needed basic information, telling the proponents of unitization just how far they have traveled along their difficult path. If meaningful productivity comparison between unitized and nonunitized fields can be developed, it could also tell them just how worthwhile was the struggle to get this far and what may be the rewards for continuing. This might not do much to convince recalcitrant interest holders of the benefits of unitization to them personally, but it could well lend some conviction and urgency to attempts to lead state legislators down the road to earlier and easier unitization. If asking for better information seems a feeble response to the continuing problems of organizing oil and gas production, it should be remembered that it was the lack of technical knowledge that first set the industry on its wasteful path, and resistance to new knowledge, in the 1920s, that kept it there.

---

[72] Above, Ch. 9, at 292–3.

[73] Production statistics for the 100 largest fields are, however, collected and published by the Energy Information Administration: see United States. Energy Information Administration 2009: App. B.

[74] Above, Ch. 9, at 292–3.

REFERENCES

ARCHIVAL MATERIALS

Australia

National Archives of Australia, Canberra
Series A518 (Department of National Development/Department of Industry)

Western Australia State Records Office, Perth
Cons. 129
Cons. 3712, Petroleum—General (1901–1919)
Cons. 3712, Petroleum—General Vol. III (1923–1953)

United Kingdom

National Archives, Kew
FO series 104
FO series 371
POWE series 62

United States

Drake Well Museum and Archive, Titusville, Pennsylvania
Heydrick papers, DW.76.37
Stralko collection of Venango County Court papers, DW.70.06
Unclassified lease collection

Los Angeles County Records
Misc. R, Vol. 1

West Virginia and Regional History Collection, West Virginia University, Morgantown
Levassor papers, A & M No. 1363
W. C. Stiles family oil and mining company records, A & M No. 199

BOOKS, PERIODICALS, AND REPORTS

Abramowski, J. 1995. Mexican Energy Laws. *Journal of Energy and Natural Resources Law* 13: 29–39.

ACIL Consulting. 2000. National Competition Policy Review of the Petroleum (Submerged Lands) Legislation: Report to the Petroleum (Submerged Lands) Review Committee, Canberra, Australia.

Adams, J. S. 1915. The Right of a Landowner to Oil and Gas in His Land. *University of Pennsylvania Law Review* 63: 471–489.

Adelman, M. A. 1972. *The World Petroleum Market.* Baltimore: John Hopkins Press for Resources for the Future.

Aguillon, L.-C.-M. 1890. De la concessibilité du pétrole en France. *Revue de la législation des mines* 7: 65–73.

———. 1912. *Législation des mines en France.* Paris: Ch. Berenger.

American Bar Association, Section of Mineral Law. 1928. Proceedings. *Annual Report of the American Bar Association* 1928: 633–638.

———. 1929. Report of Committee on Conservation of Mineral Resources. *Annual Report of the American Bar Association* 1929: 741–770.

———. 1938. *Legal History of Conservation of Oil and Gas.* Chicago: American Bar Association.

American Petroleum Institute. 1925. *American Petroleum: Supply and Demand. A Report to the Board of Directors of the American Petroleum Institute by a Committee of Eleven Members of the Board.* New York: McGraw-Hill Book Co.

———. 1930. *Petroleum Facts and Figures.* American Petroleum Institute, [no place stated].

Anderson, O. L. 1982a. David v. Goliath: Negotiating the 'Lessor's 88' and Representing Lessors and Surface Owners in Oil and Gas Lease Plays. *Rocky Mountain Mineral Law Institute* 27B: 1029–1331.

———. 1982b. Compulsory Pooling in North Dakota: Should Production Income and Expenses Be Divided from Date of Pooling, Spacing, or 'First Runs'? *North Dakota Law Review* 58: 537–574.

Anderson, O. L., and E. E. Smith. 1999. The Use of Law to Promote Domestic Exploration and Production. *Institute on Oil and Gas Law and Taxation (Southwestern Legal Foundation)* 50: 2-1–2-95.

———. 2004. Exploratory Unitization under the 2004 Model Oil and Gas Conservation Act: Leveling the Playing Field. *Journal of Land, Resources, and Environmental Law* 24: 277–292.

Andrassy, J. 1951. Les Relations Internationales de Voisinage. *Recueil des Cours de l'Académie de Droit International* 79: 73–182.

Angermann, C. 1905. The Need for a Rational Oil Field Law. *Petroleum World* 3: 612–613.

Anon. 1865. Important Proceeding of Oil Producers and Landowners. *Oil City Register.* Oil City, PA, June 8, 1865.

———. 1873. Washburn on Easements (3rd ed.): Review. *American Law Review* 8: 343–346.

———. 1882. Petroleum: Chapter III. *Petroleum Age* 1(3): 84–87.

———. 1899a. The Method of Leasing Petroleum Lands in Russia. *Petroleum Review* 1: 614.

———. 1899b. Right of Support. *Harvard Law Review* 13: 299–300.

———. 1900. New Regulations for Leasing Petroleum Lands in Russia. *Petroleum Review* 3: 196.

———. 1903. Boryslaw. The Oil Field of 1903. *Petroleum World* 1: 5–6.

———. 1906. The Galician Petroleum Association in 1905. *Petroleum Review* 14: 295.

———. 1908a. The Condition of the Galician Petroleum Industry. *Petroleum Review* 19: 139–141, 181–182, 199–200, 227–228.

———. 1908b. Saratoga Springs 'Doctored,' He Says. *New York Times.* April 16, 1908.

———. 1909. [Petroleum Department in Baku.]. *Petroleum Review* 22: 216.

———. 1910. The Significance of Government Oil Land Auctions. *Petroleum Review* 23: 173–174.

———. 1927. Comment. *Texas Law Review* 5: 328–329.

———. 1929. The Story of Asphalt. *Bulletin of the Business Historical Society* 3(3): 9–14.

———. 2003. Iraq and Kuwait Vie for Control of Contested Oil Field. *World War 4 Report,* issue 70 (deleted web page on file with author).

———. 2005. Iraqis Accuse Kuwait of Stealing Oil. *World War 4 Report.* www.ww4report.com/node/868. Accessed November 2008.

———. 2010. Deepwater Horizon oil spill. http://en.wikipedia.org/wik/Deepwater_Horizon_oil_spill. Accessed June 2010.

Arkansas Oil and Gas Commission. n.d. Secondary Recovery of Petroleum in Arkansas: A Survey, Arkansas Oil and Gas Commission.

Asbury, H. 1942. *The Golden Flood: An Informal History of America's First Oil Field*. New York: Alfred A. Knopf.

Association of International Petroleum Negotiators. 2006. Model Form International Unitization and Unit Operating Agreement, Houston, Association of International Petroleum Negotiators.

Astruc, L. 1933. *Du régime légal de la propriété des sources d'eau minérales*. Doctoral thesis, Montpellier: University of Montpellier.

Australia. Department of Industry, Science and Resources. 1999. Australian Offshore Petroleum Strategy: A Strategy to Promote Petroleum Exploration and Development in Australian Offshore Areas, Canberra.

———. Department of National Development. 1967. Petroleum (Submerged Lands) Bill 1967: Explanatory Notes, Canberra.

———. Department of Resources, Energy and Tourism. 2008. Australia: Release of Offshore Exploration Areas 2008 (CD-ROM), Canberra.

———. Industry Commission. 1991. Mining and Minerals Processing in Australia, Parliamentary Papers 1991, nos. 103–106. Canberra.

Australian Petroleum Production and Exploitation Association (APPEA). 2008. *Key Statistics*. At www.appea.com.au/content/pdfs_docs_xls/Statistics/key_stats_2008_6.pdf. Accessed October 2009.

Austria-Hungary. Kommission zur Untersuchung der Betriebsverhältnisse des Erdölbergbaues in Galizien (1904). Ergebnisse der vom kk Ackerbauministerium im Jahre 1903 eingesetzten Kommission zur Untersuchung der Betriebsverhältnisse des Erdölbergbaues in Galizien. Wien.

Bainbridge, W. 1878. *A Treatise on the Law of Mines and Minerals*. London: Butterworths.

Ball, M. W. 1916. Petroleum Withdrawals and Restorations Affecting the Public Domain, Washington, U.S. Government Printing Office.

———. 1917. *Adequate Acreage and Oil Conservation*. London: McCorquodale.

Barraqué, B. 2001–2002. Le marché de l'eau et le *wheeling* en Californie. *Gestion Integrée des Ressources en Eau à l'Echelle Mondiale*. Paris: Ecole Nationale des Ponts et Chaussées.

Barringer, D. M., and J. S. Adams. 1897. *The Law of Mines and Mining in the United States*. Boston: Little, Brown and Co.

Bartley, E. R. 1953. *The Tidelands Oil Controversy: A Legal and Historical Analysis*. Austin: University of Texas Press.

Bastida, A. E., et al. 2007. Cross-Border Unitization and Joint Development Agreements: An International Law Perspective. *Houston Journal of International Law* 29: 355–422.

Bates, J. L. 1957. Fulfilling American Democracy: The Conservation Movement, 1907 to 1921. *Mississippi Valley Historical Review* (June1957): 29–57.

———. 1963. *The Origins of Teapot Dome: Progressives, Parties and Petroleum, 1909–1921.* Urbana: University of Illinois Press.

Bates, S. P. 1899. *Our County and Its People: A Historical and Memorial Record of Crawford County Pennsylvania.* [Boston?]: W.A. Fergusson and Co.

Beates, S. J. 2007. Oilyoute to Triumph Hill: A Story of the Tidioute Oil Excitement. *Oil Field Journal* 6: 56–76.

Beeby Thompson, A. 1904. *The Oil Fields of Russia and the Russian Petroleum Industry.* London: Crosby Lockwood.

———. 1906. Annual Reports 1906–1910: Pamphlet No. 12 *The Oil-Fields of Trinidad.* London: West India Committee.

———. 1961. *Oil Pioneer.* London: Sidgwick and Jackson.

Benazé, L. de 1893. *Sur le régime légal des eaux minérales ou thermales naturelles.* Paris: A. Giard et E. Brière.

Bennett, A. P. 1897. Roumania. Reports from H.M. Diplomatic and Consular Officers Abroad on Subjects of Commercial and General Interest, C. 8278: 1897 Parl. Pap. LXXXVII: 937–965.

Bennett, J. C. 2001. Ownership of Transmigratory Minerals. *Journal of Land, Resources, and Environmental Law* 21: 349–396.

Bentz, A. 1938. Germany: Organization of Production, Treatment, and Distribution of Mineral Oil and Final Products. In *Transactions Third World Power Conference: The National Power Economy.* Vol. IV. Edited by O. C. Merrill. Washington, DC: U.S. Government Printing Office, pp. 93–107.

Blackstone, Sir W. 1765–1769. *Commentaries on the Law of England.* Oxford.

Blainey, G. 2003. *The Rush That Never Ended: A History of Australian Mining.* Melbourne: Melbourne University Press.

Blair, J. M. 1977. *The Control of Oil.* London: Macmillan.

Blake, G. H., R. E. Swarbrick, et al. 1998. Hydrocarbons and International Boundaries: A Global Overview. In *Boundaries and Energy: Problems and Prospects.* Edited by G. H. Blake. London: Kluwer Law International, pp. 3–25.

Blakey, E. S. 1985. *Oil on Their Shoes: Petroleum Geology to 1918.* Tulsa: American Association of Petroleum Geologists.

Blanchard, N.C., et al., eds. 1909. *Proceedings of a Conference of Governors in the White House, Washington DC, May 13–15 1908.* Washington, DC: U.S. Government Printing Office.

Blauhorn, J., ed. 1910. *Das Recht der Rohölgewinnung in Oesterreich. Vol. 1, Die Gesetze und Ministerial-Verordnungen.* Berlin: Verlag für Fachliteratur.

Blavoux, B. 1998. La formation des gisements d'eau minérale. *Réalites Industrielles* (Mai): 8–12.

Blinn, K. W., C. Duval, et al. 1986. *International Petroleum Exploration and Exploitation Agreements: Legal, Economic and Policy Aspects.* London: Euromoney Publications.

Bliven Petroleum Company. 1865. *Prospectus.* New York.

Blumm, M. C., and L. Ritchie. 2005. The Pioneer Spirit and the Public Trust: The American Rule of Capture and State Ownership of Wildlife. *Environmental Law Review* 35: 673–720.

Boatner, Y. 1938. Legal History of Conservation of Oil and Gas in Louisiana. In *Legal History of Conservation of Oil and Gas.* American Bar Association Section of Mineral Law, Chicago: American Bar Association, pp. 60–74.

Bone, J. H. A. 1865. *Petroleum and Petroleum Wells.* Philadelphia: B. Lippincott and Co.

Borromeu de Andrade, C. C. 1989. Some Key Aspects of the Brazilian Legal Framework on Energy and Natural Resources. *Journal of Energy and Natural Resources Law* 7: 231–237.

Bouquet, J.-P. 1855. *Histoire Chimique des Eaux Minérales et Thermales de Vichy, Cusset, Vaisse, Hauterive et Saint-Yorre.* Paris: Victor Masson.

Bouvet, J.-P. 1997. *L'unité de gisement.* Doctoral thesis. Paris, University Paris 2. (Also published (2004) Paris, L'Harmattan.).

Bouvier, J. 1870. *Institutes of American Law.* Philadelphia: George W Childs.

Boyle, P. C., ed. 1898. *The Derrick's Handbook of Petroleum.* Vol. 1. Oil City, PA: Derrick Publishing Co.

———. 1900. *The Derrick's Handbook of Petroleum.* Vol. 2. Oil City, PA: Derrick Publishing Co.

BP. 2008. *BP Statistical Review of World Energy June 2008.* London: BP plc.

Bradley, R. 1996. *Oil, Gas and Government: The US Experience.* Lanham, MD; London: Rowman & Littlefield Publishers.

Brantly, J. E. 1971. *History of Oil Well Drilling.* Houston, Texas: Gulf Publishing.

Brereton, B. 1981. *A History of Modern Trinidad, 1783–1962.* London: Heinemann.

Brin, P. 1934. Comment: Oil and Gas—The Spacing Rule of the Railroad Commission— Rule 37. *Texas Law Review* 13: 119–130.

British Institute of International and Comparative Law. 1989. *Joint Development of Offshore Oil and Gas.* London: British Institute of International and Comparative Law.

Brown, R. C. 1885. *History of Crawford County, Pennsylvania.* Chicago: Warner, Beers & Co.

Bruce, J. G. 1966. The Continental Shelf Exercise: History of Departmental Experience, Department of Energy, United Kingdom National Archives, POWE 62/11.

Bryan, G. 1898. *The Law of Petroleum and Natural Gas, with Forms.* Philadelphia: George T. Bisel.

Buckland, W. W. 1963. *A Textbook of Roman Law from Augustus to Justinian.* Cambridge: Cambridge University Press.

Budd, H. 1891. The Law of Subterranean Waters. *American Law Register* 39: 237–265.

Bundy, R. K. 1995. Natural Resource Development (Oil and Gas) and Boundary Disputes. In *The Peaceful Management of Transboundary Resources.* Edited by G. H. Blake, London: Graham and Trotman/Martinus Nijhoff, pp. 23–39.

Bunter, M. A. G. 2002a. *Geopolitical, Economic, Legal and Technical Aspects of the Early Search for Hydrocarbons in Great Britain.* Dundee: University of Dundee, Centre for Energy, Petroleum and Mineral Law and Policy.

———. 2002b. *The Promotion and Licensing of Petroleum Prospective Acreage.* The Hague: Kluwer Law International.

Burner, D., et al. 2001. Calvin Coolidge. In *The Oxford Companion to United States History.* Edited by P. S. Boyer, et al. New York: Oxford University Press, pp. 160–161.

Burney, P. H., and N. J. Hyne. 1998. Hydraulic Fracturing: Stimulating Your Well or Trespassing? *Rocky Mountain Mineral Law Institute* 44: 19-1–19-63.

Buzatu, G. 1998. *O istorie a petrolului românesc.* Editura Enciclopedica, Bucharest.

Campbell, Jr, N. J. 1956. Principles of Mineral Ownership in the Civil Law and Common Law Systems. *Tulane Law Review* 31: 303–312.

Cancrin, F. L. von 1825. *Jurisprudence générale des mines en Allemagne.* Paris: chez Adrien Egron.

Carll, J. F. 1880. *The Geology of the Oil Regions of Warren, Venango, Clarion and Butler Counties.* Board of Commissioners for the Second Geological Survey, Harrisburg, PA.

Carmichael, G. 1961. *The History of the West Indian Islands of Trinidad and Tobago.* London: Alvin Redman.

Carr, W. F. 2003. Compulsory Fieldwide Unitization. *Rocky Mountain Mineral Law Institute* 49: 21-1–21-26, plus appendix.

Chambriard, P. 1998. L'embouteillage d'eaux minérales: quatre siècles d'histoire. *Réalites Industrielles* (Mai): 20–29.

———. 1999. *Aux sources de Vichy. Naissance et développement d'un bassin thermal (XIXe–XXe siècles).* St Pourçain-sur-Sioule, Bleu Autour.

Chernow, R. 1998. *Titan: The Life of John D. Rockefeller Sr.* London: Little Brown.

Churchill, R., M. Nordquist, et al., eds. 1977. *New Directions in the Law of the Sea.* New York: Oceana.

Clark, J. A., and M. T. Halbouty. 1952. *Spindletop.* New York: Random House.

Clayberg, J. N. 1915. The Law of Percolating Waters. *Michigan Law Review* 14: 119–135.

Cogan, J. P. J., and K. S. Culotta. 1992. The Eternal Triangle from a Texas Perspective. In *Energy and Resources Law '92.* International Bar Association Section of Energy and Resources Law, London: Graham and Trotman, pp. 614–626.

Cohen, J. G. 1926. *Le Régime des Mines et du Pétrole en Roumanie.* Imprimerie Moderne, Agen.

Colby, W. E. 1915. The New Public Land Policy with Special Reference to Oil Lands. *California Law Review* 3: 269–291.

Colson, D. 1993. The Legal Regime of Maritime Boundary Agreements. In *International Maritime Boundaries.* Vol. 1. Edited by J. I. Charney and L. M. Alexander. Leiden/Boston: Martinus Nijhoff, pp. 41–74.

Columbia Oil Company. 1863. Third Annual Report of the President and Directors to the Stockholders of the Columbia Oil Company, Pittsburgh.

Sir Conan Doyle, A. 1894. *The Memoirs of Sherlock Holmes.* London: George Newnes.

Cone, A., and W. R. Johns. 1870. *Petrolia: A Brief History of the Pennsylvania Petroleum Region, Its Development, Growth, Resources, Etc., from 1859 to 1869.* New York: D. Appleton and Co.

Conybeare, C. E. B. 1980. *Oil Search in Australia.* Canberra: Australian National University Press.

Cooley, T. M. 1868. *A Treatise on the Constitutional Limitations Which Rest upon the Legislative Power of the States of the American Union.* Boston: Little, Brown.

———. 1876. Incidental Injuries from the Exercise of Lawful Rights. *Albany Law Journal* 14: 57–63.

Corley, T. A. B. 1983. *A History of the Burmah Oil Company, 1886–1924.* London: Heinemann.

Coy, O. C. 1929. *The Humboldt Bay Region, 1850–1875: A Study in the American Colonization of California.* Los Angeles: California State Historical Association.

Craft, R. L. 1996. Of Reservoir Hogs and Pelt Fiction: Defending the *Ferae Naturae* Analogy between Petroleum and Wildlife. *Emory Law Journal* 44: 697–733.

Craig, D. 1991. Commentary on Unitisation: The Commonwealth Offshore Legislative Framework. *Australian Mining and Petroleum Law Association Yearbook* 1991: 481–496.

Craig, E. H. C. 1914. *Oil-Finding: An Introduction to the Geological Study of Petroleum.* London: Edward Arnold.

Crommelin, M. 1975. Government Management of Oil and Gas in Alberta. *Alberta Law Review* 13: 146–211.

———. 1986. The U.S. Rule of Capture: Its Place in Australia. *Australian Mining and Petroleum Law Association Yearbook*: 265–281.

———. 2008. Oil and Gas Management and Revenues in Australia. In *Forum of Federations Conference on Oil and Gas Management and Revenues in Federations.* Canada: Edmonton, October 10–11, 2008.

Cueto-Rua, J. 1975. Abuse of Rights. *Louisiana Law Review* 35: 965–1014.

Daddow, S. H., and B. Bannan. 1866. *Coal, Iron and Oil, or the Practical American Miner.* Pottsville, PA: Benjamin Bannan.

Daintith, T. 1978. Correlative Rights in Oil Reservoirs on the United Kingdom Continental Shelf. *European Offshore Petroleum Conference.* London.

———. 2000. A Critical Evaluation of the Petroleum (Submerged Lands) Act as a Regulatory Regime. *Australian Mining and Petroleum Law Association Yearbook*: 91–137.

———. 2006. *Discretion in the Administration of Offshore Oil and Gas: A Comparative Study.* Melbourne: AMPLA Ltd.

Daintith, T., G. Willoughby, et al. 2010. *United Kingdom Oil and Gas Law*. 3rd ed., looseleaf. London: Sweet and Maxwell.

Dal Bó, E. 2006. Regulatory Capture: A Review. *Oxford Review of Economic Policy* 22: 203–226.

Dalton, L. V. 1909. The Geology of the Baku and European Oil Fields. *Petroleum World*, 238d–240, 268–269, 300–301.

Darrah, W. C. 1972. *Pithole, The Vanished City*. [Gettysburg?], Author.

Daubree, A. 1887. *Les Eaux souterraines … 1 … A l'époque actuelle: leur régime, leur température, leur composition au point de vue du rôle qui leur revient dans l'économie de l'écorce terrestre*. Paris: Vve Ch. Dunod.

David, R. 1982. *Les grands systèmes de droit contemporains*. Paris, Dalloz.

Day, D. 1909a. The Petroleum Resources of the United States: The Natural Gas Resources of the United States. In *Report of the National Conservation Commission*. Vol. 3. Washington, DC: National Conservation Commission, pp. 446–475.

———. 1909b. The Petroleum Resources of the United States. *American Review of Reviews*, (January 1909) 49–56.

Deckelman, J. 1996. From Petroleum Exploration to Petroleum Production and Beyond: A Technical Perspective. *Australian Mining and Petroleum Law Association Yearbook*: 234–283.

DeGolyer, E. 1961. Concepts on Occurrence of Oil and Gas. *History of Petroleum Engineering*. New York: American Petroleum Institute, pp. 15–33.

de Ribier, L. 1904. *Les stations thermales et les eaux minérales en France sous l'Ancien Régime*. [no place given]: Jules Rousset.

Descroix, P. 1943. *Le régime juridique des eaux souterraines en France et à l'étranger*. A. Pedone, Paris.

Devaux-Charbonnel, J. 1987. *Droit minier des hydrocarbures: Principes et applications*. Paris: Editions Technip.

Di Stefano, G. 1973. *The Search for Oil in Queensland*. Doctoral thesis, Melbourne: Department of Economics and Commerce, Melbourne University.

Dodge, J. R. 1865. *West Virginia: Its Farms and Forests, Mines and Oil-Wells*. Philadelphia: J.B. Lippincott & Co.

Doherty, H. L. 1925. Suggestions for Conservation of Petroleum by Control of Production. *Production of Petroleum in 1924: Papers Presented at the Symposium on Petroleum and Gas, at the New York Meeting, February 1925*. New York: American Institute of Mining and Metallurgical Engineers, pp. 7–27.

Dolques, J. 2002. Eaux minérales: une ressource renouvelable mais pas inépuisable. *Ecomine* (Novembre) 2002.

Domat, J. 1850. *The Civil Law in Its Natural Order*. Tr. W. Strahan, Boston: Charles C. Little and James Brown.

Drummond, D. O., L. R. Sherman, and E. R. McCarthy, Jr. 2004. The Rule of Capture in Texas—Still So Misunderstood after All These Years. *Texas Tech Law Review* 37: 1–98.

Dubner, B. H., P. Hanks, et al. 1980. Demarcation of Authority over Coastal Waters and Submerged Lands in the United States and Australia. *Stetson Law Review* 10: 228–271.

Durandin, C. 1995. *Histoire des Roumains.* Paris: Fayard.

Eaton, S. J. M. 1866. *Petroleum: A History of the Oil Region of Venango County, Pennsylvania.* Philadelphia: J.P. Skelly and Co.

Ellickson, R. C. 1989. A Hypothesis of Wealth Maximisation Norms: Evidence from the Whaling Industry. *Journal of Law, Economics and Organization* 5: 83–97.

Ellison, J. 1968. The Mineral Land Question in California, 1848–1866. In *The Public Lands.* Edited by V. Carstensen, Madison: University of Wisconsin Press, pp. 71–92.

El-Malik, W. 1993. *Minerals Investment under the Shari'a Law.* London: Graham & Trotman.

Ely, N. 1933a. *Oil Conservation through Interstate Agreement.* Washington, DC: U.S. Government Printing Office.

———. 1933b. *The Oil and Gas Conservation Statutes (Annotated).* Washington, DC: U.S. Government Printing Office.

———. 1938. The Conservation of Oil. *Harvard Law Review* 51: 1209–1244.

———. 1949. The Government in the Capacity of Land Owner. In *Conservation of Oil and Gas: A Legal History, 1948.* Edited by B. M. Murphy, Chicago: American Bar Association, pp. 599–629.

———. 1959. The Evolution of the Interstate Compact to Conserve Oil and Gas. *Interstate Oil and Gas Compact Commission Committee Bulletin* 1: 47–54.

———. 1975. Changing Concepts of the World's Mineral Development Laws. In *World Energy Laws: Proceedings of the IBA Seminar on World Energy Laws Held in Stavanger, Norway, May 1975.* London: International Bar Association, pp. 4–46.

Enever, F. A. 1947. *The Law of Support in Relation to Minerals.* London: Solicitors' Law Stationery Society Ltd.

Epinois, B. de l'., and E. Papciak. 1998. La politique française de protection des sources. *Réalites Industrielles* (Mai): 35–40.

Epstein, R. A. 1997. The Modern Uses of Ancient Law. *South Carolina Law Review* 48: 243–265.

Essad-Bey. 1932. *Blood and Oil in the Orient.* New York: Simon and Schuster.

Eudel, P. 1911 [2007]. *Annales de la Bourboule.* Paris: Le Livre d'Histoire.

Faure, O. 1985. La vogue des eaux minérales au XIXe siécle. L'exemple de la région stéphanoise et lyonnaise. *Le Corps et la Santé.* Comité des Travaux Historiques et Scientifiques. Paris, CTHS, Vol. 1: 245–258.

————. 1994. Le Mont-Dore au début de XIXe siécle: du village à la station thermale. *Villes d'Eaux: Histoire de Thermalisme.* Comité des Travaux Historiques et Scientifiques Paris, CTHS, pp. 177–188.

Fehr, R. 1939. *Le régime juridique des recherches et de l'exploitation des gisements de pétrole en droit comparé: France, Angleterre, Allemagne.* Thesis, Rennes: University of Rennes.

Fenet, P.-A. 1827–1829. *Recueil complet des travaux préparatoires du Code civil: suivi d'une édition de ce code, à laquelle sont ajoutés les lois, décrets et ordonnances formant le complément de la législation civile de la France, et ou se trouvent indiqués, sous chaque article séparément, tous les passages du recueil qui s'y rattachent.* Paris, au dépôt, rue Saint-André-des-arcs, no. 51.

Finkelman, P. 2002. Fugitive Baseballs and Abandoned Property: Who Owns the Home Run Ball? *Cardozo Law Review* 23: 1609–1633.

Finnie, D. H. 1992. *Shifting Lines in the Sand: Kuwait's Elusive Frontier with Iraq.* Cambridge, Mass: Harvard University Press.

Fitzgerald, E. A. 1988a. The Seaweed Rebellion: The Battle over Section 8(g) Revenues. *Journal of Energy Law and Policy* 8: 253–284.

————. 1988b. The Tidelands Controversy Revisited. *Environmental Law* 19: 209–256.

Folger, H. C. J. 1893. Petroleum, Its Production and Products. *Annual Report of the Secretary of Internal Affairs, Commonwealth of Pennsylvania, XX Industrial Statistics, 1892.* Harrisburg: Edwin K. Meyers, State Printer.

Forbes, J. R. S., and A. G. Lang. 1987. *Australian Mining and Petroleum Laws.* Sydney: Butterworths.

Forbes, R. J. 1958. *Studies in Early Petroleum History.* Leiden: E.J. Brill.

————. 1959. *More Studies in Early Petroleum History, 1860–1880.* Leiden: E.J. Brill.

France. Ministère de l'Économie, des Finances et de l'Industrie. 1999. L'enjeu économique des eaux minérales, (No. 10) *1999 Energies et matières premières (lettre trimestrielle).*

————. 1998. Ministère de l'Emploi et de la Solidarité et Secrétariat de l'Etat à l'Industrie. Inventaire des sources de l'eau minérale naturelle. *Réalites Industrielles* (Mai): 74–115.

Frank, A. F. 2005. *Oil Empire: Visions of Prosperity in Austrian Galicia.* Cambridge, Mass: Harvard University Press.

Frankel, P. 1969. *Essentials of Petroleum: A Key to Oil Economics.* London: Frank Cass.

Franko, I. 1899. Poluika. *Poluika i yn'shi Boyslav'ski opovidania.* Lviv, Ukrains'ka-Rus'ka Vydavnycha Spika, pp. 3–29.

Franks, K. A. 1980. *The Oklahoma Petroleum Industry.* Oklahoma City: Oklahoma Heritage Association.

Freeman, B. L. 1975. Relinquishment of State Owned Minerals: The Agency Relationship between the Owner of the Soil and the State. *St Mary's Law Journal* 7: 62–77.

Gale, T. A. 1860. *The Wonder of the Nineteenth Century! Rock Oil in Pennsylvania, and Elsewhere.* Erie: Sloan and Griffeth.

Gamboa, F. X. de. 1830. In *Commentaries on the Mining Ordinances of Spain*. Edited by Tr. R. Heathfield. London: Longman Rees Orme Green and Brown.

Gaonac'h, A. 1999. *La Nature Juridique de l'Eau*. Paris: Johanet.

Gates, P. W. 1968. *History of Public Land Law Development*. Washington, DC: U.S. Government Printing Office.

Georgescu, V. 1991. *The Romanians: A History*. Columbus: Ohio State University Press.

German, W. P. Z. 1931. Compulsory Unit Operation of Oil Pools. *American Bar Association Journal* 17: 393–400.

———. 1938. Legal History of Conservation of Oil and Gas in Oklahoma. In *Legal History of Conservation of Oil and Gas*. Section of Mineral Law, American Bar Association, Chicago: American Bar Association, pp. 110–213.

Gerretson, F. C. 1953–1957. *History of the Royal Dutch*. Leiden: E.J. Brill.

Getzler, J. 2004. *A History of Water Rights at Common Law*. Oxford: Oxford University Press.

Gibb, G. S., and E. H. Knowlton. 1956. *History of the Standard Oil Company. Vol 2. The Resurgent Years, 1911–1927*. New York: Harper and Brothers.

Giddens, P. H. 1941. *The Beginnings of the Petroleum Industry: Sources and Bibliography*. Harrisburg, PA: Pennsylvania Historical Commission.

———. ed. 1947. Pennsylvania Petroleum, 1750–1872: A Documentary History Titusville, PA: Pennsylvania Historical and Museum Commission.

———. 1972. *The Birth of the Oil Industry*. New York: Arno Press.

Gidel, G. 1934. *Le droit international public de la mer*. Paris: Sirey.

Giebelhaus, A. W. 1980. *Business and Government in the Oil Industry: A Case Study of Sun Oil, 1876–1945*. Greenwich, Conn: JAI Press.

Gioni, V. 1984. La situation sociale-juridique de la paysannerie roumaine durant la seconde moitié du XIXème siecle et comment se reflète-t-elle dans l'oeuvre de Mihai Eminescu. *Recherches sur l'histoire des institutions et du droit (Romania)* 9: 21–38.

Goble, D. D. 2005. Three Cases/Four Tales: Commons, Capture, the Public Trust and Property in Land. *Environmental Law* 35: 807–854.

Goozee, R. 2009. The Cold(er) War. *O & G Next Generation*. Issue 9, at www.cisoilgas.com/article/The-colder-war/. Accessed October 2009.

Gould, L. L., et al. 2001. Theodore Roosevelt. In *Oxford Companion to United States History*. Edited by P. S. Boyer. New York: Oxford University Press, pp. 676–677.

Graham, S. B. J. 1975. Fair Share or Fair Game? Great Principle, Good Technology—But Pitfalls in Practice. *Natural Resources Lawyer* 8: 61–88.

Gramling, R., et al. 1995. Oil in the Gulf: Past Development, Future Prospects. New Orleans, U.S. Department of the Interior, Minerals Management Service. Gulf of Mexico OCS Region, OCS Study MMS 95-0031.

Great Britain Petroleum Department. 1938. Great Britain: The Organization of the Production, Refining, and Distribution of Petroleum and Petroleum Products. In

Transactions Third World Power Conference: The National Power Economy. Vol. IV. Edited by O. C. Merrill. Washington, DC: U.S. Government Printing Office, pp. 129–148.

Greer, D. E. 1923. Ownership of Petroleum Oil and Natural Gas in Place. *Texas Law Review* 1: 162–187.

Gueslin, A. 2003. *L'Etat, l'Economie et la Société Française XIXe–XXe siècles.* Paris: Hachette.

Gulishambaroff, S. 1902. Mr. S. Gulishambaroff on the Oil Industries of America and Russia. *Petroleum Review* 7: 81–88.

Gutteridge, H. C. 1933–35. Abuse of Rights. *Cambridge Law Journal* 5: 22–45.

Hager, D. 1915. *Practical Oil Geology: The Application of Geology to Oil Field Problems.* New York: McGraw-Hill Book Company.

Hardin, G. 1968. The Tragedy of the Commons. *Science* 162: 1243–1248.

Hardwicke, R. E. 1935. The Rule of Capture and Its Implications as Applied to Oil and Gas. *Texas Law Review* 13: 391–422.

———. 1938. Legal History of Conservation of Oil in Texas. In *Legal History of Conservation of Oil and Gas.* Section of Mineral Law, American Bar Association, Chicago: American Bar Association, pp. 214–268.

———. 1941. Oil Conservation: Statutes, Administration and Court Review. *Mississippi Law Journal* 13: 381–411.

———. 1951. Unitization Statutes: Voluntary Action or Compulsion. *Rocky Mountain Law Review* 24: 29–43.

———. 1952. Oil Well Spacing Regulations and Protection of Property Rights in Texas. *Texas Law Review* 31: 99–127.

———. 1961. *Antitrust Laws, et al. v. Unit Operation of Oil and Gas Pools.* Dallas: Society of Petroleum Engineers of AIME.

Harris, I. D. 1938. Legal History of Conservation of Oil and Gas in Kansas. *Legal History of Conservation of Oil and Gas.* Section of Mineral Law, American Bar Association, Chicago: American Bar Association, pp. 37–59.

Harrison, R. 1970. Regulation of Well Spacing in Oil and Gas Production. *Alberta Law Review* 8: 357–376.

Hartz, L. 1948. *Economic Policy and Democratic Thought: Pennsylvania, 1776–1860.* Cambridge, Mass: Harvard University Press.

Hassmann, H. 1953. *Oil in the Soviet Union: History, Geography, Problems.* Princeton: Princeton University Press.

Hatch, E. W. 1901. Property Rights in Percolating Waters. *Columbia Law Review* 1: 505–521.

Havemeyer, L. 1930. *Conservation of Our Natural Resources.* New York: Macmillan Company.

Hawkins, W. 1947. *El Sal del Rey.* Austin: Texas State Historical Association.

Helgesen, S. 1981. *Wildcatters: A Story of Texans, Oil and Money.* Garden City, NJ: Doubleday.

Henderson, K. P. 2001. A History of Oil Production in California. *Oil-Industry History* 2: 1–8.

Henry, J. D. 1905. *Baku: An Eventful History.* London: A. Constable and Co.

———. 1910. *Oil Fields of the Empire.* London: Bradbury Agnew and Co.

———. 1914. *History and Romance of the Petroleum Industry.* London: Author.

Henry, J. T. 1873. *The Early and Later History of Petroleum with Authentic Facts in Regard to Its Development in Western Pennsylvania.* Philadelphia: Jas. B. Rodgers Co.

Hibbard, B. H. 1939. *A History of the Public Land Policies.* P. Smith, New York.

Hidy, R. W., and M. E. Hidy. 1955. *History of Standard Oil Company (New Jersey). Vol. 1. Pioneering in Big Business, 1882–1911.* New York: Harper & Brothers.

Higgins, G. E. 1996. *A History of Trinidad Oil. Port of Spain.* Trinidad: Trinidad Express Newspapers Ltd.

Hill, H. H., and E. L. Estabrook. 1930. Unit Operations in the Eastern United States and Foreign Countries. *Transactions of the American Institute of Mining and Metallurgical Engineers* 1930: 17–32.

History of Butler County Pennsylvania, with Illustrations and Biographical Sketches of Some of Its Prominent Men and Pioneers. 1883. Chicago: Waterman, Watkins, & Co.

Hitchins, K. 1994. *Rumania, 1866–1947.* Oxford: Clarendon Press.

Hoffman, J. 1984. The Holland Land Company. *The Venango Intelligencer* 7(4).

Hohfeld, W. N. 1923. *Fundamental Legal Conceptions as Applied in Judicial Reasoning.* New Haven, Conn: Yale University Press.

Holloway, W. L. 1949. California, 1931–1948. In *Conservation of Oil and Gas: A Legal History, 1948.* Edited by B. M. Murphy. Chicago: American Bar Association, pp. 40–55.

Holmes, J. 2002. End the Moratorium: The Timor Gap Treaty as a Model for the Complete Resolution of the Western Gap in the Gulf of Mexico. *Vanderbilt Journal of Transnational Law* 35: 925–952.

Horwitz, M. J. 1977. *The Transformation of American Law, 1780–1860.* Cambridge, Mass: Harvard University Press.

Huber, M. 1907. Ein Beitrag zur Lehre von der Gebeitshoheit an Grenzflüssen. *Zeitschrift für Volkerrecht und Bundesstaatlichrecht* 1: 29–52, 159–217.

Huffcutt, E. W. 1903. Percolating Waters: The Law of Reasonable User. *Yale Law Journal* 13: 222–227.

Hughes, D. J. 1993. *Oil in the Deep South: A History of the Oil Business in Mississippi, Alabama and Florida, 1859–1945.* University Press of Mississippi: Jackson.

Hughes, I. W. G. 1991. *Department of Energy View on Unitization.* London: Langham Oil Conferences.

Hunt, C. D. 1989. *The Offshore Petroleum Regimes of Canada and Australia*. Calgary: The Canadian Institute of Resources Law.

Huntley, L. G. 1913. *Possible Causes of the Decline of Oil Wells and Suggested Methods of Prolonging Yield*. Washington, DC: U.S. Government Printing Office.

Hurst, J. W. 1956. *Law and the Conditions of Freedom in the Nineteenth-Century United States*. Madison: University of Wisconsin Press.

Imperial War Conference. 1918. Extracts: Minutes, London, His Majesty's Stationery Office: Cd. 9177.

Institutul Geologic al României. 1925. *Legiuirile miniere vechi şi noi ale României*. Bucharest: Institutul de Arte Grafica Eminescu.

Interstate Oil Compact Commission, Legal Committee. 1950. *A Form for an Oil and Gas Conservation Statute*. Oklahoma City: Interstate Oil Compact Commission.

Interstate Oil and Gas Compact Commission. 2004. *2004 Model Oil and Gas Conservation Act*. Oklahoma City: Interstate Oil and Gas Compact Commission.

Interstate Oil and Gas Compact Commission, Energy Resources, Research and Technical Committee, Unitization-Horizontal Drilling Subcommittee. 1999. *IOGCC Model Statute and Fieldwide Unitization References*. Oklahoma City: Interstate Oil and Gas Compact Commission.

Ise, J. 1926. *The United States Oil Policy*. New Haven, Conn: Yale University Press.

Jacobs, J. C. 1947–1948. Unit Operation of Oil and Gas Fields. *Yale Law Journal* 57: 1207–1228.

Jaffe, A. Y. 2007. Introduction and Summary Conclusions. In *The Changing Role of National Oil Companies in International Energy Markets*. James A. Baker III Institute for Public Policy, Rice University.

Johnston, D. 1993. The Production-Sharing Concept: Variations on a Theme. *Oil and Gas Law and Taxation Review* 11: 201–204.

Jones, G. 1981. *The State and the Emergence of the British Oil Industry*. London: Macmillan.

Kaveler, H. H. 1949. The Engineering Basis for and the Results from the Unit Operation of Oil Pools. *Tulane Law Review* 23: 331–344.

Keen, J. P. 1998. Commonwealth Draft Guidelines for Transboundary Unitisations and the Rule of Capture. *Australian Mining and Petroleum Law Association Yearbook* 1998: 433–451.

Kellam, R. O. 1960. A Century of Correlative Rights. *Baylor Law Review* 12: 1–42.

Kendall Freeman. 2003. *Oil and Gas Deposits at International Boundaries: Guidance Note*. London: Kendall Freeman.

Kerr, J. 1894. Mines and Minerals. *Albany Law Journal* 50: 253–256.

Khadduri, M., and E. Ghareeb. 1997. *War in the Gulf, 1990–91: The Iraq-Kuwaiti Conflict and Its Implications*. New York: Oxford University Press.

Killebrew, J. B. 1877. *Oil Region of Tennessee*. Nashville: The American Print Co.

King, A. A. 1948. Pooling and Unitization of Oil and Gas Leases. *Michigan Law Review* 46: 311–340.

King, J. O. 1966. The Early Texas Oil Industry, Beginnings at Corsicana. *Journal of Southern History* 32: 505–515.

———. 1970. *Joseph Stephen Cullinan: A Study of Leadership in the Texas Petroleum Industry, 1897–1937.* Nashville: Vanderbilt University Press for Texas Gulf Coast Historical Research Association.

Kokxhoorn, N. 1977. *Oil and Politics: The Domestic Roots of US Expansion in the Middle East.* Peter Lang; Herbert Lang, Frankfurt/Bern.

Kramer, B. M., and O. L. Anderson. 2005. The Rule of Capture: An Oil and Gas Perspective. *Environmental Law* 35: 899–954.

Kramer, B. M., and P. H. Martin. 1999. *The Law of Pooling and Unitization.* New York: Matthew Bender.

Kuntz, E. 1957. The Law of Capture. *Oklahoma Law Review* 10: 406–409.

Kursky, A., and A. Konoplyanik. 2006. State Regulation and Mining Law Development in Russia from the 15th Century to 1991. *Journal of Energy and Natural Resources Law* 24: 221–254.

Kussart, S. 1938. *The Allegheny River.* Pittsburgh: Burgum Printing Company.

Kwiatkowska, B. 1993. Economic and Environmental Considerations in Maritime Boundary Delimitation. In *International Maritime Boundaries.* Vol. I. Edited by J. I. Charney and L. M. Alexander. Martinus Nijhoff: Leiden/Boston, pp. 75–114.

———. 2005. Resource, Navigational and Environmental Factors in Equitable Maritime Boundary Delimitation. In *International Maritime Boundaries.* Vol. V. Edited by D. A. Colson and R. W. Smith, Martinus Nijhoff. Leiden/Boston, pp. 3223–3244.

Lagoni, R. 1979. Oil and Gas Deposits across National Frontiers. *American Journal of International Law* 73: 215–243.

Larson, H. M., and C. S. Popple. 1971. *History of the Standard Oil Company. Vol. 3. New Horizons, 1927–1950.* New York: Harper and Row.

Larson, H. M., and K. W. Porter. 1959. *History of Humble Oil & Refining Company.* New York: Harper and Brothers.

Lauterpacht, E., et al., 1991. *The Kuwait Crisis: Basic Documents.* Cambridge International Documents Series, Cambridge: Grotius Publications.

Lecocq, H. 1836. *Vichy et ses Environs.* Paris: aux Pyramides.

Leeuw, C., van der. 2000. *Oil and Gas in the Caucasus and Caspian: A History.* New York: St. Martin's Press.

Lender, W. 1934. *Le pétrole en Pologne.* Thesis, Caen: University of Caen.

Leshy, J. D. 1987. *The Mining Law: A Study in Perpetual Motion.* Washington, DC: Resources for the Future.

Levine, M. E. 1999. Regulatory Capture. In *New Palgrave Dictionary of Economics and the Law.* Vol. 3. Edited by P. Newman. London: Macmillan, pp. 267–271.

Libecap, G. D. 1978. Economic Variables and the Development of the Law: The Case of Western Mineral Rights. *Journal of Economic History* 38: 338–362.

———. 1979. Government Support of Private Claims to Public Minerals: Western Mineral Rights. *Business History Review* 53: 364–385.

———. 1984. The Political Allocation of Mineral Rights: A Re-Evaluation of Teapot Dome. *Journal of Economic History* 44: 381–391.

———. 1993. *Contracting for Property Rights.* Cambridge: University Press.

Libecap, G. D., and J. L. Smith. 1999. The Self-Enforcing Provisions of Oil and Gas Unit Operating Agreements: Theory and Evidence. *Journal of Law, Economics and Organization* 15: 526–548.

———. 2002. The Economic Evolution of Petroleum Property Rights in the United States. *Journal of Legal Studies* 31: S589–S608.

Libecap, G. D., and S. N. Wiggins. 1985. The Influence of Private Contractual Failure on Regulation: The Case of Oil Field Unitization. *Journal of Political Economy* 93: 690–714.

Liddell, C. 1897. The Petroleum Industry and Its Abuses. United Kingdom National Archive, FO Series 104, Vol. 135, September 7, 1897.

Lieuwen, E. 1954. *Petroleum in Venezuela.* Berkeley: University of California Press.

Lipp, A. 1870. *Verkehrs- und Handels-Verhältnisse Galiziens.* Prague: C.H. Hunger.

Livesley, K. P. 1990. The Timor Gap Treaty. In *Energy Law '90: Changing Energy Markets—The Legal Consequences.* London: Graham and Trotman and International Bar Association, pp. 61–99.

Longmuir, M. V. 2001. *Oil in Burma: The Extraction of Earth-Oil to 1914.* Bangkok: White Lotus Press.

Lucas, A., and C. D. Hunt. 1990. *Oil and Gas Law in Canada.* Toronto: Carswell.

Lueck, D. 1995. The Rule of First Possession and the Design of the Law. *Journal of Law & Economics* 38: 349–436.

———. 1998. First Possession. In *New Palgrave Encyclopedia of Economics and the Law.* Vol. 2. Edited by P. Newman. London: Macmillan, pp. 132–144.

Lund, J. W. 1993. Saratoga Springs, New York. *GHC Bulletin* 4–8 (March 1993).

Lund, T. A. 1976. Early American Wildlife Law. *New York University Law Review* 51: 703–730.

MacDonald, S. T. 2003. A Comparative Analysis of the Influence of the Law of Capture on Oil and Gas Conservation Legislation in Texas and Oklahoma. *Oil, Gas and Energy Quarterly* 52: 289–314.

MacDonald, S. T., et al. 2005. A Decision Theoretic Explanation for 'Irrational' Opposition to Unitization Agreements in the Oil and Gas Industry. *Oil, Gas and Energy Quarterly* 54: 83–96.

Magrath, C. P. 1966. *Yazoo: Law and Politics in the New Republic; the Case of Fletcher v. Peck.* Providence: Brown University Press.

Mallat, A. 1915. *Histoire des Eaux Minérales de Vichy*. Vol. 2. Paris: Georges Steinheil.

Mallat, A., and J. Cornillon. 1909. *Histoire des Eaux Minérales de Vichy*. Vol. 1. Paris: Georges Steinheil.

Marland, E. W. 1923. Need State Law to Protect Oil in Ground. *Oil & Gas Journal* (October 11, 1923): 122.

Marshall, J. H. 1938. Legal History of Conservation of Oil and Gas in California. In *Legal History of Conservation of Oil and Gas*. American Bar Association, Section of Mineral Law Chicago: American Bar Association, pp. 28–36.

Marshall, J. H., and N. L. Meyers. 1931. Legal Planning of Petroleum Production. *Yale Law Journal* 41: 33–68.

Martinez, A. R. 1989. *Venezuelan Oil: Development and Chronology*. London and New York: Elsevier Applied Science.

Marvin, C. 1887. *England as a Petroleum Power; or, The Petroleum Fields of the British Empire*. London: R. Anderson & Co.

———. 1891. *The Region of the Eternal Fire*. London: W.H. Allen.

McAfee, W. A. 1949. Ohio. In *Conservation of Oil and Gas: A Legal History, 1948*. Edited by B. M. Murphy. Chicago: American Bar Association, Section of Mineral and Natural Resources Law.

McBeth, B. S. 1983. *Juan Vicente Gomez and the Oil Companies in Venezuela, 1908–1935*. Cambridge: Cambridge University Press.

———. 1985. *British Oil Policy, 1919–1939*. London: Frank Cass.

McDonald, S. L. 1971. *Petroleum Conservation in the United States: An Economic Analysis*. Baltimore: Johns Hopkins Press for Resources for the Future.

McElwee, N. 2001. *Oil Creek ... the Beginning*. Oil City, PA: Oil Creek Press.

McGee, W. J. 1910. The Conservation of Natural Resources. In *Mississippi Valley Historical Association, Proceedings for the Year 1909–1910*. Cedar Rapids, Iowa: Mississippi Valley Historical Association, pp. 361–379.

McGowen, J. D. 1956. The Development of Political Institutions on the Public Domain. *Wyoming Law Journal* 11: 1–15.

McKain, D. L., and B. L. Allen. 1994. *Where It All Began: The Story of the People and Places Where the Oil & Gas Industry Began—West Virginia and South-Eastern Ohio*. Parkersburg, WVa: David L. McKain.

McLaurin, J. J. 1896. *Sketches in Crude Oil*. Harrisburg: Author.

McMurray, W. F., and J. O. Lewis. 1916. *Underground Wastes in Oil and Gas Fields and Methods of Prevention*. Washington, DC: U.S. Government Printing Office.

Merralls, J. D. 1979. Problems in Commonwealth-State Relations concerning Offshore Resources. In *Australia's Continental Shelf*. Edited by J. R. V. Prescott. West Melbourne, Vic.: Thomas Nelson, pp. 50–65.

Merrill, M. H. 1930. Stabilization of the Oil Industry and Due Process of Law. *Southern California Law Review* 3: 396–410.

————. 1940. *Covenants Implied in Oil and Gas Leases.* 2nd ed., St. Louis: Thomas Law Book Company.

Metcalfe, W. K. 1953. The Tidelands Controversy: A Study in Development of a Political-Legal Problem. *Syracuse Law Review* 4: 38–88.

Michel, L. 1896. *Recueil Méthodique de la Législation Minérale.* Saint Etienne: J. Thomas.

Miller, A. M. 2003. Comment: A Journey through Mineral Estate Dominance, the Accommodation Doctrine, and Beyond: Why Texas Is Ready to Take the Next Step with a Surface Damage Act. *Houston Law Review* 40: 461–497.

Miller, E. 1973. Some Implications of Land Ownership Patterns for Petroleum Policy. *Land Economics* 49: 414–423.

Miller, E. C. 1968. *This Was Early Oil: Contemporary Accounts of the Growing Petroleum Industry, 1848–1885.* Harrisburg, PA: Pennsylvania Historical and Museum Commission.

Miller, H. C. 1929. *The Function of Natural Gas in the Production of Oil.* New York: American Petroleum Institute.

Miller, J. 1955. History of the California Code of Civil Procedure. *West's Annotated California Codes* 23: 1–44, available at web.archive.org/web/20060713041612/www.sandiego.edu/lrc/ccp.html. Accessed October 2009.

Millern, A. von. 1864. *All about Petroleum and the Great Oil Districts of Pennsylvania, West Virginia, Ohio, etc.* New York: A. Spann.

Mining Laws of Los Angeles Mining District. 1865. Los Angeles County Records, Vol. I Misc. R.

Mirabeau, Comte de. 1973. *Discours.* Edited by F. Furet. Paris: Gallimard.

Mitzakis, J. 1911. *The Russian Oil Fields and Petroleum Industry.* London: Pall Mall Press.

Miyoshi, M. 1988. The Basic Concept of Joint Development of Hydrocarbon Resources on the Continental Shelf. *International Journal of Estuarine and Coastal Law* 3: 1–18.

————. 1999. *The Joint Development of Offshore Oil and Gas in Relation to Maritime Boundary Determination.* Durham: University of Durham, International Boundaries Research Unit.

Morris, E. 1865. *Derrick and Drill; or, An Insight into the Discovery, Development and Present Condition and Future Prospects of Petroleum.* New York: James Miller.

Morris, J. W. 1967. The North Sea Continental Shelf: Oil and Gas Legal Problems. *International Lawyer* 2: 191–214.

Morriss, A. P., R. E. Meiners, et al. 2006. Hardrock Homesteads: Free Access and the General Mining Law of 1872. *Journal of Energy and Natural Resources Law* 24: 255–277.

Morritt, H. 1993. *Rivers of Oil: The Founding of North America's Petroleum Industry.* Kingston, Ontario: Quarry Press.

Moses, L. 1943. Some Legal and Economic Aspects of Unit Operations of Oil Fields. *Texas Law Review* 21: 748–772.

———. 1945. Statutory Regulations in the Carbon Black Industry. *Tulane Law Review* 20: 83–97.

Mouton, M. W. 1954. The Continental Shelf. *Recueil des Cours de l'Académie de Droit International* 85: 343–465.

Mullican, W. F. III, and S. Schwartz. 2004. *100 Years of Rule of Capture: From East to Groundwater Management.* Texas Water Development Board Report 361, Austin: Texas Water Development Board.

Murphy, B. M., ed. 1949. *Conservation of Oil and Gas: A Legal History, 1948.* Chicago: American Bar Association, Section of Mineral and Natural Resources Law.

Myres, S. D. 1973. *The Permian Basin, Petroleum Empire of the Southwest. Era of Discovery, from the Beginning to the Depression.* El Paso, Texas: Permain Press.

Nadault de Buffon, H. 1877. *Considérations sur le régime légal des eaux de sources naturelles et artificielles en ce qui touche spécialement l'agriculture, l'industrie, le commerce et autres intérêts généraux* .... Paris: Maresque Aîné.

Nash, G. D. 1968. *United States Oil Policy, 1890–1964.* Pittsburgh: University of Pittsburgh.

National Conservation Commission. 1909. Report of the National Conservation Commission, Washington, DC.

Nevins, A. 1940. *John D. Rockefeller: The Heroic Age of American Enterprise.* New York: Charles Scribner's Sons.

Nivet, V. 1879. *La Bourboule: Ses Thermes et ses Eaux Minérales.* Clermont-Ferrand: G. Mont-Louis.

Noggle, B. 1962. *Teapot Dome: Oil and Politics in the 1920s.* Baton Rouge: Louisiana State University Press.

Nordhauser, N. 1979. *The Quest for Stability: Domestic Oil Regulation, 1917–1935.* New York: Garland Publishing.

Novak, W. J. 1994. Common Regulation: Legal Origins of State Power in America. *Hastings Law Journal* 45: 1061–1097.

Nutting, C. B. 1936. The Texas Anti-Trust Law: A Post-Mortem. *Texas Law Review* 14: 293–306.

O'Connor, H. 1955. *The Empire of Oil.* New York: Monthly Review Press.

Ohio Petroleum Company. 1864. Prospectus, New York.

Olien, D. D., and R. M. Olien. 2002. *Oil in Texas: The Gusher Age, 1895–1945.* Austin: University of Texas Press.

Olien, R. M., and D. D. Olien. 1984. *Wildcatters: Texas Independent Oilmen.* Austin: Texas Monthly.

———. 2000. *Oil and Ideology: The Cultural Creation of the American Petroleum Industry.* Chapel Hill, NC: University of North Carolina Press.

Oliver, E. 1930. Oil and Gas Law Responsible for Over-production and Waste. *Annual Report of the American Bar Association* 53: 712–726.

———. 1935. Modifying the Capture Law. *Transactions of the American Institute of Mining and Metallurgical Engineers* 114: 220–228.

———. 1937. Can the Rule of Capture Be Rationalized? *Transactions of the American Institute of Mining and Metallurgical Engineers (Petroleum Division)* 123: 133–154.

Oliver, E., and J. B. Umpleby. 1930. Principles of Unit Operation. *Transactions of the American Institute of Mining and Metallurgical Engineers* 1930: 105–117.

Ong, D. M. 1999. Joint Development of Common Offshore Oil and Gas Deposits: 'Mere' State Practice or Customary International Law? *American Journal of International Law* 93: 771–804.

Onorato, W. T. 1968. Apportionment of an International Common Petroleum Deposit. *International and Comparative Law Quarterly* 17: 85–102.

———. 1977. Apportionment of an International Common Petroleum Deposit: A Reprise. *International and Comparative Law Quarterly* 26: 324–337.

Ostrom, E. 1999. Self-Governance of Common Pool Resources. In *New Palgrave Dictionary of Economics and the Law*. Vol. 3. Edited by P. Newman. London: Macmillan, pp. 425–433.

Owen, E. W. 1975. *Trek of the Oil Finders: A History of Exploration for Oil.* Tulsa: American Association of Petroleum Geologists.

Payton-Smith, D. J. 1971. *Oil: A Study of War-time Policy and Administration.* London: Her Majesty's Stationery Office.

Pearton, M. 1971. *Oil and the Romanian State.* Oxford: Clarendon Press.

Peckham, S. F. 1884. *Production, Technology and Uses of Petroleum and Its Products,* Washington, DC: U.S. Department of the Interior, Census Office.

Pendleton, G. 1879. Support—Lateral and Subjacent. *American Law Register* 27: 529–539.

Penez, J. 1994. *Dans la fièvre thermale: La société des eaux minérales de Châtel-Guyon (1878–1914). Réussite et Expansion d'une Société Thermale.* Clermont-Ferrand: Institut d'Etudes du Massif Central.

———. 2004. Les réseaux d'investissement dans le thermalisme au XIXe siécle en France. *In Situ* (No. 4): 1–25.

———. 2005. *Historie du Thermalisme en France au XIXe Siècle: eau, médecine et loisirs.* Paris: Economica.

Petroleum Producers' Union, General Council. 1878. *Address to Producers of Petroleum.* Titusville, PA: Petroleum Producers' Union.

———. 1880. *A History of the Organization, Purposes and Transactions of the General Council of the Petroleum Producers' Union and of the Suits and Prosecutions Instituted by It from 1878 to 1889.* Titusville, PA: Petroleum Producers' Union.

Pettengill, S. B. 1936. *Hot Oil: The Problem of Petroleum.* New York: Economic Forum Co.

———. 1940. *Smoke Screen.* New York: Southern Publishers.

Pierce, D. E. 1983. Coordinated Reservoir Development: An Alternative to the Rule of Capture for the Ownership and Development of Oil and Gas. *Journal of Energy Law and Policy* 4: 1–80.

Pizanty, M. 1931. *Le Pétrole en Roumanie*. Bucarest: Institut Economique Roumain.

Plutarch. 1845. *Lives*. Transl. by J. and W. Langhorne. London: J.J. Chidley.

Pogue, J. E. 1938. The Economic Structure of the American Petroleum Industry. In *Transactions Third World Power Conference: The National Power Economy*. Vol. IV. Edited by O. C. Merrill. Washington, DC: U.S. Government Printing Office, pp. 221–267.

Polkinghorne, M. 2007. Unitisation and Redetermination: Right or Obligation? *Journal of Energy and Natural Resources Law* 25: 303–323.

Polo, M. 1908. *The Travels of Marco Polo the Venetian*. London: J.M. Dent.

Polston, R. W. 1994. Mineral Ownership Theory: Doctrine in Disarray. *North Dakota Law Review* 70: 541–585.

Price, P. H. 1947. The Evolution of Geological Theory in Prospecting for Oil and Gas. *Bulletin of American Association of Petroleum Geologists* 31: 673–697.

Prindle, D. F. 1981. *Petroleum Politics and the Texas Railroad Commission*. Austin: University of Texas Press.

Pruett, E., and J. Cimino. 2000. Global Maritime Boundaries Database, Fairfax, Va: Veridian, MRJ Technology Solutions.

Rampaul, I. N. 2003. Privately Owned Petroleum Rights in Trinidad and Tobago. *Oil, Gas and Energy Law Intelligence* 1(2).

Rarick, R. D. 1980. *The Petroleum Industry: Its Birth in Pennsylvania and Development in Indiana*. Bloomington: State of Indiana.

Richards, W. R., T. A. Mitchell, et al. 1994. Oil and Gas Conservation in Utah after *Cowling*: The Law of Capture Receives a New Lease on Life. *Journal of Energy, Natural Resources and Environmental Law* 14: 1–40.

Rintoul, W. 1976. *Spudding In: Recollections of Pioneer Days in the California Oil Fields*. San Francisco: California Historical Society.

Rockwell, J. A. 1851. *A Compilation of Spanish and Mexican Law, in Relation to Mines, and Titles to Real Estate, in Force in California, Texas and New Mexico*. New York: John S. Voorhies.

Rogers, A. 1864. *The Law of Mines, Minerals and Quarries in Great Britain and Ireland*. London: V. & R. Stevens Sons and Haynes.

Roggenkamp, M. M. 1991. *Netherlands Oil and Gas Law*. London: Chancery.

———. 2001. Energy Law in the Netherlands. In *Energy Law in Europe: National, EU and International Law Institutions*. Edited by M. M. Roggenkamp, A. Rønne, C. Redgwell & I. del Guayo. Oxford: Oxford University Press, pp. 629–727.

Romains, J. 1933. *Les superbes*. Paris: Flammarion.

Rønne, A. 2001. Energy Law in Denmark. In *Energy Law in Europe: National, EU and International Law Institutions*. Edited by M. M. Roggenkamp, A. Rønne, C. Redgwell & I. del Guayo. Oxford: Oxford University Press, Ch. 7.

Rose, C. M. 1990. Energy and Efficiency in the Realignment of Common Law Water Rights. *Journal of Legal Studies* 19: 261–296.

Rosetti, D. R. 1900. *Lois, réglements, décrets et index alphabétiques concernant les mines et le pétrole.* Bucuresti: Joseph Gobl.

Rotureau, A. 1859. *Des Principales Eaux Minérales en Europe: France.* Paris: Victor Masson.

Roughton, D. 2008. Rights (and Wrongs) of Capture: International Law and the Implications of the Guyana/Suriname Arbirtration. *Journal of Energy and Natural Resources Law* 26: 374–401.

Roux, E. G. 1975. *Fille de Murat-le-Quaire. La Bourboule. Naissance d'une Commune.* Clermont-Ferrand: Volcans.

Ruiz Moreno, I. 1959. Las explotaciones petrolíferas en las fronteres internacionales. *Anuario hispano-luso-americano de derecho internacional* 1: 92–98.

Sabadel, J. 1865. *Législation en vigueur sur les eaux minérales.* Montpellier: Ricard Frères.

Sansonetti, T. L., and W. R. Murray. 1990. A Primer on the Federal Onshore Oil and Gas Leasing Reform Act of 1987 and Its Regulations. *Land and Water Law Review* 25: 375–416.

Sarazin, M. 2000. Les eaux minérales de Châteldon (Puy-de-Dôme) de la fin du XVIIIe siècle à la fin du XXe siècle. *Bulletin de la Société d'Histoire et d'Archéologie de Vichy et ses Environs* 137: 25–48.

Sayers, J. B. 1949. Pennsylvania. In *Conservation of Oil and Gas: A Legal History, 1948.* Edited by B. Murphy. Chicago: American Bar Association, Section of Mineral Law, Ch. 28.

Schaetzel, S. 1938. Poland: Organization of Production, Treatment, and Distribution of Mineral Oil and Final Products. In *Transactions Third World Power Conference: The National Power Economy.* Vol. IV. Edited by O. C. Merrill. Washington, DC: U.S. Government Printing Office, pp. 153–162.

Scheiber, H. N. 1973. Property Law, Expropriation, and Resource Allocation by Government: the United States, 1789–1910. *Journal of Economic History* 33: 232–251.

Schönborn, W. 1929. La nature juridique du territoire. *Recueil des Cours de l'Académie de Droit International* 30: 81–189.

Schofield, R. 1993. *Kuwait and Iraq: Historical Claims and Territorial Disputes.* London: Royal Institute of International Affairs.

Scott, A. 2008. *The Evolution of Resource Property Rights.* Oxford: Oxford University Press.

Scott, A., and G. Coustalin. 1995. The Evolution of Water Rights. *Natural Resources Journal* 35: 821–980.

Serdaru, V. S. 1921. *Le pétrole roumain: aperçu historique, économique, politique, et législatif, chiffres et interprétations 1825–1920.* Thesis, Paris: University of Paris.

Shinn, C. H. 1885. *Mining Camps: A Study of Frontier Government.* New York: Charles Scribner's Sons.

Shippen, E. W. 2002. In the Oil Business in Pennsylvania (as Recalled in Later Years). *Oil-Industry History* 3: 87–105.

Simonton, J. W. 1921. Has a Landowner Any Property in Oil and Gas in Place? *West Virginia Law Quarterly* 27: 281–300.

Sinclair, U. 1927. *Oil!*. New York: A. and C. Boni.

Smith, E. E. 1965. The Texas Compulsory Pooling Act. *Texas Law Review* 43: 1002–1035.

———. 2008. The Growing Demand for Oil and Gas and the Potential Impact upon Rural Land. *Texas Journal of Oil, Gas and Energy Law* 4(1): 1–25.

Smith, E. E., J. S. Dzienkowski, et al. 2000. *International Petroleum Transactions*. Denver: Rocky Mountain Mineral Law Foundation.

Smith, E. E., and J. L. Weaver. 1998. *Texas Law of Oil and Gas*. Carlsbad: Calif., LEXIS Law Publishing.

Smith, H. E. 2004. Exclusion and Property Rules in the Law of Nuisance. *Virginia Law Review* 90: 966–1051.

Smith, J. C. 2008. East Texas Oil Field. In *Handbook of Texas Online*, www.tshaonline.org/handbook/online. Accessed April 2009.

Spier, J. 2005. Conclusions. *Unocal Netherlands B.V. v. Continental Netherlands Oil Co.* Supreme Court of the Netherlands (unofficial translation).

Sprankling, J. G. 2008. Owning the Center of the Earth. *UCLA Law Review* 55: 980–1040.

Stocking, G. W. 1925. *The Oil Industry and the Competitive System*. Boston: Houghton Mifflin Co.

Stone, R. B. 1926. *McKean, the Governor's County*. New York: Lewis Historical Publishing Co.

Stratton, D. 1998. *Tempest over Teapot Dome: The Story of Albert B. Fall*. Norman: University of Oklahoma Press.

Sullivan, R. E. (ed.) 1960. *Conservation of Oil and Gas: A Legal History, 1958*. Chicago: American Bar Association, Section of Mineral and Natural Resources Law.

Summers, F. P. 1937. *Johnson Newlon Camden: A Study in Individualism*. New York: G.P. Putnam's Sons.

Summers, W. L. 1919. Property in Oil and Gas. *Yale Law Journal* 29: 174–187.

———. 1938. The Modern Theory and Practical Application of Statutes for the Conservation of Oil and Gas. In *Legal History of Conservation of Oil and Gas*. Section of Mineral Law, American Bar Association, Chicago: American Bar Association, pp. 1–15.

———. 1954. *The Law of Oil and Gas*. Kansas City: Vernon Law Book Co.

Sutherland, D. A. 1899. The Petroleum History of Roumania. *Petroleum Review* 1: 95–101, 131–137.

Swanner, G. M. 1988. *Saratoga: Queen of Spas*. Utica, NY: North Country Books, Inc.

Swenson, R. W. 1968. Legal Aspects of Mineral Resources Exploitation. In *History of Public Land Law Development*. Edited by P. W. Gates, Washington, DC: U.S. Government Printing Office, pp. 699–764.

Szekely, A. 1987. The International Law of Submarine Transboundary Hydrocarbon Resources: Legal Limits to Behavior and Experiences in the Gulf of Mexico. In *Transboundary Resources Law*. Edited by A. E. Utton & L. A. Teclaff, Boulder, CO: Westview Press, pp. 253–288.

Taggart, M. 2002. *Private Property and Abuse of Rights in Victorian England: The Story of Edward Pickles and the Bradford Water Supply*. Oxford: Oxford University Press.

Tarbell, I. M. 1904. *The History of the Standard Oil Company*. New York: Macmillan.

———. 1972. Introduction. In *The Birth of the Oil Industry*. Edited by P. H. Giddens, New York: Arno Press, pp. xiii–xxxix.

Testa, S. M. 2005. The Los Angeles City Oil Field: California's First Oil Boom during the Revitalization Period (1875–1900). *Oil-Industry History* 6: 79–100.

———. 2007. The History of Oil along the Newport-Inglewood Structural Zone, Los Angeles County, California. *Oil-Industry History* 8: 9–35.

Thibault, R. P., M. A. Shelby, et al. 2008. A Modern Look at the Law of Subsurface Trespass: Does It Need Review, Refinement, or Restatement? *Rocky Mountain Mineral Law Institute* 54: 24-1–24-34.

Thoenen, E. D. 1964. *History of the Oil and Gas Industry in West Virginia*. Charleston, WVa: Education Foundation.

Tiedeman, C. G. 1886. *A Treatise on the Limitations of the Police Power in the United States Considered from Both a Civil and Criminal Standpoint*. St. Louis: F. H. Thomas.

Tiffany, H. T. 1920. *The Law of Real Property and Other Interests in Land*. Chicago: Callaghan and Co.

Timor Sea Designated Authority. 2006. Production Sharing Contract for the Joint Petroleum Development Area.

Tolf, R. W. 1976. *The Russian Rockefellers: The Saga of the Nobel Family and the Russian Oil Industry*. Stanford, CA: Hoover Institution Press.

Townsend-Gault, I., and W. G. Stormont. 1995. Offshore Petroleum Joint Development Arrangements: Functional Instrument? Compromise? Obligation? in *The Peaceful Management of Transboundary Resources*. Edited by G. H. Blake, Graham and Trotman/Martinus Nijhoff, pp. 50–76.

Toyoda, T. 2003. Oil Rush: Looking for the Land and Petroleum. *Osaka Keidai Ronshu* 54(2): 187–218.

Trabish, H. K. 2005. Scandal: A Short History of the Teapot Dome Affair. *Oil-Industry History* 6: 101–121.

Trinidad. Asphalt Industry Commission. 1902. Report of the Asphalt Industry Commission, London: Colonial Office.

Tyrrell, J. F., ed. 1865. *The Oil Districts of Canada*. New York: American News Company.

UK Energy Research Centre. 2009. *Global Oil Depletion: An Assessment of the Evidence for a Near-Term Peak in Oil Production*. London: UK Energy Research Centre.

Umbeck, J. R. 1981. *A Theory of Property Rights, with Application to the California Gold Rush*. Ames: Iowa State University Press.

Umpleby, J. B. 1930. Problems of Petroleum: Comment on Paper by J. Elmer Thomas. *Transactions of the American Institute of Mining and Metallurgical Engineers* 1930: 427–428.

———. 1933. Unit Development of Oilfields. In *World Petroleum Congress*. Vol. 1. Edited by A. E. Dunstan & G. Sell. London: World Petroleum Congress, pp. 299–303.

Union Petroleum Co. of New York. 1865. *First Annual Report of the Board of Trustees to the Stockholders*. New York: Union Petroleum Co.

United Kingdom. Department of Trade and Industry, Oil and Gas Division. 2000. *Guidance Notes and Procedures for Regulating Offshore Oil and Gas Developments*. London: Department of Trade and Industry.

———. 1918. Copy of an Agreement Made between the Minister of Munitions and S. Pearson and Sons on 10th September 1918 for Management of Petroleum Development, Cmd 9188 (Parliamentary Papers 1918, Vol. XV), London: His Majesty's Stationery Office.

United Nations. International Law Commission. 2008. Draft Articles on the Law of Transboundary Aquifers, with Commentaries, untreaty.un.org/ilc/texts/instruments/english/commentaries/8_5_2008.pdf. Accessed August 2009. To be published in 2008 *Yearbook of the International Law Commission*, Vol. II, part 2.

———. 2009a. Shared Natural Resources, Comments and observations received from Governments. United Nations General Assembly Doc. A/CN.4/607, January 29, 2009.

———. 2009b. Shared Natural Resources, Paper on oil and gas prepared by Mr. Chusei Yamada, special rapporteur on shared natural resources. United Nations General Assembly Doc. A/CN.4/608, February 18, 2009.

United Nations. Secretariat. 1950. Memorandum on the Regime of the High Seas. *Yearbook of the International Law Commission* (2): 67–113.

United States. Department of the Interior, Minerals Management Service. 1986. Oil and Gas Lease of Submerged Lands under the Outer Continental Shelf Lands Act, Form MMS-2005 (March 1986).

———. 2008. Federal OCS Oil and Gas Production as a Percentage of Total U.S. Production, 1954–2006.

———. 2009. Outer Continental Shelf Lease Sale Statistics.

United States. Energy Information Administration. 2007a. Oil and Natural Gas Market Supply and Renewable Portfolio Standard Impacts of Selected Provisions of H.R. 3221.

———. 2007b. Crude Oil Production and Natural Gas Gross Withdrawals and Production Tables (Annual) 2007, at tonto.eia.doe.gov/dnav/pet and tonto.eia.doe.gov/dnav/ng. Accessed March 2009.

———. 2009. U.S. Crude Oil, Natural Gas, and Natural Gas Liquids Reserves 2007 Annual Report, Washington, DC: U.S. Department of Energy, DOE/EIA-0216 (2007).

United States. Federal Oil Conservation Board. 1926a. Complete Record of Public Hearings, February 10 and 11, 1926, Washington, DC: U.S. Government Printing Office.

———. 1926b. Report to the President of the United States, Washington, DC: U.S. Government Printing Office.

———. 1929. Report III to the President of the United States, Washington, DC: U.S. Government Printing Office.

———. 1930. Report IV to the President of the United States, Washington, DC: U.S. Government Printing Office.

United States. Federal Trade Commission. 1952. The International Petroleum Cartel, Washington, DC: Sub-committee on Monopoly, Senate Select Committee on Small Business.

United States. House of Representatives, Committee on the Public Lands. 1897. Patenting of Petroleum Lands, House Rpt. 2655, 54th Congress, 2nd Session.

United States. Public Land Commission. 1880. *The Public Domain: Its History, with Statistics.* Washington, DC: U.S. Government Printing Office.

Vandevelde, K. J. 1980. The New Property of the Nineteenth Century: The Development of the Modern Concept of Property. *Buffalo Law Review* 29: 325–368.

Van Hise, C. R. 1910. *The Conservation of Natural Resources in the United States.* New York: Macmillan Co.

Veasey, J. A. 1920a. The Law of Oil and Gas. *Michigan Law Review* 18: 445–469.

———. 1920b. The Law of Oil and Gas, Chapter II. *Michigan Law Review* 18: 652–668.

———. 1920c. The Law of Oil and Gas, Chapter IV. *Michigan Law Review* 19: 161–189.

———. 1927. Legislative Control of the Business of Producing Oil and Gas. *Annual Report of the American Bar Association* 50: 577–630.

———. 1941. *Inquiries Leading to a Change in One Element of the Rule of Capture as It Now Obtains at Common Law to the End That the Rights of Operators to Produce Oil and Gas Shall Be Determined upon the Relativity of Reservoir Conditions Between and Among the Separate Properties in a Reservoir.* Ann Arbor, Mich.: Legal Research Library.

Verdier, S. 1993. *La Bourboule, naissance d'une station thermale (1828–1936).* Thesis, Clermont-Ferrand: University of Clermont Ferrand.

Vincent, D. 1998. *The Culture of Secrecy: Britain, 1832–1998.* Oxford: Oxford University Press.

Wade, A. 1915. The Supposed Oil-Bearing Lands of South Australia. Adelaide: Government Printer.

Walker, A. W. J. 1928. A Brief Summary of Two Important Cases on Oil and Gas Rights in Public Land. *Texas Law Review* 7: 125–128.

————. 1938. Property Rights in Oil and Gas and their Effect upon Police Regulation of Production. *Texas Law Review* 16: 370–381.

Walker, B. P. J. 1951. Discussion: A Model Oil and Gas Conservation Law. *Tulane Law Review* 26: 267–302.

Warner, C. A. 1939. *Texas Oil and Gas since 1543*. Houston: Gulf Publishing.

Weaver, J. L. 1986. *Unitization of Oil and Gas in Texas: A Study of Legislative, Administrative and Judicial Politics*. Washington, DC: Resources for the Future.

————. 1994. Unitization Revisited. *Institute on Oil and Gas Law and Taxation (Southwestern Legal Foundation)* 45: 71–752.

————. 2004. The Tragedy of the Commons from Spindletop to Enron. *Journal of Land, Resources, and Environmental Law* 24: 187–193.

Weaver, J. L., and D. F. Asmus. 2006. Unitizing Oil and Gas Fields around the World: A Comparative Analysis of National Laws and Private Contracts. *Houston Journal of International Law* 28: 3–197.

White, G. T. 1962. *Formative Years in the Far West: A History of Standard Oil Company of California and Predecessors through 1919*. New York: Appleton-Century-Crofts.

White, I. C. 1909. The Waste of Our Fuel Resources. In *Proceedings of a Conference of Governors in the White House, Washington, DC, May 13–15, 1908*. Edited by N. C. Blanchard. Washington, DC: U.S. Government Printing Office, pp. 26–37.

Wilkinson, R. 1988. *A Thirst for Burning*. Sydney: David Eli Press.

Williams, H. R. 1952. Conservation of Oil and Gas. *Harvard Law Review* 65: 1155–1184.

Williams, H. R., C. Meyers, et al. 2003. *Oil and Gas Law*. Newark, NJ: LexisNexis/ Matthew Bender.

Williamson, H. F., R. L. Andreano, et al. 1963. *The American Petroleum Industry. Vol. 2. The Age of Energy, 1899–1959*. Evanston, Ill: Northwestern University Press.

Williamson, H. F., and A. R. Daum. 1959. *The American Petroleum Industry. Vol. 1. The Age of Illumination, 1859–1899*. Evanston, Ill: Northwestern University Press.

Willoughby, W. W. 1929. *The Constitutional Law of the United States*. New York: Baker, Voorhis and Co.

Wilson, K. 1989. Conservation Acts and Correlative Rights: Has the Pendulum Swung Too Far? *Rocky Mountain Mineral Law Institute* 35: 18-1–18-34.

Woodward, M. K. 1965. Ownership of Interests in Oil and Gas. *Ohio State Law Journal* 26: 353–369.

Woolnough, W. G. 1931. Report on Tour of Inspection of the Oil-Fields of the United States of America and Argentina, and on Oil Prospects in Australia. In *Session 1929–31*. Vol. 2. Canberra, Australia: Parliament, Records of Proceedings, pp. 1715–1832.

————. 1933[?]. Notes by Dr Woolnough, Commonwealth Geological Adviser, on the Defects of the Laws of the Individual States in Relation to the Search for and Development of Potential Petroleum Resources in Australia. Canberra, National Archives of Australia. A518, A846/1/59 Part 1.

Work, H. 1927. Conservation's Need of Legal Advice. *Annual Report of the American Bar Association* 50: 556–576.

Wright, J. E. 1966. *The Galena Lead District: Federal Policy and Practice, 1824–1847.* Madison: State Historical Society of Wisconsin for the Dept. of History, University of Wisconsin.

Wright, W. 1865. *The Oil Regions of Pennsylvania.* New York: Harper & Brothers.

Wylie, J. C. W. 1986. *The Land Laws of Trinidad and Tobago.* Port of Spain: Government of Trinidad and Tobago.

Yergin, D. 1991. *The Prize: The Epic Quest for Oil, Money and Power.* New York: Simon and Schuster.

Zimmermann, E. W. 1957. *Conservation in the Production of Petroleum: A Study in Industrial Control.* New Haven, Conn: Yale University Press.

CASES

France

Badoit c. André, Dalloz Périodique 1856.2.199 (Cour impériale de Lyon, April 15, 1856).

Brosson, Recueil Général des Lois et des Arrêts (Sirey) 1844.1.664 (Cass. crim., April 13, 1844).

Cazeaux c. Ville de Bagnères, Dalloz Périodique 1884.3.50 (Tribunal des Conflits, November 25, 1883).

Commune de Varennes-les-Nevers c. Boignes, Dalloz Périodique 1861.2.149 (Cass. civ., December 4, 1860).

Dangé, Recueil Lebon 1868.1071 (Conseil d'Etat, December 19, 1868).

de Seraincourt c. Compagnie du Chemin de Fer d'Orléans, Dalloz Périodique 1878.2.222 (Cour d'Appel de Montpellier, January 9, 1877).

Dubois, Dalloz Périodique 1880.1.282 (Cass. crim., March 12, 1880).

Dubois, Recueil Lebon 1876.899 (Conseil d'Etat, December 13, 1876).

Dubois, Recueil Lebon 1886.631 (Conseil d'Etat, July 16, 1886).

Forissier c. Chaverol, Dalloz Périodique 1902.1.454 (Cour de Cassation, Chambre des Requêtes, June 10, 1902).

Larbaud, Recueil Lebon 1855.720 (Conseil d'Etat, December 13, 1855).

Larbaud, Recueil Lebon 1875.104 (Conseil d'Etat, February 5, 1875).

Lasaigne, Inventaire des Arrêts du Conseil du Roi, Règne de Louis XV, T. III, Pt. 2, 1730–1736, No. 22702 (Conseil du Roi, August 28, 1736).

Mercador c. Couderc et Lacvivier, Dalloz Périodique 1849.1.305 (Cass. civ., December 4, 1849).

Parmentier, Sirey 1832.1.643 (Cass. crim., September 8, 1832).

International

Aegean Sea Continental Shelf Case (Greece v. Turkey), Interim Measures [1976] I.C.J. 3 (International Court of Justice).

Case concerning Maritime Delimitation in the Black Sea (Romania v. Ukraine) www.icj-cij.org/docket/files/132/14987.pdf (February 3, 2009) (International Court of Justice).

Guyana v. Suriname www.pca-cpa.org/upload/files/Guyana-Suriname%20Award.pdf (September 17, 2007) (Arbitral Tribunal).

Libya v. Malta [1985] I.C.J. Rep. 13 (International Court of Justice).

North Sea Continental Shelf Case [1969] I.C.J. 3 (International Court of Justice).

United Kingdom and Commonwealth

Acton v. Blundell (1843), 12 M. & W. 324, 152 Eng. Rep. 1223 (Exchequer Chamber).

Attorney-General for New South Wales v. Attorney-General for the Commonwealth (1975), 135 C.L.R. 337 (High Court of Australia).

Attorney-General v. Eriche (1894), 1 Trinidad and Tobago Supreme Court Reports 19 (Supreme Court of Trinidad and Tobago).

Backhouse v. Bonomi (1861), 9 H.L.C. 503, 11 Eng. Rep. 825 (House of Lords).

Bocardo SA v. Star Energy UK Onshore Ltd [2010] Ch. 100 (Court of Appeal).

Borys v. Canadian Pacific Railway [1953] 2 A.C. 217 (Privy Council).

Case of Mines (1568), 1 Plowden 310, 75 Eng. Rep. 472.

Chasemore v. Richards (1859), 7 H.L.C. 349, 11 Eng. Rep. 140 (House of Lords).

Commonwealth v. Yarrmirr (2001), 208 C.L.R. 1, [2001] HCA 56 (High Court of Australia).

Humphries v. Brogden (1850), 12 Q.B. 740, 116 Eng. Rep. 1048 (Queen's Bench).

Hunt v. Peake (1860), Johnson 705, 70 Eng. Rep. 603 (Vice-Chancellor).

Mabo v. Queensland (No. 2) (1992), 175 C.L.R. 1 (High Court of Australia).

New Trinidad Lake Asphalt Co. Ltd v. Attorney-General (1900), 1 Trinidad and Tobago Supreme Court Reports 83 (Supreme Court of Trinidad and Tobago).

New Trinidad Lake Asphalt Co. Ltd v. Attorney-General [1904] A.C. 415 (Privy Council).

North-Eastern Railway Co v. Elliott (1860), 1 Johnson and Heming 145, 70 Eng. Rep. 697 (Vice-Chancellor); 10 H.L.C. 333, 11 Eng. Rep. 1055 (House of Lords).

Popplewell v. Hodkinson (1869), L.R. 4 Ex. 248 (Exchequer Chamber.).

Rylands v. Fletcher (1868), L.R. 3 H.L. 330 (House of Lords).

Salt Union Ltd v. Brunner, Mond & Co. [1906] 2 K.B. 822 (King's Bench).

St. Catherine's Milling and Lumber Co. v. Attorney-General for Ontario (1887), 13 S.C.R. 577 (Supreme Court of Canada).

Trinidad Asphalt Co. v. Ambard [1899] A.C. 594 (Privy Council).

Trinidad Lake Asphalt Co. v. Warner (1894), 1 Trinidad and Tobago Supreme Court Reports 10 (Supreme Court of Trinidad and Tobago).

U Po Naing v. Burma Oil Co. (1929), L.R. 56 Ind. App. 140 (Privy Council).

United States

Acheson v. Stevenson, 145 Pa. 228 (1892).

Alabama v. U.S. Department of Interior, 84 F. 3d 410 (11th Cir. 1996).

Allison and Evans' Appeal, 77 Pa. 221 (1875).

Amazon Petroleum Co. v. Railroad Commission of Texas, 5 F. Supp. 633 (E.D. Tex. 1934).

Ammons v. South Penn Oil Co., 47 W. Va. 610; 35 S.E. 1004 (1900).

Atlantic Refining Co. v. Railroad Commission of Texas, 162 Tex. 274, 346 S.W. 2d (1961).

Barnard v. Monongahela Natural Gas Co., 216 Pa. 362; 65 A. 801 (1907).

Barstow v. Mojave Water Agency, 23 Cal. 4th 1224, 5 P. 3d 853 (2000).

Bassett v. Salisbury Manufacturing Co., 43 N.H. 569; 32 Am. Dec. 179 (1862).

Bettman v. Harness, 42 W. Va. 433; 26 S.E. 271 (1896).

Blair v. Peck, 1 Pennypacker 247 (Pa. 1881).

Bradford Oil Co v. Blair, 113 Pa. 83, 4 A. 218 (1886).

Brewster v. Lanyon Zinc Co., 140 F. 801 (8th Cir. 1905).

Brown v. Humble Oil and Refining Co., 126 Tex. 296; 83 S.W. 2d 935 (1935); on rehearing 126 Tex. 314; 87 S.W. 2d 1069 (1935).

Brown v. Spillman, 155 U.S. 665 (1895).

Brown v. Vandergrift, 89 Pa. 142 (1875).

Burgner v. Humphrey, 41 Ohio St. 340 (1884).

Buttes Resources Co v. Railroad Commission of Texas, 732 S.W. 2d 675 (Tex. Civ. App. 1987).

Caldwell v. Fulton, 31 Pa. 475 (1853).

Champlin Refining Co. v. Corporation Commission of Oklahoma, 286 U.S. 210 (1932).

Chandler v. Hart, 161 Cal. 405, 119 P. 516 (1911).

Chatfield v. Wilson, 26 Vt. 49 (1855).

Coastal Oil and Gas Corp. v. Garza Energy Trust, 268 S.W. 3d 1 (Tex. 2008).

Colgan v. Forest Oil Co., 194 Pa. 234 (1899).

Cosmos Exploration Co. v. Gray Eagle Oil Co., 104 F. 20 (S.D. Cal. 1900).

Cowan v. Hardeman, 26 Tex. 217 (1862).

Cowling v. Board of Oil, Gas and Mining, 830 P. 2d 220 (Utah 1991).

Cox v. Robison, 105 Tex. 426, 150 S.W. 1149 (1912).

Creede and Cripple Creek Mining and Milling Co. v. Uinta Tunnel Mining Transportation Co., 196 U.S. 337 (1904).

Danciger Oil & Refining Co. v. Railroad Commission of Texas, 49 S.W. 2d 837 (Tex. Civ. App. 1932).

Dark v. Johnston, 55 Pa. 164 (1867).

Denver Producing and Refining Co. v. State, 199 Okla. 171; 184 P. 2d 961 (1947).

Desormeaux v. Inexco Oil Co., 298 So.2d 897 (La.App. 3rd Cir. 1974).

Duffield v. Rosenzweig, 144 Pa. 521, 23 A. 4 (1891).

Elliff v. Texon Drilling Co., 210 S.W. 2d 588 (Tex. 1948).

Empire Gas & Fuel Co. v. State, 121 Tex. 138, 47 S.W. 2d 265 (1932).

Erickson v. Crookston Waterworks Co., 100 Minn. 481, 111 N.W. 391 (1907).

Ex parte Elam, 6 Cal. App. 233; 91 P. 811 (Ct App. Cal. 1911).

Farmers Irrigation District v. Schumacher, 194 N.W. 2d 788 (Neb. 1972).

Fletcher v. Peck, 6 Cranch (10 U.S.) 87 (1810).

Forbell v. City of New York, 160 N.Y. 357, 58 N.E. 644 (1900) (N.Y. Ct. App.).

Frazier v. Brown, 12 Ohio St. 294 (1861).

Funk v. Haldeman, 53 Pa. 229 (1867).

Gadbury v. Ohio and Indiana Consolidated Natural and Illuminating Gas Co., 162 Ind. 9, 67 N.E. 259 (1903).

Gant v. Oklahoma City, 150 Okla. 86, 6 P. 2d 1081 (1931).

Gas Products v. Rankin, 63 Mont. 372, 207 P. 993 (1922).

Geer v. Connecticut, 161 U.S. 519 (1896).

Geo-Viking Inc. v. Tex-Lee Operating Co., 839 S.W. 2d 897 (Tex. 1992).

Green v. Putnam, 62 Mass. 21 (1851).

Greene v. Robison, 117 Tex. 516, 8 S.W. 2d 655 (1928).

Greenleaf v. Francis, 18 Pick. 117 (Mass. 1836).

Gregg v. Delhi-Taylor Oil Co., 162 Tex. 26, 344 S.W. 2d 411 (1961).

Gruger v. Phillips Petroleum Co., 192 Okla. 259; 135 P.2d 485 (1943).

Hague v. Wheeler, 157 Pa. 324; 27 A. 714 (1893).

Halbouty v. Railroad Commission of Texas, 163 Tex. 516, 357 S.W. 364 (1962).

Hall v. Reed, 54 Ky. 479 (1854).

Hammond Oil Co. v. Titus, unreported (No. 103, August Term 1865, Court of Common Pleas, Venango County, PA).

Harris v. Ohio Oil Co., 57 Ohio St. 118, 48 N.E. 502 (1897).

Hastings Oil Co. v. Texas Co., 149 Tex. 416, 234 S.W. 2d 389 (1950).

Hathorn v. Natural Carbonic Gas Co., 194 N.Y. 326; 87 N.E. 504 (1909) (N.Y. Ct. App.).

Hawkins v. Texas Co., 146 Tex. 511; 209 S.W. 2d 338 (1948).

Henderson v. Railroad Commission of Texas, 56 F. 2d 218 (W.D. Tex. 1932).

Hermann v. Thomas, 143 S.W. 2d 195 (Texas Civ. App. 1911).

Higgins Fuel and Oil Co v. Guaranty Oil Co., 145 La. 233, 82 So. 206 (1919).

Houston & Texas Central Railway Co. v. East, 98 Tex. 146, 81 S.W. 279 (1904).

Huber v. Merkel, 117 Wis. 355, 74 N.W. 354 (1903).

Huggins v. Daley, 99 F. 606 (4th Cir. 1900).

Hunter v. McHugh, 202 La. 97, 11 So. 2d 495 (1942); 320 U.S. 222 (1943).

Irwin v. Phillips, 5 Cal. 140 (1855).

James v. Emory Oil Co., 1 Pennypacker 242 (Pa. 1881).

Jameson v. Ethyl Corp., 271 Ark. 621, 609 S.W. 2d 346 (1980).

Johnson v. McIntosh, 21 U.S. (8 Wheat.) 543 (1823).

Jones v. Forest Oil Co., 194 Pa. 379, 44 Atl. 1074 (1900).

Julian Oil and Royalties Co. v. Capshaw, 145 Okla. 237; 292 P. 841 (1930).

Katz v. Walkinshaw, 141 Cal. 116; 70 P. 663 (1902), on rehearing 141 Cal. 116, 74 P. 766 (1903).

Kelley v. Ohio Oil Co., 57 Ohio St. 317, 49 N.E. 399 (1897).

Kier v. Peterson, 41 Pa. 357 (1862).

Kleppner v. Lemon, 176 Pa. 502, 35 A. 109 (1896).

Lindsley v. Natural Carbonic Gas Co., 220 U.S. 61 (1911).

Lochner v. New York, 198 U.S. 45 (1905).

Louisiana v. United States, 832 F. 2d 935 (5th Cir. 1987).

Louisville Gas Co. v. Kentucky Heating Co., 117 Ky. 71; 77 S.W. 368 (1903).

Macmillan v. Railroad Commission of Texas, 51 F. 2d 400 (W.D. Tex. 1931).

Magnolia Petroleum Co. v. Railroad Commission of Texas, 120 S.W. 2d 553 (Tex. Civ. App. 1938).

Majority of the Working Interest Owners in the Buck Draw Field Area v. Wyoming Oil and Gas Conservation Commission, 721 P. 2d 1070 (Wyo. 1986).

Manufacturers' Gas and Oil Co. v. Indiana Natural Gas & Oil Co., 155 Ind. 461; 57 N.E. 912 (1900).

Marblehead Land Co. v. City of Los Angeles, 47 F. 2d 528 (9th Cir. 1931).

Marrs v. City of Oxford, 24 F. 2d 541 (D.C. Kan. 1927); 32 F. 2d 134 (8th Cir. 1929).

McCray and Donaghy v. Kepler, Watson et al., unreported 1870 (Court of Common Pleas, Venango County, PA).

McKnight v. Manufacturers' Natural Gas Co., 146 Pa. 185, 23 Atl. 164 (1892).

Medina Oil Development Co. v. Murphy, 233 S.W. 333 (Tex. Civ. App. 1921).

Meeker v. City of East Orange, 79 N.J.L. 623; 74 A. 379 (1909).

Mining Co. v. Consolidated Mining Co., 102 U.S. 167 (1880).

Moore v. Smaw, 17 Cal. 199 (1861).

Munroe v. Armstrong, 96 Pa. 307 (1880).

Nevada Sierra Oil Co. v. Home Oil Co. 98 F. 673 (S.D. Cal. 1899).

Norman v. Giles, 148 Tex. 21, 219 S.W. 2d 678 (1949).

Ohio Oil Co v. Indiana, 177 U.S. 190 (1900).

Ohio Oil Co. v. Kelley, 9 Ohio C.C.R. 511 (1895) (Ohio Circuit Court).

Oklahoma v. Texas, 258 U.S. 574 (1922).

Oxford Oil Co. v. Atlantic Oil Producing Co., 16 F. 2d 639 (N.D. Tex. 1926); 22 F. 2d 597 (5th Cir. 1927).

Palmer Oil Corp. v. Phillips Petroleum Co., 204 Okla. 543, 231 P. 2d 997 (1951).

Panama Refining Co. v. Ryan, 293 U.S. 388 (1935).

Pasadena v. Alhambra, 33 Cal. 2d 908; 207 P. 2d 17 (1949).

Patterson v. Stanolind, 305 U.S. 376 (1939), affirming 182 Okla. 155, 72 P. 2d 83 (1938).

People v. New York Carbonic Acid Gas Co., 169 N.Y. 421; 90 N.E. 441 (1909).

People's Gas Co. v. Tyner, 131 Ind. 277, 31 N.E. 59 (1892).

Popov v. Hayashi, 2002 WL 3183371 (Westlaw) (San Francisco Superior Court, Cal. 2002).

Railroad Commission of Texas v. Bass, 10 S.W. 2d 586 (Tex. Civ. App. 1928).

Railroad Commission of Texas v. Humble Oil and Refining Co., 193 S.W. 2d 824 (Tex. Civ. App. 1946).

Railroad Commission of Texas v. Manziel, 361 S.W. 2d 560 (Tex. 1962).

Railroad Commission of Texas v. Rowan & Nichols Oil Co., 311 U.S. 570 (1941).

Rich v. Doneghey, 71 Okla. 204, 177 P. 86 (1918).

Richmond Natural Gas Co. v. Enterprise Natural Gas Co., 66 N.E. 782 (Ind. App. 1903).

Rose v. Lanyon Zinc Co., 68 Kan. 126, 74 P. 625 (1903).

Rynd v. Rynd Farm Oil Co., 63 Pa. 397 (1870).

Schechter Poultry Co. v. United States, 295 U.S. 495 (1935).

Shepherd v. McCalmont Oil Co., 38 Hun. 37 (N.Y. App. Div. 1865).

Sipriano v. Great Spring Waters of America Inc., 1 S.W. 3d 75 (Tex. 1999).

Slaughterhouse Cases, 83 U.S. 36 (1872).

Smith v. City of Brooklyn, 18 App. Div. 340, 46 N.Y. Supp. 141, 54 N.E. 787 (N.Y. App. Div. 1897).

State v. Allegheny Oil Co., 85 F. 870 (Ind. 1898).

State v. Ohio Oil Co., 150 Ind. 21, 49 N.E. 809 (1898).

Stephens County et al. v. Mid-Kansas Oil and Gas Co., 113 Tex. 160, 254 S.W. 290 (1923).

Stoughton's Appeal, 88 Pa. 198 (1878).

Texas Co. v. Daugherty, 107 Tex. 226, 176 S.W. 717 (1915).

Texas Co. v. Vedder, unreported (Superior Ct., Los Angeles 1930).

Texas Pacific Coal and Oil Co. v. Comanche Duke Oil Co., 274 S.W. 193 (Tex. Civ. App. 1925).

Texas v. Secretary of Interior, 580 F. Supp. 1197 (E.D. Texas 1984).

Tidewater Oil Co. v. Jackson, 320 F. 2d 157 (10th Cir. 1963).

Townsend v. State, 147 Ind. 624, 47 N.E. 19 (1897).

Tyler v. Wilkinson, 24 Fed. Cas. 472 (1827).

Tyner v. People's Gas Co., 131 Ind. 408, 31 N.E. 61 (1892).

Tysco Oil Co. v. Railroad Commission of Texas, 12 F. Supp. 195 (S.D. Tex. 1935).

United Carbon Co. v. Campbellsville Gas Co., 18 S.W. 2d 1110 (Ky. App. 1929).

United States v. California, 332 U.S. 19 (1947).

United States v. Louisiana, 339 U.S. 699 (1950).

United States v. Louisiana, 363 U.S. 1 (1960).

United States v. Maine, 420 U.S. 515 (1975).

United States v. Midwest Oil Co., 236 U.S. 459 (1915).

United States v. Southern Pacific Co., 251 U.S. 1 (1919).

United States v. Southern Pacific Co., 260 F. 511 (S.D. Cal. 1919).

United States v. Standard Oil, 221 U.S. 1 (1911).

United States v. Sweet, 245 U.S. 563 (1918).

United States v. Texas, 339 U.S. 707 (1950).

Walls v. Midland Carbon, 254 U.S. 300 (1920).

Westmoreland & Cambria Natural Gas Co. v. De Witt, 130 Pa. 235, 18 A. 724 (1889).

Wheatley v. Baugh, 25 Pa. 528 (1855).

Williamson v. Jones, 39 W. Va. 231, 19 S.E. 436 (1894).

Winkler v. Anderson, 104 Kan. 1, 177 P. 171 (1919).

Wood County Petroleum Co. v. West Virginia Transportation Co., 28 W. Va. 210 (1886).

Wood Oil Co. v. Corporation Commission, 205 Okla. 537, 239 P.2d 1023 (1950).

Woods Exploration and Producing Co. v. Aluminum Co. of America, 438 F. 2d 1286 (5th Cir. 1971).

Young v. Forest Oil Co., 194 Pa. 243, 45 A. 21 (1899).

Other

Unocal Netherlands B.V. v. Continental Netherlands Oil Co., Case C04/127HR, October 14, 2005, Hoge Raad (High Court of the Netherlands).

PRINCIPAL LAWS, REGULATIONS, AND TREATIES CITED

Australia

Commonwealth

Petroleum (Submerged Lands) Act 1967, No. 118.

Petroleum (Australia-Indonesia Zone of Co-operation) Act 1990, No. 36.

Offshore Petroleum and Greenhouse Gas Storage Act 2006, No. 14 (as amended and renamed).

Queensland

Mining for Coal and Mineral Oil Act 1912, 3 Geo. V, No. 6.

Petroleum Act 1915, 6 Geo. V, No. 23.

Petroleum Act 1923, 14 Geo. V, No. 26.

Petroleum and Gas (Production and Safety) Act 2004, No. 25.

South Australia

Mining Act 1893, 56 & 57 Vict., No. 587.

Victoria

Mines (Petroleum) Act 1935, Act No. 4359.

Western Australia

Mining Act Amendment Act 1920, 11 Geo. V, No. 50.

Petroleum Act 1936, 1 Edw. VIII, No. 36.

Petroleum Act 1967, No. 72.

Papua New Guinea

New Guinea Petroleum (Prospecting and Mining) Ordinance 1938 (No. 43 of 1938).

Papua Petroleum (Prospecting and Mining) Ordinance 1938, No. 13 of 1938, as amended, in Papua Petroleum (Prospecting and Mining) Ordinances 1938–1939, *The Laws of the Territory of Papua, 1888–1945* (annotated), Vol. III.

Austria-Hungary

Allgemeines Bürgerliches Gesetzbuch (Civil Code), June 1, 1811, J.G.S. Nr. 946.

Allgemeine Burggesetz (General Mining Law), May 23, 1854, Nr. 146 R.G.B.

Naphtha-Reichsgesetz (Imperial Petroleum Law), May 11, 1884, Nr. 71 R.G.B.

Naphtha-Landesgesetz (Galician Petroleum Law), December 17, 1884, L.G.B. für Galizien Nr. 35 ex 1886.

Naphtha-Landesgesetz (Galician Petroleum Law), March 22, 1908, L.G.B. für Galizien Nr. 61; Blauhorn 1910: 16–102.

France

Déclaration du Roi portant Etablissemen d'une Commission Royale de Médecine, pour l'Examen des Remèdes Particuliers et la Distribution des Eaux Minérales (establishment of Royal Medical Commission) (1772). Mallat and Cornillon 1909: 151–60.

Loi des 12–29 juillet 1791 relative aux mines (Mines Law). Lois et Actes du Gouvernement 1789–1794, Vol. 3, 414.

Arrêté (du 21 avril 1800) relatif à la location et à l'administration des établissmens d'eaux minérales (leasing and administration of mineral water establishments). Mallat et Cornillon 1909: 201–203.

Code Civil (Civil Code) 1804. Current text in English at www.lexinter.net/ENGLISH/civil_code.htm, in French at textes.droit.org/code/civil/.

Loi du 21 avril 1810 concernant les mines, les minières et les carrières (Mining Code), Bulletin des Lois No. 285.

Ordonnance du Roi du 18 juin–7 juillet 1823 portant règlement sur la police des Eaux minérales (mineral water regulation). Bulletin des Lois du Royaume de France, Vol. 16, 522; Rotureau 1859: 896–899.

Loi du 17 juin 1840 relative aux mines de sel gemme et aux sources d'eau salée (salt mines and salt springs). Bulletin des Lois du Royaume de France, Vol. 20, 347; Michel 1896: 583–596.

Décret du 8–10 mars 1848 relatif aux sources d'eaux minérales (mineral water sources). Bulletin des Lois No. 89, Dalloz Périodique 1848.4.45.

Loi du 14–22 juillet 1856 sur la conservation et l'aménagement des sources d'eaux minérales (mineral water sources). Bulletin des Lois No. 3827, Dalloz Périodique 1856.4.85, Rotureau 1859: 907–914.

Décret impérial des 8–20 septembre 1856 (application of Law of July 14–22, 1856). Bulletin des Lois No. 4017, Dalloz Périodique 1856.4.137; Rotureau 1859: 903–906.

Décret impérial de 28 janv.–15 fev. 1860 concernant la conservation et l'aménagement des sources d'eaux minérales (protection and improvement of mineral water sources). Bulletin des Lois No. 7331, Dalloz Périodique 1860.4.13.

Loi du 4 février 1943 relative aux permis exclusifs de recherches d'hydrocarbures liquides ou gazeux (exclusive oil and gas exploration permits). Journal Officiel de la République Française, February 10, 1943: 386.

Décret 81-374 du 15 avril 1981 (approving standard terms for oil and gas concessions). Journal Officiel de la République Française, April 18, 1981: 1111.

Indonesia

Government Regulation No. 35 of 2004 on upstream oil and gas business activities (State Gazette No. 123 of 2004).

Netherlands

Mijnwet 1810 (Mining Law = French Mining Code, April 21, 1810, above).

Mijnwet Continentaal Plat (Continental Shelf Mining Act) of September 23, 1965, Stb. 428.

Besluit tot Uitvoering van art. 12 Mijnwet Continentaal Plat (Continental Shelf mining regulations) of April 27, 1967, Stb. 24.

Wet Opsporing Delfstoffen (Mining Exploration Act) of May 3, 1967, Stb. 258.

Mijnwet (Mining Act) of 2003. Unofficial English translation at www.nlog.nl/resources/ENGVERTMIJNBOUW100103.pdf.

Romania

Règlement organique des principautés roumaines (Organic law of the Romanian principalities) 1831: Institutul Geologic al României: 1925: VII/1, 4–8.

Civil Code 1865: current text available at legal.dntis.ro.

Mining Law 1895: Institutul Geologic al României 1925: VII, 12f; Rosetti 1905: 4–139.

Oil Concessions Law 1905–1906: Institutul Geologic al României 1925: VII, 143–147.

Law for the regularization and consolidation of rights to exploit petroleum on private land, 1914: Institutul Geologic al României 1925: VII, 221–223.

Mining Law 1924: *Moniteur du Pétrole Roumain* 1924, No. 14, 1107–1165.

Russia

Mining Code 1893 (incorporating Oilfield Regulations 1892): Beeby Thompson 1904: App. B; Mitzakis 1912: Ch. IX.

Spain

Mining Ordinance of 1783 (trans. Rockwell 1851: 4–111).

Trinidad

Asphalt Industry Regulation Ordinance 1906 (now Asphalt Industry Regulation Act, Laws of the Republic of Trinidad and Tobago, rev. ed. 1980, Chap. 87: 50).

United Kingdom

Petroleum (Production) Act 1918, 8 & 9 Geo. V, c. 52.

Petroleum (Production) Act 1934, 24 & 25 Geo. V, c. 36.

Petroleum (Production) Regulations 1935, S.R. & O. 1935/426.

Continental Shelf Act 1964, c. 29.

Petroleum Act 1998, c. 17.

Petroleum (Current Model Clauses) Order 1999, S.I. 1999/160: in Daintith et al. 2010: paras. 5-1650 to 5-2165.

Petroleum Licensing (Production) (Seaward Areas) Regulations 2008, SI 2008/225: in Daintith et al. 2010: paras. 5-3116–5-3165.

United States

Texts of conservation statutes up to the end of 1932 are conveniently collected in Ely 1933b, though the incorporation of the statutes into codified compilations of legislative provisions sometimes obscures the date of enactment of a specific legislative change. It should also be noted that in some cases, significant amendments occurred between the original passage of the legislation and the date of the Ely compilation.

Federal

Land Ordinance 1785, 4 *Journals of the American Congress* 5207 (May 20, 1785), available at www.ambrosevideo.com/resources/documents/104.pdf.

Act for making provision for the disposal of the public lands (Lead Act) 1807, 2 Stat. 448.

Act authorizing the governor of the territory of Arkansas to lease the salt springs, in said territory, and for other purposes 1832, 4 Stat. 505.

Pre-emption Act 1841, 5 Stat. 453.

Mining Law 1872, 17 Stat. 91.

Oil Placer Act 1897, 29 Stat. 526.

Pickett Act 1910, 36 Stat. 847.

An Act providing for agricultural entry on lands … containing oil, gas … 1914, 38 Stat. 509.

Stock-Raising Homestead Act 1916, 39 Stat. 864.

Mineral Leasing Act 1920, 41 Stat. 437, amended inter alia by Act of April 30, 1926, 44 Stat. 373; Act of March 4, 1931, 46 Stat. 1523; Act of August 21, 1935, 49 Stat. 678, Federal Onshore Oil and Gas Leasing Reform Act 1987, 101 Stat. 1330-256; current text at 30 U.S.C. §§ 181–287.

Continental Shelf Proclamation, Proclamation 2677 and Executive Order 9633, 10 Fed. Reg. 12303 (1945).

Submerged Lands Act 1953, 67 Stat. 29, current text at 43 U.S.C. §§ 1301–1315.

Outer Continental Shelf Lands Act 1953, 67 Stat. 462, current text at 43 U.S.C. §§ 1331–1356.

Arkansas

Arkansas Code Title 15, Ch. 72 § 309(2)(3) (unitization, current text).

California

Act of March 25, 1911 (prohibiting the unnecessary wasting of natural gas into the atmosphere): Laws 1911, Ch. 309; Ely 1933b: 53–54.

Act of June 10, 1915 (An Act to protect the natural resources of water, petroleum and gas from damage, waste and destruction): Laws 1915, Ch. 718; Ely 1933b: 56, 62–66.

Act of June 4, 1931 (well spacing): Laws 1931, Ch. 586; Ely 1933b: 80–82.

Indiana

Acts 1891, p. 55 (flambeau lights): Ely 1933b: 116.

Acts 1893, p. 300 (allowing escape of gas prohibited): Ely 1933b: 111–112.

Louisiana

Acts 268 and 270 of 1918 (gas conservation): Ely 1933b: 149–154.

Act 73 of 1920 (oil conservation): Ely 1933b: 154–157.

Act 157 of 1940 (pooling and unitization).

Louisiana Revised Statutes, Title 30 § 5.1 (unitization, current text).

Oklahoma

Gas Conservation Act 1915, Ch. 197.

Oil Conservation Act 1915, Ch. 25.

Oklahoma Statutes, Title 52 §§287.1-287.15 (unitization, current text).

Pennsylvania

Charter for the Province of Pennsylvania 1681, available at www.yale.edu/lawweb/avalon/states/pa01.pdf.

Act relating to the casing and plugging of wells 1878, P.L. 56.

Oil and Gas Conservation Act, Pennsylvania Statutes, Title 58, Ch. 7.

Texas

Reconstruction Constitution 1866, available at tarlton.law.utexas.edu/constitutions/text/-FAR07.html.

Anti-Trust Act 1889, Texas Laws 1889, Ch. 117.

Anti-Trust Act 1899, Texas Laws 1899, Ch. 146.

Oil and Gas Conservation Act 1919, Acts 1919, 36th Leg., Ch. 155; Ely 1933b: 331–334 (see Hardwicke 1938: 218 for the text as first enacted).

Relinquishment Act 1919, Acts 1919, 36th Leg., 2nd C.S., Ch. 81.

Anti-Market Demand Act 1931, Acts 1931, 42nd Leg., 1st C.S., Ch. 26; Ely 1933b: 333.

Marginal Well Act 1931, Acts 1931, 42nd Leg., Ch. 58; Ely 1933b: 357–358; (current text) Texas Natural Resources Code §§ 85.122–85.124.

Market Demand Act 1932, Acts 1932, 42nd Leg., 4th C.S., Ch. 2; Ely 1933b: 331–332.

Mineral Interest Pooling Act 1965 (current text) Texas Natural Resources Code, Ch. 102.

Utah
Utah Code §§ 40-6-7, 40-6-8 (unitization, current text).

West Virginia
Act to provide for the inspection of oil wells, and the protection of oil producers 1871, Acts of the Legislature of West Virginia 1871, Ch. 126.

Venezuela

Ley sobre Hidrocarburos y demás minerales comustibles (Petroleum Law) 1922, June 9, 1922.

International Treaties

Geneva Convention on the Territorial Sea and Contiguous Zone 1958, 516 U.N.T.S. 205.

Geneva Convention on the Continental Shelf 1958, 499 U.N.T.S. 311.

Czechoslovakia–Austria Agreement concerning the Working of Common Deposits of Natural Gas and Petroleum, January 23, 1960, 495 U.N.T.S. 134.

Netherlands–Germany, Supplementary Agreement to the Treaty concerning Arrangements for Co-operation in the Ems Estuary (Ems–Dollard Treaty), 1962, 509 U.N.T.S. 140 (1962).

United Kingdom–Norway Agreement on the delimitation of the continental shelf, March 10, 1965, 551 U.N.T.S. 218, 1965 U.K.T.S. 71.

United Kingdom–Netherlands Agreement on the exploitation of single geological structures, October 6, 1965, 595 U.N.T.S. 110 (1967), 1967 U.K.T.S. 24.

Germany–Denmark Agreement on the delimitation of the continental shelf, January 28, 1971 (1971) 10 I.L.M. 603.

Agreement between the United Arab Emirates and Iran, August 13, 1974: Churchill et al. 1977: 242.

United Nations Convention on the Law of the Sea 1982 (UNCLOS), 1833 U.N.T.S. 3: for ratifications, see United Nations, Chronological lists of ratifications of, accessions and successions to the Convention and the related Agreements. www.un.org/Depts/los/.

United Kingdom–Ireland Agreement on the delimitation of the continental shelf, November 7, 1988, 1990 U.K.T.S. 20.

Australia–Indonesia, Treaty on the Zone of Cooperation in an Area between the Indonesian Province of East Timor and Northern Australia (Timor Gap Treaty), February 9, 1991, [1991] Australian Treaty Series 9, 29 I.L.M. 46.

United States–Mexico Agreement on the Delimitation of the Continental Shelf in the Western Gulf of Mexico beyond 200 Nautical Miles, June 9, 2000, 2143 U.N.T.S. 17.

Australia–East Timor, Timor Sea Treaty, May 20, 2002, [2003] Australian Treaty Series 13, available at www.austlii.edu.au/au/other/dfat/treaties/2003/13.html.

United Kingdom–Norway Framework Agreement concerning Cross-Boundary Petroleum Co-operation, April 4, 2005: Daintith et al. 2010: paras. 2-324 to 2-372.

LEGISLATIVE DEBATES

Australia

Commonwealth of Australia, Parliamentary Debates, Canberra, Australian Government Publications Service.

Queensland Parliamentary Debates, Brisbane, Legislative Assembly.

Victoria Parliamentary Debates, Melbourne, Government Printer.

Western Australia Parliamentary Debates, Perth, State Law Publisher.

France

Le Moniteur Universel (French government gazette 1811–1868), Paris.

United Kingdom

House of Commons Debates, London, Her Majesty's Stationery Office.

House of Lords Debates, London, Her Majesty's Stationery Office.

NEWSPAPERS AND PERIODICALS

Daily News, Perth, Western Australia.

Moniteur du Pétrole Roumain, Bucharest, Romania.

Oil City Register, Oil City, Pennsylvania.

Petroleum Review, London.

Petroleum World, London.

Pittsburgh Commercial, Pittsburgh, Pennsylvania.

Titusville Morning Herald, Titusville, Pennsylvania.

INDEX

ABOUT THE AUTHOR

Terence Daintith is the former director of the University of London's Institute of Advanced Legal Studies, where he now holds a professorial fellowship. He is also a visiting professor at the University of Western Australia and the University of Melbourne. His main research interests are in oil and gas law, constitutional law, and regulation. He is joint editor of Daintith, Willoughby, and Hill's multivolume *United Kingdom Oil and Gas Law*, the basic reference in the field, and founding editor of the *Journal of Energy and Natural Resources Law*.

Professor Daintith received his law degree from the University of Oxford and subsequently taught at the University of California, Berkeley, and the University of Edinburgh, before taking up a chair at the University of Dundee, where he established the first university oil and gas law course in the United Kingdom and founded what is now the Centre for Energy, Petroleum and Mineral Law and Policy. He then spent seven years at the European University Institute in Florence, Italy, before taking up appointment in London, first as director of the Institute of Advanced Legal Studies, and then as dean of the university's multidisciplinary School of Advanced Study, a post from which he retired in 2002.